Children's Literature Review

Guide to Gale Literary Criticism Series

For criticism on	Consult these Gale series
Authors now living or who died after December 31, 1959	*CONTEMPORARY LITERARY CRITICISM (CLC)*
Authors who died between 1900 and 1959	*TWENTIETH-CENTURY LITERARY CRITICISM (TCLC)*
Authors who died between 1800 and 1899	*NINETEENTH-CENTURY LITERATURE CRITICISM (NCLC)*
Authors who died between 1400 and 1799	*LITERATURE CRITICISM FROM 1400 TO 1800 (LC)* *SHAKESPEAREAN CRITICISM (SC)*
Authors who died before 1400	*CLASSICAL AND MEDIEVAL LITERATURE CRITICISM (CMLC)*
Authors of books for children and young adults	*CHILDREN'S LITERATURE REVIEW (CLR)*
Dramatists	*DRAMA CRITICISM (DC)*
Poets	*POETRY CRITICISM (PC)*
Short story writers	*SHORT STORY CRITICISM (SSC)*
Black writers of the past two hundred years	*BLACK LITERATURE CRITICISM (BLC)*
Hispanic writers of the late nineteenth and twentieth centuries	*HISPANIC LITERATURE CRITICISM (HLC)*
Native North American writers and orators of the eighteenth, nineteenth, and twentieth centuries	*NATIVE NORTH AMERICAN LITERATURE (NNAL)*
Major authors from the Renaissance to the present	*WORLD LITERATURE CRITICISM, 1500 TO THE PRESENT (WLC)*

ISSN 0362-4145

volume 52

Children's Literature Review

Excerpts from Reviews,
Criticism, and Commentary
on Books for Children
and Young People

Deborah J. Morad
Editor

DETROIT • LONDON

Library of Congress Catalog Card Number 76-643301
ISBN 0-7876-2080-7
ISSN 0362-4145
Printed in the United States of America

10 9 8 7 6 5 4 3 2 1

Contents

Preface

Literature for children and young adults has evolved into both a respected branch of creative writing and a successful industry. Currently, books for young readers are considered among the most popular segments of publishing. Criticism of juvenile literature is instrumental in recording the literary or artistic development of the creators of children's books as well as the trends and controversies that result from changing values or attitudes about young people and their literature. Designed to provide a permanent, accessible record of this ongoing scholarship, *Children's Literature Review (CLR)* presents parents, teachers, and librarians—those responsible for bringing children and books together—with the opportunity to make informed choices when selecting reading materials for the young. In addition, *CLR* provides researchers of children's literature with easy access to a wide variety of critical information from English-language sources in the field. Users will find balanced overviews of the careers of the authors and illustrators of the books that children and young adults are reading; these entries, which contain excerpts from published criticism in books and periodicals, assist users by sparking ideas for papers and assignments and suggesting supplementary and classroom reading. Ann L. Kalkhoff, president and editor of *Children's Book Review Service Inc.,* writes that "*CLR* has filled a gap in the field of children's books, and it is one series that will never lose its validity or importance."

Scope of the Series

Each volume of *CLR* profiles the careers of a selection of authors and illustrators of books for children and young adults from preschool through high school. Author lists in each volume reflect:

- an international scope.
- representation of authors of all eras.
- the variety of genres covered by children's and/or YA literature: picture books, fiction, nonfiction, poetry, folklore, and drama.

Although the focus of the series is on authors new to *CLR*, entries will be updated as the need arises.

Organization of This Book

An entry consists of the following elements: author heading, author portrait, author introduction, excerpts of criticism (each preceded by a bibliographical citation), and illustrations, when available.

- The **Author Heading** consists of the author's name followed by birth and death dates. The portion of the name outside the parentheses denotes the form under which the author is most frequently published. If the majority of the author's works for children were written under a pseudonym, the pseudonym will be listed in the author heading and the real name given on the first line of the author introduction. Also located at the beginning of the introduction are any other pseudonyms used by the author in writing for children and any name variations, including transliterated forms for authors whose languages use nonroman alphabets. Uncertainty as to a birth or death date is indicated by question marks.
- An **Author Portrait** is included when available.
- The **Author Introduction** contains information designed to introduce an author to *CLR* users by presenting an overview of the author's themes and styles, biographical facts that relate to the author's literary career or critical responses to the author's works, and information about major awards and prizes the author has received. The introduction begins by identifying the nationality of the author and by listing the genres in which s/he has written for children and young adults. Introductions also list a group of representative titles for which the author or illustrator being profiled is best known; this section, which begins with the words "major works include," follows the genre line of the introduction. For seminal figures, a listing of major works about the author follows when appropriate, highlighting important biographies about the author or illustrator that are not excerpted in the entry. The centered heading "Introduction" announces the body of the text.

- **Criticism** is located in three sections: **Author's Commentary** (when available), **General Commentary** (when available), and **Title Commentary** (commentary on specific titles).

  - The **Author's Commentary** presents background material written by the author or by an interviewer. This commentary may cover a specific work or several works. Author's commentary on more than one work appears after the author introduction, while commentary on an individual book follows the title entry heading.

  - The **General Commentary** consists of critical excerpts that consider more than one work by the author or illustrator being profiled. General commentary is preceded by the critic's name in boldface type or, in the case of unsigned criticism, by the title of the journal. *CLR* also features entries that emphasize general criticism on the oeuvre of an author or illustrator. When appropriate, a selection of reviews is included to supplement the general commentary.

  - The **Title Commentary** begins with the title entry headings, which precede the criticism on a title and cite publication information on the work being reviewed. Title headings list the title of the work as it appeared in its first English-language edition. The first English-language publication date of each work (unless otherwise noted) is listed in parentheses following the title. Differing U.S. and British titles follow the publication date within the parentheses. When a work is written by an individual other than the one being profiled, as is the case when illustrators are featured, the parenthetical material following the title cites the author of the work before listing its publication date.

    Entries in each title commentary section consist of critical excerpts on the author's individual works, arranged chronologically by publication date. The entries generally contain two to seven reviews per title, depending on the stature of the book and the amount of criticism it has generated. The editors select titles that reflect the entire scope of the author's literary contribution, covering each genre and subject. An effort is made to reprint criticism that represents the full range of each title's reception, from the year of its initial publication to current assessments. Thus, the reader is provided with a record of the author's critical history. Publication information (such as publisher names and book prices) and parenthetical numerical references (such as footnotes or page and line references to specific editions of works) have been deleted at the discretion of the editors to provide smoother reading of the text.

- Centered headings introduce each section, in which criticism is arranged chronologically; beginning with Volume 35, each excerpt is preceded by a boldface source heading for easier access by readers. Within the text, titles by authors being profiled are also highlighted in boldface type.

- Selected excerpts are preceded by **Explanatory Annotations,** which provide information on the critic or work of criticism to enhance the reader's understanding of the excerpt.

- A complete **Bibliographical Citation** designed to facilitate the location of the original book or article precedes each piece of criticism.

- Numerous **Illustrations** are featured in *CLR*. For entries on illustrators, an effort has been made to include illustrations that reflect the characteristics discussed in the criticism. Entries on authors who do not illustrate their own works may also include photographs and other illustrative material pertinent to their careers.

Special Features: Entries on Illustrators

Entries on authors who are also illustrators will occasionally feature commentary on selected works illustrated but not written by the author being profiled. These works are strongly associated with the illustrator and have received critical acclaim for their art. By including critical comment on works of this type, the editors wish to provide a more complete representation of the artist's career. Criticism on these works has been chosen to stress artistic, rather than literary, contributions. Title entry headings for works illustrated by the author being profiled are arranged chronologically within the entry by date of publication and include notes identifying the author of the illustrated work. In order to provide easier access for users, all titles illustrated by the subject of the entry are boldfaced.

CLR also includes entries on prominent illustrators who have contributed to the field of children's literature. These entries are designed to represent the development of the illustrator as an artist rather than as a literary stylist. The illustrator's section is organized like that of an author, with two exceptions: the introduction presents an overview of the illustrator's styles and techniques rather than outlining his or her literary background, and the commentary written by the illustrator on his or her works is called "illustrator's commentary" rather than "author's commentary." All titles of books containing illustrations by the artist being profiled are highlighted in boldface type.

Other Features: Acknowledgments, Indexes

- The **Acknowledgments** section, which immediately follows the preface, lists the sources from which material has been reprinted in the volume. It does not, however, list every book or periodical consulted for the volume.

- The **Cumulative Index to Authors** lists all of the authors who have appeared in *CLR* with cross-references to the biographical, autobiographical, and literary criticism series published by Gale Research. A full listing of the series titles appears before the first page of the indexes of this volume.

- The **Cumulative Index to Nationalities** lists authors alphabetically under their respective nationalities. Author names are followed by the volume number(s) in which they appear.

- The **Cumulative Index to Titles** lists titles covered in *CLR* followed by the volume and page number where criticism begins.

A Note to the Reader

CLR is one of several critical references sources in the Literature Criticism Series published by The Gale Group. When writing papers, students who quote directly from any volume in the Literature Criticism Series may use the following general forms to footnote reprinted criticism. The first example pertains to material drawn from periodicals, the second to material reprinted from books.

[1]T. S. Eliot, "John Donne," *The Nation and the Athenaeum,* 33 (9 June 1923), 321-32; excerpted and reprinted in *Literature Criticism from 1400 to 1800,* Vol. 10, ed. James E. Person, Jr. (Detroit: Gale Research, 1989), pp. 28-9.

[1]Henry Brooke, *Leslie Brooke and Johnny Crow* (Frederick Warne, 1982); excerpted and reprinted in *Children's Literature Review,* Vol. 20, ed. Gerard J. Senick (Detroit: Gale Research, 1990), p. 47.

Suggestions Are Welcome

In response to various suggestions, several features have been added to *CLR* since the beginning of the series, including author entries on retellers of traditional literature as well as those who have been the first to record oral tales and other folklore; entries on prominent illustrators featuring commentary on their styles and techniques; entries on authors whose works are considered controversial; occasional entries devoted to criticism on a single work or a series of works; sections in author introductions that list major works by and about the author or illustrator being profiled; explanatory notes that provide information on the critic or work of criticism to enhance the usefulness of the excerpt; more extensive illustrative material, such as holographs of manuscript pages and photographs of people and places pertinent to the careers of the authors and artists; a cumulative nationality index for easy access to authors by nationality; and occasional guest essays written specifically for *CLR* by prominent critics on subjects of their choice.

Readers who wish to suggest authors to appear in future volumes, or who have other suggestions, are cordially invited to contact the editor. By mail: Editor, *Children's Literature Review,* The Gale Group, 27500 Drake Road, Farmington Hills, MI 48331-3535; by telephone: (800) 347-GALE; by fax: (248) 699-8065.

Acknowledgments

The editors wish to thank the copyright holders of the excerpted criticism included in this volume and the permissions managers of many book and magazine publishing companies for assisting us in securing reproduction rights. We are also grateful to the staffs of the Detroit Public Library, the Library of Congress, the University of Detroit Mercy Library, Wayne State University Purdy/Kresge Library Complex, and the University of Michigan Libraries for making their resources available to us. Following is a list of the copyright holders who have granted us permission to reproduce material in this volume of ***CLR.*** Every effort has been made to trace copyright, but if omissions have been made, please let us know.

COPYRIGHTED EXCERPTS IN *CLR,* VOLUME 52, WERE REPRODUCED FROM THE FOLLOWING PERIODICALS:

The ALAN Review, v. 10, Spring, 1983; v. 10, Winter, 1983. Both reproduced by permission.—***Best Sellers,*** v. 29, January 1, 1970. Copyright 1970, by the University of Scranton. Reproduced by permission.—***Book Window,*** v. 6, Winter, 1978; v. 8, Winter, 1980. © 1978, 1980 S.C.B.A. and contributors. Both reproduced by permission. —***Booklist,*** v. 76, April 15, 1980; v. 77, February, 15, 1981; v. 77, April 15, 1981; v. 78, May 1, 1982; v. 78, August, 1982; v. 80, May 1, 1984; v. 82, January 1, 1986; v. 83, January 15, 1987; v. 84, November 1, 1987; v. 85, February 15, 1989; v. 85, April 1, 1989; v. 88, September 1, 1991; v. 88, April 1, 1992; v. 89, December 15, 1992; v. 89, February 1, 1993; v. 89, March 15, 1993; v. 89, May 1, 1993; v. 89, May 15, 1993; v. 90, November 15, 1993; v. 90, February 1, 1994; v. 91, July, 1995; v. 92, January 1, 1996; v. 92, March 1, 1996; v. 92, April 1, 1996; v. 93, October 15, 1996; v. 93, April 1, 1997. Copyright © 1980, 1981, 1982, 1984, 1986, 1987, 1989, 1991, 1992, 1993, 1994, 1995, 1996, 1997 by the American Library Association. All reproduced by permission.—***The Booklist,*** v. 67, November 15, 1970; v. 67, January 1, 1971; v. 67, May 1, 1971; v. 68, January 1, 1972; v. 70, October 15, 1973; v. 70, July 15, 1974; v. 72, October 15, 1975. Copyright © 1970, 1971, 1972, 1973, 1974, 1975 by the American Library Association. All reproduced by permission.—***The Booklist and Subscription Books Bulletin,*** v. 61, July 1, 1965; v. 65, February 1, 1969. Copyright © 1965, 1969 by the American Library Association. Both reproduced by permission.—***Books for Keeps,*** September, 1987; January, 1992. © School Bookshop Association 1987, 1992. Both reproduced by permission.—***Books for Young People,*** v. 1, June, 1987 for reviews of "Zanu" and "The Fusion Factor" by Leslie McGrath; v. 1, December, 1987 for a review of "Lisa" by Kenneth Oppel; v. 2, February, 1988 for a review of "Me, Myself and I" by Adele Ashby. All reproduced by permission of the respective authors.—***Books for Your Children,*** v. 14, Summer, 1984; v. 21, Spring, 1986; v. 24, Spring, 1989; v. 27, Autumn-Winter, 1992. © *Books for Your Children* 1984, 1986, 1989, 1992. All reproduced by permission.—***Books in Canada,*** v. 16, March, 1987 for "Back to the Future" by Mary Ainslie Smith; v. 17, April, 1988 for "Doers and Seekers" by Welwyn Wilton Katz; v. 18, December, 1989 for "A Boatload of Babies" by Linda Granfield; v. 22, October, 1993 for "Roads to Maturity" by Pat Barclay; v. 23, December, 1994 for "Inspired Lessons" by Pat Barclay; v. 25, October, 1996 for a review of "The Primrose Path" by Olga Stein. All reproduced by permission of the respective authors.—***Bulletin of the Center for Children's Books,*** v. XVII, June, 1964; v. XVIII, September, 1964; v. XVIII, June, 1965; v. 19, September, 1965; v. 22, January, 1969; v. 22, May, 1969; v. 23, February, 1970; v. 23, April, 1970; v. 24, November, 1970; v. 25, January, 1972; v. 27, March, 1974; v. 28, November, 1974; v. 28, February, 1975; v. 29, January, 1976; v. 30, December, 1976; v. 32, May, 1979; v. 33, December, 1979; v. 34, February, 1981; v. 35, September, 1981; v. 36, September, 1982; v. 36, March, 1983; v. 37, December, 1983; v. 37, April, 1984; v. 40, July-August, 1987; v. 44, January, 1991; v. 46, November, 1992; v. 46, April, 1993. Copyright © 1964, 1965, 1969, 1970, 1972, 1974, 1975, 1976, 1979, 1981, 1982, 1983,1984, 1987, 1991, 1992, 1993 by The University of Chicago. All reproduced by permission. / v. 47, February, 1994; v. 47, May, 1994; v. 48, December, 1994; v. 48, June, 1995; v. 49, April, 1996; v. 49, July-August, 1996; v. 50, February, 1997. Copyright © 1994, 1995, 1996, 1997 by The Board of Trustees of the University of Illinois. All reproduced by permission.—***Canadian Children's Literature,*** n. 50, 1988; n. 59, 1990; v. 20, Spring, 1994; v. 20, Fall, 1994; v. 22, Summer, 1996; v. 23, Summer, 1997. Copyright © 1988, 1990, 1994, 1996, 1997 Canadian Children's Press. All reproduced by permission.—***Canadian Literature,*** n. 116, Spring, 1988 for "Real Issues" by David W. Atkinson; n. 117, Summer, 1988 for "Social Conscience" by Gwyneth Evans. Both reproduced by permission of the respective authors.—***Catholic Library World,*** v. 53, September, 1981; v. 54, November, 1982. Both reproduced by permission—***Children's Book Review,*** v. IV, Spring, 1974. © 1974 by Five Owls Press Ltd. All rights reserved. Reproduced by permission.—***Children's Book ReviewService Inc.,*** v. 2, October, 1973; v. 23, Spring, 1995; v. 24, Spring, 1996; v. 25, March, 1997. Copyright © 1973, 1995, 1996, 1997 *Children's Book Review Service Inc.* All reproduced by permission.—***Children's literature in education,*** v. 13, Summer, 1982 for a review of "This School Is Driving Me Crazy" by Geoff Fox. © 1982, Agathon Press, Inc. Reproduced by permission of the publisher and the author.—***The Christian Science Monitor,*** October 14, 1980 for a review of "Professor Noah's

Spaceship" by Kristina L. C. Lindborg; July 1, 1981 for a review of "Does This School Have Capital Punishment?" by Rosalie E. Dunbar. © 1980, 1981 by the author. Both reproduced by permission of the respective authors. / June 24, 1965; November 7, 1968; July 3, 1974; November 6, 1974; December 4, 1978. © 1965, 1968, 1974, 1978 The Christian Science Publishing Society. All rights reserved. All reproduced by permission from *The Christian Science Monitor.* / May 10, 1956; May 9, 1957; November 5, 1959. © 1956, renewed 1984; © 1957, renewed 1985; © 1959, renewed 1987 The Christian Science Publishing Society. All rights reserved. All reproduced by permission from *The Christian Science Monitor.* —***CM: A Reviewing Journal of Canadian Materials for Young People,*** v. XVI, July, 1988; v. XVIII, May, 1990; v. XX, May, 1992; v. XX, September, 1992; v. XXII, May-June, 1994. Copyright 1988, 1990, 1992, 1994 The Canadian Library Association. All reproduced by permission of the Manitoba Library Association.—***English Journal,*** v. 59, December, 1970 for a review of "Touching" by John W. Conner; v. 61, February, 1972 for a review of "Sleep Two, Three, Four!" by John W. Conner. Copyright © 1970, 1972 by the National Council of Teachers of English. Both reproduced by permission of the publisher and the author. / v. 58, May, 1969. Copyright © 1969 by the National Council of Teachers of English. Reproduced by permission.—***The Five Owls,*** v. III, August, 1989. Reproduced by permission.—***Growing Point,*** v. 5, July, 1966 for a review of "The World of Jazz" by Margery Fisher; v. 12, January, 1974 for a review of "The Pushcart War" by Margery Fisher; v. 18, November, 1979 for a review of "Hunter and His Dog" by Margery Fisher; v. 20, March, 1982 for a review of "Bear's Adventure" by Margery Fisher; v. 23, July, 1984 for a review of "Daisy" by Margery Fisher; v. 24, March, 1986 for a review of "The Day They Came to Arrest the Book" by Margery Fisher; v. 25, May, 1986 for a review of "Does This School Have Capital Punishment?" by Margery Fisher; v. 25, January, 1987 for a review of "Goat's Trail" by Margery Fisher; v. 28, November, 1989 for a review of "A Christmas Story" by Margery Fisher; v. 30, January, 1992 for a review of "Animal Tricks" and "Animal Seasons" by Margery Fisher. All reproduced by permission of the Literary Estate of Margery Fisher.—***The Horn Book Guide to Children's & Young Adult Books,*** v. VI, Fall, 1996; v. VIII, Spring, 1997. Copyright, 1996, 1997, by The Horn Book, Inc., 11 Beacon St., Suite 1000, Boston, MA 02108. All rights reserved. Both reproduced by permission.—***The Horn Book Magazine,*** v. XL, August, 1964; v. XLI, October, 1965; v. XLII, October, 1966; v. XLV, April, 1969; v. L, October, 1974; v. LVII, February, 1981; v. LVII, August, 1981; v. LVIII, December, 1982; v. LX, August, 1984; v. LXII, January-February, 1986; v. LXIII, May-June, 1987; v. LXIV, March, 1988; v. LXV, May-June, 1989; v. LXVII, January-February, 1991. Copyright, 1964, 1965, 1966, 1969, 1974, 1981, 1982, 1984, 1986, 1987, 1988, 1989, 1991, by The Horn Book, Inc., 11 Beacon St., Suite 1000, Boston, MA 02108. All rights reserved. All reproduced by permission. / v. XXXII, April, 1956; v. XXXIII, June, 1957; v. XXXVI, June, 1960; v. XXXVI, October, 1960. Copyright, 1956, renewed 1984; copyright, 1957, renewed 1985; copyright, 1960, renewed 1988 by The Horn Book, Inc., 11 Beacon St., Suite 1000, Boston, MA 02108. All rights reserved. All reproduced by permission.—***Interracial Books for Children Bulletin,*** v. 14, 1983 for a review of "The Day They Came to Arrest the Book" by Albert V. Schwartz. Reproduced by permission of the author.—***Journal of American Culture,*** v. 10, Winter, 1987. Copyright © 1987 by Ray B. Browne. Reproduced by permission.—***The Junior Bookshelf,*** v. 30, June, 1966; v. 37, December, 1973; v. 41, June, 1977; v. 42, June, 1978; v. 43, February, 1979; v. 43, August, 1979; v. 45, April, 1981; v. 45, June, 1981; v. 46, February, 1982; v. 50, February, 1986; v. 51, February, 1987; v. 53, February, 1989; v. 54, February, 1990; v. 57, August, 1993; v. 58, February, 1994; v. 58, December, 1994. All reproduced by permission.—***Kirkus Reviews,*** v. XXXVII, October 15, 1969; v. XXXVIII, October 15, 1970; v. XXXIX, August 15, 1971; v. XLI, August 1, 1973; v. XLII, July 15, 1974; v. XLIII, November 15, 1975; v. XLVI, December 15, 1978; v. XLVII, February 1, 1979; v. XLVIII, January 1, 1980; v. XLIX, February 15, 1981; v. XLIX, October 1, 1981; v. L, September 15, 1982; v. LI, April 15, 1983; v. LI, June 15, 1983; v. LII, March 1, 1984; v. LV, July 1, 1987; v. LVII, November 15, 1989; v. LVIII, October 15, 1990; v. LX, September 15, 1992; v. LXII, January 1, 1994; v. LXII, November 15, 1994; v. LXIII, May 15, 1995; v. LXIII, September 15, 1995; v. LXIV, December 15, 1996; v. LXIV, April 15, 1996. Copyright © 1969, 1970, 1971, 1973, 1974, 1975, 1978, 1979, 1980, 1981, 1982, 1983, 1984, 1987, 1989, 1990, 1992, 1994, 1995, 1996 The Kirkus Service, Inc. All rights reserved. All reproduced by permission of the publisher, *Kirkus Reviews* and Kirkus Associates, L.P.—***Kirkus Service,*** v. XXXVI, October 15, 1968; v. XXXVI, November 1, 1968. Copyright © 1968 The Kirkus Service, Inc. All rights reserved. Both reproduced by permission of the publisher, *Kirkus Service* and Kirkus Associates, L.P.—***Kliatt,*** v. 32, July, 1998. Copyright © 1998 by Kliatt Paperback Book Guide. Reproduced by permission.—***Language Arts,*** v. 70, March, 1973 for a review of "The Girl Who Loved Caterpillars" by Junko Yokota; v. 60, September, 1983 for a review of "Pelican" by Ronald A. Jobe. Copyright © 1973, 1983 by theNational Council of Teachers of English. Both reproduced by permission of the publisher and the respective authors.—***Library Journal,*** v. 94, July, 1969. Copyright © 1969 by Reed Publishing, USA, Division of Reed Holdings, Inc. / v. 89, July, 1964 for a review of "The Pushcart War" by Harriet B. Quimby; v. 96, June 15, 1971 for a review of "How Many Kids Are Hiding on My Block?" by Cary M. Ormond; v. 98, July, 1973 for a review of "Freddy's Book" by Pamela D. Pollack; v. 98, October 15, 1973 for a review of "For All the Wrong Reasons" by Cynthia Harrison. Copyright © 1964, 1971, 1973 by Reed Publishing, USA, Division of Reed Holdings, Inc. All reproduced by permission of the respective authors.—***The Lion and the Unicorn,*** v. 1, 1977; v. 3, Winter, 1979-80. © 1977, 1980. Both reproduced by permission of The Johns Hopkins University Press.—***The New England Quarterly,*** v. 41, June, 1968 for "Transcendentalism for American Youth: The Children's Books of Kate Douglas Wiggin" by Fred Erisman. Copyright 1968 by *The New England Quarterly.* Reproduced by permission of the publisher and the author.—***The New***

York Herald Tribune Book Review, November 11, 1951. Copyright 1951, renewed 1979 by The New York Times Company. Reproduced by permission. / May 6, 1956; May 26, 1957; November 1, 1959; November 13, 1960. Copyright © 1956, renewed 1984; copyright © 1957, renewed 1985; copyright © 1959, renewed 1987; copyright © 1960, renewed 1988 by The New York Times Company. All reproduced by permission.—***The New York Times Book Review,*** July 12, 1964; May 9, 1965; November 3, 1968; May 4, 1969; October 26, 1969; November 16, 1969; November 29, 1970; December 6, 1970; November 7, 1971; January 30, 1977; January 14, 1979; July 26, 1981; March 6, 1983; May 21, 1989; December 2, 1990; May 17, 1992. Copyright © 1964, 1965, 1968, 1969, 1970, 1971, 1977, 1979, 1981, 1983, 1989, 1990, 1992 by The New York Times Company. All reproduced by permission. / March 2, 1957; April 3, 1960; May 8, 1960. Copyright © 1957, renewed 1985; copyright © 1960, renewed 1988 by The New York Times Company. All reproduced by permission.—***Publishers Weekly,*** v. 192, November 20, 1967; v. 194, September 2, 1968; v. 196, December 29, 1969; v. 200, September 20, 1971; v. 200, November 1, 1971; v. 203, May 28, 1973; v. 204, October 29, 1973; v. 206, July 8, 1974; v. 210, August 16, 1976; v. 210, November 22, 1976; v. 214, September 20, 1978; v. 214, December 25, 1978; v. 215, April 2, 1979; v. 217, January 11, 1980; v. 218, December 26, 1980; v. 220, October 2, 1981; v. 223, March 25, 1983; v. 223, June 10, 1983. Copyright © 1967, 1968, 1969, 1971, 1973, 1974, 1976, 1978, 1979, 1980, 1981, 1983 by Xerox Corporation. All reproduced from *Publishers Weekly,* published by R. R. Bowker Company, a Xerox company, by permission. / v. 228, September 20, 1985; v. 230, August 22, 1986; v. 231, June 12, 1987; v. 235, February 10, 1989; v. 238, September 13, 1991; v. 239, February 10, 1992; v. 239, October 12, 1992; v. 240, January 25, 1993; v. 240, April 19, 1993; v. 240, September 6, 1993; v. 241, October 17, 1994; v. 242, May 29, 1995; v. 243, February 12, 1996; v. 243, April 15, 1996; v. 244, January 13, 1997. Copyright 1985, 1986, 1987, 1989, 1991, 1992, 1993, 1994, 1995, 1996, 1997 by Reed Publishing USA. All reproduced from *Publishers Weekly,* published by the Bowker Magazine Group of Cahners Publishing Co., a division of Reed Publishing USA.—***Quill and Quire,*** v. 57, October, 1991 for a review of "The Race" by Anne Louise Mahoney; v. 58, September, 1992 for a review of "The Girl Who Loved Caterpillars" by Joanne Schott; v. 59, February, 1993 for a review of "Daniel's Story" by Kenneth Oppel; v. 59, October, 1993 for a review of "Safari Adventure in Legoland" by Fred Boer; v. 60, December, 1994 for a review of "Of Two Minds" by Joanne Findon; v. 61, November, 1995 for a review of "The Primrose Path" by J. R. Wytenbroek; v. 62, October, 1996 for a review of "After the War" by Teresa Toten; v. 63, March, 1997 for a review of "The Freak" by Sarah Ellis; v. 63, September, 1997 for a review of "The Garden" by Gwyneth Evans. All reproduced by permission of the respective authors. / v. 60, February, 1994; v. 61, February, 1995. Both reproduced by permission.—***Resource Links,*** v. 1, April, 1996; v. 3, October, 1997; v. 3, December, 1997. Copyright © 1996, 1997, Council for Canadian Learning Resources. All reproduced by permission. http://acs6.acs.ucalgary.ca/˜dkbrown/rl/.—***The School Librarian,*** v. 14, July, 1966; v. 27, December, 1979; v. 30, March, 1982; v. 32, March, 1984; v. 34, June, 1986; v. 37, February, 1989; v. 38, May, 1990; v. 42, November, 1994; v. 45, February, 1997. All reproduced by permission.—***School Library Journal,*** v. 10, May, 1964; v. 12, November, 1965; v. 13, October, 1966; v. 16, January, 1969; v. 16, February, 1970; v. 16, April, 1970; v. 17, October, 1970; v. 17, November, 1970; v. 17, December, 1970; v. 18, October, 1971; v. 18, December, 1971; v. 19, September, 1972; v. 20, September, 1973; v. 20, May, 1974; v. 23, February, 1977; v. 25, February, 1979; v. 27, April, 1981; v. 28, August, 1982; v. 29, August, 1983; v. 30, September, 1983; v. 30, August, 1984; v. 32, October, 1985; v. 32, January, 1986; v. 33, March, 1987; v. 34, September, 1987; v. 35, February, 1989; v. 35, May, 1989; v. 35, October, 1989; v. 36, December, 1990; v. 38, September, 1992; v. 39, January, 1993; v. 39, December, 1993; v. 40, January, 1994; v. 40, April, 1994; v. 40, September, 1994; v. 41, July, 1995; v. 41, October, 1995; v. 42, February, 1996; v. 42, May, 1996; v. 42, July, 1996; v. 42, October, 1996; v. 42, November, 1996; v. 43, May, 1997. Copyright © 1964, 1965, 1966, 1969, 1970, 1971, 1972, 1973, 1974, 1977, 1979, 1981, 1982, 1983, 1984, 1985, 1986, 1987, 1989, 1990, 1992, 1993, 1994, 1995, 1996, 1997. All reproduced from *School Library Journal,* a Cahners/R. R. Bowker Publication, by permission.—***Science Books: A Quarterly Review,*** v. 8, May, 1972. Copyright 1972 by AAAS. Reproduced by permission.—***The Times,*** London, December 19, 1989 for"Loss of Innocence" by Brian Alderson. © 1989 by Brian Alderson. Reproduced by permission of the author.—***The Times Educational Supplement,*** n. 3369, January 16, 1981 for "Tiger Cubs Wrestle" by Peter Fanning; n. 3460, October 22, 1982 for "Nursery Joke" by Naomi Lewis. © The Times Supplements Limited 1981, 1982. Both reproduced by permission of the respective authors. / n. 4144, December 1, 1995. © The Times Supplements Limited 1995. Reproduced from *The Times Educational Supplement* by permission.—***The Times Literary Supplement,*** n. 3351, May 19, 1966; n. 3915, March 25, 1977; n. 4069, March 27, 1981; n. 4308, October 25, 1985; n. 4313, November 29, 1985. © The Times Supplements Limited 1966, 1977, 1981, 1985. All reproduced from *The Times Literary Supplement* by permission.—***Virginia Kirkus' Service,*** v. XXXIII, March 1, 1965. Copyright © 1965 The Kirkus Service, Inc. All rights reserved. Reproduced by permission of the publisher, *Virginia Kirkus' Service* and Kirkus Associates, L.P.—***Voice of Youth Advocates,*** v. 5, October, 1982; v. 5, February, 1983; v. 10, April, 1987; v. 18, October, 1995; v. 19, June, 1996; v. 19, February, 1997; v. 20, June, 1997; v. 21, October, 1998. Copyrighted 1982, 1983, 1987, 1995, 1996, 1997, 1998 by *Voice of Youth Advocates.* All reproduced by permission.—***Wilson Library Bulletin,*** v. 51, April, 1977 for a review of "Sunday Father" by Michael McCue and Evie Wilson; v. 55, March, 1981 for a review of "The Young Adult Perplex" by Patty Campbell; v. 62, March, 1992 for a review of "The Snow Country Prince" by Donnarae MacCann and Olga Richard; v. 63, June, 1993 for a review of "Carousel" by Donnarae MacCann and Olga Richard; v. 69, October, 1994 for a review of "Jack and the Meanstalk" by Donnarae MacCann and Olga Richard. All reproduced by permission of the respective authors.

COPYRIGHTED EXCERPTS IN *CLR,* VOLUME 52, WERE REPRODUCED FROM THE FOLLOWING BOOKS OR PAMPHLETS:

Arbuthnot, May Hill. From ***Children and Books***. Scott, Foresman, 1947. Copyright 1947 by May Hill Arbuthnot. Renewed 1974 by Scott, Foresman and Company.—Bloom, Harold. From ***Blake's Apocalypse: A Study in Poetic Argument***. Doubleday & Company, Inc., 1963. Copyright © 1963, renewed 1971 by Harold Bloom. All rights reserved. Reproduced by permission of Doubleday, a division of Random House, Inc. In the British Commonwealth by permission of the author.—Bowra, C. M. From ***The Romantic Imagination***. Cambridge, Mass.: Harvard University Press, 1949. Copyright 1949 by the President and Fellows of Harvard College. Renewed © 1977 by the Literary Estate of Cecil Maurice Bowra. All rights reserved. Reproduced by permission of the publishers.—Damon, S. Foster. From ***A Blake Dictionary: The Ideas and Symbols of William Blake***. Brown University Press, 1965. Copyright © 1965 by Brown University. All rights reserved. Reproduced by permission.—Darton, F. J. Harvey. From ***Children's Books in England: Five Centuries of Social Life***. Second edition. Cambridge at the University Press, 1958. Reproduced with the permission of Cambridge University Press.—David, Michael. From ***William Blake: A New Kind of Man***. University of California Press, 1977. Copyright © 1977 Michael Davis. All rights reserved. Reproduced by permission.—Frye, Northrop. From ***Fearful Symmetry: A Study of William Blake.*** Princeton University Press, 1947. Copyright 1947 by Princeton University Press. Renewed 1974 by Northrop Frye. All rights reserved. Reproduced by permission.—Gillham, D. G. From ***Blake's Contrary States: The "Songs of Innocence and of Experience" As Dramatic Poems***. Cambridge at the University Press, 1966. © Cambridge University Press 1966. Reproduced with the permission of Cambridge University Press.—Hirsch, E. D., Jr. From ***Innocence and Experience: An Introduction to Blake.*** Yale University Press, 1964. Copyright © 1964 by Yale University Press. All rights reserved. Reproduced by permission of the author.—Holloway, John. From ***Blake: The Lyric of Poetry***. Edward Arnold (Publishers) Ltd., 1968. © John Holloway 1968. Reproduced by permission.—Jones, Cornelia and Olivia R. Way. From ***British Children's Authors: Interviews at Home***. American Library Association, 1976. Copyright © 1976 by the American Library Association. Reproduced by permission.—Leader, Zachary. From ***Reading Blake's "Songs."*** Routledge & Kegan Paul, 1981. Copyright © Zachary Leader 1981. Reproduced by permission.—Lincoln, Andrew. From an introduction to ***Songs of Innocence and of Experience,*** by William Blake. Edited by Andrew Lincoln. The William Blake Trust / The Tate Gallery, 1991, William Blake Trust/Princeton University Press, 1991. © 1991 The Tate Gallery and the William Blake Trust. Reproduced by permission.—Lister, Raymond. From ***William Blake: An Introduction to the Man and to His Work,*** G. Bell and Sons, Ltd., 1968. Copyright © 1968 by G. Bell and Sons, Ltd. Reproduced by permission.—MacLeod, Anne Scott. From "The 'Caddie Woodlawn' Syndrome: American Girlhood in the Nineteenth Century," in ***A Century of Childhood: 1820-1920.*** Edited by Mary Lynn Stevens Heininger & others. The Margaret Woodbury Strong Museum, 1984. Copyright © 1984 by The Margaret Woodbury Strong Museum. All rights reserved. Reproduced by permission of Strong Museum, Rochester, NY.—Moore, Annie E. From ***Literature Old and New for Children: Materials for a College Course***. Houghton Mifflin Company, 1934. Copyright, 1934, by Annie E. Moore. Renewed 1961 by Dan S. Hammock, Jr. Reproduced by permission of Houghton Mifflin Company.—Norton, Sybil, and John Cournos. From ***Famous BritishPoets***. Dodd, Mead & Company, 1952. Copyright, 1952, by John Cournos and Sybil Norton. All rights reserved.—Thwaite, Mary F. From ***Primer to Pleasure in Reading***. The Horn Book, Inc., 1972. Copyright © 1963 by Mary F. Thwaite. All rights reserved.—Townsend, John Rowe. From ***Written for Children: An Outline of English-Language***. Sixth edition. Scarecrow Press, 1996. Copyright © 1965, 1974, 1983, 1987, 1990, 1995, 1996 by John Rowe Townsend. All rights reserved.

ILLUSTRATIONS APPEARING IN *CLR,* VOLUME 52, WERE REPRODUCED FROM THE FOLLOWING SOURCES:

Blake, William, illustrator. From an illustration in ***English Romantic Writers,*** edited by David Perkins. Harcourt Brace, 1967. © 1967 by Harcourt Brace Jovanovich, Inc.—Blake, William, illustrator. From illustrations in ***William Blake at the Huntington,*** by Robert N. Essick. Harry N. Abrams Inc., Publishers, and The Henry E. Huntington Library and Art Gallery, 1994. Copyright © 1994 The Henry E. Huntington Library and Art Gallery.—Gillespie, Jessie, illustrator. From an illustration in ***The Birds' Christmas Carol,*** by Kate Douglas Wiggin. Houghton Mifflin, 1941. Copyright, 1941, by Houghton Mifflin Company.—Grose, Helen Mason, illustrator. From illustrations in ***Rebecca of Sunnybrook Farm,*** by Kate Douglas Wiggin. Houghton Mifflin Company, 1925.—Waldman, Neil, illustrator. From an illustration in ***The Tyger,*** by William Blake. Harcourt Brace & Company, 1993. Illustrations © 1993 by Neil Waldman. Reproduced by permission of Harcourt Brace & Company.—Wildsmith, Brian, illustrator. From an illustration in ***The Circus,*** by Brian Wildsmith. Oxford University Press, 1970. © Brian Wildsmith 1970. Reproduced by permission of the illustrator.—Wildsmith, Brian, illustrator. From an illustration in ***Goat's Trail,*** by Brian Wildsmith. Oxford, 1986. Copyright © 1986 by Brian Wildsmith. Reproduced by permission of Oxford University Press.—Wildsmith, Brian, and Rebecca Wildsmith, illustrators. From an illustration in ***Whose Hat Was***

That? by Brian Wildsmith and Rebecca Wildsmith. Oxford, 1993. Copyright © 1993 by Brian and Rebecca Wildsmith. Reproduced by permission of Oxford University Press.—Wildsmith, Brian, illustrator. From an illustration in ***Saint Francis,*** by Brian Wildsmith. Oxford, 1995. © 1995 Brian Wildsmith. Reproduced by permission of Oxford University Press.

PHOTOGRAPHS APPEARING IN *CLR,* VOLUME 52, WERE REPRODUCED FROM THE FOLLOWING SOURCES:

Blake, William, engraving. Corbis-Bettmann. Reproduced by permission.—Hentoff, Nat, photograph. Reproduced by permission of Nat Hentoff.—Matas, Carol, photograph by Peter Tittenberger. Reproduced by permission of Carol Matas.—Merrill, Jean, photograph by R. G. Seilbart. Reproduced by permission of Jean Merrill.—Neufeld, John, photograph. Reproduced by permission of John Neufeld.—Wiggin, Kate Douglas, photograph.—Wildsmith, Brian, photograph. Reproduced by permission of Brian Wildsmith.

Children's Literature Review

William Blake

1757-1827

English author, poet, painter, illustrator, and engraver.

Major works include *Poetical Sketches* (1783), *Songs of Innocence,* (1789), expanded edition printed as *Songs of Innocence and of Experience* (1794), *The Marriage of Heaven and Hell* (1793), *Milton: A Poem in Two Books* (1804), *Jerusalem: The Emanation of the Giant Albion,* (1804).

Major works about the author include *The Life of William Blake, Pictor Ignotus* (by Alexander Gilchrist, 1863), *William Blake* (by Algernon Charles Swinburne, 1867), *Fearful Symmetry: A Study of William Blake* (by Northrop Frye, 1947), *The Complete Writings of William Blake* (edited by Geoffrey Keynes, 1957), *Blake's Apocalypse: A Study in Poetic Argument* (by Harold Bloom, 1963), *William Blake: An Introduction to the Man and His Work* (by Raymond Lister, 1968), *William Blake: A New Kind of Man* (by Michael Davis, 1977), *William Blake: His Life* (by James King, 1991).

The following entry presents criticism on Blake's *Songs of Innocence and of Experience.*

INTRODUCTION

Famed English writer, visionary poet, and illustrator during the Romantic period, Blake is best known for his *Songs of Innocence and of Experience,* which he not only wrote but designed, engraved on copper, printed, bound, and hand-colored himself, thus establishing him as a pioneer picture book creator par excellence. Although Blake did not write or draw specifically for children, he has become a pivotal presence in contemporary interpretations of early children's literature. Blake was, as Alan Richardson commented in *Dictionary of Literary Biography,* a "brilliant adapter and implicit critic of the writing for children available in his time," and "an exemplar of what children's poetry and picture books could become." Diverging from such contemporaries as clergyman Issac Watts, whose moralistic writing advocated diligence and warned children against idleness, Blake endorsed the freedom for children and adults alike to imagine and dream. Although he was little recognized during his own lifetime, Blake has garnered praise for his skillful craftsmanship as an engraver and artist and for the visual and lyrical force of his "illuminated" poetry. His primary theme is the possibility of salvation, with a firm conviction in the redeeming qualities of one's imagination, and his language is rich with biblical symbolism. His denunciation of the harsh treatment of poor, working-class children by their so-called benefactors is an example of his unconventional social and political views. His *Songs of Innocence and of Experience* have been esteemed as models of prosody and his works have influenced later poets, such as William Butler Yeats. Blake's poetry continues to be recognized today in such new forms as Ellen Raskin's two-volume *Songs of Innocence* with her own woodcut prints and musical score (1966), Nancy Willard's Newbery and Caldecott award-winning *A Visit to William Blake's Inn: Poems for Innocent and Experienced Travelers* (1981), and Neil Waldman's picture book *The Tyger* (1993), not to mention the countless anthologies of poetry for children in which his poems appear.

Biographical Information

Blake was born in London on November 28, 1757, the second son of James and Catherine Blake's seven children. His father was a moderately successful hosier, selling stockings, gloves, and other accessories for men. Blake had visions of winged angels as a child that continued into his adulthood as visitations from Biblical personalities and poets. Taught to read and write at home, he was sent to drawing school at the age of ten, then apprenticed to an engraver at fourteen. Subsequent artwork and poetry were undoubtedly inspired by the Gothic atmosphere of Westminster Abbey, where the young William was sent to sketch tombstones for his master. In 1782, Blake married Catherine Boucher, whom he taught to read, write, and make prints of his engravings. Upon his father's death in 1784, Blake used part of his inheritance to start a print shop, which soon went out of business. After his beloved youngest brother Robert died, Blake had a vision that Robert visited him and showed him the technique of relief-etching or "illuminated writing," the method Blake used for all his books beginning with *There Is No Natural Religion* in 1788. The following year he wrote, illustrated, and printed his first book considered appropriate for children, the fantasy *The Book of Thel.* He also produced *Songs of Innocence,* while engraving for numerous other books and magazines on commission. He was hired by Mary Wollstonecraft to engrave drawings for a children's book, *Original Stories from Real Life,* in 1791, and he drew and engraved his own *For Children: The Gates of Paradise,* based on his brother Robert's sketchbook, in 1793. In 1794, Blake expanded his *Songs of Innocence* with more poems, calling the new book *Songs of Innocence and of Experience.*

In 1800, Blake moved to the seaside town of Felpham in Sussex at the invitation of poet William Hayley, who obtained engraving commissions for him. There, Blake taught himself Greek, Latin, Hebrew, and Italian so he could read the classics in their original language. He wrote his epic poem *Milton,* and in 1803, no longer able to endure Hayley's potboiler commissions and restrictions on his original work, he returned to London where he engraved and printed *Milton* together with *Jerusalem: The Emanation of the Giant Albion.* Several lean years followed, during which Blake received few engraving assignments—unable to gain acceptance for his artwork and often ridiculed as insane. In 1818, he met John Linnell, a young artist who helped him financially and created fresh interest in his work. A new patron, Thomas Butts, commissioned Blake for a series of watercolors on the *Book of Job,* which were engraved and printed in 1825 and won high acclaim. He was further commissioned to design illustrations for Dante's *Divine Comedy* but died before its completion. Although not widely recognized by his contemporaries, Blake achieved acclaim after the publication of Alexander Gilchrist's *Life of William Blake: Pictor Ignotus* in 1863. He has been hailed as an artist, a poet, and a prophet by such literary figures as A. C. Swinburne, Dante Gabriel Rossetti, and William Butler Yeats and has often been regarded by scholars as a forerunner in the children's picture book tradition. "William Blake," Anne Carroll Moore asserted in *New Roads to Childhood,* "was the first to see children, to feel childhood, and to so illuminate the record of what he saw and felt as to give children a place in the world they never held before."

Major Characteristics

Blake's *Songs of Innocence and of Experience* was originally composed of twenty-three illustrated, short lyric poems. It is considered an exemplar of the Romantic movement for its artistic championship of individuality and imagination and its condemnation of rationalist philosophy and social blight. Although Blake adopts the style of children's poetry, he betrays the seemingly straightforward form of the verses through his use of irony, symbolism, implied narrators, and other complicated devices. The work is prefaced with a subtitle page stating as its purpose, to show "the Two Contrary States of the Human Soul." It is subdivided into "Songs of Innocence" that generally reflect on the beauty of nature and the simple joys of childhood and the "Songs of Experience" that reveal the often sterner reality of eighteenth-century urban life. Each poem and its accompanying illustration was etched in relief on a single copper plate using a corrosive agent, such as nitric acid, and then hand-painted with watercolors that Blake mixed himself. Blake apparently did not find an absolute division between innocence and experience, and transferred four individual poems from the first section to the second. Scholars have noted that *Songs* evinces Blake's conviction that neither a wholly innocent nor experienced perspective is complete enough to understand the complexities of human life; rather, both are needed, as each balances the other, leading to a more comprehensive, imaginative vision.

The sequence begins with a wandering, pipe-playing young shepherd-poet who is inspired by a child, who appears to him perched on a cloud, to write a series of songs. Children are the main characters in three pairs of companion poems, both poems in each pair having the same title—one appearing in "Songs of Innocence" and the other in "Songs of Experience." These poems are "The Chimney Sweeper," "A Little Boy Lost," and "Holy Thursday." These and other "contraries" in Blake's sequence express two opposing perspectives of the same subject: one perspective relaying the simple joys (the enduring love of God and parents, pleasant dreams, the beauty of nature) and fears (losing a parent, darkness, coldness) of innocence and the other questioning social injustices, acknowledging the human repression and cruelty associated with experience. Best known of all the collection are "The Lamb" in "Songs of Innocence" and "The Tyger" in "Songs of Experience." "The Lamb," with its religious connotations of Jesus as child or sacrificial lamb, recalls such children's poems as Isaac Watts's *Divine Songs, Attempted in Easie Language for the Use of Children* (1715) and contemporary hymns. As for Blake's "Tyger," he not only represents experience as opposed to innocence, but exemplifies the infinite variety and power of creation and Christianity. In another vein, "The Little Black Boy," "London," and "On Another's Sorrow" take up issues of slavery, child labor, the urban poor, and restrictive conventions, representative of the socially conscious writers of the day. Blake has gained historical and critical significance, according to Alan Richardson, "as a creator of poems in children's forms virtually unrivaled for their high aesthetic standards, compelling rhythms and imagery, and subtle complexities."

COMMENTARY

Henry Crabb Robinson

SOURCE: A conversation with William Hazlitt in March, 1811, in his *Henry Crabb Robinson on Books and Their Writers,* Vol. 1, J. M. Dent and Sons Limited, 1938, p. 25.

[The following commentary is taken from Robinson's record of his conversation with William Hazlitt concerning Blake's Songs of Innocence and of Experience. *Hazlitt is considered one of the most important commentators of the Romantic age.]*

I showed Hazlitt Blake's *Young* ***[Songs of Innocence and of Experience]****.* He saw no merit in them as designs. I read him some of the poems. He was much struck with them and expressed himself with his usual strength and singularity. 'They are beautiful,' he said, 'and only too deep for the vulgar. He has no sense of the ludicrous, and, as to a God, a worm crawling in a privy is as worthy an object as any other, all being to him indifferent. So to Blake the Chimney Sweeper, etc. He is ruined by vain struggles to get rid of what presses on his brain—he attempts impossibles.' I added: 'He is like a man who lifts a burden too heavy for him; he bears it an instant, it then falls on and crushes him.'

Henry Crabb Robinson

SOURCE: "An Early Appreciation of William Blake," translated by K. A. Esdaile, in *The Library,* Vol. V, No. 19, July, 1914, pp. 255-56.

[Robinson, a journalist and later barrister by profession, is important to literature for his diaries and correspondence published on Blake, William Wordsworth, and other writers whose friendship he cultivated. Robinson first met Blake in 1825, drawing out his opinions on such topics as religion and literature and recording their conversations in his diary. Robinson's interest in Blake predates their meeting, however, as indicated by the following article, published in 1811 in the German periodical Vaterländisches Museum, *in which he briefly surveys* Songs of Innocence and of Experience *for the German public.]*

Of all the conditions which arouse the interest of the psychologist, none assuredly is more attractive than the union of genius and madness in single remarkable minds, which, while on the one hand they compel our admiration by their great mental powers, yet on the other move our pity by their claims to supernatural gifts. Of such is the whole race of ecstatics, mystics, seers of visions and dreamers of dreams, and to their list we have now to add another name, that of William Blake.

This extraordinary man, who is at this moment living in London, although more than fifty years of age, is only now beginning to emerge from the obscurity in which the singular bent of his talents and the eccentricity of his personal character have confined him. . . .

[A] more remarkable little book of poems by our author exists, which is only to be met with in the hands of collectors. It is a duodecimo entitled ***Songs of Innocence and Experience,*** *shewing the two contrary states of the human soul. The Author and printer W. Blake.* . . . It is not easy to form a comprehensive opinion of the text, since the poems deserve the highest praise and the gravest censure. Some are childlike songs of great beauty and simplicity; these are the ***Songs of Innocence,*** many of which, nevertheless, are excessively childish.

The ***Songs of Experience,*** on the other hand, are metaphysical riddles and mystical allegories. Among them are poetic pictures of the highest beauty and sublimity; and again there are poetical fancies which can scarcely be understood even by the initiated.

Samuel Taylor Coleridge

SOURCE: A letter to H. F. Cary on February 6, 1818, in his *Collected Letters of Samuel Taylor Coleridge: 1815-1819,* Vol. IV, edited by Earl Leslie Griggs, Oxford at the Clarendon Press, Oxford, 1959, pp. 832-34.

[Considered one of the greatest literary critics in the English language, Coleridge was central to the English Romantic movement as a poet and a critic. In the following letter addressed to H. F. Cary, Coleridge comments upon his first reading of Songs of Innocence and of Experience.*]*

I have this morning been reading a strange publication—viz. Poems with very wild and interesting pictures, as the swathing, etched (I suppose) but it is said—printed and painted by the Author, W. Blake. He is a man of Genius—and I apprehend, a Swedenborgian—certainly, a mystic *emphatically*. You perhaps smile at *my* calling another Poet, a *Mystic;* but verily I am in the very mire of common-sense compared with Mr Blake, apo- or rather ana-calyptic Poet, and Painter!

Charles Lamb

SOURCE: A letter to Bernard Barton on May 15, 1824, in his *The Letters of Charles Lamb,* Vol. II, edited by Alfred Ainger, A. C. Armstrong & Son, 1888, pp. 104-06.

[Lamb, a nineteenth-century English essayist, critic, poet, dramatist, and novelist, is chiefly remembered for his "Elia" essays, a series renowned for its witty, idiosyncratic treatment of everyday subjects. Under Lamb's auspices, Blake's poem "The Chimney Sweeper" *from* Songs of Innocence *was reprinted in an 1824 collection entitled* The Chimney

Sweeper's Friend, and Climbing Boy's Album. *The poem stirred the curiosity of Bernard Barton, whose request for information concerning Blake yielded the following response from Lamb.]*

Blake is a real name, I assure you, and a most extraordinary man, if he be still living. He is the Robert [sic] Blake, whose wild designs accompany a splendid folio edition of the "Night Thoughts," which you may have seen. . . . He paints in water colours marvellous strange pictures, visions of his brain, which he asserts that he has seen. They have great merit. He has *seen* the old Welsh bards on Snowdon—he has seen the Beautifullest, the strongest, and the Ugliest Man, left alone from the Massacre of the Britons by the Romans, and has painted them from memory (I have seen his paintings), and asserts them to be as good as the figures of Raphael and Angelo, but not better, as they had precisely the same retro-visions and prophetic visions with themself. . . . The painters in oil (which he will have it that neither of them practised) he affirms to have been the ruin of art, and affirms that all the while he was engaged in his Water paintings, Titian was disturbing him, Titian the Ill Genius of Oil Painting. . . . His poems have been sold hitherto only in Manuscript. I never read them; but a friend at my desire procured the **"Sweep Song."** There is one to a tiger, which I have heard recited, beginning—

> Tiger, Tiger, burning bright,
> Thro' the desarts [sic] of the night,

which is glorious, but, alas! I have not the book; for the man is flown, whither I know not—to Hades or a Mad House. But I must look on him as one of the most extraordinary persons of the age.

Edward Fitzgerald

SOURCE: A letter to W. B. Donne on October 25, 1833, in his *Letters and Literary Remains of Edward Fitzgerald,* Vol. I, edited by William Aldis Wright, Macmillan and Co., 1889, pp. 20-1.

[In the following letter addressed to W. B. Donne, English writer Fitzgerald responds to Blake's Songs of Innocence, *focusing on the relationship between Blake's genius and his madness.]*

I have lately bought a little pamphlet which is very difficult to be got, called ***The Songs of Innocence,*** written and adorned with drawings by W. Blake (if you know his name) who was quite mad: but of a madness that was really the elements of great genius ill-sorted: in fact, a genius with a screw loose, as we used to say. I shall shew you this book when I see you: to me there is particular interest in this man's writing and drawing, from the strangeness of the constitution of his mind. He was a man that used to see visions: and make drawings and paintings of Alexander the Great, Caesar, &c. who, he declared, stood before him while he drew. . . .

James John Garth Wilkinson

SOURCE: An excerpt from the Preface to *William Blake: The Critical Heritage,* edited by G.E. Bentley, Jr., Routledge & Kegan Paul, 1975, pp. 57-60.

[Wilkinson edited the first conventionally published edition of Songs of Innocence and of Experience, *issued in 1839. In the preface to that work, excerpted below, he focuses on Blake's deviations from the standards of spiritual and Christian vision, yet expresses hope that* Songs *will promote a greater awareness of the spiritual essence of reality.]*

[Songs of Innocence and of Experience] contains nearly all that is excellent in Blake's Poetry; and great, rare, and manifest, is the excellence that is here. The faults are equally conspicuous, and he who runs may read them. They amount to an utter want of elaboration, and even, in many cases, to an inattention to the ordinary rules of grammar. Yet the ***Songs of Innocence,*** at least, are quite free from the dark becloudment which rolled and billowed over Blake in his later days. He here transcended Self, and escaped from the isolation which Self involves; and, as it then ever is, his expanding affections embraced universal Man, and, without violating, beautified and hallowed, even his individual peculiarities. Accordingly, many of these delicious Lays, belong to the Era as well as to the Author. They are remarkable for the transparent depth of thought which constitutes true Simplicity—they give us glimpses of all that is holiest in the Childhood of the World and the Individual—they abound with the sweetest touches of that Pastoral life, by which the Golden Age may be still visibly represented to the iron one—they delineate full-orbed Age, ripe with the seeds of a second Infancy, which is 'the Kingdom of Heaven.' The latter half of the Volume, comprising the ***Songs of Experience,*** consists, it is true, of darker themes; but they, too, are well and wonderfully sung; and ought to be preserved, because, in contrastive connexion with the ***Songs of Innocence,*** they do convey a powerful impression of 'the two contrary states of the Human Soul.'

If the Volume gives one impulse to the New Spiritualism which is now dawning on the world:—if it leads one reader to think, that all Reality for him, in the long run, lies out of the limits of Space and Time; and that Spirits, and not bodies, and still less garments, are men;—if it gives one blow, even the faintest, to those term-shifting juggleries, which usurp the name of 'Philosophical Systems,' (and all the energies of all the forms of genuine Truth must henceforth be expended on these effects,) it will have done its work in its little day; and we shall be abundantly satisfied, with having undertaken to perpetuate it, for a few years, by the present Republication.

Alexander Gilchrist

SOURCE: An excerpt from *Life of William Blake,* Vol. 1, revised edition, Macmillan and Co., 1880, pp. 116-19.

Title page from Songs of Innocence and of Experience, *1794. Written and illustrated by William Blake.*

[Critics generally agree that significant scholarly interest in and understanding of Blake's thought began with the publication of Gilchrist's Life of William Blake, "Pictor Ignotus." *Gilchrist died in 1861 without completing his book. The unfinished* Life *was subsequently completed by Anne Gilchrist, Dante Gabriel Rossetti, and William Michael Rossetti and published in 1863. In the following excerpt from that work, Gilchrist praises the lyricism and naturalness of* Songs of Innocence and of Experience.*]*

First of the Poems [in ***Songs of Innocence***] let me speak, harsh as seems their divorce from the Design which blends with them, forming warp and woof in one texture. It is like pulling up a daisy by the roots from the greensward out of which it springs. To me many years ago, first reading these weird Songs in their appropriate environment of equally spiritual form and hue, the effect was as that of an angelic voice singing to oaten pipe, such as Arcadians tell of; or, as if a spiritual magician were summoning before human eyes, and through a human medium, images and scenes of divine loveliness; and in the pauses of the strain we seem to catch the rustling of angelic wings. The Golden Age independent of Space or Time, object of vague sighs and dreams from many generations of struggling humanity—an Eden such as childhood sees, is brought nearer than ever poet brought it before. For this poet was in assured possession of the Golden Age within the chambers of his own mind. As we read, fugitive glimpses open, clear as brief, of our buried childhood, of an unseen world present, past, to come; we are endowed with new spiritual sight, with unwonted intuitions, bright visitants from finer realms of thought, which ever elude us, ever hover near. We encounter familiar objects, in unfamiliar, transfigured aspects, simple expression and deep meanings, type and antitype. True, there are palpable irregularities, metrical license, lapse of grammar, and even of orthography; but often the sweetest melody, most daring eloquence of rhythm, and what is more, appropriate rhythm. They are *unfinished* poems: yet would finish have bettered their bold and careless freedom? Would it not have brushed away the delicate bloom? that visible spontaneity, so rare and great a charm, the eloquent attribute of our old English ballads and of the early Songs of all nations. The most deceptively perfect wax-model is no substitute for the living flower. The form is, in these Songs, a transparent medium of the spiritual thought, not an opaque body. . . .

These poems have a unity and mutual relationship, the influence of which is much impaired if they be read otherwise than as a whole. . . .

Who but Blake, with his pure heart, his simple exalted character, could have transfigured a commonplace meeting of Charity Children at St. Paul's, as he has done in the **"Holy Thursday"?** A picture at once tender and grand. The bold images, by a wise instinct resorted to at the close of the first and second stanzas and opening of the third, are in the highest degree imaginative; they are true as only Poetry can be.

How vocal is the poem **"Spring,"** despite imperfect rhymes. From addressing the child, the poet, by a transition not infrequent with him, passes out of himself into the child's person, showing a chameleon sympathy with childlike feelings. Can we not see the little three-year-old prattler stroking the white lamb, her feelings made articulate for her?—Even more remarkable is the poem entitled **"The Lamb,"** sweet hymn of tender infantine sentiment appropriate to that perennial image of meekness; to which the fierce eloquence of **"The Tiger,"** in the ***Songs of Experience,*** is an antitype. In **"The Lamb"** the poet again changes person to that of a child. Of lyrical beauty, take as a sample **"The Laughing Song,"** with its happy *ring* of merry innocent voices. This and **"The Nurse's Song"** are more in the style of his early poems, but, as we said, of far maturer execution. I scarcely need call attention to the delicate simplicity of the little pastoral, entitled **"The Shepherd":** to the picturesqueness in a warmer hue, the delightful domesticity, the expressive melody of **"The Echoing Green":** or to the lovely sympathy and piety which irradiate the touching **"Cradle Song."** More enchanting still is the stir of fancy and sympathy which animates **"The Dream,"** that

Did weave a shade o'er my angel-guarded bed;

of an emmet that had

Lost her way,
Where on grass methought I lay.

Few are the readers, I should think, who can fail to appreciate the symbolic grandeur of **"The Little Boy Lost"** and **"The Little Boy Found,"** or the enigmatic tenderness of the **"Blossom"** and the **"Divine Image"**; and the verses **"On Another's Sorrow,"** express some of Blake's favourite religious ideas, his abiding notions on the subject of the Godhead, which surely suggest the kernel of Christian feeling. A similar tinge of the divine colours the lines called **"Night,"** with its revelation of angelic guardians, believed in with unquestioning piety by Blake, who makes us in our turn conscious, as we read, of angelic noiseless footsteps. For a nobler depth of religious beauty, with accordant grandeur of sentiment and language, I know no parallel nor hint elsewhere of such a poem as **"The Little Black Boy"**—

My mother bore me in the southern wild.

We may read these poems again and again, and they continue fresh as at first. There is something unsating in them, a perfume as of a growing violet, which renews itself as fast as it is inhaled.

One poem, **"The Chimney Sweeper,"** still calls for special notice. This and **"Holy Thursday"** are remarkable as an anticipation of the daring choice of homely subject, of the yet more daringly familiar manner, nay, of the very metre and trick of style adopted by Wordsworth in a portion of those memorable 'experiments in poetry,'—the *Lyrical Ballads,*—in *The Reverie of Poor Susan,* for instance (not written till 1797), the *Star Gazers,* and *The Power of Music* (both 1806). The little Sweep's dream has the spiritual touch peculiar to Blake's hand. . . .

The tender loveliness of these poems will hardly reappear in Blake's subsequent writing. Darker phases of feeling, more sombre colours, profounder meanings, ruder eloquence, characterise the ***Songs of Experience*** of five years later. . . .

The designs, simultaneous offspring with the poems, which in the most literal sense illuminate the ***Songs of Innocence,*** consist of poetized domestic scenes. The drawing and draperies are grand in style as graceful, though covering few inches' space; the colour pure, delicate, yet in effect rich and full. The mere tinting of the text and of the free ornamental border often makes a refined picture. The costumes of the period are idealized, the landscape given in pastoral and symbolic hints. Sometimes these drawings almost suffer from being looked at as a book and held close, instead of at due distance as pictures, where they become more effective. In composition, colour, pervading feeling, they are lyrical to the eye, as the ***Songs*** to the ear.

On the whole, the designs to the ***Songs of Innocence*** are finer as well as more pertinent to the poems; more closely interwoven with them, than those which accompany the ***Songs of Experience.***

In the ***Songs of Experience,*** put forth in 1794, as complement to the ***Songs of Innocence*** of 1789, we come [on more lucid writing than the prophetic books ***The Gates of Paradise, Visions of the Daughters of Albion,*** and ***America: A Prophecy],***—writing freer from mysticism and abstractions, if partaking of the same colour of thought. ***Songs of Innocence and Experience, showing the Two Contrary States of the Human Soul: the author and printer, W. Blake,*** is the general title now given. The first series, quite in keeping with its name, had been of far the more heavenly temper. The second, produced during an interval of another five years, bears internal evidence of later origin, though in the same rank as to poetic excellence. As the title fitly shadows, it is of grander, sterner calibre, of gloomier wisdom. Strongly contrasted, but harmonious phases of poetic thought are presented by the two series.

One poem in the ***Songs of Experience*** happens to have been quoted often enough (first by Allan Cunningham in connection with Blake's name), to have made its strange old Hebrew-like grandeur, its Oriental latitude yet force of eloquence, comparatively familiar:—**"The Tiger."** To it Charles Lamb refers: 'I have heard of his poems,' writes he, 'but have never seen them. There is one to a tiger, beginning—

Tiger! tiger! burning bright
In the forests of the night,

which is glorious!'

Of the prevailing difference of sentiment between these poems and the ***Songs of Innocence,*** may be singled out as examples **"The Clod and the Pebble,"** and even so slight a piece as **"The Fly"**; and in a more sombre mood, **"The Garden of Love," "The Little Boy Lost," "Holy Thursday"** (antitype to the poem of the same title in ***Songs of Innocence),*** **"The Angel," "The Human Abstract," "The Poison Tree,"** and above all, **"London."** One poem, **"The Little Girl Lost,"** may startle the literal reader, but has an inverse moral truth and beauty of its own. Another, **"The Little Girl Lost, and Little Girl Found,"** is a daringly emblematic anticipation of some future age of gold, and has the picturesqueness of Spenserian allegory, lit with the more ethereal spiritualism of Blake. Touched by

The light that never was on sea or shore,

is this story of the carrying off of the sleeping little maid by friendly beasts of prey, who gambol round her as she lies; the kingly lion bowing 'his mane of gold,' and on her neck dropping 'from his eyes of flame, ruby tears;' who, when her parents seek the child, brings them to his cave; and

They look upon his eyes,
Filled with deep surprise;
And wondering behold
A spirit armed in gold!

Well might Flaxman exclaim, 'Sir, his poems are as grand as his pictures,' Wordsworth read them with delight. . . . Blake himself thought his poems finer than his designs. Hard to say which are the more uncommon in kind. Neither, as I must reiterate, reached his own generation. In Malkin's *Memoirs of a Child,* specimens from the ***Poetical Sketches*** and ***Songs of Innocence and Experience*** were given; for these poems struck the well-meaning scholar, into whose hands by chance they fell, as somewhat astonishing; as indeed they struck most who stumbled on them. But Malkin's *Memoirs* was itself a book not destined to circulate very freely; and the poems of Blake, even had they been really known to their generation, were not calculated in their higher qualities to win popular favour,—not if they had been free from technical imperfection. For it was an age of polish, though mostly polish of trifles; not like the present age, with its slovenliness and licence. Deficient finish was never a characteristic of the innovator Wordsworth himself, who started from the basis of Pope and Goldsmith; and whose matter, rather than manner, was obnoxious to critics. Defiant carelessness, though Coleridge in his Juvenile Poems was often guilty of it, did not become a characteristic of English verse, until the advent of Keats and Shelley; poets of imaginative virtue enough to cover a multitude of their own and other people's sins. The length to which it has since run (despite Tennyson), we all know.

Yet in this very inartificiality lies the secret of Blake's rare and wondrous success. Whether in design or in poetry, he does, in very fact, work as a man already practised in one art, beginning anew in another; expressing himself with virgin freshness of mind in each, and in each realizing, by turns, the idea flung out of that prodigal cornucopia of thought and image, "Pippa Passes":—'If there should arise a new painter, will it not be in some such way by a poet, now, or a musician (spirits who have conceived and perfected an ideal through some other channel), transferring it to this, and escaping our conventional roads by pure ignorance of them?' Even Malkin, with real sense, observes of the poet in general,—his mind 'is too often at leisure for the mechanical prettinesses of cadence and epithet, when it ought to be engrossed by higher thoughts. Words and numbers present themselves unbidden when the soul is inspired by sentiment, elevated by enthusiasm, or ravished by devotion.' Yes! ravished by devotion. For in these songs of Blake's occurs devotional poetry, which is real poetry too—a very exceptional thing. Witness that simple and beautiful poem entitled **"The Divine Image,"** or that **"On Another's Sorrow."** The ***Songs of Innocence*** are in truth animated by a uniform sentiment of deep piety, of reverent feeling, and may be said, in their pervading influence, to be one devout aspiration throughout. The ***Songs of Experience*** consist rather of earnest, impassioned arguments; in this differing from the simple *affirmations* of the earlier ***Songs of Innocence,***—arguments on the loftiest themes of existence.

After the ***Songs of Experience,*** Blake never again sang to like angelic tunes; nor even with the same approach to technical accuracy. His poetry was the blossom of youth and early manhood.

Algernon Charles Swinburne

SOURCE: An excerpt from *William Blake: A Critical Essay,* revised edition, Chatto & Windus, 1906, pp. 123-40.

[An English poet, dramatist, and critic, Swineburne is recognized by Blake scholars as the author of the first full-length critical study of the poet. In the following excerpt from the 1906 edition of William Blake: A Critical Essay *(1867), Swineburne declares* Songs of Innocence and of Experience *the most accessible of Blake's works, and perceives its central theme to be the championship of human instinct.]*

These poems are really unequalled in their kind. Such verse was never written for children since verse-writing began. Only in a few of those faultless fragments of childish rhyme which float without name or form upon the memories of men shall we find such a pure clear cadence of verse, such rapid ring and flow of lyric laughter, such sweet and direct choice of the just word and figure, such an impeccable simplicity; nowhere but here such a tender wisdom of holiness, such a light and perfume of innocence. Nothing like this was ever written on that text of the lion and the lamb; no such heaven of sinless animal life was ever conceived so intensely and sweetly.

And there the lion's ruddy eyes
Shall flow with tears of gold,
And pitying the tender cries,
And walking round the fold,
Saying *Wrath by His meekness*
And by His health sickness
Is driven away
From our immortal day.
And now beside thee, bleating lamb,
I can lie down and sleep,
Or think on Him who bore thy name,
Graze after thee, and weep.

The leap and fall of the verse is so perfect as to make it a fit garment and covering for the profound tenderness of faith and soft strength of innocent impulse embodied in it. But the whole of this hymn of **"Night"** is wholly beautiful; being perhaps one of the two poems of loftiest loveliness among all the ***Songs of Innocence.*** The other is that called **"The Little Black Boy"**; a poem especially exquisite for its noble forbearance from vulgar pathos and achievement of the highest and most poignant sweetness of speech and sense; in which the poet's mysticism is baptized with pure water and taught to speak as from faultless lips of children, to such effect as this.

And we are put on earth a little space
That we may learn to bear the beams of love;
And these black bodies and this sunburnt face
Are like a cloud and like a shady grove.

Other poems of a very perfect beauty are those of **"The Piper," "The Lamb," "The Chimney-Sweeper,"** and **"The Two-Days-Old Baby"**; all, for the music in them, more like the notes of birds caught up and given back than the modulated measure of human verse. One cannot say, being so slight and seemingly wrong in metrical form, how they come to be so absolutely right; but right even in point of verses and words they assuredly are. Add fuller formal completion of rhyme and rhythm to that song of **"Infant Joy,"** and you have broken up the soft bird-like perfection of clear light sound which gives it beauty; the little bodily melody of soulless and painless laughter.

Against all articulate authority we do however class several of the ***Songs of Experience*** higher for the great qualities of verse than anything in the earlier division of these poems. If the ***Songs of Innocence*** have the shape and smell of leaves or buds, these have in them the light and sound of fire or the sea. Entering among them, a fresher savour and a larger breath strikes one upon the lips and forehead. In the first part we are shown who they are who have or who deserve the gift of spiritual sight: in the second, what things there are for them to see when that gift has been given. Innocence, the quality of beasts and children, has the keenest eyes; and such eyes alone can discern and interpret the actual mysteries of experience. It is natural that this second part, dealing as it does with such things as underlie the outer forms of the first part, should rise higher and dive deeper in point of mere words. These give the distilled perfume and extracted blood of the veins in the roseleaf, the sharp, liquid, intense spirit crushed out of the broken kernel in the fruit. The last of the ***Songs of Innocence*** is a prelude to these poems; in it the poet summons to judgment the young and single-spirited, that by right of the natural impulse of delight in them they may give sentence against the preachers of convention and assumption; and in the first poem of the second series he, by the same "voice of the bard," calls upon earth herself, the mother of all these, to arise and become free: since upon her limbs also are bound the fetters, and upon her forehead also has fallen the shadow, of a jealous law: from which nevertheless, by faithful following of instinct and divine liberal impulse, earth and man shall obtain deliverance.

Hear the voice of the bard!
  Who present, past, and future sees:
Whose ears have heard
The ancient Word
  That walked among the silent trees:
Calling the lapsèd soul
  And weeping in the evening dew;
That might control
The starry pole
  And fallen, fallen light renew!

If they will hear the Word, earth and the dwellers upon earth shall be made again as little children; shall regain the strong simplicity of eye and hand proper to the pure and single of heart; and for them inspiration shall do the work of innocence; let them but once abjure the doctrine by which comes sin and the law by which comes prohibition. Therefore must the appeal be made; that the blind may see and the deaf hear, and the unity of body and spirit be made manifest in perfect freedom: and that to the innocent even the liberty of "sin" may be conceded. For if the soul suffer by the body's doing, are not both degraded? and if the body be oppressed for the soul's sake, are not both the losers?

O Earth, O Earth, return!
  Arise from out the dewy grass!
Night is worn,
And the morn
  Rises from the slumberous mass.
Turn away no more;
  Why wilt thou turn away?
The starry shore,
The watery floor,
  Are given thee till the break of day.

For so long, during the night of law and oppression of material form, the divine evidences hidden under sky and sea are left her; even "till the break of day." Will she not get quit of this spiritual bondage to the heavy body of things, to the encumbrance of deaf clay and blind vegetation, before the light comes that shall redeem and reveal? But the earth, being yet in subjection to the creator of men, the jealous God who divided nature against herself—father of woman and man, legislator of sex and race—makes blind and bitter answer as in sleep, "her locks covered with grey despair."

Prisoned on this watery shore,
  Starry Jealousy does keep my den;
Cold and hoar,
Weeping o'er,
  I hear the father of the ancient men.

Thus, in the poet's mind, Nature and Religion are the two fetters of life, one on the right wrist, the other on the left; an obscure material force on this hand, and on that a mournful imperious law: the law of divine jealousy, the government of a God who weeps over his creature and subject with unprofitable tears, and rules by forbidding and dividing: the "Urizen" of the "Prophetic Books," clothed with the coldness and the grief of remote sky and jealous cloud. Here as always, the cry is as much for light as for licence, the appeal not more against prohibition than against obscurity.

Can the sower sow by night,
Or the ploughman in darkness plough?

In the ***Songs of Innocence*** there is no such glory of metre or sonorous beauty of lyrical work as here. No possible effect of verse can be finer in a great brief way than that given in the second and last stanzas of the first part of this poem. It recalls within one's ear the long relapse of recoiling water and wash of the refluent wave; in the third and fourth lines sinking suppressed as with equal pulses and soft sobbing noise of ebb, to climb again in the fifth line with a rapid clamour of ripples and strong ensuing strain of weightier sound, lifted with the lift of the running and ringing sea.

Here also is that most famous of Blake's lyrics, **"The Tyger"**; a poem beyond praise for its fervent beauty and vigour of music. It appears by the MS. that this was written with some pains; the cancels and various readings bear marks of frequent rehandling. One of the latter is worth transcription for its own excellence and also in proof of the artist's real care for details, which his rapid instinctive way of work has induced some to disbelieve in.

> Burnt in distant deeps or skies
> The cruel fire of thine eyes?
> Could heart descend or wings aspire?
> What the hand dare seize the fire?

Nor has Blake left us anything of more profound and perfect value than **"The Human Abstract"**; a little mythical vision of the growth of error; through soft sophistries of pity and faith, subtle humility of abstinence and fear, under which the pure simple nature lies corrupted and strangled; through selfish loves which prepare a way for cruelty, and cruelty that works by spiritual abasement and awe.

> Soon spreads the dismal shade
> Of Mystery over his head;
> And the caterpillar and fly
> Feed on the Mystery.
>
> And it bears the fruit of Deceit,
> Ruddy and sweet to eat;
> And the raven his nest has made
> In the thickest shade.

Under the shadow of this tree of mystery, rooted in artificial belief, all the meaner kind of devouring things take shelter and eat of the fruit of its branches; the sweet poison of false faith, painted on its outer husk with the likeness of all things noble and desirable; and in the deepest implication of barren branch and deadly leaf, the bird of death, with priests for worshippers ("the priests of the raven of dawn," loud of lip and hoarse of throat until the light of day have risen), finds house and resting-place. Only in the "miscreative brain" of fallen men can such a thing strike its tortuous root and bring forth its fatal flower; nowhere else in all nature can the tyrants of divided matter and moral law, "Gods of the earth and sea," find soil that will bear such fruit.

Nowhere has Blake set forth his spiritual creed more clearly and earnestly than in the last of the ***Songs of Experience.*** **"Tirzah,"** in his mythology, represents the mere separate and human nature, mother of the perishing body and daughter of the "religion" which occupies itself with laying down laws for the flesh; which, while pretending (and that in all good faith) to despise the body and bring it into subjection as with control of bit and bridle, does implicitly overrate its power upon the soul for evil or good, and thus falls foul of fact on all sides by assuming that spirit and flesh are twain, and that things pleasant and good for the one can properly be loathsome or poisonous to the other. This "religion" or "moral law," the inexplicable prophet [Blake] has chosen to baptize under the singular type of "Rahab"—the "harlot virgin-mother," impure by dint of chastity and forbearance from such things as are pure to the pure of heart: for in this creed the one thing unclean is the belief in uncleanness, the one thing forbidden is to believe in the existence of forbidden things. . . . For the present it will be enough to note how eager and how direct is the appeal here made against any rule or reasoning based on reference to the mere sexual and external nature of man—the nature made for ephemeral life and speedy death, kept alive "to work and weep" only through that mercy which "changed death into sleep;" how intense the reliance on redemption from such a law by the grace of imaginative insight and spiritual freedom, typified in "the death of Jesus." Nor are any of these poems finer in structure or nobler in metrical form. . . .

In these hurried notes on the ***Songs*** an effort has been made to get that done which is most absolutely necessary—not that which might have been most facile or most delightful. Analytic remark has been bestowed on those poems only which really cannot dispense with it in the eyes of most men. Many others need no herald or interpreter, demand no usher or outrider: some of these are among Blake's best, some again almost among his worst. Poems in which a doctrine or subject once before nobly stated and illustrated is re-asserted in a shallower way and exemplified in a feebler form, require at our hands no written or spoken signs of either assent or dissent. Such poems . . . have places here among their betters: none of them, it may be added, without some shell of outward beauty or seed of inward value. The simpler poems claim only praise; and of this they cannot fail from any reader whose good word is in the least worth having. Those of a subtler kind (often, as must now be clear enough, the best worth study) claim more than this if they are to have fair play. It is pleasant enough to commend and to enjoy the palpable excellence of Blake's work; but another thing is simply and thoroughly requisite—to understand what the workman was after. First get well hold of the mystic, and you will then at once get a better view and comprehension of the painter and poet.

Osbert Burdett

SOURCE: An excerpt from *William Blake,* The Macmillan Company, 1926, pp. 41-9, 61.

[In the following excerpt, Burdett praises Songs of

Innocence and of Experience *as a celebration of emotion, imagination, and simplicity.]*

[In] 1789 Blake issued the ***Songs of Innocence,*** his first example of Illuminated Printing. This, like all Blake's books except the earlier ***Poetical Sketches,*** to be appreciated in all its beauty needs to be read in the original form in which it came from his own hand and press. Since this is not possible except for those who visit museum libraries, the method must be faithfully described. In the words of Mr. John Sampson:

> The text and the surrounding design were written in reverse [a painfully laborious method], in a medium impervious to acid upon small copper plates about 5" by 3" which were then etched in a bath of aqua-fortis until the work stood in relief as in a stereotype. From these plates, which to economise copper were, in many cases, engraved upon both sides, impressions were printed, in the ordinary manner, in tints made to harmonise with the colour scheme afterwards applied by the artist.

The text and the illustration are thus interwoven into a harmonious whole, and as the colour can be varied no two copies need be exactly alike. Little but the use of a press distinguishes the books so made from illuminated manuscripts, and the etching in reverse together with the press makes the new method even more laborious than the old. The consequence has been that Blake has had no successors in the art which he invented, nor can his originals be copied without great difficulty and expense. Only those who have compared his originals with the printed pages in which his poems are ordinarily read are fully aware of the loss now suffered by his writings, which require to be read as much by the eye as by the mind on pages suffused with life and colour. Blake evidently adopted the method by preference and artistic choice, and because his hand could not write so much as a word without the impulse to trace designs upon the paper. He wished to indulge both his gifts at the same time, and did not marry them because he desired and could not find a publisher. . . .

A necessary effect of the Illuminated Printing was to restrict his readers to the few, in the manner of an artist who displays not books but pictures. Blake often painted in words, and should be judged rather as an artist than an author. Mr. Sampson does not think it probable that "the whole impression of the ***Songs*** issued by Blake exceeded the twenty-two" that he describes. It is hardly surprising, therefore, that Blake's writings were little known. Absorbed in his invention, however, Blake eventually issued from Lambeth a prospectus defending his method and advertising the ***Songs of Innocence*** and the ***Songs of Experience*** at five shillings each: "If a method (he thus wrote in 1793) which combines the Painter and the Poet is a phenomenon worthy of public attention, provided it exceeds in elegance all former methods, the author is sure of his reward". As Mr. Symons has said:

> Had it not been for his lack of a technical knowledge of music, had he been able to write down his inventions in that art also, he would have left us the creation of something like an universal art. That universal art he did, during his lifetime, create; for he sang his songs to his own music; and thus, while he lived, he was the complete realisation of the poet in all his faculties, and the only complete realisation that has ever been known.

His combination of talents is his real defence against particular criticism. . . .

The imagination of the man who wrote the ***Songs of Innocence*** had not outgrown the simplicity of the child. Blake might be an inspired child writing for children, and these songs are nursery rhymes of pure poetry which children and their elders can equally love. . . .

He had shown that he could rival the Elizabethan lyrists, that he could transmute nature into the spirit of the earth, and from first to last the imagination itself was his principal and characteristic theme. In these songs Blake sings neither of love, nature, religion, nor sorrow, but of the imagination which, to be communicable, sees itself reflected, especially on the faces of children, in experiences such as these. The lamb, the shepherd, the infant, the cradle, the laughter of childish voices at play, are pretexts for a music as fresh, tender, awkward, soothing, merry as their original selves. For the first time in nursery poetry we feel that the grown-ups are listening, and that it is the child who is telling its mother about the lamb and God. The way in which the simplicities of feeling are conveyed and false sentiment avoided is miraculous. There is nothing quite to equal **"Infant Joy"** anywhere:

> "I have no name:
> I am but two days old."
> What shall I call thee?
> "I happy am,
> Joy is my name."
> Sweet joy befall thee!

"The Lamb", the **"Laughing Song"**, the almost monosyllabic lines to **"Spring"**, which seem as if they issued from a cradle, the lovely **"Nurse's Song"**, in which the nurse becomes the eldest of her charges for a moment, and the voice of play seems naturally to sing, are absolutely childlike. All poetry becomes young again in them, and artless utterance for the first and last time finds its proper music. There are others, however, in which the poet allows a glimpse of his hand to appear, as in **"The Divine Image"** and the haunting stanzas to **"Night"**, which Swinburne declared to be of the "loftiest loveliness". There are poems which tell stories and poems which speak of religion, taking a child's feelings about sorrow and pain for their simple lessons. So finely are they adjusted to their end that we hardly know whether the mother or her infant is reflecting, and indeed the second childhood of humanity is the blessing of those who have children of their own and are not strangers to them.

Perhaps only a poet who had read no fine literature but

as a child reads could have written such things. There is in them an innocence of heart that is not to be found in Shakespeare. A few have the quality of children's hymns, in which God appears a really loving Father, and mercy, pity, peace, and love, the virtues of childhood at its rare best, become the lineaments of His "divine image". The occasional moral, as at the end of **"The Chimney Sweeper",** is transformed by the poetry into an exquisite platitude of the world, as this is represented to children in the school-room. Its presence is an abstraction of nurse and completes the nursery atmosphere. Note, too, that the shepherd, the sheep, the cradle, and the rest are nursery symbols, thus enabling Blake to pass from the lamb to "Him who bore its name" without any change of key. The emotions aroused by this poetry are instinctive and almost as characteristic of animals as of men. Indeed, it celebrates the life, motions, and feelings of all young things, with the apparent artlessness of a lamb's bleat or the cry of a bird, a baby's shout of astonishment or pleasure. By returning to these poetry seems to return to its own infancy, and the language is almost as free from meaning, apart from emotion, as a child's prattle.

Both meaning and observation, even of social life, appear in ***Songs of Experience,*** the companion volume of 1794, though not the next to be written. These darker songs, sometimes on the same themes, and the group often called Ideas of Good and Evil, or the Rossetti MS., are a convenient bridge between the simple lyric poetry with which Blake began and the complex prophecies that were to follow. The scene tends to shift from the nursery to the school-room, from the green to the church, from the open country to the city. We pass from feeling to observation, and the poems that touch on love reveal its troubles. Jealousy and prohibitions, whether personal or ecclesiastical, are named in them. Mr. Ellis has reconstructed a situation that would explain the references to those who are curious of Blake's erotic life. The famous **"Tyger"** is of course here, and with Mr. Sampson's aid we can trace every variant in its gradual composition. The number of revisions reminds us of the care that Blake would still spend upon his form, and which he claimed to have spent later on his prophecies, where the ending of his lines can, in fact, be shown to depend upon the decoration surrounding them. In his own work poetry was to yield to decoration, and there can be no doubt that design was the principal preoccupation of his mind. The first ecstasy of conscious life is complicated with a growing knowledge of good and evil, and the music of the verse will bear the burden of this trouble without caring to assign a cause. Such lines as:

> Ah, sun-flower! weary of time,
> Who countest the steps of the sun,

are the music of heaviness of heart, as the lines to the lamb and the infant had been the music of gladness. When he observes his fellow-men fallen into the bonds of cold reason and dull experience, he wonders

> How can the bird that is born for joy
> Sit in a cage and sing?

And he finds the explanation not in their circumstances but in themselves:

> In every cry of every Man,
> In every Infant's cry of fear,
> In every voice, in every ban,
> The mind-forg'd manacles I hear.

All forms of external control were to Blake the enemy of imagination, and he was right in so far as the dictates of wisdom even have little use for us until we have made them by personal experience our own. All the rest is morality, which, so long as it remains repressive and external, is always accompanied by secret satisfactions and deceit. In the age of experience, as Swinburne finely puts it, "inspiration shall do the work of innocence", and the **"Introduction"** to the ***Songs of Experience*** tells us that it is by listening to the Voice of the Bard that innocence can be renewed. It is, in fact, the inspiration to be derived from Blake, and not the particular instructions in which he sometimes phrased the call, that we should take from him. The loved disciple is not he who slavishly mimics any master, but one who by embracing his master's example is inspired to make the most of his own gifts and to follow the way of his own understanding. The best of the second group of songs present us with rudiments of thoughts dissolved in music, and it is the strange magic of this music, by leading us to think for ourselves, that we should carry away from them. Their intellectual fascination consists in suggesting rather than in defining their meaning. They make the intellect a thing of beauty by lending it the twilight that it should not possess, and the commentators like bats awakened by the falling shadows find in the gloaming the opportunity for the most crooked of their flights. Blake loved to put his feelings into intellectual forms, but he is really great when he is content with imaginative images, and can haunt our imaginations with lines like:

> When the stars threw down their spears
> And water'd Heaven with their tears.

> The lost traveller's dream under the hill.

> Nor is it possible to thought
> A greater than itself to know,

or the splendid:

> For a tear is an intellectual thing,
> And a sigh is the sword of an angel king,
> And the bitter groan of a martyr's woe
> Is an arrow from the Almighty's bow.

All Blake's emotions, and many of his images, were "intellectual things" to him, but for the reader who would do the poet justice, it is the poetry and not the cloudy forms in which it is often presented that is the truth of Blake's writings. Here is the vital energy that was the foundation of Blake's creed, and for this essence to be separated and praised in poetry it was indispensable that it should not be limited to the very bonds and definitions that are more coherent than itself. Blake's way of attempting to defend intellectually a vitality that is its own defence has misled his less lyrical readers, who forget his relation to his age and the fact that he was protesting against an overintellectual tradition. Law was his particular enemy, and to apply anything like logic to his lyrics, or to the lyrical prose that was soon to overflow them, is to confuse his tactics with his genius. Blake was to stand or fall by his own inspiration, and there are very blank lines here and there. The reader should not shut his eyes to them, though quotation would be ungracious, for they will lead him to study the almost verbal revisions of **"The Tyger,"** the only example we have of Blake's tireless revision of verse. That this was abundantly rewarded, and that Blake remained still to the end impatient even of self-criticism, shows how much his mind and work suffered from being always in revolt.

When we consider the body of Blake's lyrical poetry, we see that he desired a language that should lie on the further side of meaning, all music, all symbol, with none or the slightest foothold on the earth. Thought and meaning were to become wholly lyrical, and yet to use the language of ideas. So far as his aim was attainable by mortal man, he came nearest to it in the ***Songs of Innocence and Experience,*** songs which no doubt afterward seemed to him but feathers from the phoenix to be born from the ashes of the prophetic books.

"Infant Joy," from Songs of Innocence, *1789. Written and illustrated by William Blake.*

Annie E. Moore

SOURCE: "Makers of Poetry for Children: William Blake," in *Literature Old and New for Children: Materials for a College Course,* Houghton Mifflin Company, 1934, pp. 281-86.

The first clear musical note in poetry for children came from William Blake (1757-1827) in his ***Songs of Innocence,*** written in early manhood. These lyrics represent the first body of poetry produced by a writer of power, speaking from his own pure spirit to the unsullied heart of childhood. Probably these poems were not written especially for the young. Blake was an idealist, and the sweet innocence and confiding nature of children appealed to him just as lambs and all tender young things did. Whatever the poet's underlying plan, it brought into this group of poems a quality which renders them equally well suited to the immature and to a developed taste in poetry. From beginning to end, merry boys and girls fill the pages and sing the songs, smiling babies stretch out their hands, and a few less happy children make their wistful appeal.

William Blake was a mystic, a dreamer of dreams, a visionary in the literal sense of the word—one who saw visions and claimed to talk face to face with heavenly visitants. He believed that he was inspired and guided by some of the prophets of old and that his brother came back from heaven to reveal to him new and effective processes in art. There were indications in childhood of nervous instability, and life's severe buffetings produced in his sensitive nature a condition bordering at times on madness. His most sympathetic friends thought him "a little mad" in his later years, but they agree that the unusual mental state was of a type which served to inspire very original and noble expression in etching, painting, and poetry. He had, too, an insight into human needs which was more than sane—it was prophetic of social reform.

From early childhood, Blake resisted physical restraint and drooped under it. He was the son of a London hosier living in the outskirts of the city, and during his boyhood, field and woodland were not far from his home. He wandered there almost at will, for his parents soon discovered that he could not endure the hard, cold regimen of school. They did not understand the child, but they were alarmed and dismayed at certain manifestations—daydreams, visions which he reported at about eight years of age, but which had begun at four, the "lies" which he continued to tell, the outbursts of passion which greeted punishment or the torment of teasing companions. Freed from school, the child fed on the sights and sounds of the country which constantly filled him with wonder, and he began to write verse at about eleven years of age. Almost incidentally he acquired a liberal education in literature. His art education was more systematic, but in this field also, he refused to be dominated by tradition and his genius expanded along independent and original lines.

This sketch is of necessity far too brief to permit the tracing of Blake's remarkable career as an artist although his peculiar gifts in that field and in poetry are fundamentally inseparable. A knowledge of his many-sided life, private as well as artistic, is necessary to a full understanding of his marked traits of character and disposition, his passions and loyalties, the things that stirred his soul and came out in freshness and beauty in creative expression.

Ardent desire for freedom of body and soul, love of his fellowman and other living creatures, and belief in the inherent goodness and worth of man's original nature, pervade his thought and stir his emotions. He craved freedom not only for his own fulfillment but cried out in fiery aphorism at the sight of caged and suffering animals, and of children cribbed, confined or cruelly treated.

A robin redbreast in a cage
Puts all heaven in a rage.

Each outcry of the hunted hare,
A fibre from the brain does tear.

A skylark wounded in the wing,
A cherubim does cease to sing.

He who shall hurt the little wren
Shall never be beloved by men.

The quickened humanitarian spirit of the age flowed in Blake, and he turned his "bow of burning gold" and his "arrows of desire" against hypocrisy, cruelty, cold selfishness, and false standards of life.

Most of these ideas began to take shape in early youth but ***Songs of Innocence,*** first printed in 1789, expresses the softer, less agitated and denunciatory attitude of that period. In children and in the innocent creatures of field and wood, Blake saw the unspoiled handiwork of Divine love. He anticipated Wordsworth's "Ode on the Intimations of Immortality," for he presents with equal clearness, though in smaller compass, the ideal conception that the newborn come from some purer realm "trailing clouds of glory." To Blake, this was not merely a poetic idea, it was a philosophic conviction. He also felt that oneness and accord between the spirit of man and the face of nature which, a little later, Wordsworth was to express much more fully. He epitomizes this harmony in four memorable lines which remind us of "Flower in the crannied wall":

To see the world in a grain of sand,
  And a heaven in a wild flower,
Hold infinity in the palm of your hand
  And eternity in an hour.

"Infant Sorrow," from Songs of Experience, *in* Songs of Innocence and of Experience, *1794. Written and illustrated by William Blake.*

And now we come to the pure and melodious ***Songs,*** a few of which will never be forgotten if the stream of human life offers any continuity in things of the spirit. To Blake, children were not little sinners to be warned and frightened, nor were they wax tablets awaiting the imprint of worn tradition; instead, they were the happy possessors of a joyous inner wisdom out of our lost Eden—a wisdom which might be communicated to a responsive ear. And so the **"Introduction,"** which is the first poem in ***Songs of Innocence,*** is dictated by a dream-child, a laughing child "on a cloud," who sets the key of sweet rural joy which pervades this group of poems.

Piping down the valleys wild,
Piping songs of pleasant glee,
On a cloud I saw a child,
And he laughing said to me:—

"Pipe a song about a lamb:"
So I piped with merry cheer.
"Piper, pipe that song again:"
So I piped; he wept to hear.

"Drop thy pipe, thy happy pipe,
Sing thy songs of happy cheer:"
So I sung the same again,
While he wept with joy to hear.

"Piper, sit thee down and write
In a book that all may read—"
So he vanish'd from my sight;
And I plucked a hollow reed,

And I made a rural pen,
And I stained the water clear,
And I wrote my happy songs
Every child may joy to hear.

And in this strain, Blake continued to write of lambs and shepherds, of children dancing on the green, of flowers and spring, of "painted birds" and of

Sweet dreams of pleasant streams
By happy, silent, moony beams.

It is hard to resist giving a number of these poems in full. A few must be especially mentioned because of some feature significant in the development of verse for children. **"Laughing Song"** is one of the merriest, gayest things ever written, with its "sweet chorus of Ha, ha, he!" from "Mary and Susan and Emily." Isn't this the first time that little children have laughed aloud in English poetry?

Blake is noted also for originality of rhythm and stanza pattern and the fitness of these to the spirit of his songs. He discovered and used poetic forms which were inevitably right for a particular mood:

SPRING

Sound the flute!
Now it's mute.
Birds delight
Day and night;
Nightingale
In the dale,
Lark in sky,
Merrily,
Merrily, merrily, to welcome in the year.

Note how in **"Infant Joy"** the poet catches and frames in miniature the smiling mystery of infancy, and the tender benediction that wells up in its presence.

I have no name,
I am but two days old.
What shall I call thee?
I happy am,
Joy is my name.
Sweet joy befall thee.

Pain and sadness are sometimes hinted in this collection but their sharp portrayal comes in the next group of poems called ***Songs of Experience,*** printed in 1794. Today, Blake's fame as a poet rests very largely on these two groups, but it is from ***Songs of Innocence*** that selections especially designed for children are chiefly drawn. His famous "Tiger, tiger, burning bright," is in ***Songs of Experience,*** placed there by Blake because it raises a profound and insoluble question of faith and philosophy.

Sympathy for the oppressed and disinherited is beautifully expressed in **"The Little Black Boy," "The Chimney-Sweeper,"** and **"Holy Thursday."**

William Blake made four notable contributions to English poetry and, in particular, to children's poetry:

He added a substantial amount to the world's store of sheer beauty and delight.

He turned his back on everything prosaic, artificial and purely formal.

He found his themes in nature and in the lives of simple people, and created a style in harmony with these.

He gave beautiful and startling expression to a higher social creed which was just beginning to emerge.

There was no immediate successor to make flute-like music for children on a shepherd's pipe, but the strains never died out and have been picked up at intervals by kindred spirits for nearly a century and a half.

Northrop Frye

SOURCE: An excerpt from *Fearful Symmetry: A Study of William Blake,* 1947. Reprint by Beacon Press, 1962, pp. 236-37.

[A Canadian-born critic, Frye exerted tremendous influence in the field of twentieth-century literary scholarship, primarily through his study Anatomy of Criticism *(1957), in which he contends that literary criticism should be an autonomous discipline similar to the sciences. In the following excerpt, taken from the 1947 edition of* Fearful Symmetry, *Frye asserts that* Songs of Innocence *and* Songs of Experience *satirize each other.]*

Childhood to Blake is a state or phase of imaginative existence, the phase in which the world of imagination is still a brave new world and yet reassuring and intelligible. In the protection which the child feels from his parents and his evening prayer against darkness there is the image of a cosmos far more intelligently controlled than ours. The spontaneity of life which such protection makes possible is the liberty of the expanding imagination which has nothing to do but complete its own growth. No one can watch babies, kittens, puppies or even the first green shoots of plants for very long without beginning to smile; and the smile is a partial vision of the state of existence which this infant life is in. It was to the same vision that Jesus was appealing when he put a child in the midst of his disciples.

However, the course of life in this world indicates that there is a higher world to attain to, and that is the world of the Providence and Father itself, which is looked up to in the infantile state. The dawn of imaginative puberty will make one at once impatient with it: one is then no longer a creature but a creator. At twelve Jesus ran away from home, and though his parents sought him as the searching parents in **"A Little Girl Lost"** do, he was now about his Father's business, ready to become one with his Father. But outgrowing the child's world does not imply abandoning what it stands for. In every attempt of an adult to console a crying child there is a reminder of the fact that as long as a single form of life remains in misery and pain the imagination finds the world not good enough.

The reader needs no commentary to help him understand the terrible indictment of this latter world in the ***Songs of Experience.*** Contempt and horror have never spoken more clearly in English poetry. But Blake never forgets to see behind all the cruelty of man the fact of his fall. Just as no one can watch a baby without smiling, so no one can see a child tortured for its own "good" or neglected for someone else's: no one can see its parents, blackened and twisted by the St. Anthony's fire of moral virtue, stumbling out of a darkened church and blinking like bats in the sun: no one can see prostitution or war or race hatred or poverty, without groping for some cause of what seems to be utterly pointless evil. The reason can supply irrefutable proofs that in such things the world is behaving illogically and contrary to its own best interests. The reason will not take us far. Only vision helps us here, and vision shows us the tree of mystery and morality growing inside the human skull; it shows us the prophet calling to the earth to redeem herself and earth answering with a groan to be delivered; it shows us our accusing enemy who frightens us out of Paradise behind the menacing blaze of a tiger's eyes.

This is the only world the child can grow into, and yet the child must grow. The ***Songs of Experience*** are satires, but one of the things that they satirize is the state of innocence. They show us the butcher's knife which is waiting for the unconscious lamb. Conversely, the ***Songs of Innocence*** satirize the state of experience, as the contrast which they present to it makes its hypocrisies more obviously shameful. Hence the two sets of lyrics show two *contrary* states of the soul, and in their opposition there is a double-edged irony, cutting into both the tragedy and the reality of fallen existence.

The actual makes the ideal look helpless and the ideal makes the actual look absurd.

May Hill Arbuthnot

SOURCE: "Singing Words: William Blake," in *Children and Books,* Scott, Foresman and Company, 1947, pp. 134-39.

Blake was the first Englishman to write a book of poems for and about children—***Songs of Innocence,*** which is a landmark in English literature as well as in children's literature. The average child may not particularly enjoy some of the more difficult poems, but he will enjoy many of them if he hears them read aloud naturally and rhythmically by someone who likes their melodies. For Blake's poems are indeed songs, as full of cadences and lovely sounds as music. . . .

For us, ***Songs of Innocence*** marks a turning point in English poetry. The classical school had run thin; Wordsworth was already writing, but the Romantic Movement had not yet become consciously articulate. Then, suddenly, ***Songs of Innocence*** appeared—fresh, simple, unique. ***Songs of Experience*** was not published until five years later, but between the two collections of ***Songs*** came many of those poems Blake called his works of prophecy. Their mysticism and their incoherence led many people to judge Blake insane. This judgment was reversed even during Blake's lifetime, and today—however people regard his visions and his more confused writings—the best of Blake's poems are ranked among England's finest lyric poetry and a large proportion of his illustrations among the world's greatest engravings.

C. M. Bowra

SOURCE: "Songs of Innocence and Experience," in *The Romantic Imagination,* Cambridge, Mass.: Harvard University Press, 1949, pp. 25-50.

[In the following excerpt, Bowra provides an overview of Songs of Innocence and of Experience, *emphasizing the work's theme of creativity and imagination.]*

It is perhaps not surprising that in recent years scholars have tended to neglect the ***Songs*** for the prophetic books; for the ***Songs*** look limpid and translucent, while the prophetic books are rich in unravelled mysteries and alluring secrets. But the ***Songs*** deserve special attention if only because they constitute one of the most remarkable collections of lyrical poems written in English.

Blake made in practice a distinction between poetry and prophecy. In the first place, he recognized and maintained a difference of form. In the ***Songs*** he uses the traditional metres of English songs and hymns without even repeating the experiment, made in ***Poetical Sketches,*** of lyrical blank verse; in the prophecies, modelling himself on the Bible and Ossian, he uses what is in fact free verse, . . .

In the prophecies Blake speaks as an orator and needs an orator's freedom: in the ***Songs*** he sings and needs the regular measures of song. In the second place, Blake's purpose differs in the ***Songs*** and in the prophecies. In the prophecies he had a great message for his generation, an urgent call to awake from its slothful sleep, a summons to activity and to that fuller life which comes from exerting the imagination. . . .

This is not the spirit in which Blake begins the ***Songs of Innocence*** with a poem significantly called **"Introduction":**

> Piping down the valleys wild,
> Piping songs of pleasant glee,
> On a cloud I saw a child,
> And he laughing said to me:
> "Pipe a song about a Lamb!"
> So I piped with merry chear.
> "Piper, pipe that song again;"
> So I piped: he wept to hear.

These are the words of a poet who sings because he must, not of a prophet whose first wish is to summon his generation to a new life.

The differences of form and intention between the ***Songs*** and the prophetic books are paralleled by comparable differences in the presentation of material. When he completed the ***Songs,*** Blake had already written some of his prophetic books and begun that remarkable system of myths and symbols which gives them so special a character. In the ***Songs*** there is almost no trace of Blake's mythical figures. Though he wrote ***Tiriel*** and ***The Book of Thel*** at the same time as the ***Songs of Innocence,*** their characters do not appear in the ***Songs.*** And this is all the more remarkable since the experience in these prophetic books is ultimately not very dissimilar from that in the ***Songs*** and belongs to the same important years of Blake's life. In the ***Songs*** Blake pursued a more traditional and more lyrical art, because some deep need in him called for this kind of expression. It is therefore dangerous to try to explain the ***Songs*** too exactly by the prophetic books. There are undeniable connections between the two, but the ***Songs*** go their own way in their own spirit. In them Blake speaks of himself from a purely personal point of view. It is true that he uses his own remarkable symbols, but not quite in the same way as in the prophetic books, and certainly not with the same desire for a new mythology to supplement or correct that of the Bible.

It is possible to read the ***Songs*** and to be so enchanted by them that we do not stop to ask what in fact they mean. Such a procedure has the formidable approval of A. E. Housman, who says of them [in his *Name and Nature of Poetry*] that "the meaning is a poor foolish disappointing thing in comparison with the verses themselves." This is of course true. The mere meaning, extracted from the poems and paraphrased in lifeless prose, is indeed a poor thing in comparison with what Blake wrote. The poems succeed through the magnificence of their poetry, and no analysis can take its place. At the same time, it is almost impossible to read and enjoy poetry without knowing what it means, for the good reason that the meaning is an essential part of the whole and makes an essential contribution to the delight which the poems give. To acquiesce in ignorance of the meaning is more than can reasonably be asked of us. Human curiosity and the desire to gain as much as possible from a work of art reject this limited approach and force us to ask what the subjects of the poems are. Nor does this destroy our pleasure in them. When we know what Blake means, we appreciate more fully his capacity for transforming complex states of mind into pure song and for giving to his most unusual thoughts an appeal which is somehow both intimate and rapturously exciting.

That Blake intended his readers to understand what he said and to pay an intelligent attention to it is clear from his title-page, which describes the songs as "showing the two contrary states of the human soul." Blake groups his verses under two main headings, and there is plainly a great difference of character between the two parts. In so arranging his work, Blake followed his own maxim that "without Contraries is no progression." The contrast meant much to him, and we neglect it at the risk of misunderstanding his intention. So emphatic a division is not to be found in the prophetic books and shows that, when he chose, Blake could impose a fine architectural order on his work. Perhaps he was able to do this because the material and manner of the songs fall more easily into a definite shape than does the various stuff of the prophetic books. In the ***Songs*** Blake limits himself to a special section of material which is relatively clear in its outlines and limits. He has distilled his thoughts into the shape of song, and his appeal is more direct and more immediate than it can be in the more complicated technique of prophecy.

The two sections of Blake's book, the songs of innocence and the songs of experience, are contrasted elements in a single design. The first part sets out an imaginative vision of the state of innocence: the second shows how life challenges and corrupts and destroys it. What Blake intended by this scheme can be seen from the motto which he wrote for the book but did not include in it:

> The Good are attracted by Men's perceptions,
> And think not for themselves;
> Till Experience teaches them to catch
> And to cage the Fairies and Elves.
>
> And then the Knave begins to snarl
> And the Hypocrite to howl;
> And all his good Friends shew their private
> ends,
> And the Eagle is known from the Owl.

This little poem shows how the ***Songs*** are related to some of the most persistent elements in Blake's thought. Since for him the primary reality and the only thing that matters is the active life of the creative imagination, he has nothing but contempt for empiricist philosophers who build their systems on sense-perceptions instead of on vision. Blake believes that the naturally good are deceived by such theories and so corrupted by them that they cease to think for themselves, and restrict those creative forces which he calls "fairies and elves." When this happens, knavery, hypocrisy, and self-seeking enter into the soul, and the state of innocence is lost; but for those who have eyes to see, the free, soaring spirit of the eagle is visible in all its difference from the sleepy, night-ridden owl. This is the main theme of the ***Songs.*** In the first part Blake shows what innocence means, in the second how it is corrupted and destroyed.

Blake's state of innocence, set forth in symbols of pastoral life akin to those of the Twenty-third Psalm, seems at first sight to have something in common with what Vaughan, Traherne, and Wordsworth say in their different ways about the vision of childhood which is lost in later life, and it is tempting to think that this is what concerns Blake. But he is concerned with the loss not so much of actual childhood as of something wider and less definite. For him childhood is both itself and a symbol of a state of soul which may exist in maturity. His subject is the childlike vision of existence. For him all human beings are in some sense and at some times the children of a divine father, but experience destroys their innocence and makes them follow spectres and illusions. Blake does not write at a distance of time from memories of what childhood once was, but from an insistent, present anguish at the ugly contrasts between the childlike and the experienced conceptions of reality.

With a book which deals with so poignant a subject, it is tempting to look in Blake's own life for some event or circumstances which forced this issue so powerfully on him. That he was deeply troubled by it is clear not merely from the agonized poems of ***Songs of Experience*** but from the prophetic books, ***Tiriel*** and ***The Book of Thel,*** which seem to have been written in 1788 and 1789. In Thel Blake presents a symbolical figure who lives in an Arcadian state of innocence but finds herself appalled and helpless before the first appearances of reality; in ***Tiriel*** he makes his chief figure die when he realizes that he has erred in substituting the deadening rule of law for the free life of the imagination. Both books are, in a sense, concerned with the tragedy of innocence. Just as Thel is unable to endure reality when she sees it and flies back into eternity, so Har and Heva, who represent an innocence which has outlived its real strength, are unable to help Tiriel in his great need. The problems suggested in these two books are not the same as in the ***Songs,*** but there seems to be a common basis of experience, something which, even when he was writing the ***Songs of Innocence,*** deeply troubled Blake and forced him to think about this issue in more than one way.

When he composed the ***Songs of Experience,*** Blake seems to have passed through a spiritual crisis. He, who was in many ways the healthiest of men, wrote in 1793: "I say I shan't live for five years, and if I live one it will be a wonder." Something had shaken his trust in himself and in life. What this was we can only guess, and such clues as are available point to a combination of different causes. The trouble was already there in 1788 when he wrote ***Tiriel,*** but it seems to have grown and to have preyed more insistently on his mind in the following years. It did not in the least interfere with his creative powers. Indeed, at this time he did an astonishing amount of work both as a poet and as an artist, and most of it is as good as anything that he ever did afterwards. But Blake's genius was not discouraged by trouble and anxiety, and that he had these in full measure is beyond reasonable dispute. In the first place, his rapturous hopes in the French Revolution, expressed in his prophetic book called after it and written in 1791, were soon replaced by the recognition that events were taking a course not to his liking. The English Government was hostile to the Revolution, and Blake's own friends, like Thomas Paine, whom he saved from arrest by a timely warning in 1792, were in danger. What such a disillusionment meant to a visionary like Blake can be seen from his ***Visions of the Daughters of Albion,*** with its passionate denunciations of oppression and slavery. He was brought down with a terrible shock from his visions of reformed humanity to a realization of what political events really were.

In the second place, Blake's domestic life seems at this time to have passed through a strange phase. His excellent wife did not sympathize with his idealistic views of free love and resolutely opposed them. To Blake at first this was an unforeseen denial of the spirit, and it shook him deeply. It seems even for a time to have broken his trust in himself. He found his solution soon enough, and the rest of his life was spent in unclouded happiness with his wife. But what he felt at the moment can be seen from his strange poem **"William Bond,"** and especially from three verses in it:

> He went to Church in a May morning
> Attended by Fairies, one, two and three;
> But the Angels of Providence drove them away,
> And he return'd home in misery.
>
> He went not out to the Field nor Fold,
> He went not out to the Village nor Town,
> But he came home in a black, black cloud,
> And took to his Bed, and there lay down.
>
> And an Angel of Providence at his Feet,
> And an Angel of Providence at his Head,
> And in the midst a Black, Black Cloud,
> And in the midst the Sick Man on his Bed.

Since by "fairies" Blake means the impulses of the creative imagination, it is clear that in this crisis his inner life has received a terrible blow from "Angels of Providence." In his language they are the forces of legality and moralism in which he saw the most sinister enemies of the free life of the imagination. He, who had put all his trust in this free life, found himself frustrated and depressed by the forces which he most condemned. Partly in politics, partly in domestic life, partly no doubt in other matters, Blake seems to have discovered that his central and most cherished beliefs were not shared by others but were the object of hatred and persecution. At some date in these years the common world was revealed to him, and he found it more frightening than he had ever suspected. From this discovery the ***Songs*** were born.

Blake's crisis takes place in a spiritual order of things and involves spiritual values, and for this reason he has to speak of it in symbols. What he describes are not actual events as ordinary men see and understand them, but spiritual events which have to be stated symbolically in order that they may be intelligible. In the ***Songs of Innocence*** Blake's symbols are largely drawn from the Bible, and since he makes use of such familiar figures as the Good Shepherd and the Lamb of God, there is not much difficulty in seeing what he means; but in the ***Songs of Experience*** he often uses symbols of his own making, and his meaning is more elusive. Indeed, some poems in this section are fully understandable only by reference to symbols which Blake uses in his prophetic books; and since the meaning of most symbols tends to be inconstant, there is always a danger that we may make his meaning more emphatic or more exact than it is, especially since, as Blake grew older, he developed his symbols and by placing them in precise contexts gave them a greater definiteness. But in both kinds of song it is clear that Blake anticipates those poets of a hundred years later who forged their own symbols in order to convey what would otherwise be almost inexpressible, since no adequate words exist for the unnamed powers of a supernatural world. Blake's own view of his method can be seen from a letter to Thomas Butts:

> Allegory addressed to the Intellectual powers,
> while it is altogether hidden from the Corporeal
> Understanding, is My Definition of the Most
> Sublime Poetry.

Since by "Corporeal Understanding" Blake means the perception of sense-data, and by "Intellectual powers" the imaginative spirit which is the only reality, it is clear that in his view poetry is concerned with something else than the phenomenal world, and that the only means to speak of it is what he calls "allegory." It is true that elsewhere he sometimes speaks disparagingly of allegory, but that is because he distinguishes between true and false allegory. For him allegory in the good sense is not the kind of "one-one correspondence" which we find in *Pilgrim's Progress,* but a system of symbols which presents events in a spiritual world.

In the ***Songs of Innocence*** the symbols convey a special kind of existence or state of soul. In this state human beings have the same kind of security and assurance as belongs to lambs under a wise shepherd or to children with loving parents. Nor is it untrue to say that both the shepherd and the father of Blake's poems is God. It is He who is Himself a lamb and becomes a little child, who watches over sleeping children and gives his love to chimney-sweepers and little black boys. In the fatherhood of God, Blake's characters have equal rights and privileges. But by it he means not quite what orthodox Christians do. Blake, despite his deeply religious nature, did not believe that God exists apart from man, but says expressly:

> Man is All Imagination. God is Man and exists
> in us and we in him . . . Imagination or the
> Human Eternal Body in Every Man . . . Imagination
> is the Divine Body in Every Man.

For Blake, God and the imagination are one; that is, God is the creative and spiritual power in man, and apart from man the idea of God has no meaning. When Blake speaks of the divine, it is with reference to this power and not to any external or independent godhead. So when his songs tell of God's love and care, we must think of them as qualities which men themselves display and in so doing realize their full, divine nature. For instance, in **"On Another's Sorrow,"** Blake says:

> Think not thou canst sigh a sigh,
> And thy Maker is not by;
> Think not thou canst weep a tear,
> And thy Maker is not near.
>
> O! He gives to us His joy
> That our grief he may destroy;
> Till our grief is fled and gone
> He doth sit by us and moan.

Blake means that every sigh and every tear evoke a response from our divine nature and through this are cured and turned to joy. Compassion is part of man's imaginative being, and through it he is able to transform existence. For Blake, God is the divine essence which exists potentially in every man and woman.

The power and appeal of this belief appear in **"The Divine Image."** The divine image, of course, is man, but man in part of his complex being and seen from a special point of view. Blake speaks quite literally and means to be taken at his word when he says:

> To Mercy, Pity, Peace, and Love
> All pray in their distress;
> And to these virtues of delight
> Return their thankfulness.
>
> For Mercy, Pity, Peace, and Love
> Is God, our father dear,
> And Mercy, Pity, Peace, and Love
> Is Man, his child and care.
> For Mercy has a human heart
> Pity a human face,
> And Love, the human form divine,
> And Peace, the human dress.
>
> Then every man, of every clime,
> That prays in his distress,
> Prays to the human form divine,
> Love, Mercy, Pity, Peace.
>
> And all must love the human form,
> In heathen, turk, or jew;

Where Mercy, Love, and Pity dwell
There God is dwelling too.

The divine qualities which Blake enumerates exist in man and reveal their divine character through him. Though Blake says of man's imagination that "it manifests itself in his Works of Art," he spread his idea of art to include all that he thought most important and most living in conduct. In mercy, pity, peace, and love, he found the creed of brotherhood which is the centre of his gospel. He knew that by itself love may become selfish and possessive and needs to be redeemed by other, generous qualities. It is in the combination of these that man is God. In the state of innocence, life is governed by these powers, and it is they which give to it its completeness and security. That is why Blake calls his ***Songs of Innocence*** "happy songs" and says that every child will joy to hear them.

In his prophetic books Blake presents something like the state of innocence in what he calls Beulah, a kind of lower paradise, inferior indeed to the highest state of the active imagination which he calls Eden, but superior to the lower states in which reason inhibits and kills the imagination. . . .

There can be little doubt that even when he wrote the

"The Divine Image," from Songs of Innocence, *1789. Written and illustrated by William Blake.*

Songs of Innocence, Blake had formed some of these ideas. He saw that though this state of childlike happiness, which he seems to have enjoyed in his first manhood, is wonderfully charming, it is not everything, and it cannot last. To reach a higher state man must be tested by experience and suffering. This is the link between the two sections of Blake's book. Experience is not only a fact; it is a necessary stage in the cycle of being. It may in many ways be a much lower state than innocence, and this Blake stresses with great power, but it is none the less necessary. The difference between the two states is reflected in the quality of Blake's poetry. Sweet and pure though the ***Songs of Innocence*** are, they do not possess or need the compelling passion of the ***Songs of Experience.*** In dealing with innocence Blake seems deliberately to have set his tone in a quiet key to show what innocence really means in his full scheme of spiritual development. He was careful to exclude from the first part of his book anything which might sound a disturbing note or suggest that innocence is anything but happy. That is why he omitted a striking verse which he wrote in the first version of **"A Cradle Song":**

O, the cunning wiles that creep
In thy little heart asleep.
When thy little heart does wake,
Then the dreadful lightnings break.

The illusion of childhood and of the human state which resembles it must be kept free from such intruding suggestions, and there must be no hint that innocence is not complete and secure.

From innocence man passes to experience, and what Blake means by this can be seen from some lines in ***The Four Zoas:***

What is the price of Experience? do men buy it
  for a song?
Or wisdom for a dance in the street? No, it is
  bought with the price
Of all that a man hath, his house, his wife, his
  children.
Wisdom is sold in the desolate market where
  none come to buy,
And in the wither'd field where the farmer plows
  for bread in vain.

Blake knew that experience is bought at a bitter price, not merely in such unimportant things as comfort and peace of mind, but in the highest spiritual values. His ***Songs of Experience*** are the poetry of this process. They tell how what we accept in childlike innocence is tested and proved feeble by actual events, how much that we have taken for granted is not true of the living world, how every noble desire may be debased and perverted. When he sings of this process, he is no longer the piper of pleasant glee but an angry, passionate rebel. In **"Infant Sorrow"** he provides a counterpart to his **"Introduction"** and shows that even in the very beginnings of childhood there is a spirit of unrest and revolt:

My mother groan'd! my father wept.
Into the dangerous world I leapt:
Helpless, naked, piping loud:
Like a fiend hid in a cloud.

Struggling in my father's hands,
Striving against my swadling bands,
Bound and weary, I thought best
To sulk upon my mother's breast.

At the start of its existence the human creature feels itself a prisoner and, after its first efforts to resist, angrily gives up the struggle.

When experience destroys the state of childlike innocence, it puts many destructive forces in its place. To show the extent of this destruction Blake places in the ***Songs of Experience*** certain poems which give poignant contrasts to other poems which appear in the ***Songs of Innocence.*** For instance, in the first **"Nurse's Song"** he tells how children play and are allowed to go on playing until the light fades and it is time to go to bed. In this Blake symbolizes the care-free play of the imagination when it is not spoiled by senseless restrictions. But in the second **"Nurse's Song"** we hear the other side of the matter, when experience has set to work:

When the voices of children are heard on the
 green
And whisp'rings are heard in the dale,
When days of my youth rise fresh in my mind,
My face turns green and pale.

Then come home, my children, the sun is gone
 down,
And the dews of night arise;
Your spring and your day are wasted in play,
And your winter and night in disguise.

The voice that now speaks is not that of loving care but of sour age, envious of a happiness which it can no longer share and eager to point out the menaces and the dangers of the dark. It sees play as a waste of time and cruelly tells the children that their life is a sham passed in darkness and cold, . . .

The first and most fearful thing about experience is that it breaks the free life of the imagination and substitutes a dark, cold, imprisoning fear, and the result is a deadly blow to the blithe human spirit.

The fear and denial of life which come with experience breed hypocrisy, and this earns some of Blake's hardest and harshest words. For him hypocrisy is as grave a sin as cruelty because it rises from the same causes, from the refusal to obey the creative spirit of the imagination and from submission to fear and envy. He marks its character by providing an antithesis to **"The Divine Image"** in **"The Human Abstract."** In bitter irony he shows how love, pity, and mercy can be distorted and used as a cover for base or cowardly motives. Speaking through the hypocrite's lips, he goes straight to the heart of the matter by showing how glibly hypocrisy claims to observe these cardinal virtues:

Pity would be no more
If we did not make somebody Poor;
And Mercy no more could be
If all were as happy as we.

In this corrupt frame of mind, selfishness and cruelty flourish and are dignified under false names. This process wrecks the world. Harsh rules are imposed on life through what Blake calls "Mystery," with its ceremonies and hierarchies and its promise of "an allegorical abode where existence hath never come." It supports those outward forms of religion which Blake regards as the death of the soul:

Soon spreads the dismal shade
Of Mystery over his head;
And the Catterpiller and Fly
Feed on the Mystery.

And it bears the fruit of Deceit,
Ruddy and sweet to eat;
And the Raven his nest has made
In its thickest shade.

The Gods of the earth and sea
Sought thro' Nature to find this Tree;
But their search was all in vain:
There grows one in the Human Brain.

So Blake re-creates the myth of the Tree of Knowledge or of Life. This tree, which is fashioned by man's reason, gives falsehood instead of truth and death instead of life.

Perhaps the worst thing in experience, as Blake sees it, is that it destroys love and affection. On no point does he speak with more passionate conviction. He who believes that the full life demands not merely tolerance but forgiveness and brotherhood finds that in various ways love is corrupted or condemned. In **"The Clod and the Pebble"** he shows how love naturally seeks not to please itself or have any care for itself, but in the world of experience the heart becomes like "a pebble of the brook" and turns love into a selfish desire for possession:

Love seeketh only Self to please,
To bind another to Its delight,
Joys in another's loss of ease,
And builds a Hell in Heaven's despite.

The withering of the affections begins early, when their elders repress and frighten children. In **"Holy Thursday"** Blake shows what this means, how in a rich and fruitful land children live in misery:

And their sun does never shine,
And their fields are bleak and bare,
And their ways are fill'd with thorns:
It is eternal winter there.

The horror of experience is all the greater because of the contrast, explicit or implicit, which Blake suggests between it and innocence. In **"The Echoing Green"** he tells how the children are happy and contented at play, but in **"The Garden of Love,"** to the same rhythm and with the same setting, he presents an ugly antithesis. The green is still there, but on it is a chapel with "Thou shalt not" written over the door, and the garden itself has changed:

And I saw it was filled with graves,
And tomb-stones where flowers should be;
And Priests in black gowns were walking their
rounds,
And binding with briars my joys and desires.

In the state of experience, jealousy, cruelty, and hypocrisy forbid the natural play of the affections and turn joy into misery.

Blake's tragic appreciation of the restrictions which imprison and kill the living spirit was no purely personal thing. It was his criticism of society, of the whole trend of contemporary civilization. His compassionate heart was outraged and wounded by the sufferings which society inflicts on its humbler members and by the waste of human material which seems indispensable to the efficient operation of rules and laws. In **"London"** he gives his own view of that "chartered liberty" on which his countrymen prided themselves, and exposes the indisputable, ugly facts:

I wander thro' each charter'd street,
Near where the charter'd Thames does flow,
And mark in every face I meet
Marks of weakness, marks of woe.

In every cry of every Man,
In every Infant's cry of fear,
In every voice, in every ban,
The mind-forg'd manacles I hear.

How the Chimney-sweeper's cry
Every black-ning Church appalls;
And the hapless Soldier's sigh
Runs in blood down Palace walls.

But most thro' midnight streets I hear
How the youthful Harlot's curse
Blasts the new born Infant's tear,
And blights with plagues the Marriage hearse.

The child chimney-sweeper, the soldier, and the harlot are Blake's types of the oppressed—characteristic victims of a system based not on brotherhood but on fear. Each in his own way shows up the shams on which society thrives. The chimney-sweeper's condemned life is supported by the churches; the soldier's death is demanded by the court; and the harlot's calling is forced on her by the marriage-laws. The contrasts between truth and pretence, between natural happiness and unnatural repression, are stressed by Blake in these three examples, and through them we see the anguish in which he faced the social questions of his time.

The astonishing thing about the ***Songs of Experience*** is that, though they were inspired by violent emotions and have a merciless satirical temper, they are in the highest degree lyrical. Indeed, no English poet, except Shakespeare, has written songs of such lightness and melody. Yet Blake's subjects are not in the least like Shakespeare's. He writes not about fundamental matters like spring and love and death, but about his own original and complex views on existence; and the miracle is that in presenting themes which might seem to need comment and explanation, he succeeds in creating pure song. His words have an Elizabethan lilt, a music which emphasizes their meaning and conforms exactly to it. Despite his strong emotions and his unfamiliar ideas, Blake keeps his form miraculously limpid and melodious. This success is partly the result of a highly discriminating art. Blake made many changes in his texts before he was satisfied with a final version, and these show how well he knew what he was doing, how clear an idea he had of the result which he wished to reach. But this art was shaped by a creative impulse so powerful that it can only be called inspiration. Blake indeed believed that his words were often dictated to him by some supernatural power. As he wrote to Thomas Butts about a prophetic book, "I may praise it, since I dare not pretend to be any other than the Secretary; the Authors are in Eternity." In the strange workings of the creative mind there is a point at which words come with such force and intensity that they have a more than human appeal. Though the poet may not receive them all at once but gradually find, as Blake did, the exact words which he needs, yet these songs are miracles because their creation cannot be explained and because with them we feel ourselves in the presence of something beyond the control of man.

Two examples must suffice to illustrate Blake's art of song, and each is equally wonderful. The first is **"The Sick Rose"**:

O Rose, thou art sick!
The invisible worm
That flies in the night,
In the howling storm,

Has found out thy bed
Of crimson joy,
And his dark secret love
Does thy life destroy.

This illustrates in an astonishing way Blake's gift for distilling a complex imaginative idea into a few marvellously telling words. If we ask what the poem means, we can answer that it means what it says, and that this is perfectly clear. It conjures up the vision of a rose attacked in a stormy night by a destructive worm, and so Blake depicts it in his accompanying illustration. But, as in all symbolical poems, we can read other meanings into it and make its images carry a weight of secondary associations. We may say that it refers to the destruction of love by selfishness, of innocence by experience, of spiritual life by spiritual death. All these meanings it can bear, and it is legitimate to make it do so. But the actual poem presents something which is common and fundamental to all these themes, something which Blake has distilled so finely from many particular cases that it has their common, quintessential character. And this Blake sees with so piercing and so concentrated a vision that the poem has its own independent life and needs nothing to supplement it. If we wish to know more about Blake's views on the issues at which the poem hints, we may find them in his prose works and prophetic books. But here he is a poet, and his thoughts are purified and transfigured in song.

My second example is **"Ah! Sun-flower!"**:

> Ah, Sun-flower! weary of time,
> Who countest the steps of the Sun,
> Seeking after that sweet golden clime
> Where the traveller's journey is done:
>
> Where the Youth pined away with desire,
> And the pale Virgin shrouded in snow
> Arise from their graves, and aspire
> Where my Sun-flower wishes to go.

This raises questions similar to those raised by **"The Sick Rose."** Again a complex thought is distilled into two verses, and again what matters is the imaginative presentation which transports us in intense, excited delight. Here Blake's theme is not quite so single as in **"The Sick Rose."** He has transposed into this song his central ideas and feelings about all young men and young women who are robbed of their full humanity because they are starved of love. Because of this, the youth pines away with desire and the pale virgin is shrouded in snow. It is the pathos of their earthbound state that the song catches and makes significant through Blake's deep compassion. The central spring of the poem is the image of the sun-flower. The flower which turns its head to follow the sun's course and is yet rooted in the earth is Blake's symbol for all men and women whose lives are dominated and spoiled by a longing which they can never hope to satisfy, and who are held down to the earth despite their desire for release into some brighter, freer sphere. In this poem Blake expresses an idea which means a great deal to him, but he does not explain or elaborate it. He assumes that his poem will do its work by itself, and his reward is that **"Ah! Sun-flower"** belongs to that very rare and small class of poems in which inspiration carries words to a final enchantment. The ***Songs of Experience*** are more powerful and more magical than the ***Songs of Innocence*** because they are born of a deep anguish, from a storm in the poet's soul. Blake knows that one kind of existence is bright with joy and harmony, but he sees its place taken by another which is dark and sinister and dead. But Blake was not content simply to complain or to criticize. He sought some ultimate synthesis in which innocence might be wedded to experience, and goodness to knowledge. That such a state is possible he reveals in the first poem of ***Songs of Experience,*** where he speaks with the voice of the bard and summons the fallen soul of earth to some vast apocalypse:

> O Earth, O Earth, return!
> Arise from out the dewy grass;
> Night is worn,
> And the morn
> Rises from the slumberous mass.
>
> Turn away no more;
> Why wilt thou turn away?
> The starry floor,
> The wat'ry shore,
> Is giv'n thee till the break of day.

The world is still wrapped in darkness, but the stars which pierce the night are a sign of other things to come, and the sea of eternity beats on the narrow shore where mankind lives. The "break of day" is Blake's symbol for the new life in which both innocence and experience are transformed, and the soul passes in its cycle to a fuller, more active life in the creative imagination. As Blake says in a note written on a page of ***The Four Zoas:***

> Unorganiz'd Innocence: An Impossibility.
> Innocence dwells with Wisdom, but never with Ignorance.

The true innocence is not after all that of the ***Songs of Innocence,*** but something which has gained knowledge from the ugly lessons of experience and found an expanding strength in the unfettered life of the creative soul. Beyond experience Blake foresees this consummation and hints that it will come, even though he is concerned with the dark hither side of it.

Blake knows well that such a consummation will not come simply from good will or pious aspirations and that the life of the imagination is possible only through passion and power and energy. That is why he sometimes stresses the great forces which lie hidden in man and may be terrifying but are none the less necessary if anything worth while is to happen. He sees that the creative activity of the imagination and the transformation of experience through it are possible only through the release and exercise of awful powers. He chooses his symbols for these powers in violent and destructive things, as when in his **"Proverbs of Hell"** he says, "The wrath of the lion is the wisdom of God," or "The roaring of lions, the howling of wolves, the raging of the stormy sea, and the destructive sword, are portions of eternity, too great for the eye of man." It was in such elemental forces that Blake put his trust for the redemption of mankind, and he contrasted them favourably with the poor efforts of the human intelligence: "The tigers of wrath are wiser than the horses of instruction." The wrath which Blake found in Christ, his symbol of the divine spirit which will not tolerate restrictions but asserts itself against established rules, was the means by which he hoped to unite innocence and experience in some tremendous synthesis.

The poetry of this desire and of what it meant to Blake can be seen in **"The Tyger."** Here, too, enraptured song conveys in essential vision some themes which Blake presents elsewhere in more detail. This is the pure poetry of his trust in cosmic forces. The images of **"The Tyger"** recur in the prophetic books, but in the poem, detached from any very specific context, they have a special strength and freedom. The tiger is Blake's symbol for the fierce forces in the soul which are needed to break the bonds of experience. The "forests of the night," in which the tiger lurks, are ignorance, repression, and superstition. It has been fashioned by unknown, supernatural spirits, like Blake's mythical heroes, Orc and Los, prodigious smiths who beat out living worlds with their hammers; and this happened when "the stars threw down their spears," that is, in some enormous cosmic crisis when the universe turned round in its course and began to move from light to darkness—as Urizen says in ***The Four Zoas,*** when he finds that passion and natural joy have withered under his rule and the power of the spirit has been weakened:

> I went not forth: I hid myself in black clouds of
> my wrath;
> I call'd the stars around my feet in the night of
> councils dark;
> The stars threw down their spears and fled
> naked away.

If we wish to illustrate **"The Tyger"** from Blake's other works, it is easy to do so, and it adds much to our understanding of its background and its place in Blake's development. But it is first and last a poem. The images are so compelling that for most purposes they explain themselves, and we have an immediate, overwhelming impression of an awful power lurking in the darkness of being and forcing on us questions which pierce to the heart of life:

> Tyger! Tyger! burning bright
> In the forests of the night,
> What immortal hand or eye
> Could frame thy fearful symmetry?
>
> In what distant deeps or skies
> Burnt the fire of thine eyes?
> On what wings dare he aspire?
> What the hand dare sieze [sic] the fire?
>
> And what shoulder, and what art,
> Could twist the sinews of thy heart?
> And when thy heart began to beat,
> What dread hand? and what dread feet?
>
> What the hammer? what the chain?
> In what furnace was thy brain?
> What the anvil? what dread grasp
> Dare its deadly terrors clasp?
> When the stars threw down their spears,
> And water'd heaven with their tears,
> Did he smile his work to see?
> Did he who made the Lamb make thee?
>
> Tyger! Tyger! burning bright
> In the forests of the night,
> What immortal hand or eye,
> Dare frame thy fearful symmetry?

Just as early in the ***Songs of Innocence*** Blake sets his poem about the lamb, with its artless question,

> Little Lamb, who made thee?
> Dost thou know who made thee?

so early in the ***Songs of Experience*** Blake sets his poem about the tiger with its more frightening and more frightened questions. The lamb and the tiger are symbols for two different states of the human soul. When the lamb is destroyed by experience, the tiger is needed to restore the world.

In the ***Songs of Innocence and Experience*** there are only hints of the final consummation which shall restore men to the fullness of joy. The poems are concerned with an earlier stage in the struggle and treat of it from a purely poetical standpoint. What Blake gives is the essence of his imaginative thought about this crisis in himself and in all men. When he completed the whole book in its two parts, he knew that the state of innocence is not enough, but he had not found his full answer to his doubts and questions. From this uncertainty he wrote his miraculous poetry. Against the negative powers, which he found so menacingly in the ascendant, he set, both in theory and in practice, his gospel of the imagination. Strange as some of his ideas may be to us, the poetry comes with an unparalleled force because of the prodigious release of creative energy which has gone to its making. The prophet of gigantic catastrophes and celestial reconciliations was also a poet who knew that poetry alone could make others share his central experiences. In the passion and the tenderness of these songs there is something beyond analysis, that living power of the imagination which was the beginning and the end of Blake's activity. In ***A Vision of the Last Judgment*** he says:

> "What," it will be Question'd, "When the Sun rises, do you not see a round disk of fire somewhat like a Guinea?" O no, no, I see an Innumerable company of the Heavenly host crying, "Holy, Holy, Holy is the Lord God Almighty."

Because Blake pierced beyond the visible world to these eternal powers and made them his daily company, he was able to give to his poetry the clarity and the brightness of vision.

Sybil Norton and John Cournos

SOURCE: "William Blake: Mystic and Poet," in *Famous British Poets,* Dodd, Mead & Company, 1952, pp. 65-70.

In 1789, the year of the French Revolution, William Blake's first original songs were issued. These ***Songs of Innocence*** were the first volumes to be produced in Blake's new manner of illuminated printing. His object appears to have been primarily ethical. For the first time his mystical aspect of thought merges with his own peculiar lyrical gift. The essence of all being, as he conceives it, is contained in such a poem as **"The Divine Image"**:

To Mercy, Pity, Peace and Love
All prayer in their distress;
And to these virtues of delight
Return their thankfulness.

For Mercy, Pity, Peace and Love
Is God, our Father dear,
And Mercy, Pity, Peace and Love
Is man, His child and care.

For Mercy has a human heart,
Pity a human face,
And Love the human form divine,
And Peace, the human dress.

Then every man of every clime,
That prays in his distress,
Prays to the human form divine,
Love, Mercy, Pity, Peace.

And all must love the human form,
In heathen, Turk, or Jew;
Where Mercy, Love and Pity dwell
There God is dwelling too.

To William Blake, God and the imagination were the same thing; that is, he conceived God as the spiritual power in man; apart from mankind he could find no meaning in God. He took pains to show that when he speaks of God's love and care he means these qualities as displayed by men and contained in men themselves.

In 1794, when Blake was thirty-seven, his ***Songs of Innocence*** and ***Songs of Experience*** were combined in one volume. . . .

He was a pleasant sociable fellow and a witty talker, keen in argument and sometimes violent as he had been from his youth. William Blake well knew the power of the tiger in man. His poem on that subject is perhaps the most popular he ever wrote:

Tiger! Tiger! burning bright
In the forests of the night,
What immortal hand or eye
Could frame thy fearful symmetry

"The Poison Tree," "The Garden of Love," "The Little Boy Lost" and many other lyrics were also included among ***Songs of Experience.***

F. J. Harvey Darton

SOURCE: "The Moral Tale: (ii) Persuasive; Chiefly in Verse," in *Children's Books in England: Five Centuries of Social Life,* second edition, Cambridge at the University Press, 1970, pp. 182-204.

[The following excerpt was originally published in Children's Books in England: Five Centuries of Social Life, *1958.]*

Blake, when he produced—literally produced: wrote, drew, engraved and put forth—his ***Songs of Innocence*** (1789, dated) and ***Songs of Experience*** (1794), was himself, in a spiritual sense, a child happy on a cloud, singing and desiring such songs as few but he could write. But he was also setting down what a child had thought, setting it down as an expression of human nature as he saw and had observed it—as innocent experience recorded, not as an offering to innocence; and the Introduction, to that extent, explains the very root of that experience, the immediate ecstasy of joy without shadow or reflection.

A great imaginative writer had, in fact, broken into this narrow library that others were toiling so laboriously to fill for children. Those others, the Edgeworths, the Watts's, the Taylors, the Lambs, the Trimmers (for they are all in the same gallery in this task), had their ideals, high, practical, long, severe, whatever you like to call them. But they never dreamt of knocking at the gate of heaven or playing among the tangled stars. At best they could only laugh a little and break a few weak chains of solemnity. They never saw the strange distance that is sometimes lifted up almost into sight beyond the clear clean horizon of sunset. They were never taken out of themselves. They always were themselves in a world of selves mutually communicable. Blake did not fit into their library, excellent though its accommodation was beginning to be. But today it is his spirit that its poets would like to recapture.

Harold Bloom

SOURCE: An excerpt from *Blake's Apocalypse: A Study in Poetic Argument,* Doubleday & Company, Inc., 1963, pp. 129, 136-45.

[Bloom is one of the most prominent American critics and literary theorists. In the following excerpt, Bloom denies that Songs of Experience *is a lamentation for lost innocence, asserting that the poems therein subtly call for a holistic integration of the spiritual and mundane components of human existence.]*

Blake wrote the ***Songs of Experience*** between 1789 and 1794, engraving them in the latter year but probably not often as a separate work. . . . Blake clearly wanted ***[Songs of Innocence*** and ***Songs of Experience]*** to be read (and viewed) together. The title of the 1794 engraved work is ***Songs of Innocence and of Experience, Shewing the Two Contrary States of the Human Soul,*** and the ***Songs of Experience*** do not in fact exist for us in a single copy without the preceding work.

Magnificent as the best of the ***Songs of Experience*** are, it is unfortunate that they continue to usurp something of the study that should be given to Blake's more ambitious and greater works. Their relative conventionality of form has made them popular for some of the wrong reasons, and they frequently tend to be misread. It is as though Milton were to be esteemed for *Lycidas* alone, and *Lycidas* to be read as a tormented mystic's outcry against the harshness of an existence that devastates the dreams of childhood. Even learned readers, who can laugh at such a possibility, are willing to see the ***Songs of Experience*** as Blake's greatest achievement, and to see it also as a lamentation for lost Innocence.

Songs of Experience begins with a powerful **"Introduction"** addressed to Earth by a Bard, and follows with **"Earth's Answer."** This Bard of Experience has considerable capacity for vision, and has much in common with Blake, but he is not Blake, and his songs are limited by his perspective. They are songs of the state of Experience, but Experience is hardly Blake's highest and most desired state of existence.

We can see the distance between the Bard of Experience and Blake in the second stanza of the **"Introduction."** The first stanza tells us that the Bard sees the "Present, Past & Future," but this is not the statement that will be made later in ***Jerusalem:*** "I see the Past, Present & Future existing all at once Before me." The later statement is true vision, for it makes the prophetic point that compels clock time to become imaginative or human time: If not now, when? The Bard of Experience sees what is, what was, and what is to come, but he does not necessarily see them all as a single mental form, which is the clue to his tragic mental error throughout the **"Introduction."** His ears *have heard* the Holy Word that *walk'd* among the ancient trees, but he does not hear that Word now. This is made altogether clear when he refers to the Soul as having lapsed:

> Calling the lapsed Soul,
> And weeping in the evening dew;
> That might controll
> The starry pole,
> And fallen, fallen light renew!

The Holy Word is God-as-Man, Jesus, who once walked in the Garden of Eden "in the cool of the day." The Word calls and weeps, and if the Word were heeded, the Fall could be undone, for "the lapsed Soul" still has the potential that might control nature. But the Bard, though he sees all this, thinks of man as a "lapsed Soul," and Blake of course does not, as the ***Marriage*** has shown us. Blake knows that when man is raised, he must be raised as a spiritual body, not as a consciousness excluded from energy and desire.

The Bard's error takes on an added poignancy as he emulates Milton, in deliberately echoing the desperation of the prophet Jeremiah. He tries to tell the very soil itself what her inhabitants are deaf to, urging the Earth to hear the word of the Lord and to return:

> O Earth, O Earth, return!
> Arise from out the dewy grass;
> Night is worn,
> And the morn
> Rises from the slumberous mass.

In this precisely worded stanza, Earth is being urged to arise literally out of herself; to abandon her present form for the original she has forsaken. If the morn can rise in its cycle, cannot Earth break the cycle and be herself at last?

> Turn away no more;
> Why wilt thou turn away?
> The starry floor,
> The wat'ry shore,
> Is giv'n thee till the break of day.

What the Bard urges is what ought to be, but Earth can no more arise "from out" the grass than man's "lapsed soul" can rise from the "slumberous mass" of his body. The Bard's dualism, traditional in orthodox Christian accounts of apocalypse, divides still further an already dangerous division. If Earth returns it must be in every blade of grass, even as man must rise in every minute particular of his body. The starry roof of the spatially bound heavens ought to be only the floor of Earth's aspirations, just as the wat'ry shore marking Earth's narrow border upon chaos ought to be a starting point of the natural, and not its end. But it is again a not fully imaginative hope, to believe that a world of matter is given to Earth only until the apocalyptic break of day. Blake's heaven, unlike the Bard's, is a radical renewal of *this* world, an Earth more alive to the awakened senses than the one that so fearfully turns away.

The Bard is neither the prophetic Devil nor the timeserving Angel of the ***Marriage,*** but the ancestor of and spokesman for a third class of men in Blake, the almost imaginative, who will later be termed the Redeemed. The parallel names for Devil and Angel will be the Reprobate and the Elect respectively, and clearly all three names are as ironic as Devil and Angel. The Reprobate are the prophets who appear reprobate to society; the Elect are dogmatists of societal values, as self-deluded as the Calvinist chosen; the Redeemed are those capable of imaginative redemption who still stand in need of it. The central irony of the ***Songs of Experience*** has proved too subtle for most of Blake's readers; the songs sung directly by the Bard are only in the Redeemed, and not the Reprobate category. That is, just as most of the ***Songs of Innocence*** are trapped in the limitations of that vision, so are many of the ***Songs of Experience*** caught in the dilemmas implicit in that state. The Bard's songs are, besides the **"Introduction,"** notably **"The Tyger," "A Poison Tree,"** and **"A Little Girl Lost."** Blake's own songs, in which he allows himself a full Reprobate awareness, are **"Holy Thursday," "Ah! Sun-Flower," "London," "The Human Abstract,"** and the defiant **"To Tirzah."** The remaining poems in ***Songs of Experience*** belong to various other Redeemed speakers.

One of this group is **"Earth's Answer"** to the Bard. A Reprobate prophet would take a tone less optimistic than that of the Bard, and Earth is too experienced to react to optimism with less than an immense bitterness. Earth is . . . dominated by a "stony dread" of what Jupiter or "Starry Jealousy" may yet do to her, though that Nobodaddy has already done his worst [Bloom describes Nobodaddy as the God who is "the nobody's father of Experience," in contrast with the loving father of Innocence; Nobodaddy connotes an association of sexuality and sin]. Grimly, Blake's Earth refers to her jealous jailer as "the Father of the ancient men," a title Blake would never grant him. Earth is in despair, and will not believe that the oppressive sky-god is merely a usurper of power. . . .

The issue between the Bard and Earth intensifies in Earth's last stanza:

> Break this heavy chain
> That does freeze my bones around.
> Selfish! vain!
> Eternal bane!
> That free Love with bondage bound.

The Bard sought to put the burden upon nature, urging Earth to turn away no more. Earth gives the burden back to whom it belongs: the Bard, and all men, must act to break the freezing weight of Jealousy's chain. If they can free Love, then nature will respond, but the sexual initiative must be taken by and between humans, for they need not be subject to natural limitations.

The themes announced in these two introductory poems are the principal themes of the entire song cycle. **"The Clod & the Pebble"** opposes two loves, the Clod's of total sacrifice, and the Pebble's of total self-appropriation. The irony is that the opposition is a negation, for neither love can lead to the progression of contraries that is a marriage. The Clod joys in its own loss of ease; the Pebble in another's loss, but there is loss in either case. Heaven is being built in Hell's despair, Hell in Heaven's despite. Both Clod and Pebble are caught in the sinister moral dialectic of exploitation that is a mark of Experience, for neither believes that any individuality can gain except at the expense of another.

This dialectic of exploitation expands to social dimensions in **"Holy Thursday,"** which matches the earlier **"Holy Thursday"** of Innocence. But the ambiguity of tone of the earlier song has vanished:

> Is this a holy thing to see
> In a rich and fruitful land,
> Babes reduc'd to misery,
> Fed with cold and usurous hand?
> Is that trembling cry a song?
> Can it be a song of joy?
> And so many children poor?
> It is a land of poverty!

Two contrary readings of the first **"Holy Thursday"** [are] equally true, but from the stance of Experience only one reading is possible. This second poem goes so far as to insist that the charity children live in an "eternal winter" without the fostering power of nature's sun and rain, since the dazed mind cannot accept poverty as natural. **"The Chimney Sweeper"** of Experience has the same childlike logic, with the peculiar rhetorical force that "because" takes in this context:

> Because I was happy upon the heath,
> And smil'd among the winter's snow,
> They clothed me in the clothes of death,
> And taught me to sing the notes of woe.

The second **"Nurse's Song"** affords a remarkably instructive contrast to the first. The Nurse of Experience reacts to the sound of children's voices on the green by recalling her earlier vision, and her face "turns green and pale," as well it might, in comparing the two states, for the movement is from:

> Come, come, leave off play, and let us away
> Till the morning appears in the skies.

to:

> Your spring & your day are wasted in play
> And your winter and night in disguise.

This is neither realism nor cynicism replacing Innocence, but an existence both lower and higher, less and more real than the undivided state of consciousness. The morning does not appear again, and so the generous expectations are self-deceptions. But the wisdom of Experience is at its best too much the wisdom of the natural heart, and we cannot altogether accept that the play was wasted. Nor are we meant to forget that the final waste will be in the disguise of death, which is the culmination of the cruder deceptions of Experience. . . .

With the greatest of these poems, **"The Tyger,"** the Bard of Experience returns, in all the baffled wonder of his strong but self-fettered imagination:

> Tyger! Tyger! burning bright,
> In the forests of the night:
> What immortal hand or eye
> Could frame thy fearful symmetry?

Nobody staring at Blake's illustration to this would see its Tyger as anything but a mild and silly, perhaps worried, certainly shabby, little beast. . . . The Tyger of the design is not in the forests of the night, but in the open world of clear vision. The forests are "of" the night in belonging to it; the Bard of Experience is in mental darkness. He sees a burning beast against a bordering blackness, and his own mortal eye is framing the Tyger in a double sense: creating it, and surrounding it with an opaque world. But from the start he desires to delude himself; the first of his rhetorical questions insists on a god or demon for its answer.

Blake evidently derived the notion of confronting a mythic beast and having it serve as the text for a series of increasingly rhetorical questions that will help to demonstrate an orthodox theodicy from the Book of Job. The Tyger is a precise parallel to the Behemoth and the Leviathan, emblems of the sanctified tyranny of nature over man. The Bard's Tyger is also "the chief of the ways of God: he that made him can make his sword to approach unto him."

Fearful and awed, the Bard learns the logic of Leviathan: "None is so fierce that dare stir him up: who then is able to stand before me?" Jehovah proudly boasted of Leviathan that he was a king over men, those deluded children of pride. Though he worships in fear, the Bard also is proud to reveal the Tyger's power. Melville's Moby Dick is another Tyger, but Ahab strikes through the mask, and asserts [Promethean defiance]. The Bard of Experience is confused, because this world in many of its visible aspects seems to have been formed both in love (the Lamb) and fright (the Tyger). The Bard is one of the Redeemed, capable of imaginative salvation, but before the poem ends he has worked his frenzy into the self-enclosure of the Elect Angels, prostrate before a mystery entirely of his own creation.

To trace this process of wilful failure one need only notice the progressive limitation of the poem's questionings. The second stanza asks whether the Tyger was created in some "distant deeps" (Hell) "or skies" (Heaven). If a mortal were the creator in either case he must have been an Icarus ("On what wings dare he aspire?") or a Prometheus ("What the hand dare sieze the fire?"), both punished by the sky-gods for their temerity. Behind the Tyger's presumably lawful creation must be the blacksmith god who serves as a trusty subordinate to the chief sky-god. His furnace, and not the human brain, wrought the Tyger's deadly terrors, including that symmetry so surprisingly fearful. What Blake called "Deism" is entering the poem, but inverted so that an argument from design induces a question that the Bard cannot wish to have answered:

> When the stars threw down their spears
> And water'd heaven with their tears:
> Did he smile his work to see?
> Did he who made the Lamb make thee?

We will come upon this image later in Blake, but its Miltonic background is enough for our understanding. When the fallen Angels were defeated, when their tears and weapons alike came down as so many shooting stars, did the same god, who is now taken to be an answer to the poem's earlier questionings, smile at his victory? And is that god, clearly the creator of the tyrants of Experience, Tyger and Leviathan, also the god of unsundered Innocence, of which the Lamb is emblematic? The Bard abandons the issue and plunges back into the affrighted awe of his first stanza, but with the self-abnegating change of "Could frame thy fearful symmetry" to "Dare frame." I do not think that Blake meant it to remain an open question, but also he clearly did not want a premature answer. All deities, for him, resided within the human breast, and so, necessarily, did all Lambs and Tygers.

The ironies of apprehension mount in the remaining ***Songs of Experience.*** The reader learns in time that what these poems demand is a heightened awareness of tonal complexities. . . .

E. D. Hirsch, Jr.

SOURCE: An excerpt from *Innocence and Experience: An Introduction to Blake,* Yale University Press, 1964, pp. 244-52.

"The Tyger," from Songs of Experience, *in* Songs of Innocence and of Experience, *1794. Written and illustrated by William Blake.*

[In the following excerpt, Hirsch explicates the poem "The Tyger," from Songs of Innocence and of Experience.*]*

[The] greatest of Blake's poems displays his most distinctive characteristic as a lyric poet: the contrast between his vividly simple language and his immense complexity of meaning. If **["The Tyger"]** is a richer poem than **"The Lamb,"** it is not because its language is more difficult. Verbally, the most daring phrase of **"The Tyger"** is "forests of the night," which is not different in kind from "clothing of delight" in **"The Lamb."** The great distinguishing mark of **"The Tyger"** is the *complexity* of its *thought and tone.*

Like **"The Lamb,"** which it satirizes, it begins with a question about the Creator:

> **["The Lamb"]**
> Little Lamb, who made thee?
> Dost thou know who made thee?
> Gave thee life, & bid thee
> By the stream & o'er the mead
>
> **["The Tyger"]**
> Tyger, tyger, burning bright,
> In the forests of the night:
> What immortal hand or eye.
> Could frame thy fearful symmetry?

While **"The Lamb"** answers the questions it poses, **"The Tyger"** consists entirely of unanswered questions. In this simple fact lodges much of the poem's richness. The questions it asks are ultimate ones, and while the answers are implicit in the poem, they cannot be pat answers because, no matter how the reader construes its implications, the poem remains a series of questions. The way each question is formed makes it also an answer, but still the answer is formed as a question, and neither is resolved into the other. All the complexities of the poem are built on this doubleness in its rhetoric, and every aspect of the poem partakes of this doubleness.

Blake's first intention in forming such a poem was no doubt to satirize the singlemindedness of **"The Lamb,"** a poem which excluded all genuine terror from life and found value only in what is gentle, selfless, pious, and loving. It is true that the ***Songs of Innocence*** as a whole do not exclude cruelty and terror. In **"Night,"** "wolves and tygers howl for prey," and in other poems there is a sufficiency of pain and tears. But cruelty and terror are presented as aspects of life that are to be finally overcome and therefore have no permanent reality or value. In **"Night"** the lion is ultimately transformed into a loving guardian; in Eternity he lies down with the lamb. Thus, while ***Innocence*** acknowledges tigerness, it entertains two reassuring ideas about it: that it is temporary and transcended, and that it is directly opposite to true holiness, which consists entirely of the lamblike virtues of Mercy, Pity, Peace, and Love. These are the two ideas that **"The Tyger"** satirizes as illusions. To the idea that the terrors of life will be transcended, the poem opposes a tiger that will *never* lie down with the lamb. He is just as fundamental and eternal as the lamb is. To the idea that only lamblike virtues are holy, the poem opposes a God who is just as violent and fiery as the tiger himself. He is not a God whose attributes are the human form divine, but a God who is fiercely indifferent to man. Thus, to the singlemindedness of **"The Lamb," "The Tyger"** opposes a double perspective that acknowledges both the human values of Mercy, Pity, and Love, and, at the same time, the transhuman values of cruelty, energy, and destructiveness.

For this reason **"The Tyger"** is not primarily a satirical poem. It submerges its satire beneath its larger concerns. It counters **"The Lamb"** by embracing both the lamb and the tiger, and it accomplishes this by embracing two attitudes at once. That is the brilliant service performed by the device of the question. The first stanza, for example, really makes two statements at once. The speaker's incredulity when confronted by a tiger who is just as fundamental as a lamb is the incredulity of one who is still close to the standpoint of ***Innocence.*** Could *God* have made this ferocity? Is there, after all, radical evil in the world? Can it be that the God who made the tiger is a tiger-God? The speaker's astonishment is that of a man who confronts for the first time the possibility that what is divine may not be what is reassuring in terms of human values, may indeed be entirely evil from the exclusively human perspective. All sympathetic readers of the poem have experienced this evocation of an evil that in human terms remains evil. Blake meant us to experience this, as we know from such phrases in the first draft as "cruel fire," "horrid ribs," and "sanguine woe."

Nevertheless, Blake canceled these phrases because they interfered with an equally powerful affirmative motif in the poem. This is easily seen when the moral astonishment of the question is transformed into something quite different by converting the question to a statement:

> Tyger, Tyger burning bright
> In the forests of the night
> None but immortal hand or eye
> Could frame thy fearful symmetry.

That would simplify the poem quite as much as "horrid ribs" and "sanguine woe," but it would also show that the *language* of the poem makes an affirmation that is just as powerful as its horrified confrontation of radical evil.

That is because the tiger is not simply burning; he is burning bright. His ferocity and destructiveness are not diminished by his brightness, but transfigured by it. His world is the night—dangerous, and deadly—but "forests," like "bright" transfigures all that dread. Blake's usual word for a tiger's habitat was "desart" (**"The Little Girl Lost"**) and it was the word normally used by Blake's contemporaries, if we may judge from Charles Lamb's misquotation of the line [in a 15 May 1824 letter]: "In the desarts of the night." "Forests," on the other hand, suggests tall straight forms, a world that for all its terror has the orderliness of the tiger's stripes or Blake's perfectly balanced verses. The phrase for such an animal and such a world is "fearful symmetry," and it would be a critical error to give preponderance either to that terror or that beauty.

Nor should we regard the image summoned up by the incantation of the first line as anything less than a symbol of all that is dreadful in the world. For the terror of the vision corresponds to the terror of the created thing itself—the *felis tigris*. No other animal combines so much beauty with so much terror. The symbol of the natural fact is grounded in the natural fact. The speaker's terror thus constitutes an insight that is just as profound as the poet's admiration of the tiger's beauty, and to disregard that terror is to trivialize the poem. **"The Tyger"** is not about two modes of looking at a tiger but about the nature of the creation.

In the **"Proverbs of Hell,"** Blake had celebrated the divinity of natural strife and energy, and in the revision of ***There Is No Natural Religion*** he had stated quite unambiguously: "He who sees the Infinite in *all* things sees God." There can be no doubt that **"The Tyger"** is, among other things, a poem that celebrates the holiness of tigerness. This aspect of the poem is reminiscent of one of the Proverbs of Hell: "The roaring of lions, the howling of wolves, the raging of the stormy sea, and the destructive sword, are portions of eternity too great for the eye of man." But the poem is a far greater statement of this religious faith than the proverb, because the mere assertion that the terrors of creation have a holiness transcending the human perspective is too complacent to be believed. How can this confident assertion be too great for the eye of man? Though the raging of the sea may be holy, it is merely terrible to the man at sea, unmitigably evil and malignant. Blake's accomplishment in **"The Tyger"** is to preserve the divine perspective without relinquishing the human. The union of terror with admiration makes the general tone of the poem that of religious awe, but this general tone is compounded of two attitudes that never altogether collapse into one another.

In the second stanza, Blake continues to evoke the doubleness of the tiger in images which suggest equally God and the Devil:

> In what distant deeps or skies
> Burnt the fire of thine eyes?

Is the tiger's fire from the deeps of Hell or the heights of Heaven? Whether good or evil, the fire has a provenance beyond the realm where human good or evil have any meaning.

> On what wings dare he aspire?
> What the hand dare sieze the fire?

Did the immortal dare to fly like Satan through chaos? Did he dare like Prometheus to bring the fire from Heaven?

As the God begins to form the tiger, the immensity of his power takes precedence over the daring of his exploit:

> And what shoulder and what art
> Could twist the sinews of thy heart?

The twisting shoulder of the god forms the twisting sinews of the tiger's heart. This imaginative identification of the tiger and the god carries the same kind of double-edged implication as the preceding images. The identification of the tiger and his creator turns the god into a tiger: if that shoulder could make that heart, what must be the heart of the god? The divine artist plays with ferocity out of ferocity. Yet if the god is a tiger, then the tiger is a god. The fire of those eyes is the spark of divinity. As the astonished and uncertain mind of the speaker shifts alternatively from god to tiger he lapses into an incoherent confusion that makes no literal sense (the couplet is an unassimilated vestige from an earlier draft) but makes good dramatic sense:

> And when that heart began to beat
> What dread hand and what dread feet?

Finally, the creation of the tiger is seen not as an act of ruthless physical daring and power but as an act of fiery craftsmanship in a fantastic smithy. This is Blake's favorite image for artistic creation, whether it be the creation of a tiger, a world, a religion, or a poem. The fiery forge is a place where incandescent energy and artistic control meet, just as they meet in the fearful symmetry of the tiger. As the rhythmic pulses of the verse fall like hammer blows, the speaker looks alternatively at the maker and the thing made, in an ecstasy of admiration and empty horror:

> What the hammer? What the chain?

[The hammer is wielded by the god, the chain is beaten by the hammer.]

> In what furnace was thy brain?
> What the anvil? What dread grasp
> Dare its deadly terrors clasp?

The staccato beats of controlled fury are succeeded by a stanza of immense calm that enormously widens the imaginative range of the poem. It is a highly compressed and difficult stanza, but it is perhaps the finest moment in Blake's poetry:

> When the stars threw down their spears,
> And water'd heaven with their tears,
> Did he smile his work to see?
> Did he who made the Lamb make thee?

The effect of the last two lines is to throw into clear relief the unresolved conflict between the divine perspective that has been implied all along in the poem, and the speaker's terrified and morally affronted perspective. The god smiles, the man cowers. (Of course, God smiled, and the answer to both questions is, "Yes!" The entire stanza is formed from traditional biblical and Miltonic imagery, and within that tradition, "God saw everything that he had made and behold it was very good.") But while the man cowers, he has a growing sense of the reason for God's smile. It could be a satanic and sadistic smile, but it could also be the smile of the artist who has forged the richest and most vital of possible worlds, a world that contains both the tiger and the lamb.

This broader perspective is introduced in the first two, highly compressed, lines of the stanza. "When the stars threw down their spears" is an allusion to the angelic fall as presented by Milton [in *Paradise Lost,* Book VII]:

> They astonisht all resistance lost,
> All courage, down their weapons dropt.

The defeat of the rebellious angels is followed by their being cast into Hell, which is followed in turn by the creation of the world. That moment of the angelic defeat is therefore a decisive moment in the divine plan. The fall of the angels is the prelude to the fall of man, and in the tradition it is thus the prelude to the bringing of death into the world and all our woe. This moment begins the catalogue of evil and cruelty that will include the tiger. Yet the angelic fall was also "his work." To smile at that is to smile at the tiger.

But why does Blake call the rebellious angels "stars"? His reason belongs to the central conception of the poem, and it is given in the next line: "And watered heaven with their tears." The defeat of the angels caused them to weep tears, and these tears, left behind as they plummeted to Hell, became what we now call the stars. The angels are named "stars" proleptically to explain the name now given to their tears. The immediate result of the angelic defeat was therefore the creation of the stars, just as its indirect result was the creation of the world. No doubt, the God whose "work" was the angelic fall is a terrible and inscrutable God, but however terrible his work is, it is sanctified by vitality, order, and beauty. The stars of night are part of the same awesome design as the forests of the night and the fearful symmetry of the tiger. When, therefore, the poet repeats the questions of the first stanza, it is with no less terror but with increased awe. The question is no longer how *could* a god—physically and morally—frame such *fearful* symmetry, but how *dare* God frame such *fearful symmetry.* The last line now emphasizes the artistic daring inherent in a creation that is incredibly rich, and terrifyingly beautiful, and is like God himself beyond human good or evil.

While **"The Tyger"** expresses a religious affirmation that is common to all of Blake's poetry in the 90s, it is the most comprehensive poem Blake produced in that period. . . . It celebrates the divinity and beauty of the creation and its transcendence of human good and evil without relinquishing the Keatsian awareness that "the miseries of the world Are misery." For all its brevity, its spiritual scope is immense.

S. Foster Damon

SOURCE: An excerpt from *A Blake Dictionary: The Ideas and Symbols of William Blake,* Brown University Press, 1965, p. 378.

[An American poet, critic, and biographer, Damon established himself as the American pioneer of Blake studies with the publication of William Blake: His Philosophy and Symbols (1924). *In the following excerpt from his later Blake* Dictionary, *he identifies dichotomy as the central underlying structural and thematic principle of* Songs of Innocence and of Experience.*]*

[Songs of Innocence and of Experience:] "Innocence" was the technical word for the state of the unfallen man;

"The Lamb," from Songs of Innocence, *1789. Written and illustrated by William Blake.*

"Experience" was used by Blake to indicate man's state after the Fall. The idea of a single work of two contrasting parts was doubtless suggested by Milton's *L'Allegro* and *Il Penseroso,* which together form a single cyclical work: where either ends, the other begins. But where Milton contrasted gaiety and thoughtfulness, Blake contrasted ecstasy and despair; and he anticipated not repetition but progress to a third state.

Blake's obvious parallels are limited to comparatively few of the poems: the two **"Chimney Sweepers,"** the two **"Nurse's Songs,"** the two **"Holy Thursdays"**; there are also contrasting titles: **"Infant Joy"** and **"Infant Sorrow," "The Divine Image"** and **"A Divine Image."** Some parallel titles are not real contrasts, but different subjects: thus **"The Little Girl Lost"** deals with the death of a child, while **"A Little Girl Found"** describes her first love affair; and **"The Little Boy Lost"** describes the child's agony at being misled, while the second poem with a similar title tells of his martyrdom for having his own ideas.

Other poems are contrasted only by subject. Thus **"The Lamb"** (God's love) is to be paired with **"The Tyger"** (God's wrath); **"The Blossom"** with **"The Sick Rose"**; and probably **"The Ecchoing Green"** with **"The Garden of Love,"** and **"The Shepherd"** with **"London."** Beyond this, the reader may make his own conjectures, because Blake was not mechanically systematic.

The first poem in the book, the **"Introduction"** to the ***Songs of Innocence,*** indicates the two Contrary States when the piper plays his tune twice: the first time, the child laughs, and the second time, he weeps. But at the third performance (this time with words) the child weeps with joy—the third stage where the contraries are synthesized. The last poem of the book, **"To Tirzah"** (added about 1795), is a fitting conclusion, as it expresses the third stage—revolution. The lad becomes himself by rejecting the maternal authority, using Jesus' own words to Mary: "Woman, what have I to do with thee?" But the sense goes deeper; for in rejecting the mother, the lad also rejects what his mother gave him: his mortal body, with its closed senses and the misery of sex. When that is transcended, "it is Raised a Spiritual Body."

Ethel L. Heins

SOURCE: A review of *Songs of Innocence,* in *The Horn Book Magazine,* Vol. XLII, No. 5, October, 1966, p. 577.

[The following review focuses on Ellen Raskin's music and illustrations for Songs of Innocence, *1966.]*

In 1789 the English mystic-artist-poet published his revolutionary ***Songs of Innocence,*** accomplishing alone the complete manufacture—printing, engraving, hand-coloring, and binding. Blake's intense spirituality and idealism pervade the twenty-two poems which capture the true spirit of childhood—its curiosity, responsiveness, wonder, and its immaturity, uncontaminated by experience. Stylistically as well, the poems are innocent and childlike in their utter simplicity of language and form, and in the directness of their ideas and images. To have made new illustrations following Blake's unique style would have been ludicrous; Ellen Raskin has interpreted the poetry sensitively and personally with strong yet graceful and serene woodcuts handsomely colored in blue, olive, brick red, and mustard yellow on well-designed pages.

It is known that Blake sang the ***Songs of Innocence*** to his own music, which has not survived. In a companion volume, uniform in size and format, Ellen Raskin presents her musical settings of the poems—simple, melodic lines, some as artless as old nursery tunes, all with easy-to-play piano and guitar accompaniments. To accommodate the music (beautifully printed on pages that open freely) the illustrations in the second book are somewhat altered in size and position, and the double-spreads of the first book have been reduced to single-page pictures.

School Library Journal

SOURCE: A review of *Songs of Innocence,* in *School Library Journal,* Vol. 13, No. 2, October, 1966, p. 222.

[The following review focuses on Ellen Raskin's music and illustrations for Songs of Innocence, *1966.]*

These two volumes of Blake's ***Songs of Innocence*** are beautiful examples of bookmaking. The first volume contains the poems alone, illustrated with magnificent woodcuts (many of them small) printed in harmonious colors (russet, mustard, pale olive, pale aqua). The second volume contains the same 21 songs set to music with a simple melody line composed by Miss Raskin. The music will be easy to play on the piano and has chords for guitar. The design of the books is elegant; the delicate type is a perfect counterbalance to the strong woodcuts. The placement of the poems on the pages together with the illustrations displays a refined instinct for presenting a beautiful and unified visual image. The two volumes are boxed together. For purchase by anyone who wants to own a lovely picture-book edition of Blake.

D. G. Gillham

SOURCE: An excerpt from *Blake's Contrary States: The "Songs of Innocence and of Experience" As Dramatic Poems,* Cambridge at the University Press, 1966, pp. 1-7.

[Gillham is a South African educator and critic. In the following excerpt, he contends that Songs of Innocence and of Experience *requires only straightforward, close study of each poem in the context of the work as a whole rather than interpretation informed by historical, biographical, or oeuvre-related issues.]*

Most Blake studies are based on the assumption that the poet requires allowances to be made for his unusual manner of writing. The ***Songs of Innocence and of Experience*** most decidedly do not require a special critical technique. . . . Blake's intention may best be discovered by a patient reading of the poems themselves without forcing on to them assistance that only a specialized knowledge can give. . . . [The ***Songs of Innocence and of Experience***] explain themselves if they are read together. Each poem must be read for its own sake, but it may most adequately be read by a mind that is informed by the remainder of the poems.

No period of history is very remote when seen through the eyes of a poet, and Blake is very much our contemporary because we are still attempting to come to terms with the rationalism that, by stimulating his antagonism, provoked his complex insight. Though we do not need the help of a special knowledge in order to understand the problems of our poet, [it is useful to note intellectual developments] of Blake's own time. This is not done on the supposition that the poetry can be explained in terms of influences that were brought to bear upon Blake, but in order to remind us of our own problems, and to throw into relief the qualities of Blake's peculiar genius in meeting those problems.

During the twentieth century a great deal has been written about Blake; most commentators have had something to say about the ***Songs,*** but for a number of reasons the commentaries on these short poems have been disappointing. Perhaps Blake is, himself, partly to blame for this. His 'Prophetic Books', by their obscure and involved construction, invite a ponderous and mysterious explanation, and the ***Songs,*** regarded as an adjunct of the 'Prophecies', are crushed beneath the weight of an exegesis they cannot bear. . . .

Much careful research has gone into tracing the influence on Blake's verse of various philosophers, of writers in the Hermetic tradition, and of the tensions and events of his day. For the reader of the ***Songs,*** however, the fruits of this research are not very helpful, and may even obscure the poetry by demanding a kind of attention that is not warranted. Blake so radically transformed the material he used, it became so very much subordinated to his own way of looking at things, that a knowledge of its origins usually seems irrelevant.

The complicated 'mythology' of Blake's later works and the idiosyncratic manner in which he chose to write them have both militated against the ***Songs*** receiving what they most need: a careful appreciation of their tone. Overwhelmed by the apparent need for a special exegetical apparatus, the reader is distracted from applying to the poems the sort of sensitivity that would be given poetry found in a less unusual setting. The ***Songs*** themselves are not idiosyncratic, but it is supposed that they should be, and the accepted tools of the reader are abandoned. Normally, we realize very soon whether a poet is speaking on his own behalf (through the mouth of an imagined character, perhaps) or is presenting us with a persona (with some character whom we cannot take as being the poet's direct representative). In lyrical poetry, it is true, we may very often take the sentiments offered as being the poet's very own, but this is not always so. In the ***Songs*** this decidedly cannot be the case, certainly not always—there is too marked a diversity in the attitudes presented.

One would expect the reader of the ***Songs,*** on making this discovery, to take all the poems with some caution; to wonder, when reading every one of them, if Blake is speaking in his own voice, or if he is presenting a possible attitude for our inspection. The outcome of such an examination should be the realization that none of the ***Songs*** can be taken simply as a direct personal utterance. Innocence is not self-aware in a way that allows it to describe itself, and the poet must stand outside the state. From the mocking tone of many of the ***Songs of Experience*** it is clear that the poet does not suffer from the delusions he associates with that condition. Again, the poet stands beyond the state depicted. Blake, in short, is detached from the conditions of awareness imposed on the speakers of his poems.

Blake's critics do not follow the clue given by his tone, however, and, although the best commentaries all have glimpses of the detachment, the insight is sporadic and soon set aside. The poet is identified with one selection from the ***Songs*** or another, or, in an attempt to make them all emanate from the poet, it is stated that we may take the ***Songs of Innocence*** to belong to an earlier and hopeful period while the ***Songs of Experience*** belong to a later condition of disillusionment. The critics have been determined that Blake should commit himself in some part of the ***Songs,*** and this determination is understandable. The poems are obviously the work of a thinker, and this thinker identifies himself, sometimes, with the prophet, which suggests that he might wish to lay down some definite guide to conduct. The philosopher and the prophet are usually men with a message, are men with formed and finalized ideas, and the poet appears to resemble them, particularly a poet with the decided manner of speaking shown by Blake. . . .

In **"London"** Blake does not express his despair of the human condition, but depicts a condition of despair, not necessarily his own. All the songs depict 'states of the soul', as the title-page tells us, and Blake's own voice is detected in the purpose that governs the assembly of the ***Songs*** rather than in any particular utterance.

Blake has no message, or 'philosophy', and would not be more worth reading as a poet if he had. He offers something better: a serious and responsible consideration of the ways in which human energy may manifest itself. In the course of his study he touches on various ideas of the nature of man, but not because he regards any of them as absolutely true, as saying the last word on what we are. His concern is a moral one and he makes (or implies) a judgement of the positions he describes, though he does not dispute their truth. Any -ism is true for the person who believes it to be so, though it does not follow that all such truths may be said to reflect a decent condition of the mind. They are to be judged according to the fullness of the life that (it may be inferred) supports them. Although he refers us to various dogmas in his description of the states, Blake subscribes to no one of them, he presents no ultimate truths but leaves us to forge our own. He does attempt to awaken us to the responsibility of becoming alive to the best truths of which we are capable, but the poet detaches himself from the task of saying what those truths should be.

There was a strong tendency during the eighteenth century to view man simply as the outcome of education and conditioning. He was seen as an intelligent animal, but the intelligence itself was conceived as a calculating faculty, enabling him to make use of his experience to civilize himself. There were no fundamental impulses in the individual that could properly be called moral, but men could estimate that it would serve them well to behave according to an accepted morality. In the course of the ***Songs of Experience*** Blake often presents us with this conception of human nature, and implies that it may appear true to those who have lost their benign impulses. They need control from without and the restraint of self-interested conformity if they are to behave well. In the ***Songs of Innocence,*** however, Blake presents us with beings who cannot be accounted for on this explanation. These songs do not present us with persons equipped with premeditated or formulated moral notions, it is true, but we are shown individuals with affectionate and sympathetic impulses that dispose them to benign forms of conduct.

In ***Songs of Experience*** Blake allows some of his characters to affirm the values and theories of rationalism, but he emphasizes that these are valid for the mind working in a superficial way only, and he describes the alternative mentality of Innocence. This alternative is not put forward as an original character or as a stage in the development of man, but as a condition of perfection, a completeness and harmony of being. Because we usually recognize this in children, we associate it with ignorance—the child shows its simple faith and whole-hearted vitality because it knows so little, has not entered into the cares of a more responsible time of life. Blake is not setting up an ideal of childishness, however, and his Innocents are not all children. All men have their innocent moments, though what constitutes an innocent poise at one time of life will not be proper at another, and what will indicate perfection of balance for one person will not do so for some other. What is important is that we have known the perfection of Innocence, and though we can no more induce a state of perfection in ourselves than we can return to childhood, we are provided, by this knowledge, with a measure of the success of our more deliberate activities.

The measure is an inarticulate one, is an intuition of the sort of thing we can hope for and not a programme we can follow, but it does provide us with a more fundamental and constant guide than convention or rational argument can offer. One convention can drive out another and arguments are subject to endless amendment, but as they pass into the mind they come under the control of a being who has known affection, sympathy, fascination and delight, and who, therefore, has a touchstone (a sort of conscience) which, without our being able to give a detailed and explicit account of what it is, directs our more articulate and deliberate impulses. By introducing us, in the ***Songs,*** to the concept of Innocence Blake shows a dimension of the mind which the eighteenth century chose to ignore because there was no formula for it.

John Holloway

SOURCE: An excerpt from *Blake: The Lyric of Poetry,* Edward Arnold (Publishers) Ltd., 1968, pp. 20-76.

Wherever one turns in Blake's lyrics, the impress of popular verse tradition is inescapably clear. It shows in the most unexpected places. . . . Here it is perhaps not out of place to remark, in passing, how the metre of Blake's most vehement, impassioned lyric is the same as that of a light-hearted nursery rhyme. It is difficult to think this is an accident, moreover, when the actual visual Gestalt is so much the same:

> Tyger, tyger, burning bright
> In the forests of the night . . .
>
> Twinkle, twinkle, little star . . .
> Like a diamond in the sky.

Perhaps there is here even some conscious reversal, on Blake's part, of the mood of the earlier piece. If so, it is not (as will transpire) by any means the only case of that.

The clearest instance of how Blake drew on the traditions of our popular literature relates to **"My Pretty Rose Tree"** in ***Songs of Experience.*** As with **"Tyger, tyger"** the connexion is one of thought, not words alone; but in this case it so much creates Blake's poem as a whole, that that had better be quoted in full:

> A flower was offer'd to me,
> Such a flower as May never bore;
> But I said 'I've a Pretty Rose-tree,'
> And I passed the sweet flower o'er.
>
> Then I went to my Pretty Rose-tree,
> To tend her by day and by night;
> But my Rose turn'd away with jealousy,
> And her thorns were my only delight

Blake has reversed the sexes, but in that poem the movement of thought, the imagery, and (one might add) the metre, are close indeed to one of our most beautiful folk-songs:

> I sowed the seeds of love,
> 'Twas early in the spring,

In April and May, and in June likewise,
The small birds they do sing . . .

My gardener he stood by,
I asked him to choose for me,
He chose me the violet, the lily and the pink,
But these I refused all three.

The violet I forsook
Because it fades so soon.
The lily and the pink I did overlook
And I vowed I'd stay till June.

For in June there's a red rosebud,
And that's the flower for me,
So I pulled and plucked at the red rosebud,
Till I gained the willow tree . . .

My gardener he stood by,
And he told me to take good care;
For in the middle of the red rosebud
There grew a sharp thorn there.

I told him I'd take no care
Until I felt the smart.
I pulled and I plucked at the red rosebud
Till it pierced me to the heart.

Again, one ought perhaps to insist that there is no question of imitation or borrowing merely at the verbal level. Among his other gifts, Blake had access to the popular mode of vision and expression *as wholes* . . . .

One must take stock of how firmly Blake's poems belong to traditions of composition that run back through the eighteenth century and indeed before it; . . .

Take a simple point first: it is the hymn which provides a perspective for one of the most immediately striking things in the lyrics, their varied use of metres, and the way in which, to a reader coming from the "literary" verse of the eighteenth century, these metres seem highly original. But at the same time, this originality is entirely different from that, say, of Herbert. Blake's *'Songs'* are *songs*. Every lyric (save **"The Voice of the Ancient Bard"**, appended to ***Songs of Innocence*** long after the collection was completed) is stanzaic, as if it were truly to be set to a repeated melody. There is only one poem, **"The Little Black Boy"**, in ten-syllable lines, and none of the metres lends itself less to a lyrical than to a thoughtful or discursive tone. Cases where the sense is not complete, or substantially so, by the line-end, are extraordinarily rare. What we have is remarkable variety of a kind that goes with great simplicity and in a sense transparency of both structure and meaning. . . . Blake in one respect departed from what was at least most usual in contemporary hymn-writing, and followed a practice common enough in the lyric throughout the whole of the eighteenth century, in that he made frequent use of triple rhythms. But for the most part he did this so that the triple rhythms combined freely with rhythms that were iambic or trochaic:

How can a bird that is born for joy
Sit in a cage and sing?
("The School Boy")

Lark in Sky
Merrily
Merrily, merrily, to welcome in the Year.
("Spring")

He very often has trochaic rhythms in short lyrics, and this is very like the hymns of his time (or indeed of later time). Blake drew a great deal on his own invention, in using or combining such varied metres, and in creating such a variety of stanza patterns. But the metrical and stanzaic variety of the hymns themselves was much greater than in lyric poetry in Blake's time. This came about because there were many varied, traditional, and well-loved melodies, and these gave their own shape to words written for them: hymn-writing was largely not the setting of words to music, but the writing of words for it.

Perhaps one clear way to show how much hymn metric has to do with Blake is to review the ***Songs of Innocence*** poems in order.

"Introduction" ("Piping down the valleys wild,/Piping songs of pleasant glee"), and **"A Dream"** ("Once a dream did weave a shade/O'er my Angel-guarded bed"), are both in the four-line seven-syllable trochaic measure of, for example, Charles Wesley's:

Christ the Lord is ris'n today,
Sons of men and angels, say . . .

"The Little Girl Lost" (beginning "In futurity/I prophetic see . . . "), and its companion piece **"The Little Girl Found"** are, metrically, trochaic versions of the first part of Wesley's stanza in "Rejoice, the Lord is King" or of John Byrom's "My spirit longs for thee". **"The Lamb"** is printed as three stanzas, each one different, in Keynes' edition; but if stanzas 2 and 3 are combined, and the lines are indented as in stanza 1, the whole poem becomes one composed of two identical stanzas, each with ten three- or four-stress lines; and then each may easily be seen as a much expanded version of the common hymnodic "Short Metre". Next comes **"The Blossom"**; and here one encounters something of a surprise. Replace an iambic by a trochaic rhythm, and the stanza of the poem is the same (save for being one line short in the second half) as the stanza-form of doubtless the best-known of all eighteenth-century hymns: "God Save the King". (It was not, presumably, this particular example of the form which most endeared itself to Blake.)

The next poem in the collection is **"The Ecchoing Green"**:

The Sun does arise,
And make happy the skies;
The merry bells ring
To welcome the Spring . . .

But suppose that the poem is rearranged to print two lines as one:

> The Sun does arise, and make happy the skies;

—and so on. There is then a very clear similarity to a well-known near-contemporary hymn by Reginald Heber:

> Brightest and best of the sons of the morning,
> Dawn on our darkness and lend us thine aid . . .

and it has really no significance that Heber's stanza is four lines long, while Blake's, if re-printed in this way, would be five.

Next come **"The Divine Image",** in hymnal Common Metre, and **"The Chimney Sweep",** an anapaestic version (rarely used in hymns) of Long Metre. **"Infant Joy",** the next poem, looks little, metrically speaking, like a hymn:

> "I have no name:
> "I am but two days old."
> What shall I call thee?

"The Shepherd," from Songs of Innocence, *1789. Written and illustrated by William Blake.*

> "I happy am,
> Joy is my name."
> Sweet joy befall thee!

But in fact, this is one of the poems nearest to hymn metre, and indeed to the most usual one, Common Metre, at that. Blake has simply re-set, and in doing so of course brought out the particular rhythms of, the following Common-Metre stanza:

> "I have no name: I am but two
> Days old." What shall I call thee?
> "I happy am, Joy is my name."
> Sweét jóy befáll thee!

The next poem, **"The Shepherd",** is in four-line triple rhythm. **"Night",** which follows it, is metrically most unusual and striking among the lyrics. Here is stanza 5 of the poem:

> And there the lion's ruddy eyes
> Shall flow with tears of gold,
> And pitying the tender cries,
> And walking round the fold,
> Saying "Wrath in his meekness,
> "And by his health, sickness
> "Is driven away
> "From our immortal day."

But this is a variant of the old "Proper Metre", as in Doddridge's Hymn 100, which begins:

> Amazing beauteous change:
> A world created new!

—and of course it is at once clear that in this particular case, substance as well as metre may be to the point. Here is stanza 5 of Doddridge's hymn:

> The tyrants of the plain
> Their savage chase give o'er:
> No more they rend the slain,
> And thirst for blood no more:
> But infant hands
> Fierce tigers stroke,
> And lions yoke
> In flowery bands.

Next comes **"A Cradle Song",** basically in Long Metre (with stanzas of four four-stress lines); and **"The Little Boy Lost", "The Little Boy Found",** and **"Nurse's Song",** which are all close to Common Metre, though in the last of these Blake's triple rhythms are insistent. The seven-stress lines of **"Holy Thursday"** ("'Twas on a Holy Thursday, their innocent faces clean" and so on) of course mean that each two lines of the poem make a four-line stanza in Common Metre.

After this comes **"On Another's Sorrow":**

> Can I see another's woe,
> And not be in sorrow too?

Can I see another's grief,
And not seek for kind relief? . . .

This, in both metre and rhyme, is again identical with hymns like Wesley's 'Jesu, lover of my soul':

Jesu, lover of my soul,
Let me to Thy bosom fly,
While the nearer waters roll
While the tempest still is high . . .

At first glance the next poem, **"Spring"**, seems quite remote from hymnody:

Sound the flute!
Now it's mute.
Birds delight
Day and Night;
Nightingale
In the dale,
Lark in sky,
Merrily,
Merrily, merrily, to welcome in the year.

But leave aside the refrain (which echoes Shakespeare's "Merrily, merrily, shall I live now,/Under the blossom that hangs on the bough"), and one eighteenth-century hymn, at any rate, is remarkably close—in more, once again, than metre only. It is by John Newton, and its first stanza is printed below in eight lines instead of the usual four:

Kindly spring
Again is here,
Trees and fields
In bloom appear;
Hark! the birds
In artless lays
Warble their
Creator's praise.

If we append Blake's refrain to this, we could slip the whole nine lines (though I am far from claiming the result as an embellishment) into Blake's poem. . . .

"The School Boy" is in Common Metre with an extra (fifth) three stress-line at the end of the stanza; it must be admitted that the rhythms of this poem are somewhat distinctive, with many free deviations from its own basic pattern. **"Laughing Song"** is in Long Metre, but triple instead of double rhythm:

When the green woods laugh with the voice of joy . . .

—and **"The Little Black Boy"**, which begins:

My mother bore me in the southern wild . . .

is in exactly the metre of such well-known hymns as 'Abide With Me' (though this particular example of the metre was composed after Blake had written his poem). This short review of ***Songs of Innocence*** in the context of hymn-metres therefore reaches a striking conclusion. Metrically, these lyrics make as clear a parallel with eighteenth-century hymns, as they make a contrast with eighteenth-century lyric (such as it was) viewed as a whole. Nor should one think for a moment that if one admits such licenses and deviations as I have noted from time to time, or allows stanzas to be re-set as I re-set **"Infant Joy"** or **"Spring"**, in order to bring out their metrical affinities, anything may then be made to look like anything. A few minutes' attempt to do for Donne's lyrics, say, or for Herbert's, what has been done here for Blake's, will suffice to show that their cases are totally different. To relate their work to hymn-metre in anything like the same way is simply out of the question.

But if the continuity between Blake's lyrics, and the hymns of his time, is to be taken any further than this, we must have regard not to the hymns in general, but now to one kind in particular: the hymn for children. ***Songs of Innocence*** is a collection of poems written, as Blake says in the introductory poem, so that "every child may joy to hear". But while other or earlier writers use the preposition "for" (Mrs. Barbauld, *Hymns in Prose for Children,* 1787; Christopher Smart, *Hymns for the Amusement of Children,* 1775; Charles Wesley, *Hymns for Children,* 1763; Isaac Watts, *Divine and Moral Songs for the Use of Children:* the first of many editions was dated 1715) Blake's preposition is "of". This detail has a surprising relevance, and I shall return to it. . . .

The last poem which calls for detailed attention in this context is **"The Tyger"**:

Tyger! Tyger! burning bright
In the forests of the night,
What immortal hand or eye
Could frame thy fearful symmetry?

In what distant deeps or skies
Burnt the fire of thine eyes?
On what wings dare he aspire?
What the hand dare sieze the fire?

And what shoulder, & what art,
Could twist the sinews of thy heart?
And when thy heart began to beat,
What dread hand? & what dread feet?

What the hammer? what the chain?
In what furnace was thy brain?
What the anvil? what dread grasp
Dare its deadly terrors clasp?
When the stars threw down their spears,
And water'd heaven with their tears,
Did he smile his work to see?
Did he who made the Lamb make thee?

Tyger! Tyger! burning bright
In the forests of the night,
What immortal hand or eye
Dare frame thy fearful symmetry?

No one, probably, fails to sense that the penultimate verse of this poem is somehow intrinsic to its whole effect; as also, that the stars in the dark sky, and the "tyger" burning in the dark forest, are somehow one; and that those same stars, which gave up their battle and fell into grief, are one as well with the rebel angels. But what has the tiger really to do with Satan or his host? The poem may be taken back ultimately to *Revelations* XXII, 16, where Christ says, "I am the bright and morning star". Since Satan was also identified with the morning star (cf. *Isaiah* XIV, 12), the passage has a curious ambiguity; though its link with an ambiguity, or at least a two-sidedness, central to Christianity, is doubtless accidental. Watts has one hymn which gives as reference *Job* XXXV, 22: "With God is terrible majesty". "Great God how terrible thou art" it begins. Its most memorable line is

God is a bright and burning fire.

One senses, I believe, a nearness already to Blake's poem, but Watts's hymn goes on:

his *eye*
Burns with *immortal* jealousy

By now the conclusion, surprising as it is, cannot be missed. It becomes impossible not to believe that when he wrote his poem about the terrors of the tiger, Blake had in mind [Isaac] Watts's piece on the terrors of God.

In the final version of the poem, as against the drafts of it in the 1793 ***Notebook,*** Blake altered the line "Did he who made the lamb make thee?", and turned "lamb" into "Lamb". It was no matter of mere eighteenth-century capitalization; and if it is said that this merely matches the capital for "Tyger", one has to say that that clinches the point. The tiger in the poem is no simple creation of the deity; he *is* the deity: if God is what the pundits have said, if he could have seen the Fall of the angels he himself made, and viewed this benignly, as he viewed each day's work of creation, then God is himself a tiger. Just as there is a question to answer, how could one God have created both the tiger and the lamb, so (the poem implies) there is a prior question: what "immortal hand or eye" could have created—or to put the question more literally, how could there be—a God who is at once a God of love, and one of terrible jealousy?—a "Tyger" and a "Lamb"? In this poem also, Blake is continuing the hymn tradition, and at the same time inverting it and challenging it. Contrary to his predecessors, he saw—or perhaps one should say supposed—that the God-of-Love-God-of-Terror formula was not a sacred mystery of religion, but a stupefying fraud.

At this point, surely, one cannot but revert to Blake's distinctive preposition: Songs *of* Innocence, where all his predecessors wrote songs *for* children; and one can see the force and newness of the closing lines of his introductory poem:

And I wrote my *happy* songs
Every child may *joy* to hear.

Or one may put this another way. Blake, in ***Songs of Innocence,*** was writings songs such that, in a sense, they could come spontaneously from children; the others were arranging an adult vision and an adult morality in such a form as might be imposed down upon them. . . .

There is a certain kind of lyric poetry—perhaps the most essentially lyrical in kind—which appears to require some bond with popular poetry and with the traditional literary heritage of the common people, if it is to exist. After the medieval period, there seem to have been only three English poets who have achieved greatness in this way: Shakespeare whose link as a lyric poet is with the folk-song (though here there is much more to say, of course); [William] Wordsworth whose was with the ballad in one of its kinds or another; and Blake who drew upon the wealth of the English Bible and the Protestant hymn. In Wordsworth's lyrical ballads there is sometimes a strangeness, a sense of the mysterious and uncomprehended, to which Blake's more decided mind seems to have been closed; but Blake was before Wordsworth, and his lyrical work has a fullness and variety, and also a whole-heartedness and absence of the reflective and diluted moralizing, which is not to be found in Wordsworth. He has come slowly to be seen for what he is; but it is now surely clear that it was he, more than any other poet of his period or just after, who recovered the lyric powers that had largely been lost between Traherne's time and his own. Moreover, Blake has only [Thomas] Hardy as something of a successor in English. Perhaps this is because England is now a country virtually without a rich literature of the common people such as it had in the past. Hardy aside, the only great poet of a kind comparable to Blake has been [William Butler] Yeats, whose work belongs to another country where popular culture still held the place it lost in our own.

But lyricism such as Blake's is not a technical success. It arises out of a certain sense—buoyant, joyous and yet serene—of life itself; and of course, from one point of view, the lyric product of that sense of life veritably constitutes what it embodies. It is this sense of life which I value most of all in Blake, and why I should therefore put ***Songs of Innocence,*** as a whole, above ***Songs of Experience.*** There is another point of view, though, and its strength shouts to be seen. Blake not only had that vision; he smarted under a searing awareness of how the great ones of the world rejected it or never glimpsed it. As a result, despite how the cruel time he lived in stifled his work, he is incomparably our most important poet of social and political comment. Here again, he has had (this point was adverted to earlier on) no real followers: and our literature, and our present resources for writing, are lamentably the poorer for that fact. On all these counts, Blake's value and importance are such that they warrant the highest praise. It is not easy to think of a half-dozen English poets whose work is more precious than his: or of many more than that, who are his equals.

In Golden Square, there is nothing to commemorate Blake. Of all things, the central place is occupied by a statue of George II. Nothing could have a sharper irony, or more confirm what he himself thought of the Powers That Be or what the English cultural scene has for so long been like. But on my last visit there, I found something else as well:

Cockle shells,
Wedding bells,
Evie, ivy, evoe (!)
Mother's in the kitchen
Doing her knitting,
How many stitches can she do . . . ?
Five, ten, fifteen, twenty . . .

and so on. This was what the children sang as they played a skipping game. One of them was what Blake would have called "A Little Black Girl". Blake's memorial was a living one, and better than the king's.

Raymond Lister

SOURCE: "Dawning Vision," in *William Blake: An Introduction to the Man and to His Work,* G. Bell and Sons, Ltd., 1968, pp. 14-36.

Songs of Innocence, which was completed in 1789, was the first of Blake's successful illuminated books. . . .

Songs of Innocence are happy evocations of the innocence and joys of childhood. There is little here to remind us of the contrary state of Experience; that will be evoked in the later ***Songs of Experience.*** Here, in a state of Innocence, the child may be seen using his intuitive imagination to comprehend the world around him. The spirit of the work is set in its **"Introduction:"**

Piping down the valleys wild,
Piping songs of pleasant glee,
On a cloud I saw a child,
And he laughing said to me:

"Pipe a song about a Lamb!"
So I piped with merry chear.
"Piper, pipe that song again;"
So I piped: he wept to hear.

"Drop thy pipe, thy happy pipe;
"Sing thy songs of happy chear:"
So I sung the same again,
While he wept with joy to hear.

"Piper, sit thee down and write
"In a book that all may read."
So he vanish'd from my sight,
And I pluck'd a hollow reed,

And I made a rural pen,
And I stain'd the water clear,
And I wrote my happy songs
Every child may joy to hear.

This is an apparently simple poem; yet it is something more, for it shows the basis of Blake's philosophy as expressed in these ***Songs.*** If we look for a moment below its surface, we can perceive how, in the course of even the first verse, the poet changes from an almost pagan joyful abandon to Christian symbolism. From "Piping down the valleys wild" he is asked by a spiritual child on a cloud to "Pipe a song about a Lamb", and when he is asked to repeat this song, the child "wept to hear", showing that his ***Songs*** are not merely pretty pastorals, but are capable of touching deeper chords, of expressing the perennial symbolism inherent in the pastoral scene. The child tells him to write down his songs "In a book that all may read", and vanishes, for he is a vision symbolising the poet's imagination. Whereupon the poet writes his

. . . happy songs
Every child may joy to hear.

It is a perfect introduction, with its themes of piping, laughter, and tears, which moves from the near-pagan glee of the opening lines to the Christian joy of its last lines. The book itself carries throughout a similar pattern: an apparent simplicity of surface structure, often expressed in a bitter-sweetness at once close to joy and sadness, clothes a deep underlying symbolism. Much of this may be seen in the most famous of all the ***Songs of Innocence:***

Little Lamb, who made thee?
Dost thou know who made thee?
Gave thee life, & bid thee feed
By the stream & o'er the mead;

Gave thee clothing of delight,
Softest clothing, wooly, bright;
Gave thee such a tender voice,
Making all the vales rejoice?
Little Lamb, who made thee?
Dost thou know who made thee?

Little Lamb, I'll tell thee,
Little Lamb, I'll tell thee:
He is called by thy name,
For he calls himself a Lamb.
He is meek, & he is mild;

He became a little child.
I a child, & thou a lamb,
We are called by his name.
Little Lamb, God bless thee!
Little Lamb, God bless thee!

In this the child addresses the Lamb and, through Christ, identifies himself with it. This is simple enough, yet there is a hint of the sacramental quality of life in it, too, for the Lamb has been given food, life and "clothing of delight" by his maker, who became incarnate in the form of a child and thus child and Lamb are identified in a deeper sense. In other words, the Lamb of God, sacrificed as the Lamb will be sacrificed, has provided the Lamb and the child with a measure of innocent joy, and so they are both blessed, both called by his name.

It has been said that Dr. Isaac Watts's *Divine Songs* (1715), the first hymn book for children, suggested the idea of ***Songs of Innocence*** to Blake. This may have some truth in it, but Watts's thought was shallow, his philosophy often downright blasphemous; if there was any such influence it must have been transitory or at most mechanical. It is inconceivable that Blake could, for instance, have written anything like this hymn of Watts's:

Whene'er I take my walks abroad,
  How many poor I see!
What shall I render to my God,
  For all his gifts to me?

Not more than others I deserve,
  Yet God hath giv'n me more;
For I have food while others starve,
  Or beg from door to door.

How many children in the street
  Half naked I behold,
While I am cloth'd from head to feet,
  And cover'd from the cold!

While some poor wretches scarce can tell
  Where they may lay their head;
I have a home wherein to dwell,
  And rest upon my bed.

While others early learn to swear,
  And curse, and lye, and steal;
Lord, I am taught thy name to fear,
  And do thy holy will.

Are these thy favours day by day
  To me above the rest?
Then let me love thee more than they,
  And try to serve thee best.

Blake's regard for his fellow men is expressed in less self-congratulatory terms, as in **"The Little Black Boy."** Well may his child on a cloud have wept with joy to hear it.

My mother bore me in the southern wild,
And I am black, but O! my soul is white;
White as an angel is the English child,
But I am black, as if bereav'd of light.

My mother taught me underneath a tree,
And sitting down before the heat of day,
She took me on her lap and kissed me,
And pointing to the east, began to say:

"Look on the rising sun: there God does live,
"And gives his light, and gives his heat away;
"And flowers and trees and beasts and men receive
"Comfort in morning, joy in the noonday.

"And we are put on earth a little space,
"That we may learn to bear the beams of love;
"And these black bodies and this sunburnt face
"Is but a cloud, and like a shady grove.

"For when our souls have learn'd the heat to bear,
"The cloud will vanish; we shall hear his voice,
"Saying: 'Come out from the grove, my love & care,
"'And round my golden tent like lambs rejoice.'"

Thus did my mother say, and kissed me;
And thus I say to little English boy.
When I from black and he from white cloud free,
And round the tent of God like lambs we joy,

I'll shade him from the heat, till he can bear
To lean in joy upon our father's knee;
And then I'll stand and stroke his silver hair,
And be like him, and he will then love me. . . .

A word concerning the designs in which Blake set his ***Songs of Innocence*** is necessary. Printed apart from these designs the ***Songs*** lose an essential dimension, though some of the designs are more profound than others. That for **"The Lamb"** is a simple illustration, in which the Lamb is depicted, just apart from the flock, with its head raised to the child, whose arm is stretched out towards it. The child is naked, itself a symbol of innocence. Behind the flock are a cottage and a tree. The verses are surrounded with the branches of two slender trees, around which tendrils grow, symbolising, perhaps, the intertwining relationship of the Lamb and child.

In Blake's designs for **"Spring"**, we may see additions to the dimension of the poem. The poem itself is a song both to welcome in the New Year and, in another sense, to symbolise rebirth:

Sound the Flute!
Now it's mute.
Birds delight
Day and Night;
Nightingale
In the dale,
Lark in Sky,
Merrily,
Merrily, Merrily, to welcome in the Year.

Little Boy,
Full of joy;
Little Girl,
Sweet and small;
Cock does crow,
So do you;
Merry voice,

Infant noise,
Merrily, Merrily, to welcome in the Year.

Little Lamb,
Here I am;
Come and lick
My white neck;
Let me pull
Your soft Wool;
Let me kiss
Your soft face:
Merrily, Merrily, we welcome in the Year.

Many overtones may be discerned in this little poem. One writer, for example, has seen in its opening two lines, and in the cock crow, a pastoral prophecy of the last trumpet. The Lamb, too, may be seen as a symbol of the Lamb of God, and it is this idea which is expressed in the poem's two designs (for it is printed from two consecutive plates). On the first the child is shown, standing on his mother's lap, his hands stretched out in a benediction-like gesture towards a flock of sheep, symbolising innocence (the child is again naked) yearning for spirituality (symbolised by the sheep). In the second the child lies with some sheep and a lamb, at whose wool he tugs. Here he has reached Eternity, the true spiritual state, and communes with the Lamb. His mother is no longer there.

The design in which the **"Introduction,"** "Piping Down the Valleys Wild", is contained is of special interest in showing what was doubtless one of Blake's visual sources. The verses are contained within a border formed by branches entwined so as to form a series of little oval spaces, in each one of which a scene is drawn. It is a device common in illuminated manuscripts, and . . . concerning the relationship between Blake's illuminated books and early coloured printed books (themselves but a remove from illuminated manuscripts), the comparison is of considerable significance.

These few examples must suffice to show what riches the ***Songs of Innocence*** hold in store for the reader. They may, it is true, be read with enjoyment as simple uncomplicated lyrics, but to appreciate their true value a little trouble and imagination must be used. In many ways the ***Songs*** are an emblem book, that is one in which engravings of emblems are accompanied by an appropriate text, often in verse, commenting, usually in esoteric terms, on their significance. Blake's books, however, differ from emblem books in which the designs are subservient to the text, and are purely literary in scope and intention. In ***Songs of Innocence*** the designs add a new dimension to the poems, expressing their ideas in purely pictorial form.

Mary F. Thwaite

SOURCE: "The Dawn of Imagination: Songs of Innocence," and "Flood Tide—The Victorian Age and Edwardian Aftermath: Songs of Innocence," in *From Primer to Pleasure in Reading,* The Horn Book, Inc., 1972, pp. 81, 129-30.

Before the end of the eighteenth century the reaction against the rule of reason had begun, but in books for children it came later than in literature for their elders. The voice of prophecy and revolt was most clearly raised by that isolated genius, William Blake (1757-1827), whose book of lyric poems, ***Songs of Innocence*** (1789), was the bright if unheeded sunrise of a new era.

Blake was poet, artist and visionary. For him the mechanistic universe of Newton and Locke was dead and meaningless. The perception of truth and reality lay behind the corporeal world in the creative power of the imagination, 'the Divine Body in Every Man . . . ' It was this revolutionary idea of the transcending importance of the imagination which was to produce the Romantic movement and to change fundamentally the whole conception of the nature and needs of the child during the coming century, with a consequent deep influence on the writing of children's books. The idea of the child as a being with a vision of his own, not as an ungrown man or woman to be quickly moulded to fit into an adult world, found vivid expression in these **Songs,** 'Every child may joy to hear', wherein Blake expressed his vision of youth unsullied by society. . . .

[But before] the eighteenth century was ended, a poet of genius was to take poetry for children into the realm of pure literature. The work of William Blake (1757-1827) was outside the main stream of children's literature, and his lyric poems, ***Songs of Innocence*** (1789), like much of the best poetry for the young, was not specially addressed to them. They were little known until about the middle of the nineteenth century. Then these verses, now so highly valued, began to find their way into anthologies for young people—especially **"The Piper", "The Lamb", "The Little Black Boy"** and **"Night".** Children's editions of 'These songs of happy chear' have now been interpreted by other artists, but in 1789 Blake put his poems into a book of his own making, etching it on copper by his own method, and encircling the verses, so full of light and laughter and tenderness, with leafy tendrils and curling flame, merging into marginal pictures of pastoral beauty. ***Songs of Experience*** came out five years afterwards in 1794. Here the imaginative vision of innocence has been darkened and transformed by life and suffering. But, from this later volume, children's poetry gained at least one great lyric—'Tyger, Tyger, burning bright'.

Blake was a rebel against the conventional theology of his day, and his unorthodox, profoundly-felt views, which moulded his life and art, shine out especially in **"The Divine Image"** in his ***Songs of Innocence.*** He reveals God as Mercy, Pity, Peace and Love, with these qualities universal in man also.

And all must love the human form
In heathen, turk or jew;

Where Mercy, Love and Pity dwell
There God is dwelling too.

Michael Davis

SOURCE: "Revolutionary: 1787-93," in *William Blake: A New Kind of Man,* University of California Press, 1977, pp. 33-61.

In [*Songs of Experience*] Blake explores the problems of good and evil. He balances individual poems and the whole series against ***Songs of Innocence,*** so 'Shewing the Two Contrary States of the Human Soul.' He combined both series of songs in one volume, moving a few poems from ***Innocence*** to ***Experience*** and varying the order of the fifty-four plates in different copies of the book, which he continued to print and colour, when commissioned by customers, until the end of his life. The essence of his thought on life before and after the Fall is condensed into the complete ***Songs.*** The Fall is experienced by every person. It occurs in each individual's life at adolescence and changes Innocence into Experience. So Blake's frontispiece to the whole book, which shows Adam and Eve against flames expelling them from Eden, tells the story of everyone. The frontispiece to ***Songs of Experience*** shows a youth advancing. In Blake's symbolism, the right hand and foot usually act spiritually, the left materialistically: this youth's right foot is forward because his journey into Experience is spiritual. On his head he balances the Covering Cherub of corrupt selfhood. Beside him, baleful ivy climbs up a tree. The title-page shows two young people mourning beside the corpses of their parents, while loving figures above are parted by spiky leaves.

Blake introduces the songs with 'the voice of the Bard', the prophet. God called to Adam in Eden: the Bard calls to fallen man in the modern world to awake from materialism and, in the free life of imagination, forsake the 'starry floor' of reason and the 'wat'ry shore' of time and space. Then day will break. Earth answers despairingly, imprisoned by reason and by restrictions on free love. The jealous creator of the material world, who brutally separated man from the divine unity and marked him for death, freezes the bones of earth in a heavy chain.

The paradox of love, in its selfless Innocence and selfish Experience, is condensed into the dozen lines of **"The Clod & the Pebble"** in ***Songs of Experience.*** . . . Some of the ***Songs of Experience*** are brilliantly condensed and show Blake as a master of lyric poetry. **"The Sick Rose"** conveys, in eight short lines, the agony and ecstasy of love in a material world. The other flower lyrics are comparably disquieting. They sum up the frustrations of love beset by envy and hypocrisy. In **"My Pretty Rose Tree"** the poet tells how he was offered the flowers of extra-marital love: he refused them, but nevertheless his wife—his pretty rose-tree—was jealous and reproachful. **"The Lilly"** shows a more perfect love than **"The Modest Rose"**. These symbols, and the stories of discord that they imply, provide no adequate basis for believing that the childless married love of the Blakes was beset by any unusual torments, complexities or frustrations.

It is tempting, however, to read **"A Poison Tree"** as a fragment of Blake's mental autobiography. A man ill-suited to repress anger, he contrasts in this poem the curative relief of wrath expressed, with the fatal hypocrisy of wrath concealed. The manuscript of this poem is ironically entitled **"Christian Forbearance"**. . . .

Blake's sense of social outrage is allied to his scorn of priest and king in **"The Chimney Sweeper"**. This little child, unlike his counterpart in ***Songs of Innocence,*** though still happy at times, knows that he is the victim of hypocritical parents. They are smugly in church, praising the Establishment which approves of clothing him 'in the clothes of death'—rags and soot—and of sending him out to cry ''weep, 'weep!' in the snow. Among the most wretched children in London were those whose parents (perhaps gin-sodden) sold them to chimney-sweeps. . . .

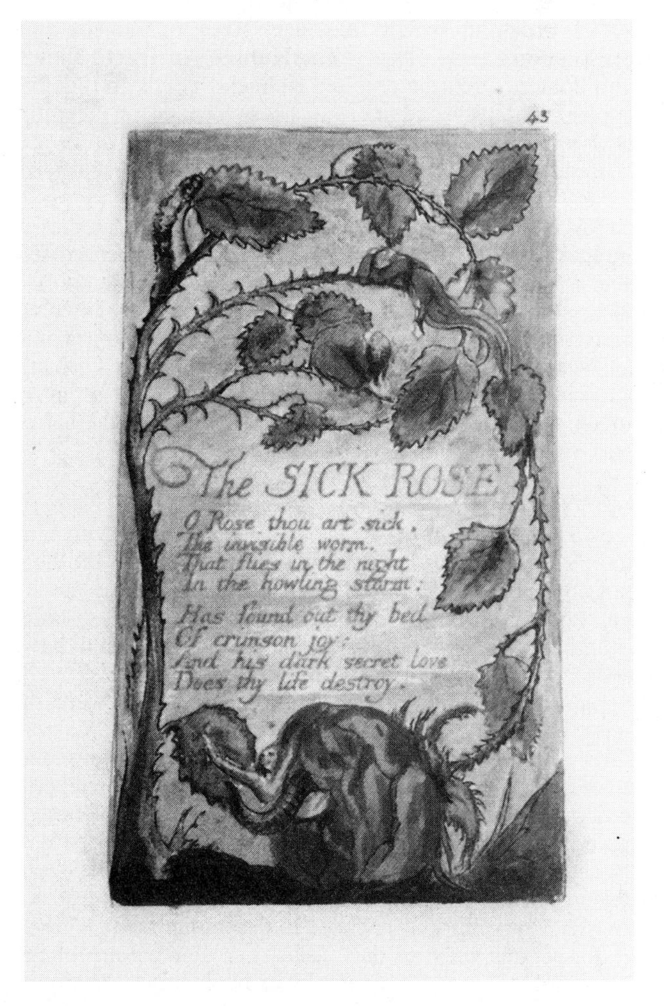

"The Sick Rose," from Songs of Experience, *in* Songs of Innocence and of Experience, *1794. Written and illustrated by William Blake.*

The plight of all poor children in a city of cold charity moved Blake to write **"Holy Thursday"** in ***Songs of Experience.*** This poem is a stark attack on the wealthy country that allowed such wretchedness. To house the many unwanted children abandoned in the streets, and illegitimate children handed over to parish officers, charity-schools were crammed. In some of these unhappy boarding-schools, six or eight children had to share a bed. In all charity-schools there was pressure to keep the children subservient to those who were not the objects of charity. School uniform was constantly worn. At church twice on Sundays and at the Holy Thursday service the children sang hymns from their special books.

In **"London",** Blake expressed his concern for every Londoner, condemned to the 'charter'd' city where all life is ruled by business, itself the product of crippled minds. Blake looked below the surface of life to the essential miseries of mankind and he condensed them into horrifying images that should destroy complacency in Church and State. While 'the hapless Soldier's sigh Runs in blood down Palace walls' and pleads for an end of war, 'the youthful Harlot'—blasting the 'Infant's tear' and blighting 'the Marriage hearse'—invokes a purer social order in which marriage gives fulfillment and prostitution has no place. **"The Human Abstract"** shows how fear of life's uninhibited richness breeds 'religious' approval of pity and mercy. These depend on keeping others unhappy. Hypocrisy of this sort was shown in the training of children from the workhouse for services of the lowest kind. The callous apprenticeship of some parish children was as inhumane as allowing others to die in infancy. Little girls, especially vulnerable, were often sent in their early teens as drudges, or domestic slaves, to the worst families. For instance, at the age of twelve a certain Anne Barnard was bound apprentice to a woman who cried old clothes in the street while her husband worked in a Lambeth pothouse. They lived in a garret in Westminster. Anne, left alone there to mind the baby, was raped by an inmate of the house.

In **"The Tyger"** Blake moves entirely into the visionary world. By superb artistry, he takes his readers with him to question the source of good and evil, and of their possible reconciliation. The enigmatic picture of the tiger below the poem is ferocious in some copies, tame in others, realistic in none—though Blake could have seen a live tiger had he wished, for animal shows were popular in London. In his youth, three tigers were on view in the Tower of London, and the entrance fee was threepence or a dog or cat as food for the lions and tigers. The roar of the tiger in Pidcock's menagerie could be heard in the Strand, and Stubbs's celebrated painting, 'The Tiger', was on view when Blake was a twelve-year-old pupil at Pars's. However Blake's Tyger came into his vision, he saw it 'Within the dark horrors of the Abysses': but he chose to depict the beast without the ravenous appetite that makes his later picture of the Ghost of a Flea, for example, a frightening creation.

In other ***Songs of Experience,*** Blake contrasts exultant

"London," from Songs of Experience, *in* Songs of Innocence and of Experience, *1794. Written and illustrated by William Blake.*

freedom with repression by priest, father, nurse and schoolmaster. He considers how body is related to soul, and life to death. **"The Voice of the Ancient Bard",** a poem which Blake moved from ***Songs of Innocence,*** concludes the sequence with a harp-song of affirmation calling to 'Youth of delight'. The new age is dawning. Doubt and 'clouds of reason' are dispelled, conflict is ended. Although many casualties have fallen by the way, the 'Image of Truth' is 'new born', and all survivors can exult in its nativity.

Zachary Leader

SOURCE: An excerpt from *Reading Blake's "Songs,"* Routledge & Kegan Paul, 1981, pp. 37-59.

[In the following excerpt, Leader studies Blake's illustrations for Songs of Innocence and of Experience, *insisting that they are intrinsic to the work and as carefully and thoughtfully executed as the poems.]*

This [essay] begins with a familiar refrain, since critical studies of Blake's verse continue to appear which ignore his visual art, or pay it only lip service: Blake meant the poems and designs of his Illuminated Books to remain together. When picture and poem are separated the result is 'Loss of some of the best things.' The designs, he writes, turning the equation around, 'perfect accompany Poetical Personifications and Acts, without which poems they never could have been Executed.' Nor would he have approved of readers who treat the designs as so much attractive but irrelevant decoration. Painting, he believed, ought to be 'as poetry and music are, elevated to its own proper sphere of invention and visionary conception.' Pictures ought to be studied as closely as poems:

> I intreat that the Spectator will attend to the Hands and Feet the Lineaments of the Countenances they are all descriptive of Character and not a line is drawn without intention and that most discriminate and particular <as Poetry admits not a Letter that is insignificant so Painting admits not a Grain of Sand or a Blade of Grass <insignificant> much less an Insignificant Blur or Mark>.

Explicit statements of this sort are backed by great personal sacrifice. Critics who fail to read the poems in light of the designs forget how high a price Blake paid to create his illuminated pages '—in time, money, patronage, friendship and spiritual energy' [Jean H. Hagstrum, *William Blake: Poet and Painter*]. 'I know myself both Poet and Painter,' Blake insists, defying those (often, as in this case, important patrons) who would prevent his 'more assiduous pursuit of both arts.' Only a few sympathetic contemporaries understood the nature of the designs: [Samuel Taylor] Coleridge spoke of 'Blake's poesies, metrical and graphic'; [Henry Crabb] Robinson mentions 'poetic pictures of the highest beauty and sublimity'; the anonymous author of 'The Inventions of W. B., Painter and Poet' finds 'The figures surrounding and enclosing the poems . . . are equally tinged by a poetical idea'; to Allan Cunningham, writing in the same year, 1830, text and design are 'intertwined . . . so closely in his compositions, that they cannot well be separated.'

This [essay] takes as one of its starting points a somewhat more timid version of David Erdman's 'working assumption' [in *The Illuminated Blake*] that 'every graphic image has its seed or root in the poetry': almost every graphic image bears some relation to—colors if it does not, in fact, grow out of—the poetry. It argues that we cannot properly appreciate the larger meaning or 'vision' of ***Songs*** without a knowledge of the designs, and in a few cases it even questions the extent to which certain poems can stand alone. **"Spring,"** from ***Innocence,*** provides a case in point. Robert Gleckner complains [in his ***The Piper and the Bard***] that in the poem's last stanza 'the "I" is not identified, except possibly as Blake himself, [and] the lamb's appearance is unprepared for.' But in the scene at the bottom of the second plate we are shown a child petting (or 'pulling') the 'soft wool' of a 'little lamb.' We notice lamb and child as soon as we turn the page (before we read the last stanza) and we identify them with similar figures on the first plate. When we turn then to the last stanza we realize at once that the child (not Blake) must be the poem's speaker and that the lamb he refers to is pictured in the designs. Text and design 'cannot well be separated.' . . .

Designs of a more abstract nature can affect our readings in equally complex and subtle ways. On the first plate of **"A Cradle Song,"** for example, the text (a mother's lullaby to her sleeping child, sung in response to the child's smiles, moans and sighs) is set against a night sky and surrounded by a tangle of flame-like vegetative forms and tiny human figures. Our initial reaction to the design is uncomplicated. The decoration, we feel, neatly captures the poem's dominant note of security and protection. Delicate intimations of identity between mother, child, and all creation are echoed in the swirling continuity of text, vegetation and human form. To [Geoffrey] Keynes, 'the dreamy tangles of falling vegetation . . . suggest the feeling of the first line: "Sweet dreams form a shade."' He also points to the 'soft female form with arms stretched out in benison' above and to the right of the second stanza who 'seems suggested by . . . "Sweet sleep Angel mild, / Hover o'er my happy child"' [Keynes, ed., ***Songs of Innocence and of Experience***]. Erdman writes of 'Suggestive, indeterminate vegetable and human forms of dreams, smiles, sweet moans, and sighs which fill the verdure backed by night sky.' When comparing this plate with other examples of flame-plant decoration, continues Erdman, 'we see that the lullaby form of energy and desire thins into "pleasant streams" and "happy silent moony beams."'

But the poem is not all gentle sweetness and content. Its delicate beauty, like that of Coleridge's "Frost at Midnight," is faintly disturbing and enigmatic. We wonder, for example, at the ease with which the mother overcomes her sense of Christ's sorrows. . . .

The mother's steady, unvarying tone fails to dispel the darker implications of moans, sighs and tears. A gap opens between what we feel and what the mother's tone would make us feel—a gap anticipated in the design on the first plate. What Erdman sees as 'pleasant streams' and 'happy silent moony beams,' others see quite differently. Wagenknecht, for example, writes of the 'terribly twisted and dark vegetation which winds against a dark background like seaweed . . . in one place tinged with red which suggests flesh as well as vegetation' *[Blake's Night: William Blake and the Idea of Pastoral]*. Vague premonitions of threat and danger soon complicate any initial impression of exuberant organic life. This vegetation, we realize, is thicker, darker and heavier than the light curlicues and intertwinings found elsewhere in ***Innocence***. The more we look at its swirling strands, the less likely we are to associate them with the dream-formed 'shade' of line 1. 'The hedging of each stanza,' writes Eben Bass, 'implies protection for the cradled child, but the stanzas are also, in fact, nearly oppressed by the design.' The decoration begins to affect the way we read. Bass wonders if '"Sweet dreams form a shade" could imply the mother's clouding, as well as protective, influence' ["*Songs of Innocence and of Experience:*

The Thrust of Design" in *Blake's Visionary Forms Dramatic,* Erdman and Grant, eds.]. Words like 'hovers' and 'beguiles' take on new and more ambiguous meanings. As the thinning strands of vegetation work their way into the text, tiny ripples of doubt disrupt the reassuring flow of the mother's words. We turn to the second plate secure in our sense of a world bounded and fused by the loving identity of mother and child, but we are also vaguely troubled. The design catches out and alerts us to subtle intimations of threat and danger in the text—even as it sounds the poem's dominant note of protection and contentment . . . .

Even when a design seems awkward, crude, or perfunctory we ought not to dismiss the impressions it makes upon us. The second plate of **"A Cradle Song"** provides a convenient example. Our first impulse is to seek some extraliterary excuse for its unpleasant appearance. . . .

Why . . . does the child's appearance disturb us? There is no mistaking the design's unpleasantness. The stark backdrop of dark, draped cloth is like nothing else in ***Innocence.*** Its strong, straight lines are of a piece with the 'hard outlines' of the chair, the large, hooded cradle, and the folds of the mother's dress. The ground's dark mottled colors suggest a patterned carpet, but the patterns lack definition or outline. Like much else in the design, it reminds us of a similarly enclosed scene in **"Infant Sorrow,"** a poem about the stifling, oppressive weight of parental influence. The hooded wicker cradle looks coffinlike, in part because of its length. Is this an accident, the wholly fortuitous result of Blake's habitual 'clumsiness' with perspective? And what of the mother? Why does she look so much less attractive and appealing than the mother on the first plate of **"Spring"**? 'Amply, almost redundantly gowned,' (Wagenknecht), with a headdress like a wimple, she is stiff and awkward as she bends over her child. . . .

'Is it chance that wraps the child's bedclothes around him as tightly as a cocoon? Why not attribute their unpleasant, 'threatening' appearance to the mother, a woman whose own clothing wholly conceals the curves of her body?

'The cradle's hood,' writes Bass, 'and the draped cloth behind are the mother's way of sheltering her child from cold and drafts, but both testify as much to danger and mortality as they do to protection.' Our doubts about the poem's concluding stanzas increase as we look at the second plate. The world, it seems, is not as benevolent as the mother's words would have us believe; protection takes on the appearance of something more threatening. We worry again about 'hovers' and 'beguiles.' Maternal affection is frequently ambiguous in ***Innocence:*** nurture slides easily into dependency, protection tightens into possessiveness. On **"The Blossom"** plate, for example, a tiny child is almost totally obscured by the embrace of a winged female dressed in green, presumably its mother. She faces *against* the cycle of generation traced by the other figures in the design.

The designs to **"A Cradle Song"** hint at the dangers implicit in the mother's easy passage from tears to smiles. Innocence must be protected, enclosed against an outside world whose threatening harshness is figured in the acanthus-shaped leaves at the top of the second plate or the nightmarish tangles of plate 1. But the domestic scene offers its own dangers. The disturbingly 'uncompromising' nature of the design on the second plate is no accident. Blake was a careful and conscious craftsman with a professional engraver's eye for detail. He thought seriously about technique, and knew how to adapt his style to different moods. No artist who supported himself by illustrating or engraving other men's works could have 'missed' or 'overlooked' the design's want of delicacy. Had he been displeased with the harsh outlines on the original copper-plate, Blake could have softened them with color, as he did in earlier copies. When a design seems crude or perfunctory, the impressions it makes upon us ought not to be dismissed too quickly. Blake has flaws, both as poet and as painter—the pictorial language of his designs is, at times, as in the case of ***Tiriel,*** inappropriate—but his visual art deserves the same respectful scrutiny as his poetry. . . .

In some plates, though, Blake seems subject to purely technical or formal limitations. The text of **"The Chimney Sweeper"** in ***Innocence,*** for example, fills almost the whole plate. Blake, we feel, has no choice but to squeeze his design into a half-inch strip along the bottom of the plate. As a result, sweep-heaven seems neither airy, light, nor particularly pleasant. . . .

Failed or flawed designs in ***Songs*** are the product less of carelessness or incompetence than of ambition. Some simply ask too much of us. The oddly inoffensive creature on **"The Tyger"** plate provides a notorious case in point. Blake might easily have drawn a fearful or ferocious tiger. 'He had no trouble drawing a fearful werewolf,' Erdman reminds us [in his *Blake: Prophet against Empire*], 'or for that matter a fearful flea.' And on the sixth page of the Notebook (or 'Rossetti Manuscript'), another page of which contains a draft of the poem, we find two genuinely ferocious beasts, one unmistakably a tiger. Yet in none of the extant copies of *Songs* is there a creature remotely comparable to the picture created by the poem's awestruck speaker. 'Comical,' 'inquisitive,' 'simpering,' 'quaint,' 'gentle,' 'tame,' 'patient,' 'worried,' 'fatuous,' 'supercilious'—these are the adjectives critics use to describe the visual equivalent of the poem's bright burning beast. . . .

Once we accept the obvious discrepancy between poem and design, a whole range of possibilities opens: the design is Blake's attempt 'to portray the smile of the Deity on its [the tiger's] lips, and to show the ultimate "humanity divine" of Nature's most terrific beast'; or it is 'a mask, deriding those who expect upon a mortal page the picture of the Deity at work' (Wicksteed); or a depiction of 'the final tiger, who has attained the state of organized Innocence as have the adjacent lions and tigers of **"The Little Girl Lost"** and **"The Little Girl Found"**' (Erdman), or a joke, not so much on us as on 'the awestruck questioner, or the Tyger, and perhaps on the Creator himself' (Grant, 'The Art and Argument of the "Tyger",' *Discussions of William Blake,* John E. Grant, ed.).

I tend towards the last of these possibilities. Blake and the poetic voice ought not to be confused, especially in a Song of Experience. Much of what the awestruck questioner says implies a world (and a way of looking at it) that Blake would have found unnecessarily limited and limiting. He might well have sought to undermine the speaker by domesticating or defanging his tiger, just as he cuts Behemoth and Leviathan down to size (Paley [in his *William Blake*] calls them 'household pets') in plate 15 of the *Illustrations to the Book of Job.*

But an 'explanation' of this sort makes the design no less jarring or unsatisfactory. Hagstrum is still right, the tiger *is* 'unworthily illustrated,' even if Blake thinks the speaker's celebration of its fierce majesty wrong or misguided. The poem is simply too powerful to be undercut so brutally. We have neither time nor inclination to make the necessary adjustments of perspective the design demands of us. . . .

The design to **"The Tyger"** is marred by a comparable lack of restraint. Blake is so eager for us to see the whole, so delighted with the ease with which he can expose his speaker, that he momentarily loses his sense of tact. The reader is much too abruptly wrenched out of the mood of the poem. . . .

John Rowe Townsend

SOURCE: "Part II: 1840-1915: Writers in Rhyme," in *Written for Children: An Outline of English-Language Children's Literature,* sixth edition, Scarecrow Press, 1996, pp. 98-9.

[The following excerpt was originally published in Written for Children: An Outline of English-Language Children's Literature, *1987.]*

William Blake's intention in writing his ***Songs of Innocence*** (1789) was clearly expressed in the introductory poem, 'Piping down the valleys wild', which concludes:

> And I made a rural pen,
> And I stain'd the water clear,
> And I wrote my happy songs
> Ev'ry child may joy to hear.

Reversing the familiar process by which work intended for the general reader finds its way to the children's list, the ***Songs of Innocence*** have found their place as part of the general heritage of English poetry. This is right and proper, although in poem after poem Blake is unmistakably addressing himself to children.

The movement of the ***Songs of Innocence*** out of accepted children's literature probably has much to do with their natural pairing with the ***Songs of Experience.*** These came five years later and contained less of the joy of childhood; brightness had fallen from the air. Yet I would hesitate to say that the elusive border between children's and general literature passes between the ***Songs of Innocence*** and the ***Songs of Experience;*** in fact the Blake poem which above all others stirs the imagination of children is in the latter book: 'Tyger, Tyger, burning bright . . . '

Brian Alderson

SOURCE: "Loss of Innocence," in *The Times, London,* No. 63581, December 19, 1989, p. 18.

Two hundred years ago this autumn, a little book was published at No. 28 Poland Street. Its like had never been seen before: ***Songs of Innocence 1789,*** ran the words on the title-page; "The Author & Printer W. Blake".

There was not much of it—a versified Introduction about a piper "piping down the valleys wild" and 22 simple lyrics—but it has claim to its own high revolutionary status. As an harbinger of Romanticism it is more significant than the much-vaunted *Lyrical Ballads* published by Wordsworth and Coleridge nine years later, and as an example of manifold creativity it is unparalleled.

For the "Author & Printer" did not simply write his poems and run them through an Adana press on his kitchen table. Every page was made up of a complex design of words and images, etched and printed by a technique Blake himself had invented. This enabled him to print from the surface of an etched metal plate instead of from lines etched below the surface. Blake claimed that he had been instructed how to do it by his dead brother Robert, who came to him in a vision. Working out the technology of the process took more than a dream, and ***Songs of Innocence*** was a first triumphant demonstration of the perfected method.

In addition to all this, the book is also one of the greatest contributions to English children's literature, the more so for being without precedent. A familiar case has been made out for Blake knowing such widely-approved works as Isaac Watts's *Divine Songs Attempted in Easy Language for the Use of Children,* first published in 1715, or Mrs Barbauld's *Hymns in Prose* of 1781. There are echoes of their phrasing in ***Songs of Innocence,*** but their conventional philosophy may have acted as irritant rather than influence. Nor did these writers have the self-assurance to address the reader with Blake's uninhibited directness or to give such an imaginative density to their texts.

Even the hackneyed "Little Lamb who made thee / Dost thou know who made thee" has more to say for itself than may be recognized by those of us who had to chant it in the school-hall. Such exploitation wrecks the fragile unity which Blake has brought to the mixed modes of pastoral, nursery rhyme and spiritual song, and which, in the original, is enhanced by pictorial illumination: in this case a quaint rural scene over-arched by wind-blown trees straight from Eden.

The illustrations develop a symbolic charge. Possible interpretations abound, and these are multiplied when the ***Songs of Innocence*** are set beside the "contrary states" expressed in the ***Songs of Experience*** which Blake published four years later. **"The Lamb"** takes on a strange incandescence alongside **"The Tyger"; "The Divine Image"** finds a bitter reflection in **"The Human Abstract"**.

However, such splendours and subtleties had little influence. The 18th-century public ignored Blake's ***Songs.*** It is true that Wordsworth copied some of the poems into his commonplace book (reflecting meanwhile on the author's lack of sanity); that Charles Lamb sent **"The Sweep Song"** to a charity publication *The Chimney Sweeper's Friend,* and that one or two of the ***Songs*** appeared in anthologies, but the books were as good as lost for 70 years, until the publication in 1863 of Alexander Gilchrist's biography of Blake, which was significantly subtitled "Pictor Ignotus". (By way of supplement it included 16 electrotype reproductions made from the original plates of the ***Songs,*** now lost.)

But this still did not lead to recognition of Blake as a poet for children. PreRaphaelites, radicals and cabbalists all welcomed him as their own, but apparently no edition of ***Songs of Innocence*** for children was published until Wells Gardner, Darton & Co brought one out in 1899, 110 years after the original. This version appeared in the publisher's "Midget Series", a miscellany of little books, just 3 x 21/2 in, and was illustrated with designs by Celia Levetus which are considerably closer to Kate Greenaway than to William Blake. All the poems from ***Songs of Innocence*** were included, with some fillers from ***Songs of Experience,*** including, inevitably, **"The Tiger"** *(sic)* and the ferociously contrary **"Nurse's Song".**

As a children's book, ***Songs of Innocence*** was persistently subverted by editors, publishers and illustrators who saw it in terms of suburban whimsy. Words almost failed the great Blake bibliographer G.E. Bentley when he came to annotate these editions and their illustrations for his *Blake Books* of 1977. Honor Appleton (1911) was "distressing"; Charles and Mary Robinson (1912) were "lamentable"; Jacynth Parsons (1927) was "dreadful", and so on to the present time. (He does not record Celia Levetus, and someone seems to have shielded him from an edition in "The Gravure Series", the frontispiece of which shows a naked cherub lying on a cloud of exhaust fumes.)

Perhaps the only illustrative response to the texts that is in any way adequate is that by Maurice Sendak in a little selection from ***Songs of Innocence*** issued by The Bodley Head in 1967. This, however, is almost as rare as the poet's own books, since it was printed in a severely limited edition for the publisher to give to his friends at Christmas.

What surprises me is that, despite all these adaptations, no one has attempted to publish a good reproduction of Blake's original illuminated texts, edited for the readers he had in mind—children. Some not very convincing arguments have been advanced: that the words of the poems are enough in themselves, or that it would be too difficult or expensive to reproduce the coloured etchings in facsimile.

Blake once remarked in a letter that his *Visions* had been "elucidated by children, who have taken a greater delight in contemplating my Pictures than I even hoped". With a bit of confidence and trust, we might find that elucidation and delight are, after 200 years, still possible.

Andrew Lincoln

SOURCE: Introduction to *Songs of Innocence and of Experience,* by William Blake, edited by Andrew Lincoln, The William Blake Trust / The Tate Gallery, 1991, pp. 9-24.

Blake's 'Contrary States' of Innocence and Experience illuminate many areas of thought and feeling. Among other things, they direct attention to dualities at the heart of the Christian tradition. In the Bible there are many contrasting ideas and images which interpreters usually seek to harmonise. Divine power is associated with terror and with joy. God is presented as a transcendent being who demands obedience to moral law, and as a loving merciful being who becomes human. If the opening chapters look back to a lost intimacy with the Lord in a garden, others celebrate an ever present relationship with Him as a good shepherd. There are visions of a universal resurrection at the eventual termination of history, and of individual regeneration as a present reality. Redemption is associated with the death of the Saviour, and with His birth. In the ***Songs*** Blake presents comparable contrasts, not as elements of a coherent and unified system of belief, but as aspects of two contrary modes of vision that illuminate each other dialectically.

There is no definitive text of the ***Songs,*** and as some poems were transferred from Innocence to Experience general comments about either 'State' have to be related to particular arrangements of the poems. In the copy reproduced in this edition, all of the songs that feature a 'bardic' voice appear in Experience. The poems of Innocence focus on joyful and protective relationships, on the sense of common identity between individuals. In the awareness of shared happiness—present, remembered or anticipated—innocents triumph over loss, deprivation and the steady passage of time. Divinity here is an innate presence that becomes visible in the human form, a personal saviour 'ever nigh' who comforts the distressed. The landscape of Innocence is typically common ground: pastoral fields, valleys wild, the village green. But although this state of being is apparently idyllic, it is not without its limitations. Its ever ready comfort and security involve passivity, dependence, even at times a feeling of resignation. The possibility that Innocence might lead to entrapment is never confronted directly in the poems, but can often be sensed. In **"On Another's Sorrow"** the conviction that the divine comforter sits 'both night & day / Wiping all our tears away' anticipates the spiritual stalemate of some Experience poems, in which fears are increased and made habitual by weeping 'both night & day'.

In contrast to the steady faith of Innocence, Experience is a state of disillusionment in which distress breeds anger and a new kind of hope. In this state the prophetic consciousness appears, with its vision of a past 'Age of Gold' from which humanity has fallen, its tormented awareness of present error and cruelty, its hope of a universal resurrection 'In futurity'. While the Innocence poems dwell on pleasure and consolation, the poems of Experience emphasize the fearful selfishness of the human heart, and the confusion and tyranny that grow from attempts to rationalize this selfishness. A typical setting of Experience is the garden, the enclosed space in which the individual, withdrawn from the larger community, cultivates private desires. The garden of Experience inevitably recalls the myth of Eden, which in this perspective can be seen as the expression of a severely limited and limiting attitude to life. If the divinity of Innocence becomes 'an infant small' in order to bring comfort and joy to the world, the divinity of Experience is usually a figure of dread, a distant father who presides over repressive institutions and ideologies. The satirical drive of Experience thus strikes at the roots of 'ancient' tradition. But in doing so it exposes its own limitations. In Experience hope and repression seem intimately related: both spring from the conviction that humanity is fallen. The Holy Word who urges earth to arise has begun to sit in judgment on 'the lapsed Soul'. The prophetic consciousness seems bound by the conditions it strives with. The seer who anticipates the transformation of the 'desart wild' accepts 'a garden mild' as his ideal.

The ***Songs of Innocence and of Experience*** rarely offer simple choices—as between moral absolutes—but tend to emphasize the relativity of particular images and points of view. 'Mercy Pity Love and Peace' can reveal the innate divinity in human life, or mask the selfishness of the natural heart. To accept one view and refuse the alternative would be to turn away from an unpleasant truth or to accept a reductive view of human feeling. Some poems contain contradictory views within them, and as we shall see, Blake's technique generates ambiguities that repeatedly complicate interpretation. Few books offer such challenges with such a disarming appearance of simplicity. . . .

Songs of Innocence was first issued as a separate work, in 1789 according to the title-page. The process of composition must have extended over several years, as the collection includes three poems that first appeared in **"An Island in the Moon"**, and one that was transcribed in a copy of ***Poetical Sketches.*** The **"Introduction"** announces the work as a book for children:

[So I wrote]
Every child may joy to hear

Blake had already become involved in the rapidly expanding market for children's books. Early in his professional career he was commissioned to engrave designs for *The Speaker* (c. 1780), an anthology designed to 'facilitate the improvement of Youth in reading and Writing', and for Mrs Barbauld's *Hymns in Prose for Children* (1781). He probably had little sympathy with the educational aims of these books, or indeed with much of the children's literature written for the polite market. But he seems to have known the market well. As many critics have noted, in the variety of its contents ***Songs of Innocence*** invites comparison with a range of other children's books available at the time, including collections of hymns for children, such as those by Isaac Watts, Charles Wesley or Anna Barbauld; educational playbooks such as William Ronksley's *The Child's Week's Work,* 1712; and emblem books such as John Wynne's *Choice Emblems . . . for the Improvement and Pastime of Youth,* 1772.

In the later eighteenth century, children's books were often illustrated, usually with an engraving or simple woodcut. Some pictures were even coloured with watercolours. Many of the visual images in Blake's work have their counterparts in contemporary books: the shepherd with his pipe, the seated woman who shows a book to two children, the vine growing around the tree, the child lost in a wood, the mother watching her baby in its cradle, and—of course—children at play. But Blake's integration of text and design goes far beyond the capacities of conventional printing methods. The relief etching process seems to have encouraged him to avoid blank spaces, to fill his margins with decorative motifs, to add the tiny leaves and figures that appear in or around the text of his songs. This embellishment invites close exploration of each plate, and helps to make the hand coloured copies of the work look more like illuminated manuscripts than printed books.

In the poems there is a comparable transformation of familiar conventions. The references to the shepherd, the Lamb, and to the 'maker' who comforts the distressed may recall the hymns of Charles Wesley and others, but there is no mention of sin or divine punishment. Several poems develop variations on the Christian theme 'Whoso dwelleth in love dwelleth in God'. But the theme is approached without conventional qualifications, in a way that tends to dissolve the traditional distinction between the human and the divine. Children's unselfconscious innocence is sometimes used to expose the limitations of adult perspectives. Indeed, the childlike vision of the poems may even challenge contemporary assumptions about poetic argument. The reader is drawn into a world in which ambiguous syntax and elusive ironies at once invite and frustrate a search for definite conclusions.

As the sequel to the Innocence series, ***Songs of Experience*** differs considerably in mood and perspective. We can see the work taking shape in the notebook Blake inherited from his brother Robert, who died in 1787. Most of the poems of ***Experience*** . . . are not accompanied by their designs, although at least three of the Experience designs (for the title-page, **"My Pretty Rose Tree"** and **"London"**) were derived from a series of emblems sketched in the notebook under the title 'Ideas of Good and Evil'. The last poem in the notebook sequence is a long lyric **"Let the Brothels of Paris be opened"** which, as David Erdman [in *Prophet against Empire*] has shown, alludes to events surrounding the career of La Fayette between 1789 and the late summer of 1792. There are clear thematic relationships between some of the ***Experience*** poems and the other illuminated books offered for sale in the 1793 prospectus. The bitterly ironical references to 'God & his Priest & King' show a new outspokenness in Blake's work, a new drive to expose the social consequences of error, which was no doubt prompted by the course of events in revolutionary France, and by the political turmoil in England. In reading through the notebook sequence and studying the revisions one can trace, as Michael Phillips says, [in "William Blake's *Songs of Innocence and of Experience*: from Manuscript Draft to Illuminated Book"] 'the vision of ***Experience*** becoming sharper, more penetrating and more uncompromising with each stage'. But Blake's concern with social and religious tyranny here is an extension of his interest in the habits of thought that imprison individuals in 'the same dull round'. The notebook includes a 'Motto to the Song of Innocence & of Experience':

> The Good are attracted By Mens perceptions
> And Think not for themselves
> Till Experience teaches them to catch
> And to cage the Fairies & Elves
>
> And then the Knave begins to snarl
> And the Hypocrite to howl
> And all his good Friends shew their private ends
> And the Eagle is known from the Owl

Cruelty and repression are seen to be rooted in mental passivity; the conventional association of goodness with conformity and restraint is seen as both a symptom and a source of error. The Motto wasn't used, but its presence among the notebook poems gives a clear indication of how Blake saw the combined work. The use of 'Contrary States' was intended to make readers think 'for themselves'.

The Experience poems were printed in a format which parallels that of Innocence, with contrasting lettering (generally pseudoitalic as opposed to the upright roman miniscule usually found in Innocence). Some were apparently etched on the back of Innocence plates. The designs, like those of the earlier series, include motifs that appear in contemporary children's books—the game of shuttlecock and battledore, the sooty sweep walking through a street. The illustration for **"Nurses Song"** is comparable to one Blake designed and engraved for Mary Wollstonecraft's *Original Stories From Real Life* (1791). The disarming resemblance to children's books quite belies the scope and complexity of the Experience poems.

In the combined work [***The Songs of Innocence and of Experience***] the parallel between the two series helps to focus attention on the differences: Innocence poems may be linked to their counterparts in Experience by identical or contrasting titles, while visual contrasts reinforce those in the text. The designs of Innocence make more use of flowing, curving lines, protective spaces, exuberant vegetation; in Experience spaces are often defined and fractured by bare branches. The etched images on the Innocence plates are usually delicate and finely detailed: the textures of fleeces, bark, furnishings and leaves are clearly represented, large surfaces are lightened by fine lines or stippling, while distance may be suggested by variations in shading or width of line. . . .

The style of Experience is generally heavier and flatter.

Blake's conception of the ***Songs*** seems to have evolved through several stages. In the prospectus of October 1793, ***Songs of Innocence*** and ***Songs of Experience*** were advertised as separate works. Perhaps Blake assumed they would be easier to sell individually, although in practice it seems that the Experience poems were usually sold in combination with their Innocence counterparts. When Blake combined the two series into a single collection in 1794, he transferred **"The Little Girl Lost"** and **"The Little Girl Found"** from Innocence to Experience. These plates seem to have been printed with the other poems of Innocence, and as they were printed back-to-back, two other poems that normally appear in Innocence were transferred to Experience with them: **"A Dream"** and **"Laughing Song"**. These transfers give a clear indication that the boundaries between the two 'States of the Human Soul' were not hard and fast in Blake's view.

Publishers Weekly

SOURCE: A review of *The Tyger,* in *Publishers Weekly,* Vol. 240, No. 36, September 6, 1993, p. 91.

[The following three reviews focus on Neil Waldman's 1993 adaptation of Blake's "The Tyger."*]*

Sophisticated illustrations of the roaming "tyger" amid the "forests of the night" accompany Blake's famous poem. Shadowy black-and-gray spreads feature window-like insets of the dazzling color compositions for which Waldman is noted, and each of these highlights one particular image—stars shooting across the skies; a woolly blue lamb; red-gold and velvet-black tiger stripes. The effect is a little like a lightning flash illuminating one small patch within a field of murky darkness. A naïve stillness renders the creatures and their landscape symbolic, not quite real, vaguely mysterious. A full-color pull-out spread has special impact. Blake's poem is difficult in itself and, unfortunately, these stylized illustrations do little to bring his imagery within children's

From The Tyger, *written by William Blake. Illustrated by Neil Waldman.*

comprehension. Adults may be intrigued by Waldman's interpretation, but it does not work hand-in-hand with the text.

Hazel Rochman

SOURCE: A review of *The Tyger,* in *Booklist,* Vol. 90, No. 6, November 15, 1993, p. 620.

"The Tyger," by revolutionary eighteenth-century poet William Blake, remains one of the most anthologized of all poems today. Even young readers are caught by the fiercely physical opening lines ("Tyger, Tyger, burning bright / In the forests of the night") and by the pounding beat. You may not be at all certain what the poem means, but the sudden astonishing question—"Did he who made the Lamb make thee?"—confronts you with the elemental mystery of creation and of human nature. Waldman's acrylic paintings extend that sense of wonder. Within each double-page spread of dark swirling forest, he sets one stanza of the poem and one small frame of brilliant color. These frames are like a window or a lens; we see how the artist works to give shape to exploding energy. Some frames show a part of the tiger—the shoulder or the "dread feet" with their curving stripes. Some frames show a gentler pastoral scene or a wide view of sky and sea. At the end, a double-page spread of the whole tiger in black and white opens out to a four-page full-color panorama that includes all the parts we have seen. The huge, snarling tiger is at the center of a world that includes the lamb, the serpent, the curves of tree and flame, the eye of the artist, and the hand of God. As animal poem, as creation myth, and as introduction to the music of poetry, this book makes a stirring read-aloud.

Ruth K. MacDonald

SOURCE: A review of *The Tyger,* in *School Library Journal,* Vol. 40, No. 1, January, 1994, p. 118.

Both the darkness of the night and the brightness of the Tyger are addressed in this outstanding picture-book version of Blake's classic poem. Its antiquity is preserved in the calligraphic typeset, which resembles the poet's handwritten text for his illustrated works. Waldman's acrylic artwork, however, is modern, highly painterly, and formal. A full-color mural of the Tyger is revealed at the end, in a fold-out spread that spans four pages. Each double-page spread leading up to it is a section of the larger canvas done in black and shades of gray; a couplet appears on each verso, and is faced by a corresponding element of the painting on the recto, framed and in full color. Readers see the brilliantly colored beast—first in parts, such as paw or tail; then its face; then in totality. The lamb of the verse is also pictured in a full-color frame. The focus on individual portions of the whole gives readers an opportunity to study **"The Tyger"** carefully, and to discuss the artist's interpretation. Even the eye and hand of God are shown, pictured as mystical and disembodied metaphoric manifestations. An excellent choice for anyone studying the poem.

Additional coverage of Blake's life and career is contained in the following sources published by Gale Research: *Concise Dictionary of British Literary Biography, 1789-1832; Dictionary of Literary Biography,* Vols. 93, 163; *DISCovering Authors, DISCovering Authors: Modules; Major Authors and Illustrators for Children and Young Adults; Poetry Criticism,* Vol. 12; and *Something about the Author,* Vol. 30.

Nat(han Irving) Hentoff

1925-

American author of fiction and nonfiction; editor, journalist, and jazz critic.

Major works include *Jazz Country* (1965), *This School Is Driving Me Crazy* (1976), *Does This School Have Capital Punishment?* (1981), *The Day They Came to Arrest the Book* (1982), *American Heroes* (1987).

For more information on Hentoff's career prior to 1966, see *CLR,* Vol. 1.

INTRODUCTION

A long-time critic and authority on jazz music, Hentoff's passion for jazz, coupled with his penchant for social causes, infuses his fiction for young adults. He is renowned for his novels that exhibit his extensive knowledge and experience of jazz, as well as his love and respect for the artists who played it. His first novel, *Jazz Country,* reflects the devotion of the jazz artist and the demands and difficulties he encounters in a world of nightlife and city clubs—a world that Hentoff experienced firsthand. Exposing injustice and defending civil rights also became ongoing pursuits for both his fiction and nonfiction. As a champion of the First Amendment, Hentoff instills in young readers the importance and sacredness of the Bill of Rights in American society and the fragility of these rights if gone unprotected. "Of all my obsessions," Hentoff explained, "this is the strongest. . . . If children do not get the sense that the Constitution, including the Bill of Rights, actually belongs to them, they will grow up indifferent to their own—and other's—liberties and rights. And if enough of the citizenry are careless in these matters, those liberties and rights will be suicidally lost." Noted by reviewers as compelling, spirited, and moving, Hentoff's writing takes on a virtuoso performance. The prose of his jazz stories, regarded as "wondrously rhythmic," reflects the music itself. His thought-provoking and insightful discussions of timely themes generate awareness, fixing in youthful minds the value of expressing and debating their own ideas and opinions.

Biographical Information

Born in 1925, Hentoff was raised in Boston by Jewish parents. When he was eleven he discovered jazz and made it an integral part of his life and, later, his writing. He loved the inherent passion, emotion, and individual freedom found in the music and, as he grew older, he sought after-hour places where it was played. Growing up Jewish amidst widespread anti-Semitism and antagonistic literature, Hentoff empathized with minority groups, women, and other outsiders who suffered discrimination and violation of their civil rights. He also became distrustful of persons in power, and meaningless words without action. His fervor for civil liberties emerged in college when he became editor of a student-run paper at Northeastern University. Under his direction, student reporters began to investigate corruption in city government. A struggle emerged between the university administration and the student journalists when Hentoff outlined a controversial story about the university's trustees. The president gave the staff a choice to back off the story or resign; Hentoff and the entire staff quit the paper. Hentoff's firsthand experience with censorship became one of several First Amendment topics that later fueled his fiction and nonfiction. After earning a Bachelor of Arts with high honors, he did graduate work at Harvard University in 1946 and at the Sorbonne in 1950. While in graduate school Hentoff hosted a jazz radio show at WMEX in Boston and interviewed such great musicians as Charlie Parker and Duke Ellington. He also immersed himself in the jazz world when he became a critic for *Down Beat*, a leading jazz magazine. In 1965, he published his first novel for young adults,

Jazz Country, which reflects his enthusiasm for the music and his knowledge of the jazz culture.

Major Works

Jazz Country portrays an untutored, teenage white boy attempting to play his trumpet in a black musician's jazz world in New York City. The novel details the hard work that accompanies success and introduces young readers to a realm of disciplined musical creativity. Hentoff explained, "I wanted to show all kids how rich and deep this music is." His enthusiasm for and experience with the jazz scene gives his first young adult novel an authentic and realistic grounding. Carolyn Heilbrun commented that *Jazz Country* "renders the experience of jazz with passion . . . [and] presents its Negro characters with honesty and dignity. . . ." A critic for *Kirkus Reviews* noted that Hentoff "incorporates some lessons in jazz appreciation and captures a sense of the abrasive realities of being black in New York." Hentoff's second young adult novel, *This School Is Driving Me Crazy,* features young Sam Davidson who reluctantly attends a school where his father is headmaster. The sequel, *Does This School Have Capital Punishment?,* follows Sam to a new school where the headmaster wrongly accuses him of a misdeed another student has committed. Peripheral student voices call attention to the responsibilities of teachers and administrators and the misuse of power. In this manner Hentoff becomes the advocate for student rights that have been neglected by persons in positions of authority. A. R. Williams pointed out that *This School is Driving Me Crazy* has "pace, racy dialogue . . . and examines the many-sided problems found in large schools."

In a similar fashion, *The Day They Came to Arrest the Book* voices Hentoff's ardor for the First Amendment through young characters who object to removing *The Adventures of Huckleberry Finn* from their high school library. Hentoff draws clear lines on the issue of censorship. He sets a narrow-minded principal, a black parent, and a young female student, who claim the novel racist and sexist, against the school newspaper editor, a teacher, and a librarian who defend free speech and see the redeeming human values honored in *Huckleberry Finn.* Reviewers have remarked that the characters who favor the banning of *Huckleberry Finn* are represented by reasonable arguments, despite their political defeat. "There is no question of sitting on the fence," claimed P. Thompson, adding that the novel "forces the brain into action." Lee Golda predicted the novel would "engage young readers in a timely conflict which has no easy resolution." In *American Heroes*, a nonfiction work, eight people, including a number of high school students, share true stories of standing up for their rights in the face of opposition and disapproval of peers. One student refuses to say the pledge of allegiance and another opposes the principal's censure of the school paper. Hentoff provides clear and inspiring stories capable of stirring a young audience to follow by example and defend their right to a free press, free speech, freedom of religion, and the right to privacy. *American Heroes* also describes the struggle and success of two librarians who bravely fight censorship. Hentoff clearly defines issues as he explains the Bill of Rights, its abuse, and misuse. Steve Matthews praised Hentoff as an author "strongly committed to freedom," while a *Kirkus Reviews* critic credited his "contemporary portraits" for "bringing alive the dated phrases of the Bill of Rights."

Awards

Hentoff received the Children's Spring Book Festival Award from the *New York Herald Tribune* and the Nancy Block Award, both in 1965 for *Jazz Country.* In 1966, *Jazz Country* also won the Woodward Park School Award.

AUTHOR'S COMMENTARY

Nat Hentoff

SOURCE: "The Rise and Fall of a Writer for Young Readers," in *Booklist,* Vol. 92, No. 13, March 1, 1996, p. 1129.

I had heard of Ursula Nordstrom—the legendary orchestrator of books for young readers—from a friend of mine. Maurice Sendak. But I never expected to hear *from* her.

One day in 1964, she called. Would I be interested in writing a children's book for what was then Harper & Row? I demurred. I would have to make the words short, the ideas simple, and take care not to offend any librarian or parent. I would let this cup pass from me, I told her.

"Write what you want to write," Ursula said. "Don't censor yourself."

The result was ***Jazz Country,*** a novel about a white high-school trumpeter trying to break into the black world of jazz. Published in 1965, it's still being read, judging from letters I get from youngsters, and for reasons that are not clear to me, the book continues to be very popular in Japan.

Encouraged, I wrote other YA novels—among them, ***I'm Really Dragged but Nothing Gets Me Down, This School Is Driving Me Crazy*** (a title provided by my younger son), ***Does This School Have Capital Punishment?*** and ***The Day They Came to Arrest the Book.***

What I particularly enjoyed was hearing from readers around the country. I've written a number of books for adults but seldom hear from anybody but reviewers. Kids, however, have strong opinions. "You didn't make the father real." "That book was about me. I get in trouble a lot, too."

There was another response. The head of the children's division at the New York Public Library told me that ***Jazz Country*** was the most stolen book in her collection. That was more satisfying to me than any prize.

I also learned a lot about censorship. At an International Reading Association conference in Chicago, two librarians from Atlanta told me how sad they were that ***This School Is Driving Me Crazy*** had just been banned in their district. Rambunctious boys with reading problems, they told me, had latched onto the novel, probably because the main character—a decent, intense boy—had problems "relating" from the time he woke up in the morning. (I'd had no intention of writing the book especially for such boys.)

The book was banned because some parents object to the use of *damn* and *hell.*

Others of my books have been challenged. Among them, ***The Day They Came to Arrest the Book,*** which tells of a concerted attack on *Huckleberry Finn* in a high school by black parents, feminists, and some Christian parents (Huck never goes to Sunday school and comes from a decidedly dysfunctional family). In Charlottesville, Virginia (a place not unknown to Thomas Jefferson), the book was attacked "because it offers inflammatory challenge to authoritarian roles."

They got that right.

Over the years, I have been invited—because of my YA books—to speak at more than 20 state meetings of school librarians, media specialists, and public librarians. I learn a lot at those sessions about attempts, some of them successful, to remove books and other curriculum materials, and I then turn the information into columns for the *Washington Post* and the *Village Voice.* I also find out that books I wrote 25 and more years ago are still being checked out of libraries and talked about in classes. I can't say that about most of my adult books.

In recent months, I've spoken to conferences of librarians in Illinois, Oregon, and upstate New York. Some of them ask when my next YA novel is coming, and at that point, I become the Ancient Mariner, telling them that no one wants to publish my next book. I've tried more than a dozen publishers, including some who have my novels on their lists and keep sending me royalty checks. The last check was for almost $5,000 for two novels that by now have been out in the country for a long time.

What I tell librarians and media specialists is that I have been banned as a YA author because apparently today's book publishers have become cautious as to certain issues that might create unpleasantness.

The novel for young readers that I want to write is based on what I've seen over 10 and more years in visits to middle and high schools and colleges in many cities. There is tribalism—bristling separatism—in the schools. There are black tables and white tables and Asian tables in the lunchrooms. The self-segregation continues at various school events and in classrooms. The result is that what Horace Mann called "the common school" is practically obsolete. The divisions and the bitter mythologies mirror the state of race relations on the outside. This is not education. It is pandering to prejudice on the part of school officials. Rather than learning how to break down these barriers, timid educators do not get involved in the separatism and thereby encourage it.

My novel about this deterioration of learning how to deal with differences will be—like my other books—partly comic and partly serious, disturbingly serious. It will not be a tract. No one willingly reads tracts. It is a story populated by a range of kids, black and white, who surprise themselves—and the writer—as the story goes on. I learned long ago that a novel that does not entertain will have a very brief life. This one will both entertain and get its readers into thinking, actually thinking, about what kind of people they are—and want to be.

It is a novel, however, that exists only in my mind. I wish Ursula Nordstrom were still here. She believed that an editor without courage ought to be in some other field. Like politics.

TITLE COMMENTARY

JAZZ COUNTRY (1965)

Virginia Kirkus' Service

SOURCE: A review of *Jazz Country,* in *Virginia Kirkus' Service,* Vol. XXXIII, No. 5, March 1, 1965, p. 252.

16 year old white boys from New York's east 70s don't gain an easy admittance to the jazz country of Negro band leaders like Moses Godrey. Tom Curtis was tolerated at first because he was earnest about playing the trumpet and could take everything Godfrey and his musicians handed out. Tom gradually found himself "inside" with growing respect for the arrogant, honest Godfrey; Tom had begun to learn what jazz, and maybe life, was all about. "You've got to find your own 'thing,'" they told him. "You've got to tell your own story." The author, a well known jazz critic, writes of Tom in the first person. He manages to sustain the tone of a young boy's viewpoint in the vivid idiom of Negro jive talk, coherently used. He incorporates some lessons in jazz appreciation and captures a sense of the abrasive realities of being black in New York. Some of the other characters too often sound like mouthpieces for a crusade rather than people; the intensity and bitterness of the race situation have been caught without the harsh laughter that usually accompanies it as a safety valve.

Tom himself is never phony and Godfrey, though idealized, is a complex and memorable man. Here is a book with something important to say about the sacrifices demanded of the artist in a way that makes a strong appeal to boys—and that's a rare combination.

Carolyn Heilbrun

SOURCE: "Life in Safe Doses," in *The New York Times Book Review,* May 9, 1965, p. 3.

Look at ***Jazz Country.*** It is the best of the teen-age books I have read. Not only does it render the experience of jazz with passion, with what strikes an uninformed reader as veracity; it presents its Negro characters with honesty and dignity, capturing well the white boy's longing to partake of the Negro experience in order, as he thinks, to produce great jazz. Yet it is precisely in so far as it is tailored for teen-agers that the book fails. Its teen-age hero is cardboard, its plot an outrageous tissue of coincidences which do not, as coincidences should, mirror inner compulsions of the characters. The setting is New York, but the hero keeps tripping over people he knows as though he were strolling around a town of 500 people. What reality the hero has he has caught from Holden Caulfield, a character in a book not written for teen-agers.

Zena Sutherland

SOURCE: A review of *Jazz Country,* in *Bulletin of the Center for Children's Books,* Vol. XVIII, No. 10, June, 1965, p. 150.

In several ways, a most unusual book: honest, perceptive, and sophisticated. Tom Curtis plays jazz trumpet, and he describes the people whose influence shape his life and his decision to go to college—at least to start—rather than to join a band. Most of the jazzmen he meets are Negroes, and Tom discovers that no phonies are accepted, racially or musically. To be rebuffed because he is white is startling—but he is dealing with people who make no pretenses. A good story about New York, a wonderfully candid story about racial attitudes, and a fine book about jazz.

Frederick H. Guidry

SOURCE: A review of *Jazz Country,* in *The Christian Science Monitor,* June 24, 1965, p. 7.

Jazz critic Nat Hentoff has put into the form of a short novel what might otherwise have been a series of essays on problems of the United States jazz musician. His hero is a white high-school senior, undecided whether to go to college or to become a professional jazz trumpet player. Most of the other characters are Negro musicians—mythical but typical—living in New York. Although much of the book has a journalistic tone—no more creative than an ordinary magazine interview—the ideas under discussion are contemporary and stimulating. In Mr. Hentoff's jazz country, race relations are never long out of a conversation.

The Booklist and Subscription Books Bulletin

SOURCE: A review of *Jazz Country,* in *The Booklist and Subscription Books Bulletin,* Vol. 61, No. 21, July 1, 1965, p. 1025.

Set in New York City this is the first-person story of sixteen-year-old Tom Curtis, son of a well-to-do white lawyer, who wants to be a jazz musician. Becoming acquainted with a group of professional jazzmen, Tom gradually breaks through the racial barrier and learns a great deal about the world of the Negro artist in America. He also finds that he has not yet lived and felt enough to tell anything worth hearing on his trumpet, and decides to go on to college. By a well-known jazz historian and critic, an unusually fine teen-age novel, written with honesty, appreciation, and perception.

Margaret C. Scoggin

SOURCE: A review of *Jazz Country,* in *The Horn Book Magazine,* Vol. XLI, No. 5, October, 1965, p. 517.

Seventeen-year-old Tom Curtis, a white Anglo-Saxon Protestant, wants to be a jazz musician and wants to be accepted by the Negro jazz musicians he most admires. He is not sure he has real talent and he doesn't know whether or not he should go on to college. He haunts the jazz spots in Greenwich Village. He finds it is not easy to be accepted but gradually the musicians do befriend him and he is able to make his own decision about college. He realizes that he doesn't yet have enough "to say" to be a first-rate jazz musician. The scene is authentic (one can recognize a few real people), the jazz feeling excellent and up-to-date. Hentoff knows his music and his musicians and this will be of interest to any jazz fan or young adult curious about jazz.

Times Literary Supplement

SOURCE: "Top of the Pops," in *Times Literary Supplement,* No. 3351, May 19, 1966, p. 442.

Jazz Country is the story of sixteen-year-old Tom Curtis who wants to be a jazz musician. By any standard—and surely these days books for the 14-year-old upwards ought to stand up as adult fare—this is an excellent novel. Not only does Nat Hentoff show with great perception the development of one boy's understanding of other people, but without any strain, without recourse to either hip jargon or learned explanations, he opens for the uninitiated the significance of the world of jazz. As jazz critic of *The New Yorker* one would expect him to know the score, but this is virtuoso playing.

Tom is a nice guy, making good grades at school and with the kind of calm, sympathetic parents every teenager must long to have. The narrative comes clearly and straightforwardly from his lips. "Your life has been too easy for you to be making it as a jazz musician", the Negro bass player in the great Moses Godfrey's band tells him after hearing his talented but heartless trumpet playing. "And too white", adds his militant wife, Mary. By the end of the book Tom knows a lot more about life and how difficult it is to be both a jazz musician and black. The race relations material in ***Jazz Country*** is not a crude emotional appeal for togetherness because we all like music. We see the white cops beating up the black man for no better reason than because he is black, but we are also made to visualize the dilemma of the educated Negro whose sole desire is to live his own life as an individual but who constantly feels guilty that he is not a champion of his race at its time of destiny.

Marcus Crouch

SOURCE: A review of *Jazz Country,* in *Junior Bookshelf,* Vol. 30, No. 3, June, 1966, pp. 195-96.

Authorities on Jazz may not agree entirely with the thesis which is the basis of young Tom Curtis' efforts to find himself as a jazz player in this short novel for young people, but his experiments and experiences make stimulating reading. Tom discovers that there are human and personal undercurrents to the Jazz scene unsuspected by the amateur who never thinks of stepping across the borderline of professional music-making. The significance of colour in a man is explored, as well as the prejudices it arouses—usually in reverse of the common order of such things. Alongside are examined the normal problems of growing up and deciding on a career. There is no doubt the author knows his subject; working on *Down Beat* not only equips him but entitles him to put forward cogent and developed ideas in this fictional form.

Margery Fisher

SOURCE: A review of *Jazz Country,* in *Growing Point,* Vol. 5, No. 2, July, 1966, p. 748.

Young Tom Curtis has two ambitions—to be a real jazz trumpeter and to be a genuine accepted friend of negroes. Both these ambitions are helped along when he meets the great Moses Godfrey and establishes a real liking between them. He shares the perennial problem of youth; he must decide whether to earn money with his music, as it improves, or whether to take some time at college first. The problem is stated not in stiff terms but vigorously in terms of the story, which is interesting and tolerably realistic. It is a novel written specifically for the young but with no idea of making life seem rosy, and will serve as a good starting-point from which to look at adult books on the same musical theme.

David Churchill

SOURCE: A review of *Jazz Country,* in *The School Librarian,* Vol. 14, No. 2, July, 1966, p. 223.

The rather obvious dust jacket and the fact that the first eight pages were repeated, upside down, at the back of my copy prejudiced me against this book. The contents, however, won me over and I shall not hesitate to include the book in the senior half of my school library. It portrays a white youth with the personal problem of either continuing his education and getting a safe job or leaving school and trying to achieve recognition as a jazz trumpeter. Tom becomes involved with a group of coloured musicians who encourage him to develop his own identity and to make his own decisions. Jazz and jazzmen are not glamorized, entertaining slang is used, but no swear words, and all the right human attitudes are shown. Tom is an exceedingly well-balanced boy, and his father, who gives him complete freedom, is amazingly wise. The simplification does not detract from this skilful and fascinating book.

I'M REALLY DRAGGED BUT NOTHING GETS ME DOWN (1968)

Publishers Weekly

SOURCE: A review of *I'm Really Dragged But Nothing Gets Me Down,* in *Publishers Weekly,* Vol. 194, No. 10, September 2, 1968, p. 59.

A few years ago Nat Hentoff wrote a fine book for young people, ***Jazz Country.*** Now he has written another book for them—a book that could be put in a time capsule to be read by sociologists 20 years from now, for it records all the social problems that the young are facing currently—the draft, the generation gap, the lack of communication between generations, Vietnam, marijuana, integration. They're all here. What isn't here is a novel. There are no people here—there are just names attached to the tracts. Mr. Hentoff gives the names in order to verbalize. It could be a useful tract to current parents faced with young people faced with these problems.

John Weston

SOURCE: "Hang-ups Do Happen," in *The New York Times Book Review,* November 3, 1968, pp. 2, 66.

Nat Hentoff's ***I'm Really Dragged But Nothing Gets Me Down*** treats an important dilemma: how best can a young man serve his country and himself and retain his sense of morality? Jerome Wolf, 18, and his friends must face the issues of the draft. Refusing to register means a prison sentence, a loss of five years out of life; accepting a draft card, in their view, means accepting a sellout to murder; capitalizing on their opportunity for deferment by attending college means that the dumb and the poor must take their places. Mr. Hentoff attempts to present all sides of the question, concluding with the only unarguable decision—that, through education (in this case, draft counseling) each potential draftee must make his own peace and that a larger peace begins at the one-to-one human level.

Although timely and important in theme, the book falls short as a novel for basic reasons. It lacks driving power; it becomes, instead of a story that moves the reader, a philippic that instructs. The welding of a moral and philosophic discussion to a dramatic form is never easy to do but done well that is precisely what makes great books great. Because the surface of this one remains so flat, the characters so blurred, the arguments so objective, the impact of Mr. Hentoff's theme is largely ineffective.

Zena Sutherland

SOURCE: A review of *I'm Really Dragged But Nothing Gets Me Down,* in *Bulletin of the Center for Children's Books,* Vol. 22, No. 5, January, 1969, pp. 78-9.

Jeremy Wolf is a high school senior. His father doesn't understand him and Jeremy doesn't understand his father; the only girl he likes isn't interested; above all, he is in conflict about the draft—he doesn't want to kill, and he doesn't have the courage to take action. Endlessly, painfully, Jeremy and his friends talk about their responsibilities and goals, and just as painfully Jeremy and his father argue about their differences. The vitality of Hentoff's style and the scope of his perception and understanding give the book an impact that comes from the importance of its concepts rather than the drama of its action.

Lisa Melamed

SOURCE: "Between the Lines of Fire: The Vietnam War in Literature for Young Readers," in *The Lion and the Unicorn,* Vol. 3, No. 2, Winter, 1979-80, pp. 76-85.

I'm Really Dragged But Nothing Gets Me Down is not an overwhelming novel. It is not a gutwrenching work; rather, it is a piece of literature-verité that sometimes slips in the verité department. But Hentoff's triumph comes in the ways he deals with the issues. For all of the work's stylistic blandness and occasional tendencies toward cliché, it deserves consideration and some acclaim because the author has developed a forum about the Vietnam war and has dealt with the many sides of the questions, "Should I fight?" and "What does it all mean?"

Thankfully, this story is not set on the battlefields of Saigon, but in New York City. The characters are not soldiers; they are high school seniors in 1968, puzzling over their futures made uncertain by the ongoing war. These young people have found themselves faced with the task of choosing the right option, the lesser evil, and trying to live with it. Hentoff shows young men—boys, really—tossing their ideas around between album cuts and tokes of grass, and sets these conflicts against another conflict, the generation gap as it affects one father and his son.

The characters are distinguished by their differing philosophies, almost to the point where they cannot converse without expounding. Their tirades feel false, for all of the truths they contain, because they do not grow naturally from the exchanges. A difficulty with this book, eleven years after its publication, is that the kids seem to be reciting the catchphrases and metaphors of the late sixties which, because they are now historically familiar, may sound clichéd. Peter talks about "what kind of head you want to be," declaring that "the whole world is a head shop." Jeremy tells his father, "I know some things very clearly. That this country talks about peace and makes war. That this country talks about freedom but tries to run things where it can." Perhaps in 1968 the dialogue sounded remarkably relevant, but now it seems stylized. ***I'm Really Dragged . . .*** is a book that captured the immediacy of its time, without a doubt, but it is not powerful enough to outlive its topicality. I suspect that certain passages were even too much sixties rap for a sixties-rapper; even the title suggests that Mr. Hentoff was trying just a touch too hard.

It is unfortunate that ***I'm Really Dragged . . .*** is not better written because it contains many valuable insights. The war discussions are not grandiose political seminars, but reflect the attitudes and conflicts about the war as it affected its potential "members." Hentoff takes on the moral debate as well as the more peripheral, but no less important, matters. Jeremy, the most confused of the group, questions his friend early on: "It doesn't bug you being able to stay in school while kids who can't make it or don't have the money get sent off?" A discussion of this follows. It is nowhere as lovely or as striking as James Michener's treatment of this issue in *The Drifters,* but it's acknowledged. Both the idealists and the realists get the chance to say their piece, and there is some strong dialogue in this area. A physicist who was involved in World War Two speaks to a classroom full of students in varying states of emotional confusion and tells them, "My concern is not remaining pure but being relevant." His belief that acts of violence can be legitimized if they save lives in the long run is a challenge to the students, and their responses to this perplexing but somehow not so far fetched idea are expressed with powerful conviction. Other paradoxes of war are expressed; it is clearly absurd when Jeremy's uncle blurts out, "A murderer can be rehabilitated, but who would hire a draft-dodger?"

As a whole this work is unsatisfying and ironically some of the reader's dissatisfaction stems from Mr. Hentoff's understanding that there are no easy answers. When the book ends or, more accurately, stops, the reader is left feeling that while the characters are stronger for having explored many viewpoints, nothing has been solved. The war goes on. The conflicts continue from without and from within. Issues and emotions have been stirred, but not settled. This is honest, and to the extent that it is disturbing, it should be. What is more disturbing is that the mild impressions that the characters might have made on the reader dissipate very quickly. It is more effective to get a reader worked up about an issue by engaging her or him through a powerful or sympathetic character. But in this work, the characters are, for the most part, used as proponents of this side of the conflict or that, and the people get overshadowed by their ideologies. Young readers of the sixties, for whom this was immediately relevant, undoubtedly brought a lot of personal feelings into their experience of the work. But readers today have much less reason for concern about the issues raised, except in a theoretical sense, and will approach the book with less fervor. For them, ***I'm Really Dragged But Nothing Gets Me Down*** may prove to be enlightening, but not particularly fulfilling.

JOURNEY INTO JAZZ (1968)

Publishers Weekly

SOURCE: A review of *Journey into Jazz,* in *Publishers Weekly,* Vol. 194, No. 10, September 2, 1968, p. 59.

This is a fine, straight, clear explanation of jazz—the finest, the straightest, the clearest your reviewer has ever read. Ever *seen* would be more accurate, for its pictures lead you by the hand through the progressive steps of Nat Hentoff's definition. And they illuminate the joy that brightens his clear definition of jazz.

Kirkus Service

SOURCE: A review of *Journey into Jazz,* in *Kirkus Service,* Vol. XXXVI, No. 20, October 15, 1968, p. 1157.

In a picture book format, and told as if it were a matter of learning to tie shoelaces—just one discouragement after another—is the retraining of Peter Parker and his trumpet: his technique is perfect but he doesn't dig jazz. Lured by the sound of a band nearby, he tries to join in, finds he doesn't fit, trudges home to listen to trumpet players on records; tries again, still doesn't fit because he can't play with people, trudges home to listen this time to what the other players are doing; tries again, still doesn't fit because he doesn't play what he feels; trudges home angry and plays "raw and ugly," then triumphant, then happy. The next time he belongs, there's no more to know. Besides the trudgery, some improvisation ("he poked his trumpet into string quartets and he chatted with oboes") and an explosion of sharp pink and blue and yellow. Wild, man, and wildly inappropriate for any conceivable audience.

Melvin Maddocks

SOURCE: "Country Slickers," in *The Christian Science Monitor,* November 7, 1968, p. B4.

Nat Hentoff has squarely faced up to (1) the city and (2) the 20th century in ***Journey into Jazz.*** His boy-protagonist consorts with pink transistor radios rather than white foxes. The lessons are social rather than solitary. The young trumpet player begins by putting a sign on his door: MUSIC IS BEING MADE. DO NOT ENTER. At the end of the story, after music has been revealed to him as participation, the sign has been changed: MUSIC IS BEING MADE—COME ON IN. A nice point, made as lightly as a trumpet obbligato.

Mary Ann Wentroth

SOURCE: A review of *Journey into Jazz,* in *School Library Journal,* Vol. 16, No. 2, January, 1969, pp. 72-3.

Originally written as part of a musical work for a children's concert at the first International Jazz Festival, this text may well have been very effective when it was complemented by the music of Gunther Schuller. In picture-book format, it seems unlikely to satisfy, as the brief story of Peter Parker who progresses in musical ability and feeling as he grows from toddler to young teen has almost nothing to say to young children. The message that "You just have to keep on being yourself" to be successful in playing jazz will have meaning to serious young musicians, but they will be put off by the extreme simplicity of the presentation. Non-readers, at the 6th and 7th grade levels, interested in the subject might constitute an audience for it; they will certainly respond to the sketches by David Martin in black and white with bright wash of pink, blue and yellow, which strikingly and successfully suggest the sound and rhythm of jazz.

IN THE COUNTRY OF OURSELVES (1971)

Publishers Weekly

SOURCE: A review of *In the Country of Ourselves,* in *Publishers Weekly,* Vol. 200, No. 18, November 1, 1971, p. 55.

It is doubtful whether Nat Hentoff's theme of revolutionaries, reformers, non-activists and pacifists in a contemporary high school will appeal to young people, right wing or left wing, or even to adults trying to understand the problems. Mr. Hentoff makes some realistic observations—he is well aware of vital issues among young people—but at times the story line is confusing and the characters no more than spokesmen for the various political viewpoints.

Jack Forman

SOURCE: A review of *In the Country of Ourselves,* in *School Library Journal,* Vol. 18, No. 4, December 1971, p. 64.

In the short novels ***Jazz Country*** and ***I'm Really Dragged But Nothing Gets Me Down,*** Hentoff wrote about what it's like to be a contemporary urban high school student. ***In the Country of Ourselves*** is also a short novel about being in high school today, but it displays even more of an awareness of the complexities of this situation than did the two earlier novels. Here, mutually suspicious black and white radical students, with the aid of a concerned teacher and an apparent New Left sympathizer in the local police force, attempt to disrupt order in the high school they attend. Opposing them is a stubborn, authoritarian, yet concerned and dedicated principal. Unfortunately, some of the episodes are a bit strained, and the responses of the characters are occasionally overdrawn in an attempt to make the philosophies they espouse clear. Nevertheless, most of the kids behave believably—and, thankfully, not always predictably—and the book is very wittily written. All in all, it's one of the fairest and most entertaining titles available about politically aware young teens today.

Zena Sutherland

SOURCE: A review of *In the Country of Ourselves,* in *Bulletin of the Center for Children's Books,* Vol. 25, No. 5, January, 1972, p. 74.

A novel of unrest and rebellion in a high school, the trouble fomented by a group of students and encouraged by a radical teacher. A student strike and a police roundup result in a shift of power within the group, the dismissal of Scanlan, the teacher, and the emergence of a stronger position for the principal, Rothblatt. But it is clear that the battle will go on, and the implication is that the young people of conviction, black and white, will continue to press after the agitators have been sloughed off. The characters are developed well, yet each seems a type, without being a stereotype, that represents a point of view—so that the fate of each seems less important than the solution and resolution of their cause.

Sally C. Estes

SOURCE: A review of *In the Country of Ourselves,* in *The Booklist,* Vol. 68, No. 9, January 1, 1972, p. 391.

Hentoff takes a cast of stereotypes, puts them in a contemporary high school setting, and follows their predictable course of action. The students involved include a radical, a black, a pacifist, and an apolitical boy; other main characters are a Machiavellian radical teacher who uses his students to his own ends and the school principal, a well-intentioned strict disciplinarian. By touching on so many bases in so few pages Hentoff does not fully develop either characterizations or plot, but he has written a fast-paced if superficial story of high school unrest that may lead teenagers to contemplation of the problems introduced.

THIS SCHOOL IS DRIVING ME CRAZY (1976)

Denise M. Wilms

SOURCE: A review of *This School Is Driving Me Crazy,* in *The Booklist,* Vol. 72, No. 4, October 15, 1975, p. 302.

Sam Davidson's continual push to attend a different school gets him nowhere at first. His father, headmaster of Bronson Alcott School, reasons first of all that a good headmaster can handle such a situation, and secondly, that Bronson Alcott is the best school in the city and sending Sam elsewhere would harm his education. Those well-intentioned, if headstrong, assumptions are put to a severe test when a student in trouble accuses Sam of running a school shakedown racket. Though he is innocent, his irrepressible cheek and penchant for mischief make him a plausible culprit, and only when Sam's friends pressure an extortion victim to talk are the real thieves exposed. As the viewpoints of father and son are developed, the contentions of each gain legitimacy; this strengthens their portrayals and compensates for some mouthpiece peripheral characters who seem clearly designed to convey ideas on the responsibilities of teachers and school administrators. The story line's smooth (almost too easy) development and its success in generating interest and peer group identification smooth over the spots where Hentoff's messages overcome the medium of his story.

Kirkus Reviews

SOURCE: A review of *This School Is Driving Me Crazy,* in *Kirkus Reviews,* Vol. XLIII, No. 22, November 15, 1975, p. 1296.

It seems at first that Hentoff, with his characteristically heavy hand, must be setting you up for an indictment of the anachronistic, dictatorial school that Sam's father heads and Sam, twelve, reluctantly attends. But if you know Hentoff's views on education you won't be surprised when Sam comes round in the end: "I guess he is a pretty good headmaster. . . . I mean, he really does take charge when he has to. And he's fair in school. . . . " His father gives a little too, allowing Sam to attend a different school next year "where I'll be just another kid"—but "It's funny. I almost want to stay here now." It's still a setup in any case, with the conversations of parents, teachers and kids (one is black) all contrived to represent different views and approaches. As for the plot, Sam is accused of shaking down a little kid but the real villains—three tough tenth graders who have been victimizing a number of younger boys—break down with such alacrity upon confrontation in the office that it's clear even the author isn't all that interested in his individuals and events.

Zena Sutherland

SOURCE: A review of *This School Is Driving Me Crazy,* in *Bulletin of the Center for Children's Books,* Vol. 29, No. 5, January, 1976, p. 78.

Sam Davidson is a bright, energetic boy with a Big Problem: he doesn't want to attend the school of which his father is headmaster. Father insists. Sam, always in some minor scrape or up to some mischief, is his teachers' despair. When a smaller boy, lying, accuses Sam of being the bully who forced him to steal, matters come to a head; the trio of real bullies is unmasked and expelled, the attitudes of teachers are exposed, and the relationship between Sam and his father improves—with Sam's impending transfer decided on by the end of the story. Sam is an engaging character, and the writing style—in particular the dialogue—is pungent. And a good thing, too, because the messages almost overbalance the narrative. Hentoff is concerned not only about the relationship between father and son, but about the role of the school, the responsibility of the teacher, and relationships between students and teachers. To make his points, he has overdrawn some characters, such as the adamantly hostile teacher Kozodoy or the glib, mendacious brother of one of the three expelled. Yet the issues affect all children in school, public or private, and the minor imbalances of the book are more than compensated for by humor, action, and setting. Note for the shockable: the language is what you might expect in a school for boys.

A. R. Williams

SOURCE: A review of *This School Is Driving Me Crazy,* in *Junior Bookshelf,* Vol. 42, No. 3, June, 1978, p. 155.

Of course it is a bit much to be a pupil at an American High School when the headmaster is your father. Nat Hentoff reminds the reader that life, in such circumstances, can be just as difficult for father and mother. Sam, unfortunately, has a gift for wrong-footedness, which does not help matters. What plot there is has no outstanding novelty, and the teachers are nothing special either, but the story has pace, racy dialogue, and at least a superficial appreciation of the problems that arise on all sides in large schools. Sam might just double as an updated William (the William of Richmal Crompton's books, not of the television series) and his parents certainly provide a suitable domestic frame.

Book Window

SOURCE: A review of *This School Is Driving Me Crazy,* in *Book Window,* Vol. 8, No. 1, Winter, 1980, p. 28.

The story of an American teenager, Sam, who faces the problem of having to attend the school of which his father is the headmaster, this is an absorbing and exciting novel. Sam's problems and the ways in which he tries to solve them will readily invoke the sympathies of teenagers in the middle range of secondary school, while the main plot line, involving Sam's dilemma when he uncovers the activities of a gang of bullies, but feels unable to tell his father about them, provides a tension and excitement which holds the reader's attention throughout. One might perhaps quibble about the ending, in which Sam is allowed to take what seems to be the easy way out by going off to a different school, but on the whole this is a well-written novel aimed mainly at the 14-15 age range.

Geoff Fox

SOURCE: A review of *This School Is Driving Me Crazy,* in *Children's literature in education,* Vol. 13, No. 2, Summer, 1982, p. 57.

The American boys' private school has had a bad press in recent times. John Knowles's *A Separate Peace* and Robert Cormier's *The Chocolate War* uncovered tensions and animosities of peculiar cruelty. Nat Hentoff's Alcott School is seen from a more comic standpoint, but the plot still turns upon bullying and extortion in the corridors and cloakrooms.

Sam Davidson is amusingly scatter-brained, highly articulate, given to thoughtless horsing around and basically a good kid; as is the way of many post-Zindel heroes in American novels. His lack of personal organisation would matter less if the headmaster of Alcott were not also his father. Through his silent loyalty to a victim of some blackmailing school heavies, Sam falls under threat of expulsion himself. The headmaster's high principles dictate that justice be visibly done, and only some swift thinking by Sam's friends eventually sets things to rights. There are no easy reconciliations, however, and Sam does finally leave Alcott to try another school.

Nat Hentoff's dialogue is particularly lively and the scenes between the boys are thoroughly entertaining. The headmaster's problems about Sam (to the despair of his wife, he is unable to show his supportive love to his son) might seem implausible to the layman. In practice, headmastering regularly throws up circumstances where the public mask sits uncomfortably, threatening to mould the features beneath.

Sam is the target for criticism from other members of staff, and it is here that the book is least convincing. Teachers, absorbed in their community, may indeed lose a sense of perspective, but the personal animosity which drives Mr. Kodozoy to try to destroy Sam and weaken the head's influence is difficult to credit; as indeed is Mr. Davidson's vindictive pleasure in determining to increase Kodozoy's teaching load next year as retribution.

Very many readers will find the underworld of school, flourishing beyond the knowledge of the staff, all too believable, and the text's energy and hilarity should sweep readers along. Mr. Hentoff does not exactly tell it like it is, but he has that nicely judged sense of the slightly larger than it is, so satisfying to the inmates of the institutions he describes.

THE FIRST FREEDOM: THE TUMULTUOUS HISTORY OF FREE SPEECH IN AMERICA (1980)

Kirkus Reviews

SOURCE: A review of *The First Freedom: The Tumultuous History of Free Speech in America,* in *Kirkus Reviews,* Vol. XLVIII, No. 1, January 1, 1980, pp. 46-7.

Not a history of free speech in the marketplace, which might be intermittently "tumultuous," but a review of more or less famous court cases—on the assumption that free speech must constantly be fought for. Hentoff groups the cases under headings of church and state, the free press, sedition, and education; and though issues in each of these areas have generated intense, often violent political struggles between opponents, Hentoff's gaze remains fixed on the courtroom. Decision after decision batters the reader, all adding up to Hentoff's position that freedom of speech must be steadfastly generalized—i.e., broadened—in order to protect everyone; and for Hentoff, like the ACLU in which he is active, the acid test becomes the court case over the attempted march of Nazis in Skokie, Ill. The First Amendment, he maintains, becomes strengthened through its use by everyone, including those whose views are considered repugnant. But Hentoff's narrow legalistic approach ignores important questions of shared values and loss of community—questions which render speech problematic in the first place. In focusing on the courtroom, Hentoff has presented a brief for the ACLU and missed an opportunity to consider fundamental social and political issues.

Publishers Weekly

SOURCE: A review of *The First Freedom: The Tumultuous History of Free Speech in America,* in *Publishers Weekly,* Vol. 217, No. 1, January 11, 1980, p. 81.

Hentoff's fact-filled survey traces the controversies and court cases surrounding the First Amendment from its adoption in 1791 to the present. Stressing the relevance of free speech to young people, the author examines major recent instances of book censorship, control of the student press, and political dissent involving students, librarians and teachers. He describes the evolution of the First Amendment and recounts the significant challenges its guarantees have faced—most notably, from state legislatures, mobs and individuals in the 19th century, and from federal efforts to safeguard national security in the Civil War, the world wars, and Vietnam. Hentoff writes clearly and concisely about recent Supreme Court and other decisions (on libel, obscenity, free press versus fair trial, and other issues) and brings alive such controversies as the Pentagon Papers case and the Nazi march in Skokie, Ill. A staff writer for *The Village Voice* and *The New Yorker,* the author is a board member of the New York Civil Liberties Union.

Stephanie Zvirin

SOURCE: A review of *The First Freedom: The Tumultuous History of Free Speech in America,* in *Booklist,* Vol. 76, No. 16, April 15, 1980, p. 1195.

After a brisk, attention-grabbing consideration of censorship cases involving today's schools, Hentoff fills in background on events leading up to the adoption of the Bill of Rights. His focus, however, is on shifts in Supreme Court interpretations of the First Amendment that have broadened or narrowed the scope of its guaranteed freedoms. He lucidly reviews a wealth of court cases that point out past threats to freedoms and demonstrate such current dilemmas as those revolving around censorship, separation of church and state, judicial gag orders versus fair trials, national security, protection of journalists' confidential sources, libel, obscenity, and offensive speech. A choice work for general readers as well as for high school political science students.

Voice of Youth Advocates

SOURCE: A review of *The First Freedom: The Tumultuous History of Free Speech in America,* in *Voice of Youth Advocates,* Vol. 10, No. 1, April, 1987, p. 13.

The First Freedom: The Tumultuous History of Free Speech in America by Nat Hentoff is as good an introduction to the First Amendment for young adults as we can hope to have. Hentoff writes with passion and verve about a topic that is dear to his heart. He covers current issues, particularly student rights, as well as historical struggles such as the Alien and Sedition Acts. This is one title that should be required reading followed by, no doubt, heated discussions.

DOES THIS SCHOOL HAVE CAPITAL PUNISHMENT? (1981)

Stephanie Zvirin

SOURCE: A review of *Does This School Have Capital Punishment?,* in *Booklist,* Vol. 77, No. 16, April 15, 1981, p. 1147.

Beginning his first year in high school, Sam Davidson almost immediately falls seriously afoul of school administrators when Jeremiah, a fellow student, refuses to clear Sam and a friend when drugs are found in their possession. Things look bleak, until Major Kelley, an elderly jazz musician Sam knows, gets Jeremiah to tell the truth. Hentoff fashions two very different worlds for Sam—a structured everyday existence, along with a world of music for which Hentoff's prose takes on a wonderfully rhythmic quality. Although he fails to mesh the two smoothly and his focus-switch from Sam to Jeremiah near the story's close is too abrupt and too contrived, Hentoff's follow-up to ***This School Is Driving Me Crazy*** is filled with humor and sharp characterizations.

Rosalie E. Dunbar

SOURCE: A review of *Does This School Have Capital Punishment?,* in *The Christian Science Monitor,* July 1, 1981, p. 18.

As a new student at exclusive Burr Academy, Sam Davidson is eager to do well. Things go along pretty smoothly at first. He begins his interviews of Major Kelley, a legendary black jazz trumpet player for his oral history course, and he makes some friends. Then he and his best buddy, Rob, are falsely accused of possessing marijuana cigarettes, an infraction that leads to automatic expulsion.

The real culprit, Jeremiah Saddlefield, refuses to confess because he fears that his father, a hardboiled newspaper tycoon and the boy's only parent, will disown him. Mr. Monk, the headmaster of Burr, recognizes that Sam and Rob are not likely to be drug users. But the evidence is against them. Monk decides to delay his decision, hoping that more facts will come to light.

Distraught, Sam tells his problem not just to his parents, but also to Major Kelley, who offers to help, though he refuses to tell how. Through his own sources, Kelley learns that Saddlefield is a lonely and neglected child and decides to befriend him. Before long, Saddlefield is visiting the clubs where Kelley plays.

After one performance, the boy is so overcome by the contrast between the powerful beauty of the music and his feeling of rottenness over what he has done to Sam and Rob that he confides in Kelley. The musician points out that Saddlefield can either keep his secret and allow it to poison everything he does, or he can confess and take the chance that his father won't cut him off. When Saddlefield at last confesses to his father the boy is surprised to learn the businessman knew all along but didn't think the boy had sufficient backbone to confess. This change in his son alters the father's attitude toward him and gives them a new start.

When Saddlefield tells all to the headmaster, he receives a similar response. Mr. Monk says, "This ought to be your last day here. . . . But . . . I find it very difficult to banish from this place someone who so clearly shows that redemption is indeed possible."

A short plot summary can't begin to share the many true-to-life incidents experienced by these perfectly believable characters. Sam is wonderfully disorganized, but sincere; Rob is a classic hothead, and Saddlefield is a creep's creep until he sees the light. The lesser characters are equally well drawn.

Only one scene—where a businessman has a nervous breakdown on his way to work and is reduced to making animal-like sounds—doesn't ring true; the man has no connection with the school or the plot, a minor flaw in an otherwise delightful book.

The author's descriptions of jazz are especially beautiful and vivid. The power of music is an important element in the outcome, too. As Major Kelley says to Sam after Saddlefield has confessed at school, "This music is a mighty powerful force, and it zapped that boy at the right time. Nothing more need be said."

Of this book that exalts integrity and shows in a realistic and enjoyable way that justice can prevail, nothing more need be said either, except that it's well worth reading.

Annie Gottlieb

SOURCE: A review of *Does This School Have Capital Punishment?,* in *The New York Times Book Review,* July 26, 1981, p. 13.

Nat Hentoff's new book (the first was ***This School Is Driving Me Crazy***) about Sam Davidson, a good kid who can't stay out of trouble, is a sentimental fantasy, complete with good guys who need to learn compassion, bad guys who turn out to have soft hearts and a fairy godfather in the form of a great old black jazz musician.

It is improbable, to say the least, that a renowned trumpeter named Major Kelley would travel from New York to Chicago to help a bright, smart-alecky white kid beat an unfair accusation of marijuana possession—and then buy a cake inscribed "INNOCENT" to celebrate the victory for the boy (who had approached the jazzman for an oral history project). But then almost everything in this book is a little unreal. Both kids and teachers at tough, exclusive Burr Academy are impossibly clever; Major Kelley is often impossibly oracular; and any character can in an instant become a mouthpiece for a minilecture (thoroughly worthy, mind you) on why jazz should be taught in the schools or why it feels better to tell the truth. The creepy kid who pins the bum rap on Sam is impossibly victimized by a newspaper-tycoon father who's a moustache-twirling capitalist villain . . . and so on.

The whole mix might appeal only to urban preppies were it not for Mr. Hentoff's virtuoso writing on jazz, which soars out of its silly setting like a silver phoenix.

This book is worth reading just to meet a clarinetist with a "sound like hot spice," to learn that jazz can "bring you back from the dead" and to hear about an era in the Kansas City of the 1930's when "the air, the air itself, moved in jazz time." And Major Kelley and his ancient father are grand characters, despite the mawkish roles they are made to play vis a vis Sam and friends.

Zena Sutherland

SOURCE: A review of *Does This School Have Capital Punishment?,* in *Bulletin of the Center for Children's Books,* Vol. 35, No. 1, September, 1981, p. 10.

In a sequel to ***This School is Driving Me Crazy*** Sam Davidson, whose father is headmaster in a private school, is now enrolled at another school; he gets off to a bad start when he uses a friend's expired subway pass, is caught, and has to go to court. On probationary status, Sam is warned by his new headmaster that his record must be impeccable—and then Sam and another boy are framed, accused of smoking pot by the classmate who had actually been the culprit. This plot line then merges with another, Sam's new friendship with an elderly black jazz musician, Kelley, who is the real hero of the story. Kelley goes to a great deal of trouble and expense to prove Sam's innocence and to help the boy who got Sam in trouble; both boys have become enchanted by their introduction, via Kelley, to jazz. The merging of the plots is smooth and enables Hentoff to focus on two of his long-expressed interests: jazz and education. As with the first book, there is some exaggeration of character (the director of the high school, a man whose philosophy is contrasted with that of the headmaster) to make the author's point about teaching and teachers' attitudes, but the characterization on the whole is vivid and credible; the dialogue is witty, with humor inherent in situations rather than in action. Like the first book, this is a better-than-average school story, both in the sense of being provocative and being an enjoyable read.

Holly Willett

SOURCE: A review of *Does This School Have Capital Punishment?,* in *The Horn Book Magazine,* Vol. LVII, No. 4, August, 1981, pp. 432-33.

Despite his good intentions, Sam Davidson, brilliant but hapless, falls into trouble almost immediately upon entering Burr Academy for his freshman year. Using a friend's expired subway pass results in his first encounter with the law. Sam defends himself successfully in court, but when the unpopular Jeremiah causes Sam and his friend Rob to be unfairly accused of possessing marijuana at school, it is much more difficult to "'beat the rap.'" Sam's most powerful ally is Major Kelley, a Black jazz trumpet player who has been Sam's subject for an oral history assignment and on whom much of the story is focused. Sam's parents and the headmaster are sure Sam and Rob are innocent, but they need proof; it is Major Kelley who brings about an outcome favorable to all three boys. Without using an over-abundance of slang, the author creates believable teenage dialogue. Sam is both funny and earnest in his ironic observations; conversation reveals the character of the adults, too. The contemptuous school director and Jeremiah's callous father are antagonists, and—realistically—neither of them is completely vanquished at the conclusion. The relationships between the fathers and the sons are central to the plot, yet none are explored to a satisfying depth. Most of the personalities are vivid and distinctive, but they need more room in which to interact. Jazz is described so lyrically the reader regrets that Major Kelley is merely a fictitious character. Contemporary and entertaining, the novel offers humor and a bridge over the generation gap.

Margery Fisher

SOURCE: A review of *Does This School Have Capital Punishment?,* in *Growing Point,* Vol. 25, No. 1, May, 1986, p. 4613.

Headmasters are fair game in junior fiction and Mr. Levine-Griffin, director of New York's prestigious Burr Academy, is a splendid example of the pompous dominie, reminiscent of Stalky's 'Jelly-bellied flag-flapper' in his self-consciously slangy, mercurial, ultra-patriotic discourses. It is unfortunate for young Sam that his first year at the school, described in ***Does this School Have Capital Punishment?*** should place him in situations which his impetuous nature and liberal upbringing hardly equip him to deal with. He has friends, though, in Mrs. Wolf, a tough but intuitive teacher, and in 'Major' Kelly, a trumpeter apprenticed many years before in the New Orleans jazz scene and wise in his understanding of adolescent vagaries. Both these people help Sam when a fellow-student in far greater need of help contrives to throw the blame for drug-pushing on him. Forceful in its picture of one kind of urban high school, the story has an oddly artificial air about it; dominated as it is by the moral issues of truth and politics, candour and neurotic frustration, it carries conviction as a social treatise rather than a novel based on character.

THE DAY THEY CAME TO ARREST THE BOOK (1982)

Zena Sutherland

SOURCE: A review of *The Day They Came to Arrest the Book,* in *Bulletin of the Center for Children's Books,* Vol. 36, No. 1, September, 1982, p. 11.

A censorship crisis is precipitated when an angry parent attacks the use of Mark Twain's *Huckleberry Finn* as required reading for a history class. Soon both the town and the high school are in a state of conflict; parents are divided, as are students and teachers. The case goes to a review committee, and then to the school board and it gets national media coverage. The censors lose; the book stays. Much of the credit for the victory goes to the school librarian. These are the bones of the story, with Hentoff using all the arguments that have been used on both sides in real life. Only the fact that Hentoff is a capable writer keeps this from being a case history, but he has done a fine job of bringing both the characters and the issues to life.

Kirkus Reviews

SOURCE: A review of *The Day They Came to Arrest the Book,* in *Kirkus Reviews,* Vol. L, No. 18, September 15, 1982, p. 1060.

A fictionalized airing of the book censorship issue, set in a high school with a weak, oily principal, a strong and principled English teacher, and a new librarian. (The old one quit over the principal's underhanded appeasement of censors; the last straw was his attempt to remove a Dickens novel and his quickly rescinded suggestion that the librarian tear certain pages from the Bible.) Hentoff avoids the predictable alliances by making the complainant a black parent who objects to the use of "nigger" in *Huckleberry Finn.* Before the book issue emerges, Hentoff sets the stage with a guest debate, for an American history class, between an articulate conservative and an equally articulate if less smooth young ACLU lawyer. Later the conservative sides with the black father, as does Kate, an aggressive feminist student who objects to Mark Twain's treatment of women. They are joined by the usual guardians of morality shocked by Huck and Jim's nudity and the message that "a child ought to decide for himself what's right and wrong." Hentoff allows both sides persuasive arguments at the school board hearing that results in the book being restricted but not removed altogether, and again at the second meeting where a black student testifies to his ability to "tell when the word nigger is directed at me." This time the review committee reconsiders and lifts the restrictions. What the anti-censorship forces learn is that it's best to bring such conflicts into the open. There are other twists to this conflict: the principal schemes behind the scenes in the interest of his own career; the school paper editor backs down on an editorial attacking the principal, but later publishes a more damning interview. Hentoff, however, stages no inner agonizing, sticks in no personal subplots, and doesn't bother to pass off the various mouthpieces as characters or personalities. Even more than his other novels, this issue "novel" is all issue, without pretense or apology. As such it's accessibly well-reasoned, timely once more despite the ancient heritage of all the arguments, and probably better off without the extracurricular padding.

Paul Heins

SOURCE: A review of *The Day They Came to Arrest the Book,* in *The Horn Book Magazine,* Vol. LVIII, No. 6, December, 1982, pp. 657-58.

When Nora Baines, who taught American history at the George Mason High School, assigned *Huckleberry Finn* as required reading, she aroused the ire of one of her black students. To avoid trouble with black parents, Mr. Moore, the jovial yet temporizing principal of the school, would gladly have removed the book from the curriculum or even limited its use in the library, but the issue of book banning became public. In the school auditorium, representatives of the Citizens' League for the Preservation of American Values and the American Civil Liberties Union debated the question "Is Individual Freedom Getting Out of Hand?" Parents, teachers, students, and school board discussed the significance of the content of *Huckleberry Finn,* which ultimately seemed to rest on a correct reading of Mark Twain as well as on the nature of intellectual freedom. Despite the outspoken, breezy style, the author earnestly presents the arguments of students and adults on both sides of the question, embodying their expression in passionate outbursts or sly innuendos. A novel in the sense that a crucial contemporary academic and political situation has been dramatized, the book balances satire and serious concern.

Lee Galda

SOURCE: A review of *The Day They Came to Arrest the Book,* in *The ALAN Review,* Vol. 10, No. 2, Winter, 1983, p. 17.

Hentoff combined his interest in the First Amendment with his talent as a young adult writer to produce ***The Day They Came to Arrest the Book.*** The book in question is *Huckleberry Finn,* and those who want it removed from the school library include blacks, who think it's racist; women, who think it's sexist; and a parents' group, who think it's immoral. This problem is complicated by a school principal who has a history of censoring books, the editor of the school newspaper who is determined to expose him, and the school librarians who believe in freedom of speech. As more people get involved, the community becomes polarized and the tension mounts.

Hentoff effectively provides information about the problems and procedures involved in censorship cases and engages young adult readers in a timely conflict which has no easy resolution.

Mary K. Chelton

SOURCE: A review of *The Day They Came to Arrest the Book,* in *Voice of Youth Advocates,* Vol. 5, No. 6, February, 1983, pp. 36-7.

The Adventures of Huckleberry Finn is challenged by a Black parent who objects to the use of "nigger" throughout the book, and Hentoff's novel discusses the pros and cons of this censorship attempt in a school with a new but feisty librarian, an old but feisty social studies teacher, an oily principal who would censor anything he could get away with (in violation of his own school policy often), and a group of interested kids on both sides of the fence. The review committee at first recommends limited access to the book and its removal from "required" classroom reading lists, but the school board overturns this decision and allows the book to remain a classroom experience. Readers are left wondering, though, what Mr. McLean is going to do next, and whether a political change in the composition of the school board will result in more censorship ultimately. Unfortunately, this is a very boring book, because the story is hopelessly bogged down in pro and con First Amendment rhetoric. The sheer talkiness of it all is inimical to the teen novel formula, and the abstractions necessary to approach the topic will be above any early adolescent who is still a concrete-operational thinker, whereas the packaging of the book will probably prevent older adolescents from picking it up. As is common in all of Hentoff's YA novels except ***Jazz Country,*** all the characters represent a point of view in the argument rather than real-life people. Despite the importance of the topic, by the standards set by Cormier and Arrick, for example, this is really minimal storytelling. It is doubly unfortunate that four courageous women who have defended intellectual freedom are immortalized in the dedication of such a bad book. John Neufeld's *Small Civil War* and Susan Pfeffer's *Matter Of Principle* are both better books on the same theme, and intended for the same audience.

Saul Maloff

SOURCE: A review of *The Day They Came to Arrest the Book,* in *The New York Times Book Review,* March 6, 1983, p. 30.

At the end, when the good triumph and the wicked get theirs, the villainous, craven, despotic high school principal Mighty Mike Moore stands reverently before a large photograph of the heroic John Wayne and unpacks his heart—his hopes, his dreams, his devious schemes.

George Mason High School and the community have just emerged from bloody struggle between the forces of darkness seeking to censor *Huckleberry Finn* and the forces of light. By a dramatic last-minute shift the latter have won a precarious victory, and Moore is already plotting to unleash another assault when the balance on the school board is tipped.

The new members include a black "activist" for whom the great novel comes down to that single unspeakable six-letter epithet, a right-wing zealot and moralizer who wants God established and sin cast out and others of his persuasion gathered together in such organizations as Save Our Children From Atheist Secular Humanism (SOCASH). Against them stand an attractive, intelligent, principled librarian, the teacher passionately committed to democratic rights who assigned the book for reading alongside Tocqueville, and other admirable people and good kids.

Nat Hentoff, himself well known for his devotion to the First Amendment, makes honorable efforts to give the most unsavory characters their due, such as it is. He is also fairly merciless in his portraiture. The black parent is obsessional, dogmatic, pompous; the mealy-mouthed white ultrist is wily, slithery, unctuous; Moore has further distinguished himself by excising from the school Bible some of the more awkward episodes (see II Samuel 13 and Judges 19).

Mr. Hentoff takes such scrupulous care that in places he almost makes it seem that there are indeed two rational positions on the novel from which we are all descended, and that is no small achievement, especially considering his own uncompromising partisanship. If the book is less a novel than a morality play, the arguments are lucidly and forcefully laid out—though we are never in doubt that Mr. Hentoff is steadfastly on the side of the seraphim.

Albert V. Schwartz

SOURCE: A review of *The Day They Came to Arrest the Book,* in *Interracial Books for Children Bulletin,* Vol. 14, No. 6, 1983, pp. 18-19.

In a November, 1977, article in *School Library Journal* Nat Hentoff inveighs against literature that "stiffens into propaganda (no matter how nobly intended)." Judging by his newest book, however, he doesn't really mind one-sided message books as long as he can select the message.

The Day They Came to Arrest the Book is purportedly about censorship in a high school. Hentoff's protagonist states: "Fiction is imagination. The novelist can suppose, and so he can get inside people's heads." Unfortunately, this novelist's "people" are one-dimensional characters spouting simplistic messages.

Hentoff presents his personal concepts of political liberalism and First Amendment absolutism through the events at fictional George Mason High School (George Mason, one of the drafters of the Declaration of Independence, fought for freedom of the press). Here censors of the left and right—feminists, Black militants and Moral Majority types—join in an attempt to "arrest" *Huck Finn* (*i.e.,* remove it) from a high school history curriculum. In Hentoff's simplistic schema, characters who absolutely love and accept all books are "good." Characters who criticize books are "bad."

Also among the "good" are: the hero Barney Roth, editor of the school paper; Nora Baines, a social studies teacher who uses lots of supplementary reading, including *Huck Finn;* Deidre Fitzgerald, the new librarian; Karen Salters, the exlibrarian who quit her job rather than accept the principal's censorious policies.

Among the worst "baddies" are: Michael Moore, the super-evil principal, who not only removes books from the library but has actually cut lascivious parts out of the Bible; Kate, a feminist student; and Gordon McLean, a Black militant student who, along with his father, institutes the attack on *Huck Finn.*

Hentoff uses little conversations and large debates to advance his ideas. A little conversation, for instance, shows that liberals trust children: Gordon McLean, the Black militant student, complains, "My parents don't trust me for a second." When Barney says his parents "take an interest, you know, but they're not all over me," Gordon answers:

> Barney, I'd like you to come home to dinner some night . . . and tell my folks just that. Just that one thing. You got to be near the top of the class, you're the editor of the paper, and you never get into hassles with any of the teachers of anybody else. So you are a walking advertisement for the freedom way of life.

Score 1 for the good guys.

Of the word "nigger" in *Huck Finn,* Barney informs us: "That's the way people talked then. Mark Twain is just showing the way it was." Another student adds, "Some people are too damn sensitive. Nobody's calling *them* that. The book was written a long time ago." So much for racism. Score 2.

A young Black student gets in his digs:

> I do not believe that all of the people complaining about this book have read it all. If they had, and if they *can* read, they wouldn't have been saying what they said about it. Second, many of those complaining about this book say they want to protect *me,* as a black person, from certain words in this book. Well, it is too late to do that for *me.*

Score 3.

Words like "Ms." and "chairperson" produce "scores" too. When the villainous principal uses the address, "Ms. Baines," the good teacher reacts with: "If you're going to call me anything, Mr. Moore, please call me *Miss.* That other thing sounds as if you were a yardman asking me if there were any other chores for you to do." She tells her social studies class, "Just watch out that you don't fall into such deformities of language as 'clergyperson' or 'policeperson' or 'chairperson.' I will not accept such genderless abominations in any paper in this class." (Home run for Hentoff's team.)

Hentoff scores (sometimes with cheap shots) for his side, but doesn't let the other side get to first base. He obviously doesn't trust young people far enough to allow them to hear any of the real views of the opposition. This makes for a dull and witless book.

Margery Fisher

SOURCE: A review of *The Day They Came to Arrest the Book,* in *Growing Point,* Vol. 24, No. 6, March, 1986, pp. 4581-82.

Concepts of justice, of prejudice, and of communal responsibility [in ***The Day They Came to Arrest the Book***] demand reconsideration when the editor of the school newspaper decides the time has come to expose the blackmail tactics of the venal headmaster and his bigoted views on education. The immediate occasion is the decision to ban *Huckleberry Finn* from the school library after certain parents have condemned the book as racist and un-American. The 'trial' takes the form of discussions—between parents and pupils, between members of the staff—in which opinions about the classic tale (a set book, in fact, for a senior class) reflect far wider issues of human rights and definitions of freedom relevant to the state of society today. The conclusion of the story is, inevitably, a compromise, leaving the opponents of censorship uneasily aware that the headmaster has made only a token gesture to majority opinion. It is not a happy nor a reassuring conclusion but readers in the mid-'teens will recognise its essential honesty and will have no difficulty in relating the story to the world they live in, a world in which they will soon take up decisive positions. This is justifiable propaganda, well adapted to a novelistic framework.

P. Thomson

SOURCE: A review of *The Day They Came to Arrest the Book,* in *Books for Your Children,* Vol. 21, No. 1, Spring, 1986, p. 19.

If you are the kind of family which likes to discuss books together, this is likely to be the most provoking book you have come across for a long time. There is absolutely no question of sitting on the fence. It forces the brain into action. A school is asked to ban *Huckleberry Finn* on the grounds that the language is offensive to black people. Two sides quickly form and the whole town gets involved in the issue of censorship. The author ultimately makes his decision but it is not easy for the characters or the reader. The opening is a little slow, and particular to the States, but this is soon eclipsed by the immediacy and challenge of the debate. A book to remember and maybe even to act upon.

Dorothy Nimmo

SOURCE: A review of *The Day They Came to Arrest the Book,* in *The School Librarian,* Vol. 34, No. 2, June, 1986, pp. 166, 169.

Huckleberry Finn is on trial at George Mason School. For the defence, Nora Baines (History, a brisk, chunky blonde woman), Deidre Fitzgerald (Librarian, tall, slender with long lustrous brown hair), and Barney (Editor of the school newspaper). For the prosecution, Kate the feminist (a thin, crisp girl with jet-black hair), Mr. McClean (a black parent), and various members of the school board. Michael Moore (Headmaster, a large man in his mid-forties with a magnificent mane of prematurely white hair) tries to appear neutral. The arguments are set out. *Huckleberry Finn* is racist, the word nigger is used repeatedly and offensively; it is sexist, the women are all ciphers; and it is obscene. But it is a work of genius, it is about moral education, it is of its time. The verdict, after Mr Moore has been discovered in devious behaviour, including censoring the Bible, is 'Not Guilty'. As journalism this is fine, fair and spirited, a good basis for discussion. For literature you would do better to reread *Huckleberry Finn.*

AMERICAN HEROES: IN AND OUT OF SCHOOL (1987)

Publishers Weekly

SOURCE: A review of *American Heroes: In and Out of School,* in *Publishers Weekly,* Vol. 231, No. 23, June 12, 1987, p. 87.

Most of this volume by the noted civil libertarian lives up to the promise of the title. These are the compelling, true stories of high school students who endure censure by adults they'd been taught to obey and the taunts of friends and peers who ostracize them. Hentoff does not present both sides of issues, but instead offers the reader inspirational tales of ordinary youngsters who feel they must stand up for First Amendment principles. Nearly as moving are the stories of the librarians who battled evangelists and small-minded politicians in the name of the free exchange of ideas. Midway through the book, however, Hentoff shifts gears, devoting two chapters to a minibiography of Joan Baez as a nonviolent activist, and two more chapters to the horrors of corporal punishment in the schools, which bogs down the book with too much detail and exhortation. But readers will likely find the first half of the book stirring.

Kirkus Reviews

SOURCE: A review of *American Heroes: In and Out of School,* in *Kirkus Reviews,* Vol. LV, No. 12, July 1, 1987, pp. 992-93.

Eight case studies and two long biographical profiles introduce real-life teen-agers and adults who have lived the Bill of Rights.

The cases involving high-school students feature both popular and unpopular causes, including a school newspaper editor whose editions were confiscated by the principal, a young woman who refused to stand for the Pledge of Allegiance, and a freshman who was stopped from distributing anti-abortion pamphlets. Although each is briefly presented, Hentoff clearly defines the issues, often citing revealing quotations from judicial decisions. Censorship issues are discussed by profiling two librarians, Jeanne Layton of Utah and Kathy Russell of Virginia, both of whom successfully defended their libraries from local censors. In the longer profiles, Hentoff writes with great admiration about folksinger Joan Baez, who has lived her nonviolent beliefs in word and deed, and teacher Adah Mauer, who has spent years trying to abolish corporal punishment in schools.

These contemporary portraits will be extremely useful to teachers as discussion starters, bringing alive the dated phrases of the Bill of Rights for 20th-century kids.

Zena Sutherland

SOURCE: A review of *American Heroes: In and Out of School,* in *Bulletin of the Center for Children's Books,* Vol. 40, No. 11, July-August, 1987, p. 209.

Hentoff discusses court cases instigated by American citizens, some of whom are adolescents, in defense of their civil liberties, especially in the areas of civil rights and free speech. In addition, he cites the long record of such activists as Joan Baez or Adah Maurer, a longtime foe of corporal punishment in the schools. As the title indicates, the author does not remain aloof from the issues; he is enthusiastically sympathetic to his heroes. This results, although Hentoff is a capable writer, not in distortion but in a laudatory note that tends at times to vitiate the impact of what courage and tenacity he is recording. An informative book, and a useful one to stimulate group discussion. A bibliography is included.

Steve Matthews

SOURCE: A review of *American Heroes: In and Out of School,* in *School Library Journal,* Vol. 34, No. 1, September, 1987, p. 201.

In the last chapter of [***American Heroes: In and Out of School***] Hentoff states that "In addition to the basics, . . . there is no more important work to be done in our schools than to make freedom personal." Here he personalizes the Bill of Rights for high-school students through case studies of real people fighting for their civil rights. The issues presented include censorship of books in a public library, the right of a student not to say the pledge of allegiance, and the rights of students not to be searched at random at school. Hentoff is strongly committed to personal freedom, and he presents his "heroes" with fervor and clarity. Whether readers agree or disagree with the stances of the subjects, they should find the reading involving and thought-provoking. Each story provides insight into individual rights and the Bill of Rights and would serve as an effective tool to stimulate discussion on the vital questions presented.

Hazel Rochman

SOURCE: A review of *American Heroes: In and Out of School,* in *Booklist,* Vol. 84, No. 5, November 1, 1987, p. 465.

In a vivid, informal style, Hentoff dramatizes and explains basic principles of the Bill of Rights, using examples of individuals who have stood up in their daily lives for freedom of speech, press, and religion, and for the right to privacy. He begins with students—such as a girl who refused to salute the flag, a school newspaper editor who fought his principal's censorship, and a student who distributed anti-abortion literature at school—and in later chapters includes "the necessary bravery of librarians," Joan Baez's lifelong advocacy of nonviolence, and Adah Maurer's fight to end corporal punishment in schools. He devotes much space to the case of the young Indiana student subjected to a search by police dogs and then a strip search by police. Hentoff shows that taking a stand—whether on the left or the right—is often unpopular and that courage, stamina, and intelligence are required to oppose powerful authority and social pressure. In each case he follows the personal drama with a clear, jargon-free discussion of the issues involved. The style is sometimes hortative (Joan Baez is presented as a saint with a sense of humor), and more documentation would have been helpful so that readers could pursue some of the debates in depth instead of having to rely on Hentoff's summary of the arguments. But the account will provide readers with information and encouragement and will stimulate them to think about heroism without violence and the responsibilities of citizenship in a democracy.

Margaret A. Bush

SOURCE: A review of *American Heroes: In and Out of School,* in *The Horn Book Magazine,* Vol. LXIV, No. 2, March, 1988, p. 223.

Hentoff's heroes are teenagers, parents, teachers, and librarians who have fought various free speech and civil rights battles related to experiences of students at school. In this time of great attention to the origins of the Constitution the author very successfully highlights the contemporary relevance of that important document in the lives of young people. He begins by narrating the events and implications of several freedom of speech cases, including student refusal to sing the national anthem or salute the flag; expressions of unpopular viewpoints in yearbooks, school newspapers, and pamphlets; and the censorship of books in libraries. These descriptions are followed by two troubling civil rights areas with unique implications for children and teenagers—search and seizure practices in schoolrooms and corporal punishment, which remains a legal practice in all but nine states. Hentoff is unabashed in his admiration of certain public figures and so devotes considerable attention to Joan Baez's many activities on behalf of pacifism and nonviolent revolution and the efforts of California activist Adah Maurer, who continues to be a leading force in lobbying for the elimination of corporal punishment throughout the country. Provocative questions and unsettling bits of information emerge throughout these accounts. First of all, it is clear that many adults do not consider the legal protection afforded by the Bill of Rights to apply equally to children. Then, sadly, most of those young people who press for their rights fight a lonely battle; the popular support of the system rather than the individual or the principle of justice is a strong theme in these accounts. One hopes that Hentoff's explication of the importance of constitutional mandates and democratic freedoms will inform young people and bolster both tolerance and moral courage. As constructed the volume is an informative introduction and a superb vehicle for stimulating conversation.

Additional coverage of Hentoff's life and career is contained in the following sources published by Gale Research: *Authors and Artists for Children and Young Adults,* Vol. 4; *Contemporary Authors New Revision Series,* Vol. 25; *Contemporary Literary Criticism,* Vol. 26; *Major Authors and Illustrators for Children and Young Adults;* and *Something about the Author,* Vol. 69.

Carol Matas

1949-

Canadian author of fiction and plays; scriptwriter.

Major works include *Lisa* (1987; U.S. edition as *Lisa's War*), *Jesper* (1989; U.S. edition as *Code Name Kris*), *Daniel's Story* (1993), *The Burning Time* (1994), *After the War* (1996).

INTRODUCTION

A prolific author of historical and realistic fiction, fantasy, and plays for primary and middle graders and young adults, Matas is considered one of the most important contemporary Canadian authors of juvenile literature. A Jewish writer who is profoundly concerned about social issues and awareness, Matas is best known for creating historical fiction set during or just after World War II that reflects the experiences of Jewish youths caught up in the war and its aftermath. In addition, she has written contemporary fiction, science fiction, and fantasy as well as historical fiction set in the sixteenth and nineteenth centuries. Her works are lauded as exciting, insightful, and thought-provoking stories that inform and entertain young readers while challenging them to examine moral issues and questions of faith. Although she often addresses the events of the past, Matas also is concerned with the present and future. Her science fiction, for example, presents the consequences of nuclear war and what happens when a society gives itself over to consumerism, while her realistic fiction explores such topics as the abuse of power and the workings of the Canadian political system. She is credited with introducing her readers to some less familiar aspects of Jewish history such as the Danish and French resistances, the shtetls of nineteenth-century Russia, and the beginnings of the Arab/Israeli conflict. She is further acknowledged for the historical accuracy of her books as well as for the power of her themes and the success of her characterizations. Although she employs both male and female protagonists, Matas is especially noted for her portrayals of strong, resourceful young women in both historical and contemporary settings. Her characters often confront life-and-death situations in which instances of horror and atrocity are combined with examples of heroism and compassion. Matas's protagonists are forced to make difficult choices about themselves, both physically and spiritually; through their experiences, these young characters discover their personal strength and achieve self-awareness, qualities that lead them to socially responsible actions. Throughout her fiction, Matas attempts to show young people that they can make a difference in the world at any time in history.

Matas is often praised for her skill as a storyteller and for the dramatic quality of her prose. A playwright and former actress, she uses a spare, straightforward style that depends heavily on dialogue and first-person narration. Matas also is recognized as a starkly realistic writer: her books include murder, suicide, torture, kidnapping, betrayal, sexual abuse, and pedophilia as well as authentic depictions of the Nazi death camps. Although occasionally accused of preaching and for including an excess of historical information, Matas is usually regarded as a writer of moving, ultimately hopeful books that succeed as good stories and incisive explorations of social values. Writing about the Holocaust in *Canadian Children's Literature,* Graham Caie said, "[S]ome parents might ask about the value of keeping such bitter memories alive for yet another generation, but I believe that Carol Matas's objective and healthy treatment of the subject provides the most sensible approach for children today." Marie Campbell echoed this sentiment, noting that in Matas's hands "historical fiction is an uncompromising and painfully vivid thing. . . . The way Matas tells it, there's empowerment as well as sadness to be taken from history. In fact, with her quicksilver dialogue and breathless pacing, the way Matas tells it is the way historical fiction should be told."

Biographical Information

Born in Winnipeg, Manitoba, the setting for several of her books, Matas did not originally intend to be a writer. After graduating with a degree in English from the University of Western Ontario, she trained for two years at Actor's Lab in London, England, then returned to Canada to pursue a theatrical career in Winnipeg and Toronto. The friends that Matas made in Toronto were aspiring writers, and they often read their stories to her. When a friend read her an original fantasy he had written, Matas was prompted to write her own story about the adventures of children shrunk to miniature size by a magic teapot. Encouraged by her friends' favorable responses, she kept on writing as a hobby. In 1977, Matas married Per K. Brask, a theater professor of Danish descent; the stories that Brask told his wife about his father and grandfather in the Danish Resistance would inspire her to create her first book of historical fiction, *Lisa.* Matas began writing seriously when she was pregnant with her first child, Rebecca, who was later to become the model for the heroine of Matas's science fiction stories; Matas and Brask also have a son, Sam. During her pregnancy, a period in which she stopped acting, Matas wrote her first full-length book, the unpublished fantasy *Carstan and Kaspar.* After Rebecca was born, Matas stayed at home to take care of her and to write the first "Rebecca" book, *The Fusion Factor* (1986). In her autobiographical essay in *Seventh Book of Junior Authors and Illustrators,* Matas noted, "I believe it was one of the first books in Canada to deal with the topic of nuclear war, and publishers were a bit afraid of the subject matter. In my file I have about twenty rejection slips for it." *The Fusion Factor* was eventually published in 1986 and republished as *It's Up to Us* in 1991. In 1982, Matas wrote another "Rebecca" book, *The DNA Dimension*, a novel about genetic engineering that was immediately accepted for publication; the series also includes *Zanu* (1986) and *Me, Myself, and I* (1987). In an interview in *Canadian Children's Literature* with Perry Nodelman, an author and critic with whom she collaborated on the young adult fantasies *Of Two Minds* (1994) and *More Minds* (1996), Matas noted, "It wasn't until I wrote my first novel that I specifically focused on children as an audience. . . . I have to admit I wrote those books with children in mind and with their minds in mind, specifically. In fact, dare I admit this, I wanted to change them. . . . I wanted to make them into young people who would think for themselves." She added, "As I progressed in my writing I settled into children's writing because I felt that it was an area in which I could make a difference."

When Matas heard the story of the Danish Resistance from her husband, it came as a revelation to her. She told Nodelman, "I figured, as a fairly well-educated Jew, if I hadn't heard it, probably most children hadn't heard it either. So I felt I *had* to write it." After the positive reception of *Lisa,* which was published in the United States as *Lisa's War,* and its sequel *Jesper,* which was published in the United States as *Code Name Kris,* Matas was contacted by the United States Holocaust Memorial Museum in Washington, D.C. to write a book to complement its exhibit "Daniel's Story: Remembering the Children." The resulting work, *Daniel's Story,* describes a boy who thumbs through his photo albums—literally and imaginatively—on his way to several concentration camps. In her interview with Nodelman, Matas recalled that *Daniel's Story* was "the most painful and difficult book I've ever had to research. In a way, although obsessed by the evil of the Holocaust, it was also a topic I actively avoided because I got depressed just thinking about it. This book forced me to look at the worst, most evil thoughts and deeds, and I could not flinch." After completing *Daniel's Story,* Matas began to wonder what might happen to children who survived the war. Later books such as *After the War* and its sequel *The Garden* (1997) depict the anti-Semitism encountered by these young survivors as they returned home as well as their attempts to create new lives for themselves in Palestine. Although she no longer acts, Matas is still involved in theater. She wrote an original play, *The Escape,* that was produced in 1993, adapted her novel *Sworn Enemies* (1993) for a dramatic reading, and turned her book *Telling* (1998) into a radio play. Matas and her husband have also adapted her novels *Lisa* and *Jesper* for the stage. In addition to her work as an author and playwright, Matas has taught adult education courses in creative writing at the University of Winnipeg, has been a visiting professor and writer-in-residence at schools in both Canada and the United States, and tours frequently as a lecturer on writing.

In her essay in *Seventh Book of Junior Authors and Illustrators,* Matas said, "No matter what I'm working on, there has always been only one compelling reason for me to write—I love to tell a good story." Matas told Nodelman, "I have to have a reason for writing, and I desperately want to tell a story that is unputdownable!" She added, "I'm trying to open a question, a dialogue, give my reader food for thought. . . . [W]hat I'm trying to do is to present this world, in all its complexities, to my readers. And hope they are both challenged and entertained." Matas concluded, "Often I place my characters in a situation where their assumptions are challenged or where they are forced to challenge others. I hope their dilemma will challenge the reader in a similar way. And if my point of view does come through then I hope it's one the reader at least finds interesting—maybe it's something that they hadn't considered before, a new, different way of seeing the world."

Major Works

Matas's first historical novel, *Lisa,* describes how the twelve-year-old heroine, a Danish Jew, becomes involved in the underground resistance during the Nazi occupation of Copenhagen during World War II. Over a three-year period in which she kills a German soldier and contributes to the destruction of a factory, Lisa helps to evacuate hundreds of Jews by boat to neutral Sweden. At the end of the novel, Lisa and her family also must escape to Sweden to avoid being sent to the Nazi death camps. Lisa's romance with Jesper, a friend of her older brother's, and her ruminations about her role balance the book's action. *Lisa* is considered an exciting book that calls attention to an important part of war history. Called "an unsettling, important novel" by a critic in *Publishers Weekly,* the U.S. edition, *Lisa's War,* has been noted by Freda Klienburd to be "the only children's book to present this dramatic episode from the point of view of the endangered Jews rather than their Christian rescuers." Edith Milton further concluded that *Lisa's War* poses "sophisticated concerns with an honorable simplicity rare even in adult fiction." Lisa's love interest, seventeen-year-old Jesper, is the focus of the sequel bearing his name. Jesper, who has been captured and tortured by the Germans and is awaiting execution, chronicles the events that led up to his capture, including his actions as a saboteur. Matas also includes a romantic triangle—Jesper, Lisa, and Janicke, a fellow member of the resistance—and portrays Jesper's confusion about a former mentor who has become a Nazi. On the eve of Jesper's execution, a Royal Air Force bombing raid liberates him. Calling *Jesper* "a really good teenage novel," Graham Caie commented that Matas "manages to convey an important historical lesson while telling an exciting story." Ellen Fader concluded that throughout *Jesper* "runs the theme of the Danes' tremendous courage and the knowledge that one must stand up for what one believes to be right; that is why this novel, written, like its predecessor, after much research and consultation with Danish survivors, is so gripping and unforgettably exciting."

In order to create the title character of *Daniel's Story,* a book that depicts a Jewish teenager's struggle to survive the horrors of a series of Nazi death camps, Matas created a composite of children who were housed in concentration camps. Daniel and his family are sent to the Jewish ghetto in Lodz, Poland, before being transferred to Auschwitz in 1944. Daniel and his father, the only surviving members of their family, are then transported to Buchenwald, where they live in fear before being liberated by the Allies. At the end of the novel, Daniel and his girlfriend Ruth prepare to begin a new life in Palestine. Kenneth Oppel noted, "Carol Matas, as always, shows a deft hand with historical material," concluding that *Daniel's Story* "is never less than gripping. It is a book all children should read." Matas considers post-Holocaust life in *After the War* and *The Garden.* In the first novel, fifteen-year-old Ruth, a Buchenwald survivor, joins a Zionist group after encountering anti-Semitism when she returns home to Poland. Joining an underground organization, she leads a group of Jewish orphans across Europe and then to Palestine. Hazel Rochman commented, "The climatic scene in which Ruth finds the brother she feared was dead. . . is something you want to read over and over again; it is a miracle." *The Garden* describes Ruth's life in Palestine during the following year. As a Palmach soldier dedicated to defensive action, Ruth is forced to kill in the guerrilla conflicts that marked the beginning of the Arab/Israeli War; however, as the novel ends Ruth begins to see the garden that she tends on her settlement as a symbol of hope for her new homeland. Ann W. Moore concluded, "*The Garden* is a riveting, relevant novel that raises tough questions—and provides no easy answers." Gwyneth Evans added, "Matas here takes on a topic of central importance to international affairs in the 1990s—the existence of the state of Israel and the conflict between Arabs and Israelis." Matas also addresses the Nazi occupation in *Greater than Angels* (1998), a novel that focuses on Anna, a young woman transported to a concentration camp in Vichey, France who is saved by the villagers of Le Chambon-sur-Signon, humanitarians who have since been recognized for their exceptional rescue work during the war.

Matas's other historical novels also explore the topics of discrimination and persecution. In *Sworn Enemies,* she addresses the fine line between heroism and villainy in a story about two Jewish boys set in czarist Russia during the nineteenth-century. Aaron, a young Talmudic scholar, is kidnapped by Zev, a street urchin hired to kidnap his fellow Jews in order to fulfill the Czar's military quotas. Later, when Zev himself is forced into the army, he and Aaron come face to face with each other. At the end of the novel, Aaron, who escapes to France, has converted to Christianity to stay alive, but Zev has triumphantly remained a Jew through bravado and bribery. Matas underscores her story with ethical and theological questions about the true nature of Judaism and why bad things happen to the undeserving. Betsy Hearne noted, "It's unusual to have religious issues explored without thematic didacticism. This is the kind of book that will challenge readers to wonder what they would have done under the circumstances; their absorption of historical information in vivid detail is a valuable bonus."

In *The Burning Time*, fifteen-year-old Rose relates how her widowed mother Suzanne, a gifted healer and midwife, is accused of witchcraft in sixteenth-century France. When Suzanne refuses the sexual advances of a local priest and is charged with the death of her sister-in-law, she is imprisoned and tortured as a witch before her daughter, at her mother's request, gives her poison to commit suicide. After Suzanne's death, Rose, who realizes that her mother's only crime has been to be a woman, comes home to take her mother's place as a healer. Marie Campbell commented that *The Burning Time* "is a story entirely ripe for telling in our day, and Matas is unflinching in her handling of this explosive historical material." In addition to her historical fiction, Matas is the creator of well-received realistic fiction for young adults. *The Race* (1991) uses the frame of Canadian politics to describe how a fourteen-year-old girl, the daughter of the front-running candidate for the Liberal Party, proves her individualism. *The Primrose Path* (1995) describes how a teenage girl confronts the Orthodox Jewish rabbi who has taken sexual liberties with herself, her mother, and a group of young female followers. *The Freak* (1997) outlines how a fifteen-year-old with psychic powers learns to accept her gift after saving her synagogue from bombing by an anti-Semitic group. Matas is also recognized for her works for younger children, such as the fantasies that she wrote with Perry

Nodelman about enterprising Princess Leona and her former fiancé Prince Coren, and *The Lost Locket* (1994), realistic fiction about an eight-year-old girl who faces her fears to confront the school bully who has taken her most prized possession.

Awards

Lisa received the Geoffrey Bilson Award for Historical Fiction for Young People in 1988; it was also named a Sydney Taylor Award honor book by the Association of Jewish Libraries in 1989 and an "Our Choice" Memorable Book for Young People by the Canadian Children's Book Centre in 1991. *Jesper* was named a runner-up for the Young Adult Canadian Book Awards and a Mr. Christie's Award honor book, both in 1990, while *The Race* was named a notable book by the Canadian Library Association in 1992. In 1993, *Daniel's Story* received the Silver Birch Award, was nominated for the Governor General's Literary Award and the Ruth Schwartz Award, and was designated a Mr. Christie's honor book. *Sworn Enemies* won the Sydney Taylor Award in 1993 while *The Burning Time* won the "Our Choice" Award from the Canadian Children's Book Centre and was nominated for the Governor General's Literary Award in 1994.

In 1995, *The Primrose Path* was named Outstanding Book of the Year by the Canadian Children's Book Centre and was nominated for Manitoba Book of the Year. Several of Matas's works have been named as notable books by the *New York Times Book Review, School Library Journal, Voice of Youth Advocates,* and the National Council for the Social Studies and Children's Book Council, among others; Matas has also received several child-selected awards for her works.

AUTHOR'S COMMENTARY

Carol Matas with Perry Nodelman

SOURCE: "Good, Evil, Knowledge, Power: A Conversation between Carol Matas and Perry Nodelman," in *Canadian Children's Literature*, Vol. 22, No. 82, Summer, 1996, pp. 57-68.

PERRY: Carol, we've had some interesting but random conversations about various aspects of children's literature over the years, in the course of my reading early drafts of your work, and particularly in the process of collaborating on the two children's novels we've written together. But most of these have been in the context of hasty phone calls in the midst of other matters, and we've never actually sat down and had a formal, organized conversation about the subject. Nor are we ever likely to, as we pursue our two different careers and separate lives across town from each other. Hence this discussion-by-fax, devoted specifically to exploring your views about children's literature. . . .

I'd like to talk to you particularly about the darker aspects of life as depicted in your work—simply because they tend to be darker than a lot of people seem ready to see as appropriate in the context of literature for children. As you and I both know, many people like to believe that children are, or ought to be, innocent—that they aren't capable either of doing much evil themselves or of understanding the evil others do. Many other people aren't sure that children can't understand evil, but would still prefer that they didn't; as many parents and teachers often say to me, "They'll find out soon enough—why bother them with all that awful stuff when they're so young?" Your books do often bother children with all that stuff—and therefore distress the many adults who might prefer that they didn't. So I'll start with the BIG question: considering your obvious interest as a writer in depicting the darker aspect of existence, and considering the boundaries that writing for children seems to put on authentic and complete descriptions of those darker aspects, what led you to choose specifically to become a children's writer?

CAROL: When I read your question, my first reaction was—uh oh, he's asked me the wrong question, because I never "intended" to become a children's writer. I sort of stumbled into it, writing stories at the beginning with children as the central characters, which I assumed people of all ages would read. It wasn't until I wrote my first novel that I specifically focused on children as an audience. And here, I'd like to take back my question over your question, although it puts me in a nasty spot. I have to admit I wrote those books with children in mind and with their minds in mind, specifically. In fact, dare I admit this, I wanted to change them (oh, how politically incorrect, does this have to be public knowledge?). I wanted to make them into young people who would think for themselves. So I challenged them to see how the future might turn out if pollution is allowed to go unchecked (***Zanu***), if a nuclear war should happen (***It's Up to Us***). I wanted them to have the fun adults were having in reading a time travel book (***Me, Myself and I***) and I wanted them not ever to completely trust those in charge (***The D.N.A. Dimension***). Of course reviewers immediately accused me of preaching. Funnily enough, that never occurred to the young people reading the books. They liked them as straightforward action/adventure—and sometimes they did make them think, as evidenced by the many letters I received, one from a group in Ontario that literally revolutionized the entire county recycling program after reading ***Zanu*** and forming an organization called the Zanu group.

As I progressed in my writing I settled into children's writing because I felt that it was an area in which I could make a difference. You know, catch them when they're young and before they've solidified their views, become rigid. I also, and this is of equal importance, wanted to give them a wonderful reading experience. I *loved* to read when I was young for the sheer pleasure of it—and is there anything wrong with trying to deliver a pleasurable experience to children? I hope not.

PERRY: Me either. But I'm interested in the two different goals you suggest here—and the ways in which the two might be seen to be contradictory, perhaps even opposite to each other. You want to entertain children, AND you want to challenge them or even change them. Are you assuming that children find it entertaining to be changed, or at least to have someone or some book try to change them? Or do you see these as two separate things your books are doing, offering entertainment in order to sneak the message across? I guess I'm asking, what do you see as the pleasure your books, or reading in general, offer? And does it have anything to do with the challenge to think, or is that something separate from reading pleasure?

CAROL: Perry, you fiend, that's a hard question.

PERRY: I know. That's why I asked it. (*Imagine fiendish laughter.*)

CAROL: And it's a question that has many different answers, I think. Let me start with a basic response: I can only write if I have a reason to do so. This was apparent when we worked on ***Of Two Minds*** together. I felt it was about women, and power, and imagination, and how women would deal with power—you refused to consciously think about anything but the story.

PERRY: There *is* something else beside the story in ***Of Two Minds***?

CAROL: Of course there is, you dolt. And I need both. Equally, I have to have a reason for writing. and I desperately want to tell a story that is unputdownable! What I hope for is that the reader will have 1), a good read (yes, that is number 1) and 2), *if* they want to, will also be challenged by the material. If both happen, wonderful. The disaster would be that it was only a book *about* something—a dull, pedantic, unimaginative text.

Which brings me to the pleasure of reading. For me, the greatest pleasure is to read a book that is compelling *and* substantive. Doris Lessing, for instance, is the epitome of this kind of writing. I guess that's what I aim to do. I don't try to sneak a message in—that's not at all how I'd describe it. (In fact I hate that description.) I have themes I want to explore, characters I want to explore, ideas I want to challenge. Naturally it comes from my own point of view, that's a given. But I'm not trying to preach a message—quite the opposite. I'm trying to open a question, a dialogue, give my reader food for thought, challenge assumptions. And for me as a reader, as I've said, that *is* part of the pleasure of reading.

I like to read for pure entertainment too. And sometimes, as a pure challenge. So I think there's a place for all kinds of books—young people should be no more confined in their choices than us old guys.

Let me talk about my motivation more specifically. ***The Burning Time*** describes the witch burnings of Europe in the 1600s, France. So often these days I hear young girls distressed by my kind of feminism, determined to be apolitical. I felt I had to acquaint young women with their history—show them how women's power was systematically taken away, bring up issues of power and sex and how the male establishment, ruled by fear, used sexual repression to demonize women. After all, these mindsets are still operational today—if a women dresses a certain way, she is "asking" for it, if she behaves aggressively she's accused of being a witch etc. We can't understand our present if we don't understand our past.

Interestingly, some reviewers in the U.S. (The book got raves in Canada) were horrified, one reviewer calling it feverish, which I take to be another word for hysterical. And yet I had to leave the worst out—it was far too horrible. Other reviewers, fortunately, saw what I was trying to do and were very appreciative, but more importantly, young women who write me now list it as one of their favourite books (my reward).

PERRY: Well, Carol, I'm not surprised they like it. "Intense" and "exciting" are also other possible words for "feverish," and I think ***Burning Time*** is an intense and exciting book—and pretty scary, even if you did leave the worst stuff out. That's what *I* like about it—and what I admire about a number of your books. They tell exciting, suspenseful, involving stories—and as you said, that's *all* I like to think about myself when I'm writing fiction (I think it's because I'm always conscious of the other hat I wear as, not only a literary critic, but a specialist specifically in children's literature: I'm afraid that if I start thinking about the meanings of my novels as I write them, I'll end up overloading them with all the complex theoretical stuff I think I know, and as a result they'll just collapse under the weight, and be dead on arrival. Instead, I'd rather trust that if the characters say the right things and the plot takes the right turns, then the meanings or morals, whatever they are, will be there without my having to consciously worry about it.) But that takes me back to my original question, about how the serious concerns in your books relate to the pleasure they offer. I have a sense that you're right in suggesting the two go together, and that ***Burning Time*** would be much less involving if the issues weren't as serious as they are. But at the same time, I get a little worried when you tell me that you want to show your readers how women's power was systematically taken away, or to bring up issues of power and sex and so on. I worry, because that *does* sound to me like preaching a message. And yet when I read the novel it doesn't feel that way to me. I don't sense preaching going on at all. Not that there aren't moral and intellectual issues in the air—there are lots of those. But I get the sense when I read your books that the characters are being placed in moral or ethical dilemmas that they have hard times solving, if they actually ever do solve them at all—and that you're careful not to make the solutions to those dilemmas clear or obvious. I take this to mean that if you're preaching, you're always preaching the same message: that when it comes to defining human values there are no easy answers, that there are always at least two sides to every question, that only a fool would leap at one of the sides and be content with a total commitment to it. Is that a fair reading of the books? Is your concern with meanings perhaps a matter of raising questions rather than providing answers?

CAROL: You've said it so well that I'm not sure what I can add—but I won't let that stop me! Your question has forced me to actually consider what it is I do. Of course, thanks to you, I'll probably never write another word, now that I have to examine my writing process.

PERRY: The unexamined life is not worth living. Proceed.

CAROL: I will. Most books put forth a point of view, don't they? The question is, *how* is that point of view expressed—as a simple message, which does end up preaching, or in a context where the character is placed in a situation which challenges the character's assumptions and hopefully the readers assumptions as well? I hope I do the latter—and you're right, I don't like pat answers.

For example, in ***Sworn Enemies*** I wanted to explore the issues of faith, idealism and religion. Zev and Aaron are both religious, and at the beginning of the book, neither questions their faith. But as the story develops we see that Zev uses his religion to justify anything, even kidnapping. Aaron is forced to question his faith, God, anything he ever believed in. Both boys must convert or die. Zev refuses to convert, Aaron gives in. Does that mean Zev is a better person? Or just a fanatic? In a way, the book itself is a reflection of my attitude, my point of view. Zev is the character who represents the simple message; Aaron is the character who challenges all assumptions, who questions everything, who in the end is the moral one because he goes into the unknown with no fixed rules of right and wrong, only his own conscience to guide.

To complicate matters further, I ask a larger question: how does one live morally in an immoral world? Zev is also a victim—forced to be a kidnapper by the leaders of the Jewish community, who in turn are forced by the Tsar to send a quota of boys every year to the army. The reader must question the choices all these characters make, yet view them in the context of the greater world they live in. A modern parallel, of course, is the war in Vietnam.

Often I place my characters in a situation where their assumptions are challenged, or where they are forced to challenge others. I hope their dilemma will challenge the reader in a similar way. And if my point of view does come through then I hope it's one the reader at least finds interesting—maybe it's something that they hadn't considered before, a new, different way of seeing the world.

PERRY: Let me pick up on that "different way of seeing." What you've said about ***Sworn Enemies*** suggests some themes or interests—or obsessions?—that seem to me to appear in a number of your books. One is a concern with the ways in which people use or misuse their authority over others—particularly people who claim to represent the will of God. In ***Burning Time,*** in ***Sworn Enemies***, in ***Primrose Path***, religious, theoretically good people act badly in ways that seriously harm others. And meanwhile, theoretically good characters like Aaron or like Lisa herself in ***Lisa*** find themselves having to do theoretically evil things, things they themselves find morally obnoxious, in order to survive or to defend what they believe to be right. I find this particularly fascinating since it implies a way of seeing good and evil quite different from the simplistic opposition often present in children's books. Could you talk a bit about your way of seeing or understanding good and evil—particularly evil? What is evil? And what draws you to focus on this kind of a problem so often? What leads you to be so interested in the evil potential of good people and the good potential of evil ones?

CAROL: Perry, the questions get tougher and tougher, you evil fellow! No, I don't mean that. Because, in fact, in my definition of evil you wouldn't qualify at all, not being a control freak. Someone, (I wish I could remember who) once said evil is the desire to control other human beings. I think that's a pretty good definition and have adopted it as my own. From Hitler down to the class bully this definition seems to apply.

You see, Zev *likes* having power over Aaron. The priests in ***The Burning Time*** *like* to have power, ultimate power over women; the rabbi in ***Primrose*** is all about power and control. My supposedly "good" characters don't really want to control anyone, but *are* forced by circumstances to sometimes kill, lie, etc. And sometimes, a part of them *wants* to do it, but a bigger part finds it abhorrent. And I guess that my view of "evil" is that there is the potential for good and bad in all of us and that like form and shadow, they co-exist. It is the people who never acknowledge their "dark side" who are in danger of being overtaken by it. Hitler put all his darkness onto others and this is typical—Zev blames everyone for his misfortune, *never* taking responsibility. Aaron does take responsibility for his actions, he also sees his dark side, and, in the end, learns to live with it. That's what I consider courageous, honest, and yes, even "good."

PERRY: This all raises two questions for me, and I can't seem to choose which one to ask—there's a joke about being "of two minds" in here somewhere, but I'm not sure exactly what it is. Anyway, I'm going to ask you both of the questions at once. You may answer in turn, or together, or as you wish.

The first question is about specific episodes in two of your novels that clearly relate to this question about good people being evil and evil people being good—episodes that often puzzle and even upset students when I've discussed your work with them in the children's literature courses I teach. One episode is the moment in ***Lisa*** when Lisa shoots and kills in cold blood—and only thinks about the implications of her doing so afterwards. Some students worry that this conveys a message that being a murderer is sometimes okay. The other episode is the scene in ***Jesper*** in which Jesper discovers that the Nazi in charge of his fate is an old friend from his past, and must deal with conflicting feelings about a friend who is also an enemy—and furthermore, a Nazi who, rather than being a despicable monster like the Nazis we usually see in movies, is someone Jesper always looked up to, an idealist with a strong belief in the positive moral value of what he believes in. Here, students wonder why you made this all so complicated—wouldn't it confuse children and make them think that maybe fascism isn't so bad after all? I wonder how you would respond to their concerns.

The second question relates to that one, sort of. It's about the idea of evil as control. It occurs to me that Frederik's profound idealism about Nazism suggests his need for a system of ideas to believe in and feel secure about and shape his behaviour—in other words, a sort of religion. Because isn't much of what many religions (and especially the religion of the background both of us share, Judaism) offer believers exactly the feeling of being safely controlled by forces outside oneself, of having rules to follow and superiors to obey? Is this, perhaps, why you seem to be drawn so often to stories involving uses and misuses of religious authority? Do you see your books as being concerned with what it means to have faith or be religious? Is the fact of your own Jewish background of any significance in shaping this aspect of your writing? (Incidentally: I hate it when people ask me personal questions like this. You may refuse to answer if you want.)

CAROL: Perry, your students' comments that Lisa's shooting a German soldier in cold blood is a message that murder is OK makes my blood boil! This is really ignorant thinking.

First of all, Lisa is a character. As I said before she's not there to convey a message, but her action *hopefully* will make people think (not *not* think, like these students!). Secondly, she *does* react, it isn't a cold blooded act—she sweats, her heart pounds, she shakes, she throws up afterwards. Any intelligent reader can see that, in fact, she's *very* upset. Finally, she has to kill the soldier or *all* the fifty people counting on her will certainly be captured, and probably killed. She has no choice. She does the hard thing, the right thing, at that moment: to put her own scruples and feelings above the welfare of those she's caring for would be irresponsible.

Re[garding] your question about Jesper and why it's all so complicated. Again, the very question frustrates me—after all, that's the whole point of the book. To say it's complicated is to miss the whole point, which is it *is* complicated. Frederick *does* believe in what he's doing, he *is* an idealist, but surely that doesn't mean fascism is good? Just because someone believes in it? People believe all sorts of things but that doesn't make those things true? And those people are often idealists—and ideologues, like Newt Gingrich, for instance. I think ideologues are *always* the most dangerous types. In Canada Brian Mulroney was a perfect example of that, and so are Preston Manning and Mike Harris.

Which brings me to your last question about control. I think I am more concerned with the political ideologues than I am with religious ideologues, because in this day and age religious ideologues have less power. But in the times I've been writing about, they often had a lot of power—i.e ***Sworn Enemies, The Burning Time***. Even so, I hope the parallels will be apparent to the reader—those that believe in a system which has all the answers are in danger of handing over their decision-making power to someone else. And that someone, whoever it is, should *never* be given absolute power because absolute power corrupts absolutely. This is all too obvious in ***The Primrose Path***.

How do my convictions affect those themes? Well, they must, I suppose. I dislike any kind of "orthodoxy" in any religion, for the reasons stated above. They give too much power to one person and not enough to the individual. Very rarely do we see people in those positions of power using it wisely. The Pope's shocking silence about the massacres of Jews in World War II is still a scandal the church has not fully addressed. He very well might have slowed it, even stopped it, had he used the full weight of his office. Why didn't he? Is it an accident that the worst atrocities happened in countries where the Catholic church had encouraged anti-Semitism for hundreds of years? It is no accident that ***Primrose Path*** is set in an orthodox synagogue rather than a reform synagogue, because, again, Orthodoxy sets out all the rules and regulations and then puts one *man* (never a woman) in charge of it all.

Now that I've managed to insult just about everyone, let me move on to the more personal side of your question about my upbringing. I was not brought up in a religious household, but in a household where it mattered what happened to others, where community large and small was considered our responsibility. What I hate most about the right wing agenda is the emphasis on the individual as removed from his or her community. All decisions are based solely on how things affect the individual. I hate to break this news, but eventually the larger community impinges on all of us—the person who has been made homeless by welfare cuts may have kids that will one day knock on your nice townhouse door and blow you away. Never mind the moral issues of leaving people to suffer like that!

Also I'd like to clarify here—because first I spoke of the importance of the individual thinking for him or herself. Then I spoke of the importance of the community. I don't think these are contradictory ideas—but ideas which have to be balanced. After all, in communism we saw community overwhelming the individuals. In the U.S. right now we see the individual overwhelming community. It is the balance of these which forms a healthy society.

In terms of your *very* personal question about my own beliefs. I am a very spiritual person, but not religious. And I'm not sure how that affects my writing except that it makes me pretty skeptical about all formal religion.

PERRY: I'd like to pursue this whole business of the parallels between the religious ideologues and the political ones a little further, because I find it intriguingly paradoxical—and it also engages the matters of control and of communal obligation rather than individual ones that you've been talking about. Let me lead up to a question by way of some other things I know people have said about your work.

First, another student in one of my classes, this one of German background, expressed deep distress that your characters called those who invaded Denmark in ***Lisa*** "Germans" and not specifically "Nazis." To her, it suggested that *all* Germans were evil, and encouraged prejudice against Germans in the past and in the present. I couldn't persuade her that all these particular Nazis in the book were, indeed, not only German, but employees of the German government of the time, representatives of Germany—that it was an historic fact. That mattered less to her than the potential damage she imaged to the reputation of her people. Second: I know that a school board official somewhere in southern Ontario, this one of Jewish background, proposed the banning of ***Sworn Enemies*** because it suggested that some Jews in the past might have been bad people—thus confirming the prejudices of anti-Semites and damaging the reputation of her people. And third: there was also a similar decision recently to ban you from discussing ***The Primrose Path*** at a synagogue here in Winnipeg, wasn't there?

What intrigues me about all these responses is what they have in common—that people worry that your work might give comfort to those whom they perceive as their enemies. And yet the enemies are anti-German in one case, anti-Semitic in the others. That not only seems to confirm the presence in your work of the parallel between religious ideologues and political ones—it also suggest how that idea does bother at least some adults, who happily acknowledge the potential for evil for others but not in their own group or community. They want, also, to control things—to preserve one-sided orthodoxies? And they clearly believe that the welfare of their community as a whole is more important than the facts and your individual right to tell about the facts.

Now, finally, my question. Am I misreading all this? Because if I'm not, I wonder how you respond in this case as the individual a community is trying to condemn or to silence (and perhaps particularly, as a Jew being condemned or silenced for the good of the Jewish community)? How does that relate to or impinge upon your idea (which, incidentally, I fervently agree with) that we've currently overbalanced in favour of individual rights over communal responsibilities? Is this a contradiction, or a paradox? Or how exactly do you imagine a balanced way of walking through these particular minefields?

CAROL: Perry, you *are* reading it dead on. And in answer to your question, as an individual the community is trying to silence, I'd say, it's neither a contradiction or a paradox because, as I said earlier, it's a question of balance. Without the individual's voice, speaking what people often don't want to hear, we get fascism. The individual is all important. And yet, if the individual speaks only for his/her self, you get the "me" society that cares for no one and buzz words like "personal responsibility" which no longer mean that, but mean every man for himself.

As for walking through minefields—if you mean me as a writer, I will be responsible to my material and my audience to the best of my ability. And to me, that means being honest, being a mirror to our society, and inevitably some people won't like what they see.

PERRY: Mirrors are like that, right? But I started all this asking you about your interest in depicting the darker aspects of life—and we've talked quite a bit about responses to various of your novels which confirm the fact that some people—most of them adults—don't like what *you* see and know of the world and want to show to children. I suspect this response is at its most intense in terms of the novels you've written about various aspects of the Holocaust and its aftermath. There's ***Lisa, Jesper, Daniel's Story***—and now two new books, ***After the War*** and ***The Garden,*** about a girl who survives her horrific experience in a concentration camp and moves on to Israel, not always without facing new horrors. That's a lot of novels centring around the same moment in history—and to me, it suggests a fascination, a commitment, even an obsession. (I promise you that all of those, even the obsession, strike me as being good things, not bad ones—for surely the best writing comes out of a commitment to the things that matter most intensely to writers?) I wonder if you could say a little about your interest in this particular time in history. What led you to write about the Jewish experience in World War II in the first place? And why do you keep coming back to it so often?

CAROL: I have always been obsessed by the Holocaust, you're right. I admit it. And I guess it's because of what we've covered already—the issue of evil. After all, the Holocaust *is* evil, and to study it is to study the very worst in human nature.

But I came to write about it by a different path. My husband Per began to tell me stories of what his own father and grandfather had experienced during World War II in Denmark. The stories were so exciting I began thinking about writing a novel for young people which told the story of a boy in the resistance. At that point, I was given a book on the rescue of the Jews in Denmark and was amazed to discover a story I'd never heard before. I figured, as a fairly well-educated Jew, if I hadn't heard it, probably most children hadn't heard it either. So I felt I *had* to write it. I must admit it was as much for the drama of the story, as for the theme I wanted to explore. Also, it was an uplifting story, a story which said this didn't have to happen the way it did, look at what happened in Denmark.

That's how I came to write ***Lisa***. So you see, I kind of fell into World War II. I never said, "I'm going to write a series of World War II books!" ***Jesper*** was, of course, the book I originally thought of, about a boy in the resistance. So it was quite natural for me to write that after I finished ***Lisa***.

Now, ***Daniel's Story*** was something quite different. I was asked to write that by the U.S. Holocaust Memorial Museum as a complementary piece to their children's exhibit. (Not a novelization, as some reviewers mistakenly stated.) And with their backing, I felt comfortable delving into that material.

But I must say, it was the most painful and difficult book I've ever had to research. In a way, although obsessed by the evil of the Holocaust, it was also a topic I actively avoided because I got depressed just thinking about it. This book forced me to look at the worst, most evil thoughts and deeds, and I could not flinch. And it wasn't only the litany of horrors that was hard to stomach—the detailed descriptions of atrocity after atrocity. Some images, like the German soldiers throwing babies out of hospital windows while their colleagues on the streets below played the game of seeing how many they could catch on their bayonets, will never leave me. (By the way, although I included that scene I left out the part about the bayonets, because the image is *too* horrible for anyone, including children.) But always I was plagued by the *lack* of good, what could have been, why didn't the US bomb the train tracks which took the victims to the death camps. They could have but had "more important" targets. Why did townsfolk watch as Jews were marched by them, pretending to see nothing? Why was the Pope silent? Isn't the absence of good also a form of evil?

My two new books, ***After the War*** and ***The Garden,*** deal with the illegal immigration to Israel after the war, and the subsequent fight for a Jewish state. In ***After the War,*** the characters are survivors of the atrocity, the death camp. What kind of people were they when it was all over? What had happened to their own humanity? What were they willing to endure to find a place that could be called home? How had their encounter with evil affected them, moulded them? These are the questions of ***After the War. The Garden*** deals with survivors who want only peace, quiet, who are still afraid, now confronted with annihilation by the Arab nation surrounding them. They must fight but at least now they can fight, they are no longer victims. And yet, having to kill as they were once killed is a terrible moral dilemma, so the questions raised here are all to do with idealism and what one must do to survive. Apparently, when Golda Meir and Anwar Sadat made peace, Golda said that she could forgive him for all the Jewish lives he had taken but could never forgive him for turning the children into killers. That is the issue I'm trying to work through in ***The Garden***.

As you know, I'm now proposing at least two new books set in World War II. Again, I suppose this time offers an incredible wealth of dramatic stories as well as an opportunity to explore issues and to put my characters in life and death situations where moral dilemmas have to be faced.

PERRY: "Moral dilemmas that have to be faced," you say. And earlier, you spoke about how ***Daniel's Story*** forced you to look at difficult things and that you couldn't flinch—and within the novel, Daniel himself often reiterates how important it is for him to take his pictures of the horror that surrounds him, to look and not flinch, to be a witness. As I remember my reading of ***Daniel's Story*** and think about what you've been telling me in this conversation, I'm fascinated by the ways in which you so often bring questions of evil and knowledge together—how important it is for you yourself to know evil, to witness it, how important it is for characters to do so, how important it is for your young readers to do so. In fact, as I think back on it, this question of knowing evil seems to be the thread that connects all the different things we've talked about in this conversation. Is that a fair assessment?

CAROL: Perry, I agree with your assessment. I guess I believe that old cliché, knowledge is power. Children without knowledge are powerless. This has become very clear to me in my writing of ***The Primrose Path***. And one of the main reasons I wanted to write it. Perhaps if children have thought about these issues, have thought about how charismatic leaders work, how they slowly try to suck you in using trust and friendship as their weapons, perhaps they will be able to avoid such situations. But a child who is "innocent" which, to me, means ignorant, has *no* choice.

Similarly with ***Daniel's Story***: perhaps reading about the devastation will put them on their guard, and if someone talks to them about becoming a skinhead they will *know* what that means. Educators and parents who are afraid of letting their children read this material because it might upset them should think about how upset their children would be once they were made a victim of a child abuser or once they were complicit in far worse things than the act of reading a book.

Sworn Enemies talks about moral choice, the difference between self interest and larger moral issues. Surely these are things worth considering.

I spoke earlier about evil being the need to control. While in New York recently I saw Terence McNally's play, *Master Class*. In it, the lead character based on Maria Callas spoke of how one *must* dominate a stage, be in control of the audience, and I suddenly realized that even with a concept like control there is *no such thing* as a clear answer. And maybe this is the best way to end this discussion—to agree that the world is a complex place and that what I'm trying to do is present this world, in all its complexities, to my readers. And hope they are both challenged *and* entertained.

PERRY: As one of your readers, I am both. And I know lots of children and other adults that are too. Thanks for talking to me about this.

GENERAL COMMENTARY

Mary Ainslie Smith

SOURCE: "Back to the Future," in *Books in Canada,* Vol. 16, No. 2, March, 1987, pp. 37-9.

Strange encounters with the supernatural or with life in another time and place are features of a number of recent books for children. In two science-fiction books by Carol Matas the same heroine, Rebecca, travels through time to two different futures. She remains in Winnipeg, her home in the present, but in both stories it is a Winnipeg changed beyond her recognition.

The Fusion Factor takes Rebecca to a complex underground city where the genetically damaged survivors of a nuclear war hope to rebuild civilization by kidnapping healthy children from the past for breeding purposes. In ***Zanu,*** she is transported to what seems to be a much happier future. War and disease are gone and everyone lives in a glamorous world of beautiful clothes and exciting shopping centres, with robots and computers providing every comfort at home.

However, Rebecca soon discovers the extreme pressures in this seemingly perfect society. Zanu is a corporation, a big business that has entirely taken over the world, eliminating all other governments. Citizens, even children Rebecca's age, must conform and fulfil daily quotas of buying and selling to support the corporate structure. If they don't, they are "cut loose"—banished from the perfect city to a wilderness dead from industrial pollution where there seems to be no chance of survival.

Both books offer bleak views of the future, but Matas suggests some hope in each case. . . .

In both of Matas's books the only hope offered is for Rebecca to escape and return to our present time. Then, with her added knowledge, she can perhaps make even a small change—like the death of Bradbury's butterfly—that will prevent disaster. Rebecca, spunky and ultimately optimistic, wants to believe that one person can make such a difference. Her determination to work for a better world should get some healthy ideas stirring in the minds of the readers of these two books.

Leslie McGrath

SOURCE: A review of *Zanu* and *The Fusion Factor,* in *Books for Young People,* Vol. 1, No. 3, June, 1987, pp. 9-10.

Carol Matas, whose earlier novel ***The DNA Dimension*** appeared in Gage's Jeanpac Series, has two new works from Fifth House. ***The Fusion Factor*** and ***Zanu*** are the first books in the promising new Fifth Perception series, which consists of "action packed science fiction-adventure stories dealing with contemporary issues".

Both stories are set in Winnipeg and involve time travel to the year 2080. ***The Fusion Factor*** introduces the heroine, 12-year-old Rebecca, whose courage and loyalty quickly win the reader's sympathy. She follows a kidnapped friend through a time-travel machine into a nightmarish, post-nuclear-war underground colony, where scientists and military madmen dream of repopulating the world with unwanted children stolen from the past. Rebecca and her friend succeed in escaping, together with some refugees from the future, and, safely back in the present, they vow to work towards preserving the world from nuclear destruction.

In ***Zanu,*** which takes place the following summer, Rebecca is given a glimpse of another possible future when she is accidentally transported to ultra-modern Winnipeg in 2080, or 40 R.C.E. (Real Corporate Era). Here, everything (people and objects alike) is owned and controlled by the world-wide Zanu corporation. The inhabitants appear happy and glamorous, but Rebecca becomes aware of the more frightening aspects of a completely consumption-oriented society. Again, Rebecca escapes, after helping the anti-Zanu underground, but she carries a searing vision of the results of corporate irresponsibility and human negligence with her.

These stories are, as promised, action-packed, with lots of suspense. The tone is serious, but ultimately hopeful. The younger characters are more convincing than the adults; most modern parents wouldn't dismiss a child's frightened account of a friend's being kidnapped as a "dream", and the police would surely ask some pertinent questions about the vehicle, etc. Also, in spite of the differences in time and circumstance, there is virtually no disparity between the language of 1986 and that of 2080/40 R.C.E. On the whole, however, the stories flow and are well written. Individual readers and class groups (grades 7-9) will find ***The Fusion Factor*** and ***Zanu*** enjoyable and thought provoking.

Sandra Odegard

SOURCE: A review of *Zanu, The Fusion Factor,* and *Lisa,* in *Canadian Children's Literature,* No. 50, 1988, pp. 79-80.

A group known as "Manitoba Educators for Social Responsibility" endorses the second [***The Fusion Factor***] of these adventure stories as a vehicle for promoting classroom discussion of the nuclear threat and for stimulating and encouraging its readers. While the subject matter of the other two stories is not the nuclear threat, clearly in all three Carol Matas is interested in promoting the idea in her young readers that they do have a responsibility to other people, at family, community, national and world levels, and in encouraging them to believe that they have the power to make significant changes. The adolescent protagonists are placed in circumstances where their present way of life is threatened, and they bravely, in the face of death, struggle against powerful regimes and succeed in changing the course of history. Each story centres on a spirited girl with a quick temper and a willingness to enter into physical combat, who at considerable risk to herself, engages in a mission of rescue—thus breaking across the old stereotype of the male as rescuer.

In ***Zanu*** and ***The Fusion Factor,*** the same protagonist, Rebecca, a 12-year-old Winnipeg girl, by actively following up on her concern for another person—one a stranger, the other her school enemy—is accidentally propelled into the future through a time machine. The two books present a future world of sterility, computerized surveillance, and pollution.

Matas emphasizes that the future scenarios she depicts are not unalterable. At the conclusion of each of these two books, Rebecca returns to the present time firmly resolved to do all she can to change the way things are. In ***Zanu,*** before she leaves, she is involved in establishing an underground network of people determined to overthrow the totalitarian regime. In ***The Fusion Factor,*** on her return from the underground city of the future she helps set up a peace group aimed at preventing nuclear holocaust. These children, and Matas's readers, learn that they are not powerless and that they can alter their own world; indeed, that their world is in its present shape because of decisions made by individuals and because of the passivity of the majority of people. These stories warn young readers about the possible results of a consumer-oriented society dominated by the ethics of profit-making, or of the build-up of nuclear weapons. Matas suggests that challenging the established power structure of any society calls upon physical, as well as moral, courage.

Lisa is historical, rather than speculative, fiction. This story from the past upholds the vision of ***Zanu*** and ***The Nuclear*** [*Fusion*] ***Factor.*** The "Afterword" of the book tells how in Denmark approximately 6,500 Jews were saved from the Nazis because of the courage of a Nazi informant and the daring and compassion of some Danish people who sheltered their Jewish neighbours and helped them to escape to Sweden. The heroine of the story, a young Jewish girl living in Copenhagen when Denmark fell to the Germans, becomes involved in the underground resistance movement. She is 12 in 1940, when the story begins, and 15 at its conclusion, and like anybody of her age, she is concerned about school assignments and dances, her relationship with her friend, Suzanne, and her romantic feelings for her co-conspirator, Jesper. She is no larger-than-life hero, but an ordinary girl who bravely determines to fight for the freedom of her country and to help others.

In all three of these stories, the family, community and country are shown as being the potential sources of strength and safety, rather than as centres of exclusivity. Since ***Lisa*** is based on history, Matas demonstrates here that the ideals she encourages not only can, but do, change the course of events at personal and political levels.

TITLE COMMENTARY

FUSION FACTOR (1986; U.S. edition as *It's Up to Us,* 1991)

David W. Atkinson

SOURCE: "Real Issues," in *Canadian Literature,* No. 116, Spring, 1988, pp. 143-45.

[In ***The Fusion Factor,***] Matas brings attention to the causes and consequences of nuclear war, even while delivering the hopeful message that humankind's extinction is not inevitable. . . .

The Fusion Factor begins with Rebecca partnered with Lonny for a school project. Lonny, she learns, is trouble, but when she sees him kidnapped and no one believes her, Rebecca feels she has a responsibility to investigate. What Rebecca discovers is beyond her wildest dreams: a time machine which is used to kidnap children to an underground shelter, where in the year 2040 a few survivors of nuclear war continue to live. The reason for the kidnappings is one of monumental proportions, and in large measure seems to justify what would otherwise be an unacceptable action. As most of the children born after the bombing are retarded, young, healthy children are needed to allow for the continuation of the underground community and, it is hinted, of the human race itself.

As well as recounting Rebecca's efforts to get herself and the other kidnapped children back to their own time so that somehow the nuclear holocaust can be avoided, Matas's novel is a depiction of life after nuclear war. While there is mention of the obvious things—fallout, radiation sickness, nuclear winter—these do not make the greatest impression on Rebecca or on the reader. Rather it is the greyness of life underground, the lack of spontaneity in children who have known nothing else, the awareness that the world Rebecca so much takes for granted is gone. It is a frightening reality made even more horrifying when Rebecca and Lonny encounter mutants from the surface who are neither animal nor human. The point is that the people living in the underground shelter are no more human than the mutants, in that they are denied the opportunity to grow in the world. . . .

Matas understands that social awareness is not achieved overnight; rather it is always evolving, and must therefore be part of the educational process. Too often, young people see themselves as having little influence; ***The Fusion Factor*** makes clear that young people can matter, as Rebecca and her friends return to their own time intent on working for peace. . . .

There are, needless to say, a few things with which one might quibble. That in ***The Fusion Factor*** Catherine and Lewis are so easily accepted into Rebecca's family stretches believability, although Matas does allow that the adjustment is not going to be an easy one. Arguments at the breakfast table start the second day. Matas overlooks, too, an inevitable problem encountered in time travel. If the children are to make a difference because of their experiences in the future, then the future which they experienced will never actually occur. While Matas might be wise to avoid the problem of tampering with history, it is certainly an issue for any regular reader of science fiction.

ZANU (1986)

Gwyneth Evans

SOURCE: "Social Conscience," in *Canadian Literature,* No. 117, Summer, 1988, pp. 158-60.

Zanu, an anti-Utopian fantasy, uses the device of time travel for a didactic purpose; like the prototype of its genre, H. G. Wells's *The Time Machine,* ***Zanu*** gives an admonitory vision of the future, in which present threats have become realities. In Winnipeg in 2085, synthetic comforts temporarily cushion city-dwellers from awareness of the devastation outside, created by acid rain, other forms of pollution, and the "greenhouse effect." The eponymous Zanu, a giant corporation which has taken over the world, enforces the spending of money and consumption of goods as the chief duty of all citizens. Children must leave school at the age of 10 to join the work force as producers and consumers; they have money, cars; and fashionable clothes, but not the opportunity to continue to be school children, and no contact with what we now think of as nature.

Matas borrows largely and rather too casually from stock science-fiction gadgets, while her characters seem to be merely colour-coded—distinguishable by the descriptions of their hair and clothing rather than by any genuine individuality. What makes her vision unusual within North American writing for young adults, however, is its child's-eye vision of a world wholly given over to consumerism, and its direct ascription of social evils to the corporate and individual greed of our own society. Matas leaves implicit a realization of how far we have already moved towards the compulsive and compulsory shopping mania of this future world, but her scene in the Winnipeg mall of 2085 is both prophetic and eerily familiar. More overtly, the novel stresses personal choice and responsibility as the means of preventing such a future. Unlike most popular fiction for teenagers, Matas's book challenges some very basic North American social values, and shows what damage our own comfort-seeking can do. It's a pity that such important subject matter is not embodied in a more carefully conceived and better-written story.

LISA (1987; U.S. edition as *Lisa's War,* 1989)

Kenneth Oppel

SOURCE: A review of *Lisa,* in *Books for Young People,* Vol. 1, No. 6, December, 1987, p. 6.

Set in Copenhagen during the Nazi occupation, Carol Matas's ***Lisa*** is the story of a Jewish girl's involvement in the Danish Resistance. Though Lisa is only 12 when German troops sweep through her country, she quickly realizes the frightening implications the invasion holds for the Jewish community. With the help of her older brother, Stefen, Lisa joins the Resistance movement and begins distributing leaflets throughout the city. As the occupation stretches on and German atrocities increase, Lisa's involvement becomes more zealous: she helps destroy a factory and later is forced to kill a German soldier. When the Resistance learns that the Nazis are planning to raid synagogues during Rosh Hashanah, Lisa, now 15, plays a vital role in evacuating hundreds of Jews, by boat, to Sweden.

Interwoven with the central story of Lisa's heroism is a more personal story, which addresses her close relationship with her family and friends, her first romantic stirrings, and also her misgivings both about her role in the Resistance and her gradual desensitization to the violence she witnesses daily.

Lisa narrates the story as a flashback, in the present tense—as if it were being told orally. Her language, appropriately, is colloquial and engaging, and her sense of humour provides some refreshing relief from the intense drama of the story. Lisa is a particularly sympathetic and authentic character, and her actions are motivated by adolescent rather than by adult sensibilities. Less convincing is the character of Stefen, who often speaks with too much maturity for his young years. A tightly paced story with a truly harrowing climax, ***Lisa*** is compelling reading for both boys and girls age 11 and up.

Welwyn Wilton Katz

SOURCE: "Doers and Seekers," in *Books in Canada,* Vol. 17, No. 3, April, 1988, p. 36.

The title character in ***Lisa,*** by Carol Matas, is a Jewish teen-ager growing up in Copenhagen under Nazi occupation. The story covers three years, from the night the Germans invade until Lisa and her family must leave Denmark to escape being sent to the Nazi death camps. At 12, Lisa joins the Danish resistance, progressing from passing out leaflets to helping blow up factories and aiding with other escapes. Eventually, Lisa comes to fear that in its violence the resistance could become as bad as the Nazis; yet in the end, she kills a man herself. There are many violent acts in ***Lisa,*** but the book is made less dark by the characters' desire to move beyond them.

The book is necessarily episodic (because of the long time span) but still moves quickly and is exciting and suspenseful. Matas writes with the verve she showed in her other books but with more control and less confusion. Still, there are technical flaws. One problem is that Matas writes in the present tense and the first person, a diaristic style that gives immediacy but is hard to accept in action scenes (one can't imagine Lisa with pen in hand recording the events as they happen); it also makes it easy to get lost in the flashbacks. I had a disorienting sense of not always knowing when *now* was.

Publishers Weekly

SOURCE: A review of *Lisa's War,* in *Publishers Weekly,* Vol. 235, No. 6, February 10, 1989, p. 73.

Matas offers a powerful account of a young Jewish girl who fights back after the Germans invade Denmark in 1940. Lisa, 12, and her brother Stefan join the Danish resistance when the Germans invade Copenhagen. Stefan is deeply involved in the movement, undertaking missions to sabotage German-run factories, while Lisa and her friend Susanne distribute pamphlets published by the resistance. When Susanne's parents are killed by the Germans, Lisa, too, becomes as involved as Stefan. Over the three-year period that this book documents, thousands of Danish Jews must flee their country to save themselves; Lisa and Stefan risk their own lives helping hundreds of Jews escape safely to Sweden. Lisa describes her experiences in the first-person present tense, creating a potent immediacy. Through the riveting narration, the rising tension in the country is effectively conveyed. An unsettling, important novel.

Denise Wilms

SOURCE: A review of *Lisa's War,* in *Booklist,* Vol. 85, No. 15, April 1, 1989, p. 1387.

This novel about the German occupation of Denmark and the escape of Danish Jews to Sweden takes the form of an adolescent girl's first-person narrative. When Denmark falls, Lisa is 12 and a clear-eyed observer of those around her. Her older brother, Stefan, is bitter because Denmark has given in without a fight. He's soon involved in resistance activities, which Lisa begs to be part of. Her first outing nearly ends in disaster when she upchucks in sheer terror after several German soldiers enter her streetcar. Two years later, her fears have been conquered, but conditions are worse. A baby now lives with the family, its mother shot at the hospital where Lisa's physician father works; Lisa's friend Susanne also lives with them, following her parents' death in a bombing raid. With the news that the Germans are rounding up Jews, Lisa and her family flee, their journey made possible by the resistance and the quiet cooperation of friends. The flight itself is harrowing. Lisa, who has stayed behind with her brother to aid other refugees, shoots a German soldier, and afterward, she and Stefan join other refugees in rowing to Sweden. Though similar in theme to Lowry's *Number the Stars,* the titles carry different flavors—Lowry's shows a quicker pace and more concessions to plotting, while Matas's tends toward introspection and a somber tenor. Events rather than characters take precedence here, though Lisa herself projects an authentic voice. An absorbing, fictional look at a significant piece of World War II history.

Susan M. Harding

SOURCE: A review of *Lisa's War,* in *School Library Journal,* Vol. 35, No. 9, May, 1989, pp. 127-28.

Lisa is 12 years old when the Nazis invade Denmark. Angered at her country's surrendering without a fight, Lisa and her family each join the resistance, doing their part for their country while trying to hide their activities from the others. Lisa starts with a small assignment of delivering some pamphlets (and finds that frightening enough), but by the end she is helping to organize a mass evacuation of Danish Jews to Sweden. As a counterpoint to Lisa's family's activist attitudes is her cousin Erik and his family, whose complacent "it can't happen here" attitude is shattered by Gestapo raids on Rosh Hashanah. Despite the dramatic plot, the characters (and therefore the book) never quite come to life. Readers may feel a chill of horror when Lisa's father describes a delivery room massacre which spares only the newborn infant, or pity Erik's parents when they are forced finally to face the reality that they've been denying for so long, but Lisa does not earn the emotional investment required to anchor the novel.

Edith Milton

SOURCE: "Escape from Copenhagen," in *The New York Times Book Review,* May 21, 1989, p. 32.

Two novels this spring concern themselves with a single small corner brightening the general darkness of the Holocaust the remarkable rescue of Jews from Nazi-occupied Denmark to neutral Sweden in the fall of 1943. Denmark had made tolerance of its 8,000 Jewish citizens a condition for not resisting coexistence with its German invaders and bemused, the Germans seemed more or less to have agreed.

When word leaked out on Sept. 29 that the Jews were, after all, to be rounded up by Oct. 1, put onto transport vessels and taken to their almost certain death, no one was prepared. But in a matter of a few days, a few hours, in fact, the Danish resistance, with extraordinary cooperation from the general population and even the Danish police, managed to arrange a few private pleasure boats, some cargo ships and a great many fishing vessels to spirit 7,000 Jews to safety. The story makes irresistible fiction. . . .

Lisa, who thinks she is too big and too clumsy, and disguises her admiring affection for her older brother Stefan in withering scorn, makes a totally convincing narrator. Majestically self-disparaging, she delights in the ironies and ambiguities of the world around her. In the three years the novel covers, between invasion and exodus, she grows from sardonic 12-year-old to courageous adolescent, joins the Copenhagen resistance, takes on dangerous missions and, though she is losing patience with her cousin Erik's refusal to confront danger or count himself as Jewish, still puzzles over questions about her own Jewish identity and about the morality of killing people because they threaten to kill you.

Lisa's War poses such sophisticated concerns with an honorable simplicity rare even in adult fiction. And at the same time it builds a great deal of excitement, as the German menace spreads and intensifies, growing from a sinister fear to lethal reality. As it does, Lisa's involvement in the resistance also grows from a first, comically terrified attempt to leave contraband leaflets on the streetcar to a central role in guarding her fellow Jews as they wait to go to Sweden.

Many things are admirable in this story: its humor, its heroine's complex, feisty and irreverent intelligence, the realism of its characters as they are seen through her eyes. Carol Matas, a Canadian writer, makes real the pervasive atmosphere of fear and disruption. But she places these distortions of an extreme time in the context of normal human standards, so that Lisa can marvel at how necessary it has become for members of her family to lie to each other so as to spare each other.

The book's impulse is against stereotype and facile conclusions. For instance, Lisa's father, a surgeon, is small, delicate and rather tender, while his daughter is large and bent on action; the Germans, loosing their most devastating atrocities almost at random, seem most often murderously inane; the resistance is not a heroic monolith but a group of frightened individuals acting from rage and necessity. And however one approaches it, as history, as adventure or simply as a story about growing up, ***Lisa's War*** is enthralling.

Mary M. Burns

SOURCE: A review of *Lisa's War,* in *The Horn Book Magazine,* Vol. LXV, No. 3, May-June, 1989, pp. 377-78.

Written for the adolescent audience, ***Lisa's War*** offers additional insight into Hitler's impact on the Jewish populations of occupied countries by focusing on Denmark, where, with few exceptions, the entire nation rallied to thwart the "Final Solution." Based on research and on interviews with survivors of that time, the novel achieves a sense of immediacy through use of the first person. Lisa, the narrator, is twelve at the beginning of the story, fifteen at its conclusion. Before her thirteenth birthday she has already become part of the resistance movement, despite the initial objections of her older brother, Stefan. Theirs is not a romantic venture, for they realize that they have placed their lives in double jeopardy—as Jews and as underground fighters for freedom. As they progress from distributing leaflets to executing informers, Lisa shudders at the change in all their lives, thinking, "These Germans are dragging us all down to their level." Then, having learned of the Nazi plot to arrest and "relocate" all Danish Jews during the celebration of Rosh Hashanah, Lisa and her family, along with thousands of other Jews, manage to escape to safety in Sweden. The style is terse, the tone of the dialogue changing as Lisa grows older. . . . The compounding of images—Germans bursting into a hospital operating room and machine gunning its occupants as "a warning," a Danish father killing his children so that they will not suffer in a concentration camp—makes the issues clear. These images serve as grim reminders that ***Lisa's War*** is not an adventure story with war as a backdrop but an account of events that irrevocably changed the lives of human beings.

Freda Kleinburd

SOURCE: A review of *Lisa's War,* in *The Five Owls,* Vol. III, No. 6, July-August, 1989, p. 93.

Less than a handful of novels for young people have dealt with Denmark's extraordinary rescue of the Danish Jews during World War II. ***Lisa's War,*** which the author has based on eyewitness testimony, is a suspenseful and thought-provoking addition to this group, especially as it is the only children's book to present this dramatic episode from the point of view of the endangered Jews rather than their Christian rescuers.

Lisa is twelve when the German army invades Denmark in 1940. Although the Nazis place no immediate restrictions on the Jews, Lisa and her family live in constant fear, as they know about the persecutions of the Jews in other Nazi-occupied countries. Longing to be involved in the growing Danish resistance movement, Lisa joins her brother Stefan in distributing anti-Nazi leaflets and, eventually, sabotage against the Germans. When the Nazis' plans to deport the Danish Jews are discovered on the eve of Rosh Hashanah in 1943, Lisa and her family join over 7,000 other Jews in escape to Sweden, aided by the exceptional combined effort of the resistance and almost the entire population of Denmark. (Of the 474 Jews captured during the roundup, most returned home to Denmark from the Theresienstadt ghetto in 1945, due to the unrelenting interest shown for their welfare throughout the war by the Danish government, which prevented their transfer to the death camps.)

The reader is immediately involved in the story through the first-person narration of the spunky and determined Lisa, who slowly discovers the depths of her courage as her involvement in the resistance grows and, ultimately, as she must shoot a German in order to protect the Jews during their harrowing escape to Sweden. Aside from the usual adolescent worries over physical appearance and first love, Lisa must also grapple with more unforeseen moral issues that imbue the narrative with poignancy and complexity: Should Lisa's father, a surgeon, continue to treat the very Germans who may eventually deport him, or should he break his oath to medicine and provide them with inferior care? Has Lisa's friend Susanne, whose parents have been killed by a German bomb, become debased by her desire for revenge at any price?

Although the publisher recommends ***Lisa's War*** for ages twelve and up, the novel's brevity and reading level make it accessible to a slightly younger audience. Even though the Nazi's grim plans for the Jews are clearly spelled out, and a few scenes of horror are briefly described (the machine-gunning of innocents in an operating room, the murder-suicide attempt of a young Jewish family afraid of capture), there is surely more violence than this depicted in other books about the Holocaust deemed appropriate for upper-elementary school readers. The title, cover art, and relatively large print do not indicate that this is a work for junior high readers, so it is to be hoped that this fine account of a relatively little known episode will find an appreciative audience.

ME, MYSELF AND I (1987)

Adele Ashby

SOURCE: A review of *Me, Myself and I,* in *Books for Young People,* Vol. 2, No. 1, February, 1988, p. 10.

In this, the third title in the Fifth Perception series, Rebecca is back from her time-travels to the year 2080 and a future world run by a big business called Zanu, but she has returned to present-day Winnipeg on the wrong day. Because it is three days earlier than it should have been, another Rebecca is still in her room studying, and the event that transported her to the future has not even happened yet.

Meanwhile, in another future in 2080, Jonathan keeps having bad dreams in which the same young girl appears again and again. With the help of Rebecca's new brother and sister, Jonathan's great-grandmother, and a time machine, Rebecca's two selves are reunited and Jonathan meets the girl of his dreams.

If this sounds confusing, it is (it's enough to send Rebecca's mother to bed with Tylenol), but reading the book's two predecessors, ***Fusion Factor*** and ***Zanu,*** helps. Matas only partially succeeds in lifting the book out of the realm of the superficial by introducing issues such as pollution, but the central issue of what constitutes identity is never really dealt with. And isn't there someone at Fifth House who knows how to spell Hans Christian Andersen's and Alan Garner's names? This is a time-trip for die-hard science-fiction fans only.

Nadiya Blaine

SOURCE: A review of *Me, Myself and I,* in *CM: A Reviewing Journal of Canadian Materials for Young People,* Vol. XVI, No. 4, July, 1988, p. 130.

Me, Myself and I is the third book in the "Fifth Perception" series. This science fiction series for young readers is different in that, apart from being exciting and entertaining, it encourages young people to consider how the present could affect the future.

Me, Myself and I is about Rebecca, who returned from the future a week earlier than when she left—and finds that there are now two of her. How she handles the situation and gets herself back together make an interesting story. Matas also offers several alternate looks into the future—from a violent world to a seemingly utopian one.

With adventure, time travel and surprise twists, this book and the series should catch the attention and interest of young readers. I strongly recommend this series for the elementary school library.

JESPER (1989; U.S. edition as *Code Name Kris,* 1990)

Linda Granfield

SOURCE: "A Boatload of Babies," in *Books in Canada,* Vol. 18, No. 9, December, 1989, pp. 19-23.

The pictures of the Second World War rendered by Wilson and Pearson seem fit for the nursery set when the reader encounters Carol Matas's ***Jesper.*** The opening lines deliver a punch: "I am to be executed. It will be soon. The Nazis are getting desperate, and as they get more desperate they get meaner." Within a few paragraphs describing the horrible tortures carried out in the prison, the reader learns that the speaker is a teenager. ***Jesper*** is a companion novel for Matas's award-winning ***Lisa;*** indeed, Lisa is recalled in this book as an influence in Jesper's life, his first love as well as his fellow soldier.

This story of the Danish resistance is compelling. The narration is swift, as Jesper moves back and forth between "then" (why he was arrested and what he did for the Resistance) and "now" (the time spent awaiting execution). This device would have been confusing in less skilled hands; Jesper's recounting of his story to keep his mind occupied while he painfully awaits the unknown is masterfully executed. Matas convincingly portrays the turmoil of adolescence: love, embarrassment, audacity, and fear are portrayed with vigour. Scenes continue to shock the reader out of a careless reading. How unfortunate, however, that the major confrontation scene between Jesper and his executioner suffers from a surfeit of coincidence. Matas spoiled her readers with earlier, better-shaped scenes. Still, one cannot deny the power and vigour of the subject matter and plot of this fine stylist.

Graham Caie

SOURCE: A review of *Jesper,* in *Canadian Children's Literature,* No. 59, 1990, pp. 85-7.

This work is a sequel to Carol Matas's ***Lisa*** which won the Geoffrey Bilson Prize for Historical Fiction for Young People in 1988. ***Lisa*** was about a Danish Jewish girl caught in occupied Denmark during the Second World War, along with her older brother Stefan and his friend Jesper. ***Jesper*** continues the story of young teenagers in the Danish underground movement after Lisa's and Stefan's departure. Jesper recalls early experiences with them in a series of flash-backs from his cell in Shell House, Copenhagen, where he is imprisoned by the Gestapo towards the end of the war. The 14-year-old boys begin with relatively simple acts of sabotage, such as making German trucks inoperative, and progresses to more dangerous assignments. Later Jesper becomes involved in an underground resistance newspaper and is closely attached to the young people producing and distributing it. On one occasion he is caught and nearly shot. While he is interrogated, he recognizes an old friend, Frederick, now a Nazi officer. Throughout the novel Jesper wishes to believe that Frederik is an undercover resistance agent posing as a Nazi.

The concluding chapters are particularly exciting: Stefan returns to Denmark on a special assignment in order to free a resistance leader. Stefan secures Jesper's aid in this dangerous rescue operation, which provides a fascinating conclusion to a really good teenage novel.

Carol Matas manages to convey an important historical lesson while telling an exciting story. She must be complimented for her meticulous research on the Danish resistance and her ability to convey the mood of the Danish people in these dark years, which provide much more than a backcloth to a thriller: it is an historically sound account of the Danish resistance. Many of the details she gives are well-known to all Danes and have become part of their national heritage, e.g., the king's daily rides throughout the city to encourage his people and how he informed the Germans that he and all his people would wear a star of David if the Jews were forced to do so. Likewise the tragedy of the accidental bombing by the Allies of the French School, the attack on Shellhuset, the bombs in Tivoli and the general strike are well known and give this historical novel greater credibility and depth.

The author manages to steer a course between glorifying the resistance and dwelling on the cruelties of the Gestapo. Just sufficient details of the torture are given (Jesper has his fingernails painfully removed) to suggest the greater persecution, while the fear and discomfort of the resistance members detracts from any romantic sense of heroism. Even today the topic is one of great sensitivity in countries like Denmark and Holland. At a period of the reunification of Germany and the unification of Europe some parents might ask about the value of keeping such bitter memories alive for yet another generation, but I believe that Carol Matas's objective and healthy treatment of the subject provides the most sensible approach for children today. It makes them aware that mankind is capable of such atrocities. In addition it keeps alive the memories of the brave resistance fighters of all ages who risked their lives to liberate their country.

The author also provides a subtle portrayal of her hero's development between 14 and 18 years old. He has to grow up very quickly, as he is soon separated from his parents, and we follow him through his teenage love for Lisa and later infatuation with Janicke, a colleague who is two years his senior. More confusing is his realization that even his hero, Frederik, has shifted his loyalty and betrayed him, so that everything becomes uncertain: "Ever since the Germans took over, that has been at the forefront of our lives—uncertainty. Nothing is sure. Nothing is safe. Is your neighbour a friend or an enemy? Before we could look our fellow Dane in the eye—now we don't know if we are looking at a friend or an enemy".

P. J. Hammel

SOURCE: A review of *Jesper,* in *CM: A Reviewing Journal of Canadian Materials for Young People,* Vol. XVIII, No. 3, May, 1990, p. 129.

Carol Matas's latest novel ***Jesper*** is the sequel to her earlier book ***Lisa,*** which won the Geoffrey Bilson Prize for Historical Fiction for Young People. Readers of ***Lisa*** will remember that, while fighting in the Danish resistance movement during World War II, she met and fell in love with another young resistance fighter named Jesper. This novel provides an exciting account of Jesper's activities fighting the Nazis after Lisa has escaped to Sweden.

Matas opens the story with Jesper in a German prison; repeated torturings have left him in constant pain as he awaits execution by his captors. In flashbacks, he reveals his adventures as a journalist and saboteur. On the eve of his execution, a daring RAF bombing raid signals not only the end of the German occupation of Denmark but also Jesper's liberation.

This is an unusual presentation. The story is one that early teens would enjoy. There are exciting action scenes, a love interest and even some rather mature curse words—all of interest to those who are beginning to feel the imminence of young adulthood. ***Jesper*** is unusual, however, in that the reading level, according to Frey's scale, measures out at the grade 4 level. This latter would seem to suggest that the story was written to serve as high interest/easy reading material for the low-achieving teenager.

Kirkus Reviews

SOURCE: A review of *Code Name Kris,* in *Kirkus Reviews,* Vol. LVIII, No. 20, October 15, 1990, p. 1458.

In a strong sequel to ***Lisa's War,*** Jesper continues his activities with the Danish resistance after Lisa and her brother Stefan depart in 1943 with the other Jewish refugees. Chiefly, he's involved in putting out an underground newspaper, and—especially after Stefan's eventual return—he also engages again in hair-raising acts of sabotage.

From its opening ("I am to be executed": Jesper has been caught and tortured by the Gestapo, and relates his adventures from prison), this is a gripping story that includes a fascinating range of resistance activities and coherently relates them to events in the war and the way Danish society evolved under the Nazis. While it doesn't offer new insights, the earlier story's themes are powerfully reiterated: in the end, Jesper recoils from the hate and violence the Nazis have elicited from him. And Matas skillfully holds attention by leaving the reader to wonder until the end whether Jesper will survive and by introducing a Danish member of the Gestapo who may or may not be a double agent. Fine historical fiction.

David A. Lindsey

SOURCE: A review of *Code Name Kris,* in *School Library Journal,* Vol. 36, No. 12, December, 1990, pp. 121-22.

This sequel to ***Lisa's War*** opens with 17-year-old Jesper in a cell awaiting execution at the hands of the Gestapo. Recalling the events that brought him there, he attempts to put it all "in order" to keep from despairing. As a result of helping his Jewish friends Lisa and Stefan escape to Sweden in 1943, he had gone underground in the Danish Resistance, bearing the code name "Kris" and becoming involved in clandestine newspaper operations and sabotage. Jesper/Kris relates how events brought his friend Stefan back to Denmark, and the anti-Nazi activities that led to the young men's capture. Matas, in sparse, understated, and somewhat dispassionate prose, effectively depicts what life was like in occupied Denmark and in the Danish Resistance. Without being didactic, she informs readers about the Resistance's organization, day-to-day activities, and special operations as well as the dangers and fears its members faced. All of this is woven into an easily read, interest-holding story of bravery, loyalty, and patriotism. The author doesn't stoop to unduly bashing the Germans and their collaborators but simply states what happened. The ending is perhaps a bit too pat, but this flaw is more than offset by Matas's storytelling and characterizations.

Ellen Fader

SOURCE: A review of *Code Name Kris,* in *The Horn Book Magazine,* Vol. LXVII, No. 1, January-February, 1991, pp. 74-5.

This novel continues the story of ***Lisa's War,*** which concluded with the escape of siblings Stefan and Lisa to Sweden to avoid a Nazi plan to round up Denmark's Jews in October 1943. In ***Code Name Kris,*** numerous first-person flashbacks from a prison cell tell seventeen-year-old Jesper's story of continued serious involvement with the Danish resistance movement. Because he is not Jewish, Jesper is able to remain in Denmark after his friends are smuggled out, but he finds he must go underground for fear of endangering his family's lives. From a series of safe houses, he participates in the production of an underground newspaper as well as in other acts of sabotage against the Germans. But Jesper, who had fallen in love with Lisa, feels torn because he is now attracted to one of his co-workers in the movement; he then discovers that his best friend, Stefan, who has returned to take on a special assignment, is also interested in Janicke. This is a grim and serious novel, not at all lightened by the romantic triangle: young people are given their own machine guns and training in how to use them; Jesper is tortured by having all his fingernails pulled out; people take frightening risks, and many of them are killed. Yet through it all runs the theme of the Danes' tremendous courage and the knowledge that one must stand up for what one believes to be right; that is why this novel, written, like its predecessor, after much research and consultation with Danish survivors, is so gripping and unforgettably exciting.

THE RACE (1991)

Anne Louise Mahoney

SOURCE: A review of *The Race,* in *Quill and Quire,* Vol. 57, No. 10, October, 1991, p. 35.

Fourteen-year-old Ali Green, a youth delegate at a Liberal leadership convention in Calgary where her mother is the frontrunner, has a lot of problems: a huge zit on her chin, a major lack of interest in politics, a crush on her mother's main opponent's 15-year-old son, Paul, and some inside information that could tarnish her mother's name later on down the road. But Ali's not the type to let things like that get her down, and by the end of the four-day convention she proves herself to be not only her mother's daughter, but her own person.

The Race, the latest novel from the talented Carol Matas, is fast-paced and exciting. While the author is careful not to overburden the reader with information about the Canadian political system, she does manage to inform as well as entertain. She fills the story with the energy, enthusiasm, and nail-biting anticipation found in a good leadership convention. With rumours and backroom deals flying across the convention floor, the reader has no idea who will win until the very end (but you can bet that Ali has something to do with it).

Ali is a truly likable character: her first-person narrative is full of humour and teenage angst, and brings a fresh perspective to politics and life in general. Her mother, while obviously a capable and intelligent lawyer and politician, does step out from behind the calm, professional image once in a while. And Paul, Ali's love interest, is a surprisingly sensitive and expressive guy. He makes a tough decision that could have serious personal repercussions, and is the better for it. While Matas manipulates the plot in a way that may strike adults as unrealistic, younger readers will warm to Ali and get swept up in the action-packed and quite unpredictable race.

Gordon Heasley

SOURCE: A review of *The Race,* in *CM: A Reviewing Journal of Canadian Materials for Young People,* Vol. XX, No. 3, May, 1992, p. 168.

Set at a Liberal leadership convention, ***The Race*** is an engaging young adult narrative that artfully combines the stories of a questioning adolescent and the elaborate political process of a leadership race.

Ali Green, the narrator, is a somewhat shy, maturing fourteen-year-old who has worked extremely hard to get herself elected as a junior delegate to the Liberal leadership convention in Calgary. Her mom is Rosaline Green, member of Parliament for Winnipeg South, a sincere, hard-working idealist running for party leader.

Beginning at 11:00 a.m., July 5, just as the wheels of the plane touch down on the runway, ***The Race*** begins a chronological movement through the five days of the convention. The dialogue and the energy of a well-written story hook our interest and maintain it.

The Calgary airport is a beehive of activity as volunteers direct delegates to various buses. Here Ali meets up with Paul James, son of her mom's main leadership opponent, by accidentally dropping a suitcase on his foot. The romantic plot begins as Ali and Paul fall for each other and begin a secretive and then much publicized relationship. Then, when Ali and Paul overhear Paul's dad take a political pay-off, things become even more complex.

The Race offers short descriptive passages explaining the whole process of the leadership struggle. The opposition party's role, for example, is to "criticize the government, point out their mistakes and suggest a better way of doing things." Even such issues as image creation, dirty play, media coverage and bias, and the importance of "winning Quebec" are discussed.

Ali's mom succeeds, as does Carol Matas's latest book. The mastery of ***The Race,*** however, should come as no surprise to anyone who has followed Matas's career.

Marie Campbell

SOURCE: A review of *The Race,* in *Canadian Children's Literature,* Vol. 20, No. 73, Spring, 1994, p. 79.

It's a clever structural device, and one that could have easily backfired in less-skilled hands. Carol Matas opens ***The Race,*** her compulsively readable story of fourteen-year-old Ali Green, as Ali's plane touches down in Calgary for the first day of a Liberal leadership convention. The novel wraps up, but for a brief epilogue, four days later as the convention concludes its business—having narrowly elected Ali's mother as leader. The action—and there's a lot of it—is fast-paced and compelling. Matas neatly capitalizes on the built-in tension and momentum of a high-powered competition for political power. She manages also to inform her readers, ever so casually and unobtrusively, about the intricacies of the Canadian political process. These details could have hijacked the narrative or overwhelmed Ali's character; they don't. ***The Race*** could have been yet another classroom lesson unimaginatively disguised as a novel; it isn't.

There is danger, too, in compressing a novel's action into a mere four days: characters can experience, learn, and mature only so much in a long weekend. Matas does not sacrifice verisimilitude, however, or falter in her dead-on treatment of fourteen-year-old concerns (how to deal with a "zit" that "will soon rival the Rockies in size;" how to remain cool while falling in love for the first time). Ali comes to a few new realizations in the course of the novel, but not unconvincingly: she may find politics a little more interesting by the end of the novel, but not nearly so involving as the son of her mother's chief rival.

Ali's one moment of rapid, painful maturation comes as she realizes, sadly, that "[e]verything used to seem so clear, so black and white. It doesn't anymore." Matas creates a world shaped largely by wealth and influence, and she is relentless in her treatment of the news media: "This is something I'm learning about the media," Ali says. "They can really slant a story the way they want." While this could be little more than a dose of political cynicism, 1990s style, Matas is careful to provide her audience with a means of defense: read critically and carefully. (This applies even to her own text. Ali's first-person narrative, with its characteristically teenage naïvete

and self-absorption, is as unreliable as any journalist's report.) And although Ali comes to understand that life really is about making choices—the central event of the novel forces her to wrestle with some pretty complex ethical issues—Matas highlights the empowering edge of that weighty responsibility: individuals *have* choices. That means that individuals, even fourteen-year-old girls who are slightly insecure, can make a difference. And that they should.

ADVENTURE IN LEGOLAND (1992)

Lorrie Ann Clark

SOURCE: A review of *Adventure in Legoland,* in *CM: A Reviewing Journal of Canadian Materials for Young People,* Vol. XX, No. 4, September, 1992, p. 204.

Most of the characters in this story are stiff, plastic and artificial. However, this is not a complaint about the book, as most of the characters are made of Lego pieces and have trouble with mobility.

Adventure in Legoland involves a little boy named Aaron, who is summoned one night to return to Legoland, where he and his family had just spent the day visiting. His mission is to save the prince of the Lego castle, who has been kidnapped by a bad piece of lego named Bad Bart.

There is apparently a real Legoland in Copenhagen, Denmark. The author uses this setting to spin her story. After I read this story to a class, we were all anxious to visit this particular spot.

Carol Matas writes a good tale and, with the right combination of a real-life setting, drama, suspense and interesting characters, she is able to keep the attention of her readers. Her main character, Aaron, is very well developed. He is an active, loud, bright little boy I am sure several young readers could relate to.

I recommend this story for young readers, as it will keep them anxious to find out what is going to happen in each new chapter. The illustrations [by Mark Teague] sprinkled throughout add to the imagination and enhance the story.

DANIEL'S STORY (1993)

Kenneth Oppel

SOURCE: A review of *Daniel's Story,* in *Quill and Quire,* Vol. 59, No. 2, February, 1993, p. 35.

Published in conjunction with the United States Holocaust Memorial Museum, ***Daniel's Story*** is the harrowing account of a Jewish teenager's struggle to survive Nazi persecution, culminating in his enslavement in Auschwitz and Buchenwald. Daniel's family has lived in Germany for centuries, but once Hitler is appointed Chancellor in 1933, all Jews are instantly demoted to second-class citizens and quickly stripped of their civil rights.

Carol Matas, as always, shows a deft hand with historical material, skillfully depicting the horrific acceleration of Jewish persecution, the events filtered through the eyes and voice of her young protagonist. Matas is also adept at showing how even Daniel's ill-timed childhood enjoys its moments of joy and normalcy—a testament both to the human spirit and to the resilience of the Jewish community. But following the outbreak of World War II, Daniel and his family are deported to the Jewish ghetto in Lodz, Poland, and are put to work for the Nazi war effort; those too weak to work are taken away in trucks. After the D-Day landings in 1944, the Jews are shipped like cattle to Auschwitz. Only Daniel and his father survive to be transported to Buchenwald, which is shortly liberated by the Allies.

The historical material itself is so powerful here that it['s] impossible not to become intensely emotionally involve[d]; it would be difficult to invent antagonists more villai[n]ous than the Nazis, or develop a situation with great[er] dramatic tension than a boy's struggle to survive in [a] concentration camp. All this could have easily swamp[ed] the characters but, to Matas's credit, we never lose sig[ht] of Daniel as an authentic teenager even as, increasing[ly] (and understandably), his survival instinct dominates [his] character. Daniel, apparently a composite of real chi[ld]ren who endured the Holocaust, does assume allegori[cal] status in the novel, but the human voice of a child [is] always there. Despite a rather self-conscious openi[ng,] ***Daniel's Story*** is never less than gripping. It is a bo[ok] all children should read.

Betsy Hearne

SOURCE: A review of *Daniel's Story,* in *Bulletin of [the] Center for Children's Books,* Vol. 46, No. 9, M[ay,] 1993, p. 289.

Published in conjunction with the U.S. Holocaust M[e]morial Museum, this is based on scenes from an exh[ibit] about a boy who serves as a "carefully researched co[m]posite of the many children who lived through the H[o]locaust." Unlike Matas' involving portrayals in ***Lis[a's] War*** and ***Code Name Kris,*** the novel never seems [to] take on a fictional life of its own but remains almos[t a] descriptive explanation of Jewish suffering at the ha[nds] of the Nazis. The distance is partially due to the dev[ice] of Daniel's rumination over photographs, stressing lo[ng] passages of narrative over action ("But how differen[t] be running from one warm house to another than to [be] trapped day and night in an unheated school when [the] temperature is twenty-five degrees and people are s[uf]fering from frostbite and malnutrition"). Daniel's re[la]tionship with a first love is interrupted by exposit[ory] comments ("By the time the ghetto was sealed off fr[om] the rest of the world, in April 1940, there were 160,

people there. By 1943 there were around 80,000 of us left, the rest having died or been sent away in one of the many transports"). Even dramatic moments are vague; when Daniel steps off the train at Auschwitz, we learn that "many in the car are dead" but not how or why. Dialogue often seems contrived: "'It was all that nettle soup they fed us,' I answer. 'Little did they realize that it was just chock-full of vitamins and minerals and everything.'" The book is unarguably well-informed and well-intentioned, and reading it will certainly add to the impact of attending the museum exhibit; but it's paradoxically true that particular individuals' stories such as Leitner's ***The Big Lie*** convey a more universally effective sense of experience than generalized situations such as this one.

Kay Weisman

SOURCE: A review of *Daniel's Story,* in *Booklist,* Vol. 89, No. 18, May 15, 1993, p. 1688.

In this book created as a companion piece to "Daniel's Story: Remember the Children," an exhibit at the new U.S. Holocaust Memorial Museum, Matas's fictional hero becomes an archetypal figure symbolizing the millions of young people who suffered and died under Adolph Hitler's regime. As Daniel views a collection of photographs representing his life, he remembers his happy childhood in Frankfurt before the rise of anti-Semitism; his family's deportation to the Lodz ghetto; the horrors of his imprisonment at Auschwitz, Bergen-Belsen, and Buchenwald; and his eventual liberation in 1945. Matas's technique—flashbacks based on pictures from the exhibit that are described but never shown—is interesting but not entirely successful. Though Daniel emerges as a convincing narrator, and readers will be able to visualize the photos, the narrative vehicle distances readers from the intensity of the topic, and only rarely will they be able to lose themselves in the story. Despite this flaw, the story is an important one that will appeal to young readers and be useful as part of Holocaust teaching units.

Pat Barclay

SOURCE: "Roads to Maturity," in *Books in Canada,* Vol. 22, No. 7, October, 1993, pp. 57-8.

Teenaged angst pales beside the challenges faced by 14-year-old Daniel of Frankfurt, Germany, however. The year is 1941; Hitler is in power and is deporting Jews to Poland. By 1944, Daniel's mother and sister are presumed dead and he and his father are imprisoned in Auschwitz, where they experience unforgettable horrors. ***Daniel's Story,*** by Carol Matas, was written to coincide with an exhibit at the United States Holocaust Memorial Museum in Washington, D.C. Although Daniel is a fictional character, his story unsparingly recreates, for a new generation, the dreadful realities of Nazi Germany.

> If we forget, we will once again be defenseless against evil. If we forget how bestial, how brutal . . . clean, upstanding citizens became, if we forget, then we too could become that way.

Matas has Daniel say, in justification of a book that could give some of its young readers nightmares. This is strong medicine, to be taken with caution.

SWORN ENEMIES (1993)

Ilene Cooper

SOURCE: A review of *Sworn Enemies,* in *Booklist,* Vol. 89, No. 11, February 1, 1993, p. 977.

The enemies in Matas's story, set in czarist Russia, are Aaron, a young Jewish scholar, and Zev, a *Khapper,* hired to kidnap his fellow Jews to fulfill military quotas. Told alternately from the perspectives of Aaron and Zev, this describes the hardships that Jews suffered once they were conscripted into the army—one goal was to have them convert—as well as the antipathy the young men have toward one another. Zev kidnaps Aaron because he is so jealous of Aaron's life and especially of the young woman to whom Aaron is betrothed, but a twist of fate finds Zev ordered into the army, too, where he must come face to face with the young man he has tried to destroy. For his part, Aaron, the pious Jew, has to deal with the murderous rage he feels toward Zev. Although philosophical questions are posed—Where is God? and What does he require of us?—they get lost in the action. Too bad, because the book obviously aims to be provocative. Still, there's plenty here to interest readers, especially those with a taste for the historical or the psychological.

Betsy Hearne

SOURCE: A review of *Sworn Enemies,* in *Bulletin of the Center for Children's Books,* Vol. 46, No. 8, April, 1993, p. 258.

It's a sign of fine writing when a historical novel asserts the impact of here-and-now fiction, and Matas has achieved just such an effect with this alternating first-person narrative of two sworn enemies in nineteenth-century Russia. Aaron is an upright, gifted Yeshiva student whose father has paid to keep him out of the army, but Zev, jealous of Aaron's betrothal to a girl they both love, has him kidnapped to fill the Czar's military quota. Then Zev himself is snared by recruiters, and the two end up on a forced march that nearly kills them both. The brutal anti-Semitism is only a background here for the moral dilemmas more fully developed through portrayals of each character's inner conflicts. Ultimately, a hero and a villain do emerge, but their motivations and ambiguities—all revealed through urgently paced action—seem as important as the choices they have made. It's unusual to have religious issues

explored without thematic didacticism. This is the kind of book that will challenge readers to wonder what they would have done under the circumstances; their absorption of historical information in vivid detail is a valuable bonus.

J. R. Wytenbroek

SOURCE: A review of *Sworn Enemies,* in *Canadian Children's Literature,* Vol. 20, No. 75, Fall, 1994, pp. 70-1.

An historical novel for young adults, Carol Matas's newest book, ***Sworn Enemies,*** is a glimpse into the life of the Jews under Czarist repression in the early nineteenth century. Telling the tale alternatively are Aaron, privileged scholarly son of a wealthy Jew, and Zev, embittered child of a poor family, who makes extra money by kidnapping other Jewish boys for the Czar's army. Zev's hatred for Aaron creates the plot as well as fuelling the characters in a manner that creates coherence and consistency throughout the novel, somewhat coincidental though the plot may seem at times. However, the very differences between the boys sets up a black-and-white counterpoint that weakens the novel.

Aaron is a young but already respected scholar, betrothed to the beautiful Miriam, with whom he is fortunately also in love. He is even exempt from army service because his comparatively wealthy father can pay the bribes necessary to keep him free. Yet after he is kidnapped by Zev and impressed into the Czar's army, Aaron goes through his own soul-searching, as he learns to eat non-kosher foods and even externally converts to Christianity to survive. However, despite his change of lifestyle, his new experiences and his new doubts, Aaron remains a basically admirable character. He is admittedly bitter against Zev, and certainly desires revenge against him, but he never takes that revenge. His doubts and soul-searching have mainly to do with his faith. While these doubts add interest to the story, they are not likely to really engage the modern reader who may know very little about Jewish beliefs.

Zev is utterly despicable from beginning to end, from his desire and play for Miriam *after* he has kidnapped Aaron, to his repeated refusal to face what he has done, constantly condoning his increasingly repulsive behaviour with an assurance that God would want him to act this way. While unfortunately realistic, Zev is so utterly unlikable that he, like Aaron, is unlikely to engage the reader.

The themes in the novel are interesting. Matas asks questions about good and evil, including why bad things happen to the innocent or fundamentally good. However, overall this novel does not work because the characters are too black-and-white, too unambiguous. Further, the horrific details of the ugly army-life for Jewish boys in Russia in the 1800s are gruesome and although linked to the theme of racial discrimination, seem a little excessive. Matas has taken potentially powerful material here and written a competent history but not a compelling novel.

SAFARI ADVENTURE IN LEGOLAND (1993)

Fred Boer

SOURCE: A review of *Safari Adventure in Legoland,* in *Quill and Quire,* Vol. 59, No. 10, October, 1993, p. 43.

This sequel to ***Adventure in Legoland*** returns to Denmark's Legoland amusement park, and once again features Aaron Samuel answering a call for help from his tiny fairy friend, Prince Aryeh. This time, the prince has lost a valuable trophy in the middle of the dangerous "Safari Park," where life-sized Lego animals come alive after dark. He needs the help of Aaron and a Lego hunter named Safari Bill to recover the trophy—in a hurry. Although the connection with the Lego Amusement Park and frequent references to Lego Blocks make this book sometimes seem like an advertisement, beginning readers will find it entertaining. The plot of ***Safari Adventure in Legoland*** is more straightforward and exciting than that of the earlier book, and it occasionally generates some real suspense.

Jennifer Johnson

SOURCE: A review of *Safari Adventure in Legoland,* in *CM: A Reviewing Journal of Canadian Materials for Young People,* Vol. XXII, No. 3, May-June, 1994, p. 76.

Adventure in Legoland introduced Aaron, on holidays from his home in Winnipeg. Answering a call for help, the eight-year-old set off to rescue Prince Aryeh. Shrunk to Lego size by a magic formula, Aaron proceeded into the exhibits.

In ***Safari Adventure in Legoland,*** Carol Matas continues her exploration of this amusement area by taking Aaron and Aryeh into the Safari Park. This time the two boys work together to recover a lost trophy in the midst of animals both life-size and alive. They are joined by Safari Bill, who has to be restrained from offering his well-meant but dubious help, and successfully negotiate the return of the prize by enacting an old trick on a troop of monkeys.

Matas has shown her strong writing skills and ability to create sympathetic characters in her young adult novels. In her Legoland novels she illustrates that her writing and emotional range is wide. She creates a world of undeniable appeal for her younger readership in choosing a well-loved toy as a basis for both setting and action. The exotica of the fairy palace, rodeo villains and jungle animals, and the appeal of being able to play in rather than with Legos make the setting eminently attractive. The boys' stresses with parents and their need to gain independence are well realized.

Matas necessarily writes a very spare plot. The addition of Safari Bill is a distraction here, and, while he adds an element of humour, readers may want to just get on with the story.

On the whole, Matas has created an accessible, exciting tale with strong appeal to younger fiction readers and for older students who are not fluent readers but who are being asked to make the move into chapter books.

THE LOST LOCKET (1994)

Marie Campbell

SOURCE: A review of *The Lost Locket,* in *Quill and Quire,* Vol. 60, No. 2, February, 1994, p. 39.

Designed to turn browsers into buyers, promotional blurbs on book jackets should hide every weakness and hype every strength. What they shouldn't do is give away more than half of the book's plot. From the title of ***The Lost Locket,*** we ascertain that eight-year-old Roz *does* misplace her prized heirloom, although that doesn't actually happen until the end of Chapter One. But from the back-cover buzz, we also learn which of Roz's classmates took it. Why give away the first 38 pages of what is only an 80-page book?

Because there really isn't much else that happens in this slim-plotted story, Scholastic's Shooting Star series, designed with short chapters and large type for early readers, occupies a middle range that is difficult to work—how to be simple but not simplistic? Despite her obvious talents, Matas doesn't succeed brilliantly here.

Without the camouflaging effects of a suspenseful plot, the "lessons" Roz learns in the course of recovering her locket overwhelm the narrative. Roz's world is realistically drawn—mistrust and violence play their roles—but there is, apparently, a catch-all solution. "You just need more confidence," her mother says. That, and a good karate flip, allow Roz to confront Curtis, the class bully, and demand her locket's return.

Yet however pat the resolution to Roz's life problems may seem, to Matas's credit, she has once again created convincing child characters. She is particularly good at developing relationships between children and at acknowledging the rigid schoolyard rules by which they live: it is equally understood that Roz must neither snitch on Curtis nor wear her embarrassing hood at recess.

Dinah Gough

SOURCE: A review of *The Lost Locket,* in *Canadian Children's Literature,* Vol. 23, No. 86, Summer, 1997, p. 57.

Against her mother's wishes, Matas's Roz wears an heirloom locket to school where it is promptly stolen by the school bully, leaving Roz to figure out how to retrieve it before she gets into trouble at home. Language is competently used and dialogue is believable. Interesting new words (conundrum, ogle, flabbergasted) are blended in. The story moves forward crisply. Family dynamics are well drawn; readers will easily identify with Roz's resentment of her parents' indulgence of her younger brother, her distress at having to follow through with the karate lessons she begged for but now dreads, and her efforts to conceal her disobedience in order to avoid punishment. Less believable is the ultimate confrontation at which Roz suddenly masters her elusive karate skills and vanquishes the bully.

THE BURNING TIME (1994)

Publishers Weekly

SOURCE: A review of *The Burning Time,* in *Publishers Weekly,* Vol. 241, No. 42, October 17, 1994, p. 82.

"'I dreamed a fire consumed us all!' Mine. Trembley shook her gnarled finger at us and screamed." Such are the portentous opening lines of this feverish novel about a witch hunt in 16th-century France. Through no fault of her own, Rose Rives's mother has earned the enmity of many neighbors: the doctor bitterly resents her midwifery skills, which far surpass his own; the priest hates her for spurning his sexual advances; her late husband's brothers want control over her land; jealous wives accuse her of bewitching their husbands. When a judge arrives in town demanding the names of witches, Mama's is among the first submitted. As she did in ***Daniel's Story,*** Matas insists on casting her protagonist in every scene, and she seeks out the extreme: Rose watches the vicious torture of her mother, eavesdrops on the judge's deliberations with the lewd priest, sneaks in and out of her mother's jail cell. The overweening injustice of it all may grab YA audiences; however, Matas limits her impact with her inability to convey historical drama through any but the crudest filters.

Kirkus Reviews

SOURCE: A review of *The Burning Time,* in *Kirkus Reviews,* Vol. LXII, No. 22, November 15, 1994, p. 1538.

Matas depicts the persecution of women accused of witchcraft in a 16th-century French village. When a witch-hunter with full power to condemn arrives, Rose's mother, Suzanne, is the first suspect. She's a healer who has earned the local doctor's enmity by saving the countess in childbirth. Rose's father, whose mercantile prosperity has aroused his peasant neighbors' envy, has just died in a fall from a horse and his pretty, independent widow has rejected sexual overtures from both her brother-in-law, who covets her inheritance, and the parish priest.

After Suzanne is imprisoned, Rose (with the help of a friend at the castle) secretly visits her cell. Forced to hide in another room before she can leave, she witnesses Suzanne's torture and confession; later, accused herself, Rose returns with a suicide potion for her doomed mother, then escapes.

The historical injustice resonates, but Matas's earnest dramatization is sabotaged by an excess of unlikely contrivances; and though her details are plausible, there are too few particulars to make the milieu more than generically medieval, while the focus on Suzanne's torment borders on sensationalism.

Betsy Hearne

SOURCE: A review of *The Burning Time,* in *Bulletin of the Center for Children's Books,* Vol. 48, No. 4, December, 1994, p. 139.

Seizing dramatic moments in history is Matas's specialty, and here the experience of a sixteenth-century French girl whose mother is accused of witchcraft becomes almost an adventure tale. There's little subtlety or ambiguity about the characters, but readers will be compelled by the action, which includes harrowing scenes of Rose's witnessing her mother's torture and then administering a fatal potion to save her from further pain. Through historical documentation and fictionalization, the dynamics of witch hunting have become well known, and this story is a model of the social conflicts classic to such situations. The first-person narrative is accessible and easier to read than more substantial novels we've seen on New England's victims (*The Witch of Blackbird Pond, Tituba of Salem Village*), while the protagonist's romance and escape will draw kids who are reluctant to read.

Marie Campbell

SOURCE: A review of *The Burning Time,* in *Quill and Quire,* Vol. 61, No. 2, February, 1995, p. 37.

The Burning Time is haunted by laughter, but it's not of the mirthful kind. There's the laugh that escapes the lips of Madame Rives, newly widowed, after she rejects the sexual advances of the powerful local priest. There's the laugh of adolescent narrator Rose Rives when, following her father's death, an oafish hired man crudely proposes marriage and offers his "protection." These near-hysterical outbursts betray that Rose and her mother, on their own in a 16th-century French village, are living on the edge of their nerves. They also plunge both mother and daughter, who dare to mock male authority, into mortal danger when the village is gripped by witch-hunt fever.

In the hands of award-winning Winnipeg writer Carol Matas, historical fiction is an uncompromising and painfully vivid thing. ***Lisa*** and ***Daniel's Story*** were set against the Holocaust; ***Sworn Enemies*** witnessed Jewish boys brutally converted to Christianity in 1827 Russia. ***The Burning Time*** visits Europe at a time when any woman—especially a gifted healer and midwife like Madame Rives—could be accused of witchery and be burned at the stake.

It is a story entirely ripe for telling in our day, and Matas is unflinching in her handling of this explosive historical material. Rose comes to some harsh realizations—her mother's death, she concludes, is punishment for no other crime than that of being a woman—but the tone and action of the novel are skillfully balanced. Rose suffers the abuses of power, but she is also able to survive and to effect tentative change in her community. The way Matas tells it, there's empowerment as well as sadness to be taken from history. In fact, with her quicksilver dialogue and breathless pacing, the way Matas tells it is the way historical fiction should be told.

OF TWO MINDS (with Perry Nodelman, 1994)

Pat Barclay

SOURCE: "Inspired Lessons," in *Books in Canada,* Vol. 23, No. 9, December, 1994, p. 57.

Of Two Minds, by Carol Matas and Perry Nodelman, is ostensibly a rollicking fantasy about a princess who can make real whatever she imagines and a prince who can read any mind. About to be married, they are diverted instead into a world ruled by a benevolent dictator who condemns whole races of beings (elves, trolls, fairies, etc.) to invisibility. Though relentlessly sprightly and flippant in tone, ***Of Two Minds*** is actually an allegory about democracy vs. dictatorship and what happens when a people gives too much power to its leader. The message that a dictator lives in each of us also comes through loud and clear.

Joanne Findon

SOURCE: A review of *Of Two Minds,* in *Quill and Quire,* Vol. 60, No. 12, December, 1994, p. 33.

The arranged marriage between Lenora, the stubborn young princess of Gepeth, and the shy and clumsy Prince Coren of Andilla seems doomed from the start. Lenora's ability to turn her imaginative musings into reality is constantly getting her into trouble, while Coren shuns his own inherited talent for reading other people's minds, hoping for a dull, stable life. Yet Coren is drawn to Lenora in spite of himself, and he agrees to the wedding. Just as Coren and Lenora are about to exchange vows before the Keeper of the Balance, however, they are sucked out of their own world and into that of the alluring despot Hevak, whose ability to erase individual will gives him frightening power over his adoring followers. Only by combining their innate powers can Lenora and Coren escape Hevak's control.

Of Two Minds is an appealing secondary-world fantasy that grabs the reader's attention and never lets it go. The story of a shy boy and a willful girl whose mutual loathing turns to love is nothing new, but Carol Matas and Perry Nodelman revitalize this familiar narrative type through the use of off-kilter plot twists and a liberal dose of humour. The alternating perspectives of the two characters allow for the sympathetic portrayal of both. (The two dovetail nicely, as do the writing styles of Matas and Nodelman, whose unusual dual authorship of this book is surprisingly successful.) And the unexpected climax, as Lenora and Coren discover who Hevak *really* is and what his world represents, adds a layer of deeper meaning to the story.

Of Two Minds will not revolutionize the genre of young-adult fantasy, but it certainly is a ripping yarn that will keep readers turning the pages.

Kirkus Reviews

SOURCE: A review of *Of Two Minds,* in *Kirkus Reviews,* Vol. LXIII, No. 18, September 15, 1995, p. 1354.

A strong joint effort by Matas and Nodelman. Headstrong, independent Lenora is endowed with the gift of giving life to her imaginings, but somehow she is unable to imagine away her arranged marriage to staid mind-reader Coren. When she spies a fantasy land beckoning to her on her wedding day, she recklessly jumps in—unaware that Coren is right behind her. The two end up without their powers in a brave new world ruled over by the charismatic (and devastatingly handsome) Hevak. At first Lenora seems perfectly content with the loss of her powers—more than made up for by Hevak's attentions—but when she finally asserts herself, Hevak has her thrown into the dungeons, where she is reunited with Coren. Together, Lenora and Coren destroy Hevak—whose true identity provides a neat twist—and return to their own world where they decide to postpone the wedding and just date. The collaboration offers no added dimension to the book; the authors' voices meld coherently and well. The result is a solid fantasy about thinking for oneself, thinking other people's thoughts, and the power of imagination.

Lisa Denis

SOURCE: A review of *Of Two Minds,* in *School Library Journal,* Vol. 41, No. 10, October, 1995, p. 136.

This collaboration begins with elements borrowed from traditional fairy tales, then offers an original, unpredictable twist; fresh, well-rounded characters; and an ambiguous, thought-provoking ending. The complex plot follows the adventures of Lenora, a headstrong princess with the power to make anything she imagines real, and Coren, the shy prince chosen by her parents to be her husband. Trapped in a strange land and stripped of their powers (Coren had been able to read the thoughts not only of humans, but also of animals and objects), the two must work together to overthrow the tyrannical Hevak, restore harmony to the country, and return home safely. Their triumph is particularly impressive and meaningful because it involves learning self-mastery (Lenora) and self-confidence (Coren) rather than simply overcoming an outside challenge through brute force. That the happy ending comes with no guarantees (and no imminent wedding bells) makes it even more believable and satisfying. The story moves swiftly and the writing is consistently smooth, with sophisticated vocabulary and challenging concepts. Matas and Nodelman have themselves done a heroic job of melding their two voices to create a kaleidoscope of character, cultures, and events that offers both entertainment and enrichment to young readers.

Lynne McKechnie

SOURCE: A review of *Of Two Minds,* in *Canadian Children's Literature,* Vol. 23, No. 86, Summer, 1997, p. 82.

Carol Matas and Perry Nodelman are well-established, award-winning authors whose experience and skill has undoubtedly contributed to meeting the challenges of joint authorship. ***Of Two Minds*** flows seamlessly and it has two equally strong protagonists. Princess Lenora of Gepeth can make things real simply by imagining them. Prince Corin of Andilla can read minds. Their parents, hoping to bring the two kingdoms closer together, arrange for their marriage. Just as Lenora and Corin are to exchange vows they are whisked away to a strange land ruled by a despot named Hevak whom they manage to overcome by working together. Lenora and Corin's supernatural powers, shared by all in their kingdoms, seem not as compelling as those which differentiate and accentuate Cora Taylor's Julie *(Julie)* or Janet Lunn's Mary *(Shadow in Hawthorn Bay)* within their families and communities. While ***Of Two Minds*** clearly communicates the dangers associated with the abuse of institutional and especially individual power, readers are likely to enjoy more the humour and adventure which pervade this light epic fantasy for young teens.

THE PRIMROSE PATH (1995)

J. R. Wytenbroek

SOURCE: A review of *The Primrose Path,* in *Quill and Quire,* Vol. 61, No. 11, November, 1995, p. 45.

In Carol Matas's new novel, ***The Primrose Path,*** the characterization of Debbie, the fourteen-year-old hero, is excellent. Early on, the reader comes to understand how her mind works, and gets caught up in the turmoil of her emotions. The story becomes completely riveting when Debbie moves to a new school and finds herself happily involved with a group of new girlfriends and their charismatic Rabbi. Her innocent crush on the handsome Rabbi turns to discomfort and then active fear as he takes advantage of his position of trust. Debbie's confusion and sense of betrayal are horribly real.

Matas handles a delicate subject in a very sensitive manner. Moreover, she does not oversimplify the problem. Debbie's friends withdraw from her as she makes public the Rabbi's betrayal of trust, and the Rabbi manipulates Debbie and the other girls into lying for him. This is echoed by the sub-plot in which the Rabbi seduces Debbie's mother and then subsequently denies it. In this way, the social and personal ramifications of exposing abuse are treated wisely but honestly.

Because Matas involves the reader with the primary characters so convincingly, the story is powerful. The only weakness lies in the first couple of chapters where the reader is launched a little too quickly into Debbie's woes before having a chance to get to know her. As well, the dialogue is stilted and laboured here. However, by the third chapter, both of these problems disappear and the novel rapidly becomes absorbing. Few authors can make history come alive for young people the way Matas has in other novels. In ***The Primrose Path,*** she proves that she can handle contemporary problems convincingly as well.

Resource Links

SOURCE: A review of *The Primrose Path*, in *Resource Links* Vol. 1, No. 4, April, 1996, p. 177.

This novel is informative and entertaining, in that order. Matas clearly has two strong didactic impulses in this story of a rabbi who uses his authority and charisma to molest teenage girls and seduce their mothers. She conveys a warning about good touching and bad touching and at the same time purveys a substantial quantity of information about different branches of Judaism.

When Debbie's grandmother dies, her family moves to eastern Canada. Her mother, searching for help in dealing with her own mother's death and with a troubled marriage, attaches herself to an Orthodox synagogue much to the family's surprise, and decides to send Debbie to the associated school. Debbie is horrified at first at the strictures of Orthodoxy, especially the attitude towards women. Soon, however, she makes friends with a group of girls who are the Rabbi's special pets. At first, Debbie takes his tickling and fooling around as signs of affection; her faith in him is reinforced by her mother who is completely under his spell. Her gradual unease eventually leads to a confrontation. Matas is careful not to tie up every loose end, but the change in Debbie's own family is achieved rather speedily and conveniently.

Surprisingly, the book manages to be moderately gripping despite its overload of earnest instruction. The plot, of course, has its own primal appeal: will enough people be prepared to step forward and testify against a leader beloved by his congregation? Specifically, will enough females tell their humiliating stories to a synagogue board which is nearly all male and very unsympathetic?

This book will undoubtedly appeal to many teenagers who will empathize with Debbie's conflicting emotions and probably learn a little bit about the Jewish faith along the way (though I wonder how members of that faith will respond to Matas's explanations). It would be a better story, however, if the author's didactic agendas were less obvious.

Olga Stein

SOURCE: A review of *The Primrose Path,* in *Books in Canada,* Vol. 25, No. 7, October, 1996, p. 30.

The Primrose Path is not a story about the usual afflictions of adolescence: crippling insecurity, alcohol or drug addiction, and sexual peer pressure. Debbie Mazer's life is marred by something far more disturbing and sinister, something that even the author of this book refrains from naming outright. I shall name it for her: it is sexual abuse and pedophilia. Admittedly, this is not something new. We are no longer shocked, or should I say surprised, by stories of sexual molestation of children. And yet I was shocked. Carol Matas has managed to be very original by creating a setting for this tale of sexual aberrance that is unlike any I have ever encountered. It is this context which lends the story the strength to keep its reader captive—repelled and at the same time fascinated. It is this same context that ultimately weakens the story and may alienate many readers from what is essentially a well-written and thoughtful book.

The Primrose Path is about a fourteen-year-old Jewish girl (beautifully brought to life by Carol Matas) who, along with her parents and baby brother, moves to a new city and finds herself unexpectedly part of a small Orthodox community. The founder, mover, and shaker of this community is Rabbi Werner. He is both the principal of the Orthodox school that his synagogue houses, and Debbie's teacher. He is also a practised sexual molester, who touches and strokes his students' bodies under pretext of tickling them and being otherwise physically demonstrative. Needless to say, this backdrop of Jewish Orthodoxy is what makes this story so different.

Carol Matas is unquestionably a very capable writer. Debbie Mazer is a living breathing adolescent whose preoccupations and concerns—about school, friends, and her parents' troubled marriage—elicit genuine empathy from the reader. Matas's writing is generally effective by virtue of its simplicity and directness. It is the premise of this book, not her skills as a writer, that I would like to take issue with.

Her objective is, I believe, to reinforce the message that

sexual abuse and molestation can happen in the most unexpected places; the perpetrator may be an accomplished and respected individual. Our refusal to believe that such a person is guilty can be almost as damaging to a child as the abuse itself. Stressing this point is certainly worthwhile. However, Matas's decision to use an Orthodox rabbi to convey her message has unfortunate ramifications. To a large extent this is due to the fact that Rabbi Werner is the focal point of Matas's Orthodox setting; and it is Werner who spearheads Debbie's and her mother's conversion to Orthodoxy. Another strong character representing Orthodoxy might have served Matas well by counter-acting some of the negative associations with Orthodoxy that Werner's centrality evokes.

Matas does attempt to demonstrate that Rabbi Werner's conduct is not an aspect of Orthodoxy. For example, the reader learns from one of the minor characters that physical contact between an Orthodox man and a girl over the age of three is not permitted. Similarly, Debbie's father insists that we are dealing here with "two different issues. Orthodoxy and the Rabbi. After all, Orthodox rabbis don't behave this way." I would argue, however, that Matas's efforts to protect the image of Orthodoxy do not go far enough. What we hear, when all is taken into account, are a few weak and scattered denials that simply do not amount to much in the face of the insidious and overwhelming ugliness of Werner's behaviour, his abnormal predilection for young girls, and his manipulativeness and hypocrisy. Moreover, Matas undermines her own effort to isolate Werner from both Orthodoxy and Judaism in general, by allowing Debbie's mother (who is also victimized by Werner) to lose all interest in observance. "Mom won't set foot in any synagogue," Debbie Mazer tells us. In other words, however faulty her logic, Debbie's mother has made a connection between religion and Werner's reprehensible conduct, a connection that Matas should not have allowed her to make. Everything she has learned about Orthodox Judaism—rules relating to the observance of the Sabbath, the kosher preparation of food, etc. (there is truly so much beauty and wisdom in Judaism)—loses its appeal (and, perhaps, its validity) because it was Werner who instructed her. This is what I find so objectionable about this book. By assigning Rabbi Werner the dual role of charismatic mentor (the source of this newly acquired knowledge about Judaism) and despicable villain, Matas has unwittingly permitted Orthodoxy to sustain considerable damage.

Debbie's aunt's assertion that Rabbi Werner's congregation is a cult supports this conclusion. This is an interesting statement, one that may prompt the reader to wonder whether there is any real difference between a cult and a congregation whose members are governed by a strict set of rules that have a far-reaching effect on their everyday lives. Here I would like to say that any religious congregation distinguishes itself from a cult by virtue of the voluntary nature of its members' association. Rabbis have traditionally assumed the role of teachers and counsellors, when it was asked of them, but their role in Jewish communities, though a highly respected one, has been of a limited nature.

I am acquainted with a Lubaviche (Orthodox) rabbi who never forgets a face or the name of its owner. He is also one of the most tolerant people I know. Whenever we meet he asks good-naturedly when my family and I will at last move to the vicinity of a Lubaviche school so that my children can attend it. I am certain he realizes that this might never happen, but the question itself (and his manner of asking) is a gentle effort to give us direction; by no means does it constitute coercion or any other attempt at bullying. As for Carol Matas's book, the premise—a rabbi who can't keep his hands off young girls, and who gets away with it in public—strikes me as highly improbable. I have never seen an Orthodox man touch a woman other than his wife; rules forbidding such contact are very strict and are strictly observed. Can I say with absolute certainty that what Matas describes in her book is impossible? I cannot, and that may be the exact point Matas is trying to make.

AFTER THE WAR (1996)

Betsy Hearne

SOURCE: A review of *After the War,* in *Bulletin of the Center for Children's Books,* Vol. 49, No. 8, April, 1996, pp. 271-72.

The author of several other novels set during World War II, Matas casts this docudrama into the form of a story related by Ruth Mendenberg, a fifteen-year-old survivor of the Ostroviec ghetto, Auschwitz, Buchenwald, and post-war Polish anti-Semitic pogroms. Italicized flashbacks give us a glimpse of her horrific memories as she joins a Zionist group that makes its way across dangerous borders, with the goal of illegal entry into Israel. Although their ship is attacked by the British and Ruth is taken to a refugee camp in Cyprus along with her companions, she does find one of her brothers (nearly eighty members of her family are dead) and escapes with her boyfriend to the promised land. The action is fast paced and the history well researched, but too much information has been loaded onto the dialogue and first-person narrative. In addition to having an unbelievably broad perspective on the European/Middle Eastern political panorama ("Betar is aligned with the Irgun in Palestine, a militant group which launches attacks on the British to try to help them decide to leave Palestine"), Ruth has a self-conscious flippancy ("Of course, I can't swim, they don't give lessons in concentration camps") that seems to belong more to a 1990s suburban middle-schooler than to a 1940s victim of the Holocaust. What's realized well is not the traumatic experiences themselves—which seem almostgenerically packed into stories within a story here—but the day today anxiety of loners trying to connect with each other; despite the expository tone, Matas's re-creation of life on the run acquires some authentic urgency.

Hazel Rochman

SOURCE: A review of *After the War,* in *Booklist,* Vol. 92, No. 15, April 1, 1996, p. 1361.

Matas's docunovel is about young Jews trying to reach Palestine after the war. The story is told in the present tense by 15-year-old Ruth, who returns, alone, from Buchenwald in 1945. In the first scene she tries to go back to her home in Poland, but she is chased off by the people who have taken her house. She joins an underground organization and helps lead a group of children with false documents on a dangerous journey across Europe and then on a boat that tries to evade the British blockade of Palestine. Woven into the action are stark vignettes of what Ruth is trying to forget and of what the children tell her—of ghettos, roundups, transports, camps, massacre. A teenage boy crawled out alive from a mass grave; an eight-year-old cared for his infant brother in the forest; Ruth last saw her mother and sister marched off to the gas chamber in Auschwitz, where "a red glow from the furnaces covered everything." The young people remember, and they argue about God, about Zionism, about guilt.

It's unrealistic that Ruth and even the young children should be so articulate about their feelings. ("I'm sick of this numbness, but I know it's too dangerous to wake up.") And as Ruth begins to allow herself to feel again, there's not only adventure but also romance with a brave, good, perfect young leader. However, the historical incidents are true, and Matas has retold them and shaped them into a tightly edited drama far from the rambling and repetition of authentic oral history. The climactic scene in which Ruth finds the brother she feared was dead—hears his voice, then finds him on the deck of the ship, and touches his face while the hushed crowd watches—is something you want to read over and over again; it is a miracle.

Robyn Nicoline Ryan

SOURCE: A review of *After the War,* in *School Library Journal,* Vol. 42, No. 5, May, 1996, p. 135.

Matas's historical novel shows that the persecution of Europe's Jewish population did not end with their liberation from the Nazi death camps. She tells the story of Ruth, 15, who makes her way back from Buchenwald to her Polish homeland to discover that Jews are still viewed by others with suspicion and hatred. Desperate and alone, she meets Saul, who persuades her to join a group of refugees planning to emigrate to Palestine. Historically, the book is accurate and references to actual events are interwoven neatly into the narrative. The author does oversimplify the position of the British and their decision to stop Jewish immigration to Palestine, and this is a definite weakness. Nonetheless, the story is strong and compelling and the use of descriptive language creates a mood of desperation and hope combined with a commitment to survival. The use of flashbacks is effective and serves to sustain the mood as well as add depth to Ruth's character. ***After the War*** is a thought-provoking novel that offers great insight into the current problems in the Middle East and the passion with which the Jewish people will fight to protect what they perceive to be rightfully theirs.

Teresa Toten

SOURCE: A review of *After the War,* in *Quill and Quire,* Vol. 62, No. 10, October, 1996, p. 49.

Weary and broken, 15-year-old Ruth Mendenberg struggles back to her family home in Poland. Though she's somehow survived Buchenwald concentration camp, Ruth fears that most of her family was slaughtered at Auschwitz. Still, she dares hope. A contemptuous former maid greets her at the door: "I thought you were all dead. Didn't the gas ovens finish you all off?" And the door slams shut.

Winnipeg author Carol Matas is an accomplished writer of fictional history. ***After the War*** is exhaustively researched and cleanly written. She packs a powerful wallop of post-war and family history without ever taking her eyes off the story.

Like her biblical namesake, Ruth embarks on a life-transforming journey. A young sabra (a native Israeli) convinces her to help lead 20 Jewish orphans on an illegal and dangerous quest through half of Europe to their new homeland, Israel. Miraculously, surviving the carnage and persecution of post-war Poland, the children steal away in the night, on trucks, in trains, and often on foot, across hostile borders. They are encouraged to tell their shredded histories to Ruth who, at first, cannot bear to hear them. But Matas doesn't flinch. We hear the screams of children being torn from their mothers, and smell the decay of the mass graveyards. Yet, each atrocity is juxtaposed against acts of heart-stopping courage and compassion. Evil walks this earth, but Matas's young heroes are not powerless against it.

For much of the journey, Ruth is, quite understandably, functionally comatose. Since Matas tells her story in first person present, this leaves Ruth somewhat removed from us and muffles her eventual reawakening. On the plus side, this dry recounting style may be helpful to young readers trying to digest Ruth's personal terror and the tension of the quest itself. Certainly, as with most great adventure stories, readers might wish it were longer.

As it is, ***After the War*** is a compelling and important story, fashioned from horror and redeemed by hope. Ruth Mendenberg's journey will travel with thousands of young readers, and may very well pack up a trunk full of awards along the way.

MORE MINDS (with Perry Nodelman, 1996)

Lisa Dennis

SOURCE: A review of *More Minds,* in *School Library Journal,* Vol. 42, No. 10, October, 1996, p. 148.

The rebellious Princess Lenora and her cautious, clairvoyant fiancé, Coren, return. Once again, the princess is bored with the predictable pace of life in Gepeth and seeks adventure, this time searching for a giant who is terrorizing the land. She escapes her parents' scrutiny by creating an idealized version of herself and inadvertently creates a second Coren as well (this one is a swashbuckling adventurer). These two "shadow" characters add both humor and meaning to the tale, exemplifying the ways in which stereotypes limit personal growth. As the four young people seek to discover the source of the problems plaguing Gepeth, they are thrust into many odd situations. Although their views on free-will, personal power, and the importance of balancing diverse needs and abilities are intriguing, Matas and Nodelman occasionally allow these themes to intrude upon the story. Another (minor) weakness is the sheer number of characters and events crammed into the tale. While all are potentially interesting, none are as fully developed as those in the previous book, and the conclusion, while ironically funny, also suffers in comparison to the thought-provoking shocker of the first novel. Despite these quibbles, however, this second collaboration will be welcomed by those who enjoy challenging fiction, told with humor and energy.

Amy E. Brandt

SOURCE: A review of *More Minds,* in *Bulletin of the Center for Children's Books,* Vol. 50, No. 6, February, 1997, p. 214.

After rescuing the Gragians from the existential mind manipulation of the dictator Hevak in ***Of Two Minds,*** Princess Lenora of Gepeth is not content to sit quietly at home contemplating her trousseau. When a giant invades the north, headstrong Lenora sneaks off to imagine him out of existence. However, she soon discovers that the Balance, which sets limits to the Gepethians' ability to turn their imaginings into reality, has been disrupted and imagination/reality becomes seriously out of control. Lenora finds herself battling chaos on behalf of the order she had rebelled against before. The story is hampered by excessively long scenes, and it's stretched out by super-explanatory dialogue, surreal descriptions of Balance-less life, and relentless bickering. Fiancé Prince Coren is the only character who betrays any emotional depth, reacting to illogical events with sensitivity and occasional spirit, while Lenora turns anger, elation, and impatience on and off like hot and cold water faucets. Young readers who appreciate enterprising princesses may enjoy Lenora, who certainly knows how to get what she wants.

Mary Ann Capan

SOURCE: A review of *More Minds,* in *Voice of Youth Advocates,* Vol. 20, No. 2, June, 1997, p. 119.

This slight story brings back the people and world created in ***Of Two Minds*** and it will be most easily understood by those who have read the prequel. However, it will be those same readers who will be disappointed. As the story begins, chaos reigns everywhere. A destructive giant has appeared in the north, the weather is out of control, and people's thoughts are running amok. With wedding plans in full swing, Princess Lenora creates a duplicate of herself to continue planning the wedding while she slips away unnoticed to save the kingdom. Lenora does this with some assistance from Prince Coren, her husband-to-be, and they all will live happily ever after.

This book is certainly much different from the first in tone, style, characterization, and plot. The reader must plod through a silly story that has no real substance to get to the point of the book: for all of her life, Lenora has resisted the quiet Balance in the royal land of Gepeth. In the end, Lenora realizes that she herself imagined and created the Balance—a perfect world—that she has rebelled against for all of her life. It's the same as when young adults just out of their teen years finally realize that their parents, who were so "stupid" while they were teenagers, have suddenly become so "smart." Amazing. The character of Lenora, however, is still too immature to come to this conclusion, as evidenced at book's end when she sets off to save the world from itself. Rest assured, headstrong Lenora will be seeking more adventures in the future. The explicit theme, "Nothing works out the way you expect" and the ending leave open the possibility of a third book in which Lenora will strive to humanize the Balance.

THE FREAK (1997)

Sarah Ellis

SOURCE: A review of *The Freak,* in *Quill and Quire,* Vol. 63, No. 3, March, 1997, p. 79.

Jade, 15, living in Winnipeg, recovers from a life-threatening attack of meningitis to discover that she is changed. She now has flash visions of the future, can read people's thoughts, and has the ability to see coloured auras. At first, she predicts only minor disasters such as an exploding science experiment, but when she starts to sense in advance the acts of anti-Semitic violence occurring in her community, her distress over her abilities becomes acute. At this point, the plot changes gear from the psychological-psychic with a subplot of teen romance to the detective thriller, as Jade plants a hidden microphone at the home of a war criminal, outwits the police, and saves the synagogue from a bomb attack.

This story is based on an appealing, inventive idea and the action rolls along smoothly enough, but given the intensity of the material—mental breakdown and hate crimes—the effect is not as strong or engaging as might be expected. ***The Freak*** is not a subtle book and it has some problems: the narration does not remain consistently first person; Jade has a habit of explaining matters to the readers. And in the opening chapters of the book, Jade remains in a confused state about what's happening to her for too long; readers will have long since figured out that she can predict the future. Although Jade's confusion may be psychologically realistic, it slows things down and delays us from jumping wholeheartedly into the altered world. When it comes to writing style, "kinda" and "sorta" substitute for any real attempt to capture the diction and cadence of adolescent speech. And when a character is described as "attractive" (that generic word), the author is skating close to the language of series romance.

In one respect, however, ***The Freak*** is fresh, even groundbreaking. Matas chooses to see Jade's dilemma as not just psychological or even ethical, but as having a spiritual and religious dimension. Religious questions are of deep interest to many young adults, yet these issues are remarkably absent from their literature. The existence and nature of God, the conflict between free will and determinism, and the problem of evil are all questions of importance for young adults. It is when Jade thinks about these questions, and when she discusses them with other characters, that she deepens into a real person and her genuine voice comes through. I just wish I had encountered this person more consistently throughout the whole story.

Resource Links

SOURCE: A review of *Freak*, in *Resource Links*, Vol. 3, No. 1, October, 1997, p. 36.

The initial premise of this novel is interesting. Fifteen-year-old Jade nearly dies of meningitis, and when she recovers she finds she has psychic powers—she can see people's auras, and knows what they're thinking. Her new ability makes her feel like a freak. But when she manages to track down the source of a flood of anti-Semitic hate literature and save her synagogue from a bomb on Yom Kippur, she accepts her unusual skills.

This novel is young adult fiction in the sense that no one but an undemanding teenage reader world settle for it. Matas keeps what might be a fantasy firmly in the territory of realistic fiction by providing simplistic scientific explanations for Jade's unusual experiences: an understanding psychiatrist and a grandmotherly psychic reconcile Jade to her unwanted gift. The inflexible first-person present-tense narrative, and the shallow reflections on religion that make Jade seem much younger than 15, made me feel I was reading New Age Judy Blume.

THE GARDEN (1997)

Hazel Rochman

SOURCE: A review of *The Garden,* in *Booklist,* Vol. 93, No. 15, April 1, 1997, p. 1322.

In this sequel to the fine docunovel ***After the War,*** 16-year-old Holocaust survivor Ruth Mendelson is on a kibbutz in Palestine in 1947, caught up in the war against the Arabs, a reluctant combatant—and killer—in the guerrilla conflict. Ruth's first-person, present-tense narrative tells of brutal action, including massacre by Arabs and Jews. She tells it quietly, trying to be fair to different Jewish views about the war, caught herself between her brother's extremism and those who fight only in self-defense. She is trying to make a home, trying to forget ("All I want is to live in peace"). This is not as strong as the first book. Each character seems to be here to represent a viewpoint, and the story is purposive, more political warfare than fiction.

Ann W. Moore

SOURCE: A review of *The Garden,* in *School Library Journal,* Vol. 43, No. 5, May, 1997, pp. 137-38.

In ***After the War,*** Matas related the story of a 15-year-old concentration camp survivor, Ruth Mendelson, and told of her journey from Poland to Palestine. ***The Garden*** is set in and around Kibbutz David, where Ruth now lives. It is November 1947, and the United Nations is preparing to vote on a plan to partition Palestine into Jewish and Arab lands. Ruth describes the difficulties the kibbutzniks face as British troops stand by and Arabs attack. She struggles with conflicting feelings about armed confrontation and longs for peace and security. Ruth is a courageous, sensitive young woman whose actions, ideas, and ideals are genuine and thought-provoking. Her first-person, present-tense narration is engrossing and unaffected. The other characters are well delineated, particularly Ruth's wisecracking boyfriend. ***The Garden*** is a riveting, relevant novel that raises tough questions—and provides no easy answers. It will be useful in units on war and conflict, but it's also a truly good read.

Gwyneth Evans

SOURCE: A review of *The Garden,* in *Quill and Quire,* Vol. 63, No. 9, September, 1997, p. 75.

In this novel, Carol Matas takes up the story of her character Ruth Mendenberg from November 1947 to April

1948, the uncertain period leading up to the establishment of a Jewish state. It's the sequel to ***After the War,*** the story of Ruth's journey as a concentration-camp survivor from ravaged postwar Europe to a new homeland in Israel.

Deeply concerned about social issues, Matas here takes on a topic of central importance to international affairs in the 1990s—the existence of the state of Israel and the conflict between Arabs and Israelis. The information and points of view presented in this novel come from the perspectives of the main characters, who are Jewish; there are no Arab spokespeople. Nonetheless, Matas dramatically presents the conflicting positions of the Jews themselves, on the issues of self-defence versus aggression, violence versus passive resistance, and the central question of entitlement. There are no absolutes in this novel, and even the heroism of the central characters comes at great cost. "I don't want to be a heroine for killing people. . . . I had no choice," says Ruth.

In the present tense, the voice of 16-year-old Ruth describes the raids she goes on and attacks she suffers as a Palmach soldier, dedicated to defensive rather than aggressive action. Woven into the dramatic events of the story are her speculations about the future of Israel, brief memories of the horrors of the camps and the loss of her family, and worries about the escalating violence around her, her own role as a fighter, and her one surviving brother who has joined a terrorist group. The question for the young Jewish characters of the novel is how they can act justly and yet survive.

Ruth, who has planted and loves a garden on her kibbutz, desperately wants peace, but as tensions build, the missions on which her unit is sent become increasingly violent. Determined to survive and not to let her people be driven from this longed-for homeland, Ruth makes hard choices. The garden itself is an image of the fertility and harmony she hopes Israel might offer; trampled by soldiers' boots, the garden is replanted and offers the possibility of renewed life. Although the characterizations are sketchy and Ruth's inner monologues not always convincing, ***The Garden*** is a fast-paced yet thoughtful novel that gives insight into an important and topical subject.

Resource Links

SOURCE: A review of *The Garden* in *Resource Links*, Vol. 3, No. 2, December, 1997, pp 87-8.

The young Holocaust refugees who escaped from Poland in Carol Matas's novel ***After the War*** attempt to rebuild their shattered lives on a kibbutz in Palestine. As the United Nations votes to partition Palestine to create the State of Israel, Ruth Simon, Zvi and the others know that the homeland they long for will not be easily won. ***The Garden*** spans the period from November, 1947 to May, 1948, when the escalation of violence makes an Arab-Israeli war inevitable.

Matas uses the metaphoric garden of the title well to evoke the mythic, biblical call to a peaceful homeland. At Kibbutz David, Ruth tends her literal garden for therapy, desperate to call this land her own. Alongside the roses, however, she plants smuggled guns, guns that seem necessary for the establishment of this earthly state.

Matas is at her best exploring the complex moral world of these Jewish refugees: having been victimized by unspeakable evil, they resolve never again to be so helpless. In their determination to gain a secure homeland, however, are they similarly victimizing Palestinians? Jewish characters in ***The Garden*** represent the spectrum of moral positions, from Karl's left-wing group hoping for peaceful co-existence without partition, to the Haganah's reliance on defensive strikes only, to Simon's Irgun terrorists who vow "an eye for an eye". Ruth, though attempting to adhere to the middle ground, participates in the escalation of violence and faces the horrifying parallel between Nazi attacks on Jews and an Irgun attack on defenseless Arabs.

An afterword and glossary provide a sense of historical accuracy. But one omission is troubling. The Palestinian perspective is told through Jewish eyes, not shown through Arab sensibilities; the one Arab character is purely functional, illustrating the Jewish moral dilemma and the peaceful intentions of some Arabs. Unfortunately, Matas's acknowledgments of historical sources include no mention of Palestinian sources. A novelist is under no obligation to tell historical stories through all participants' eyes; nevertheless, given the current penchant for treating historical novels as social studies texts, as well as the continuing volatility of the Arab-Israeli situation, this caution may be worth noting.

GREATER THAN ANGELS (1998)

Claire Rosser

SOURCE: A review of *Greater Than Angels,* in *Kliatt,* Vol. 32, No. 4, July, 1998, p. 52.

Matas has written other memorable books explaining to today's young people through the medium of fiction what it must have been like for young people faced with the Nazi occupation, the Holocaust, and its aftermath. ***Greater than Angels*** focuses on Anna, who is transported by the Nazis to a camp in Vichey France, and later saved by the humanitarians living in Le Chambon-sur-Lignon, a small village that has since been recognized for its amazing rescue work during WW II.

The first camp in France that Anna, her family and Jewish neighbors were placed in, Gurs, was little better than the infamous camps with more familiar names. In fact, as the war went on, eventually the Jews at Gurs were shipped north in cattle cars to the death camps.

Before that happened, there was an opportunity for the Jewish adolescents at Gurs to relocate to the village that saved their lives. Through this story of the vibrant Anna, her friend Klara, Klara's brother Rudi, and Peter, who becomes Klara's boyfriend, we learn how these Protestant villagers took in the children, respected their faith, and risked their own safety to protect them.

I'm glad Matas has included the many questions of faith that the Holocaust forced upon Jews, such as "If there is a loving God, how could He possibly allow these horrors?" The young people argue these theological points realistically and intelligently, coming to somewhat different conclusions among themselves. The title of the book reflects the religious element of the story, as the villagers are respected as being the kind of humans God meant us to be.

Patricia J. Morrow

SOURCE: A review of *Greater than Angels* in *Voice of Youth Advocates*, Vol. 21, No. 4, October, 1998, p. 275.

Anna Hirsch is deported from Mannheim along with her grandmother, mother, and aunt to Gurs, a refugee camp under Vichy control in southern France, where they struggle to survive. Tragedy strikes as the grandmother sinks into unreality and dies. Given a chance to live in the village of Le Chambon-sur-Lignon, Anna and her friends Klara, Rudi (Klara's brother), and Peter relocate and continue school. As Anna tells her story, her sense of humor—a litany of Jewish jokes—and dramatic flair lighten many situations. Rudi surprises Anna with his involvement in the underground and she begins to help him deliver forged identity documents for escapees. Anna gets passes to visit her family at Gurs only to see them boarded on cattle cars bound east.

As German control spreads, Rudi convinces Anna to take Klara to safety and the girls leave, along with Peter, on a harrowing mountain journey. They cross the Swiss border only to be sent back to French authorities and the camp at Rivesaltes. When Germany takes final control, students and political prisoners are set free and the trio returns to Chambon. Germans begin to round up the Jews, and Klara, Peter, and Anna again attempt to get to Switzerland, this time successfully. At the end, we feel that Anna will return to join Rudi and the resistance.

Matas has again brought us a finely crafted novel about young people's experiences that broadens readers' understanding of the Holocaust throughout Europe and recognizes the strengths of young people and their ability to survive with their humanity intact. Survivors of Chambon have continued their relationship with those who helped them, as noted in the afterword. A nice addition to the book is a map of the French region during the war.

Additional coverage of Matas's life and career is contained in the following sources published by Gale Research: *Authors and Artists for Young Adults*, Vol. 22; *Contemporary Authors*, Vol. 158; and *Something about the Author*, Vol. 93.

Jean (Fairbanks) Merrill

1923-

American author of fiction, poetry, plays, and retellings.

Major works include *The Superlative Horse* (1961), *The Pushcart War* (1964), *The Toothpaste Millionaire* (1972), *Maria's House* (1974), *The Girl Who Loved Caterpillars* (1992).

INTRODUCTION

Widely respected as a prolific and creative writer, Merrill is best known for the unusual diversity of her work. Writing for an audience ranging from preschoolers to middleschoolers, Merrill presents a variety of characters and themes in many genres and styles, including picture books, poetry, fantasies, folktales, and novels. Praised for her "rhythmic style" and beauty of language, Merrill has a unique ability to pull readers into her story and have them live the adventures. She creates characters that speak with the vivid and natural dialogue used by children every day, making her works more accessible to less proficient readers. She often writes with a moral theme—the struggle of the small and weak against the strong and mighty, the triumph of honesty over deceit, the misuse of power—but never with a heavy touch. Reviewers have lauded her honest presentation of comtemporary themes such as death and grieving, human rights, multiculturalism, and cultural barriers, and have regarded her outlook as ahead of its time. Humor is an important leavening agent in many of her works. Like the Far East tales she admires, Merrill's works exhibit a reverence for life and a kinship with the natural world. With an understanding that what we read as children often "colors our perception and expectation of the world," Merrill professed that writers for children should be "uncompromising enemies of the shoddy, meretricious, or sentimental in our work." More than a diversion, writing could also be, as she once explained, "a centering on the most deeply felt of our experiences as human beings."

Biographical Information

Born in Rochester, New York, Merrill and her family moved to an apple and dairy farm near Lake Ontario when she was eight years old. In the country she developed a passion for the outdoors that was matched by the intense pleasure she found in reading. Starting her education in a one-room country school, Merrill went on to Allegheny College, where she studied English and theater. She later received a master's degree from Wellesley College and studied Indian folklore at the University of Madras as a Fulbright scholar. Merrill spent several years as a writer and editor with *Scholastic* magazines in New York City. Her assignments included writing stories and plays, as well as conducting interviews with celebrities like aviator Jacqueline Cochran, actress Julie Harris, diplomat Chester Bowles, and Nepalese Sherpa Tenzing Norkey. After dividing her time between New York City and the Vermont countryside for many years, Merrill now lives full-time in Vermont, spending her winters in town and her summers in a rustic farmhouse.

Major Works

Merrill's keen interest in Asian folklore is evident in the several tales she has adapted for young readers. *The Superlative Horse*, for example, tells about a Chinese ruler who loves horses and seeks out a man who can find the superlative horse—one that raises no dust and leaves no tracks, something as elusive as thin air. In his search the ruler learns that real worth is not measured by outward appearances but by inner qualities. In *The Girl Who Loved Caterpillars*, Merrill retells a twelfth-century Japanese story about Izumi, a strong-willed girl who is pressured by her family and friends to adopt the social graces that will make her an acceptable wife for a nobleman. But Izumi follows her own ideas: instead of painting her face and learning music and poetry, she eagerly studies insects, especially caterpillars, and befriends scruffy-looking boys who bring her the insects. Although the ancient tale is a fragment and its end remains a mystery, Izumi's passion and imagination make the story satisfying and timeless.

While adept at retelling ancient tales, Merrill also has had great success in creating modern tales with moral themes. *The Pushcart War,* often called a modern classic, traces the outbreak of hostilities between truck drivers and pushcart peddlers in New York City when overcrowding brings traffic to a standstill. People blame the trucks; the truckers blame the pushcarts; factions form and strategies develop. Tension mounts as news of New York City's traffic problem begins to spread across the world. Describing this book as her personal David and Goliath fantasy, Merrill was inspired by the contrast she saw between the huge "menacing" trucks in New York City and the "friendly" farm trucks she remembered from her youth. The story, combining a core of wisdom about the uses of power with genuine humor, is bolstered by its mock-serious tone. *The Pushcart War* "is one of the funniest and most satisfying triumphs of small-and-clever I know," observed Noel Perrin. "It can be read in [many] different ways, and they all are funny."

In *The Toothpaste Millionaire,* Merrill entertains and educates her readers with a moral theme. Kate, a sixth-grade student, tells the story of her classmate Rufus who creates a million-dollar business by selling inexpensive homemade toothpaste and promoting it with honest advertising. Along the way, Rufus learns the economics of running a business, including production costs, profit margin, and taking out a business loan. Rufus's problems in business math are an engaging part of the story. In a similar vein, *Maria's House* presents the story of another talented youngster. With the help of her mother who irons shirts at a laundromat during the night, young Maria is able to attend Saturday art classes at a museum. When her art teacher asks the class to draw pictures of their homes, Maria, ashamed to recreate the tenement she lives in, draws a picture of the typical suburban home where her classmates likely reside. When her mother tells her that the drawing is not true, Maria must wrestle with her embarrassment to finally produce a drawing that is both honest and satisfying.

Awards

The Superlative Horse and *The Pushcart War* won the Lewis Carroll Shelf Award in 1963 and 1965, respectively. *The Pushcart War* also received the Boys' Clubs of America Award in 1965. *The Toothpaste Millionaire* was selected for the Dorothy Canfield Fisher Memorial Children's Book Award in 1976 and the Sequoyah Children's Book Award in 1977.

TITLE COMMENTARY

HENRY, THE HAND-PAINTED MOUSE (1951)

Virginia Kirkus' Bookshop Service

SOURCE: A review of *Henry, the Hand-Painted Mouse,* in *Virginia Kirkus' Bookshop Service,* Vol. XIX, No. 17, September 1, 1951, p. 480.

Although the style is often a bit arch and self-consciously uninhibited, this is a tantalizing story with an amusing twist about a wistful and sentitive mouse and his artist friend. The mouse, called Henry the 8th because he lived on the eighth floor of a tall building, was depressed and sad because he was lonely and none of the interesting people in the lofts below him paid any attention to his hopeful visitations. But when an artist who creates hand-painted ties comes to live with Henry and accidentally paints Henry in the process, Henry's life and philosophy undergo a happy change. The illustrations by Ronni Solbert are wonderfully spirited and imaginative.

The Horn Book Magazine

SOURCE: A review of *Henry, the Hand-Painted Mouse,* in *The Horn Book Magazine,* Vol. XXVII, No. 5, September-October, 1951, p. 320.

Henry the 8th was a small grey mouse who lived on the eighth floor until The Artist came to live there too and absent-mindedly, and with entirely satisfactory results, wiped his brushes on Henry. The Artist was forced to paint neckties because "people don't have time for pictures unless they are accidentally there. . . . For pictures hanging quietly on the wall people haven't time." The story and line drawings have some sophisticated touches that only adults will appreciate, but they have originality and humor that will appeal to children too. ***Henry*** makes me feel that here is a new author-illustrator team worth watching.

Anne Izard

SOURCE: A review of *Henry, the Hand-Painted Mouse,* in *Library Journal,* Vol. 76, No. 18, October 15, 1951, p. 1710.

There is the lilt and touch of gay originality in this story of a mouse who looked like a "fluff of dust in the corner" until an artist moves into the loft and changes his mode of life by accident. Pictures and text practically beg for color but there is none of it in the book. The black-and-white outlines will present an almost irresistible temptation to the reader. Perhaps the librarians should hand-paint their copies before circulating.

Louise S. Bechtel

SOURCE: "Big Doings for Small Boys," in *The New York Herald Tribune Book Review,* November 11, 1951, p. 32.

"Henry the 8th" lived in a loft building and knew what odd work went on, on all the floors below his own, the 8th of course. He shinnied up and down the elevator chute to watch and was very lonely until an artist moved in who made hand-painted neckties. Talking happily with Henry about his art, absent-mindedly he painted him. Then every one on all floors had to notice Henry and his life never was lonely again.

This rather sophisticated little story has real charm. The big black and white pictures, clever and modern, have distinction. It will appeal as a gift book and might even be put with the right person's new gift necktie.

BOXES (1953)

Virginia Kirkus' Bookshop Service

SOURCE: A review of *Boxes,* in *Virginia Kirkus' Bookshop Service,* Vol. XXI, No. 17, September 1, 1953, p. 578.

A wonderful flight of fancy is also a serious comment on economics. Bernard and Boris Zorn are brothers in the box business. Their little shop is fairly thriving, but when they go to a Business Man's Convention nobody seems much impressed with their trade and the Zorns are so depressed that their business comes to a standstill. But demand being what it is, the citizens object, the Mayor takes cognizance of the shortage and the Zorns are feted into producing again. All shapes, sizes and categories of boxes and people in the humorous lines of Ronni Solbert's colored pictures.

Bulletin of the Center for Children's Books

SOURCE: A review of *Boxes,* in *Bulletin of the Center for Children's Books,* Vol. VII, No. 2, October, 1953, p. 15.

The Zorn brothers own a box factory of which they are inordinately proud until one day at a businessmen's convention they learn, to their dismay, that no one is interested in boxes as such. The brothers, becoming discouraged, stop work and allow orders to pile up until a crisis is reached when there are no longer any boxes in which to put things. The brothers are finally persuaded that theirs is an important business and they then return happily to work. Both the text and the illustrations are too adult and sophisticated for the picture book age. As fantasy the story falls flat, and too many misconceptions are created for it to serve as a book to show young children the inter-dependence of businesses.

THE TRAVELS OF MARCO (1955)

Virginia Kirkus' Bookshop Service

SOURCE: A review of *The Travels of Marco,* in *Virginia Kirkus' Bookshop Service,* Vol. XXIV, No. 4, February 15, 1956, p. 122.

Marco is a pigeon from New York's lower east side, "born in a rooftop coop, pleasantly situated in a grove of television aerials". But a big electric sign for the Jewish daily, *Forward,* gets him thinking—why keep returning to the coop?—and off he goes. His flight leads him to upper Manhattan and thrilling new experiences. However he finds no solid meal. He is just thinking he will have to return when Bingo, a Central Park boy, promises him peanuts every day—and Marco finds his new life at last. Grey and orange, well composed drawings by Ronni Solbert complement a story that makes a very valid point.

Jennie D. Lindquist

SOURCE: A review of *The Travels of Marco,* in *The Horn Book Magazine,* Vol. XXXII, No. 2, April, 1956, p. 106.

Marco, the pigeon, could see from his roof in New York a sign bearing the name of a well-known newspaper: *Forward.* "What does *Forward* mean?" he asked the older pigeons and they told him that it meant "upward and onward" and "to travel." "'Why don't we travel?' asked Marco. . . . 'Buckwheat,' said the older pigeons. 'That's why. If we didn't return to the coop, what would we eat?'" The answer did not satisfy Marco; everyone else must eat, too, he thought, and perhaps what they ate was better than buckwheat! He decided to find out. Story and pictures in red and black on soft gray tell of his adventures in the city as he met many new friends and sampled all sorts of things from bagels to spaghetti, and finally found the most delicious food of all and the happiest place for a pigeon to live. This is, I think, the best of the books by this author-artist team and the most childlike in its appeal.

Booklist

SOURCE: A review of *The Travels of Marco,* in *Booklist,* Vol. 52, No. 17, May 1, 1956, p. 368.

A feeling for New York City and its inhabitants is evident in both story and drawings in this entertaining picture book. Inspired by a big sign that said "Forward" to get out of his circle-flying rut and to travel and learn what there was to eat besides buckwheat, Marco the pigeon left his Lower East Side rooftop coop and headed due north. As he traveled uptown Marco made friends and sampled their favorite foods but not until he reached Central Park did the hungry pigeon find a delicious food—peanuts—pleasing to both him and his new-found friends.

Margaret Sherwood Libby

SOURCE: A review of *The Travels of Marco,* in *The New York Herald Tribune Book Review,* May 6, 1956, p. 9.

Amusing, characterful drawings in black with bright splashes of red on pale gray paper will appeal to the older group in the picture-book crowd, those that can read to themselves but still want the big page with only a few lines on each. For them Jean Merrill has written a neatly rounded story of Marco, an adventurous New York pigeon who is inspired to explore the city by an advertising sign that says "Forward." Tired of eating buckwheat and of flying in circles, he roams through streets of push-carts and of paper kites, tastes many strange foods and makes many friends. None of the foods from the bagel of Mrs. Kovarsky to the frozen peas of Bingo Brown quite suit Marco until . . . Well, New York is a remarkably varied city and Marco discovers one place and one food that he and all his new friends find delightful.

Mary Handy

SOURCE: A review of *The Travels of Marco,* in *The Christian Science Monitor,* May 10, 1956, p. 13.

[This is] a fable in appreciating people of many different races and colors. It's also a delightful picture story of a pigeon who flies his coop. Through the big, friendly pictures we follow Marco through many sections of New York—nibbling bagels with a Jewish lady, spaghetti with an Italian man, black olives from a Greek store, watermelon with a little colored boy, rice with a Chinese girl.

In the end Marco finds all his new friends as well as his favorite food in the park in the middle of the city. Like a very sensible pigeon he seems to realize that springtime in a park with new leaves and flowers and friends is hard to beat!

Bulletin of the Center for Children's Books

SOURCE: A review of *The Travels of Marco,* in *Bulletin of the Center for Children's Books,* Vol. 9, No. 10, June, 1956, p. 116.

Marco is a pigeon living in a rooftop coop in New York City. Every day he flies around with the twenty-four other pigeons from the coop and then returns to the rooftop for a meal of buckwheat. One day he notices the large sign on one of the buildings advertising the newspaper, *Forward,* and decides to follow its advice. He flies to various sections of the city, sampling food on the way—bagels, fried rice, ripe olives, frozen peas—and rejecting each in turn until he discovers Central Park and peanuts. There he settles down to the perfect life and the perfect food for pigeons. A picture story book with an unobtrusive lesson in the bird's eye view of different people and their different tastes.

THE TREE HOUSE OF JIMMY DOMINO (1955)

Bulletin of the Center for Children's Books

SOURCE: A review of *The Tree House of Jimmy Domino,* in *Bulletin of the Center for Children's Books,* Vol. 9, No. 9, May, 1956, pp. 97-98.

Jimmy Domino lives happily alone in his tree house until the day when he is visited by a large black dog, a tramp with a guitar, and a motherly woman who likes to cook. By the time Jimmy has had a chance to think about each of the three and to grow lonesome, they have each decided to return to his tree house and join him in his care-free life. The straight-faced, understated manner of the telling gives a feeling of possibility to a wholly improbable story that will have appeal for young children who would like to share Jimmy Domino's freedom and who are old enough to appreciate the pleasures of both solitude and companionship. Not for the literal-minded. Although the text is written at an upper second grade reading level, the size of type and amount of text to a page make the book best suited to reading aloud, and its enjoyment as read aloud material will be further enhanced by the rhythmic style and beauty of language.

A SONG FOR GAR (1955)

Virginia Kirkus' Bookshop Service

SOURCE: A review of *A Song for Gar,* in *Virginia Kirkus' Bookshop Service,* Vol. 25, No. 1, January 1, 1957, p. 2.

Boxes and ***The Travels of Marco*** were the first two books by this able author-artist team and both were about city people. Now comes a story of Eastern mountain folk in which both text and pictures give a feeling of the gaiety of the Marvells, a musical family who live on Sour Cherry Ridge. Though Absalom, the youngest of six boys, has a scratchy voice, it is he who makes up the song with which his elder brother Gar wins the contest and prize money that allows him to marry pretty Camden Pride. With its tricks and catches and the song all written out, the process is engaging. Ronni

Silbert's drawings in ink and blue tints have a jaunty playfulness.

The Booklist and Subscription Books Bulletin

SOURCE: A review of *A Song for Gar,* in *The Booklist and Subscription Books Bulletin,* Vol. 53, No. 14, March 15, 1957, p. 388.

How the ballad-type song evolves is shown in an entertaining and flavorsome story of hill people. In hopes of winning the $100-purse so he could marry his redheaded girl, Absalom's brother Gar was going to enter the Song Swapping—if he could find a likely song to sing. When the family failed to agree on an appropriate song, worried Absalom, singing his thoughts to his pet coon, came forth with a song of his own making with which Gar won the prize. Verses and musical score for the song are included.

Ellen Lewis Buell

SOURCE: "On Sour Cherry Ridge," in *The New York Times Book Review,* March 24, 1957, p. 42.

It's a sorry thing to be the only untalented member of a family. All the Marvells who lived on Sour Cherry Ridge, somewhere in the southern Appalachians, were known for their fine singing voices—all except Absalom. But although this youngest of six brothers had a voice "as rackety as a coon's" it was he who unwittingly found just the right song for brother Gar to sing at the Swapping Song Contest. This meant that Gar could marry the girl of his choice and all the Marvells were happy.

The pleasant joke of this lively, regional story is that Absalom never realized he was making up a song—he was just singing his thoughts to his coon. It's a cheerful thing, set to the tune of Polly-Wolly-Doodle. Groups ought to have a good time singing along with Absalom as he adds verse after verse until he has proved unknowingly that "it takes more than a sweet voice to make a good song."

The Christian Science Monitor

SOURCE: A review of *A Song for Gar,* in *The Christian Science Monitor,* May 9, 1957, p. 18.

Absalom lived with his Ma and Pa and five big brothers on Sour Cherry Ridge, and all his brothers had sweet voices. But Absalom had a scratchy voice, and a pet coon named Barbary Allen, who didn't seem to mind his scratchy voice at all. How he helped his brother Gar win the prize at the Song Swapping contest is a lovely story, with plenty of mountain atmosphere. Even so distinguished a mountain poet as Jesse Stuart commends it for its "flavor of hill music and dancing feet."

Margaret Sherwood Libby

SOURCE: A review of *A Song for Gar,* in *The New York Herald Tribune Book Review,* May 26, 1957, p. 11.

Ronni Solbert has made very attractive black and white pictures touched with blue crayon for Jean Merrill's gay and simple tale of a mountain family living on "Sour Cherry Ridge." The faces have character, all six of the Marvell boys and their parents, and even Absalom Marvell's pet coon, Barbary Allen, has an especially pert look. Absalom, the youngest, was the only Marvell with a scratchy voice, but he was the most anxious of all for his big brother Gar to win a song contest and have enough money to marry his red-headed girl, Camden Pride. The trouble was none of them could agree on the "likeliest song." It had to be strong, pretty, funny, and serious. When Absalom was puzzled he used to lie on the grass and sing to his coon and this led to the most surprising inspiration for Gar. His song that had "everything" is part of the text, to be sung to "Polly Wolly Doodle," and the primaries, whether they have scratchy voices like Absalom or not, will sing it and dance to it too and get the feel of a hill music festival.

Virginia Haviland

SOURCE: A review of *A Song for Gar,* in *The Horn Book Magazine,* Vol. XXXIII, No. 3, June, 1957, p. 215.

Absalom Marvell, youngest of six boys in a Southern Mountain family, tried his best to find a good song for Gar, his oldest brother, to sing in the big Song Swapping. They all knew that such songs as "Barbara Allen" were too familiar. Fortunately, Absalom, in spite of his poor, scratchy voice, liked to sing to his pet coon. Gar heard him and decided to make these new verses his entry. The spontaneous evolution of this ballad-type song (sung to the tune of "Polly-Wolly-Doodle") suggests how any folk song might be born. The book will be interesting to some children for this reason, as well as for its natural story of a contest with a happy outcome. All the verses and the music are included, with delightful sketches.

THE VERY NICE THINGS (1959)

Virginia Kirkus' Bookshop Service

SOURCE: A review of *The Very Nice Things,* in *Virginia Kirkus' Bookshop Service,* Vol. 27, No. 3, July 1, 1959, p. 439.

One of the very nicest things is this fantasy of an elephant and an owl by the author-illustrator team of ***The Travels of Marco.*** When William Elephant comes upon a swimmer's clothes he is enchanted. They are very nice things, indeed. The hat will do splendidly as a bath tub for Owl, the shoes will do ideally as salt shakers, the shirt will make a perfect sail. Even the swimmer cannot deny the efficacy of William's arrangement and bequeaths his wardrobe to the inventive animal. Whimsical illustrations by Ronni Solbert in gray and pink complement this text which will invite delight from all those readers, children and parents, who are fond of "very nice things".

Bulletin of the Center for Children's Books

SOURCE: A review of *The Very Nice Things,* in *Bulletin of the Center for Children's Books,* Vol. 13, No. 1, November, 1959, p. 50.

William Elephant found some very nice things one day while he was walking in the woods; although he and his friends didn't know what the things were for, uses were found for all the items. Along came a man and put the things (all articles of clothing) on to show how he used them, but the elephant liked his own way. The bland text has a gravity that makes the improbable events very humorous. Technique and color in the illustrations are softly pleasing, and the brevity of the story fits well the slightness of theme.

Margaret Sherwood Libby

SOURCE: A review of *The Very Nice Things,* in *The New York Herald Tribune Book Review,* November 1, 1959, p. 3.

No matter how odd things are they have their uses. William Elephant was determined to think up uses for some things he found in the forest. They were such "very nice things," he said, as he made a birdbath, a sail, salt and pepper shakers and trunk and head warmers out of them. His friend Old Owl did not think he was using them for what they were intended, but Willie Elephant was satisfied. He was even more satisfied when a man came along and dressed up in them, actually using them as clothes, as shirt, pants, shoes and socks and a hat. The man looked very nice, but both Willie and Old Owl were sure it was absurd to think that the man had any idea what the "very nice things" were for. Willie's solution was far superior. This is the best short tale Jean Merrill has written. She has created a very funny situation in her brief text, one which small children should laugh at gleefully and Ronni Solbert's pictures in black, gray, gray green and pink crayon are just right, expressing with great simplicity of line William and Old Owl's wide range of thought, puzzlement, scorn, satisfaction and triumph.

Rod Nordell

SOURCE: "For Looking at and Listening to," in *The Christian Science Monitor,* November 5, 1959, p. 2B.

This book is a bit like the alleged British preference in humor—not a lot of different jokes but the same joke repeated in slightly different ways. For the 4-8s who get the joke, even though it does not end entirely as expected, the title of ***The Very Nice Things*** is apt. They may identify the things William Elephant finds hanging on a tree before he does (if he ever does), and when they're sure he puts them to the wrong uses, they may be surprised at what the man in the book does about it. However they approach the idea of the joke, they should find the picturing of it hard to resist, especially that plump, pastel pachyderm who starts it all.

BLUE'S BROKEN HEART (1960)

Viginia Bookshop Service

SOURCE: A review of *Blue's Broken Heart,* in *Virginia Kirkus' Bookshop Service,* Vol. XXVIII, No. 2, January 15, 1960, p. 48.

Blue, a little dog, has a broken heart. He goes ruefully to Dr. Thomas, the veterinary, in order to have it mended. Here he meets his friends, the giraffe with the broken neck, the elephant who has grazed his legs, the crocodile with the injured jaw, the kangaroo on crutches. All the animals seem comfortable under the expert care of Dr. Thomas, but Blue's wound will take some time to heal, but heal it does, with love and the opportunity to help others. Ronni Solbert's menagerie are no less winning than they are instructive in this tender and purposeful little fantasy. A simple vocabulary conveys a story which is attractive and compelling.

Alberta Eiseman

SOURCE: "A Sad Dog," in *The New York Times Book Review,* April 3, 1960, p. 40.

A broken-hearted little dog named Blue went to see Thomas, the animal doctor. Thomas was an expert fixer of giraffes' necks, hippopotamus' noses, elephants' knees, even snakes' tails, but he had never before mended a broken heart, and he was most concerned. He wound a bandage around Blue's middle and warned him that it would have to be changed every day, so Blue had better stay with him a while. And Blue did, with the happiest results. This is a wistful little story, told in quiet tones, and the gently humorous drawings make all the characters appealing, snake and kangaroo alike. Certainly no child will find it a wildly exciting experience, yet it was received by one of Zorro's stanchest fans with rapt attention and very misty eyes.

Elvajean Hall

SOURCE: A review of *Blue's Broken Heart,* in *Library Journal,* Vol. 85, No. 10, May 15, 1960, p. 2029.

Blue, an appealing Scottie whose master was dead, found

that the animal doctor really did know how to "fix" a broken heart as well as the usual broken tails, legs, and paws. Unusually appealing illustrations by Ronni Solbert help carry the story for young readers. Unusually good for reading aloud. Recommended for school and public libraries.

SHAN'S LUCKY KNIFE: A BURMESE FOLK TALE (retold by Merrill, 1960)

Virginia Kirkus' Bookshop Service

SOURCE: A review of *Shan's Lucky Knife: A Burmese Folk Tale,* in *Virginia Kirkus' Bookshop Service,* Vol. XXVIII, No. 7, April 1, 1960, p. 289.

Shan was a country boy from the Burmese hills. He longed to find a way to earn some money, but refused staunchly to part with the kan his father taught him to play and the bag his mother made him. At last he was offered a job as boatman on Ko Tin's boat to Rangoon. People warned him that Ko Tin would trick him, but Shan thought he was smart too. But it took two trips and the loss of his bag and his kan and his wages before he learned that only a trick would serve to pay back the crooked Ko Tin. Here's a folk tale from Burma, in a story of a country boy pitted against a city merchant. One finds oneself on the side of Shan, even if the issue is cloudy. Effective line and wash drawings by Ronni Solbert.

The Booklist and Subscription Books Bulletin

SOURCE: A review of *Shan's Lucky Knife: A Burmese Folk Tale,* in *The Booklist and Subscription Books Bulletin,* Vol. 56, No. 17, May 1, 1960, p. 548.

A country boy from the hills of Burma hires out to a boatmaster from Rangoon despite the warnings that Ko Tin is greedy and a clever trader and will undoubtedly try to take advantage of him. On the first trip Ko Tin, true to his reputation, tricks Shan out of his wages and his two prize possessions, but on the second trip Shan cleverly outwits Ko Tin, recovering his own property and winning Ko Tin's boat and everything on it. Well told and handsomely illustrated, this diverting story is based on a Burmese folk tale heard by the author and artist in Burma.

The New York Times Book Review

SOURCE: A review of *Shan's Lucky Knife: A Burmese Folk Tale,* in *The New York Times Book Review,* May 8, 1960, p. 32.

Ko Tin was the craftiest boatmaster on the Irrawaddy, and when young Shan joined his crew it looked as though the boy would be at the mercy of the rogue's tricks. And so he was on the first trip, but not the second. In fact, by a neat trick of his own, Shan shrewdly turns the tables on his master—a particularly satisfying feat, since the hero is a very likable lad.

Virginia Haviland

SOURCE: A review of *Shan's Lucky Knife: A Burmese Folk Tale,* in *The Horn Book Magazine,* Vol. XXXVI, No. 3, June, 1960, p. 216.

An entirely satisfying picture-story book, combining the suspense and humor of a folk-tale plot with pictures arranged in flowing doublespreads which have uncluttered movement and plenty of free white space. Shan, the story's hero, a country boy from the hills of Burma, makes his chance to row down the Irrawaddy to the Rangoon bazaar on a trading boat and manages by a clever trick to outwit the wily boatmaster who would cheat him of his just pay. Captures the flavor of Burmese river life and city trading.

Augusta Baker

SOURCE: A review of *Shan's Lucky Knife: A Burmese Folk Tale,* in *Library Journal,* Vol. 85, No. 12, June 15, 1960, p. 2472.

Ko Tin, the sly boatmaster on the Irrawaddy River, outtrades Shan, boy from the Burmese hills, by conniving trickery. In the end, however, Shan proves he can outtrick Ko Tin. Simple but effective adaptation of a Burmese folk tale which the author and artist (Ronni Solbert) heard on a visit to Burma. Illustrations, many are full-page and double-spread, make this a colorful picture book. One minor criticism: Shan's bag in the pictures is orange, although the text constantly refers to it as a red bag. Nevertheless, an attractive book with a well-told tale.

EMILY EMERSON'S MOON (1960)

Virginia Kirkus' Bookshop Service

SOURCE: A review of *Emily Emerson's Moon,* in *Virginia Kirkus' Bookshop Service,* Vol. XXVIII, No. 13, July 1, 1960, p. 493.

Emily Emerson is a lucky little girl because she has a father who can do most anything. And so she is not the least surprised when her doting parent promises her the moon. How he keeps his promise is told in this playful story with its moon-pale illustrations. The author's new approach to the familiar situation and its expected solution endow Emily's predicament with just the right amount of suspense and freshness required for the nursery reader.

Siddie Joe Johnson

SOURCE: A review of *Emily Emerson's Moon,* in *Junior Libraries,* Vol. 7, No. 1, September, 1960, p. 58.

A new angle on the girl-wants-moon theme, not quite so enchanting as "Many Moons," but with a nice little picture-book flavor all its own. Story is told in rhyme. Illustrations by Ronni Solbert have a European folk touch. Splashes of blue and yellow are added to the black and white. Emily would have no balloon substitute for the moon, but, had she not been teased, would have settled for a sunflower on her lapel. However, the moon in the pond seems at last to be the answer. For large picture-book collections.

The Booklist and Subscription Books Bulletin

SOURCE: A review of *Emily Emerson's Moon,* in *The Booklist and Subscription Books Bulletin,* Vol. 57, No. 1, September 1, 1960, p. 31.

Had it not been for her scornful older brother Emily Emerson might have settled for a sunflower instead of the sun and a ribbon of six colors in place of the rainbow. As it was Emily held her gently teasing father to his promise to get her the moon. The ingenious way in which he fulfilled his promise, to Emily's complete satisfaction, is told in a playful, endearing picture book with rhymed text and amusing colored drawings.

Virginia Haviland

SOURCE: A review of *Emily Emerson's Moon,* in *The Horn Book Magazine,* Vol. XXXVI, No. 5, October, 1960, p. 399.

Little Emily Emerson converses alternately with her doting father and with her deflating brother Avery—all most engagingly, on the subject of getting the moon or perhaps a scrap of rainbow. She believes in Daddy's offers, although Avery scoffs in brotherly fashion. Daddy has to think harder: "How did a man get hold of a moon?" The young listener will find the solution acceptable and the relationships wholly natural. It is the latter that give the book its special charm. The blue-and-yellow drawings capture childlike feelings.

Margaret Sherwood Libby

SOURCE: A review of *Emily Emerson's Moon,* in *The New York Herald Tribune Book Review,* November 13, 1960, p. 3.

> "Emily Emerson"
> Said Emily's father,
> "What would you like today?
> Shall I climb up
> And get you the moon.
> Or a piece of the milky way?"

Naturally Emily Emerson was pleased but she made the mistake of boasting about it to her brother Avery who said, "Daddy's teasing I bet. The moon's too high. In the top of the sky. For even Daddy to get." This put Daddy on the spot, and Emily was not one to drop the matter. Neither was Avery. Every stop-gap Daddy provided was jeered at by Avery while Emily Emerson kept on rooting for her father. Avery said, "It couldn't be done. But Daddy would do it. She knew it." ***And he did.*** Not in any of the ways Emily thought of but in a fashion wholly satisfactory to the nursery-age children who will enjoy the little poem, and the expressive blue and yellow, crayon-like drawings. A new version of the "Many Moons" theme planned for a younger group than James Thurber's charming story.

TELL ABOUT THE COWBARN, DADDY (1963)

Zena Sutherland

SOURCE: A review of *Tell About the Cowbarn, Daddy,* in *Bulletin of the Center for Children's Books,* Vol. XVII, No. 10, June, 1964, p. 160.

A picture book that shows in its illustrations the scenes described from memory rather than the scene taking place, which is a bedtime dialogue between a small boy and his father. The conversation will, in pattern rather than in subject, evoke a sympathetic feeling in the reader, since it is clear that father and son have had the same conversation before. "Daddy, tell about . . ." What else? What about the silo?" the child prompts. As father describes the barn of this boyhood, quite a few facts about cows, barns, and farms emerge—painlessly.

HIGH, WIDE AND HANDSOME AND THEIR THREE TALL TALES (1964)

Arlene Mosel

SOURCE: A review of *High, Wide and Handsome and Their Three Tall Tales,* in *School Library Journal,* Vol. 10, No. 9, May, 1964, p. 86.

High the monkey, Wide the pig, and Handsome the fox meet Rolling Stone a slick, well dressed hound dog from the city. The three friends challenge the stranger to a storytelling contest in which the winner will get the loser's clothes. Outwitted by sly trickery, the country connivers lose their clothes and learn a lesson. This is a fine Burmese version of a traditional folk tale theme. The four stories within the story are cleverly written and illustrated. Pictures are vivid with reds and orange. A truly humorous book that can be read to younger child-ren; third-graders will want to read it for themselves.

Ethel L. Heins

SOURCE: A review of *High, Wide and Handsome and Their Three Tall Tales,* in *The Horn Book Magazine,* Vol. XL, No. 4, August, 1964, p. 371.

Three lazy rustics—High, a monkey; Wide, a pig; and Handsome, a fox—meet Rolling Stone, an elegant hound wearing an embroidered jacket, brocaded trousers, a feathered hat, and "red velvet slippers turned up at the toes." Conniving to win the fine clothes for themselves, they challenge Rolling Stone to a storytelling contest. Inevitably the clever dog outwits the three fools, but not until four impossibly exaggerated tales have been told. A delightful book—equally inviting to storytellers and to young readers—with amusing illustrations on handsomely designed pages that are warm with tones of coral and yellow-orange. Only the jacket blurb asserts that "This is a Burmese version of an old folk tale"; the author herself might have stated the source.

Zena Sutherland

SOURCE: A review of *High, Wide and Handsome and Their Three Tall Tales,* in *Bulletin of the Center for Children's Books,* Vol. 19, No. 1, September, 1965, p. 14.

Delightfully illustrated, a Burmese version of a folk tale in which there are four tall tales, each of which is told by one of the animal characters. High, Wide, and Handsome are a monkey, a pig, and a fox; they are lazy: they "liked to hang around the rest house, because there was always the chance that a traveler would treat them to a palm toddy or a nice dinner in return for a story." When a flashily dressed dog drives up, the three friends decide to trick him with a tall-tale contest. Their tales are brief and nonsensical, but the wily dog easily bests the three hopeful connivers.

THE PUSHCART WAR (1964)

Harriet B. Quimby

SOURCE: A review of *The Pushcart War,* in *Library Journal,* Vol. 89, No. 13, July, 1964, pp. 2878-79.

The outbreak of a war in 1976 between truck drivers and pushcart peddlers brings to the attention of both the city of New York and the world the nuisance value of traffic. This is a satire on almost every conceivable aspect of modern urban life: the city politician, the union, children, secret weapons, mechanization, and ever so much more. It is flawless. Each incident, each personality is subtly drawn, from Frank the Flower, accused of flattening 18,000 truck tires, to Big Moe of Mammoth Moving. Minute detail, matter-of-fact humor, and the ridiculous situations that young people appreciate hold the story together. The author has truly captured the rhythmic pattern of New York speech ("Pin money we'll need"). To some it may seem slow at the onset; to all it should be funny; and to many it will have a disturbing ring of truth. Peopled primarily with adults, it will appeal to the older reader and certainly to adults. The illustrations are just right.

Alberta Eiseman

SOURCE: A review of *The Pushcart War,* in *The New York Times Book Review,* July 12, 1964, p. 18.

The year was 1976. New York City had become so crowded that, one day, all traffic on the streets stopped completely. Most people blamed the trucks, which had grown too large and arrogant. The Three, owners of the largest trucking companies in the city, knew they must find a scapegoat—and pushcarts seemed an easy target. So began the pushcart war, the only war in recent years—says the learned foreword—which was uncomplicated enough for a peace-loving modern person to understand. It's a delightful notion, and an utterly captivating book. Never shedding the mood of mock seriousness, the author has detailed each step of the hostilities, creating a foreword, an introduction, footnotes, original documents—all the paraphernalia of scholarly tomes. The characters on both factions are many and memorable; the satire cuts deep into some of our most hallowed institutions. Best of all, the dialogue and situations are irresistibly funny. Possibly the book is too long, but it would be hard to suggest which episode should be sacrificed. It's rare indeed to find a book for young people with both a point of view and a sense of the ridiculous.

Ruth Hill Viguers

SOURCE: A review of *The Pushcart War,* in *The Horn Book Magazine,* Vol. XL, No. 4, August, 1964, p. 378.

The definitive history of New York's war between the pushcarts and the trucks is one of those rarities—a book that is both humorous and downright funny. The humor is in the satire of the straight-faced reporting and the many surprising little interpolations. The nonsense arises from making the most of every funny, sometimes slapstick, situation. The war started when Mack, driving a Mighty Mammoth, ran down a pushcart belonging to Morris the Florist. Trucks, constantly growing more huge and more numerous, were becoming a great problem in the city; and when the pushcart peddlers devised a scheme to immobilize the trucks, they had the people's sympathy. With the arrest of Frank the Flower the peddlers had to desist, but children all over the city carried on. As the war progressed and the politicians became involved, the outcome seemed almost hopeless. But then the Battle of Words began, letters poured into the newspapers, the tide turned, and, at the Pushcart Peace Conference, the Flower Formula solved the crisis. Such a lively book will need little introducing; once a boy or girl discovers it, the news will spread. Very amusing illustrations and attractive format.

Zena Sutherland

SOURCE: A review of *The Pushcart War,* in *Bulletin of the Center for Children's Books,* Vol. XVIII, No. 1, September, 1964, pp. 15-16.

An imaginative conception is delineated with a light touch and a good deal of craftsmanship. In an unusual story set in the near future, the pushcart owners of New York City fight and win the war against the truckers. By 1976 the trucks are enormous, the drivers are arrogant, the traffic is completely snarled. The Pushcart Army is composed of a small, brave band of brothers—and General Anna—whose weapons are unusual and whose strategy is inspired. Although the writing style is restrained, the story has good pace, delightful ingenuous humor, bland burlesque of the social and political facts of life, and a New York atmosphere so solid you can eat it with a spoon.

C. Martin

SOURCE: A review of *The Pushcart War,* in *The Junior Bookshelf,* Vol. 37, No. 6, December, 1973, p. 394.

The all-American setting and language of this book might at first deter readers, though as they read on they may find the idiomatic dialogue of New York's mixed community curiously endearing. And, although the story is set in New York, it could easily be transferred to London or any other city or town in this congested world, since the villain of the piece is the monster we know as the juggernaut whilst the hero is the humble citizen who is prevented from going about his lawful business, and who is here represented by the New York barrow-boys. The book was first published in America nearly ten years ago, and as the events chronicled are due to happen in 1976, we are evidently almost there; which adds immediacy to a story which quickens in pace as it goes along, the whole episode being exciting in itself, never mind the moral which is implied rather than preached and never holds up the action. The whole book is nicely produced and can be recommended to those of eight upwards who love a victory of the Davids over the Goliaths of this world.

Margery Fisher

SOURCE: A review of *The Pushcart War,* in *Growing Point,* Vol. 12, No. 7, January, 1974, pp. 2317-18.

Comic fantasy has to establish its mood and mode quickly; the reader must be put into the right frame of mind to accept absurdity. The sudden opening of ***The Pushcart War*** catches the attention at once. Morris the Florist is carrying on his lawful trade in the street when a Mighty Mammoth truck driven by the impetuous and conscience-less Albert P. Mack runs him down and flattens his barrow. He and his mates start a campaign against the juggernauts, using in the first place a weapon (nails shot into tyres by pea-shooters) so simple that for some time it goes undetected. More sophisticated methods follow. There are street fights, demonstrations, conferences, discussions with the Mayor, ending in victory for the Small Man against Big Business. The nightmare we all share about huge vehicles may not be exorcised by this blithe piece of satire but it is certainly brought into daylight. Told in a beautifully sustained deadpan manner, the story is given credence by its framework. It purports to be told by a newspaperman in 1986; he is working from his recollection of the happening, in 1976, referring for documentary evidence to Professor Lyman Cumberly's scholarly work, *The Large Object Theory of History,* which was itself inspired by the Pushcart War, and making good use of the Portlette Papers, named for Miriam Portlette, an office cleaner who by chance overheard some of the plotting of The Three and managed to purloin their documents. Dry, witty dialogue and smooth narrative pull us along at speed, ensuring that we appreciate the point cheerfully rather than gloomily. This is made still easier by Ronni Solbert's gorgeously eccentric pictures.

Margot Petts

SOURCE: A review of *The Pushcart War,* in *Children's Book Review,* Vol. IV, No. 1, Spring, 1974, pp. 19-20.

Writing in 1986 of an event which took place in 1976, the author uses a deadpan style which is both traditionally journalistic and hilariously Runyonesque. The event is the war, fought on the streets of New York City, between the pushcart peddlars and the truck drivers—the latter relying on the unsubtleties of sheer weight and numbers, the former on a 'secret weapon', pea-shooters and pins. There had already been a number of minor skirmishes, but the war began in earnest on the day that Mack, driving a truck for Mammoth Moving, met Morris the Florist and his pushcart in a confined space:

'"Look, I got to unload ninety dozen piano stools before five o'clock," Mack said.'

'"I got to sell two dozen bunches of daffodils" Morris replied. "Tomorrow they won't be so fresh."'

'"In about two minutes they won't be so fresh" Mack said.' This was the lead-up to what the history books now call 'The Daffodil Massacre'.

Mack and Morris, though important, are only two of the dozens of New Yorkers who battle their way through the streets. Ranged on one side or other of the barricades are such characters as Wenda Gambling, a well-known film star, later to play herself in the cinema version of the war; Walter Sweet and Lovie Livergreen of (respectively) Tiger Trucking and LEMA (Lower Eastside Moving Association); Mayor Emmett P. Cudd; and Mr. Posey of Posey's Pea Co. ('By the Ounce, By the Pound, By the Ton').

In one of the most inventive stories to have come my way (we have had to wait nine years after its appearance in America), Jean Merrill draws from both the credit and debit sides of the human account, which contributes greatly to her credibility, *and* produces a fascinating solution to the problem known to posterity as 'The Flower Formula', which should be submitted, presto, to the

Department of the Environment, the London Transport Executive and the EEC. 'Genuinely funny' black and white illustrations by Ronni Solbert should help to clarify any uncertainties for English readers.

The New York Times Book Review

SOURCE: A review of *The Pushcart War,* in *The New York Times Book Review,* January 14, 1979, p. 37.

An account of a war staged in New York City's streets between truck drivers and pushcart peddlers that satirizes both the inurbanities of modern urban life and the curious ways of tome writers, for it is buttressed with all manner of scholarly paraphernalia. Ronni Solbert's illustrations add to the amusement. Our reviewer called it "an utterly captivating book" for readers 11 years and older.

Ann Welton

SOURCE: A review of *The Pushcart War,* in *Booklist,* Vol. 88, No. 1, September 1, 1991, p. 67.

The Pushcart War began on the streets of New York City when a mover named Mack ran down a pushcart belonging to Morris the Florist. The war between the trucks and the pushcarts, escalating from the so-called Daffodil Massacre, builds in a lucid and humorous manner that, with the added enhancement of frequent pen-and-ink illustrations, will leave readers with a clear understanding of how wars begin and grow and how they can be prevented.

THE ELEPHANT WHO LIKED TO SMASH SMALL CARS (1967)

Publishers Weekly

SOURCE: A review of *The Elephant Who Liked to Smash Small Cars,* in *Publishers Weekly,* Vol. 192, No. 21, November 20, 1967, p. 56.

How W. C. Fields, whose dream, as Corey Ford remembers in his *Time of Laughter,* was to smash other cars with his car—how Fields would have relished the beginning of this book as a small elephant demolishes small cars! And how frustrated Fields would have been at its finale, when the small elephant's fun is spoiled by big cars; so frustrated a magnum of martinis wouldn't have silenced his grumblings. Children won't grumble; they'll relish it all.

THE BLACK SHEEP (1969)

Natalie Babbitt

SOURCE:A review of *The Black Sheep,* in *The New York Times Book Review,* October 26, 1969, p. 42.

On an island in the North Sea lives a commune of single-minded sheep who spend the time exclusively in clipping their own wool and knitting it into sweaters which they wear to keep warm. Alas—enter The Black Sheep who prefers gardening to knitting and his own shaggy coat to a sweater. He's nice about it, too, and that's always unforgiveable in a nonconformist. A law is passed against gardening and The Black Sheep is imprisoned. But one restrictive law begets another, and soon the sheep have legislated themselves right down to the chaos of nothing-to-do-but-think. Only The Black Sheep knows how to deal with thinking, and in the end he saves them from themselves. Jean Merrill brings off a difficult thing very well with the assistance of Ronni Solbert's carefully careless, waggish drawings. Her fable is a satisfying sandwich in which the peanut butter, sticky and nourishing, slides down with ease due to judicious use of jelly.

Publishers Weekly

SOURCE: A review of *The Black Sheep,* in *Publishers Weekly,* Vol. 196, No. 25, December 29, 1969, p. 67.

It's refreshing to come upon a fable with a moral that comes right out in the daylight and declares it *is* a fable with a moral. And when it is written by Jean Merrill (the ***Pushcart War***) and illustrated by Ronni Solbert, who illustrated her ***The Elephant Who Liked to Smash Small Cars,*** among other books, the result is a contemporary fable, rich in humor and satire. And wisdom.

Zena Sutherland

SOURCE: A review of *The Black Sheep,* in *Bulletin of the Center for Children's Books,* Vol. 23, No. 8, April, 1970, p. 131.

An entertaining fable about our organized and conforming society, written with sharp wit. Into a rigidly-structured community of white sheep there is born a black lamb who grows up to be a pacific rebel. He will not wear a sweater, when the whole focus of the group is the perpetual knitting of sweaters, with accompanying rituals of shearing, carding, et cetera. The black sheep wears his own shaggy coat and is perfectly comfortable, and he wastes all his time growing gardens, enjoying the color and scent. In fact, being useless. As the society becomes increasingly compulsive, some of its members wonder about the black sheep, now a pariah; the story ends with a mass realization of the futility of the established pattern, and a new order based on the simple, gentle way of life of the black sheep. Sly but not acid, pointed but not minatory.

Margaret A. Dorsey

SOURCE: A review of *The Black Sheep,* in *School Library Journal,* Vol. 16, No. 8, April, 1970, p. 123.

This deftly fable-styled story, in which the non-conformist triumphs over his regimented society, is a comic standout among sober titles with similar themes. Basalt is the only black sheep on a self-sufficient island of white sheep; worse, he refuses to be shorn to provide wool for the island industry—knitting sweaters to keep the shorn sheep warm; worst of all, he spends all his time gardening. The other sheep's reactions progress from puzzlement to disdain to irritation to fear to imprisonment of Basalt and the uprooting of his gardens. Sheep society becomes increasingly repressive to eradicate all traces of Basalt's influence until the whole structure breaks down under "a series of unnatural occurrences": no spring lambs are born, the knitting-needle-providing porcupines disappear, it snows in July. On the verge of mass suicide, the sheep are brought to their senses by discovery of Basalt's prison garden and his ability to cope with the terror of new ideas by relating them to gardening. Third- to fifth-grade readers should relish this delightful tale, while younger listeners can be charmed by a good story gracefully, wittily told.

A FEW FLIES AND I: HAIKU BY ISSA (written by Issa Kobayashi, selected by Merrill and Ronni Solbert from translations by R. H. Blyth and Nobuyuki Yuasa, 1969)

Polly Longsworth

SOURCE: A review of *A Few Flies and I: Haiku by Issa,* in *The New York Times Book Review,* May 4, 1969, p. 46.

"A haiku is a little like a telegram. It carries an important message in a very few words." So Jean Merrill tells us in her introduction to this delightful collection of haiku by Issa, the 18th-century Japanese poet who wrote seven thousand of the 17-syllable poems in his lifetime.

A Few Flies and I is itself a little like a telegram. Its well-chosen, happily balanced selections convey at least two important messages to young people. First, at a time when violence is prevalent in our nation, we marvel at Issa's reluctance to harm so much as a flea:

> I'm going to turn over;
> Mind away,
> Cricket.

Beyond this, Issa's life was devoted to making perceptive observations about a wide range of humble creatures. His kindly acknowledgments of the right to existence of man and beast, insect and flower, reminds modern man of his place in a balanced environment. Issa gently corrects our lordly tendency to think ourselves directors and chief inhabitants of creation.

> The flying butterfly:
> I feel myself
> A creature of dust.

Cherie Zarookian

SOURCE: A review of *A Few Flies and I: Haiku by Issa,* in *Library Journal,* Vol. 94, No. 13, July, 1969, p. 2682.

This delicate collection of Issa's haiku, containing 94 of the 200-year-old poems, concerns nature's smaller creatures (fleas, crickets, cicadas, sparrows, snails, etc.) and the feelings of the poet himself. A simple introduction by Jean Merrill discusses haiku as a form of poetry, Issa's philosophy, and his life. The format is lovely: tiny, very simple soft drawings ornament tinted pages and enhance the subtle yet often piquant observations, making this total effort a very graceful, appealing success.

MARY, COME RUNNING (1970)

Marilyn R. Singer

SOURCE: A review of *Mary, Come Running,* in *School Library Journal,* Vol. 17, No. 2, October, 1970, p. 149.

Refreshing heterodoxy is ***Mary, Come Running*** by Jean Merrill and Ronni Solbert. Joseph is a delightfully human, blustering old goat as represented by an indomitable, equally memorable old gypsy, Rom, who tells the nativity story as it would have been had the Romanies been there. They came to Bethlehem to steal from everyone, taxpayers, especially tax collectors; they even took chocolate off the donkey of a man named Joseph. "'Mary,' he calls, 'Mary, come running! Gypsies have entered. Gypsy rogues with the faces of sheep! And they're eating up all the chocolate!'" Mary, however, calms him down and tells him to make them some hot chocolate to drink. He flies off the handle again when he thinks the gypsy women are stealing the swaddling clothes off their new baby. Then people start coming into the stable, drawn by the star, and they say the child is a king. Even the Romanies—who recognize no king but their own—agree, and they honor him because he was born "poor as any Rom" and lived "begging his bread like a Rom." The story is based on an old Spanish carol, the words and music for which are supplied in the beginning of the book. The puckish illustrations, nondoctrinaire as the story, are the shapes of smooth stones and the colors of fine silks.

Zena Sutherland

SOURCE: A review of *Mary, Come Running,* in *Bulletin of the Center for Children's Books,* Vol. 24, No. 3, November, 1970, p. 46.

An unusual Christmas story based on an old Spanish carol and illustrated with small, brilliantly-colored pictures of the Nativity, the stiff little figures suggesting the grouping in a crèche. An old gypsy tells a small boy how the gypsies came, too, to Bethlehem. They stole from everybody, old Rom explains, but only so much as each good man would have given gladly; from the tax collectors they stole as much as they could. Joseph was worried. "Mary, come running," he called, when he saw the gypsies taking some chocolate. But Mary serenely made hot chocolate and just as calmly let the gypsy women hold the Babe. Like a queen, the gypsies felt, she welcomed them with grace; with the same dignity she accepted the gifts of the Magi. The vitality and humor of the story have no note of irreverence. A good choice for reading aloud to younger children.

George A. Woods

SOURCE: A review of *Mary, Come Running,* in *The New York Times Book Review,* December 6, 1970, p. 58.

"There are as many stories," reads the beginning of ***Mary, Come Running*** "about the birth of the Christ Child as there are story-tellers. . . . No one has heard them all." No one has heard this story, told by Jean Merrill, in which Old Rom, "oldest of Romanies," relates the true happenings behind the words of a Spanish carol which has for its refrain "Mary, come running! Come flying!/For gypsies are stealing his clothes."

The gypsies did come to Bethlehem to steal, Old Rom admits, but only a little from each man, "only as much as a good man would have given us gladly, had he known of our need. Except for the tax collectors. From them we stole *everything.*" And in the end they stayed to adore. Ronni Solbert's colorful, sophisticated primitive illustrations help prove that with this book there is indeed something new under the stars.

Booklist

SOURCE: A review of *Mary, Come Running,* in *Booklist,* Vol. 67, No. 9, January 1, 1971, pp. 373-74.

Suggested by an old Spanish carol that records the presence of gypsies at the stable in Bethlehem, this is a fresh and charming picture-book story of the Nativity. Old Rom, oldest of the gypsies, recounts to a small boy the events of that first Christmas Eve and the part played by the Romanies who came to steal whatever they could but stayed to worship the child. In the spirit of the carol the text portrays Joseph as a distraught husband and Mary as a calm, hospitable wife and the delightful paintings in colors appropriate to the locale are folklike in character yet reverent in tone.

HERE I COME—READY OR NOT! (1970)

Booklist

SOURCE: A review of *Here I Come—Ready or Not!* in *Booklist,* Vol. 67, No. 6, November 15, 1970, p. 270.

Two children playing hide-and-seek find wonderful hiding places in the barn. The game itself is fun for the reader of this picture book but even more interesting is the view of the interior of the barn, the farmyard, farm buildings, and farm animals afforded by the ordinary but agreeable detailed three-color drawings. The brief text is sufficiently lively and easy to read. The book should be useful with urban children.

Trevelyn Jones

SOURCE: A review of *Here I Come—Ready or Not!* in *School Library Journal,* Vol. 17, No. 4, December, 1970, p. 68.

Pure fun is Jean Merrill's ***Here I Come—Ready or Not!*** In a barnyard setting, Katy and Tony play hide and seek, On each page, one of the two is well hidden and readers will take great pleasure in looking for them. Uncluttered illustrations by Frances Gruse Scott in reds and yellows are perfect for preschoolers as well as for first-grade readers.

HOW MANY KIDS ARE HIDING ON MY BLOCK? (1970)

Booklist

SOURCE: A review of *How Many Kids Are Hiding on My Block?* in *Booklist,* Vol. 67, No. 17, May 1, 1971, p. 749.

What the author and the artist's ***Here I Come—Ready or Not*** did for the country scene this book does for the city. Unpretentious, pleasantly detailed three-color drawings and a brief adequate text depict a group of children in an integrated urban neighborhood playing hide-and-seek, hiding in such places as a trash can, a discarded bathtub, a pile of tires, a mannequin-filled show window, and a telephone booth.

Cary M. Ormond

SOURCE: A review of *How Many Kids Are Hiding on My Block?* in *Library Journal,* Vol. 96, No. 12, June 15, 1971, p. 2126.

Ten kids hiding on a busy city block. One by one, they are found and join in the hunt, with diminutive Annabel Lee eventually winning the prize by outwitting the others. Reds, browns and blacks enforce the warmth of the pencil drawings, and intriguing urban details (e.g., demolition work, second-hand stores, a hot-dog cart) provide a lively background for the multi-racial children. Eagle-eyed viewers or readers will relish the care with which each individual child is given a particular shock of hair or striped shirt so as to be identifiable from start to finish. The text is simple and there is satisfying repetition as each succeeding child is found and joins the seekers. A book to be savored by those who have it read to them, as well as by second-graders who read it for themselves.

PLEASE, DON'T EAT MY CABIN (1971)

Science Books: A Quarterly Review

SOURCE: A review of *Please, Don't Eat My Cabin,* in *Science Books: A Quarterly Review,* Vol. 8, No. 1, May, 1972, p. 62.

This lavishly illustrated little book informs the reader and the preschool listener about some of the smaller animals of the woods in such a way that they may become familiar with creatures that they might only come into contact with in a zoo. A young boy, Adam, takes his pet star-nosed mole and spends a summer at his grandmother's camp in the woods and during this time tames a woodchuck, an owl, a field mouse, and a porcupine who is the star attraction. Adam overcomes his grandmother's dislike and lack of trust in porcupines who have on past occasions tried to chew up her cabins, tables, etc. When a porcupine is killed leaving a motherless baby, Adam befriends it, calls it "Q," hides it for 2 weeks in his cabin where he feeds it an array of leftover foods from his meals, and finally convinces grandmother that the little fellow is not out to eat any cabins after all. To satisfy their new pet's craving for the taste of salt and wood, salty water is poured over unwanted tree stumps. Many interesting bits of information about animals and some insights into little boys and their eternal fascination with little creatures are woven into this story for children.

Patricia Vervoort

SOURCE: A review of *Please, Don't Eat My Cabin,* in *School Library Journal,* Vol. 19, No. 1, September, 1972, p. 70.

The author of ***The Pushcart War*** and ***The Black Sheep*** has written a gentle story about young Adam and the animals he tames into well-behaved pets. Adam is invited to visit Tessie, his grandmother, at her summer camp in the forest. In the first month, Adam tames a field mouse, a baby owl and a woodchuck, and Tessie draws pictures of the animals. However, Tessie isn't pleased with one of Adam's new pets—a destructive baby porcupine—until the day they make ice cream and the porcupine is found gnawing the stump over which salty ice water had been poured. Tessie had been tripping over that stump for a long time. Unfortunately, the task of taming wild animals is made to appear a simple one and the special care needed by these animals is not mentioned. Still, this effectively conveys a grandparent-child relationship where each cooperates and yet can pursue his own interests, and the muted yellow and grey illustrations complement the quiet, slow-paced story.

THE TOOTHPASTE MILLIONAIRE (1972)

The Christian Science Monitor

SOURCE: A review of *The Toothpaste Millionaire,* in *The Christian Science Monitor,* July 3, 1974, p. 7.

A delightfully upbeat story about a young genius named Rufus Mayflower, who discovers how to turn business ethics and tubs of homemade toothpaste into a multimillion-dollar operation. There are many lessons in this slim little book, including a hefty collection of math problems, but all tucked so expertly and unobtrusively into the story that they only heighten the reader's enjoyment.

Booklist

SOURCE: A review of *The Toothpaste Millionaire,* in *Booklist,* Vol. 70, No. 22, July 15, 1974, p. 1254.

Merrill's idealistic construct of how to succeed in business without really trying functions both as a light story and as an explication of free enterprise mechanics. Rufus, a sixth grader, is disgusted at the high cost of toothpaste and decides to make his own with bicarbonate of soda as the main ingredient. His goal is low-cost production with a penny profit on each unit, and he begins marketing his product to neighborhood customers at three cents a jar. Publicity increases orders, and Rufus takes out a loan to rent a factory and the machinery needed to keep up with ever growing demand. At the end of it all, costs have driven the price up to 15 cents a tube, (still lower than any competition), but the penny profit margin remains. Rufus is splendidly ahead, an ethical, self-made millionaire who has survived a price war, a hired bomber, and the IRS. Farfetched but engaging instruction. Soft line drawings punctuated with warm colors highlight the text.

Virginia Haviland

SOURCE: A review of *The Toothpaste Millionaire,* in *The Horn Book Magazine,* Vol. L, No. 5, October, 1974, p. 137.

It requires exceptional talent to make engrossing a story with so plain a purpose, but in ***The Pushcart War*** the author demonstrated her gift for writing about an everyday problem. Of smaller compass, this work of fiction focuses on the overpricing of a commodity. The teller of the tale is a classmate of brilliantly inventive sixth-grade Rufus Mayflower, who "doesn't seem to mind that I'm white and he's black." Rufus makes and markets an extraordinarily inexpensive toothpaste—which still sells at a low price even when stockholders, promotion, and all the necessary apparatus of a growing business introduce expenses. The narrative is breezy and fast-moving, and becomes most amusing when Sparkle, Dazzle, and Brite try to meet the competition after *Consumer's Friend* has proclaimed Rufus' toothpaste the best buy.

Zena Sutherland

SOURCE: A review of *The Toothpaste Millionaire,* in *Bulletin of the Center for Children's Books,* Vol. 28, No. 3, November, 1974, p. 49.

Kate tells the story, which is laden rather heavily with arithmetic and business details, but rises above it. She had just moved to East Cleveland, and Rufus was the first friendly sixth-grader she met; he didn't even seem to mind that she was white, and he quickly impressed her as being a genius. Sensible and sharp, Rufus had decided that toothpaste was unnecessarily expensive, so he mixed his own and sold it for three cents a tube. Honest commercials popularized the product (which was just called "Toothpaste") and forced competitors out of business, a plant was soon in operation, and Rufus soon had stockholders and a board of directors. He also grew bored. And the last Kate heard of him was a postcard, while he was on vacation, asking her to investigate the cost of blow-up rafts and 100-pound bags of dried soup. "If America hadn't already been discovered," Kate concludes, "it wouldn't surprise me at all if that was what Rufus had in mind." The illustrations are engaging, the style is light, the project interesting (with more than a few swipes taken at advertising and business practices in our society) and Rufus a believable genius.

MARIA'S HOUSE (1974)

Publishers Weekly

SOURCE: A review of *Maria's House,* in *Publishers Weekly,* Vol. 206, No. 2, July 8, 1974, p. 75.

Maria looks forward to art class each week until her assignment is to bring a drawing of her house. How can she draw the ugly tenement, with its fire escapes, spilled garbage, milk cartons, stray cats and graffiti? But Mama insists that real art has to be true, so Maria takes real art to class. The teacher, Miss Lindstrom, calls the class to gather around and view "the nicest thing you've done this year." Maria is pleased until the teacher asks her to draw her *own* house instead of a street scene next week. She is truly Mama's daughter when she replies, "But that *is* my house." The author of some 30 children's books has written a touching, simple story, beautifully illustrated by a newcomer [Frances Gruse Scott] to children's books.

Kirkus Reviews

SOURCE: A review of *Maria's House,* in *Kirkus Reviews,* Vol. XLII, No. 14, July 15, 1974, p. 743.

Maria's Mama irons shirts for the Overnite Laundry to pay Maria's tuition at the Museum's Saturday morning art classes, but she knows as much about art as anybody. And when Maria is ashamed to draw her own house as specified in a class assignment, Mama encourages her to "tell the truth" and show the rundown tenement, complete with scrawled graffiti and milk cartons on the windowsill. Maria's embarrassment at the poverty of her home soon fades into pride in her artistry, though it's hard to be sure whether her teacher (who at first says, "Maria didn't quite understand the assign ment . . . I'd meant for you to draw your own house") is naive or just trying to be tactful. In any case, it's a more reticent treatment of the situation than one might expect nowadays, but Maria's close relationship with Mama and distant idolatry of her tall blond teacher capture her ambivalence neatly. And though young readers will wish they could see the picture Maria drew, Scott's sketches of street scenes and Mama's kitchen have a comparable feeling for homely detail.

Booklist

SOURCE: A review of *Maria's House,* in *Booklist,* Vol. 71, No. 1, September 1, 1974, p. 45.

To Maria art classes at the museum are wonderful; she works intently on her drawings and hopes for words of praise from her idolized teacher. But her happiness is clouded by a take-home assignment to sketch her own house, because she is ashamed of her crowded, rundown tenement. Her mother, telling her that art must be true, urges her to draw what she sees. Maria's decision to follow this advice not only yields a sensitive drawing but leads her toward the confidence to admit to her teacher the way she lives. Simply told, although sometimes too obvious, this warm story provides food for thought.

David K. Willis

SOURCE: A review of *Maria's House,* in *The Christian Science Monitor,* November 6, 1974, p. 11.

The best children's books are adult books as well, from *Alice in Wonderland* to *Winnie-the-Pooh.* They are so good, and so universal in theme, that they appeal to the best in all of us.

Which is why one unobtrusive-looking new book this season, accompanied by plain black and white line drawings, stands head and shoulders above most books this reviewer has looked at in the past several years.

Maria's House starts out to be the story of a little girl (aged about ten, one guesses) with a gift for drawing, whose mother irons shirts for a laundry late into the night so that Maria can attend art classes every Saturday at the museum, a whole shining world away from her lower-class tenement district.

It ends as the triumph of honesty over deceit, of love over selfishness.

Maria usually lives for Saturday mornings, and for what they mean: a clean smock, a bus ride across town, the grandly spacious entrance hall of the museum—and Miss Lindstrom, the art teacher. On one particular Saturday, Maria shrinks from her class. Miss Lindstrom has told the children to draw the house they live in—and Maria feels she just cannot draw her own 15-family tenement, with its broken window panes, and the milk cartons put out on the window ledge of one apartment to keep cool (the electricity keeps being cut off when the bills aren't paid).The other children in the class live in suburban houses which only have one family in them. And what would Miss Lindstrom say. . . . Maria draws a magazine picture of an idealized suburban home. But Mama says it isn't "true," . . . and Maria must wrestle with herself as she watches Mama iron. Miss Lindstrom likes the eventual drawing very much, but assumes it is not of Maria's own home. It would be so easy not to tell her that it actually is.

After finishing the book while riding into the office in a car-pool one morning, this reviewer could hardly wait to share it with his own six- and five-year-old daughters. They sat still for half an hour, listened to it all, found the drawings clear and satisfactory, smiled with satisfaction at the ending . . . and confirmed that Miss Merrill, author of some 30 other children's books, has a rare gift for creating real characters and letting them develop.

Zena Sutherland

SOURCE: A review of *Maria's House,* in *Bulletin of the Center for Children's Books,* Vol. 28, No. 6, February, 1975, p. 97.

Maria loved Miss Lindstrom, who taught the Saturday art class at the museum, but she hated the latest assignment: drawing a picture of your house. Nobody at art class knew that Maria was poor and lived in a tenement, and she didn't want them to know, so she had drawn a big white house set among large lawns. It looked like a magazine picture, Mama said, but it wasn't true, and art must be true. Maria loved Mama and knew how much she gave up so that there could be art lessons—and so she tore up the picture and drew her own house. And Miss Lindstrom thought it was beautiful. A slight vehicle, but it speaks clearly of the integrity and sense of values that a child can absorb from her parents, it's nicely structured and simply written.

MARAH (1981)

Kirkus Reviews

SOURCE: A review of *Marah,* in *Kirkus Reviews,* Vol. XLIX, No. 19, October 1, 1981, p. 1250.

A happy-hearted, frisky, podgily sentimental romantic adventure set in the sulphurous East London slums circa 1900. Dewy waif Marah, slavey to the formidable Miss Slaughter (Temperance-preaching director of the East London Mission), first sees languid Lord Malgrave while she's dragging a harmonium through fog and mud on one of Miss Slaughter's anti-tavern assaults. But Miss Slaughter explains that Lord Malgrave is a "Fornicator. Lecher. Dissolute rapscallion. Landlord of the whole district, etc., etc." Furthermore: "His father murdered his mother." So Marah, product of a Foundling Asylum, tries to resist the ubiquitous Malgrave's attentions: he dines her in his fine home, buys her new clothes, takes her to a sinister socialist meeting. (After all, the meeting notice appeared in the Mission paper—for which Marah herself composes such high-minded tales as "Drowned Through Their Own Fault" and "Ruined by Rank.") But Marah prefers nice printer Mr. Cawthorne, who's researching the mystery of Marah's birth and the ring—bearing something akin to a Malgrave coat-of-arms!—found on her baby person. Meanwhile, Malgrave is sleuthing the socialists (who look forward to the Royal Family cleaning sewers and stringing up such as Malgrave). And Marah snoops too, when a Mission disciple is framed for burglary and when a local courtesan dies bizarrely: in disguise, she visits Mr. Cawthorne's awful mother; there are free-for-alls in the Mission and on the street, with avuncular interventions by Malgrave (whose Tory heart is pure taffy); Marah is hurled from a window by the villain; her parentage-secret is aired; and all hands are paired off nicely . . . with Miss Slaughter regally crocked. Upbeat juvenilia, but—like old Disney-movies—it moves briskly and offers innocent merriment.

Publishers Weekly

SOURCE: A review of *Marah,* in *Publishers Weekly,* Vol. 220, No. 14, October 2, 1981, pp. 100-01.

Set amid the murk and gloom of a squalid London slum in the 1890s, this historical romance revolves around young Marah Michaelmas, abandoned as a baby on the steps of a foundling asylum. She now assists Miss Slaughter, director of the East London Halfpenny Mission (dedicated to crusading against the evils of alcohol), having been chosen from the orphanage to serve as an unpaid lackey. Marah begins to unravel the mystery of who her parents were, and finds herself with two admirers who seem equally interested in her origins: the handsome printer Mr. Cawthorne, and Lord Malgrave, landlord of the slums she has grown up in. Merrill has written an intricately plotted story that transports well across the Atlantic. Marah is a sympathetic and engaging heroine, minor characters add plenty of color and zest and Merrill's wry touches of humor, liberally sprinkled throughout, make her novel all the more enjoyable.

THE GIRL WHO LOVED CATERPILLARS (1992)

Joanne Schott

SOURCE: A review of *The Girl Who Loved Caterpillars,* in *Quill and Quire,* Vol. 58, No. 9, September, 1992, p. 78.

The unusual and tantalizing source for this book is a 12th-century Japanese story about court life whose promised second chapter—which may contain the conclusion to the heroine's tale—has either been lost or was never written. Izumi's father hoped she might marry a nobleman, but she dashes these hopes and embarrasses her parents with her thorough nonconformity. She refuses to pluck her eyebrows or dress her hair, and makes friends with the rough boys who deliver the caterpillars and other insects she loves to study. The Captain of the Stables is intrigued nevertheless, and he watches Izumi from outside her window. The two exchange notes, but his final correspondence—to which Izumi does not reply—claims that "no man exists sensitive and brave enough to tune his life" to a girl who loves caterpillars.

Merrill's prose is dignified and suits the story, contrasting Izumi's way of life with the expectations of the court, and revealing a delightful, original, and very likeable heroine. Floyd Cooper's sensitive paintings are beautifully executed in warm and subtle colours, full of detail in costume and setting. He introduces a note of poignancy to the Captain and his portrayal of Izumi is as richly individual as the text demands.

Kate McClelland

SOURCE: A review of *The Girl Who Loved Caterpillars,* in *School Library Journal,* Vol. 38, No. 9, September, 1992, p. 269.

A retelling of a Japanese story believed to date from the 12th century. Izumi is the privileged and pretty daughter of a provincial inspector in the emperor's court; she refuses to conform to standards of beauty and decorum. Preoccupied with the study of "the original nature of things," Izumi particularly loves caterpillars, and most enjoys the company, not of noblemen, but of low class boys who supply her with caterpillars to study. She attracts the admiration of a young nobleman who concludes he is not good enough for her; the story thus ends abruptly for, as an author's note explains, the rest of it has been lost. The retelling of this curious fragment is graceful and competent. Cooper's warm, beautiful oil wash paintings are in his familiar, appealing style, but they are flawed by inaccuracy of detail in both costume and setting, reflecting a period hundreds of years later than the story's setting. Still, this unusual piece will find use in classrooms; literally unfinished, it is a natural for creative writing assignments and, teamed with Cole's *Dragon in the Cliff,* could lead to discussion of the difficulties faced by women with a passion for science.

Ilene Cooper

SOURCE: A review of *The Girl Who Loved Caterpillars* in *Booklist,* Vol. 89, No. 1, September 1, 1992, p. 54.

Twelfth-century Japan was hardly an era of feminism, but this story retells a tale, found on a scroll, of a strong girl with ideas of her own. Izumi's parents have high hopes for her—perhaps she will become a lady-in-waiting at the Emperor's court. But unlike the exquisite noblewoman who lives next door, Izumi has no interest in butterflies, or lute playing, or writing poetry. Her attention is focused on the creepy crawlies, especially caterpillars, from which others recoil. So Izumi spends her time playing with scruffy common boys who bring her the creatures, following her passion for nature and being the object of the neighbors' gossip. Even though she does not blacken her teeth, as is the fashion, or trim her bushy eyebrows, she attracts the attention of the Captain of the Stables. Their correspondence ends, however, when he responds to the mores of his time and writes Izumi that her world is too strange for him. Izumi resumes feeding her caterpillars. In an afterword, Merrill reports that the original account had a traditional ending, "What happened next will be found in the second chapter," but the chapter has been lost. The drama of the story is stunningly captured by Cooper's soft oil-wash paintings. Edging the narrow bands of text, the artwork takes center stage. With medieval Japan in the background, Izumi, her friends, and her caterpillars are the focus of scenes that pulse with life and beauty. Izumi herself almost takes the reader's breath away, so real is she; her life-affirming determination electrifies every page. Truly, a timeless story.

Kirkus Reviews

SOURCE: A review of *The Girl Who Loved Caterpillars,* in *Kirkus Reviews,* Vol. LX, No. 18, September 15, 1992, p. 1191.

A 12th-century Japanese story, adapted from three credited translations, about a young woman of respectable rank who defies convention by refusing to pluck her eyebrows or blacken her teeth; more significantly—unlike "the Perfect Lady" next door, who collects butterflies and flowers—she's fascinated by small creatures like insects and frogs. Ragged boys who bring her insects are Izumi's friends. She also has an admirer who values her true worth; he sends her an ingenious mechanical snake, and they exchange some subtle verse, but he goes on his way, "amused and wondering." Perhaps, Merrill suggests, what followed has been lost. What remains is an intriguing glimpse of an independent-minded woman, deplored but not thwarted by her family. Merrill's adaptation is dignified and energetic, with touches of humor. Cooper's three-quarter-spread paintings (the text is nicely accommodated at one side) feature subtle, beautifully modeled portraits and exquisite fabrics against impressionistic, elegantly composed backgrounds in glowing, mellow earth tones. A lovely, unusual book.

Publishers Weekly

SOURCE: A review of *The Girl Who Loved Caterpillars,* in *Publishers Weekly,* Vol. 239, No. 45, October 12, 1992, p. 78.

Delicate, luminous oil paintings illustrate this 12th-century Japanese tale about an unconventional girl. Unlike other gentle flowers of her age, Izumi prefers collecting insects and caterpillars with "some scruffy-looking boys" to dressing fashionably and plucking her eyebrows. Her frustrated parents fear no respected suitor will want such a headstrong wife, but Izumi's reputation captures the fancy of both a nobleman and a captain, either of whom may eventually ask for her hand. Merrill's retelling has a slow, almost laborious pace. And though the story is culled from scholarly sources, its abrupt ending and question-raising afterword fail to satisfy. Cooper's glowing portraits of Izumi, with her "eyebrows like caterpillars," breathe life and imagination into the text. The book's becoming design makes the most of his striking artwork, which occupies three-quarters of each spread—text is arranged in vertical columns against the remaining space. Silken Japanese robes, indigenous flora and architecture imbue the paintings with an authentic Eastern flavor. Although Izumi's independence holds much appeal, young readers may be eager for more information about her fate.

Betsy Hearne

SOURCE: A review of *The Girl Who Loved Caterpillars,* in *Bulletin of the Center for Children's Books,* Vol. 46, No. 3, November, 1992, p. 82.

Adapted from an anonymously written twelfth-century Japanese tale, this story of an independent girl has a surprisingly contemporary tone, perhaps because it's part of an unfinished manuscript. Izumi refuses to follow the fashions her socially ambitious parents hope will attract a wealthy husband. Instead, she remains absorbed in her study of caterpillars, worms, toads, and insects, often brought to her by poor boys whom she rewards with expensive possessions which she cares nothing about. Finally her reputation attracts a witty nobleman who admires her for her unique nature. They exchange amusing, mutually admiring notes, but this is not a romance; the nobleman leaves her garden forever, as she calls for her scruffy friends to bring fresh leaves for her caterpillars. Merrill's adaptation is cleanly yet elegantly styled, as are Cooper's pastel double spreads, which elaborate on the many vivid images in the story, including Izumi's furry eyebrows—she will not pluck them into a fine line as the court ladies do. While the art is soft-edged, it's not sentimental but is instead sustained by sturdy drafting and muted colors. The suspended ending, which may leave some younger listeners puzzled, will provide primary graders with an intriguing take-off for discussion.

Junko Yokota

SOURCE: A review of *The Girl Who Loved Caterpillars,* in *Language Arts,* Vol. 70, No. 3, March, 1993, p. 218.

A conflict that young women of various cultures face is that of independent choice versus societal expectations. In this case, the society is 12th-century nobility in Japan, a country and a time period that held rigid expectations for female nobility. Izumi chooses not to model the highly regarded behavior of The Lady Who Loves Butterflies, who epitomizes the appropriate lifestyle of ladies of the Heian period Japanese court. Instead, Izumi prefers to study and play with caterpillars. She prefers the insects the local boys bring her to the expensive gifts of courting noblemen. Throughout the story, Izumi exemplifies independent decision making. Illustrator Floyd Cooper brings to life the story Jean Merrill adapted from 12th-century scrolls.

Additional coverage of Merrill's life and career is contained in the following sources published by Gale Research: *Contemporary Authors New Revision Series,* Vol. 38; *Major Authors and Illustrators for Children and Young Adults;* and *Something about the Author,* Vol. 82.

John (Arthur) Neufeld

1938-

(Also writes as Joan Lea) American author of fiction and screenplays.

Major works include *Edgar Allan* (1968), *Lisa, Bright and Dark* (1969), *Touching* (1970; published as *Twink,* 1971), *Freddy's Book* (1973), *Gaps in Stone Walls* (1996).

INTRODUCTION

Neufeld is best known for groundbreaking novels for young adults which confront such sensitive subjects as racism, sex, and mental illness. His frank, matter-of-fact treatment of controversial issues was uncommon in works for adolescents when he published his first novel in 1968, and since then he has continued to write openly and honestly on matters of interest to teens and preteens. In his best works, critics note, Neufeld combines a compelling story and believable characters with an objective look at the issue at hand; in addition, he often leaves the resolutions of his works ambiguous, giving readers a chance to place themselves in the situation and come to their own conclusions. Neufeld also allows adult characters to have significant roles in his works, presenting a more realistic portrayal of how teens must deal with difficulties than is usually found in the genre. Even with adult assistance, however, his young characters must often come to their own terms with their problems, whether they stem from family concerns—such as divorce, pregnancy, and illness—or social issues—such as censorship, homelessness, and political oppression. Neufeld has said that his goal is to "introduce young readers to situations they themselves might meet. If they read how a contemporary has handled a difficult conflict, the aloneness of facing that identical crucible is mitigated. That," Neufeld argues, "is one of the great values of literature for children."

Biographical Information

Neufeld was born in Chicago in 1938 but was raised in Des Moines, Iowa. An avid reader, he quickly graduated to adult novels and was writing his own stories by his teens. After attending a prep school in New Hampshire, Neufeld graduated from Yale University in 1960, travelled through Europe, and was drafted into the Army. Upon completing two years' service, the book lover moved to New York, where he hoped to become an editor; however, after a series of publicity jobs, Neufeld discovered he preferred working on his own plays and stories. He was attending a publishing conference in California when he heard the story of a white family who had been forced by community pressure to give up their adopted black child. The story stuck with Neufeld and formed the basis for his first novel, *Edgar Allan.* "I didn't set out to write juveniles," he once explained. "I only wanted to write a simple story, easily understood."

Nevertheless, the critical and popular success of *Edgar Allan* gave Neufeld an instant reputation as an author for young people, one solidified by his second work, *Lisa, Bright and Dark.* Neufeld's treatment of such formerly taboo issues as racism, mental illness, teenage sex and pregnancy, and children's curiosity about profanity led him to be pegged by critics and publishers as an author of "problem novels." After the publication of *Sharelle* in 1983, Neufeld took a break from writing for young adults, finding little inspiration in a field that he saw as having been exhausted by the flood of problem novels published in the 1970s, and turned to adult novels. He focused his energies on a teaching career in Los Angeles. It wasn't until a stint as a volunteer in a day-care center for homeless children that Neufeld was again inspired to write for juveniles. The result was *Almost a Hero* (1995), and Neufeld followed that work with his first historical novel, *Gaps in Stone Walls.* Although Neufeld still sees himself as an adult author, he has said that as long as he finds issues that inspire him, he will continue to share his work with young readers: "As a child, I thought I could learn more about life by reading fiction than nonfiction," he once wrote. "I still believe this to be the case with good children's books."

Major Works

Neufeld's critically acclaimed debut novel, *Edgar Allan,* established the standard for his future fiction; in this work, a white minister's family adopts a three-year-old black child, only to find themselves faced with prejudice from both the outside community and their own family. The novel is narrated by the family's fourteen-year-old son, who attempts to deal with the resentment his sister feels about the adoption as well as the aftermath of his father's eventual capitulation to the forces urging him to give up the child. With its combination of personal and political themes, *Edgar Allan* proved a successful look at a significant issue; critic Richard Horchler noted that it "offers an experience in the growth of compassion and understanding." *Lisa, Bright and Dark* was another forthright examination of a sensitive topic, as three teens try to deal with the progressing mental illness of their friend, whose attempts at seeking help have been spurned by the adults around her. Physical impairments are the focus of adolescent efforts at understanding in *Touching,* in which a sixteen-year-old boy attempts to learn more about his new stepsister Twink, who has suffered from cerebral palsy since birth. Neufeld's stark portrayal of the girl's condition, including an unflinching description of an operation she receives, disturbed some critics who felt it might be too much for children; other reviewers, however, believed the novel effectively portrayed Twink, making her a human character rather than an object of pity. Neufeld turned to science fiction with *Sleep, Two, Three, Four!* (1971), a futuristic thriller with a political edge in which a group of teens battle a fascistic American government that is reminiscent of the Nixon administration.

Another groundbreaking yet controversial work was *Freddy's Book,* in which a young preteen tries to discover the meaning of a profanity he sees on a bathroom wall. Attempts by peers and adults to explain to Freddy what the word means give him an education in both misconceptions and truths about sex. Critical reaction was mixed, although critic Robert J. Lacampagne noted that the work was pioneering in that "its technical and clinical discussions of sex are combined with consistent and appealing humor." Other Neufeld books of the late 1970s and early 1980s were less successful with reviewers; dealing with issues such as teen marriage, divorce, and pregnancy, they were often faulted for being more message than fiction, even if well-written. One of the more successful works from this period was *A Small Civil War* (1982), a remarkably balanced story of a school censorship battle, originally published in 1982 and later revised in 1995. When Neufeld resumed writing young adult works with *Almost a Hero* (1995), critics noted that he had lost none of his ability to engage his audience in this story of a boy whose volunteer work at a homeless shelter leads him to learn that life is more complex than it seems. A murder mystery with an ambiguous ending forms the center of the historical work *Gaps in Stone Walls,* set in a nineteenth-century New England community where twenty percent of the population is hearing impaired. Reviewers praised Neufeld's ability to portray a unique historical setting, as well as his treatment of his deaf protagonist and her community. As Jennifer Fleming noted, Neufeld "has once again proven himself an unflinching student of the human heart, and has illuminated a revealing aspect of American history."

Awards

Both *Edgar Allan* and *Lisa, Bright and Dark* earned "Book of the Year" citations from the *New York Times* and American Library Association in 1968 and 1969, respectively; *Edgar Allan* was similarly cited by *Time* magazine in 1968. *Gaps in Stone Walls* was nominated for an Edgar Allan Poe Award from the Mystery Writers of America in 1996.

AUTHOR'S COMMENTARY

John Neufeld

SOURCE: "Young Adult Propaganda and Change," in *The ALAN Review,* Vol. 10, No. 3, Spring, 1983, pp. 1-2, 40.

Over the past fifteen years, I have been asked by many well-meaning (I assume) people why I write as often as I do for Young Adults. I've had, therefore, a lot of time to formulate an answer. It is only *my* answer. I would not presume to imagine any other writer's response.

It certainly isn't, or wasn't, for the money. My first novel, ***Edgar Allan,*** brought me a total advance of $750. Divide that in half—half on signing, half on delivery—and you have a very thin year, indeed. (For ***Lisa, Bright and Dark,*** the advance was identical.)

It wasn't for recognition. All authors are subject to the same cocktail party exchange: "Oh? Would you have written anything I might know?" My answer: "Probably not. Millions of people don't . . . unless you have children."

It wasn't for awards and honors, or for opportunities to teach. I've had none of the former, although I admit to yearning for a chance to do the latter.

If not for fame and fortune, why?

To be felt. To make oneself felt at a vulnerable moment in someone else's life. To present ideas to readers young enough not to have immediate experience of the subject and yet to arm them, so that if ever they find themselves in situations about which they might have read, they have some sort of experience upon which to draw.

Because I feel strongly about certain things, I want other people—young people, especially—to know about them.

Admittedly, I feel strongly as an adult. The subjects of my books are not taken from my own memories of growing up. Rarely is autobiographical detail included. But the inequalities, unfairnesses, injustices that exercise me as a voter, as a member of any community, as an ordinary human being are those that I want to present to others.

The fact that I choose a particular topic, I imagine, uncovers my own particular bias in each case.

In ***Edgar Allan,*** for example, neither the family nor the problem of interracial adoption was my own. But I felt, and do still, that the process can be successful, healthy, and happy. There may and probably will be problems. But these can be overcome with honesty and good-will and affection. That Edgar Allan is given away, that the Ficketts failed is their peculiar story. I felt it was an honest portrayal of a situation, but it need not have ended as it did. *That* is the point.

What could I hope for in writing a story that on its outside seemed pessimistic and saddening? That young people would calmly consider the choices made and the paths taken and be able to think what they might do in the same instance. And that they would *agree* with me—it need not have turned out so.

For that is the ultimate aim of the stories I tell. I *want* agreement. I want it early. I want it to last. And I purposely choose to present my theories and feelings to people whose own experiences and sensations are necessarily somewhat more embryonic and limiting than my own.

In short, ***Edgar Allan*** is a novel of propaganda. And so is ***Lisa.*** And ***Sleep Two, Three, Four?*** And almost every other project that's ever seen daylight.

Is this taking unfair advantage of willing minds? Am I subverting youthful independence and investigation? Am I lobbying unfairly?

I don't think so.

I have often—most recently, on the publication of ***A Small Civil War***—been criticized for trying to be too even-handed at the expense of tension and character in a story.

That's a danger of which I'm always aware, and which I try mightily to skirt, not always with success.

But as a moral propagandist—i.e., I feel a responsibility to put a *whole* case before the public, not a one-sided one—I don't see any alternative. The best I can hope to do is present arguments for and against a certain point of view, and work hard to make the reader come down on *my* side. (There *is* an alternative: greater skill. I'm *trying!*)

In ***A Small Civil War***—a story of book censorship in a small Iowa community—clearly I opt for the forces that believe reading is beneficial, not harmful, to its practitioners. Reading *anything*.

When I was in college, for instance, my sister announced one evening at dinner that there was nothing in the house to read. She was under eleven at the time. I was dumbfounded. I challenged. Had she read Dickens? Yes. All of him. What about something more current, Nicholas Monsarrat's *The Cruel Sea?* Yes, that, too. Reaching even further, I grinned and asked about that season's salacious and notorious best-seller, *The Chapman Report.* She'd read that, as well.

Well!

The point is that as far as I can tell, her behavior was altered in no lubricious fashion after having read that book, nor do I think any child's would have been. It seems to me that unless and until you have personal experience with which to measure, reading such a book becomes an exercise in pure fiction—reading for the story alone. The sexual detailing, the needs and hungers of adult characters, are obscured by whether or not the story pulls you along.

As for ***A Small Civil War,*** the book that figures as target (as it did in reality) is *The Grapes of Wrath.*

Dutifully and slowly I reread the book, twice. Once in simple admiration and awe, for it is a giant. Again, underlining and counting the number of times certain "questionable" words or phrases are used in the text. The final tally *is* huge: on an average, there are more than two instances *per page* of what people, rightly or wrongly, consider bad language, unclean thought, imagery that is either corrupting or inciting. From a particular point of view, it is possible to see why the book might upset adults hoping to protect their young from the crudities and shocks of life in the thirties, as well as in the eighties. From my own point of view, however, it is still and always what the writer says, not the particular words or phrases in which he speaks, that matter. And what one remembers of *The Grapes of Wrath* is sadness and frustration, sympathy and strength. *And* a small amount of triumph, too, in lasting, in getting to California, in hoping to stay.

What Steinbeck did so brilliantly was to replicate the speech of a certain set of people, but very carefully. If anyone wants to take the time and trouble—you'll find that Ma Joad never, ever succumbs to language that could in any way be considered censorable, despite her travails. This, I assume, was a conscious choice of the artist. Ma Joad *wouldn't* swear. She doesn't need to. She has strength, belief, patience. And she's a leader. She has other, finer, stronger tools at her command.

I don't want to presume, but I think Mr. Steinbeck was propagandizing. He wanted readers to see the wretchedness of life on the road for his Okies. He wanted us to understand and sympathize. He wanted us to care for, learn from, remember. He had his villains, too—the forces that put the Joads out of their homestead, that drove them from temporary refuges along their route back out into the wilderness again. He wanted us to feel the injustice of all this. He succeeded.

What I wanted to do in ***A Small Civil War*** was smaller-scaled, but equally pointed. I wanted people on both sides of this issue to understand each other. There were safeguards and liberties both to be considered. People's feelings, as well as individual rights, were at stake. That in this case the "wrong side" won, alas, simply corresponds with life. But the important thing is to understand, to know where one would stand if faced with identical choices. I could only hope that most readers would, in the face of the temporary defeat in these pages, know it was temporary, know that it was an outcome that could be, must be changed.

I have also been criticized for too often selecting as a point of view that of a teen-aged girl, rather than a boy.

I accept that. (Still, what about ***Edgar Allan, Touching, Sleep, Two, Three, Four!, Freddy's Book?***)

Some things in life don't seem to change much. One of them is the average reader for YA Books. It *is* a teen-aged girl: middle-class, curious, thoughtful.

If, as we so often say we believe, women are the gentling influence in life, then why not write directly to this audience? They are malleable, still; unformed and open. And if a liberal's concerns are ever to be presented and to have any sort of impact, at what better age? (That sounds unfair and manipulative. It is.)

What *has* changed, I think and hope, is the reader's and the publisher's willingness—nay, ability—to allow for the possibility that young people do not live in a vacuum in which no adult figures any more prominently than the knees of mothers and fathers in comic strips.

This was not always so. I began writing in 1968. At that time, the cardinal rule seemed to be that adults—if involved in a story at all—were to be marginal, generally well-meaning if a little blind, and were never, ever to receive equal focus or attention. Editors felt that young people wouldn't read a story in which adults figured too prominently.

This has always seemed to be specious. A child grows in an environment in which, plainly, adults do count, do rule the roosts. How can we isolate what concerns a child from his/her surroundings? (I ask this not of teachers and librarians, or parents, alone, but also of other writers who have zeroed in so tightly on a child's singular life. Children can and do ask questions of adults; they can and do come to adults for guidance and support.)

I've tried, therefore, in my own work, to put adults as much in the light as young adults. And because of this, not to mention the fact that as years progress, one is further from youth oneself, I begin to find adult characters more interesting and challenging, more varied and flawed, more central to any story that's worth telling to or about young people. After all, as I grow older, so do they—young readers. If my world is mostly that of an adult, theirs soon will be.

Which is why, I think, the character of the mother in ***Sharelle*** is so important—not simply to the story, but to me and the progress of what I write.

Without Melba Marston there is no Sharelle. Not simply in a physical sense, but metaphorically. It is Melba who provides the tension, the drive behind the story. It is she who has the sense of humor, the selfishness, the *fear* that animates the entire book. True enough, what happens in ***Sharelle*** is Sharelle's story: her problems, her solutions. But it is Melba who shapes them all.

And Melba is a wreck. She's loose. She's small-minded. She drinks. She sleeps around. There is a patina of civic-mindedness atop all this; a layer of community concern. But it is as sheer and porous as her own affection for her two daughters. On a sliding scale, Melba's efforts at motherhood would rank near the bottom. As a *liver,* Melba's right up there at the top.

I don't think young people will dismiss Melba or find her unsympathetic. They may not have women in their own lives with whom to compare, but they'll recognize her, instinctively. Just as they'll recognize Sharelle's pride and determination even if they don't agree with her life decisions.

That ***Sharelle*** is a story of responsibility and its limits, of one young woman's understanding of what adult acts lead to alongside her mother's flight from aging and loneliness, is purposeful. It *is* a dual story. People do live side by side and have to solve problems in proximity. Melba's story is somewhat more oblique than Sharelle's, necessarily. ***Her*** problems are simply not as concrete as her daughter's. Their solutions are gradual, whereas for Sharelle, solutions must be immediate. Both stories are, I think, worth telling.

I used to think that the projects I wanted to work on had to be "firsts." I did not want, for example, to take a stab at writing about a blind girl in East Harlem and incest (a suggestion once made sincerely by an editor to me). (The rejection of that idea comes more from the editor's choice of victim and circumstance more than anything else; I found it shockingly smug and stereotypical and untrue.)

But one of the ideas that seems to come clearer with age is that, truly, there are really only seventeen good stories in all the world, or variations thereon (or twelve, or two). One can't always be first. What one can be is oneself. One can learn to have faith in one's own approach to a situation. One can invent new and vivid characters to use in dealing with an old tension. From there, ideally, come new solutions to hoary problems based on characters.

I still believe in what I write. I still believe that almost everything I write is somehow political. I still want people to agree with my point of view. I still aim my darts at undersized targets—and that is not meant pejoratively. Those darts, if well and truly aimed, will stick in someone's side so that they will become part of the baggage or equipment a growing person carries into a growing and grown-up world.

That's enough for me.

John Neufeld

SOURCE: "Preaching to the Unconverted," in *School Library Journal,* Vol. 42, No. 7, July, 1996, p. 36.

In an October 29, 1995 interview in the *Boston Globe Magazine,* Anita Silvey, then editor of the *Horn Book* and now head of children's publishing at Houghton-Mifflin, addresses the value of current children's books and offers advice to parents, the Walt Disney Company, didactic authors, and writers of would-be children's classics:

Q: "So if you want to write a successful children's book, write a fantasy about animals."

A: "If you want to create a classic, that's probably right. A fantasy about animals is your best bet."

Earlier in the same interview, Silvey lays down her premise: "The books that work over time are fantasies and animal stories. *The Little Prince, The Wind in the Willows,* animal stories like *The Incredible Journey* or *Misty of Chincoteague."*

One more quotation will telegraph my dispute with Ms. Silvey. "In my view, today's authors err on the side of being too didactic. . . . They want the book to be *about* something, instead of just trying to entertain and tell a good story. They want to get children to think the way they think. If anything, what we see now is far too much preaching."

As the author of a dozen children's and young adult novels, I think Ms. Silvey is wrong.

I have often been criticized for being didactic. Sometimes that criticism has been warranted. At other times, I have felt that reviewers were unable to distinguish between information offered—valuable information for young people—and what they perceive as a Message.

At no time was I ever guilty, as most children's book authors are not, of "wanting to get children to think the way (I) think." That charge is better leveled at parents, both for good and ill. I may direct a reader's attention to, or help focus it on, an idea or problem, but I can only induce readers to decide whether that story applies to their own lives.

The Little Prince and *Misty* and *The Incredible Journey* are about something beyond the immediacy of their authors' skills at storytelling. So, for that matter, are *Charlotte's Web* and *Stuart Little* (fantasies *with* animals!). Writers of children's fiction select their stories because an idea (which is certainly about something), subject, person, or event energizes them. Without this light under our chairs we would never have sufficient drive and purpose to write.

What we *do* try to do is introduce young readers to situations they themselves might meet. If they read how a contemporary has handled a difficult conflict, the aloneness of facing that identical crucible is mitigated. That is one of the great values of literature for children.

As a child, I thought I could learn more about life by reading fiction than nonfiction. I still believe this to be the case with good children's books.

One of the qualities that helps a story approach the status of "classic" (whether or not it has animals) is exactly that which makes the author write it: a feeling of urgency.

The books that last are those that tell a story in such a way that readers want to think about what they would do in such a case. These books extend beyond the reading experience. It is crucial that children have someone to share their reading experiences with because the young readers are aflame with ideas and comparisons and insights into their own community. I think this is the best result for which any of us can hope.

To be sure, *Ferdinand* is an animal story. It is also *about* something: the Spanish Civil War, pacifism, the coming clouds of World War II, the value of staying true to oneself. *The Five Hundred Hats of Bartholomew Cubbins* has animals (the horses on which the king's entourage ride), but more than that it has wit and surprise and delight.

More recently, writers of books of great value have won notice and medals for addressing problems facing contemporary youth: *Dicey's Song,* the books of Robert Cormier, last year's Newbery winner [1995 winner *Walk Two Moons*]. There may be animals in each of these texts, but more important is always the banner of hope in the face of eternal events: death, cruelty, loss. I would bet that in the long term, books of this nature and quality will outlast three-fourths of the animal fantasies Ms. Silvey may now choose to publish.

There is another kind of "classic": those books that are

out of time (i.e., science fiction and historical fiction). With youthful heroes facing antagonists and threats to their own quality of life—and without the trappings of didacticism—*Catherine Called Birdy* and books by Lloyd Alexander and Madeleine L'Engle all ring bells in young readers' minds and hearts.

Stories *about* young people, *for* young people, are the feasts authors serve their youthful readers. I like to think that some of what we offer sticks to their bones.

TITLE COMMENTARY

EDGAR ALLAN (1968)

Kirkus Service

SOURCE: A review of *Edgar Allan,* in *Kirkus Service,* Vol. XXXVI, No. 21, November 1, 1968, p. 1226.

"This is a story about my father, and about God," begins Michael, sounding like the minister's son that he is; it is also about a family that takes in a small Negro child, and loves him, and is buffeted by pressures, and gives him back. Especially it's about what happens afterward: to fourteen-year-old Mary Nell who alone among the children resented Edgar Allan and threatened to leave unless he did, but never believed her parents would capitulate; to Father who made the decision despite his belief in a "whole man" who could not live parts of his life differently; and to Michael, a knowing twelve and a stern judge, who cannot forgive his father, and doesn't. What is left for all of them is the possibility of starting over (ironically, Father loses his church anyhow by losing the respect of his congregation), and this is not only the one acceptable outcome (Michael himself rules out others as artificial or inappropriate); it is also an affirmation that the family has resources to draw on. Quite apart from Mary Nell's coming around, there's ample evidence in the characters of parents and children and the moments of quick sympathy or quick laughter among them. As for Michael, he has guts, and he doesn't mince or multiply words. Perhaps the ultimate accolade in these topical times is that this isn't: Edgar Allan is a darling but he could have been any sort of bombshell (or any child betrayed).

Richard Horchler

SOURCE: A review of *Edgar Allan,* in *The New York Times Book Review,* November 3, 1968, p. 33.

This is a novel about a white family that adopts a Negro child. But it is not a novel about prejudice or race relations or brotherhood, or anything so simple. It is about parents and children, young people, and older people, about love and failure, loss and discovery, coming to terms with oneself and others. In short, ***Edgar Allen*** is really a novel, a serious work of art, and therefore about what it means to be a human being.

The story is told, quietly and believably, from the point of view of a 12-year-old boy. His father is a clergyman, and the family lives in a comfortable community on the California coast. The parents—good, right-thinking people—adopt a black 3-year-old orphan, or at least take him for possible adoption. Things happen. Over a few months' time, the neighbors react, the father's church congregation becomes agitated, the 12-year-old son meets racism in his school, a cross is burned on the lawn, the teenage daughter decides to leave home. And the father returns the Negro child to the orphanage.

What this meant to all of them, how they were all changed and wounded, is probed and pondered. Many of the questions raised—about the complexities of motivations, about responsibility, about judging others, about the suffering of the innocent—are not finally answered, because they cannot be. Better than easy answers, ***Edgar Allan*** offers an experience in the growth of compassion and understanding.

The Booklist and Subscription Books Bulletin

SOURCE: A review of *Edgar Allan,* in *The Booklist and Subscription Books Bulletin,* Vol. 65, No. 11, February 1, 1969, p. 594.

A white minister's family in a well-to-do neighborhood in a California town attempts to adopt a black child. Bright three-year-old Edgar Allan elicits different responses from the various members of the family: simple, loving welcome from the youngest two children; determined loyalty from the mother and from twelve-year-old Michael, who narrates the story; and fear and rejection from fourteen-year-old Mary Nell, who adds her voice to the community pressures that break down the minister's resolve to keep Edgar Allan. Psychological reactions to crisis and failure are perceptively drawn throughout the book, and the restrained action is well-paced in short chapters. Certain to challenge thought and discussion.

Virginia Haviland

SOURCE: A review of *Edgar Allan,* in *The Horn Book Magazine,* Vol. XLV, No. 2, April, 1969, p. 172.

Issues and relationships more complex than those commonly found in literature for young readers are presented in depth and with conviction. In a southern California town a minister and his wife, the parents of four children, take into their home for expected adoption a Negro child only a little younger than their three-year-old youngest, not anticipating the staunch opposition of fourteen-year-old Mary Nell—nor the cross burned on their lawn. Twelve-year-old Michael, whose recollections advance the story, resists community prejudices and supports his parents. What happens after Edgar Allan's enrollment in nursery school and Mary Nell's threat to leave home is handled provocatively—to lead young readers into thought and debate over the conflicts. It is the very provocation to argument for white children that is the value of the admittedly purposeful book.

Zena Sutherland

SOURCE: A review of *Edgar Allan,* in *Bulletin of the Center for Children's Books,* Vol. 22, No. 9, May, 1969, p. 147.

Twelve-year-old Michael tells the story of Edgar Allan, the Negro baby who is adopted by his family. Michael's father is a minister in a small California town, and he has told the adoption agency that they wanted "someone who might need help more than other children." Michael and the two younger children accept Edgar Allan, but the oldest girl, fourteen, cannot—nor can the minister's congregation. For Michael, who has a high ethical sense, the prospect of giving the child up is a betrayal of all his parents have taught him. When criticism turns to persecution, Edgar Allan is sent away, and Michael finds it difficult to forgive his father. Unhappily, he accepts the fact that society is not ready to practice the love it preaches, and that even a good man may not be strong enough to resist the pressure of society. Despite the tinge of case history, this is an important and a touching book, especially adept in portraying the conflicts and relationships within the family.

Gloria Fischer

SOURCE: A review of *Edgar Allan,* in *English Journal,* Vol. 58, No. 5, May, 1969, pp. 778-79.

When a white minister, living in a conservative California town, adopts a three-year-old black boy, he disturbs the structure of his family. Although the narrator of the story is the twelve-year-old son of the minister, his teenage sister is very much a part of the plot.

The story is about the minister and his family who return the adopted boy under pressure of the confused emotions of their adolescent daughter. It is also the story of a twelve-year-old boy who becomes painfully aware of his father's weaknesses. He comes very close to losing all respect for his behavior, especially since his father has preached idealistically. Michael's mother is also disappointed in her husband's reactions, and we feel that their relationship might never be quite the same again. His sister feels that she has overestimated the strengths of her family. Her attitude changes radically, but only when it is too late. The youngest siblings, four and six, are so shaken by the experience of losing their new brother, that they become afraid of being rejected next. These are emotionally packed concepts and situations; the family does not live happily ever after.

🕮 *LISA, BRIGHT AND DARK* (1969)

Kirkus Reviews

SOURCE: A review of *Lisa, Bright and Dark,* in *Kirkus Reviews,* Vol. XXXVII, No. 20, October 15, 1969, p. 1124.

Enter Lisa, going crazy. But, despite her overt pleas for help, the signal act of poking holes in herself with a pin, and her increasingly erratic behavior, her parents, two thoroughly selfish phonies, refuse to take the sixteen-year-old seriously. Neither will school psychologist Mr. Bernstein stick his neck out. "Adults are in many ways simply chicken," observes narrator Betsy, relating how she and managing Mary Nell and aloof Elizabeth try to textbook-diagnose, then just cushion, Lisa's violent ups and downs. From the outset both glib and ingenuous, this becomes the prototypical girls' story: Lisa's quandary could be any crisis, *how will Lisa get help* could be translated into *how will the school play be saved.* Or, perhaps, how will the Prince find Cinderella. With Betsy's father as witness, Lisa walks through a glass door, while she's hospitalized, Elizabeth summons "absolutely technicolor" psychiatrist Neil Donovan (who'd been her doctor: "There! It was out!"). After much negotiating, the good(looking) doctor arrives at Lisa's bedside, unloosing a salubrious torrent of tears. The girls celebrate and, before Lisa leaves for treatment, they're assured she'll be well enough to come home for a Christmas visit. Which might be the most precarious prognostication of any year; *I Never Promised You a Rose Garden* is far wiser.

Dorothy M. Broderick

SOURCE: A review of *Lisa, Bright and Dark,* in *The New York Times Book Review,* November 16, 1969, p. 52.

The first step toward being cured is to admit you are sick. This is fine when you are an adult and able to control your own destiny. But what happens when you are 16 and your parents believe you are faking? John Neufeld's book defines the problem without offering a solution, primarily because there is no simple answer.

Lisa Shilling is mentally ill. She knows it; so do her friends. Gradually, even the gutless, "we don't want to be involved" teachers know it. But her parents, whose egocentric world contains no room for a mentally ill daughter, refuse to recognize the truth. Even a half-hearted attempt at suicide cannot wake them.

Into this vacuum come three well-meaning friends: Betsy, the narrator and only character to see Lisa as a person; Mary Nell Fickett, the uptight 14-year-old from ***Edgar Allan,*** Neufeld's first book; and Elizabeth, a girl who has had her own psychiatric problems. Three teen-agers practicing amateur psychiatry are dangerous, as we would all agree. But what are the alternatives? To stand by and see a girl damned to live a life of terror or, worse yet, to see her succeed in committing suicide?

John Neufeld has sharpened his pen considerably since ***Edgar Allan.*** His young people may not be competent to deal with great problems, but at least they are willing to try. His adults are so busy protecting their self-images and self-interests that none has the time or energy to get angry—really angry—at the sight of a young girl being destroyed. The fact that the book ends with Lisa receiving psychiatric care does not alter the over-all message: don't count on adults for anything that will cost them something besides money or talk.

Best Sellers

SOURCE: A review of *Lisa, Bright and Dark,* in *Best Sellers,* Vol. 29, No. 19, January 1, 1970, pp. 389-90.

Lisa is losing her mind. Why can't her parents accept this and take preventive measures before she harms someone? Why won't her teachers become involved, if only to the point of alerting her family? After a horrifying incident at school, M. N., Betsy and Elisabeth realize that, if Lisa is to have any help, it must come from her friends. Armed only with their desire to help, the encyclopedia and books on mental illness available in their libraries, Lisa's "doctors" plan group therapy to allow her to open up and let off steam. Young readers will easily identify with this novel. The things Lisa and her friend care about are exactly what real life teens today are involved with, especially the lack of communication with parents and those in authority.

Zena Sutherland

SOURCE: A review of *Lisa, Bright and Dark,* in *Bulletin of the Center for Children's Books,* Vol. 23, No. 6, February, 1970, p. 103.

The story of Lisa is told by Betsy Goodman, one of a trio who are Lisa's classmates and who are concerned about the fact that she is losing her sanity. Lisa herself has said so, and her parents brush it off; the three girls set up an informal plan for therapy sessions, hoping that it will work. It doesn't. Lisa swings, pendulum fashion, from calmness to violence and depression, her parents only believing her condition when she walks through a picture window and is hospitalized. One of the girls (Elizabeth, who has been through the same thing) brings in a psychiatrist and the book ends on a hopeful note, which seems not quite warranted. There is enough girlish prattle from Betsy to keep the book from being morbid; in fact, the writing has considerable flair and vitality. Although Lisa's condition as it develops is convincingly pictured, and her parents are so characterized that their obtuseness is believable, it seems dubious that the entire faculty of the school (in which a good deal of the action takes place) would refuse to take action and that only Lisa's friends do so.

Sada Fretz

SOURCE: A review of *Lisa, Bright and Dark,* in *School Library Journal,* Vol. 16, No. 6, February, 1970, p. 90.

The story of a teen-age girl who is losing her mind and knows it, told by one of three friends who try to help her when no one else will take notice. Rebuffed by Lisa's parents, who refuse to admit that anything is wrong, effectively ignored by teachers and school psychologist who fear involvement, the girls themselves engage in a series of group therapy sessions designed to offer Lisa some support and release of tension. When Lisa finally attempts suicide, one of the girls produces her own former psychiatrist (formerly unknown to the narrator or readers) and Lisa's parents agree to his treating Lisa at a resident hospital. The story does not delve into the gruesome details of mental illness but it does present a serious subject previously untouched in children's books, and its disintegrating heroine is convincing in her desperation. Despite some faults—the adults are either shadows or stereotypes; the girls' conversations about movies, boys and diets often lack authenticity, the doctor's final emergence and acceptance by Lisa's parents constitutes too pat a solution—this story is superior to most junior novels, is skillfully constructed and more exciting than Neufeld's previous, highly praised ***Edgar Allen.***

TOUCHING (1970; published as *Twink,* 1971)

Kirkus Reviews

SOURCE: A review of *Touching,* in *Kirkus Reviews,* Vol. XXXVIII, No. 20, October 15, 1970, p. 1163.

Harry Walsh's first experience of Twink, his cerebral-palsied stepsister, is a shock and, when he finds he can divine her meaning, something of a tonic; this is not Harry's story, however, though he is the nominal narrator of half of it, but Twink's as he draws it first from his stepmother on the drive home to Chicago and then from another older stepsister, the narrative having resumed in the third person on their arrival. The mechanics defy explanation as does the desultory attempt to fictionalize a memoir akin to *Death Be Not Proud.* Twink does not die, but in her refusal to despair she is like Johnny Gunther—or would be if we had more than snatches of her, and less of her physical surroundings, her treatment and maltreatment in various institutions (little is said to be known of C.P., invalidating this for today). Whether better or worse she had always been alert and hopeful . . . right up to the ghastly brain operation, without anesthesia, that loosened her few controls and left her blind. That Harry, on meeting her, remained unaware of her blindness is a bit of duplicity on the part of the author but only incidental to the general malfunctioning. A final warning: this is a short book in large, ten-year-old type and one usually imperturbable adult found the dismemberment of Twink's brain, graphically detailed, almost too much to bear; that the operation is authentic compounds the danger of instilling in children a horror of brain surgery.

Jean C. Thompson

SOURCE: A review of *Touching,* in *School Library Journal,* Vol. 17, No. 3, November, 1970, pp. 121-22.

This short book, designed to disperse ignorance about and fear of cerebral palsy, has an enormously sympathetic central character. But it is less a novel than a personified tract, written in a distracting patchwork narrative style and featuring two-dimensional supporting characters. Although he thought himself prepared to see her, narrator Harry is shocked by the appearance of Twink, his new stepsister, afflicted with c.p. since birth. Eventually, however, at Christmastree Hill where Twink and her fellow victims reside, Harry becomes used to the effects of the disease; he learns that often someone who has c.p. can be in complete possession of his faculties even if he has difficulty controlling his movements and speech. Harry also learns how Twink spells her messages to the outside world as she asks him a modicum (it takes so long to spell) of intelligent, polite questions. Her last question, off the wall, disturbs Harry before he leaves the Hill: "Why can't people give us time?" On the way home, he hears about Twink's history from her mother, his stepmother. The point of view begins to waver at this point; Neufeld discards Harry at times for a more useful [omniscient] third-person narrator. By the time Part II begins, Neufeld is patently operating in the third person: e.g., the straightforward first paragraph ends: "Harry stood out in the hall, watching." Now Harry meets Whizzer, his other stepsister, who grew up in the presence of Twink's problem. Whizzer takes up the tale of Twink: she utilizes photos and scraps of paper from a diary to aid her memory. At the end of the day, Harry realizes that he never touched Twink physically, despite his other communications with her; he, and readers, stand powerfully accused. The portrait of a sad, superbly brave human being, not an object, has emerged here; however, Twink, the heroine and focal point, deserves a story more steadily told as well as more believable associates. Harry's occasional peripheral remarks about his life as a student aren't enough to give him completeness as a character; so too with his stepsister Whizzer, the artist. The story is replete with honesty, but lacks the stylistic integrity to make it entirely convincing.

Georgess McHargue

SOURCE: A review of *Touching,* in *The New York Times Book Review,* November 29, 1970, p. 38.

In ***Touching,*** John Neufeld reveals what happens when a cool, preppy 16-year-old, Harry Walsh, finds the abstract statistics of human suffering translated into the unpicturesque (and unsentimentalized) struggles of a newly acquired stepsister, Twink, also 16. Twink is a victim of cerebral palsy who faces her life with impressive courage and determination. But even more than on Twink, the story centers on Harry's reaction to a person who can neither speak coherently, nor walk, nor feed herself. In one intense day, Harry passes through a painful and unanticipated revulsion at Twink's alien physical presence toward an understanding of his own fears and prejudices concerning the handicapped.

The first part of the narrative (for it is not quite a novel) has the force, economy, and strongly realized characters which marked the author's noteworthy first novel, ***Edgar Allan.*** But Part Two, in which we learn of the harrowing operations which added blindness to Twink's other difficulties, is oddly compressed and unsatisfying. Taking the form of a scrapbook of Twink's childhood, as captioned for Harry by her older sister, this section is inherently rather relentlessly informative. Though the book's humanity indicates it has aimed at being much more, this near-perfunctory sparseness, reduces ***Touching*** to the level of dramatized socio-medical documentary. As such, it is quite effective, but one regrets the limitation.

John W. Conner

SOURCE: A review of *Touching,* in *English Journal,* Vol. 59, No. 9, December, 1970, pp. 1303-04.

Occasionally a novel is so moving that this reader abandons all pretense of composure. The result of such physical catharsis is usually a second reading with emotions held severely in check to determine how the author structured the story. An exceedingly fine line separates the truly maudlin from romantic reality. I was not cheated by John Neufeld. A second reading of ***Touching*** revealed his tightly structured style and sparse but brilliant language. The author often breaks his account at the point when a reader can imagine eloquently for himself. It was at these times when my emotions took over, stimulated by the carefully chosen language of the author. This author telescopes ideas in a manner which should appeal to media-conscious adolescents. This approach created an intensely real feeling for this reader.

Touching is divided into two parts. Part One is narrated by sixteen-year-old Harry Walsh. In a fresh, casual way a reader sees Harry's family through his eyes. Part Two has an omniscient narrator. The abrupt switch bothered this reader only briefly, for the necessity for changing points of view becomes clear as you read the second part of the story.

Touching is an emotional shocker. Harry Walsh meets his stepsister for the first time. Twink is also sixteen, but she is a blind cerebral palsy victim, confined to a wheel chair. Harry is alternately fascinated and revulsed by Twink. Slowly he becomes intrigued by her mental sharpness. In Part Two Harry meets Twink's twenty-two-year-old sister. This stepsister is an attractive college graduate well established in her own career. As

Harry and Whizzer attempt to know one another the subject is still Twink, that is, Twink's story as seen through the eyes of Whizzer.

Touching is concerned with the relationships between people: the artificial relationships created by family ties, the real relationships which grow because of mutual interests and desires. It is a brief book which should be read in a single sitting, if possible. The author is a careful writer. Every word, every nuance in this tale builds to the final page of the novel. I think adolescents will be intrigued by Twink and Whizzer. And I think an adolescent reader may understand himself better because he has met Harry Walsh.

SLEEP, TWO, THREE, FOUR! A POLITICAL THRILLER (1971)

Kirkus Reviews

SOURCE: A review of *Sleep Two, Three, Four! A Political Thriller,* in *Kirkus Reviews,* Vol. XXXIX, No. 16, August 15, 1971, pp. 882-83.

Apres Nixon, le deluge. . . . The time is 1983 and one Wagenson has been President for 10 years. His secret Special Forces units directed by John Mitchell who took over the FBI when J. Edgar kicked off have put the fear of man, fellow-man, into everyone and thus insured his tenure: "The President was right," sighs the woman attacked at the startling outset; "To have elections now would only divide the country." D.J. Berryman, sixteen and one of the attackers, is divided himself, unbearably: conned into joining Unit Five which his father was blackmailed into overseeing, he wants out—but the Government has a long arm. Blacks, Indians, Japanese-Americans, the fat, the handicapped, the old, the young with homicidal proclivities—all minorities have been established in "homogenous communities"; someone later explains how Wagenson lulled the people into sacrificing freedoms, "talking softly all the time" ("' . . . a full generation of peace for our children . . . '"). Neufeld is indefatigably imaginative in creating his scenario and in profiling some splendid young people like D.J. in binds; but when he assembles them all on a protracted journey to rescue a friend from the Iowa men's detention center, the story starts losing the grimly rigorous momentum that commanded a suspension of disbelief early on. Not all of the saboteurs survive the adventure: Tank, whose tits bedazzle Never Ready, is captured while swimming nude during a sensual reverie; Elizabeth gives herself up to deflect pursuit from the others; Freddy, only nine and on the run because his bum foot was spotted by a raiding Unit, expires at the end. By the time the mission is accomplished, all that remains is a vestigial urgency—in the anticlimactic form of hope for "peace soon" and "love forever"; the book has long since become tediously bottom-heavy, increasingly disingenuous, just pseudo-apocalyptic. It may still have a lot of things going for it, but it's certainly overambitious.

Publishers Weekly

SOURCE: A review of *Sleep Two, Three, Four! A Political Thriller* in *Publishers Weekly,* Vol. 200, No. 12, September 20, 1971, p. 48.

John Neufeld's story gets off to a slow start but picks up momentum as the scene shifts from a small Iowa town, across country to a large prison complex in the middle of nowhere. The six protagonists, all young people, are underground agents who are escaping a totalitarian U.S. government in the year 1983. Their encounters and hardships along the way to free their friend in a prison camp, then join other revolutionaries, will make good reading for political science fiction buffs.

Margaret A. Dorsey

SOURCE: A review of *Sleep Two, Three, Four! A Political Thriller* in *School Library Journal,* Vol. 18, No. 2, October, 1971, p. 122.

Subtitled "A Political Thriller," this excellent future fiction opens with a scene as gripping as any in *1984*—in fact, the approximate date of the story. But the totalitarian society here is American, the protagonists are mostly between the ages of nine and 16, and prospects for defeat of the regime are decidedly gloomy, despite the teen-age heroes' enthusiasm.

Sleep's America is still involved in an Asian war; it is a society whose "pre-criminal" and handicapped children are carted off to special camps, whose citizens are forced into racially and economically homogeneous communities where they live in fear of apparently random, destructive raids by the mysterious Special Forces Units. The Units are actually a government tool for keeping people frightened enough to acquiesce in the suspension of civil rights and elections as President Wagenson enjoys his 12th year in office. Despite all this, life mostly goes on in a frighteningly "normal" way.

The plot as such concerns the resistance activities of seven teen-agers—their unsuccessful attempt to kidnap a Unit Leader and their subsequent flight to avoid arrest and to rescue a friend from a political prison. By the end of the story they have completed the rescue but lost three of their number—two captured, one dead—and are off to seek whatever underground organizations may exist. This is a chilling novel which, because of the author's skill, is all too believable from the opening paragraph. However, librarians should be aware of some of the background elements woven into the story to increase its impact: an anti-protest quote by Agnew is prominently displayed in the high school (and an anti-Agnew statement is made by one character); a speech by President Wagenson includes some familiar Johnsonian and Nixonian phrases; the powerful Attorney General—who has been in office longer than Wagenson and is "a man mostly legend, all fear"—is a certain Mr. Mitchell. Add to this an occasional justifiable profanity and a charming petting scene, and libraries in some communities may be in for some back talk on the book.

Hopefully, they will be prepared to defend it—it's eminently defensible thanks to its enormously superior plotting and characterization. Worthy of the term "Art," it's also sure to help answer teen complaints about the preachy and/or irrelevant books that fill too many library shelves.

Benjamin DeMott

SOURCE: A review of *Sleep Two, Three, Four! A Political Thriller* in *The New York Times Book Review,* November 7, 1971, pp. 3, 22, 26.

All over the country smart sensitive "young teens" are waking to contemporary political reality, catching on to school as a sorting-out place (greasers here, preppies there, freaks in the cellar, black kids nowhere), leaning toward fighting The System on behalf of an ideal. But it's a rare child who's conquered every doubt and uncertainty. How much really, does "injustice" matter? If you're "only a kid," what can you hope to accomplish by political action? Will a reputation as a high school rebel wreck you with Ivy Admissions deans? Should you give a damn if it does? People need help with such questions—and the recent determination of some authors of "problem juveniles" to try to provide it is, on the whole, admirable. Civilization begins anew with every child, and so, too, does the idea of social justice, and not to care how it begins is an act against life itself.

It's one thing to say this, though, and another to claim that the writers who've been turning to the high school political scene are as yet brilliantly successful at their job. The truth is that the job is complicated. . . .

John Neufeld's ***Sleep Two, Three, Four!*** [is] billed as a political thriller and featuring a cast of dozens of mindless schoolkids. Set a decade into the future, this tale is for most of its length a cops-and-robbers chase. (Here's the *shtick,* baby, redo *1984* and *The Silver Sword* for teenies, dig?) Brainwashed, fascistic America roars after a brave band of freedom-loving youngsters with helicopters and bloodhounds, determined to crush dissent. One chapter heats up a slugging. Another amounts to a sexy tease. ("He could feel the silk of her slip. He stopped breathing. It was soft. It was so soft. It was just like the slip, it was so soft.") Still another offers a Dad-stomping: "Mr. Berryman looked sadly at his son. 'Do I really deserve this, D.J.?' he said. 'Do you really hate me so?' 'I said shut up,' D.J. answered, pushing his father around. . . . "

Laying out a road to right political reason is tricky work, whether the travelers are young or old. At their best [authors can] provide something that can be built on; Mr. Neufeld's pretentious fantasy is a mean and dull bad trip.

John W. Conner

SOURCE: A review of *Sleep Two, Three, Four! A Political Thriller* in *English Journal,* Vol. 61, No. 2, February, 1972, pp. 305-06.

Imagine our country separated into ghettos for each race, controlled by a benevolent dictator who maintains "health camps" as disposal units for all physically handicapped persons and encourages special police units who terrorize citizens by breaking into private residences and destroying all furnishings. This is the setting for John Neufeld's dramatic new novel. The major characters are all adolescents, members of an underground group which is pledged to restore freedom for our country. One of them is a reformed member of a special police unit, another is physically handicapped; all of them are frightened by the enormous task which faces them.

Sleep Two, Three, Four! recounts their attempts to rescue one of their members from a Federal prison while being pursued by government policemen using blood hounds and helicopters in the search. Neufeld's masterful use of simple language to build suspense enhances the reading. The author rarely wastes words. His descriptions of events collide with one another or smoothly overlap, creating varying degrees of tension in a reader. Only once does the author's description of political events and feelings threaten to slow the pace of the novel. At this point Rafe, a nearly blind Indian, has provided shelter for the group in a secret cave. Rafe's explanation of political facts unknown to these young people reveals more background for their actions than the reader really needs to know.

The simple purpose of the group's journey keeps the plot trim and direct. But the author develops his characters through their contributions to the rescue attempt. Also he shows the developing affection between likeable Never Ready and plain Julie. Having admired one another secretly from afar, these two are embarrassed but secretly pleased by the chance to be near one another in flight.

Sleep Two, Three, Four! needs to be read in a single sitting. The characters plunge headlong into their adventure, too immature to fear the unknown, pursued by authority which they have been taught to trust. It is a world without customary restraints which John Neufeld has created. And in this world his characters must explore to find that which they can believe in. Adolescent readers will be entranced by the situation in ***Sleep Two, Three, Four!*** and will assess how they would react if placed in a similar situation. John Neufeld will make his readers cherish their ability to question and will make them uneasy about accepting seemingly easy solutions to sociological issues.

FOR ALL THE WRONG REASONS (1973)

Publishers Weekly

SOURCE: A review of *For All the Wrong Reasons,* in *Publishers Weekly,* Vol. 203, No. 22, May 28, 1973, p. 35.

It could just be that addicts of muted soap opera will find in this tale of teenage marriage the qualities they are looking for. But people who require of their fiction a certain vividness of characterization, intricacy of plot, originality of feeling or thought, robustness of prose, are likely to find this novel dull or plumb unreadable. When 16-year-old Tish of Princeton, N.J., (who confides her inmost thoughts to her "Dear Diary") is made pregnant by 17-year-old Peter, she steels herself for abortion; but Peter, a Catholic, decides to do the grown-up thing and marry her, despite the consequences, which include quitting high school and enraging his parents. Besides, he and Tish love each other. Peter finds, however, that the grown-up thing doesn't square with his adolescent feelings and has a breakdown. The manners of contemporary youth may be here, but only after being strained, as it were, through muslin.

Carol Starr

SOURCE: A review of *For All the Wrong Reasons,* in *School Library Journal,* Vol. 20, No. 1, September, 1973, p. 98.

Another teenage-pregnancy/early-marriage story with the obvious moral. Seventeen-year-old Tish cooly decides to lose her virginity but carefully selects the male, Peter McSweeny. When she becomes pregnant, Tish decides, independently, to have an abortion. Peter convinces her that marriage is the adult solution to the problem: since they like each other, with a child in common they will learn to love each other. Their parents object weakly, so Tish and Peter are married. They both play house until Peter begins to resent the curtailment of his freedom. Split between wanting to be responsible and wanting to be free, he has a nervous breakdown and regresses to an earlier age. Peter is more believable than Tish, whose ability to face the problems of motherhood and her husband's mental illness develops too quickly. Similar to Ann Head's *Mister and Mrs. Bo Jo Jones,* the subject is popular and is handled better here than in most other novels of the kind.

Cynthia Harrison

SOURCE: A review of *For All the Wrong Reasons,* in *Library Journal,* Vol. 98, No. 18, October, 1973, p. 3022.

At the start of this novel, Tish Davies is 16 years old, a middle-class high school student in Princeton, New Jersey in 1972, and interested primarily in losing her virginity. She quickly succeeds, and becomes pregnant. Tish wants an abortion, but the father, Peter, insists on marriage and financial independence, which they achieve in a modest way, both dropping out of school. Peter fluctuates between being super-husband and irresponsible kid, while Tish becomes more and more mature. On the day of the baby's birth, Peter has a nervous breakdown and is preemptively taken charge of by his mother. The novel is partly narrative and partly Tish's diary entries. Both the "liberated woman" and the traditional wife and mother are presented positively by minor characters, although it isn't clear why they appear. This reviewer found the plot unbelievable, respecting the denouement of the story, and Tish's very quick maturation from 16-year-old virgin to 17-year-old mother. The writing is competent.

The Booklist

SOURCE: A review of *For All the Wrong Reasons,* in *The Booklist,* Vol. 70, No. 4, October 15, 1973, p. 208.

Determined at age sixteen to "become a woman" by experiencing sexual intercourse Tish Davies approaches Peter McSweeny whom she meets at a party, achieves her aim, and embarks on a romantic-sexual relationship that soon leads to her pregnancy. To her surprise Peter is against abortion and resolves to marry her, drop out of school, and get a job. After the initial shock the parents are reluctantly cooperative, and the young couple enters into a marriage that becomes more and more stormy as Peter approaches a mental breakdown because his outward strength is belied by his inner conflicts. Told partly as third-person narrative and partly as entries from Tish's diary the story is somewhat sophomoric but will have wide appeal for the women's magazine readership.

FREDDY'S BOOK (1973)

Pamela D. Pollack

SOURCE: A review of *Freddy's Book,* in *Library Journal,* Vol. 98, No. 13, July, 1973, p. 2196.

The story of a boy's efforts to find out what "fuck" means could be a landmark at this level—instead it's a landmine. Freddy sees it on the school washroom wall, apparently lacks the usual apprehension that it's a "bad" word, and confides his ignorance to crony Johnny Norman, who tells him it's "bumping" (maybe misheard for humping?). This same sage also divulges that girls bleed through "'Their tits'" and stick Kotex in their bras until "' . . . they have a menstrual pause.'" The site is later straightened out (if kids read that far), but menopause is never mentioned again. After Freddy "bumps" his sister, Mother blushingly intercedes. She's interested in possible incestuous implications (though that was certainly never an issue), and her plug and socket analogy fails to shed light on sexual intercourse: "'The electricity that was waiting there meets the plug and comes out, when it's ready, lighting a bulb or a vacuum cleaner.

It's quite the same thing.'" Mother must be hung up on household appliances—her explanation of menstruation is "' . . . as in an old-fashioned refrigerator, the body needs to be defrosted, cleaned.'" Freddy later asks his father if sperm has to "defrost" and is told that's taken care of by wet dreams (not masturbation!). Nocturnal emissions are thus seemingly equated with menstruation. A further flash from Father is that "'God made it so that two people could get together and have sex and produce children easily.'" No biologist, he. A college student who coaches Freddy's football team drags in stranger-across-a-crowded-room romantic clichés and asserts that fucking is best when it's "'making love with someone you really love.'" Freddy decides to keep his hard-found information to himself: "' . . . what could be more fun than knowing something Johnny Norman didn't. Maybe, just every once in a while, Freddy would hint a little. Just a little. It would drive Johnny crazy.'" Neufeld's boring descriptions of dictionary and card catalog consultations are mere space fillers; the subplot—a diatribe against competitive team sports—seems tacked on; and the effect of the whole is to coyly exploit the mysteriousness of sex and compound confusion.

Kirkus Reviews

SOURCE: A review of *Freddy's Book,* in *Kirkus Reviews,* Vol. XLI, No. 15, August 1, 1973, p. 817.

There is less novel and more problem orientation in this easygoing odyssey of a boy's search for the meaning of the word "fuck" than in any of Neufeld's previous problem novels. Still, readers a step or two ahead of Freddy will be amused by his frustrating bout with the librarian and the card catalog and his bemusement in the face of his mother's electric plug analogy and his friends' misinformation (Johnny says fucking is bumping a girl—"just bumping into somebody?"—and Neil explains that "your peter goes into a lady and . . . pretty soon, a baby in there grabs hold, and comes out with it"). More important, boys in Freddy's shoes should be both reassured by the awareness that they are not alone in their perplexity and gradually enlightened along with Freddy as first his father and then his college boy coach clear up the mechanical details, explain why it's also called "making love," and assure him that yes, it's fun, but a long way in the future for him. Though perhaps undeserving of a fiction classification, this is a charmingly personalized approach to sex education, and it would probably be a big help to other Freddys to file at least a "see" card under the word they'll be looking up.

Paul E. Kaplan

SOURCE: A review of *Freddy's Book,* in *Children's Book Review Service Inc.,* Vol. 2, No. 2, October, 1973, p. 16.

This book clearly sets a new standard for children's books. It is a healthy and easy way for a child to learn about sexual behavior and is also suggested reading for adults as a means of conveying information to a child about sex. The author points out the many misconceptions a child has about his body and those of the opposite sex and tactfully and honestly dispels them. I hope this book will be openly received, for it could well become a vital part of any family or public library.

Publishers Weekly

SOURCE: A review of *Freddy's Book,* in *Publishers Weekly,* Vol. 204, No. 18, October 29, 1973, p. 36.

Freddy is frustrated. He feels he's the only boy who doesn't comprehend the four-letter word he sees scrawled everywhere and hears his classmates using casually. One boy tells him the word means bumping a girl, so Freddy deliberately bumps his sister and gets into hot water at home. His mother only confuses him further by her evasive answers to questions about sex. Luckily for the author, Freddy's father is off on an extended business trip; otherwise, Freddy would have received the information he needed sooner and there would be no story. But home he comes at last, and Freddy gets a clear, uncluttered explanation of the basics. This is an amusing and possibly helpful book for those young people like Freddy—almost pathologically ignorant about sex. Doesn't seem possible there could be many, however, in these outspoken times.

Zena Sutherland

SOURCE: A review of *Freddy's Book,* in *Bulletin of the Center for Children's Books,* Vol. 27, No. 7, March, 1974, p. 116.

Freddy, who has just come from Toronto to live in an American city, is baffled. He knows that the most popular four-letter-word graffito means *something* bad—but what, exactly? "Bumping," one of his friends says. (Bumping? When he bumps into his sister and explains it in terms of the four-letter-word, she runs screaming to their mother.) Mother's explanation further befuddles Freddy, and the librarian won't give him a sex education book without parental supervision. His father's response is informative, but it isn't until Freddy talks to his football coach that he understands that there's a connection between love and sex, and feels satisfied. Although there are some very funny moments in the book, it isn't quite convincing in constructing a situation in which so many people do a bad job of giving information; that enables the author to make a long story out of Freddy's quest, but the contrivance weakens the story, and it's noticeable that all the female characters are remarkable for their ineptitude. Although purposive, this sex education book may be of comfort to youngsters (Freddy seems to be about 11 or 12) who are embarrassed because they don't know what it's all about—but how many boys of this age don't?

Robert J. Lacampagne

SOURCE: "From Huck to Holden to Dinky Hocker: Current Humor in the American Adolescent Novel," in *The Lion and the Unicorn,* Vol. 1, No. 1, 1977, pp. 62-71.

[Around] 1920, American literature shifted from gentility to a period of increasing frankness and rebellion, of "aggressive enterprise," and this dramatically changed the literary treatment of the adolescent. Books written for the adolescent, both serious and comic, have taken longer to move in this direction, but today the term "aggressive enterprise" is an accurate description of many novels for the adolescent.

A particularly good example of aggressive enterprise and the breaking of previous taboos is John Neufeld's ***Freddy's Book.*** This novel, written on the pre- or early adolescent level, recounts Freddy's humorous attempt to find out the meaning of a most common four letter word scrawled on the wall of the boys' bathroom in his school.

> Clearly, the only thing for it was to understand what the word meant. Once. For all. If it were going to appear in strange places, if it were going to be heard from boys his own age, he would simply have to know exactly what it meant.
>
> He decided that what ever its meaning, the word couldn't be difficult to understand. There were only four letters in it.

At this pre-adolescent stage, a young person's most common source of information (read mis-) tends to be from his friends. Freddy asks his best friend, Johnny, if he knows what the word means.

> "Sure," Johnny replied. "Everybody does."
>
> "What?"
>
> "Well," Johnny said, stretching the word carefully. "What it is," he said after a minute, "is bumping."
>
> "Bumping?" Freddy was puzzled. "What do you mean?"
>
> "I don't know," Johnny admitted, "but that's what it is. I heard some older guys at school talk about bumping someone. One of the girls in their class. Bumping the hell out of her, they said."

Freddy finds out, however, that there are certain nuances of language that need more precise clarification. To check out his new found knowledge he playfully bumps against his older sister, Pru, in her bedroom.

> Pru asked. "What kind of silly game are you playing now?"
>
> "I just bumped into you."
>
> "So what?" demanded Pru.
>
> "So," Freddy said, giggling a little, "I just fucked you."
>
> "You *what?*" Pru shrieked, backing away. "You did *what?*"
>
> But before Freddy could say another word, Pru was at the door to her room, shouting into the hall.
>
> "Mother!" she called. "Mo—ther!"

Mother's subsequent explanation of how people "make babies," using the analogy of an electric plug and socket, does not clarify matters either, for Freddy notes that the male plug has two—sometimes three—prongs on it. He thinks, examining his own anatomy, that he might be missing something. His progress in learning more accurate information about intercourse, menstruation, and nocturnal emissions is told honestly and perceptively. What is rare is that its technical and clinical discussions of sex are combined with consistent and appealing humor.

SUNDAY FATHER (1975)

Publishers Weekly

SOURCE: A review of *Sunday Father,* in *Publishers Weekly,* Vol. 210, No. 21, November 22, 1976, p. 50.

Liza [Tessa] O'Connell, aged 14, is a child of divorce. She and her 11-year-old brother share a small Denver apartment with their mother and see their father only one day a week. One Sunday he announces that he is about to remarry and introduces the children to his intended. This precipitates a crisis in Liza's life, one that is predictably resolved by the passage of time and the survival instinct. An unpretentious, weightless little book, with a few charming insights into the psyche of a budding young woman.

Martin Levin

SOURCE: A review of *Sunday Father,* in *The New York Times Book Review,* January 30, 1977, pp. 24-5.

Everybody is prepared to be civilized about Daddy's impending remarriage except his 14-year-old daughter Liza [Tessa]. The O'Connells live in Denver, where Daddy has visiting privileges with Liza and her 11-year-old brother Allie. If her father remarries, it will kill the chance for reconciliation that Liza hopes for. So she digs in her heels, determined to make things difficult. Disappears for a night; acts sullen; refuses to listen to reason. These tactics might be a problem for Daddy if his daughter were in his custody, but she is not. As it is, they are serious problems only for Liza. Slight but engaging, in the manner of Sally Benson.

Michael McCue and Evie Wilson

SOURCE: A review of *Sunday Father,* in *Wilson Library Bulletin,* Vol. 51, No. 8, April, 1977, pp. 674, 687.

The impact of her parents' divorce on 14-year-old Tessa O'Connell is the subject of this popular author's latest offering. When her father announces that he is going to remarry, Tessa feels that she and her mother have been betrayed and rejected. Seen through her eyes, the difficult adjustments confronting divorced parents and their children become real and immediate. Young adults can identify with Tessa's effort to understand the role of love in each person's life. Her inner dialogues reflect Neufeld's ability to capture teenage parlance. He has depicted Tessa's conflict of loyalties and emotions with sensitivity, and the interrelationships among characters are well drawn. This contemporary novel should enjoy wide readership among YAs.

A SMALL CIVIL WAR (1982; revised, 1996)

Stephanie Zvirin

SOURCE: A review of *A Small Civil War,* in *Booklist,* Vol. 78, No. 17, May 1, 1982, p. 1154.

A heavy-handed issue book, Neufeld's latest teenage novel concerns censorship and its effects on a complacent midwestern community. Using high school senior Ava Van Buren as uncommitted observer/narrator of events, the author builds his story around a local politician's efforts to ban *The Grapes of Wrath* from the high school reading list and the community uproar that ensues. With Ava's younger sister playing a prominent role in the battle, her boyfriend involved in anticensorship activities, and her parents constantly quarreling over their differing views, Ava begins to feel impatient and puzzled at her own lack of commitment. Readers may grow impatient too, since Neufeld's characters lack strength and his plot is more a platform for the censorship question than a vehicle for Ava's personal dilemma. But the author introduces many of the arguments and problems that seem to crop up in censorship controversies, stays clear of pat solutions, and cloaks his action in enough teenage trappings to lure a less demanding audience.

Mary K. Chelton

SOURCE: A review of *Small Civil War,* in *Voice of Youth Advocates,* Vol. 5, No. 4, October, 1982, p. 45.

In teen novel form with a first-person protagonist, Neufeld describes eloquently what happens to a town and a family when *Grapes of Wrath* is deemed too dirty for the 10th-grade English classes by an ambitious city councilman seeking reelection. Ava, the protagonist, is on the school paper, and for most of the book plays the uninvolved onlooker as her younger sister Georgia organizes FIRIF (Freedom is Reading is Freedom), the anticensorship group, her father supports the banning much to the disgust of her mother and Georgia, the school librarian gets fired, and a black classmate's house is burned, as the election approaches.

Neufeld is as fair to all points of view as a writer can possibly be; if anything, the fairness slows up the plot somewhat while everybody says what they think. Georgia's radicalism is really unexplained in terms of her personality previous to the censorship attempt, and her father borders on being unbelieveable because he obviously supports her in doing what she believes in even if he does not believe in it too. One hopes parents can be like that, but one is left wondering . . .

Ava's gradual involvement in the issue is what is really interesting about the book, and this crystallizes in her dismissal of a would-be boyfriend whose very lack of involvement becomes a major barrier between them. Her perspective is also interesting because her longtime male friend is the son of the banning councilman. He moves out of his house rather than fight with his father until the election.

The ending and theme of this book make it an excellent discussion vehicle to get at issues usually avoided or presented in a severely biased way. It could also be read in comparison with [Susan Beth] Pfeffer's *Matter of Principle.*

Sally Estes

SOURCE: A review of *A Small Civil War,* in *Booklist,* Vol. 93, No. 4, October 15, 1996, p. 414.

First published in 1981, this novel has been changed considerably for its 1996 rebirth. Georgia, who was 14, is now 13; the narrative is now in the third person, with Georgia as protagonist, rather than in the somewhat breathless first-person viewpoint of older sister, Ava, whose love life was a major factor; the older twin brothers in college have been eliminated, which avoids tackling an unnecessary gay issue. Much of the dialogue remains intact; however, sometimes it is said by another character. In short, extraneous details have been vanquished and references to real-life events have been updated or generalized. All of this tightens the story and allows it to concentrate on the issue of censorship, as we follow Georgia's wrath and activism after *The Grapes of Wrath* is challenged at her high school. If you have the original, do you want this? Probably. The new version is the better book, and just think of the uses for the two together for creative-writing assignments.

Pat Scales

SOURCE: A review of *A Small Civil War,* in *School Library Journal,* Vol. 42, No. 11, November, 1996, p. 124.

"A Small Civil War" erupts in the town of Owanka, IA, when Mr. Fairchild Brady, chairman of the city council, instructs Stanley Sopwith, "a founding father of the local New Right," to report to the council on whether *The Grapes of Wrath* should be removed from the 10th-grade curriculum at Owanka High School. Thirteen-year-old Georgia Van Buren, mature beyond her years, becomes irate over the issue and leads a personal battle to make the public aware of this threat to the First Amendment rights of her fellow students. As an eighth grader, Georgia hasn't read the book, but she worries about what other titles will come under attack if these men win their fight. During the battle, the high-school librarian is forced to resign, families are split over the issue, and friendships are shattered. Originally published in 1981 under the same title, this revision has a different point of view, but the quality of the book hasn't been improved. The characters are still unbelievable, often expounding on ideas with dialogue that is fake and unconvincing. Even the little romance that develops between Georgia and 16-year-old Con Arrand is manipulated to lure teen readers into the story. While Georgia loses her battle, there is never any doubt which side Neufeld is supporting. Like Richard Peck's *The Last Safe Place on Earth* (1995), Kathryn Lasky's *Memoirs of a Bookbat* (1994), Julian Thompson's *The Trials of Molly Sheldon* (1995), and Nat Hentoff's *The Day They Came to Arrest the Book* (1983), Neufeld's plot is constructed to drive home a message about freedom of speech. While the conflict in each of these novels is timely, Hentoff still offers the most intriguing and believable story.

Judith A. Sheriff

SOURCE: A review of *A Small Civil War,* in *Voice of Youth Advocates,* Vol. 19, No. 6, February, 1997, p. 331.

When some members of the Owanka, Iowa, City Council object to *The Grapes of Wrath* and try to get it removed from the tenth-grade assigned reading list, factions in the community become involved in an escalating political war and a community referendum. If this seems familiar, it's because this is a new edition of the Neufeld novel, which was originally published in 1982. Where the previous edition told the story from introspective high school senior Ava's first-person point of view, the new version is told in third-person with firebrand younger sister Georgia (now thirteen rather than fourteen) taking center stage. A couple older brothers who existed in the first version are removed from this story. The romance which is used as a hook in both versions is now Georgia's rather than Ava's.

In short, the new edition is shorter by a quarter or so and has been rewritten with a younger audience in mind. Consequently, much of the depth has been removed, and the first version is much more successful as a coming-of-age story. While Neufeld is still good at showing the verbal and physical escalation of a censorship debate, these characters never quite come alive. Most fill stereotypical roles, and readers are told too often how to see an event or a person rather than being allowed to decide for themselves. Richard Peck's *The Last Safe Place on Earth* (1994) is more involving in raising similar issues for this audience.

Denise V. Herzberg

SOURCE: A review of *A Small Civil War,* in *The Horn Book Guide to Children's & Young Adult Books,* Vol. VIII, No. 1, Spring, 1997, p. 83.

When prominent town members agitate to get *The Grapes of Wrath* banned from the local high school, thirteen-year-old Georgia goes on a campaign to stop them. This rewritten and expanded version is balanced and shows all sides of the issue, but the story and characters are overwhelmed by a dialogue about censorship and politics, and the story often wanders from its focus on the likable, strong-willed protagonist.

SHARELLE (1983)

Publishers Weekly

SOURCE: A review of *Sharelle,* in *Publishers Weekly,* Vol. 223, No. 23, June 10, 1983, p. 64.

The author of the noted ***Lisa, Bright and Dark*** and other award-winning novels, Neufeld tells a profoundly moving story here, inspired by his experiences at San Diego's Abraham Lincoln High School. The school runs a nursery program for young mothers like the heroine, Sharelle, barely 14 when she becomes pregnant. On the night before her sister Annette's wedding, Sharelle's about-to-be brother-in-law seduces her and the girl is so unaware—innocent really—that she is into her sixth month before she realizes her plight. Neufeld describes her situation compellingly: a hard-drinking, impatient mother; kind but helpless Annette and the admirable people at the Lincoln School who see Sharelle through her crises. The reader cares for the girl and her beloved daughter and learns how a person like Sharelle endures trials, even the pain of the ultimate sacrifice, and still goes on to make life meaningful.

Kirkus Reviews

SOURCE: A review of *Sharelle,* in *Kirkus Reviews,* Vol. LI, No. 12, June 15, 1983, pp. 665-66.

A soggy, drawn-out novel, documentary in impetus (Neufeld appends a note of thanks to the kids at the high school where much of it is set) but contrived in plot and incident, about Sharelle, who becomes pregnant at an insecure 14 after passively submitting to the man who would be her brother-in-law only days later. Sharelle is just as passive about the pregnancy, so that by the time professional help presents itself it is too late for abortion. Her flighty mother flares up on hearing the news, then announces "I'm going to stand by you." When baby Renee comes, however, Sharelle finds herself doing all the cooking and housework as well as the childcare. Sister Annette also gets pregnant soon after the marriage, and when her baby is ill her husband Dallas, father to both babies, sneaks in one night to steal Renee—in a melodramatic scene that ends with the exhausted Sharelle, clutching Renee, shaking on a rescuing neighbor's floor. There's another hysterical scene when Sharelle's mother, fed up with a baby in the house, sets fire to Renee's things. There are flatter scenes at Sharelle's new high school, which has a nursery program and a parenting class (that some nice boys also take); there are long talks, which read like scripts for training films, with model members of the helping professions; there are the representative cases of other girls who aren't coping as well. ("But there is help," counsels the now remarkably mature Sharelle, who wonders how the other girls "could let life stop them this way.") Sharelle deals maturely with classmate Barney, who wants her to live with him in college so she can go on helping him with math. ("You're a dynamite man, Barney. You're fast and funny and you know what you want and where you're going. . . . What I'm trying to say is that as *I* see it, Barney, the kind of life you're talking about doesn't really have a lot of room for me in it. . . . ") She also exchanges love and understanding with Patrick, who will be a priest. (Having sex before he goes to the seminary, Patrick explains, would "cheapen me a little in God's eyes, I think.") By the time Sharelle, for everyone's sake (and not least her mother's), decides to give up Renee for adoption, readers should have their fill of wallowing in the subject matter.

Audrey B. Eaglen

SOURCE: A review of *Sharelle,* in *School Library Journal,* Vol. 29, No. 10, August, 1983, p. 79.

On the night before Dallas is to marry Annette, he seduces her 14-year-old sister Sharelle, who becomes pregnant. Upon giving birth, Sharelle brings the baby home to live with her and her fun-loving but selfish mother, Melba. But the pressures of schoolwork, keeping house for the slovenly, irresponsible Melba and taking care of an infant eventually bring her to realize that it is in both her and the baby's best interest for Sharelle to give her up to adoptive parents. This is a Message book with a capital *M,* and as such it suffers all the evils associated with didacticism in the form of a novel. Its characters are either stereotyped or cardboard, often both. Sharelle particularly is completely unbelievable and as unlikable a character as any we've seen in YA novels for years. Melba is pure stereotype but also pure tripe. Other characters are just as faceless. In short, this is a shoddy, unbelievable, heavily moralistic tract, which goes on for 298 tedious pages. It is the kind of book that gives the YA problem novel a bad name, and won't convince even its most simple-minded readers of anything.

Zena Sutherland

SOURCE: A review of *Sharelle,* in *Bulletin of the Center for Children's Books,* Vol. 37, No. 4, December, 1983, p. 74.

Left alone after a picnic with her sister Annette's fiance, Sharelle succumbs easily to his love-making; she is stunned the next day when Dallas acts as though nothing had happened. Naively, she had assumed he loved her and would reject her sister. That's the situation in which a miserable Sharelle finds she is pregnant and decides to have and keep her baby. Most of the story, written with candor, is concerned with Sharelle's problems with her shiftless and often vituperative mother, her efforts to get an education, her horror when Dallas (who has fathered a sickly legitimate daughter) declares he wants and will take Sharelle's child. Sharelle's solution (to be able to get a job and an education, to keep the baby from Dallas, and to be available to help her mother) is to have the baby adopted. Given the hostility of her mother, it is hard to find Sharelle's decision convincing; she explains to a counselor that her mother needs her and will be relieved to have the baby gone. Neufeld writes well, but the impact of the book is lessened by the fact that it is more a message than a narrative.

ALMOST A HERO (1995)

David C. Mowery

SOURCE: A review of *Almost a Hero,* in *Children's Book Review Service Inc.,* Vol. 23, No. 12, Spring, 1995, p. 142.

With this provocative, moving novel, Mr. Neufeld reenters the field after 12 years. For a class project during his spring vacation, 12-year-old Ben volunteers to help at a daycare center for children of the homeless in Santa Barbara, California. Good-natured Ben quickly has his eyes opened to the "real" world and in the process learns several important things, including: the ugly presence and effects of child abuse and neglect, to nurture the children in his care, and how to work with "the system" to correct wrongs. In his first adult adventure, Ben makes the painful discovery that some things can't be set right. Readers will be impressed with the honesty and realism of the story.

Kirkus Reviews

SOURCE: A review of *Almost a Hero,* in *Kirkus Reviews,* Vol. LXIII, No. 10, May 15, 1995, p. 714.

Ben Derby's spring vacation is preempted by a class assignment requiring students to help out in one of various social agencies. Ben, who is fond of children, decides on a daycare center for the homeless. There he meets brooding Wendell, withdrawn Stephanie, and others, but the child who steals his heart is sturdy, cheerful

Batista. When Ben sees him apparently the victim of domestic violence, he tells the authorities, and then enlists the help of his friends in a ridiculous plot to kidnap him. It fails, and Ben learns that Batista's family is a warm and loving one. There are also subplots, melodramatic and mostly unresolved.

Neufeld built his reputation on the strength of ***Edgar Allan*** (1969) and ***Lisa Bright and Dark*** (1970). This time out he provides more tract than novel, with a fairly preposterous plot, a lot of loose ends, weak characterization, and more than one message with a capital M.

Publishers Weekly

SOURCE: A review of *Almost a Hero,* in *Publishers Weekly,* Vol. 242, No. 22, May 29, 1995, p. 85.

A class assignment has Ben, almost 13, spending his spring vacation at a day care center for homeless children near his home in Santa Barbara, Calif. After his first day there, Ben sees Batista, one of his young clients, in a local grocery store—being hurled, presumably by his stern mother, across the aisles. He reports the incident to the appropriate authorities, who begin to investigate. But when another youngster from the center is beaten and thrown to his death from a welfare hotel window, Ben and his friends decide to forego bureaucratic channels to save Batista from a similar fate, and they hatch a plot to kidnap the boy. Neufeld's novel, fairly bursting with good intentions, tends toward the pedantic in its discussion of societal ills and is almost completely driven by coincidence. At the same time that Ben works at the center, he is haunted by memories of his own, long-deceased younger brother, whose mysterious death was followed by the abrupt disappearance of their mother. Also joining the story is a quietly appealing classmate of Ben's who turns out to be homeless, too. The unlikely thicket of revelations unfortunately undermines the credibility of Neufeld's examinations of homelessness and abuse.

Deborah Stevenson

SOURCE: A review of *Almost a Hero,* in *Bulletin of the Center for Children's Books,* Vol. 48, No. 10, June, 1995, pp. 355-56.

Benjamin is displeased when his history teacher assigns the class volunteer work during spring vacation: he'd planned to waste time doing normal twelve-year-old things, but instead he's working at a day-care center for homeless kids. Soon he's involved in spite of himself, and he sticks his neck out when he thinks one of his charges is being abused. While some of the book is a bit neat and predictable (Ben is wrong about his suspicions, and one of his school friends proves to be homeless himself), some of it is not: Ben doesn't adore all of the kids, and he learns that the center can't cure all problems. Neufeld, author of such classic problem novels as ***Edgar Allan*** and ***Lisa, Bright and Dark,*** proves he can still write a compelling story but can also season it with some contemporaneous ambiguity; Ben ponders some difficult questions in ways that young readers, who may face similar moral challenges themselves, will relate to.

Julie Yates Walton

SOURCE: A review of *Almost a Hero,* in *Booklist,* Vol. 91, No. 21, July, 1995, p. 1874.

Twelve years may have passed since Neufeld has written for young adults, but he still knows his audience. Ben Derby is a 12-year-old whose teacher has assigned to him a week of charitable work during spring break. Ben works at a day care center for homeless children, one of whom Ben thinks he sees being abused in the grocery store, When "the system" is too cautious in its response, Ben and his friends plan a bold rescue of the child. Ben's experience opens his eyes to the complexities of homelessness, the fine line between helping and intruding, and even the unhealed grief within his own family. With a few exceptions, Neufeld's casual writing seems to flow straight from the heart of a 12-year-old. Right on target are Ben's wry observations of adults, his frustration and his youthful impetuosity. Dealing as well with family, friends, and a potential girlfriend, too, Ben is much more than a mouthpiece for social issues—he is a rich, three-dimensional character and worthy of the title, almost a hero.

Joel Shoemaker

SOURCE: A review of *Almost a Hero,* in *School Library Journal,* Vol. 41, No. 7, July, 1995, p. 79.

Recalling that a classmate had recently been shot and killed by her best friend, Ben posits that "Seventh grade can be murder." It's a great hook, but the rest of the book, told in flashback while Ben attends his first funeral (not for the victim mentioned above), is a mixed bag. His spring break seems to be ruined by an assignment to volunteer at Sidewalk's End, a day-care provider for homeless children in Santa Barbara, but, as it turns out, he enjoys working with the kids and staff. After witnessing what he thinks is a clear case of a child abuse, and after another little boy at the center dies as a result of family violence, he and some friends execute a half-baked plan to kidnap the boy for his own protection. It turns out that Ben had jumped to incorrect conclusions, and another classmate intervenes by tackling him as he's making his getaway. He slowly begins to understand the limits of his own power to change the injustices he sees around him. He and his dad, a restauranteur, then begin to devise a plan to help a homeless classmate. The somber cover accurately portrays the emotional tenor of the book. It is true that kids are often kept in the dark about important facets of their own family's lives. But did Ben's little brother die as a result of abuse, and is that why his parents suddenly divorced? What is the cause of

Ben's initial, seemingly irrational fear of the day-care center's pet rat? These unresolved issues may be stumbling blocks, leaving readers wondering what else they might have missed.

Holly M. Ward

SOURCE: A review of *Almost a Hero,* in *Voice of Youth Advocates,* Vol. 18, No. 4, October, 1995, p. 222.

Spring vacation, a time that seventh-grader Ben Derby is looking forward to, until he learns that for a class project he will be spending his week of vacation volunteering at a local Santa Barbara community charity. Ben chooses Sidewalk's End, a daycare center for homeless children. Here Ben faces the reality of being homeless, both for the children and their parents. Ben also believes that he witnesses child abuse first hand and can't understand a system that appears to move too slowly. There is an underlying family mystery that seems to drive Ben in his quest to help this child. Ben's mystery is never spelled out, but we can definitely guess how his younger brother died and why his mother is gone. Ben also learns that being homeless can happen to anyone for many different reasons, even a classmate and friend. An easy, but realistic, look into a world that is becoming more and more a reality in all communities.

GAPS IN STONE WALLS (1996)

Sharon A. McKinley

SOURCE: A review of *Gaps in Stone Walls,* in *Children's Book Review Service Inc.,* Vol. 24, No. 12, Spring, 1996, p. 142.

Merry Skiffe is 12, intelligent, capable—and a murder suspect. There are four members of her small Martha's Vineyard town without alibis, and a lawman has been sent to investigate. Will he discover that Merry had a motive for the killing? She decides to run away. Neufeld does a good job of describing this 1880 community in which 20 percent of the inhabitants are deaf. Their lives are matter-of-fact, their use of a local sign language taken for granted. Merry's deafness is just a small part of the story, which deals with her feelings and entrapment, relationships with friends and family, her cousin's plans to elope and Mary's determination to escape with her. Its positive way of dealing with deafness is a plus, and the book should find a wide audience.

Elizabeth Bush

SOURCE: A review of *Gaps in Stone Walls,* in *Bulletin of the Center for Children's Books,* Vol. 49, No. 8, April, 1996, p. 274.

The murder of Ned Nickerson, the most despised man in Chilmark, would hardly trouble his neighbors were it not for the inevitable investigation. Twelve-year-old Merry Skiffe has particular reasons for concern—she cannot verify her whereabouts on the night of the murder, her deafness impedes communication with the investigator, and her young age hinders her clumsy efforts to flee. The tale is set in a nineteenth-century community on Martha's Vineyard, once remarkable for its high incidence of deafness among the population. Never explicitly introducing characters as deaf, Neufeld cunningly allows the reader to infer this information through the characters' interrelationships. The central murder mystery, however, is more clumsily handled, and the audience seldom empathizes with Merry's anxiety to prove her innocence. The revelation of whodunit is strained, and the fact that the killer goes free will evoke only mild puzzlement rather than relief or outrage. Those seeking a tense mystery can give it a pass, but historical fiction buffs will find much to enjoy in observing the methods of communication developed over time by this tight-knit community.

Shelley Townsend-Hudson

SOURCE: A review of *Gaps in Stone Walls,* in *Booklist,* Vol. 92, No. 15, April 1, 1996, p. 1366.

In this sharply accurate historical novel set in 1880 on Martha's Vineyard, 12-year-old Merry Skiffe, who is deaf, is one of four people suspected of murdering Ned Nickerson, a wealthy islander whom Merry despised because he made advances to her. Like a country squire, Nickerson flaunted his wealth and pilfered his neighbor's farm animals, making himself generally unpopular. As Merry schemes to leave the island, her family and her friend Simon try to vindicate her. The novel excels in its sense of place and strong characterizations, but the story loses power and coherence when it oddly switches focus to the boyfriend of Merry's cousin and the murder remains unresolved for everyone but the reader.

Kirkus Reviews

SOURCE: A review of *Gaps in Stone Walls,* in *Kirkus Reviews,* Vol. LXIV, No. 8, April 15, 1996, p. 605.

An often enthralling, not entirely satisfying, mystery, set in Martha's Vineyard in 1880, a closed community where deafness is commonplace.

Neufeld never closes the credibility gaps in this story of an unlikely murder suspect. Readers meet Merry Skiffe, 12, on the run after learning that she's one of only four people on the island without an alibi at the time of the murder of Ned Nickerson, a dishonest, dissolute man who is hated by all. Merry's extreme fear of the law is supposedly explained by her having once rebuffed Nickerson's improper advances, but that's hardly reason enough for others to believe her capable of murder. The revelation of the real culprit—who's about to elope with Merry's deaf cousin—may come as a surprise to some, but the readers who will like this best will be those with an interest in Martha's Vineyard and the historical details Neufeld deftly works into the plot.

Publishers Weekly

SOURCE: A review of *Gaps in Stone Walls,* in *Publishers Weekly,* Vol. 243, No. 16, April 15, 1996, p. 69.

A curious historical fact lends color to Neufeld's carefully researched if uneven novel: in the late 19th century, hereditary deafness affected at least one-fifth of the population of Chilmark, a town on Martha's Vineyard. Among this group is Merry Skiffe, an artistic 12-year-old whose peaceful life unravels when wealthy miser Ned Nickerson is murdered on a dark road one Saturday night and Merry finds herself among the four residents of Chilmark who have no alibi. Terrified of bringing shame on her family, the girl runs away from home, scheming to escape from the island with her eloping cousin. Merry's smoothly integrated reveries provide flashbacks that give impressive dimension to her resourcefulness in coping with her deafness. Neufeld's treatment of the murder mystery, however, is somewhat unsettling. Merry and the villagers view Nickerson as so base that he deserved to die, an impression corroborated by the author when he reveals the killer's identity only to readers and not to the other characters, allowing him to get away with his crime. Pacing, too, is problematic, with much of the novel's action unfolding as a repetitious, laborious chronicle of Merry's furtive journey across the countryside. On the other hand, Neufeld evokes the terrain she covers so vividly that readers may feel as though they are following closely behind the plucky heroine—darting through rolling pastures, creeping along stone walls and breathing in the salty air.

Jennifer Fleming

SOURCE: A review of *Gaps in Stone Walls,* in *School Library Journal,* Vol. 42, No. 5, May, 1996, p. 114.

This fast-paced crime story is also a fictionalized account of the community of Chilmark, Martha's Vineyard, in 1880, where an extraordinary number of people were born Deaf. Virtually every resident, hearing or Deaf, knew sign language. Merry Skiffe, 12, who is Deaf, is a suspect in the murder of another islander. After some dismal insights into the victim's cruel nature (especially his penchant for propositioning young girls), numerous false accusations, and more plot twists than a tiny island should have to bear, Merry is able to clear her name and return to her family. Translating the unique grammar of sign language into English text can be problematic, but it is handled well here. The use of tildes instead of quotation marks indicates conversations in sign language, with remarks made by hearing signers enclosed in quotes and tildes. Though this is distracting at first, by the time readers are a chapter into the story it seems a natural way to approach the issue. The book has some minor failings, such as Merry reminiscing about her school days, which interrupts her tense, exciting flight from the law. However, her anguish and fear are palpable, and Neufeld shows again his wonderful gift for creating sympathetic and utterly believable characters. He has once again proven himself an unflinching student of the human heart, and has illuminated a revealing aspect of American history. In ***Gaps in Stone Walls,*** he reminds readers that their ideas about "handicaps" are often as arbitrary and groundless as the claims of Merry's guilt.

Ann Welton

SOURCE: A review of *Gaps in Stone Walls,* in *Voice of Youth Advocates,* Vol. 19, No. 2, June, 1996, pp. 98-9.

One great thing about historical fiction is that it provides access points to many different areas of the curriculum. This is certainly true of ***Gaps in Stone Walls.*** The plot concerns the tribulations of twelve-year-old Merry Skiffe, who, suspect in a murder investigation, decides that she has no choice but to flee her home on Martha's Vineyard. The 1880s setting is well realized, and the narrative (despite including a tedious amount of running and hiding) will keep most readers going until the end. Merry is exonerated, and the real killer is revealed to the reader—though not to any of the characters in the story. Thus the tale finishes with a sort of "loose ends" feeling to it, an unsatisfying lack of resolution. As well, the characterization is lacking in depth. The strength of the book lies in its penetrating treatment of an historical time and an historical phenomenon. In the late nineteenth century, two towns on Martha's Vineyard, Chilmark and Squibnocket, had rates of congenital deafness that ran at 20% and 25% respectively. The high number of hearing impaired led to a culture in which virtually everyone was bilingual—English and Sign. The signing done on Martha's Vineyard little resembled the signing done at the American Asylum for the Deaf in Hartford, Connecticut, which was then a mecca for the deaf in the United States. Vineyard signing had developed earlier and in isolation. Yet the isolation tended toward a culture that assimilated the hearing impaired as normal, functioning members of society. Applicable to biology units as a study in Mendelian genetics, to social studies as a tie-in to how we deal with the hearing impaired today (and especially well suited for use with clips from *Mr. Holland's Opus*), or for composition, where the use of the quote marks before and after passages where the communication is being signed could be discussed, this period piece has a unique merit.

P. D. S.

SOURCE: A review of *Gaps in Stone Walls,* in *The Horn Book Guide to Children's & Young Adult Books,* Vol. VII, No. 2, Fall, 1996, p. 304.

Twelve-year-old Merry, a deaf girl in the late nineteenth century, is suspected of murdering the town reprobate. To avoid being falsely charged, she plots her escape. The historic setting of Martha's Vineyard, where many residents experienced hereditary deafness, is unique and well realized. The conclusion is unsatisfying, but the novel contains some of Neufeld's finest prose.

Additional coverage of Neufeld's life and career is contained in the following sources published by Gale Research: *Authors and Artists for Young Adults,* Vol. 11; *Contemporary Authors New Revision Series,* Vol. 56; *Contemporary Literary Criticism,* Vol. 17; *Major Authors and Illustrators for Children and Young Adults; Something about the Author Autobiography Series,* Vol. 3; and *Something about the Author,* Vols. 6, 81.

Kate Douglas (Smith) Wiggin

1856-1923

American author of fiction, plays, and autobiographies; editor.

Major works include *The Birds' Christmas Carol* (1887), *Cathedral Courtship, and Penelope's English Experiences* (1893), *Rebecca of Sunnybrook Farm* (1903), *New Chronicles of Rebecca* (1907; published in England as *More about Rebecca of Sunnybrook Farm,* 1930), *Mother Carey's Chickens* (1911; published in England as *Mother Carey,* 1911).

Major works about the author include *Kate Douglas Wiggin as Her Sister Knew Her* (1925) and *Kate Douglas Wiggin's Country of Childhood* (1956).

INTRODUCTION

Although during her lifetime Wiggin was known as a pioneer in the kindergarten education movement and an author of numerous works for both children and adults, today she is best remembered for her classic tale of a young girl's coming of age, *Rebecca of Sunnybrook Farm.* Like many of the author's other works, *Rebecca* was popular with children and adults alike; Wiggin's experiences as a kindergarten teacher meant that children were often featured in her works, but her books were intended for and enjoyed by a wide readership. While her writings occasionally displayed the sentimentalism prevalent in her era, Wiggin's better works were praised for their fresh and lively wit, believable characters, and realistic settings. Her books ranged from humorous travelogues to family stories to tragicomic tales in the vein of Dickens, and many of them were set in her native Maine, giving them a distinctly regional flavor similar to the stories of Sarah Orne Jewett. While *Rebecca of Sunnybrook Farm* incorporates Wiggin's knowledge of her Maine setting, it is the portrayal of the title character—lively, loving, and intelligent—that has made the work a favorite of generations of readers. "Wiggin belonged to the great age of children's literature that flourished on either side of the century's turn; she was, in fact, one of its shining lights," asserted Anne Scott MacLeod in *A Century of Childhood: 1820-1920,* adding that Wiggin "deserves her place in any critical history of literature for the young."

Biographical Information

Although Wiggin was born in Philadelphia, she spent her formative years in Maine, the setting for her most famous work, *Rebecca of Sunnybrook Farm.* She was an avid reader from an early age, primarily reading adult materials belonging to her mother and stepfather. The family's favorite author—and Wiggin's primary influence—was Charles Dickens, whom she met as a child while on a train trip, an event later recounted in her book *A Child's Journey with Dickens* (1912). Her stepfather's declining health led him to move the family to California in 1873, and after his death in 1876 the family found themselves in dire financial straits. That fall Wiggin had her first story, based on her school experiences, published in the children's magazine *St. Nicholas,* earning her one hundred fifty dollars. Although she published another story two years later, the young woman recognized that she had little else to write about at this stage in her life. She instead turned to education, learning about the kindergarten theories of Friedrich Froebel from Carolina Severance, a leading suffragette and educational advocate. After completing her training, Wiggin was selected to organize the Silver Street Kindergarten in San Francisco, the first free kindergarten established west of the Rocky Mountains. Although Wiggin left the classroom after her marriage in 1881, she continued her involvement in kindergarten education by supervising the training of new teachers, and lecturing and touring throughout the United States. Her involvement led her to return to writing, as her first book, *The Story of Patsy: A Reminiscence* (1883), was published in order to raise money for the Silver Street Kindergarten. Although Wiggin herself claimed that the tale had little literary merit, the success of this volume and her second, *The Birds' Christmas Carol,* allowed her to travel and regain her health after her husband's unexpected death in 1889. She met such noted authors as Mark Twain, Henry James, William Dean Howells, and John Masefield, and travelled to Europe. These travels served as the basis for her popular "Penelope" travelogues; she also met her second husband, George Riggs, on one of these voyages, and they married in 1895. The couple split their time between England and Maine, although Wiggin's classic novel of a Maine childhood, *Rebecca of Sunnybrook Farm,* was conceived while she was convalescing in New York. In total, Wiggin wrote or edited over thirty works for children, penned ten novels for adults, adapted several of her works for the stage, and was widely recognized as one of the country's pioneers in the education of young children. She had just completed the manuscript for her autobiography, *My Garden of Memory* (1924), when she died in Harrow-on-the-Hill, England, on August 24, 1923. Her ashes were scattered in the Saco River in Maine, over the same area that was the setting for so many of her books, including her beloved classic *Rebecca of Sunnybrook Farm.*

Major Works

Wiggin's first two novels, *The Story of Patsy* and *The Birds' Christmas Carol,* both feature sickly but saintly young protagonists in the vein of Dickens's Little Nell or Tiny Tim. Although some critics have regarded these portrayals of the sick children—the first a poor kindergartner and the second the daughter of a wealthy family—overly sentimental for modern tastes, the latter novel also includes humorous glimpses of family life and was one of Wiggin's most popular and remembered works. *Timothy's Quest: A Story for Anybody, Old or Young* (1890) and *Polly Oliver's Problem: A Story for Girls* (1893) were similarly steeped in the tradition of the nineteenth-century sentimental novel, and the former book in particular owed much to Dickens. The memorable characters and colorful setting of *Timothy's Quest* enlivened the standard Cinderella story plot, however, and the novel was very popular in Great Britain, where reviewers compared it favorably to Frances Hodgson Burnett's *Little Lord Fauntleroy*. Reviewers on both sides of the Atlantic also found favor with Wiggin's travel stories, from *A Cathedral Courtship* (1893) to the various "Penelope" volumes: *Penelope's English Experiences, Penelope's Progress* (1898), *Penelope's Irish Experiences* (1901), and *Penelope's Postscripts: Switzerland, Venice, Wales, Devon, Home* (1915). Based on Wiggin's own experiences in Europe, the stories chronicle the travels of three American women and their encounters with the various people they meet in both city and countryside. Featuring the title character's witty observations, the books were hailed for their freshness, insight, and humor, leading the British periodical *Spectator* to note that the Penelope books made Wiggin "one of the most successful of the ambassadors between America and Great Britain."

One reviewer remarked that Wiggin's masterpiece *Rebecca of Sunnybrook Farm* had the "same delightful play of wit" as her "Penelope" books; that humor, combined with the vivacious, intelligent, yet utterly believable character of Rebecca Rowena Randall, has made the novel one of America's most unforgotten classics for children. Rebecca is one of seven children of an impoverished widow, and her maiden aunts have agreed to take her in to help the family. As the girl acquires an education, she also wins the heart of her stern Aunt Miranda, and upon Miranda's death inherits her property. Rebecca is also a budding writer who keenly observes the world around her, like two heroines to whom she is often compared, Louisa May Alcott's Jo March and L. M. Montgomery's Anne Shirley. The novel is very much a product of its time; Rebecca embodies the ideals of childhood as espoused by Wordsworth, and her self-sufficiency, desire to learn, and love of nature recall the beliefs of the Transcendentalist movement, as critic Fred Erisman has observed. Rebecca returned in *New Chronicles of Rebecca,* which did not continue Rebecca's story into adulthood but instead presented new vignettes from her childhood. Although not as structurally complete as its predecessor, it contained the same believable characterizations, entertaining dialogue, and powerful setting as the first volume. Of Wiggin's later works, only *Mother Carey's Chickens* stands out, being almost as popular as the *Rebecca* books and *The Birds' Christmas Carol*. This story of another fatherless family whose attempts to make a new home endear them to their entire community was more of a fairy tale than a realistic novel, but still found favor with its audience. Although at the time of her death in 1923 Wiggin was in doubt that any of her works would survive to become "beloved . . . by generations of children," the continuing success of *Rebecca of Sunnybrook Farm*—which has had numerous adaptations and modern reworkings—attests to its enduring popularity. As Francelia Butler summarized, Wiggin "wrote with humor and had a talent for characterization. Her writings have influenced the social attitudes of generations of children and are an interesting reflection of her age."

Awards

In 1906, Wiggin received an honorary doctorate from Maine's Bowdoin College, an all-male institution which rarely conferred degrees upon women.

AUTHOR'S COMMENTARY

Kate Douglas Wiggin

SOURCE: An excerpt from *My Garden of Memory: An Autobiography,* Houghton Mifflin Company, 1923, pp. 162-354.

To take in more of the babies waiting wistfully in the back streets, I tried to replenish our treasury by writing ***The Story of Patsy*** (1882), dedicating it to Miss Crocker, thus:

To H. V. C.

In memory of gladness given
to sorrowful little lives.

I was far too close to the life I was picturing to make this book wholly worthy of its subject. I am well aware that it lacks perspective, and that it has more heart than art, but oh! how many kindergartens it brought to places that had never known one; how many girls read it and flew to the nearest training-school, unconscious, perhaps, that they were not only being fitted for teaching, but for motherhood and for life in general! It was not published, only privately printed, bound in a paper cover, and sold here and there for twenty-five cents for the benefit of the cause.

For the same reason, with no special literary impulse or ambition, I later wrote ***The Birds' Christmas Carol*** (1886), and I remember that the kindly printer remarked casually that, if I gave the profits to the Kindergarten Association, I ought at least to keep the copyright myself. I had no time to look in the dictionary and see exactly what the terms of a copyright might be, but the printer acted in my behalf and went through the necessary legal steps. (I am grateful to him for the suggestion and so, I am sure, are my publishers!)

My volume of children's songs and games (***Kindergarten Chimes***), the fruit of my daily teaching, had now also appeared under the imprint of Oliver Ditson and Company, Boston, and was soon in steady demand among kindergartners and primary teachers. The writing of these books, and of dozens and dozens of educational articles and annual reports and appeals, I never considered as the work of an author, but simply as useful propaganda and as forming a record of interesting events. . . .

The early summer of 1894 found me on my way to England again. My dear mother was inclined at first to think that these annual journeys across the Atlantic were slightly extravagant, and a pessimistic aunt said at one time: "Well, let her go, but Kate'll cross that ocean once too often!" The same aunt wrote, a few years later when I was living in an apartment eight stories above the street: "The New York elevators are fire-traps, of course, but her life is her own. If she dies a natural death, do the elevators admit the carrying down of coffins at a funeral? Kate would be sure to have a large funeral!"

My mother realized before long that the ocean voyages gave me rest after my exhausting winters, and that I always came home rejuvenated in body and mind, with a hundred new impressions valuable in a literary as well as in a financial way.

The fruits of these travels were finally: ***A Cathedral Courtship, Penelope's Experiences*** (England, Scotland, and Ireland; three volumes), ***Penelope's Postscripts*** (Wales, Switzerland, Italy), ***The Diary of a Goose Girl,*** and several short stories. . . .

I ceased at length to feel any terror of Dukes or Duchesses, Earls or Countesses, Masters of Horse, Masters of Buckhounds, Chancellors, Lord Advocates, Q.C.'s or K.C.'s or K.C.B.'s;—they all seemed an integral part of the life I was so miraculously living in their company. Not that I was for a moment unmindful of my opportunity for gathering valuable information of every sort, and of wending my way unobtrusively along roads I had never thought to travel. On the contrary, I was eager to get the different points of view and enlarge my own horizon, and continually I was asking myself: "How did I happen to be here?" I never hungered and thirsted for these opportunities, never plotted nor planned, nor harbored feverish ambitions. The experiences simply came my way and I accepted them gratefully, but, indeed, the chronicles of these later years and the varied records on the milestones of the journey must seem strange to the faithful reader of my first chapters, where the diary of the "truly" little girl depicts her life in a Maine village, where, in the opinion of the worldly-wise, nothing ever happened!

The books did it, as I have said before! The children in them opened certain hearts to me, while ***The Cathedral Courtship, The Goose Girl,*** and other international stories, with their fresh point of view concerning things immemorially old and stable, coupled with their light-hearted manner and the deep respect that underlay the nonsense, beguiled others and disarmed criticism. One can imagine that people would listen to the tone of a golden trumpet, but why they should pay any attention to the faint music breathed through a reed I can hardly understand.

I never overrated my work myself, and I never shall! I have a sense of literary values, and a camel sees himself truly when he goes under a mountain. I am much in the company of mountains and they do not encourage vanity. Nevertheless, my books have brought me such joy and such richness of compensation that I can only hope that some of it has overflowed the cup and given pleasure elsewhere, for I should always like to be a "sharing" sort of a person if I might, believing with Lowell that the gift without the giver is bare. . . .

Books appear on almost every wall in every corner of every house in which we live, but there is one particular bookcase which contains a practically complete file of my own work, and to glance at it casually would seem to give the impression that from my earliest days I had been a drudge, a slave to the pen and inkwell, which is very far from the truth.

On the top shelf stands the uniform ("Quillcote") edition of my books, ten volumes, but many more than ten stories, because the too-brief ones have been bound together, sometimes three under one cover. My old-time friend, Mrs. Frances Hodgson Burnett, wrote, as a labor of love and without my knowledge, a most beautiful tribute to this edition in the way of Introduction. . . .

My habit of work has been, generally speaking, to write what was uppermost in my mind and to stop when I had nothing more to say about it. I have done many wrong things in my life, but I have never done a long thing! This may have been discretion, but it is quite likely that it was lack of matter! . . .

As I gaze upon these various milestones set along the road of a literary life, I wonder which of them all is dearest to me. The inquiry is, happily, almost out of fashion among readers, although it sometimes occurs in unsophisticated circles of society, where an author is still considered a person of unique powers. It was always a foolish question, and an embarrassing one to answer. No one would ever think of asking a mother which one of her children she regarded as most interesting, yet, if she felt any difference and chose to reveal the secret reason of preference, she would seem to be less directly responsible for the beauty, virtues, or faults of her offspring than the author is for the children of her brain.

The author clearly has no one but himself to blame if he has written a poor book—that is, if he has spared no pains and done his conscientious best. As to his favorite, what shall he say if by chance he is confronted with the question?

There is the First Book, never to be forgotten, whether it was the flat failure that, through discouragement, led to greater concentration and effort, or the signal success that laid the foundations of the future.

Then there is the Last Book, very tenderly cherished for the moment, like an unexpected baby arriving after a considerable interval of time.

There is the Book that had the best circulation, a positively shameless and unwieldy popularity; finding itself among the "best-sellers," where the author didn't particularly wish it to be, because of the critics who invariably remark that the Walter Paters, the George Merediths, the Samuel Butlers, and the Matthew Arnolds have to content themselves with a small but select company of readers, while the best-sellers cater to an ignorant, ravening mob.

Then last of all there is the Book for which the author has an indefensible affection. Only eight or ten thousand people ever agree with him and a hundred thousand set their capricious affections elsewhere; but, if you wish to win the undying gratitude of a writer, praise that particular volume!

I have accomplished much less literary than active practical work of various kinds, yet, in temperament, desire, and passionate absorption in the task while it lasts, I feel myself, first of all, an author. From a truly literary point of view a rather negligible one (even wide circulation tells only a half truth), but still an author dyed in the wool. I see, hear, think, like an author. As to quantity of production, my life, circumstances, responsibilities, indifferent health, and several other factors too numerous to mention, have led me to write few books and brief ones. I never seem able to free myself from external activities, and therefore I lack concentration; but I am still an author, diverted for the time being from her true task, this view of things being a common and most agreeable form of vanity. If I haven't anything to write, I am just as anxious to "take my pen in hand" as though I had a message to deliver, a cause to plead, or a problem to unfold. Nothing but writing rests me; only then do I seem completely myself! And then the compensations! They exist, to be sure, in all creative work, but they are so instantaneous, so rich, so personal, so affectionate, so delicious in authorship!

There is another curious thing about an author's books, and that is connected with the places in which he writes them; the mysterious effect they have upon his work; the lively memories they evoke, so that, whenever he opens a certain volume, the scene of its creation, like a picture in a dream, makes a background for the story absolutely inseparable from it.

I have slept or tarried or lived in hundreds of rooms in years of travel abroad and at home, and I cannot recall the features of a single one save those in which I have worked. On the other hand, there is no room in which I have done any writing which ever fades from my memory. It is not only the room itself, but the carpet and every article of furniture, together with the views from the windows, that are stamped upon my brain. I think I can draw every table or desk at which I have ever written a chapter or a book, put it in the exact position it occupied when I was working, and see myself, sometimes in the very dress I wore at the time, bending over the paper.

There is no confusion in my mind as to where any particular book grew into being, although on all other points I have the most treacherous of memories. . . .

I remember a large bedroom in San Francisco—it overlooked the Golden Gate and the low green slopes of the Marin shore—where I wrote my first book, ***The Birds' Christmas Carol.*** It was not to be published, but merely printed, put between paper covers, and sold for the benefit of the Silver Street Free Kindergartens where my life-work lay at the moment. The book was a good friend to me. It earned the wherewithal to take a group of children out of the dangers of the squalid streets and transport them into a place of safety and gladness. Then it took me by the hand and led me into the crowded world where the public lives. It brought me friends in strange places, it won for me the love of mothers and children, that ever blessed little book of less than a hundred pages.

The Story of Patsy was written in that same bedroom

and for the same purpose, though later the two volumes were to prepare my entrance into the real world of publishers and reviewers, copyrights, and translations.

Marm Lisa had the same California background, and so had ***Polly Oliver's Problem,*** but both of these were written in New England. How well I recall the farmhouse in a little Maine village, unpoetically named "Spruce Swamp," where I wrote ***Polly Oliver.*** The white, green-blinded cottage lay at the end of a grass-grown lane nearly an eighth of a mile from the main road, and no lovelier solitude for work ever existed. The dear people who owned the house and took me in gave up to me the parlor. Closing my eyes I can still see the gray-painted floor with flecks of white on it, the drawn-in rugs, the whatnot in the corner, the cedar trees outside, and the enormous bed of lilies-of-the-valley underneath the window. The black haircloth sofa was cool and comfortable enough for a rest when the story "gave out," or when I had to wait for inspiration to begin again.

The first half of ***Timothy's Quest*** was written at Quillcote (Hollis, Maine), years before it became my property. I left the manuscript behind me in America and went abroad for the first time, not intending to write during a year of travel on the Continent; but a pressing letter from my publishers determined me to take up my story in time for publication that year.

Eventually, after having discarded some of the fairest spots in England, I settled down at Stratford-upon-Avon, in one of the smaller hotels. I did not beguile myself with the belief that the Muse of Shakespeare might still be haunting the river-banks of the lovely country that surrounded Anne Hathaway's cottage, but the Falcon Inn pleased me and I entered my name in the visitor's book. The landlady gave me the public sitting-room for my private use; I bade an affectionate farewell to my friends at the railway station, came back to my writing-table, and took up my pen, only to find that I had forgotten the names of some of my characters and what they had said and done in the eight or nine chapters left with my publishers in America. . . .

I cabled to my publishers asking them to send the first chapters of ***Timothy's Quest.*** Pending their arrival, I wrote another story, and then happily finished the book so inauspiciously interfered with by circumstances. The moment I re-read the manuscript, Stratford and the Muse of Shakespeare disappeared; my State o' Maine dialect came back to me and I belonged entirely to the land of my fathers. For a month I forgot that I was in an English village; the Avon became the Saco! I discerned only dimly the people and the things that surrounded me, for I was living in the blissful dream that we call "writing a book"!

My three volumes, ***Penelope's Experiences,*** in England, Scotland, and Ireland, have often been considered as filled with true incidents, whereas they are fiction almost to a page. I chose the three heroines advisedly—Penelope, the artist; Francesca, a charming and rather capricious society girl from the West; and Salemina, a delightful middle-aged spinster from Massachusetts—as giving me an opportunity to write three different love stories, each having its own background.

The English Penelope was written partly at Bramall Hall, Cheshire, and finished at North Malvern, Worcestershire, where I spent six weeks at what is generally known in England as a "village pub." "Mrs. Bobby's cottage," the picturesque and ideal retreat where Penelope is supposed to have written her Experiences, was farther along the village street. Inasmuch as the owner thereof took no boarders or lodgers, I could not settle myself on her most enchanting premises, but had to live at the wayside inn and try to make myself believe that I was dwelling somewhere else.

If I were an artist I could paint the shabby but comfortable English sitting-room, with the matchless views of the Worcestershire Hills from its windows, its open fire, its pictures of Queen Victoria, Prince Albert, the Prince of Wales, and Gladstone adorning its walls. . . .

In these backward-looking thoughts I have mentioned six characters: Carol Bird, Patsy, Marm Lisa, Polly Oliver, Timothy, and the Penelope whose ***Experiences*** in England, Scotland, and Ireland were to furnish me with work so delightful that during several years it seemed play.

Strangely enough, no unkindly criticism ever came from the countries described. Indeed, the London *Spectator* was kind enough to say that the Penelope books had made Mrs. Wiggin one of the most successful of ambassadors between America and Great Britain.

I have been asked daily, if not hourly, for more than a quarter of a century—asked by word of mouth and by letter—if these characters are real and the various experiences are true.

Even my dear old friend, Mr. Howells, assured me that I might tell him forever that I was not Penelope and he could hardly believe it; but he would not say the same of some of my other heroines, who, to him, as a realist, would doubtless seem a trifle "too bright and good for human nature's daily food."

The fact is, it is utterly impossible for me to dissect and pin to the wall any man, woman, or child whom I have ever known. It requires a different kind of art from that which is native to me. Instead of being simpler and easier for me to describe a personage I have seen, or with whom I have come in contact, it is more difficult than to imagine a character from the ground up. If Mr. Howells thought Penelope "real," it is because I might conceivably have comported myself as she did in similar circumstances. The fact is that the experiences in my book are as purely fictitious as the characters. If either of them seem "true" to my readers, it is because they are so simple and so probable.

Of course, had I not been a kindergartner in my youth

there never could have been a Patsy or a Marm Lisa; however, these are but composite photographs of the hundreds of physically and mentally pitiful children under my care. As for "incidents" and "experiences," they may be patterned on my own, but they never are my own and never will be.

One thing only I strive to make as true and as real as possible, and that is the background, whatever it may be. As for the speech of my fictitious characters, I never create a character whose mental processes and language I do not feel that I know as well as if they were my own.

The rooms and the houses in Scotland and Ireland where the imaginary Penelope wrote the various chapters of her imaginary ***Experiences*** are many in number and extraordinarily different in character.

There are but two ways to write books of travel, or dissertations upon strange countries. One is to delve deep into social, political, and racial conditions and find something new and illuminating to give the world. This is the method of the scholar and presumes a talent for national psychology. My sense of humor saved me from any vast ambitions. If anything unique or valuable was to be said about Great Britain—already somewhat familiar to the gentle reader—obviously I was not the person to say it. On the other hand, undeterred by friends who agreed with me that I could add nothing to the sum of human intelligence, and who advised me further not to till old ground lest I be dull and trivial, my pen refused to be quiet, but continually leaped from my desk and begged me to cast a happy, careless, fresh eye on the enchanting scenes amid which I was living.

If a man loves a woman he does not stop to consider how much better her relations and friends know her, nor what has already been said about her; he is never satisfied unless he can pay his own personal tribute. That was precisely my case. Nobody could delight in England, Scotland, and Ireland more than I, and to hold my tongue while I was being consumed by this inner fire of affection and interest was quite impossible. Had I been a better workman the result would have been more worth while, for no one ever had wider or more unique opportunities.

The ***Experiences*** were written before I had grown from first impressions into the deeper knowledge which is not so apt to spend itself in words; where the scenes have grown unspeakably dear and familiar and the shock of the unexpected has become less provocative. Scotland grew to be home to me, and so did Ireland in its turn, but it was while they were still strange and new to Penelope's eyes that she set down her bird's-eye views and impressions.

Once I selected the island of Iona as a fitting place to set down the ***Scottish Experiences,*** I had seen pictures of Columba's ancient cathedral; but, after taking an expensive but beautiful sea trip to the lonely island, I found but one person who could accommodate an author with meals and lodgings, the price asked being equivalent to twenty dollars a week! It transpired on inquiry that William Black had written "Macleod of Dare" on the island and raised the price of board to authors for all time.

It is extraordinary how one's own stories vanish completely from the memory in course of time, as if one had never had any part in them. During an attack of illness which seizes me at intervals—and which is never wholly unendurable, because it gives me a chance to re-read at least six volumes of Jane Austen—I took up ***Penelope's Experiences*** and had a most enjoyable day with them! Not only did I add to my stock of information, for the volumes were full of facts entirely new to me—history, romance, balladry, all delightfully blended with stories—but I smiled continuously at the pleasant humor of the text! Many times during the day I said to myself: "What delightful books!" I remember Mrs. Frances Hodgson Burnett telling me that her sister always knew when she was reading one of her own novels after a long interval, because she never looked so interested under any other circumstances!

This naïve conceit may seem repellent to the gentle reader, but I can only say that apparently it can exist side by side with the most depressing humility—a doubt of one's own powers so extravagant that the author wishes for the moment to think of her works as tied about her worthless neck and drowned with her in the most convenient ocean. . . .

Last [on my bookshelf] comes ***Rebecca of Sunnybrook Farm,*** which the world doubtless supposes to be the darling of my heart. I am not in the least a psychic person, but Rebecca's origin was peculiar to herself. I was recovering from a long illness and very early one morning I lay in a sort of waking dream. I saw an old-fashioned stage-coach rumbling along a dusty country road lined with maple and elm trees. A kind, rosy-faced man held the reins that guided two lean horses and from the little window of the coach leaned a dark-haired gypsy of a child. I was instantly attracted by her long braids floating in the breeze and by the beauty of the eyes in her mischievous face. She pushed back a funny little hat with an impatient gesture, straightened it on her head with a thump, and, with some wriggling, managed to secure the attention of the driver by poking him with a tiny frilled parasol. That was all. The picture came, and went, and returned, and finally faded away, but it haunted me, and I could recall every detail of it at will. Too weak to write, I wondered who the child was, and whither she was traveling, and whence she came. I could not content myself until I had created answers to my questions and the final answer was, indeed, the book itself. The child even named herself, for the moment I visualized her mother it seemed to me that a romantic novel-reading woman might have so loved the two heroines of *Ivanhoe* that she called her baby after both of them.

"Rebecca Rowena" came to me precisely in that fashion, by a sort of lightning express. My nurse's name was Randall, and, as she was very much a part of my waking dreams just then, she somehow became further entangled in them.

The book was begun at a Southern health resort, carried on a little during a make-believe convalescence, and finished in a sanatorium where I persuaded the doctors that the work was better out of my system than in it.

No room in the world is more vividly remembered than the quiet one looking on to distant hills and mountains, where Rebecca lived with me for a month or more, mitigating my weariness and sense of separation from active life. I could not put all I seemed to know about her into the first volume, and a year or two later wrote the ***New Chronicles of Rebecca,*** which is not a sequel, but a further "filling in" of incidents from the child's checkered existence at Aunt Miranda Sawyer's brick house in Riverboro.

Rebecca somewhat changed the current of my life-stream by bringing me into a wider fellowship and intimacy with girls of all ages. She unconsciously made me a deal of trouble, for she doubled my correspondence as suddenly and efficiently as she had leaned from the stage-window and poked Uncle Jerry Cobb with the ivory knob of her pink parasol. These letters make one glad as well as weary, for, if one cannot do the great, the memorable things in literature, there is something intoxicating in the sensation that one has chanced to create a child who seems real as well as winsome, one that other children recognize as belonging to their favorite circle.

From Rebecca of Sunnybrook Farm, *written by Kate Douglas Wiggin. Illustrated by Helen Mason Grose.*

When I feel a trifle depressed that my audience is chiefly one of girls and women, I re-read an occasional letter from men, who are not copious correspondents! Here is one, strangely enthusiastic from an author of Jack London's type. I quote it verbatim because it is an interesting revelation of the man.

Headquarters
First Japanese Army
Feng-Wang-Chu
Manchuria
May 25th, 1904

Dear Kate Douglas Wiggin:

May I thank you for ***Rebecca? Penelope's Experiences*** whiled away the hours for me the other day, but they appealed to my head, while Rebecca won my heart. Of course, I have laughed, but I have wept as well. She is real; she lives; she has given me many regrets, but I love her. I would have quested the wide world over to make her mine, only I was born too long ago and she was born but yesterday. Why could she not have been my daughter? Can't I adopt her? And, O, how I envy "Mr. Aladdin"! Why couldn't it have been I who bought the three hundred cakes of soap? Why, O, why?

Gratefully yours

Jack London

Letters from all over the world come to any author who has written an appealing book of the human sort. They come from lame, halt, blind, and deaf; from young and old, men, women, and children. They do not mean that you have written a classic; alas, no! But the classicists must long to get them sometimes just as a change from bay leaves and sonnets and laudations of critics! They simply mean that you have spoken, and your unknown public has heard and responded. Nobody can explain why people write to you in droves about one book and only by dozens and fifties about another, but these letters are among the chief compensations of the author. They will never enshrine you in a Hall of Fame; they will only make you warm to the very core of your being.

Years and years ago I said: "To write a book that two successive generations of children might love, read twice, and put under their pillows at night, oh! what joy of joys, greater than showers of gold or wreaths of laurel!" Some people would call that a humble wish, viewed from the standpoint of their own ambitions; others would deem it too great to be realized. Fortunately, I shall never know whether I have even once achieved my goal, for only the passage of years can decide the ultimate fate of a book.

GENERAL COMMENTARY

The Dial

SOURCE: A review of *Penelope's English Experiences* and *Penelope's Progress,* in *The Dial,* Vol. XXIX, No. 347, December 1, 1900, p. 426.

Mr. Charles E. Brock's capital and copious drawings form a sufficient pretext for the reissue of Mrs. Kate Douglas Wiggin's two entertaining books entitled ***Penelope's English Experiences*** and ***Penelope's Progress.*** Each volume contains fifty odd pictures which duly reflect the vivacious humor of the text. Of narratives of the foreign experiences of the American female tourist, we have had not a few of late; but we do not recall any of these that for refined humor, stingless and therefore agreeable satire, and general charm of style, are worthy to be compared with these popular stories (for such they are in form) of Mrs. Wiggin. They may be read to the best advantage, or re-read with an added zest, in this pictorial Holiday edition, in which the two volumes are boxed together as a set.

The Baron de B.-W.

SOURCE: A review of *Penelope's English Experiences* and *Penelope's Experiences in Scotland,* in *Punch,* Vol. 120, January 2, 1901, p. 2.

Were the Baron asked, "What shall I give a youth or a mere boy as a New Year's present?" he would reply, "Kind Sir, or good Madam, as the case may be, whether the youth, or mere boy, has been good, bad, or indifferent, during the past year, I should strongly recommend you to give him a Wiggin." And when the Baron thus expresses himself he would have it understood that the "Wiggin" *he* means is Mrs. Kate Douglas Wiggin, whose two works, old friends, with new faces by Mr. Charles Brock, ***Penelope's English Experiences*** and ***Penelope's Experiences in Scotland*** (Gay and Bird,—the very description for publishers of such light and airy books) will be one of the delights of his life. The Baron emphasizes them as "old friends," as they first saw the light in 1893, but "the new faces," the pictures in these books, endow them with a vitality that will considerably extend the popularity they have already achieved. The name of the artist, Mr. Charles Brock, recalls one associated with artistic brilliancy in fireworks as is that of this present artist with artistic brilliancy in apt and humorous illustration.

Anne Carroll Moore

SOURCE: "The Creative Spirit in America," in *New Roads to Childhood,* George H. Doran Company, 1923, pp. 173-92.

As I write these words, over the cable comes the sad news of the death of Kate Douglas Wiggin in England.

It is not too soon for one who knew her well and who has lived in intimate association with two generations of children from all nations who have loved both her books and her vivid personality to give ***Rebecca of Sunnybrook Farm*** and ***The Birds' Christmas Carol*** a high place in American creative writing for children.

Kate Douglas Wiggin will live in the hearts of children to come by virtue of all that is timeless in the quality of her dramatic art, and she leaves no successor in her field. The creative spirit pervaded everything that Kate Douglas Wiggin touched. Even the anthologies—***Golden Numbers*** and ***The Posy Ring,*** the collections of fairy and folk tales, ***Tales of Wonder*** and ***Tales of Laughter, Magic Casements, The Fairy Ring***—which she made in collaboration with her sister, Nora Archibald Smith, were chosen and named out of the fullness of her own strong romantic association with the things in literature she loved and wanted to share.

The true art of the story-teller, the integrity of a fine critical judgment, were behind this work, but there was more—the sure touch of one whose deep human interest in all children was founded upon a bedrock of practical experience and illuminated by a vision of their future. . . .

Fred Erisman

SOURCE: "Transcendentalism for American Youth: The Children's Books of Kate Douglas Wiggin," in *The New England Quarterly,* Vol. 41, June, 1968, pp. 238-47.

[In the following excerpt, Erisman discusses Wiggin's fiction in relation to three nineteenth-century Transcendentalist ideas: the doctrine of compensation, a high regard for individualism, and a reverence for nature.]

In her best-known works, from ***Timothy's Quest*** (1891) through the two chronicles of **Rebecca of Sunnybrook Farm** (1904, 1907), she presents a Romantic-Transcendental view of contemporary America. In this view, and in her adherence to the ideals it assumes, lies much of her importance.

Many characteristics of Transcendentalism appear in Mrs.

Wiggin's works, but three in particular stand out: the doctrine of compensation, a high regard for individualism (i.e., self-reliance), and an unwavering faith in the value of nature. The first of these, compensation, is the trait that enables her genteelly poor heroines to endure. Polly Oliver, for example, the heroine of the aptly named ***Polly Oliver's Problem*** (1893), is typical. As one of the characters observes,

> The straightened circumstances in which she [Polly] has been compelled to live have prevented her from yielding to self-indulgence or frivolity. Even her hunger for the beautiful has been a discipline; for since beautiful things were never given to her readymade, she has been forced to create them. Her lot in life, which she has always lamented, has given her a self-control, a courage, a power, which she never would have had in the world had she grown up in luxury.

The strength that Polly gains from her recognition of compensation is made explicit elsewhere in the book. Her freckles, for example, are the result of "the law of compensation. When I was younger [she says], and didn't take the boarders so much to heart, I had freckles given to me for a cross; but the moment I grew old enough to see the boarders in their true light and note their effect on mamma, the freckles disappeared." And it is the law of compensation that strengthens her after her mother's death; her loss is a great one, but from it Polly comes to a sweeter and stronger view of the world.

The same doctrine strengthens Rebecca Randall ***(Rebecca of Sunnybrook Farm)*** as she tries to cope with illness, grief, and death. Left the mistress of Sunnybrook Farm by an injury to her mother, she finds in the routine of planning meals, organizing housework, and caring for the younger children a growing unity with her mother. Of this relationship Mrs. Wiggin observes: "In this, and in yet greater things, little as she realized it, the law of compensation was working in her behalf, for in those anxious days mother and daughter found and knew each other as never before." There is nothing that to Mrs. Wiggin is wholly bad. She is able to see in all things a compensating good, echoing Emerson's conviction that calamity "permits or constrains the formation of new acquaintances and the reception of new influences that prove of the first importance to the next years; and the man or woman who would have remained a sunny garden-flower, with no room for its roots and too much sunshine for its head, by the falling of the walls and the neglect of the gardener is made the banian of the forest, yielding shade and fruit to wide neighborhoods of men." All existence is balanced; every evil brings a compensating good.

Somewhat more important to Mrs. Wiggin is individualism. All of her central characters are paragons of self-reliance: ten-year-old Timothy Jessup, of ***Timothy's Quest,*** strikes out on his own, seeking a home more desirable than the slum in which he was raised; and Polly Oliver, left without funds by her mother's death, supports herself by creating a story-telling hour for preschool children. Rebecca's self-reliance is explicit: "Necessity," Mrs. Wiggin tells us, "has only made her brave; poverty has only made her daring and self-reliant." Rebecca herself speaks to the same point, as she looks at her fellow graduates at the academy commencement: "We do our hair alike, dress alike as much as possible, eat and drink alike, talk alike,—I am not even sure that we do not think alike: and what will become of the poor world when we are all let loose upon it on the same day of June? Will life, real life, bring our true selves back to us? Will love and duty and sorrow and trouble and work finally wear off the 'school stamp' that has been pressed upon all of us until we look like rows of shining copper cents fresh from the mint?" For Rebecca, the answer to the question lies in the asking of it. She clearly has reached the time in her education to realize that imitation is suicide. She, at last, senses the vibrations of her own iron string.

If Mrs. Wiggin's characters view life self-reliantly, aware of the compensatory patterns of the universe, they also rely upon the qualities present in nature to help them over their difficulties. In nature they find the answers that civilization cannot provide; once bathed by unfettered nature, they, too, with Emerson, become "part or parcel of God." In Mrs. Wiggin's books, the urban landscape is uniformly ugly. When the city shuts out nature, the result is a slum such as Minerva Court, where

> there were frowzy, sleepy-looking women hanging out of their windows, gossiping with their equally unkempt and haggard neighbors; apathetic men sitting on the doorsteps, in their shirt-sleeves, smoking; a dull, dirty baby or two sporting itself in the gutter; while the sound of a melancholy accordion (the chosen instrument of poverty and misery) floated from an upper chamber, and added its discordant mite to the general desolation.
>
> The sidewalks had apparently never known the touch of a broom, and the middle of the street looked more like an elongated junkheap than anything else. Every smell known to the nostrils of man was abroad in the air, and several were floating about waiting modestly to be classified, after which they intended to come to the front and outdo the others if they could.

Scenes such as this contrast vividly with the pastoral landscapes of Mrs. Wiggin's New England—landscapes dotted with trees and flowers, crossed by placid and unpolluted streams, and inhabited by good (if occasionally somewhat misled) people.

Nature does many things for Mrs. Wiggin's characters, but one of its major services is the provision of peace. There is not a single bustling landscape in all of her work. Instead, one finds such vistas as that of Pleasant River: "There was a long main street running through the village north and south. Toward the north it led through a sweet-scented wood, where the grass tufts grew in verdant strips along the little-traveled road. It had been a damp morning, and, though now the sun was shining brilliantly, the spiders' webs still covered the fields; gossamer laces of moist, spun silver, through which shone the pink and lilac of the meadow grasses." This is no frantically active setting; although the road suggests the presence of civilization, it is "little-traveled," and the fields are calm enough to retain the delicacy of spiders' webs. A similar peace of nature extends year round, independent of the season. The December snows, for example, bring "a great white mantle of peace and good-will over the little town, making all ready within and without for the Feast o' the Babe." Mrs. Wiggin's nature clearly is not Darwin's, red in tooth and claw. It is, instead, Wordsworth's or Emerson's, leading man to peace through example.

Perhaps the most important function of nature in Mrs. Wiggin's books is to lead man to an understanding of himself. For example, she suggests, in a natural setting there is no need for artifice; two old spinsters, . . . find themselves talking in the forest of matters that they would never mention in the village. Similarly, Rebecca, gazing off the village bridge in a Wordsworthian reverie, becomes aware of the parallels between the vagaries of the river and the vagaries of life: "How many young hearts dreamed out their futures leaning over the bridge rail," Mrs. Wiggin remarks, "seeing 'the vision splendid' reflected there and often, too, watching it fade into 'the light of common day.' Rebecca never went across the bridge without bending over the rail to wonder and to ponder. . . . " For Rebecca, though, the greatest service of nature is its provision of hope. Returning to Sunnybrook Farm after a lengthy absence, she finds her mother frail and the youngest child, Mira, dead. The sight of her old playgrounds increases her gloom; only in nature is there solace:

> The dear little sunny brook . . . was sorry company at this season. There was no laughing water sparkling in the sunshine. In summer the merry stream had danced over white pebbles on its way to deep pools where it could be still and think. Now, like Mira, it was cold and quiet, wrapped in its shroud of snow; but Rebecca knelt by the brink, and putting her ear to the glaze of ice, fancied, where it used to be deepest, she could hear a faint, tinkling sound. It was all right! Sunnybrook would sing again in the spring; perhaps Mira too would have her singing time somewhere—she wondered where and how.

The cycles of nature parallel the cycles of man. Through this understanding, Rebecca is able to understand her own life, and look ahead to her own far-off spring. To her, as to all of Mrs. Wiggin's characters, nature brings the solutions so clearly lacking in civilization.

Throughout her works, Mrs. Wiggin accepts and utilizes the tenets of Transcendentalism; in particular, she uses compensation, self-reliance, and regard for nature to make her points. This, of itself, is of little importance. What is significant is that Mrs. Wiggin presents these qualities not in the context of the 1830s and 1840s, but in that of the period between 1890 and 1910. That she was able to do so, to the great satisfaction of her readers and her publishers, provides some suggestive insights into the nature of American life.

First, Mrs. Wiggin's view of America is blatantly slanted. Despite her credentials as a member of urban genteel society (her first husband was a successful attorney, her second a well-to-do importer), Mrs. Wiggin says nothing of the undeniable virtues of city life; instead, she invariably presents the city as low, sordid, and filthy. On the other hand, her works present rural life as idyllic, pastoral, and wholesome; she says nothing of the narrowness and crudity cited by Eggleston, Garland, or Howe. In short, she gives to her readers the picture of America that they evidently wanted to have—an America in which the city (i.e., sophistication) is bad, the country (or simplicity) good.

Moreover, her views are unrealistic. In putting forth her view of American life, Mrs. Wiggin must reconcile her ideals with reality. She must, for example, reconcile her commitment to self-reliance with mechanized, systematized urban life; she must reconcile her belief in compensation with the bleak facts of urban vice and crime; and she must reconcile her faith in redeeming nature with the relentless expansion of the city. She must do all of these things, and cannot. Her failure, though, does not disturb her, as apparently it did not disturb her readers; ***Rebecca of Sunnybrook Farm*** has been far more popular with the public than another book published in the same year, Lincoln Steffens' *The Shame of the Cities.*

Most suggestive of all is that Mrs. Wiggin presents these ideals not to adults, but to children. In the context of her Froebelian [Friedrich Froebel] background, this might imply that, in her small way, she is engaged in the perpetuation of an ideal—the ideal America in which we claim to live. This, in turn, might imply the serene stability of Americans' view of themselves. Though she writes in a time when over half of the school children in urban America had no first-hand knowledge of the flora and fauna of which she speaks so blithely, she implies that one need not be concerned with the problems of modernity. Instead, if one retains the older, natural ideals (i.e., those of a pre-Civil War, pre-industrial time), all will work out for the best. If she is less vehement in this than is Emerson, she is no less definite. This is the way, both agree, to a better society.

In one respect, though, Mrs. Wiggin goes beyond Emerson. Emerson intends his ideas for adults; although he acknowledges the superior perception of the child, it is the adult, he says, who must attempt to retain "the spirit of infancy even into the era of manhood." But Mrs. Wiggin goes to the source, the child: it is the children, she says, who will "do all we have left undone, all we have failed to do, all we might have done had we been wise enough, all we have been too weak and stupid to do." This they will learn to do from their reading, for stories, Mrs. Wiggin says, are the child's "first introduction into the grand world of the ideal in character." In her books, therefore, lies her solution to the problems of modern America. Her characters endure the present; so does she, and so must her readers. The true hope, however, lies in the future, when the children of today, grown at last to adult estate, can realize their acquired ideals and bring about their American, Transcendental utopia.

Anne Scott MacLeod

SOURCE: "The *Caddie Woodlawn* Syndrome: American Girlhood in the Nineteenth Century," in *A Century of Childhood: 1820-1920,* The Margaret Woodbury Strong Museum, 1984, pp. 97-119.

[In the following excerpt, MacLeod places Rebecca of Sunnybrook Farm *and* New Chronicles of Rebecca, *like their contemporary* Anne of Green Gables, *into the nineteenth-century tradition that romanticized the "innate joyousness of youth" and idealized the childhoods that gave their female heroines freedom.]*

Rebecca of Sunnybrook Farm (1903) by Kate Douglas Wiggin and *Anne of Green Gables* (1908) by L. M. Montgomery are assembled of virtually identical elements. Both tell stories of little girls who leave rather straitened circumstances (Anne is an orphan, Rebecca comes from a family over-supplied with children and under-supplied with the means to raise and educate them) for a new home which is by no means rich, but which can offer a chance for education. The locale in each case is a village, and the woman into whose care the child is delivered is, in both books, a crusty, exacting spinster whose heart has withered for lack of a woman's normal accoutrements; that is, husband, children, and the giving and receiving of human affection. The span of time covered is also similar in the two novels; each takes the heroine from about her eleventh to her seventeenth year, showing again the passage from childhood to young womanhood.

Both books are primarily character studies. Of the two, ***Rebecca*** is better written, more realistic, and less sentimental than *Anne,* but in all other respects the characterizations are practically interchangeable and belong firmly within the romantic tradition. Anne and Rebecca embody the idea of childhood which celebrated the child as child, and saw a child as perfect in itself, in harmony with itself and with nature; innocent, spontaneous, imaginative, loving. Each eleven years old, highly verbal, poetic, and imaginative, the little girls make a vivid contrast to the cramped and colorless adults around them. Their stories show them touching and in some cases transforming the lives of others, bringing happiness to adults who have lost the innate joyousness of childhood, and, in fact, nearly lost the knack of being truly alive. Rebecca and Anne grow, learn, and of course, suffer mishaps and correction of their childish mistakes, but they are never really wrong or bad. They have no true "faults;" they only make mistakes on the way to learning the complicated rules of adult society, which is, often as not, more truly at fault than they are, since it is less simple and natural than childhood. They are William Blake's vision of children: "Innocence! Honest, open, seeking the vigorous joys of morning light."

As romantic children, Rebecca and Anne are of a quite different order of being from the children of Alcott's books. Louisa May Alcott, born in 1833, was a full generation older than Kate Douglas Wiggin. The view of childhood in her writing for children belongs to the rationalistic, pre-romantic view that dominated children's books until the latter part of the nineteenth century. It is an attitude accepting of childhood and children, but it is not romantic. Alcott's opinion of her young heroines has none of the doting fondness of Wiggin's feeling for Rebecca or Montgomery's for Anne. Likeable as Jo March is, she cannot be mistaken for the author's idea of perfection.

The very title, *Little Women,* is indicative: to Alcott, as to most Americans of her time, children were adults-in-process, apprentices to the rigors and demands of adult life. It was not a matter of viewing children as "little adults"; that was not a nineteenth-century attitude. It is simply that Alcott, like many of her contemporaries, saw childhood primarily as a period of preparation; children were properly engaged in learning, becoming, forming a worthy character for the future; certainly they were not considered finished and wholly admirable as they were. . . .

Once romantic attitudes had penetrated the literature, however, the picture children's books presented of adult responsibility toward children altered subtly but profoundly. The right sort of adult could still act as guide and mentor to a child, but the effort had changed from molding childish character into acceptable moral and social form to easing it toward adulthood without destroying the special virtues inherent in children. In the romantic view, the best (though the least likely) adult character was one which preserved most completely the qualities of childhood. Adam Ladd, obviously Rebecca's future husband, and Miss Maxwell, her devoted teacher, had many conversations about Rebecca as she neared young womanhood, all of which centered on how she should be educated without obliterating or dampening her special personality. Or, to be more exact, they regretfully conceded the reality of Rebecca's growing up, and tried to decide how they might help her negotiate her inevitable maturity while protecting the perfection of her childhood being.

Though Montgomery's sequels to *Anne of Green Gables* carry her protagonist into adult life, it is clear that she and Wiggin alike were most entranced with their heroines as children. It was childhood that gave full scope to Rebecca's and Anne's personalities. During those years, their dramatic and poetic imaginations were not unduly constrained by consciousness of conventional expectations. They prattled on, using extraordinary vocabularies gleaned from omnivorous reading, unconsciously amusing and charming those adults perceptive enough to appreciate them. They were strong-minded and full of enterprise and too innocent yet to know that leadership was not for females. They summarized in themselves all that their authors thought attractive and promising in a child.

The question, therefore, is what became of all this as these girls neared womanhood? In the answer to that question lies a volume of commentary, whether or not the authors intended it so, on how little had changed since Louisa May Alcott looked for a satisfactory, if fictional, niche for Jo's forceful character, and since she and Sarah Woolsey could draw a close parallel between womanly virtue and physical crippling.

By the time Wiggin and Montgomery wrote, enterprising or needy girls had a few more acceptable opportunities to consider than had their mothers and grandmothers. Anne and Rebecca both acquired the education which was accessible to girls by the end of the century, though it was clear in both books that scholarships or private benevolence were necessary if girls as poor as these were to go to school past the level of the local grammar school. And both girls looked forward to paid work as teachers; they did not have to choose from the limited and distasteful array of occupations the March girls faced: governess, seamstress, companion, or (possibly, with luck, talent, and determination) a writer.

Yet the narrowness of the future choices available to Rebecca and Anne is quite apparent when one considers what expectations a boy with their talents would have had without question. In childhood, the two girls demonstrate intelligence, energy, and a capacity for leadership that their companions concede without jealousy. Such qualities in a boy would all but assure an interesting, probably a public career. Not so for these girls, as their creators tacitly concede in their descriptions of their heroines' adolescence. As the girls grow older, their personalities become less emphatic. Their colorful (and undeniably intrusive) qualities of mind and imagination dim to "dreaminess" in their midteens, while their ambition turns toward conventionally acceptable careers as teachers. They never rebel and never yearn for what they can not have; indeed, they never even recognize that there is work in the world for which they are suited by nature but from which they are prevented by social convention.

Nor does their ambition in any way interfere with their acceptance of the traditional womanly possibility to care for others if the need arises. Anne and Rebecca were openly ambitious throughout their school years; they were even, though less openly, competitive. And each won by her efforts the offer of a choice teaching position as she left high school. But before she can collect the reward of her talent and hard work by moving into a paid employment, each girl is faced with a crisis in the form of a seriously ailing relative who needs care. In both cases, the girls respond without hesitation, cheerfully shelving previous plans and undertaking a sacrificial role as a matter of course. It is as though the authors wanted to demonstrate that neither ambition nor achievement had destroyed the selfless sense of duty that was the core of the nineteenth-century womanly model. It was, too, as though these authors saw a period of self-abnegation as a necessary stage in a girl's way to womanhood, just as Alcott and Woolsey had a generation before. Less overtly than their predecessors, but still clearly enough to be understood, Wiggin and Montgomery conveyed the message that the paths a woman trod were likely to be steep and stony for a girl just leaving the freer territory of childhood.

Perhaps for this reason, Kate Douglas Wiggin declined to deal at all with Rebecca's life as an adult. In the original ***Rebecca*** book, she rounded off her story with Rebecca's graduation from high school at seventeen. Adam Ladd's interest in Rebecca as a woman is plainly enough indicated, but Wiggin was not ready to go further. Though Adam finds Rebecca "all-beautiful and all-womanly," the time is not yet: "He had looked into her eyes and they were still those of a child; there was no knowledge of the world in their shining depths, no experience of men or women, no passion, nor comprehension of it." And so the book ends, with Rebecca still a child.

New Chronicles of Rebecca does not, as readers might have expected, pick up where the first book left off. Instead, Wiggin dips back into Rebecca's young years for more anecdotes, as charming and amusing as those of the first book, of Rebecca's childhood. Once more, Wiggin brings Rebecca up to the age of seventeen, and this time also to the betrothal of her "bosom friend" of childhood. The story ends on a note of nostalgic sadness. Rebecca, watching Emma Jane and her fiancé walk away arm in arm, feels her childhood is slipping away "like a thing real and visible . . . slipping down the grassy riverbanks, . . . the summer night."

The mood is wistful, rather than passionately regretful. It is much less clear here than in *Little Women* what is being lost as childhood "slips away." Jo March knew very well what she mourned: the intact family of her childhood and the freedom to behave according to her nature rather than to a prescribed code for her sex. And Jo, within the strictures of nineteenth-century behavior (and of nineteenth-century children's books) was rebellious and resentful at her loss. Anne and Rebecca are not rebellious; their passage into adult life is made to seem gradual and free of conflict. Though their strong personalities would seem to presage a struggle over the need to trim their sails to the prevailing nineteenth-century wind, Wiggin and Montgomery will not have it so. Anne and Rebecca are romantic children, whose inborn natures are beyond reproach; not they, then, but their creators, must accommodate convention. These girls must ease into adolescence and then into maturity without strife or storm; they must become the most desirable models of young womanhood without seeming to give up any of their childhood perfection, and so they do. For all their vibrancy as children, Anne and Rebecca sail into their womanly backwaters without a murmur.

If the pattern I have described was common in the lives of nineteenth-century American girls—as I think it was—it may seem strange that only a few adult women openly revolted against it. At first glance and from the distance of our own time, a system that allowed for so much freedom at one stage of life and so little at the next, would seem destined to produce resentment and rebellion.

But human reaction is rarely so simple or so linear in its logic. Like most people who live in a reasonably coherent and consistent culture, nineteenth-century American girls accepted the view of life their culture presented to them, and with it, the view of women's proper role. Not only accepted: they absorbed and internalized it and eventually passed it on to a new generation. The books they wrote for children suggest how the processes of adaptation and accommodation actually worked. . . .

Yet to opt against an open rebellion against injustice was not quite to neutralize resentment. Pushed out of sight it might have been; obliterated, it probably was not. Women's resentment of their lot must have surfaced in dozens of ways we can only guess at. It surely emerged, as we have seen, in children's books, and often, paradoxically enough, in the very stories which were written with conscious intent to perpetuate the conventional ideal. Responses ranging from outrage to something like mourning run just under the surface of books utterly conventional in their openly asserted attitudes. At the very least, women's sense of loss fed the nostalgia for childhood that children's books often expressed. The child who read late nineteenth-century books could hardly avoid the conclusion that the end of childhood was also the end of the best part of life. Certainly a girl was unlikely to miss the message that puberty would be for her the beginning of her imprisonment in a "woman's sphere." She would surely understand that for her the central task of adolescence as defined by her culture was to trim her qualities of mind and character, whatever they might be, to fit the model society had prepared for her.

It was 1777 when Hannah More delivered herself of some profoundly dampening comments on the upbringing of girls [quoted in P.M. Spacks, *The Adolescent Idea,* 1981]

> That bold, enterprising spirit, which is so much admired in boys, should not, when it happens to discover itself in the other sex, be encouraged, but suppressed. Girls should be taught to give up their opinions betimes. . . . It is of the greatest importance to their future happiness, that they should acquire a submissive temper, and a forbearing spirit; for it is a lesson the world will not fail to make them frequently practice, when they come abroad into it, and they will not practice it the worse for having learnt it the sooner.

More than a century later, Rebecca Randall acknowledged that More's prescription had by no means passed out of date. "All of us can have the ornament of a meek and lovely spirit," she observed, and added, with her customary accuracy, "especially girls, who have more use for it than boys."

The evidence suggests that American girls often enjoyed a season of freedom before they had to face up altogether to what More and Rebecca agreed was the lot of their sex. But sooner or later, the most blithesome girl had to recognize the reality that awaited her. And whether she chose to rebel against or to accede to the demands of her culture, a nineteenth-century girl could not but realize, with all her sex, that after childhood, gender (to paraphrase Freud) was inexorably destiny.

Eve Kornfeld and Susan Jackson

SOURCE: "The Female Bildungsroman in Nineteenth-Century America: Parameters of a Vision," in *Journal of American Culture,* Vol. 10, No. 4, Winter, 1987, pp. 69-75.

[In the following excerpt, Kornfield and Jackson examine Rebecca of Sunnybrook Farm *and several other examples of what they term the "female bildungsroman"; these nineteenth-century coming-of-age novels reflected their authors' unusual lives by their "subtle subversion of the cult of domesticity."]*

By observing and imitating, adolescents try to forge a sense of self, usually by integrating aspects of the culture to which they are exposed. In writing for adolescents, an author tries to encapsulate the ideologies which she feels will be of most use to her readers in their attempt to define themselves. The moral frameworks provided by the author reflect social assumptions about behavior, including gender relations. *Little Women* was the first well-known American novel written specifically for and about adolescent girls; it depicted them as interesting characters, capable of fun and adventures. While they do enjoy themselves, however, the heroines must also learn how to "govern the kingdom" of the self by learning to be good women. Alcott's model was widely imitated in nineteenth-century America. Study of the female bildungsroman is thus particularly interesting because it was written by women and for girls, and illuminates the social expectations of female life as well as the secret hopes and dreams which might not be revealed in another format. . . .

As young girls, the heroines of *Little Women* dream impossible dreams. Jo would "have a stable full of Arabian steeds, rooms piled with books, . . . do something heroic or wonderful, . . . write books, and get rich and famous." Amy's pet wish is "to be an artist, and go to Rome, and do fine pictures, and be the best artist in the whole world." Meg wants "a lovely house, full of all sorts of luxurious things. . . . I wouldn't be idle, but do good, and make everyone love me dearly." These dreams serve two functions. They provide an outlet for young girls trying to come to terms with a prescribed adult identity, and at the same time they reveal a dissatisfaction with the prohibition against entering a male world.

This vague dissatisfaction with a society that offers so few options for women is expressed explicitly at the outset of the novel, in the heroine's wish that she were a boy: "I can't get over my disappointment in not being a boy; and it's worse than ever now, for I'm dying to go and fight with Papa, and I can only stay at home and knit, like a poky old woman." Significantly, Jo is not alone in this sentiment; each of the major examples of the nineteenth-century female bildungsroman begins in much the same vein. Even Rebecca of Sunnybrook Farm echoes the lament: "Boys always do the nice splendid things, and girls can only do the nasty dull ones that get left over." The rest of each book is devoted to the interesting adventures that the heroines have as they learn to become little women.

But they do not learn these hard lessons in the real world. The authors of these nineteenth-century books for girls created a matriarchal society—a feminine utopia. They assumed a power of womanhood not usually found in contemporary American society, and used it as a structure within which a girl could learn to survive, by assimilating the proper values. At the heart of this world, not surprisingly, was the mother. . . .

When his second daughter, Louisa, was born, A. Bronson Alcott wrote to his father-in-law: "Abba [Louisa's mother] is very comfortable, and will soon be restored to the discharge of those domestic and maternal duties in which she takes so much delight, and in the performance of which she furnishes so excellent a model for imitation." These domestic and maternal duties were what Kate Douglas Wiggin, the author of ***Rebecca of Sunnybrook Farm,*** called "the crown of womanhood." Women were to provide an example to their daughters of piety and grace, and to help them through the difficult task of reaching adulthood.

Interestingly, in these fictional female utopias, the power of the mother's benevolent influence extends beyond the female sphere. In each fictional family, the girls share their mother with male friends who have none. . . .

The authors of the nineteenth-century female bildungsromans thus created a power of womanhood not generally found in contemporary American society. The role of males in the novels is correspondingly complex. Harriet Mulford Lothrop (Margaret Sidney's real name; her father thought it improper for women to write and forced her to assume a pen name) wrote that "my judgment told me I must eliminate Mr. Pepper [who has died before *Five Little Peppers* begins] because the whole motif 'to help mother' would be lost if the father lived." This comment indicates the fragility of the matriarchal world, even in a fictional setting.

In the real world, of course, men had all of the economic power—a fact that the authors could not deny, even in a utopian situation. It is no coincidence that in each bildungsroman studied, there is a male benefactor who distinctly improves family fortunes. The authors skirt the issue of male power, however, by removing fathers through death and war, and minimizing the direct influence of the male benefactors. Men appear only when they can perform a useful function, and only after it is clear that the women can manage perfectly well on their own, even though circumstances have definitely conspired against them.

There is no room for traditional masculine qualities in this world of women. When Laurie cries with Jo over her sister's impending death in *Little Women,* Alcott editorializes, "it might be unmanly of Laurie to cry, but he couldn't help it and I'm glad of it." The only example in any of the books of a man without any womanly qualities appears in ***Rebecca of Sunnybrook Farm:***

> Mr. Simpson spent little time with his family, owing to certain awkward methods of horse-trading, or the "swapping" of farm implements and vehicles of various kinds. . . . After every successful trade he generally passed a longer or shorter term in jail: for when a poor man . . . has the inveterate habit of swapping, it follows naturally that he must have something to swap; and having nothing of his own it follows still more naturally that he must swap something belonging to his neighbors.

An abundance of "good" (feminized) men provide counter examples of behavior in these fictional worlds. Adam Ladd is visiting his aunt when he meets Rebecca of Sunnybrook Farm; his first line is, "I am the lady of the house at present . . . what can I do for you?" Rebecca proceeds to sell him three hundred cakes of soap to benefit the Simpson family, for whose well-being she feels responsible. Adam Ladd is thus doubly acceptable, because he is a thoroughly feminized philanthropist.

Since the ideal of motherhood transcended sexuality and is not necessarily considered to be a biological function, it is possible in these novels for a man to act as a mother. Jeremiah Cobb, the stagedriver who takes Rebecca to live with her aunts (her mother cannot afford to have her live at home), becomes her surrogate mother. He shares this role with his wife Sarah, whom he calls "Mother," a name which, despite her short tenure in that vocation (their only child died at seventeen months), "served at any rate as a reminder of her woman's crown of blessedness." Feminized men and women alike could teach the blessed duties of benevolence and domesticity in this utopian world. Curiously, the worship of domesticity and maternal nurture seems to have overwhelmed even traditional gender boundaries in these novels.

Coincidentally with learning her duties within the domestic sphere, a girl was inculcated in the importance of the community of women through these novels. . . .

As a girl matured, she widened her circle of female friends, but continued to turn to other women for sympathetic support. Rebecca of Sunnybrook Farm, for example, had to move in with her maiden aunts at the age of eleven because her widowed mother could not afford to care for all of her children. Rebecca's aunts are kind in their own way, and Rebecca finds many male and female friends, but she needs "somebody who not only loved but understood; who spoke her language, comprehended her desires, and responded to her mysterious longings." She finds that person in her spinster teacher at the Wareham seminary.

By the late nineteenth-century, about ten percent of all American women were spinsters; in the Northeast, the percentage may have been twice as high. Many spinsters appeared in the nineteenth-century female bildungsroman. In these novels, however, the spinsters are portrayed quite differently than in American culture in general: not bitter, disillusioned, or unfulfilled, spinsters in these female utopias are independent financially and mentally; they play an important role in the lives of the heroines and their communities. The vital and interesting role of the spinster in these novels indicates to the reader that a single woman can have a fulfilling life.

Indeed, the heroines of these female bildungsromans who marry do so only after they have established their own independence. Even Marmee, whose bliss is her daughters, proclaims, "better be happy old maids than unhappy wives, or unmaidenly girls, running about to find husbands." The authors take pains to ensure that their heroines will escape what Mary Livermore, in an advice book of 1883, *What Shall We Do With Our Daughters,* called "one of the most serious dangers to which inefficient women are liable,—the danger of regarding marriage as a means of livelihood." These authors realized that marriage could be a way of gaining financial security, but they were also aware of its drawbacks. . . .

Distanced from their own adolescence, the authors of female bildungsromans could reinvent girlhood with an eye towards perfection. The "grown-up" life of housewifery, however, could not be portrayed in such a distant, idealized manner. Kate Douglas Wiggin described Rebecca's stint as a housewife in less than glowing terms:

> [She spent] two months of steady, fagging work; of cooking, washing, ironing. . . . No girl of seventeen can pass through such an ordeal . . . without some inward repining and rebellion. She was doing tasks in which she could not be fully happy . . . and like a promise of nectar to thirsty lips was the vision of joys she had had to put aside for the performance of dull daily duty.

Perhaps it was because they realized that this was the inevitable future of their heroines that the authors shied away from having them marry; they generally did so only in sequels demanded by the public.

The drudgery of housework aside, a rather grim picture of the state of married life emerges from these novels. None of the heroines come from an "ideal" family, defined by prescriptive advice books as one in which "the husband will be the breadwinner, and the wife the bread-maker;" Mr. March does not earn a living, and the rest of the fathers are deceased. But the books all have portraits of wronged wives, such as poor Mrs. Winslow, who was left in the forest by her husband, and whose motherless son provided the impetus for the founding of the charitable Riverboro Aunts Association. Rebecca's own mother is another wronged wife: in her effort to keep her family from dissolving after her insolvent husband's death, she ends up "content to work from sunrise to sunset to gain a mere subsistence for her children, she lived in the future, not in her own present, as a mother is wont to do when her own lot seems dull and cheerless." Again and again, the authors subtly refute the notion that a woman's only place is the home, and that she should be content with that, by their inability to portray married life as interesting and rewarding.

Alcott and her successors offered something other than housework and childrearing to their readers. In their utopian, fictional world there was an opportunity for "young ladies to make themselves the mistresses of some attainment, either in art or science, by which they might secure a subsistency, should they be reduced to poverty." To some extent, their fiction reflected these authors' unusual lives. Alcott, who felt compelled to support her own family since her father could not, never married. Harriett Mulford Lothrop, the author of the *Five Little Peppers* series, married her publisher, Daniel Lothrop, when she was thirty-nine; they had one daughter. Kate Douglas Wiggin, the author of ***Rebecca of Sunnybrook Farm,*** devoted a single page of her 440-page memoir to her first husband, Samuel Wiggin, to whom she was married for eight years; all she recorded about him was that they married and he died. Her second husband was allotted eight pages, as well as numerous letters—throughout most of their marriage they lived in separate countries. Lucy Maud Montgomery, the author of *Anne of Green Gables,* was almost forty when she married. Prior to that she cared for the grandparents who had raised her. Voluntarily or not, the creators of the female bildungsroman in America lived extraordinary lives, and, consciously or not, their lives affected their fiction.

For, despite their worship of maternal nurture and family life, these novels all contain some elements subversive to the nineteenth-century cult of domesticity. Most striking, perhaps, is the curious role assigned to men in these matriarchal utopias: traditional gender boundaries are crossed frequently by "feminized" men, if not by "masculine" women; and there seems to be no appreciation for traditional "masculine" qualities. Implicitly, then, these novels contain a deep critique of the male world of money and power, within their exaltation of the value of female nurture. A subtle subversion of the cult of domesticity is also apparent in the treatment of marriage in these books: while spinsters often have positive roles and fulfilling lives, marriage (unlike motherhood) is not portrayed very positively. At least for a while in each series of novels, some alternative to domesticity is offered to the heroines and readers alike. With the bonds of womanhood supporting them, the heroines of these novels exercise some choice over the paths of their lives. . . .

The boundaries of the feminine utopia can become oppressive after the girl heroine has passed through adolescence. Although she can dream as much as she wants, duty to her family must be her first concern, even if it gets in the way of her own plans. . . .

The authors of the female bildungsromans created a utopia as a framework in which the problems of adolescence could be solved. The nature of this utopia was in part derived from the things denied to women in the real world. The matriarchal culture of nineteenth-century female bildungsromans gave their heroines the freedom of development they would not have found in a male world. They were still, however, precluded from entering this male world fully and finally.

The attraction of fiction is that it allows the author to recreate the world. When Jo March wishes that her sisters were her heroines, Alcott comments on her own position, in which her sisters are her heroines. Eventually, Jo does have "some rich relation leave [her] a fortune unexpectedly," and Amy does "go abroad and come home [married to a rich man] in a blaze of splendor and elegance." Even in the fiction, however, things happen to the characters which Alcott does not want to happen. She is bound by the constraints of domestic fiction and the need to create a credible facsimile of life. The parameters of this world are set by a social reality over which even an author cannot exercise complete control.

Perri Klass

SOURCE: "Stories for Girls about Girls Who Write Stories," in *The New York Times Book Review,* May 17, 1992, pp. 1, 36-9.

[In the following excerpt, Klass examines the long line of literary heroines—from Jo March of Little Women *to Wiggin's Rebecca to* Harriet the Spy*—who portray the young girl as a writer with a professional future.]*

[The] girl's books of the late 19th and early 20th centuries are well peopled with young women with literary talent, literary drive, literary ambitions. This is perhaps not surprising; these books are, after all, the creations of grown-up women with literary careers, looking back at childhood. Sometimes they are quite explicitly autobiographical—Louisa May Alcott (1832-88) made herself into Jo March, as she made her three sisters into Meg, Beth and Amy, in *Little Women* (1869). [Lucy Maud] Montgomery put big pieces of her own life into the Emily books. On the other hand, Kate Douglas Wiggin (1856-1923) said in her autobiography, ***My Garden of Memory,*** that ***Rebecca of Sunnybrook Farm*** (1903) was inspired by a vision of a dark-haired child rattling along in an old-fashioned stagecoach: "I wondered who the child was, and whither she was traveling, and whence she came. I could not content myself until I had created answers to my questions."

The child is called Rebecca Rowena Randall, and she is being sent away from Sunnybrook Farm by her impoverished widowed mother to be raised by her two maiden aunts, Miranda and Jane Sawyer. She is a slender, shabbily dressed child with remarkable eyes that "glowed like two stars, their dancing light half hidden in lustrous darkness." Rebecca writes poetry, she has always written poetry, she needs to write poetry. She also, the reader learns in the sequel, ***New Chronicles of Rebecca,*** keeps a Thought Book. "Write she could, write she would, write she must and did, in season and out; from the time she made pothooks at 6, till now, writing was the easiest of all possible tasks; to be indulged in as solace and balm."

Like Rebecca Randall, [Montgomery's] Anne Shirley and Emily Starr are also slender, shabby children with remarkable eyes; Jo March is introduced as very thin, and possessed of "sharp, gray eyes, which appeared to see everything, and were by turns fierce, funny, or thoughtful." As a stolid, solid (not to say plump) child with myopic eyes behind thick glasses, I was somewhat miserably aware that I did not fit this description, and perhaps also that fanciful tales of fairyland would seem incongruous coming from me, no matter how right they were coming from Emily Starr, who herself seemed to remind everyone of an elf, a sprite, a fairy.

But I understood about needing to write, about writing as solace and writing as balm. I understood being handy with words, knew how Rebecca could turn out neatly rhymed verses, one after another, to the amazement of her friends. And I also understood how Emily, when her teacher came to New Moon to complain that Emily had misbehaved in school, could take comfort in collecting impressions of the dramatic scene for later use: "Some part of her had detached itself from the rest and was interestedly absorbing impressions and analyzing motives and describing settings. She felt that when she wrote about this scene later on she must not forget to describe the odd shadows the candle under Aunt Elizabeth's nose cast upward on her face, producing a rather skeletonic effect." To this day, I sit in meetings or other gatherings where I do not really wish to be, and make tiny little notes to myself about the speeches and behavior and probable motives of other people.

In an age in which most women do not have professions, Emily and Jo and the others created identities for themselves by sheer force of authorial will. "I can write poetry," Emily says proudly when the other children taunt her on her first day at the new school, demanding to know her accomplishments. Rebecca also commands attention from her world, her fellow students and her teacher, who comments; "quaint, countrified little verses, doggerel they are, but somehow or other she always contrives to put in one line, one thought, one image, that shows you she is, quite unconsciously to herself, in possession of the secret." In a sense they make themselves up, these children, who start out stripped by their creators of family and money and other worldly advantages, left only with their verses and their remarkable eyes.

Emily and Rebecca and Jo and, for that matter, Betsy Ray of the "Betsy-Tacy" books, which were set at the turn of the century and published by Maud Hart Lovelace (1892-1980) during the 1940's, write because they are driven to write, because writing is more real to them than many aspects of real life. Emily's inspiration comes as a sudden visitation: "the flash," as she calls it. Whenever the flash comes, she has a moment of unexpected beauty and happiness, leaving her uplifted for days, inspiring poetry and fiction. Less mystically, Jo March "did not think herself a genius by any means; but when the writing fit came on, she gave herself up to it with entire abandon, and led a blissful life, unconscious of want, care or bad weather, while she sat safe and happy in an imaginary world, full of friends almost as real and dear to her as any in the flesh."

Whether they write from inspiration or because they must, these young women are not purists. They are keenly aware that a person can earn her living with her pen. They are, after all, orphans (Anne, Emily) or semi-orphans (Rebecca) or in straitened circumstances (Jo). They will need to make their way in the world—and writing offers professional opportunities, a confluence of destiny and opportunity. For an aspiring writer growing up on these books, there was a fascinating element of professionalism, a hardheaded assumption that after the "flash," the "writing fit," there were manuscripts to submit, editors to second-guess, rejection slips to rise above. . . .

For a young girl who wants to be a writer one day, these books offer a tantalizing glimpse of the marketplace, of women making talents into careers—and they were probably even more intriguing in 1869 or 1923. These are not inspired dreamers, spinning pretty poems in remote towers; they are driven and ambitious workers—again, unusual elements in girls' books of more than 20 years ago.

For the writers who created these girls, writing was indeed serious business. They were professionals, and successful professionals, and if the business aspects of their books ring true, it is because their authors cared passionately for the money and recognition and independence that writing could bring. . . .

Since most adults, especially adult males, would probably not think of ***Rebecca of Sunnybrook Farm*** as grown-up fare, it may be somewhat surprising nowadays to realize quite how celebrated these authors were for their books, written for and about young girls and, for all their sprightliness and good fun, moral in tone and language.

Consider, for example, Jack London's letter to Kate Douglas Wiggin, written in 1904 from Manchuria, where London was covering the Russo-Japanese War for the Hearst papers and where his leisure reading apparently included ***Rebecca:*** "Rebecca won my heart," he wrote. "Of course, I have laughed, but I have wept as well. She is real; she lives; she has given me many regrets, but I love her. I would have quested the wide world over to make her mine, only I was born too long ago and she was born but yesterday." Mark Twain wrote to Maud Montgomery early in this century to tell her Anne was "the dearest, and most lovable child in fiction since the immortal Alice." In fact, *Anne of Green Gables* conquered not only literary lights but also politicians; the two great rivals of British politics in the 1920's, Stanley Baldwin and Ramsay MacDonald, Tory and Labor, were both fans.

Writing is not just part of the inner life of Emily, Jo and company. Their aspirations and their literary attempts figure in the plots of all these books, creating a kind of girls' book metafiction, stories for girls about girls who write stories and who frequently usurp the narration with their Diaries and Thought Books. Each of the writers at some point comes to grief, experiences a disaster that is specifically a writer's tragedy.

Rebecca leans on the railing of a bridge to compose a poem, only to find that the railing has been recently painted and her best dress is ruined. When Jo March quarrels with her sister. Amy burns up the little book Jo has been writing, a collection of fairy tales: "She had just copied them with great care, and had destroyed the old manuscript, so that Amy's bonfire had consumed the loving work of several years." (Another lesson you can learn from *Little Women:* always keep a copy or, nowadays, back up your hard disk.) Recently, as I was reading this book aloud to my 8-year-old son, we came to this chapter and I confessed that I was not sure that in Jo's place I would ever have forgiven Amy—even with the near-fatal accident Louisa May Alcott engineers to bring about remorse and forgiveness.

And Emily—well, this was the great traumatic scene I remember from my own childhood, the passage in the book that made the most tremendous impression on me. Emily's cruel, sarcastic teacher catches her surreptitiously writing poetry in school, and reads it aloud mockingly, "in a sing-song nasal voice, with absurd intonations and gestures that made it seem a very ridiculous thing. . . . 'The Lost Diamond—A Romantic Tale,' read Miss Brownell, 'Lines on a Birch Tree—looks to me more like lines on a very dirty piece of paper, Emily.'"

There is parallel disaster in a much more recent children's book, a book that mattered to me as much as any other when I was growing up—*Harriet the Spy* (1964), by Louise Fitzhugh (1928-74). Harriet, 12 years old, who lives in Manhattan somewhere in the East 80s, is, thank heavens, not particularly slender, and nothing is ever said about her eyes. But she is a writer, and she is always going to be a writer, and she collects material by spying and making notes in her notebook. She makes honest notes about her friends and classmates, and the action of the book centers on their reactions when they read the notebook and Harriet finds herself ostracized.

I identified powerfully with the violation Harriet suffers, with her pain and misery as unfriendly eyes examine her private notes. But I also appreciated her energy and her oomph; Harriet, like her fictional forebears, aspires to professionalism. She is pulled out of her despair by the suggestion that she take some of her notes and write a story. So she spends the day typing wildly on her father's typewriter, and her comment when the story is done is this: "Enough is enough. It is time to rise and shine. Wait till The New Yorker gets a load of that story." I have read *Harriet the Spy* more times than I care to remember, and have never felt the slightest qualm that anything might distract her from her goal; as she says on page two, she is going to be a writer.

Some of the other girls, however, do get distracted. Anne marries and has six children and essentially gives up writing. Maud Montgomery herself married after she was already well known as a writer; she and her husband, a minister, had two sons. Montgomery continued to write books at quite a clip, while also fulfilling the many duties of the minister's wife and reading prodigiously. . . .

Alcott herself never married; she supported her relatives, traveled and wrote more books. Like all the other authors, she was a writer for life.

In her autobiography, Kate Douglas Wiggin wrote, "Years ago I said: 'To write a book that two successive generations of children might love, read twice, and put under their pillows at night, oh! what joy of joys, greater than showers of gold or wreaths of laurel!' Some people would call that a humble wish, viewed from the standpoint of their own ambitions; others would deem it too great to be realized. Fortunately, I shall never know whether I have even once achieved my goal, for only the passage of years can decide the ultimate fate of a book."

In fact, for all their faults, their occasional sermonizing, their twee exclamations, their frequent and lavish sunsets (Maud Montgomery had a weakness for descriptions of clouds), all of these books are in print and are read with that special engagement that is usually left behind in childhood. Certainly I know that I never read adult fiction with the devotion I brought to *Emily of New Moon* or *Harriet the Spy*. I no longer go to fiction with that same openness, that same willingness to see my life and my daydreams shaken out and rearranged, that same sense of limitless possibilities.

Emily and Jo and Anne and Rebecca and Betsy and Harriet are permanent residents of my mind, and I suspect they go on colonizing new young minds, year after year. They brought me information, details about life as a writer, vicarious triumphs and agonies. But above all they brought me reinforcement in my determination that I would grow up to write books, try to get those books published and then write more of them. I saw these stories as personal letters to me, words of advice and encouragement from authors who had once been little girls to little girls who would one day be authors. As Maud Montgomery put it, "There is a destiny which shapes the ends of young misses who are born with the itch for writing tingling in their baby fingertips."

And, speaking of baby fingertips, I have to admit that I am eager to see my own daughter, Josephine (yes, named for "Little Women"), reading these books. What will she think? Will she respond to Emily, will she shudder when Miss Brownell mocks her poems? Will she carry a spy notebook? Well, she will have her own responses and her own destiny. But I can't help wondering whether maybe she too will feel some special identification with those girls' book heroines who write because they want to be rich and famous, because they love to write and, ultimately, because they have to write. If she should indeed turn out to have that itch in her fingertips, she could do worse for a model than the lofty confidence of mission and professional practicality in 12-year-old Emily Starr's response to her Victorian aunt:

"'Don't you know that it is wicked to write novels?' demanded Aunt Elizabeth.

"'Oh, I'm not writing novels—yet,' said Emily. 'I can't get enough paper. These are just short stories.'"

TITLE COMMENTARY

THE BIRDS' CHRISTMAS CAROL (1887)

Perri Klass

SOURCE: "No Good Deed Goes Unpunished: Or, The Little Match Girl Syndrome," in *The New York Times Book Review,* December 2, 1990, pp. 7, 30.

[In the following excerpt, Klass analyzes how Wiggin's The Birds' Christmas Carol, *along with other stories of brave and pathetic children, exemplifies the nineteenth-century tradition that combined sentimentalism and realism in dealing with the death of children.]*

"It was very early Christmas morning and in the stillness of the dawn with the soft snow falling on the housetops, a little child was born in the Bird household." So begins ***The Birds' Christmas Carol*** published in 1887 by Kate Douglas Wiggin, who is best remembered as the author of ***Rebecca of Sunnybrook Farm.*** In the holiday tale about the Birds (the surname of a human family), the child is named Carol because the music of the Christmas service reaches her mother's ears. Thanks to the sentimentality and the neatness of literary construction peculiar to the 19th century, she proves worthy of her birthday and her naming. "Her cheeks and lips were as red as holly-berries, her hair was for all the world the color of a Christmas candle-flame, her eyes were bright as stars; her laugh like a chime of Christmas-bells, and her tiny hands forever outstretched in giving."

Unfortunately, when 19th-century authors created angelic children, they all too often felt the need to elevate them to truly angelic status. Even in a Christmas story intended for children little Carol's prognosis is not good.

Over the past several years, I have been reading 19th-century fiction in search of children who were sick, children who were dying. I had been writing a novel about a pediatrician who finds herself bewildered by a life frequently colored by the sufferings of her patients. She goes searching in books to see whether people living in an era of much higher infant and child mortality had found any way to integrate the harsh truth of those statistics into daily life. What she finds (that is, what I found for her, in my research) was sentimentality, the idealization of the dying child as always too good to live.

After a while, I rather prided myself on being able to judge from the first description of a child whether that particular juvenile was going to live through the book. Anyone who did anything even faintly mischievous was safe, anyone who got dirty, or showed some spunk, or answered back. Young Jane Eyre survives Lowood School and goes on to meet her destiny and Mr. Rochester, while Jane's friend, the saintly Helen, who bears with such unnatural fortitude the cruelties inflicted on her by her sadistic teacher, dies drenched in a strong odor of sanctity. Similarly, Oliver Twist escapes the workhouse, the funeral home and even the iniquities of London, but the plaintive and gentle little Dick welcomes his death in the workhouse because, he says, "I dream so much of Heaven, and Angels, and kind faces that I never see when I am awake."

In a certain sense, the images of Christmas we all know best are products of the 19th century. *The Nutcracker,* with its splendid tree and magical presents; *A Christmas Carol,* with its turkey ("What, the one as big as me?") and pudding; the poem, *A Visit From St. Nicholas* ("'Twas the night before Christmas")—these make up the secular iconography of Christmas. Even now idealized greeting-card views of the holiday are lit by gaslight, by fire-light, by candles on the tree. And these stories carry with them, always, the images of happy children, children lavished with gifts and treats, children wide-eyed before the tree, children dazzled by visions of sugar-plums or by the Sugarplum Fairy. But 19th-century literary Christmas scenes are also full of children who are less fortunate, children who are poor and hungry, set to serve as objects of charity, children who are sick and even dying, whose narrative function is sometimes to point a moral, sometimes to invoke the holy pathos of suffering innocence, and give a story poignancy and power.

Victorian fiction, both English and American, drew some of its punch from the juxtaposition of poverty and privilege, from the sufferings endured by children in the midst of plenty. Christmas provided an ideal setting for such contrasts, and also a not-to-be-missed opportunity to demonstrate the power of charity, especially holiday charity. Scrooge, after all, sets the entire elaborate machinery of *A Christmas Carol* in motion by refusing to donate money to provide the poor with holiday cheer ("Are there no prisons?"). . . .

"It was December, ten years later. . . . But Christmas in the Birds' Nest was scarcely as merry now as it used to be in the bygone years, for the little child, that once brought such an added blessing to the day, lay month after month a patient, helpless invalid, in the room where she was born."

As the Victorians pointed charitable morals in their Christmas scenes, they also often invoked the pathos of sick and dying children, reminding readers that in the midst of life, there may be death. Although there are lessons to be learned in today's Christmas stories—*Miracle on 34th Street, How the Grinch Stole Christmas*—they are usually lessons about commercialism, about family love, about the true meaning of Christmas. In this day and age, a holiday story is less likely to encompass the death of a sympathetic juvenile protagonist. We have lost the unabashed sentimentalism of the 19th century, and lost also the realistic facts-of-life attitude underlying that sentimentalism. That is, we expect children to grow up, barring disaster; the Victorians, less sheltered, could not.

The most famous coupling of childhood illness and Christmas takes place, of course, in *A Christmas Carol.* Tiny Tim enters the story borne on his father's shoulder, home from church in time for Christmas dinner. Anyone who has given any thought to the fate of saintly children in Victorian fiction must tremble for him when his father says, "He told me, coming home, that he hoped the people saw him in the church, because he was a cripple, and it might be pleasant to them to remember upon Christmas Day, who made lame beggars walk, and blind men see." Pitifully weak, nobly good of heart, victim both of the cruel fate that crippled him and of the unfeeling society that keeps his family in poverty, Tiny Tim would seem to have no chance of living through the story. In fact, Dickens makes use of that convention. His readers could remember, after all, the sad fates 'met' by other sweet, gentle, long-suffering children born into Dickens novels to suffer in a harsh world, and eventually to die. By the time *A Christmas Carol* was published in 1843, Dickens had already created and killed off not only little Dick in *Oliver Twist* (1838), but also Smike in *Nicholas Nickleby* (1839) and, most famous of all, Little Nell in *The Old Curiosity Shop* (1841).

In *A Christmas Carol,* Tiny Tim in fact gets the sad and sacred death he deserves—in Christmas Future, where Tim's mother talks sadly about how his father loved to carry him, and his father comes in briskly from his

Christmas visit to the grave, and then breaks down. "My little little child!" cries Bob. "My little child!" When he has recovered himself, he speaks to his other children about the patience and the gentleness of the dead child, and all agree that in honor of his memory, they will never quarrel. Dickens himself, in true 19th-century authorial exclamation, comments. "Spirit of Tiny Tim, thy childish essence was from God!"

But *A Christmas Carol* is a holiday story, and a holiday story with a happy ending. There is a social moral as well; there is hope even for Tiny Tim, if his poverty is alleviated, and for Scrooge, to redeem himself and to save the child. No wonder that when Dickens gave public readings of this story, "they took the line 'and to Tiny Tim who did NOT die,' with a most prodigious shout and roll of thunder."

Little Carol, in ***The Birds' Christmas Carol,*** is not so lucky. She dies on Christmas night, after spending the day entertaining the poor children next door at a fabulous party. Her death is detailed in a chapter that is a true masterpiece of the pathetic, a chapter titled "The Birdling Flies Away." Kate Douglas Wiggin was not interested in miracle cures, and little Carol was certainly no victim of poverty but the well-beloved child of well-to-do, indulgent and loving parents. The stark, realistic 19th-century truth that even parents like these could not keep a child safe is, in this book, combined with the most extravagant Victorian sentimentalism about children and the death of children—which is seen as their translation to a higher state. "Carol's mother, even in the freshness of her grief, was glad that her darling had slipped away on the loveliest day of her life, out of its glad content, into everlasting peace."

But the saddest, starkest holiday child, the strangest 19th-century combination of sentiment and social realism and holiday imagery, is without doubt Hans Christian Andersen's Little Match Girl. It is New Year's Eve when she goes wandering barefoot through the snow, afraid to go home because she has sold no matches and her father will beat her. And as she huddles against a wall, striking her matches one after the other to keep warm, the pictures that appear to her in the flames are pictures of the holiday celebrations going on around her. One match shows to her a holiday feast, complete with a roast goose stuffed with apples and prunes. The next yields a Christmas tree, alight with candles. Finally the little girl's grandmother appears, embraces her, and carries her off to heaven.

But the story doesn't end with that triumphant ascent. It ends the next morning, with the frozen dead body of the Little Match Girl found, the burnt-out matches clutched between her fingers. It ends with a reminder, even in a fairy tale, of harsh sociological reality: true, the little girl has gone to glory, but the reader must not forget, even in a fairy tale, that a child can freeze to death in the street while adults party in their warm houses.

Perhaps the very lavishness of the holiday season, as

From The Birds' Christmas Carol, *written by Kate Douglas Wiggin. Illustrated by Jessie Gillespie.*

celebrated in 19th-century fiction, demanded certain elements of pathos for contrast, for poignancy, for moral justification. In a season marked by the indulgence and gratification of children, poor children as objects of charity could point a moral, could allow themselves to be helped and thereby entitle their wealthy benefactors to enjoy holiday excess with a free conscience. Ill children, suffering bravely, could remind readers of their own good fortune. And dying children, the ultimate angels, could bless the holiday season as they ascended—or even, in one very celebrated case, could survive a destined death to preside at Christmas dinner and observe, "God Bless Us, Every One!"

A SUMMER IN A CAÑON: A CALIFORNIA STORY (1889)

The Dial

SOURCE: A review of *A Summer in a Cañon: A California Story,* in *The Dial,* Vol. X, No. 116, December, 1889, p. 223.

The golden land of California has lured many a refugee from our rigorous northern climate, and holds him with a fascination as strong as any which it threw around the old Spanish explorers. For this reason, as well as from the fact that Kate Douglas Wiggins is well known as a writer of charming stories, ***A Summer in a Cañon: A California Story*** is sure of appreciative readers. The *dramatis personae,* for there is no set hero or heroine, are a company of young men and maidens, who spend their summer in an ideal camp in Southern California. There is no plot, no love-story, and no startling incident; it is simply a charming picture of what camp-life may be for a congenial set of young people overflowing with animal spirits. It is a restful, refreshing book, and will make one feel the breezes of summer in our coldest winter days.

The Nation, New York

SOURCE: A review of *A Summer in a Cañon,* in *The Nation, New York,* Vol. 50, No. 1284, February 6, 1890, p. 118.

A Summer in a Cañon is a bright and taking little story, which does not have to be labelled "for young people." It is unmistakably theirs. The fun is infectious, and many of the situations and speeches are irresistibly comical. The bane of American youth, however, is slang, and this otherwise healthful tale does not wholly escape it. Dr. and Mrs. Winship undertake the charge of a dozen or more persons during a camping expedition on a large scale. For three months the happy party live in tents in Las Flores Cañon, under the spreading oaks and sycamores, hung with mistletoe and gray Spanish moss, which temper the perpetual sunshine of a California summer. Evidently the descriptions of the region were written *con amore*—even at the beginning occurs an almost eloquent passage expressive of the early-morning beauty of the day upon which the expedition sets forth. Some entertaining information about the old-style *rodeo,* and the early California days, is given picturesquely "round the campfire."

TIMOTHY'S QUEST: A STORY FOR ANYBODY, OLD OR YOUNG (1890)

The Baron de B.-W.

SOURCE: A review of *Timothy's Quest,* in *Punch,* Vol. 104, February 18, 1893, p. 77.

In the arid life of the book-reviewer there is sometimes found the oasis of opportunity to recommend to a (comparatively) less suffering community a book worth reading. My Baronite has by chance come upon such an one in ***Timothy's Quest,*** by Kate Douglas Wiggin. The little volume is apparently an importation, having been printed for the Riverside Press, Cambridge, Mass. It is published in London by Gay and Bird, a firm whose name, though it sounds lively, is as unfamiliar as the Author's. Probably from this combination of circumstances, ***Timothy's Quest*** has, as far as my Baronite's quest goes, escaped the notice of the English Reviewer. That is his personal loss. The book is an almost perfect idyl, full of humanity, fragrant with the smell of flowers, and the manifold scent of meadows. It tells how Timothy, waif and stray in the heart of a great city, escaped from a baby-farm to whose tender cares he had been committed; how, in a clothes-basket, mounted on four wooden wheels, cushioned with a dingy shawl, he wheeled off another waif and stray, a prattling infant; and how, accompanied by a mongrel dog named Rags, the party made its way to a distant village, nestling in the lap of green hills with a real river running through it. Here boy and baby—and Rags too—find New England friends, whom it is a privilege for *nous autres* to know. Samanthy Ann is a real live person, and so is Jabe Slocum—a long, loose, knock-kneed, slack-twisted person, of whom Aunt Hitty Tarbox (whom George Eliot might have sketched) remarked he would have been "longer yit if he hedn't hed so much turned up fur feet." ***Timothy's Quest*** is the best thing of the kind that has reached us from America since *Little Lord Fauntleroy* crossed the Atlantic.

A CATHEDRAL COURTSHIP, AND PENELOPE'S ENGLISH EXPERIENCES (1893; reprinted as *Penelope's English Experiences,* with new illustrations, 1900)

The Nation, New York

SOURCE: A review of *A Cathedral Courtship, and Penelope's English Experiences,* in *The Nation, New York,* Vol. 56, No. 1461, June 29, 1893, pp. 475-76.

Mrs. Wiggin's stories of American women's experiences in England are very amusing. Along with all the things we have found funny in the English since first the steamers began to ply between America and Liverpool, she has, with keen American scent for the different, brought to her pages many new examples of the same cause for mirth. Jokes may be so violently up to date that there is a gloss upon them as of a little boy's hair plastered down with soap for Sundays. Mrs. Wiggin's pleasantries are sometimes of this order. Among many delightfully bright observations there runs a cheaper variety which dashes the reader's enjoyment and deters him from pronouncing the whole entirely attractive. Without these drawbacks (and they are removable, being, as the surgeons say, non-malignant), the sketches would be throughout, as they are now in great part, favorable specimens of American humor.

The Catholic World

SOURCE: A review of *A Cathedral Courtship, and Penelope's English Experiences,* in *The Catholic World,* Vol. LVII, No. 341, August, 1893, p. 720.

What a relief it is to get hold of a book that is really refreshing to the mind, free from that eternal "trail of the serpent" which crawls through the vicious literature of the day, and at the same time full of delicate humor! It is as the oasis in the desert to the disgusted life-wayfarer who, because he or she *must* read for amusement, must needs take the prurient draught if they would take anything at all, so subtly have the keepers of the well mixed up its waters. We have a right to be thankful to Kate Douglas Wiggin (a name at which she herself seems to poke fun in a sly way in the course of her work), for having given us the twin volume ***A Cathedral Courtship*** and ***Penelope's English Experiences.*** They are really charming revelations of the American feminine mind, and not mere emotional bits of ingenuousness like Marie Bashkertseff's. The humor sparkles in every sentence; the necessary sentiment, where it is thrown in, is thrown in as a condiment, indispensable to the perfect making of the dish. Her narratives take the shape of friendly correspondence and diaries, and have all the *vraisemblance* of real confidences. Of course such outpourings must have a human centre and culmination, and equally of course, we may perhaps say, the centre and culmination must be the "old, old story." The way in which the inevitable is dealt with in these two delightful bits of writing show the author's deftness and discretion. She ventures upon dangerous ground in one of her sentimental chapters. The fact that such a past-master in the art as Sterne had shed inky tears over a dead ass does not deter her from endeavoring to elicit our indignation against the erratic independence of a live representative of that long-suffering tribe. However, she does it well, and we not only forgive but applaud her. We hope we shall hear from Kate Douglas Wiggin, over the same or any other name, again.

The Athenaeum

SOURCE: A review of *A Cathedral Courtship, and Penelope's English Experiences* in *The Athenaeum,* Vol. 102, No. 3432, August 5, 1893, pp. 188-89.

A Cathedral Courtship and ***Penelope's English Experiences*** are a couple of sketches that make a pleasing, bright little volume. In each there is just enough narrative to bind into a story the surface impressions produced on some clever American women by sundry aspects and phases of English life. The humour, vivacity, and freshness written on almost every page are specially noticeable on a first glance; this is probably the effect intended, for the book does not seem to take itself at all seriously. The remarks on the "manners and customs of the British race," and on our small, insular peculiarities and prejudices, show quick observation and feeling for subtle contrast, as well as a keen, not to say malicious outlook—in the pleasant sense of the word. There are amusing and original ideas on travelling manners, or their absence; on the humours of lodging-houses, lodgers, and donkeys, or rather one donkey—Jane—a somewhat typical representative of the class. The ways of "park lovers" cannot be entirely strange even to the least observant Londoner; "the dead calm of the Park embrace," "the kind of superb finish and completeness about their indifference to the public gaze," seem to us well imagined. The almost inhuman aspect of the well-trained servant has often before been recorded; here is something rather funny about powdered footmen. "I tremble," says Miss Wiggin,

> to think of what the Powdered Footman may become when he unbends in the bosom of his family. . . . I should think he might be guilty of almost any indiscretion or violence. I for one would never consent to be the wife and children of a Powdered Footman and receive him in his moments of reaction.

The author, though endowed with a good deal of ready facility of expression, has not erred on the side of providing that "too much of a good thing" which spoils so many books.

POLLY OLIVER'S PROBLEM: A STORY FOR GIRLS (1893)

The Nation, New York

SOURCE: A review of *Polly Oliver's Problem,* in *The Nation, New York,* Vol. 57, No. 1484, December 7, 1893, p. 434.

The adventures of Kate Douglas Wiggin's newest heroine (***Polly Oliver's Problem: A Story for Girls***) can hardly fail of the sympathy, not only of younger, but even of older readers, who will be apt to fancy, rightly or wrongly, they detect in them an autobiographical ring. Polly Oliver, portrait or fancy sketch as the case may be, after trials and sorrows of an intimately personal nature, makes a successful venture into a hitherto unexplored tract of activity suited to young ladies endowed with fine imagination, a little skill in music, and a pleasing personality. She is sent, in the first place, by a benevolent lady to tell tales two hours each day in the orphan asylums and Children's Hospital in San Francisco, at a salary of twenty-five dollars a month. The success of this venture is so pronounced that she presently invents the plan of telling stories, illustrated kindergarten fashion, by song and drawing, in a private house to groups of children of wealthy parents, at a charge to each child of five dollars for twenty hours. The details of the plan are all so carefully drawn out that any young girl who chooses to consult the volume may find even the toilets appropriate to the private-house story hours sketched with a *modiste's* skill. As a further development of this pretty scheme, a class for child's-nurses is also hinted at, and visions are thereby evoked of the happy future awaiting infant minds when they have been freed from the terrifying or drivelling inventions of the unaided nursery-maid. There are also some hints for ways of becoming what the charity organization societies put down as "benevolent individuals," such, for instance, as "buying up splendid old trees in the outskirts of certain New England country towns—trees that were in danger of being cut down for wood," or putting stamps on the unstamped letters displayed in post-offices and "sending them spinning on their way."

There is undoubted suggestiveness in all this, and to remark that judgment is a necessary ballast to suggestion, is merely to fall into a truism never fresher in the mind than in these days of profuse grafting of the old stock; and since it is so much easier to sit in judgment on all ideas than to suggest a new one of even the smallest value, thanks must always be due to the one who can see her way to the ounce of practicability in the hundredweight of objection.

The Athenaeum

SOURCE: A review of *Polly Oliver's Problem: A Story for Girls,* in *The Athenaeum,* Vol. 103, No. 3460, February 17, 1894, p. 211.

Mrs. Wiggin's name is well known to all those interested in the training and education of young children on both sides of the Atlantic. Her books have, moreover, secured her a public larger than her admirable developments of the Kindergarten system could in the nature of things command. ***Children's Rights*** was found pleasantly suggestive even by those strenuous modern parents whose own claims are more likely to be found sinking into abeyance than those of the rising generation, to whose improvement they devote themselves with such overwhelming and sometimes, alas! misguided zeal. ***Polly Oliver's Problem*** will not add much to Mrs. Wiggin's reputation. It is full of right feeling, of high spirits, and of that sort of nonsense which is only taking when a very nice and pretty young girl is actually giving utterance to it. Schoolgirl fun hardly bears the severe test of being recorded in black and white, and Polly Oliver, good and courageous as she is, by no means surpasses the intellectual average of a very ordinary schoolgirl. The story of her devoted struggle to make life easier for her mother, both in the Californian boarding house and out of it at San Francisco, may amuse, and ought certainly to instruct, other young persons of sixteen. She does not become more interesting as she goes on, however, and the story drags slowly on its course after Mrs. Oliver's death and her orphan daughter's adoption by the opulent and childless Mrs. Bird. Polly's discovery of her gift for telling stories may prove a useful suggestion to other girls in real life. Her friend Edgar appears to promise a touch of future romance for Polly; but she is not allowed to be precocious in this respect. The illustrations are pretty.

***PENELOPE'S PROGRESS* (1898; published in England as *Penelope's Experiences in Scotland*)**

The Athenaeum

SOURCE: A review of *Penelope's Experiences in Scotland,* in *The Athenaeum,* Vol. 112, No. 3688, July 2, 1898, p. 32.

Penelope's Experiences in Scotland, by Kate Douglas Wiggin, is a story of three Americans—"Salemina, Francesca, and I"—who stay first in Edinburgh, and then in the East Neuk of Fife. They are maiden ladies of uncertain age (Salemina at least over forty), but possessed of every grace and accomplishment; and two of them at the finish are married or going to be married, Francesca to an Established minister. There is much about ministers—some of them surely well-known living divines—churches, General Assemblies, Holyrood levees, and suchlike, so that the book, which is brightly written, may be safely recommended to Southron lovers of kailyard literature: with less confidence to native-born Scots, who will know that "Jingling Geordie" and George Heriot were identical, that the Mound is not visible from George IV Bridge, that in Scotch a potato is not a vegetable, and that cakes are *cookies,* not "goodies." Our chief quarrel, however, with Mrs. Wiggin is her portentous amount of cram; her own real experiences of Edinburgh would, we fancy, have been much more readable. No hard-working Edinburgh landlady, not even one going three times to church on a Sunday, would know anything of Anne of Denmark; and we wonder what Mrs. Wiggin herself knows of some of her "shining lights, Robert Fergusson, Adam Ferguson, Gavin Wilson, Sir Henry Raeburn, David Hume, Erskine, Lords Newton, Gillies, Monboddo, Hailes, Kames, Henry Mackenzie, and the Ploughman Poet himself."

The Critic

SOURCE: A review of *Penelope's Progress,* in *The Critic,* Vol. XXXIII, No. 854, July-August, 1898, pp. 101-02.

It will be no new news to reading Americans that they can find a delightful cicerone for their wanderings about Great Britain in the person of Mrs. Riggs—or Mrs. Wiggin, as her publishers prefer to call her, in a confusing style that is undeniably convenient; and she has been too kindly received by her English public to leave it doubtful that there are many Scottish readers who will now gladly welcome the opportunity "to see themselves as ithers see them." Surely they cannot but be pleased to find three such charming strangers as Penelope, Francesca and Salemina displaying a familiarity with their ancient ballads and an enthusiasm for Bonnie Prince Charlie hardly equalled by Mr. Black's heroines—to say nothing of their brave determination to master all the intricacies of the vernacular tongue. It is true that books of this type, with their efforts at sustained humor, are always a little difficult to read with a constantly unwearied mind; and when they proceed from feminine sources, like this and Mrs. Cotes's *American Girl in London,* there is about them a certain haunting sprightliness—the phrase is Stevenson's, and he applies it to the contemporary feminine—which makes them better not read through at a sitting.

Penelope, however, the narrator of these North British experiences, is wise in not trying to be too continuously sprightly. She can interject, here and there, tender and pathetic passages which relieve the reader; and there are a number of ways in which she shows a fine insight not only into the minds of her sex and nation, but into regions that lie beyond. One bit in particular, the chapter which describes the trio "playing Sir Patrick Spens" with some utterly captivating children, shows a penetration into "Golden-Age" habits of thought not often found in mere Olympians. Whether amid the gayeties of Edinburgh for the first half of the book, or buried for the second in the East Neuk of Fife, the three fair Americans have enough amusing adventures, interspersed with properly romantic love-passages, to reward those who pursue them to their appointed and eminently satisfactory end. Never again will Francesca walk "in maiden meditation, fancy-free"; and the sound of Penelope's wedding-bells is heard in the last pages. May they live happily ever after!

The Atlantic Monthly

SOURCE: A review of *Penelope's Progress,* in *The Atlantic Monthly,* Vol. LXXXIII, No. CCCCXCVI, February, 1899, pp. 283-84.

It must be that we read books of travel far more for the sake of the traveler's idiosyncrasies than for solid information about the lands which he or she may elect to visit; else how should we be ready and eager to accompany a dozen successive adventurers to the North Pole or the heart of Africa, scores to Russia, India, and Egypt, hundreds to Athens, and thousands to Rome? No reader can reasonably have expected that the beguiling heroine of ***Penelope's English Experiences*** would have anything new to tell him about the "land o' cakes and brither Scots" in the tartan-clad volume with the alliterative title of ***Penelope's Progress.*** But who, after having sojourned in London and "Belvern" with Penelope, would hesitate about accompanying her anywhere? She is at her very best in Scotland, with her bright audacity, her invincible good temper, and, above all, her frank and infectious laughter at herself. Her gift of unforced but unflagging high spirits is one that is becoming ominously rare in this world; and once we have yielded a minor point of old-fashioned etiquette, and conceded that one's experiences of private hospitality may properly be served over as side dishes at a public banquet, we shall find few entrées more daintily and spicily concocted than Penelope's. It would hardly be possible to win a social victory more adroitly, or to describe it less offensively, than does our witty countrywoman that of her first Edinburgh dinner party:—

> I think my neighbor found me thoroughly delightful, after he discovered my point of view. He was an earl; and it always takes an earl a certain length of time to understand me. I scarcely know why, for I certainly should not think it courteous to interpose any real barriers between the nobility and that portion of the 'masses' represented in my humble person. . . . The earl took the greatest interest in my new ancestors, and approved thoroughly of my choice. He thinks I must have been named for Lady Penelope Belhaven, who lived in Leven Lodge, one of the country villas of the Earls of Leven, from whom he himself is descended. 'Does that make us relatives?' I asked. 'Relatives, most assuredly,' he replied, 'but not too near to destroy the charm of friendship.'

> He thought it a great deal nicer to select one's own forbears than to allow them all the responsibility, and said it would save a world of trouble if the plan could be universally adopted. He added that he should be glad to part with a good many of his, but doubted whether I would accept them, as they were 'rather a scratch lot.' I use his own language, which I thought delightfully easy for a belted earl.

There is a great deal else in the book which is quite as amusing as this; and some few graver passages, like the discussion of the typical Scotch sermon and long improvised public prayer, which show both sympathy and acute penetration.

In its freshness, lightness, and candor, and in absolute lack of pretension to be other than it is, ***Penelope's Progress*** is a delightful book.

PENELOPE'S IRISH EXPERIENCES (1901)

The Nation, New York

SOURCE: A review of *Penelope's Irish Experiences,* in *The Nation, New York,* Vol. 72, No. 1873, May 23, 1901, p. 422.

Penelope and her friends here cross St. George's Channel to Ireland, in search of adventures such as, already recounted concerning England and Scotland, have delighted a large circle of readers. Whether it is that England presents a wider or was a fresher field, after perusal of the present volume we are still of the opinion that Mrs. Riggs's experiences there were the richest. The narrative reads better than when appearing in serial form. We are not compelled to centre ourselves upon particular chapters that may not please, but are left free to choose those which do. The love story intertwined to meet the general taste of readers of light literature is of the most airy character, though it does end to the strains of a bridal march in a cathedral.

The book has its faults. The domestic arrangements at Mrs. Duddy's Hotel and Knockarney House should have been hinted at, not described. Doubtless Mrs. Riggs met such in Ireland, though we never have. But, true or imaginary, they might better have been left unparticularized, like many other mundane horrors. Occasionally, in generalization, our authoress treads on delicate ground. In so far as Irishmen, high or low, may appear different from the inhabitants of other countries, it is less in the blood than in the surroundings. And Alfred Austin is a singularly unsafe guide in Irish generalizations. Mrs. Riggs was never more mistaken than when fancying that "there is scarcely a country on the map in which one could be more foolish without being found out." There are, in truth, no keener sticklers for proprieties than the Irish peasantry, and the supreme foolishness of travellers who indulge in foolish pranks in Ireland is in supposing they are not seen through.

Our author is singularly happy in the selection of snatches of Irish song and passages from Irish legends woven into her narrative. Some of her touches are inimitable, as in the scene at the railway station, where the porter solemnly announces: "This thrain never shtops! This thrain never shtops!"—or in a village, "wan of the natest towns in the ring of Ireland, for if ye made a slip in the street of it, be the help of God ye were always sure to fall into a public house!" Mrs. Riggs excels in descriptions of the natural beauties of the country:

> In dazzling glory, in richness of color, there is nothing in Nature that we can compare with this [the gorse], loveliest and commonest of all wayside weeds. The gleaming wealth of the Klondyke would make but a poor show beside a single Irish hedgerow; one would think that Mother Earth had stored in her bosom all the sunniest gleams of bygone summers, and was now giving them back to the sun king from whom she borrowed them.

She has genuine appreciation of and feeling for the people:

> All is silent, and the blue haze of the peat smoke curls up from the thatch. Lisdara's young people have mostly gone to the Big Country; and how many tears have dropped on the path we are treading, as Peggy and Mary, Cormac and Miles, with a wooden box in the donkey-cart behind them, or perhaps with only a bundle hanging from a blackthorn stick, have come down the hill to seek their fortune. . . . They are used to poverty and hardship and hunger, and, although they are going quite penniless to a new country, sure it can be no worse than the old.

Penelope must have been in Ireland but a short year ago from the date at which we write. All appeared loyalty and enthusiasm concerning the Queen. She has passed from earth. The Irish question again stands out in some of its grimmest features. It is well we have writings in "lighter vein," such as this, to enliven our thoughts concerning the "Dark Rosaleen."

The Baron de B.-W.

SOURCE: A review of *Penelope's Irish Experiences,* in *Punch,* Vol. 120, June 12, 1901, p. 430.

Penelope (Mrs. Kate Douglas Wiggin), sighing for fresh kingdoms to conquer, having flitted over England, and sped through Scotland, has alighted on Ireland. ***Penelope's Irish Experiences*** is not the least delightful of the trio of books. In some respects it is the best, since the characteristics of the Irish people appeal more strongly to her sympathies, her poetic temperament, and her keen sense of humour. She does not shirk the gay shiftlessness of the people, their indifference to cleanliness, tidiness, punctuality, and other commonplaces, observance of which adds to the comfort of the more stolid Saxon. But, as she writes, "The Irish peasants would puzzle you, perplex you, disappoint you, with their inconsistencies; keep from liking them if you can." Penelope, susceptible to the influence of her surroundings, scorns anything like system. Wandering about the Island in occasionally bewildering fashion, she comes on charming bits of nature and meets delightful natives, male and female. *More Hibernico,* the most original character in the book is the strange girl from Salem, U.S.A., who comes accidentally on the scene and figures in many of its brightest episodes. Through the pages runs a pretty love-story, ending happily as it should. Penelope herself is in love with her husband, Himself, as she terms him, filling the provoking part which the Man of Wrath does with Elizabeth in her German Garden. To crusty bachelors like my Baronite it is quite boring to have charming women perpetually flinging themselves at the feet of their absent husbands—a way of putting it which shows how infectious is the *more Hibernico* alluded to.

DIARY OF A GOOSE GIRL (1902)

The Dial

SOURCE: A review of *The Diary of a Goose Girl,* in *The Dial,* Vol. XXXII, No. 383, June 1, 1902, p. 392.

Always exquisitely humorous, Kate Douglas Wiggin (Mrs. Riggs) is at her best—and briefest—in ***The Diary of a Goose Girl.*** It is a story of English rustic life from the point of view of an intelligent and gently critical American girl, who is seeking escape from a pursuing lover by immuring herself in a small household where poultry of one sort and another is the chief interest. The story is told with reality enough to make it seem truly autobiographical, and is suitably illustrated with pen-drawings by Mr. Claude A. Shepperson, admirably according with the insistent fun in the narrative.

H. W. Boynton

SOURCE: A review of *The Diary of A Goose Girl,* in *The Atlantic Monthly,* Vol. XC, No. DXXXVIII, August, 1902, pp. 276-77.

It is a little hard to say how [Henry Harland's heroines] differ from Penelope and Mrs. Wiggin's other vivacious adventuresses. But there is a difference. It may arise partly from the fact that Mr. Harland, being a man, is in love with his own sweet ladies, while Mrs. Wiggin is, through no fault of her own, simply able to see that men might be in love with hers. Certainly her heroines do not lack the quality of sex; if they lack anything of its charm, it is because their femininity is altogether unabashed. A mere man is not sure that he enjoys this humorous exposure of the feminine point of view. He admires the idea of a neat reticence veiling the operations of the feminine mind and heart. It is right for man to blurt, but too free speech in woman connotes a certain baldness, and the glory of a woman is otherwise conditioned. The adventures of the Goose Girl at Barbury Green are of the playful Penelope sort, and her comments on life rural and urban have a familiar pungency, not to say impudence. "There is nothing on earth so feminine as a hen," says the Goose Girl unblushingly. We feel that she deserves the rebuke Celia once bestowed upon Rosalind. Rosalind knew how to be flippant at times, but she did not make a business of it.

REBECCA OF SUNNYBROOK FARM (1903)

The Dial

SOURCE: A review of *Rebecca of Sunnybrook Farm,* in *The Dial,* Vol. XXXV, No. 416, October 16, 1903, p. 264.

Mrs. George C. Riggs (Kate Douglas Wiggin) brings to her ***Rebecca of Sunnybrook Farm*** the same delightful play of wit that animated her tales of foreign travel; and her story is the pleasantest possible reading in consequence. It follows the fortune of a spirited and mischievous little girl, through her school graduation into her work as teacher in one of the bleakest parts of New England—bleakest in both a material and spiritual sense. A man of means and cultivation comes into her life very early, and at the close of the book bids fair to remain in it until the end. Rebecca can be depended upon to endear herself to the reader long before the story is done, and the general impression left by the book is one of gratefulness to the author.

H. W. Boynton

SOURCE: A review of *Rebecca of Sunnybrook Farm,* in *The Atlantic Monthly,* Vol. XCII, No. DLIV, December, 1903, pp. 858-60.

In ***Rebecca of Sunnybrook Farm,*** Mrs. Riggs introduces to us an engaging little person instinct with that genial life which has commended Penelope and the vociferous Ruggleses to so many readers. If one may venture to define by an airy distinction the cleavage of the multitude as well as the alternation of moods in the mind of the elect reader, Rebecca is likely to have the suffrages both of readers of sensibility and of readers of perception. The person of sensibility—and who of us would rebut so soft an impeachment—will find the story provocative of the most pleasurable emotions, while the person of perception will discover in its workmanship ground for interesting and instructive comment.

Rebecca Rowena Randall is one of the seven children of Aurelia Randall and Lorenzo de Medici Randall, deceased. After some years of vicarious motherhood, such as befalls a child with many younger brothers and sisters, she is sent to live with two maiden aunts in their "brick house," and it is with the story of the vicissitudes of her life here that the book has to do.

This narrative of the making of Rebecca is made to engage the reader's sympathy by the faithful portrayal of the April weather of which that young lady's life consisted. One is given to understand early in the story that from Lorenzo de Medici Randall, Rebecca inherited an artistic temperament of the intensest sort, while in the course of her "making" in the brick house, we see how its attendant irresponsibilities are one by one put by. The portrait is other than that of the typical imaginative child, for from her tenderest years Rebecca is something of a poet, and she is visited by fantasy and dream. Yet there is nothing of the prig about her, and her personality is compact of wholesome affections. We know her perfectly when we discover that she seems but a plain child when scolded in brown calico, yet quite beautiful when praised in pink gingham. A person troubled with hypertrophy of the perception might urge that when a little girl of this temperament is made to tell the story of a shrewd unhappiness with no tinge of exaggeration, the character is out of drawing. But the idealization is pleasing, nevertheless, and the person of sensibility will like it better so. In other respects the character is as convincing as it is vivid.

There are many points in Mrs. Riggs's handling of the story which lure one to comparison of her method with that of the masters in fiction. No point, perhaps, is more striking than the excellent comic treatment of the names of the characters. Lorenzo de Medici Randall as the name of the inglorious Milton of a Maine village may savor of the broader effect of farce, but when we come to consider it in relation to his forbears and his descendants, it comes to have a harmonious appropriateness in which the farcical element is perfectly fused in the comedy. There are many similar touches of curious propriety which recall the art in that kind of Dickens and, yet more precisely and oddly, of Smollett. Indeed, memories of Smollett and the quality of his art will occur more than once to the attentive reader of Mrs. Riggs's book. There is one notable passage where the honors are little short of even. Smollett's death of Commodore Trunnion is undeniably one of the great death-bed scenes of literature. Yet when Rebecca comes to the bedside of her aunt Miranda lying *in extremis* there ensues a scene which is as grimly and tragically humorous:—

> There came a morning when she asked for Rebecca. The door was opened into the dim sickroom, and Rebecca stood there with the sunlight behind her, her hands full of sweet peas. Miranda's pale, sharp face, framed in its nightcap, looked haggard on the pillow, and her body was pitifully still under the counterpane.
>
> 'Come in,' she said; 'I ain't dead yet. Don't mess up the bed with them flowers, will ye?'
>
> 'Oh, no! They're going in a glass pitcher,' said Rebecca, turning to the washstand as she tried to control her voice and stop the tears that sprang to her eyes.
>
> 'Let me look at ye; come closer. What dress are ye wearin'?' said the old aunt in her cracked weak voice.

> 'My blue calico.'
>
> 'Is your cashmere holdin' its color?'
>
> 'Yes, aunt Miranda.'
>
> 'Do you keep it in a dark closet hung on the wrong side, as I told ye?'
>
> 'Always.'
>
> 'Has your mother made her jelly?'
>
> 'She hasn't said.'
>
> 'She always had the knack o'writin' letters with nothin' in 'em. What's Mark broke sence I've been sick?'
>
> 'Nothing at all, aunt Miranda.'
>
> 'Why, what's the matter with him? Gittin' lazy, ain't he? How's John turnin' out?'
>
> 'He's going to be the best of us all.'
>
> 'I hope you don't slight things in the kitchen because I ain't there. Do you scald the coffee-pot and turn it upside down on the winder-sill?'
>
> 'Yes, aunt Miranda.'
>
> 'It's always "yes" with you, and "yes" with Jane,' groaned Miranda, trying to move her stiffened body; 'but all the time I lay here knowin' there's things done the way I don't like 'em.'

If this has not quite the reassuring amplitude of movement which in the greatest death-bed scenes in literature makes us see life steadily and whole, it is, none the less, true and fine art, and it is notably free from the overwrought pathos and uneasy sentimentalism by which such scenes may so easily be spoiled. The impressive realism of this passage is of a piece with the texture of the book. It is obviously not the realism of the critical, and, as it were, scientific observer, which is now so much with us. It is, rather, the realism of Dickens, of the creative sentimentalist;—be it said without dispraise! Yet how real it is! Rebecca's remarks to Mr. Cobb, the stage-driver, when she returns to the inside of the stage,—to take the most casual of examples,—have the genuine accent of life.

> I forgot—mother put me inside, and maybe she'd want me to be there when I got to aunt Mirandy's. Maybe I'd be more genteel inside, and then I wouldn't have to be jumped down and my clothes fly up, but could open the door and step down like a lady passenger. Would you please stop a minute, Mr. Cobb, and let me change?

The informed in such matters will recognize that this is the way little girls do talk; and any one who has lived in a house with a child addicted to lisping in numbers will know that this is the way they versify:—

> This house is dark and dull and dreer
> No light doth shine from far or near
> It's like the tomb.
>
> And those of us who live herein
> Are most as dead as serrafim
> Though not as good.
>
> My guardian angel is asleep
> At least he doth no vigil keep
> Ah! woe is me!
>
> Then give me back my lonely farm
> Where none alive did wish me harm
> Dear home of youth!"

Still endeavoring to see the book through the eyes of our reader of perception, we will notice the skillful balance of character, which, provided it be done not too artificially, is a prime source of delight to readers of both our classes. We have, for example, a suggestive contrast between the two maiden aunts,—the one the typical sour and overweening spinster, and the other the gentle maiden-lady, with a shrine in her heart, and between the thoughtful Rebecca and her bosom friend and confidante, Emma Jane, who, as Rebecca writes to her mother, "can add and subtract in her head like a streek of lightning and knows the speling book right through but has no thoughts of any kind."

Thus the reader of perception might go on, pointing out this or that evidence of clever construction and imagina-

From Rebecca of Sunnybrook Farm, *written by Kate Douglas Wiggin. Illustrated by Helen Mason Grose.*

tive felicity, but concerning a book of this sort in the end it is the voice of the reader of sensibility that prevails, and he—we say "he" without irony—will be perennially grateful for the creation of so charming a character, for the reassurance that even in bleak New England *la verginella è simile alla rosa;* and he will solicitously await further news of her.

Olivia H. Dunbar

SOURCE: A review of *Rebecca of Sunnybrook Farm,* in *The Critic,* Vol. XLIII, No. 6, December, 1903, p. 570.

The thousand pitfalls that lie in wait for those that are valorous enough to attempt to picture the life of a child are triumphantly avoided by Mrs. Wiggin in this really inspired little biography. Rebecca was an unimportant child in a commonplace Maine village; but her lustrous qualities of energy and sweetness and imagination and humor make her a more enthralling heroine than ninety-and-nine of her fellow-competitors for public attention.

It is natural that the dominating quality in the book should be its humor; and still, unintermittently funny as it is, the fun is never overdone. Rebecca's history is probably no more innocently grotesque than would be the history of any precocious little girl in incongruous surroundings,—granting, always, the medium of a Mrs. Wiggin with the sympathy to perceive and the art to describe.

What mars the beautiful child characters of classic fiction is their consistency. What makes Rebecca human and adorable are her delightful inconsistencies; nor is she ever a prig for a single paragraph, even when, in a memorable hour of renunciation, she threw her beloved pink parasol down the well, or when, while "representing the family" at a missionary meeting, she "led in prayer." In each chapter she appears in a fresh and diverting phase; yet none of the quaint episodes, with their inimitable New England background, are without a very easy range of possibility. It is the perfect naturalness of the story that makes it so appealing, whether in the adroit touches that fill out the picture of village life or in the interesting stages of Rebecca's own progression from brown gingham pinafores to the white "graduation dress" of young-ladyhood.

In her way Rebecca was something of a poet, finding verse, indeed, a more congenial medium than prose; so that when her teacher required of her a "composition" on "solitude," urging upon her at the same time the elegance of the impersonal pronoun, Rebecca reluctantly composed the following:

> It would be false to say that one could ever be alone when one has one's lovely thoughts to comfort one. One sits by one's self, it is true, but one thinks; one opens one's favorite book and read's one's favorite story; one speaks to one's aunt or one's brother, fondles one's cat, or looks at one's photograph album. There is one's work also: what a joy it is to one, if one happens to like work. All one's little household tasks keep one from being lonely. Does one ever feel bereft when one picks up one's chips to light one's fire for one's evening meal? Or when one washes one's milk pail before milking one's cow? One would fancy not.

The Nation, New York

SOURCE: A review of *Rebecca of Sunnybrook Farm,* in *The Nation, New York,* Vol. 78, No. 2012, January 21, 1904, pp. 54-5.

Pleasant reading and full of insight into the magic land of children's thoughts and ways is ***Rebecca of Sunnybrook Farm.*** It may be owned that Rebecca the young irrepressible, wearing her best gingham on second-best occasions, and flinging her precious pink parasol into the well as voluntary atonement for wholly unrelated sin, is more diverting than she of the "done-up" hair, the graduation essay, and the fairy prince. The early Rebecca is an inspired piece of portraiture—imaginative portraiture we might say, except that most of us have known just such impossibilities. Some of her youthful poetry may well stand beside Marjorie Fleming's.

Mary K. Ford

SOURCE: A review of *Rebecca of Sunnybrook Farm,* in *The Bookman,* Vol. XVIII, February, 1904, pp. 652-53.

"Angels are not just the same as seraphims. Seraphims are brighter, whiter, and have bigger wings, and I think are older and are longer dead than angels, which are just freshly dead and after a long time in heaven around the great white throne grow to be seraphims."

This masterpiece of theological definition is not taken from the writings of the Fathers, but is to be found in Mrs. Kate Douglas Wiggin's book, ***Rebecca of Sunnybrook Farm,*** an effective study of a gifted, artistic child, growing up among the unfavourable surroundings of a small New England village and under the cramping tutelage of her aunt, the typical New England spinster.

Rebecca Rowena Randall is the second child of an unsuccessful singing-school teacher and a well-to-do farmer's daughter. No better indication can be given of the romantic nature of this pair than the names they gave their children. Rebecca thus describes her family to the friendly stage-driver on her way to Riverboro, where live the two maiden aunts, her mother's sisters, who have undertaken to bring her up and educate her.

> We are all named after somebody in particular. Hannah is Hannah at the Window Binding Shoes, and I am taken out of *Ivanhoe;* John Halifax was a gentleman

in a book; Mark is after his uncle, Marquis de Lafayette, that died a twin. Jenny is named for a singer, and Fanny for a beautiful dancer, but mother says they're both misfits, for Jenny can't carry a tune and Fanny's kind of stiff-legged.

Rebecca's mother is very poor; there is the usual mortgage on the farm, and so the aunts offer to take one child and do for her. Hannah is the one asked, but she can not be spared, so Rebecca goes, and the book deals with her life in Riverboro from the day she arrives, a quick-witted, imaginative, impulsive child of ten or thereabouts, down to the time, seven years later, when her Aunt Mirandy dies, and her will reveals the fact that Rebecca had won what heart she had.

Not only is the character of Rebecca skillfully portrayed, but the minor personages are also well drawn. Miss Dearborn, the Riverboro school-teacher, who "can answer more questions than the Temperance one, but not so many as I can ask," Emma Jane, Rebecca's friend, who "can add and subtract in her head like a streak of lightning and knows the spelling book right through, but has no thoughts of any kind," Uncle Jerry Cobb, the kindly stage-driver, the forlorn Simpson family, all these are put plainly before us by means of their own acts and words and not by what we are told about them. In this respect the book is quite remarkable, for it is a trick of the incompetent writer to tell of the brilliancy of his characters without being able to prove it from their own mouths. This Mrs. Wiggin has avoided; Rebecca is convincing from first to last.

Mrs. Wiggin understands that individualism which is the keynote of American education and achievement. This she has realised, and in her description of Rebecca she has made it plain that it is her all-pervading personality which she brings to bear upon her severe New England surroundings which transforms them. Rebecca infuses a new spirit into the Friday afternoon recitations at school, furnishes the Simpson twins with a suitable "piece," gives the timid Emma Jane confidence by reciting a dialogue with her, dresses the schoolroom with flowers, and turns what was formerly considered a trying ordeal into a festive occasion.

One of the most amusing episodes is that of the banquet lamp. The forlorn Simpson family, not having enough to eat or to clothe themselves with, are fired with a desire to possess the banquet lamp offered as a premium by a soap manufacturing company to whoever should sell a certain number of cakes. Rebecca and Emma Jane volunteer to help, and the account of their trip into a neighbouring village with a horse and buggy is most entertaining. It is while on this excursion that Rebecca meets the young man who proves a staunch friend to her and furnishes the only hint of future love-making to be found in the book.

Rebecca writes poetry and encloses this gem ["Sunday Thoughts"] in a letter to her mother:

This house is dark and dull and drear
No light doth shine from far or near
Nor ever could.

And those of us who live herein
Are most as dead as seraphim
Though not as good.

This is a good description of a New England farmhouse on a Sunday afternoon, and yet it is quite the sort of thing that a clever child might write. So is the verse about the mortgage.

Rise my soul, strain every nerve
Thy mortgage to remove,
Gain thy mother's heartfelt thanks
Thy family's grateful love.

The first part of the book is perhaps the best. Rebecca's life as a child in Riverboro is more interesting than her career at the Academy at Wareham, and yet we lay the book down with regret. It naturally suggests that other study of imaginative childhood, *Sentimental Tommy,* about which opinions differed so strongly. Perhaps it is because we are more familiar with the *mise en scène* of ***Rebecca*** that it seems the better book and rings more true. Mrs. Wiggin has done nothing better than this for a long time.

R. Gordon Kelly

SOURCE: "The Child Prepared: Anticipating Adulthood in American Children's Books, 1865 to the Present," in *Catholic Library World,* Vol. 53, No. 2, September, 1981, pp. 65-9.

There is, in Kate Douglas Wiggin's **Rebecca of Sunnybrook Farm** (1903), the same sharply realized sense of village culture that can be found in Alcott and Twain. [Wiggin] traces the use of a gifted child born into circumstances which she must escape if she is to fulfill her promise. Rebecca . . . is less in need of discipleship than she is in need of opportunities to grow spiritually and intellectually. She has less to overcome than Jo March [of *Little Women*] certainly, and she rejects instinctively the meanness and pettiness and village gossip just as she later instinctively rejects the shallowness and unseemly flirtatiousness of her schoolmate Hulda Meserve, who is Wiggin's embodiment of fashionable society. And like [Louisa May] Alcott and [Thomas] Hughes, Wiggin invokes universal moral law in order to explain the meaning of experience. There is in **Rebecca of Sunnybrook Farm,** however, a reciprocity of influence that sets the book off sharply from the others. To be sure, Rebecca grows and flourishes in the care of various adults, who recognize her gifts and try to meet her needs. But a pivotal chapter, "A Change of Heart," is not about Rebecca at all but about the beginnings of change in her Aunt Miranda, who is the type of the sharp-tongued, mean-spirited New England spinster. Rebecca's influence on her aunt is salutary, softening and humanizing the bitter and disappointed old woman. Wiggin's use of this theme—the child as redeemer (which has a long history in children's books)—reminds us that the romantic view of the child (which is the foundation of modern children's literature) contains a troubling paradox. If the child is born perfect, the process of socialization is inevitably one of corruption. The subversive potential of the notion should be clear.

ROSE O' THE RIVER (1905)

The Nation, New York

SOURCE: A review of *Rose o the River,* in *The Nation, New York,* Vol. 81, No. 2111, December 14, 1905, pp. 488-89.

Rose o' the River is as slender a tale as ever walked into print on the merits of an author's name. The heroine, as might be predicted from her poetical label, has stepped forth from a valentine. She had neither brooch nor earrings, "but any ordinary gems would have looked rather dull and trivial when compelled to undergo comparison with her bright eyes." Out of the mouths of a "fool-family" and a professional braggart comes a certain amount of substance, and in the vivid scenes of logjamming on the Saco there is balm. It is worthy of notice that in York County hepatica and partridge-berries come together as—yes, of course—"sweet harbingers of spring."

NEW CHRONICLES OF REBECCA (1907; published in England as *More about Rebecca of Sunnybrook Farm*)

The Nation, New York

SOURCE: A review of *The New Chronicles of Rebecca,* in *The Nation, New York,* Vol. 84, No. 2181, April 18, 1907, p. 362.

Of ***The New Chronicles of Rebecca*** it need only be said that it is absolutely certain to enthrall those people to whom such bits as the following appear in the light of humor:

> Written language is for poems and graduations and occasions like this—like a kind of Sunday-go-to-meeting dress that you wouldn't go blueberrying in.
>
> Thirza, you mustn't chew gum at a missionary meeting; it isn't polite nor holy.

Rebecca saves a baby from the poorhouse. She organizes the little girls of her village as home missionaries, only to be routed at their first attempt upon the village cynic. She writes many poems (all of which are quoted) in the style of rustic obituaries, and keeps a diary (also quoted at length) which suggests a question. Would the readers who enjoy this artless product be pleased, or over-stimulated, if chance introduced them to Marjorie Fleming, and gave an opportunity for comparison between its genuine oddities and the somewhat labored quaintness of Rebecca? The present volume conducts Rebecca to her eighteenth year, and closes, or, rather, is left sufficiently ajar, to permit a vista of indefinitely prolonged future chronicles.

Punch

SOURCE: A review of *New Chronicles of Rebecca of Sunnybrook Farm,* in *Punch,* Vol. 143, September 18, 1912, pp. 243-44.

Contemporaneously with her introduction to the British stage (but then, of course, these little coincidences will happen!) there reaches me a slender volume called, ***New Chronicles of Rebecca of Sunnybrook Farm.*** It is published at a shilling, and I fancy there must be many admirers of Miss Kate Douglas Wiggin quite ready to pay more than that for the renewed society of her best-known heroine. Not that Rebecca, manifold as are her excellences, is a young lady for all tastes. Personally, I believe that in real life she would have bored me crazy. I hate to say it, but in all her chronicles there is to me an uneasy suggestion of the angel-child, with limelight and appropriate music, that simply ruins my enjoyment. This is perhaps unfair, as Rebecca is by no means unduly virtuous and certainly does not die in the last chapter. Still, there it is—I can't believe in her. But those who can will certainly welcome a volume that has all the qualities of its predecessor. I fancy it is more particularly what would be called "the story of the play," as many of the chronicles—that concerning the Simpson wedding-ring and others—I recognise as forming part of Rebecca's stage traffic at the Globe Theatre. Very possibly there the art of a winsome and clever little lady may invest them with a personal fascination that (for me at least) they lack on the printed page. In that case the success of the book is assured beforehand, and my humble appreciation can be dispensed with.

MOTHER CAREY'S CHICKENS (1911; published in England as *Mother Carey*)

The Nation, New York

SOURCE: A review of *Mother Carey's Chickens,* in *The Nation, New York,* Vol. 93, No. 2411, September 14, 1911, pp. 241-42.

Whether or not Mrs. Riggs has in this story, as her publishers vaunt, pictured "the ideal American mother," she has certainly written a pleasant and wholesome story for boys and girls. It deals with just the sort of impossibilities children delight in. The charming house which stands ready in its Eden for the impoverished Careys is like the sugarplum dwellings of fairyland. Such stately mansions do not really rent at sixty dollars a year even in the most abandoned parts of New England. But never mind: there are, roughly speaking, such good turns of fortune as befell the Careys in their need. And there are, we doubt not, somewhere or other such adorable family circles as that of the Careys themselves.

Mother Carey is the still young and lovely widow of an American naval officer. His death has left her almost without means; and the family must leave their city house and city way of living. Fate directs them to Beulah and the wonderful Yellow House. Its owner is an American diplomat, long an absentee. He has tender memories of the Yellow House, but his life has led him into hard and worldly paths, and he is an unlucky member of what Mrs. Riggs calls "a family rhomboid." In other terms, there is no simple warmth of relation between him and his wife and daughters. Now Mother Carey's eldest daughter, Nancy, is an enterprising chicken. Soon after the Careys take the Yellow House, Nancy writes the consul a letter which wins his heart. It is true that, coldly regarded, the letter is such as a ten-year-old might have been forgiven for—virtually a begging letter—and Nancy is fifteen. However, it wins the consul. The sixty dollars rent is eliminated, and on the Careys is bestowed virtual ownership of the Yellow House, which, with no money to do it with, they proceed to make beautiful. We ought perhaps to commend Mrs. Riggs for abstaining from the "back-to-the-soil" motive. If they had gone into some little old farmhouse, and beautified it, and halved their table expenses by keeping a cow and chickens and growing their own vegetables, their experience would have been comparatively commonplace in these days. As a matter of fact, they remain little city people gracefully condescending to rural conditions—carrying, as it were, a light into that darkness. To them the country is a place where good-hearted but rather ridiculous people live, and where trees and crimson ramblers grow in uncommon profusion. When the worst pinch comes, the girls start a little summer school, and the oldest boy becomes clerk and delivery boy in the local "store"; they have to get money to buy milk and eggs and vegetables with! And they are finally delivered from their poverty not by their own ingenuity, but by the immemorial succor of a legacy.

But the tale is, we say, a pleasant one, a frankly sentimental celebration of motherhood as it may be. All the crabbed persons turn sweet under her influence, and in the end everything is as lovely for everybody as anybody could desire. We confess to an impression of Nancy as, like all Mrs. Riggs's heroines, something of a minx.

Punch

SOURCE: A review of *Mother Carey,* in *Punch,* Vol. 141, November 8, 1911, p. 346.

You remember what the Duke in *Patience* says about the effect of a diet of unvaried toffee? Well, that is rather how I felt myself after the perusal of Kate Douglas Wiggin's latest story, ***Mother Carey.*** It is so very sweet. I know that there are persons in plenty who will go into raptures over it; who will delight in the charming children, and their adorable mother, and their kindly landlord and their perfect neighbours. All I will say is just what a nice and very much more human child of my acquaintance said of the *Swiss Family Robinson,* "They seem to have been very lucky!" Seriously, though I can take my dash of sentiment with the best, I feel that the clever author has here slightly overdone the dose. However, I suppose she knows what people like; certainly the fact that the publishers announce the book as a companion story to ***Rebecca of Sunnybrook Farm*** would seem to show that it is expected to meet a popular demand. I am sorry, because the effect produced upon me was that of real talent debased. As for the story itself, it is about a perfect mother, who, being left a young widow with several perfect children, retires to economise in a kind of barley-sugar cottage, whose landlord declines to take any rent beyond a tribute of wild flowers, and eventually marries his son to the eldest daughter. What astonished me was that nobody married Mother Carey; but perhaps that came later. I cannot help thinking that, if rural life in America is really like that, I have been strangely misinformed.

***PENELOPE'S POSTSCRIPTS: SWITZERLAND, VENICE, WALES, DEVON, HOME* (1915)**

The Nation, New York

SOURCE: A review of *Penelope's Postscripts: Switzerland, Venice, Wales, Devon, Home,* in *The Nation, New York,* Vol. 101, No. 2617, August 26, 1915, pp. 262-63.

After twenty-odd years of intermittent flow, the stream of Penelope's experiences runs rather thin and pale. The truth is, Penelope is already a trifle antiquated. Her piquancies and audacities have been possibly imitated, certainly outdone, by a multitude of feminine successors on the page of fiction. Beside them she appears retiring, almost commonplace. Conventional standards have so far shifted that she no longer appears so delightfully near the ragged edge. Her very witticisms are of a fading fashion, and we blush for the feeble limericks and anecdotes with which she is fain to enlarge these concluding pages of her confidences. At least we understand them to be concluding pages, though a Penelope would be quite as easy to resuscitate as a Sherlock Holmes or an Allan Quatermain. They certainly give us, within reasonable limits, the "ever after" of Penelope and her friends. After sundry rather perfunctory journeyings, in Venice, Switzerland, Devon, and Wales, dressed out in the whimsical manner (as far as her author can achieve it) of the Penelope of old, we get a glimpse of the wanderers at home. Francesca is married to a minister of the Established Church of Scotland, and by exceeding virtue lives down the American splendors of her clothes, before the eyes of an Edinburgh congregation; Salemina yields to a middle-aged widower whom she has loved from youth, a professor in Trinity College, Dublin. Upon Penelope herself, now Mrs. Beresford, and mother of several children, the curtain falls in an idyllic posture in a New England orchard surrounded by her adoring husband and babes.

The Dial

SOURCE: A review of *Penelope's Postscripts: Switzerland, Venice, Wales, Devon, Home,* in *The Dial,* Vol. LIX, No. 700, September 2, 1915, p. 157.

With ***Penelope's Postscripts*** we bid good-bye—but not finally, let us hope—to the trio of heroines who have smiled through two earlier volumes, shepherded by Mrs. Kate Douglas Wiggin. Like its predecessors, this smaller book maintains the idea that "the most charming knowledge is the sort that comes by unconscious absorption, like the free grace of God." But the three delightful women are now all married, and it is "ten years after," and Penelope herself writes that she and her husband are "growing old with the country that gave us birth (God bless it!) and our children growing up with it, as they always should." It is a book of peace in a sadly troubled world.

Additional coverage of Wiggin's life and career is contained in the following sources published by Gale Research: *Contemporary Authors,* Vol. 111; *Dictionary of Literary Biography,* Vol. 42; *Major Authors and Illustrators for Children and Young Adults;* and *Yesterday's Author's of Books for Children,* Vol. 1.

Brian Wildsmith

1930-

English author and illustrator of picture books and retellings.

Major works include *ABC* (also published as *Brian Wildsmith's ABC,* 1962), *Birds* (also published as *Brian Wildsmith's Birds,* 1967), *The Owl and the Woodpecker* (1971), *Cat on the Mat* (1982), *The Easter Story* (1994).

For information on Wildsmith's career prior to 1976, see *CLR,* Vol. 2.

INTRODUCTION

Called "this generation's most remarkable book-artist" by a critic in *The Junior Bookshelf,* Wildsmith is regarded as an exceptionally talented artist and gifted creator of picture books whose works inform children about concepts, values, and the natural world while introducing them to sophisticated color and form. A prolific author and illustrator noted for the variety of his subjects and techniques, Wildsmith—whose audience ranges from toddlers to readers in the upper primary grades—has published informational books, retellings of folktales and Bible stories, wordless picture books, pop-up books, books with minimal text, and longer stories. He has also provided the illustrations for books by authors such as Charles Dickens, Frances Hodgson Burnett, Rene Guillot, Nan Chauncy, Geoffrey Trease, and Daisaku Ikeda, and has drawn the pictures for texts by his brother Alan and his daughter Rebecca.

As an author, Wildsmith characteristically features animals and birds as the focal points of his stories. His works present beginning concepts for children to learn, such as the alphabet, numbers, and opposites, as well as enjoyable games such as puzzles. Riveting the attention of young readers with his eye-catching pictures, Wildsmith then teaches children basic lessons about words, numbers, or nature while providing examples of values such as compassion, honesty, and kindness. Several of Wildsmith's books reflect his strong environmental consciousness and fascination with religious subjects and themes. Wildsmith is perhaps best known for his first book, *ABC,* an energetic approach to the alphabet that pairs letters with bold, textured paintings in brilliant colors. Considered a truly original concept book as well as a striking example of illustration art, *ABC* is acknowledged as a groundbreaking title in the field of children's literature. Wildsmith is also credited for his innovation in creating wordless picture books and books with minimal text for very small children. As an illustrator, he is lauded for bringing the attributes and quality of fine art to the picture book genre while developing a particularly distinctive personal style. His art is celebrated for employing glowing, contrasting colors and geometric forms, especially the triangle, while reflecting a strong sense of composition and page design. Working in mediums such as line, watercolor, gouache, and collage, he uses full pages, half pages and split pages for his illustrations, which range from representational to abstract. Although some reviewers call Wildsmith's texts pedestrian and his pictures mannered and overly stylized, most critics praise him as one of the most brilliant artists to have created books for children during this century. Marcus Crouch called Wildsmith "one of the great masters of colour" and "a major master of the art of book design." Crouch concluded, "At his best Brian Wildsmith is the master of them all."

Biographical Information

Born in Penistone in Yorkshire, England, Wildsmith is the son of a coal miner who painted after work and a homemaker who, the author wrote in his essay in *Something about the Author Autobiography Series (SAAS),* encouraged him and his three siblings "to believe that if we were to embark on any activity. . . it would only be of value unless we put ourselves entirely to it"; Wildsmith concluded that his mother "helped us find ourselves and, by way of that, what we wanted from life." At the age of two, Wildsmith moved with his family to the small mining town of Hoyland Commons. Although he never saw any art, he loved sports, especially cricket, and excelled at playing the piano. He was also good in science, and planned on becoming a research chemist until, at the age of sixteen, he abruptly decided to go to art school. With a portfolio consisting of pictures of geometric shapes he had drawn in class and cars he drew in his free time, Wildsmith was accepted by Barnsley School of Art in Yorkshire, where he developed skill as a draftsman as well as an admiration for modern artists such as Picasso and Klee. In 1949, Wildsmith won a scholarship to the Slade School of Fine Art at University College, London, an institution that he credits with introducing him to the world of art. During his lunch hours, Wildsmith pored over the drawings and etchings of Rembrandt, da Vinci, and Michelangelo at the British Museum, which at the time allowed its patrons to handle the documents in its collection. After graduating from the Slade with a diploma in fine arts, Wildsmith fulfilled his military service requirement by teaching math at the Royal Military School of Music in Twickenham. At twenty-four, he left the army and began teaching art to young people from the ages of eleven to eighteen. He also started submitting designs for book jackets to publishers.

In 1957, Wildsmith became a freelance illustrator as well as a part-time instructor at the Maidstone College of Art. In the same year, he met editor Mabel George of Oxford University Press who, impressed with his abstract paintings, commissioned Wildsmith to design book jackets and illustrations. After providing the pictures for an edition of *Arabian Nights,* George suggested that Wildsmith illustrate an alphabet book. The resulting volume, *ABC,* was Wildsmith's first book for children as well as the first children's book to be published by Oxford University Press. Wildsmith won the Kate Greenaway Medal for *ABC* in 1962.

After creating *ABC,* Wildsmith became excited about the possibilities of working with picture books; the four children that he had with his wife Aurelie also inspired him. In an interview in *Books Are by People,* Wildsmith noted, "I realized just what an appalling gulf there was between what I knew to be good and fine in painting and illustrating and the awful damage being done to children's minds via children's books. I decided to commit myself fully to doing books for boys and girls." During the 1960s, Wildsmith retold fables and stories by the French fabulist Jean de la Fontaine, illustrated a collection of Mother Goose rhymes, and created several concept books. In 1970, Wildsmith decided, as he wrote in *SAAS,* "to span, if possible, with the use of form, colour, and words, the whole educational range of a young child from its initial introduction to our alphabet and numerical system to the foundation of sound humanitarian-based principles, necessary for the development of its responsibility towards the society in which it lives. I wanted to feed the eyes and minds of children with lusciously colourful images, representative of the potential beauty of our planet and its inhabitants." He added in *Children's Books and Their Creators,* "From the beginning, what I wanted to do above all for children's literature was to try and span the whole spectrum from an ABC to counting—through puzzles, myths, nursery rhymes, and stories." In 1971, Wildsmith published his first self-authored and illustrated title, *The Owl and the Woodpecker,* a picture book about friendship and neighborliness. In 1974, Wildsmith was invited to become the set and costume designer for *The Blue Bird,* a film adaptation of the novel by Maurice Maeterlinck that was a joint production of the United States and the USSR. His work on the movie, a star-studded film that describes two children's search for the bluebird of happiness, became a difficult experience for Wildsmith: although he had designed over a hundred costumes, he was replaced by a Russian costumer because it was decided that an Englishman should not be responsible for both costumes and sets. In 1976, Wildsmith published his own version of *The Blue Bird*, illustrated with his costume designs.

In 1982, Wildsmith attempted, as he wrote in *SAAS,* to fill "a hole in the children's book market with a set of small and very simple books" such as *Cat on the Mat, The Trunk* (1982), and *The Island* (1983). Soon thereafter, he premiered books using the split-page format of illustration, a technique in which a half-page illustration is set between each double-page spread; as the pages are turned, the two illustrations are superimposed. In the late 1980s, Wildsmith began painting seriously. He wrote in *SAAS,* "It has taken me a long time to feel ready and mature enough to approach a blank canvas and one of the reasons for this delay is the simple fact that I fell in love with children's books, finding the process exciting, ever-changing, and fully enjoyable." Wildsmith has continued to combine his creation of literature for children with his other artistic pursuits. Concluding his autobiographical essay, he wrote, "I have always been fascinated by the ability of the Great Masters to cover as many areas that the field of art encompasses. My ambition is to be able to do likewise."

Major Works

With *ABC,* an alphabet book that depicts familiar animals and objects in a rainbow of contrasting colors, Wildsmith made an auspicious debut in the field of children's literature. Most reviewers noted both the success of Wildsmith's art and the appeal of his book to the young. John Rowe Townsend commented in *Written for Children,* "The richness of [Wildsmith's] *A.B.C.* was astonishing when it first appeared in 1962; there was nothing else quite like his kettle aglow with heat or his lion on the next page aglow with sun." In *Birds,* a volume published in 1967, Wildsmith's pictures depict the group names of twelve species of birds, such as a "walk of snipe" and an "unkindness of ravens." A reviewer in *The Junior Bookshelf* noted, "Wildsmith has never drawn with greater assurance or with better control of his characteristic mannerisms. . . . Lucky children to be born into a world which has birds and Brian Wildsmith in it." With *The Circus* (1970; also published as *Brian Wildsmith's Circus*), Wildsmith created a picture book with just nine words of text and opulent pictures that, in the words of a reviewer in the *Times Literary Supplement,* "give a brilliant impression of the glamour and excitement of the sawdust ring. Anne Wood called *The Circus* "a breathtaking book," while Zena Sutherland began her appraisal with, "Who needs words?" *The Owl and the Woodpecker,* Wildsmith's first original story for children, features two birds who learn to be friends. Although critics noted that the text was less successful than the pictures, the book is considered one of Wildsmith's best. A reviewer in *The Junior Bookshelf* claimed, "No one today conveys more convincingly the texture of living things. . . ."

A devout Catholic, Wildsmith has created several works with a Christian theme. His first book of this type, *The True Cross* (1977), is a retelling of the legend of the Tree of Life, the tree that came from the Garden of Eden and served at Jesus' crucifixion before being rediscovered by St. Helena. Marcus Crouch wrote, "Mr. Wildsmith's book clearly springs from a genuine religious impulse, and is informed with his love of all living things," while a reviewer in *Publishers Weekly* said, "Wildsmith's unmistakable style makes his new book as personal as his signature." The artist has been especially praised for his two books based on the life of Christ, *A Christmas Story* (1989) and *The Easter Story*. In the first title, Wildsmith depicts the Nativity from the viewpoint of a small donkey who follows its mother—Mary's transportation—to Bethlehem. Margery Fisher said, "The artist has used all his skill in interpreting an anecdote simple in itself . . . but serving as an image for a universal myth." Hazel Townson, calling *A Christmas Story* "a magnificent production," claimed that it is "the perfect book to wake up to on Christmas morning." In *The Easter Story,* Wildsmith again uses a donkey to describe the events of Holy Week and transport Jesus into Jerusalem on Palm Sunday. A critic in *Kirkus Reviews* called *The Easter Story* a "richly complex visual feast, masterfully integrated into a reverent, unusual interpretation: Wildsmith at his best." Elizabeth Bush named it a "first choice for the Easter collection."

In the 1980s and 1990s, Wildsmith's works began to reflect both spiritual and environmental themes. For example, *Professor Noah's Spaceship* (1980), a space-age twist on the biblical story of Noah's Ark, depicts a futuristic Earth that is enveloped by pollution. When the animals go to Professor Noah for help, he builds a spaceship intended to take them to another planet for forty days and forty nights. When a dove brings back a leaf from Earth, Professor Noah realizes that he has traveled back in time to a land that is still healthy; at the end of the story, an otter comments subtly, "Thank goodness for all the rain. There seems to have been some flooding here." A reviewer in *Publishers Weekly* observed, "Wildsmith's new book is entirely different from and, in some ways, more meaty than his popular works. . . . The surprise ending deepens the import of a timely cautionary tale." Marcus Crouch noted, "A really good idea, ... [L]et us be duly grateful for such splendid riots of colour as *Professor Noah's Spaceship.*" Wildsmith also has done well-received pop-up books of *Noah's Ark* (1994) and *The Creation* (1995), as well as *Saint Francis* (1996), a picture book narrating the life of "the poor man of Assisi" in first person. A reviewer in *Publishers Weekly* concluded, "A gorgeous book and an ideal gift, Francis teaches all of us the beauty of both the natural and the spiritual world." *Brian Wildsmith's Amazing World of Words* (1996) combines many of the author/illustrator's interests: using the premise of a visiting alien that encounters the creatures and objects of Earth, the book identifies animals, birds, structures, machines, musical instruments, and other creations in such locations as a town, a jungle, a museum, an ocean, and a playground. A critic in *Kirkus Reviews* noted, "As usual with Wildsmith's work, the animals and birds are superb, but there are also some extraordinary renderings of buildings and machines. . . ," while Eunice Weech concluded, "The colorful, intricate drawings will keep browsers occupied for hours. An intriguing vocabulary builder."

Awards

Wildsmith received the Kate Greenaway Medal for *ABC* in 1962, Greenaway commended designations for *The Lion and the Rat: A Fable* and *The Oxford Book of Poetry for Children* in 1963 and *Birds* in 1967, and a highly commended designation for *The Owl and the Woodpecker* in 1971. *A Child's Garden of Verses* (illustrated by Wildsmith) received the Lewis Carroll Shelf Award in 1966 and *Brian Wildsmith's 1, 2, 3*s won the Art Books for Children Award in 1973. *Pelican* was named a runner-up for the Kurt Maschler Award in 1982 and was given a Parents' Choice citation for illustration in 1983. Wildsmith was runner-up for the Hans Christian Andersen Award and named a highly commended illustrator by the International Board of Books for Young People (IBBY) in both 1966 and 1968. He also received the Soka Eakkai Japan Education Medal in 1988 and the USHIO Publication Culture Award in 1991. In 1994, a museum devoted to Wildsmith's books and artwork was opened in Izu, Japan.

AUTHOR'S COMMENTARY

Brian Wildsmith

SOURCE: "Antic Disposition: A Young British Illustrator Interviews Himself," in *School Library Journal,* Vol. 12, No. 3, November, 1965, pp. 21-4.

Q. Mr. Wildsmith, or may I call you Brian?

A. Of course.

Q. When and where were you born?

A. 1930, Peristone, Yorkshire, England.

Q. And was that a good place to be born?

A. Well, I didn't have much choice. The Yorkshire people are hardworking, efficient, thrifty and levelheaded; they drink wine, beer, play the finest cricket and football in England, have the loveliest countryside, do the best cooking and produce most of what makes England what it is!!!

Q. I suppose you drew and painted from a very early age?

A. Yes, I was 16 years old when I started.

Q. Really?

A. Yes.

Q. Where did you receive your art education?

A. I won a scholarship to the Slade School of Fine Arts, University College, London.

Q. When you left did you start illustrating books?

A. No. I had to go into the army and teach.

Q. What? Art?

A. No. I taught mathematics, you know 2 + 2 = 4, etc.

Q. I suppose you were a very sympathetic and successful teacher, were you not?

A. Yes. Our unit held the record number of failures for the Army first-class mathematics exam.

Q. Let's leave the army and get back to art, shall we?

A. Yes. Let's.

Q. Who gave you your first assignment in black and white book illustration?

A. Oxford University Press.

Q. Who gave you your first assignment in color and what was it?

A. Oxford University Press. *Tales from the Arabian Nights.*

Q. And was this well reviewed?

A. Yes, one review began, "But the descent is steep to Brian Wildsmith's attack on the Arabian Nights. The seemingly aimless scribbles are splashed lavishly and untidily with bright smudges of paint," etc., etc.

Q. You seem to know that quote by heart.

A. Yes.

Q. Brian, after such reviews who published your second book in color?

A. Oxford University Press. It was the *ABC.*

Q. Brian, what kind of an artist would you describe yourself as?

A. Oh, about 160 pounds of solid muscle, 6'2" tall with dark wavy hair, blue eyes. I guess I could be taken for Gregory Peck.

Q. Really Brian, you're pulling my leg. Seriously, why do you illustrate young children's books?

A. Seriously, I believe in the Jesuit saying "Give me a child under seven years and he is mine forever." How often have we left all that is good and free in our culture to be brought before the child too late, when his taste has already been formed, maltreated, warped and destroyed by the everlasting rubbish that is still thought by many to be good enough for children. I hope my picture books will help alleviate this, and perhaps guide them to finer and greater paths.

Q. But how?

A. Well, I try to reconcile the beauties of form and color in pure painting with the problems of illustrating a given text. By attracting the child to the stories in picture form, consciously or subconsciously (it doesn't matter which), the shapes and colors seep into the child's artistic digestive system, and he is aroused and stimulated by them.

Q. Do you really think that young children are aware of and understand form and color?

A. Of course. Children are fascinated by color and form; whether they understand it or not I couldn't say. I don't think one *understands* the arts: one is moved, provoked, or stimulated, and one enjoys. But understand completely, no! All works of art, whatever the medium of expression, have in them some secret of creation that makes them universal and timeless. You can dissect their physical make-up—composition, form, texture, pattern, but all these are nothing without this elusive quality of creativity—"soul," if you wish.

Q. Brian, you mentioned earlier the problems of illustrating; could you elaborate?

A. Certainly. You see, working at home has its problems. One is amongst domestic upheavals that occur from time to time, and one is always on tap to look after the baby or help hang out the wash. You know what women are?

Q. No.

A. Well they are always after you to do something or fix things around the house.

Q. Looking around I don't get the impression that you do very much.

A. Ah well, I solved that problem.

Q. How?

A. I left all the lights without shades on them.

Q. What happened?

A. Oh you know what women are. These shadeless lights became an obsession with my wife and she forgot all about the other things that needed doing.

Q. But I notice that all the lights have shades.

A. Yes, that scheme lasted for four years. Now I've removed the door handles and you have to use a screwdriver to open the doors.

Q. And is this ruse working?

A. Yes, but fetching the screwdriver for my wife is driving me insane.

Q. Could we get back to the problems of illustrating.

A. Sorry, I do tend to ramble. I meant to say that there are, roughly, at a quick count, two ways of illustrating a book. The first is to give, shall we say, a diagrammatic representation of the text; the sole aim is putting the text into picture form. The other way is to enlarge on the text, to create a pictorial form that is at one with the text and yet is a thing unto itself.

Q. Is this second way difficult?

A. Yes. In the same way that one does not interpret and play Bach like Chopin, one should give a different interpretation to all one's books. Similarly, the book, in some way which even the artist does not understand, should make its own form, carve its own way through the artist's subconscious, until it has become the physical concrete expression of an idea. On the face of it the act of creativity is impossible to achieve; the miracle of art is that it can be achieved at all.

Q. But how can one work subconsciously and yet to a positive end?

A. Again, it's rather like the musician giving a performance in which he has to immerse himself completely in his music yet listen acutely to his own performance. This is achieved only by a great deal of hard work—getting to know the work, taking it apart note by note and achieving technical mastery, and finally, reconstructing the entire work and letting it flow spontaneously from the musician as though it were a part of him, as indeed it is by now.

Interpreting a book is a similar process. This of course is the ideal, if one were capable of achieving it. Indeed the real problems of art are psychological and not technical; perhaps it would be a good thing if our colleges of art were staffed not by art teachers but by psychologists.

Q. What do you think is the secret that makes for the best children's books?

A. Most of us, particularly the male, have in our make-up much of the child. The trick is to recapture this state when working. The other trick is to be able to switch it off again.

Q. Do children really appreciate good art in books?

A. I think children like most things good and bad, providing there is some *special* appeal for them. It is distressing that there is so much bad work with this appeal and not enough fine work to fascinate the child. The child is unbiased; not having been indoctrinated into what is good or bad, he is open to anything that is put before him and appreciates a thing for what it is and not what it ought to be. How often in libraries and bookshops do we see adults choosing books for children, saying (very often of good books) "No, I'm afraid little Fred won't like that," when it is the debased judgment and taste of the adult that doesn't like and can't accept it.

Many of us realize the artistic damage that was inflicted on us in our early years. The fact that some never recover is sad, for some of the deepest and most satisfying moments in our lives come to us through art. The artist illustrating for children has a special responsibility to uncover their sensibility while it is still plastic. In a way we are all artists, but it is the true performer of the arts who crystalizes, expresses and lays bare the feelings we all have.

Cornelia Jones and Olivia R. Way

SOURCE: "Brian Wildsmith," in *British Children's Authors: Interviews at Home,* American Library Association, 1976, pp. 155-66.

Books have always fascinated me, but the book publishing field seemed like a very closed shop, and I wondered how I might get a start making pictures for books. Then I read somewhere that in England 29,000 titles, on an average, are published every year. Well, it seemed that the thing to do was to design book wrappers. I reasoned out that the cost of making books must be quite expensive. The prices of illustrations and printing them would be so expensive that the publisher would be unwilling to stake this amount of money on someone without experience, such as I. I reasoned that book wrappers would be the thing because it's one picture rather than thirty or forty pictures for a book. This worked and in the end, after three years, I gave up teaching because I could make a living out of book wrappers—not a very good living, but enough. I did a reasonable amount of work for Oxford University Press. I had shown them my paintings earlier. In later years they did tell me that what they were waiting for was the right time to launch out in color books.

In 1960 they asked me to make fourteen color plates for *The Arabian Nights*. The pictures received severe negative criticism from the Times Literary Supplement in London, and I felt sure that Oxford University Press, publishers of the book, would no longer be interested in my work. "Well," I thought, "that's the end of you, Wildsmith." But I hadn't reckoned on Oxford. I think most publishers would have said "Go away," but Oxford really are publishers. They make a decision and they stick to it, and they back their decisions. I will be eternally grateful to them for it. They showed courage as well, and we've had a wonderful relationship. In a sense we trust each other. They trust my judgment and I trust theirs. So we're very happy partners.

After that they asked me for my ideas on ABC's. That really was the start. The *ABC* seemed to break the barrier, and from then on we've never looked back.

The trouble about printing these lovely full-color picture books [***La Fontaine Fables***] is the enormous cost involved. You need a fantastic amount of capital. There is a kind of saturation point, particularly in England, for the sale of some of these color books. Ideally you need international publishing among American and a few European countries.

Then you get the question of idea. What is right for one country may not be right for another country. So you need an international idea. We hit upon this idea of the La Fontaine fables which had never been illustrated in the form of a picture book before. They are timeless stories, with a beginning, middle, and end within a very few lines. They are wonderful ideas, compactly expressed. They fitted our need beautifully.

Then it was up to me. I spent a long time looking through La Fontaine, and I thought, "My goodness, there is nothing here," because some are a bit ribald, you know, and they are mostly political. I think in the end, from several hundred, I sorted out five or six that could be made into picture books for children.

In ***The Miller, the Boy and the Donkey,*** I made the donkey the main character. We go to Spain as often as we can. It is the country of donkeys, or it used to be. In fact, I took a trip across the Pyrenees looking for a donkey. A friend of mine knew a farmer who had a marvelous donkey. We got the donkey, and I got all the information from him. Contrary to most people's opinion about donkeys, they are not stupid. They are highly intelligent. We taught the donkey to do all kinds of tricks. He stood on his hind legs, and he took the children for rides on his back. He was really wonderful. I have a lovely movie film about him.

Most people think of England as a rather misty, mysterious sort of place, the colors not very bright; but really it's a very colorful place. We get the fog and the rain, but when that clears and the sun comes through, the color of the countryside is absolutely intense. Whereas, if you go abroad into the hot countries where the colors are supposed to be absolutely vibrant, it's so hot that you can't see the colors. There is sort of a heat mist and everything becomes faint; the colors fade out. But in England, the half-light brings out the intense color. I think they are very English—my books.

Brilliant colors do appeal to me, and I think they definitely appeal to children. I don't think they are necessarily more beautiful than the subdued colors. I think a professional artist should be able to work in whatever scale he feels is right for what he is doing. It is like a composer. He has to be able to pick the right key for what it is he is expressing. He's got to be able to work in the whole range and scale. Although I do think that the brilliant range in the color scale does have an attraction for children, I can work equally as well in the lower scale, but somehow, my subject seems to demand the brighter scale. A lot of picture book artists are throwing a lot of bright color together, expecting this to look beautiful. This does not necessarily happen. For example, you can have a red and a green, and they can be absolutely revolting because they act against each other, the two colors. Yet you can do it again in such a way that the amount of red and the amount of green somehow become absolutely glorious together, and they sing, one against the other. This is one of the dangers of color work.

There are some very fine artists working in picture books today, but very few very lovely picture books are being made. There is a demand for beautiful picture books, because many believe that only the very finest should be offered to young children. It's no good waiting until they are twelve before they are given a little culture. They should be brought up with it, so they can distinguish between the quality books and the mediocre, pseudo-quality books. Unfortunately, we are getting too many mediocre pseudo-quality books; they clog the market. They're coming out in thousands. The people in authority can't wade through all those books. They must rely on the reviewers. The reviews in England are in most cases very, very poor because the people who review, in my opinion, just don't know. Consequently, I think perhaps some of the worthwhile books get left behind.

There are two kinds of illustration. There is the factual,

diagrammatic type of illustration which is fine in its own right. It does its own particular job. Then there is the creative illustration. In the past few years certain artists have begun to really create for children, and their creative illustrations have caused a minor revolution in books for children.

Some kinds of books are more difficult to illustrate than others. Mother Goose presented a few problems—one in particular, for example:

> Oh, where, oh, where has my little dog gone?
>
> Oh, where, oh, where, can he be?
>
> With his ears cut short and his tail cut long,
>
> Oh, where, oh, where can he be?

I had to solve that problem. I had to solve the rhyme before I could make a picture of it. If you look in [my] Mother Goose, you'll see how it's been solved. There is that sort of problem with poetry sometimes, too.

I've always had the opinion that illustrating books should be rather like playing the piano. You don't interpret Bach in the same way you play Chopin. To each you give a different interpretation, and each book should have its own appearance which is different from any other book. The difficulty is to make the two things, the book and the picture, absolutely one. To make them so right that there is no other way it can be done.

The creative illustration for children may be a thing in its own right, standing independent of words. A book doesn't have to be a book of words. It is a book, and the language is color and form, not a written symbol.

Even if children don't react immediately to my books, somehow, I hope that I may sow a cultural germ in their artistic digestive systems which will one day flower and bear fruit.

From The Circus, *written and illustrated by Brian Wildsmith.*

GENERAL COMMENTARY

Kristina L. C. Lindborg

SOURCE: "Painter Wildsmith Hides Lessons in Vibrant Pictures," in *The Christian Science Monitor,* October 14, 1980, p. B10.

Page after page of explosive color. Dialogue that teems with rousing words like "Schazzzaam!," and "Ooomph," and "Kkaaarunchh." What youngster could resist? And that, maintains Brian Wildsmith, a British children's illustrator and author, is precisely why many children enjoy his "comic book" genre of reading material. "Wavelength is the key," he says.

Although Wildsmith believes children can appreciate good craftmanship, he feels that "well-intentioned" books for children too often fail to reach their audience, to "get in on their wavelength," while so many "comic books," no matter how crudely rendered, do appeal to a child's love of drama and vibrancy. Interviewed while on tour in the United States recently to promote his latest set of books, the author-painter spoke with the authority of experience. His award-winning books (more than 30 in print) have been translated into 14 languages. Their pages absolutely dance, clap, and sing with color and movement. Often directed toward very young children, their texts are clear and straightforward, yet without being trite or simplistic. Wildsmith manages to rivet a child's attention and then to teach basic lessons about such values as kindness, compassion, honesty, and the "beauty of the human spirit." "You're forming—in the child's subconscious mind—values, quality," he comments.

Professor Noah's Spaceship, Wildsmith's newest book, is just such a catalyst for thought. It deals with the environmental nightmare of wide-scale pollution. Professor Noah, a sort of updated biblical Buck Rogers, is dutifully outfitting and filling his spaceship-ark with the assorted flora and fauna that have been victimized by a negligent 20th-century preoccupation with technology. The plan is to whisk the ark off to a safer (and greener) part of the galaxy, to escape smog and contamination.

But, because of a miscalculation, the ark-ship hurls instead back through time to earth's past—the period before its devastation. And this time, everyone vows to respect the planet and not repeat past mistakes.

"Professor Noah is based on something fundamental in our society," Wildsmith comments, "which is the caring for it. . . . The very thing we owe our existence to we're destroying. Now, as adults we know it, but as children, well—perhaps later they become aware of it. It's the difference between knowing something and understanding it."

And what does Wildsmith see as the link between knowing and understanding? "It's usually some kind of personal experience, or a point really well made," he says, hastening to add that this usually can't be accomplished by "preaching." Then "you're defeating at the very start the purpose of what you're trying to do; who wants to hear you preaching? So you do it in a different way; you do it through beauty—color and shape and form."

For Wildsmith this doesn't mean mere sugar coating, either; he believes the unpopular topic of evil should be dealt with in children's books. He mentions his ***Python's Party*** as an example of how he treated the theme of trickery so that children could grasp its subtlety. The book tells about a sly, scheming serpent named Python, who has a dangerous appetite for the local cuisine, i.e., his fellow forest mates. He cunningly devises a plan that leads the unsuspecting animals to trip merrily down his tubular torso as if to a Sunday social. (Don't worry, they do eventually see daylight again.)

Wildsmith also sees a need for addressing the problem of drug abuse, even with very young children. "I think these are grave human problems. . . . It's our place to deal with them."

He says he also hopes his books will inspire the child to some kind of creative activity and perhaps sow an artistic seed that one day will bear fruit.

Peter Fanning

SOURCE: "Tiger Cubs Wrestle," in *Times Educational Supplement,* No. 3369, January 16, 1981, p. 34.

The sight of a Christmas card robin on the cover is certain to sway the hearts of all parents. Brian Wildsmith's ***Seasons*** is a decorative piece with lush illustrations to feast the eye and a simple commentary to match. The range of wash colours "when spring comes and wild flowers bloom in the meadows" is a constant joy. Fine, delicate lines all merge in a hectic dazzle of colour. ***Seasons*** is the best of the set and is followed closely by ***Animal Homes.***

Mr. Wildsmith's purposes are clear in these two didactic pieces. ***Animal Homes*** has a range of extraordinary beasts from the snail to the armadillo. This is indeed no commonplace zoo—and features no commonplace colouring either. Snail shells glow in tie-dye blurs like the inside of a kaleidoscope. The eagle's feathers are a rainbow of fire as they perch on their mottled mountain tops.

And here lies the rub. For in his assertion of pattern and sheet decoration, the artist has given us something so lovely and lush that it's simply too much for the five-year-old reader for whom it's intended.

Animal Games has a simpler text—and a hint that the author (but not of course artist) is starting to run short on ideas. "Chimpanzees make swings", "Bears climb trees", "Puppies chase their shadows", the jazzy line rhythms of "Tiger cubs wrestle" is patterned abstraction—abandoning any clear, clean colour line of a child's eye view.

Then in ***Animal Tricks*** and ***Animal Shapes*** the text falls completely apart. The author abandons the role of teacher and moves without pause into the Surreal—where hippos appear from a pelican's beak and a penguin balances a rhino. ***Animal Shapes*** shows the artist reverting to bold square shapes of the animal outline—broken down into something a child will recognize after the dazzling blur.

This five book set provides a fascinating browse, but the mixture is rich and the purpose bewildering. Parents, godparents and grandparents would do well to ask why they are buying this book. Is it really for a child? Or do they secretly want it themselves?

Kirkus Reviews

SOURCE: A review of *Animal Games, Animal Homes, Animal Shapes, Animal Tricks,* and *Seasons,* in *Kirkus Reviews,* Vol. XLIX, No. 4, February 15, 1981, p. 210.

Five cardboard-and-paper-bound, full-color volumes: outwardly alike, otherwise different, and altogether inconsequential. ***Animal Games*** has a brief line of text per double-page opening, imparts no information beyond what the pictures show ("Lion cubs bite tails," "Kittens play with balls"), and mixes some anthropomorphism ("Foxes play King of the Castle") into what is really a depiction of animal play—with pictures whose interest is exhausted at a quick glance. (None of these animals has more than a poster-like, emblematic reality.) ***Animal Homes*** presents a broader range of specimens (the first three are the snail, the armadillo, and the yak), interprets "homes" higgledy-piggledy to mean habitat or domicile ("Yaks live in the high mountains of Central Asia," "Kingfishers live in burrows"), and provides a few sentences on each animal's habits—which mostly have nothing to do with said animal's "home." These, meanwhile, are very offhandedly pictured—the beaver lodge, for instance, is really indistinguishable from a brushpile. ***Animal Shapes,*** on the other hand, has virtually no text—just the word "Zebra" or "Rhinoceros" accompanying a naturalistically-drawn and a schematically-drawn zebra or rhinoceros. (A few of these pictorial pair-ups are of some slight interest as object-lessons in abstracting form.) ***Animal Tricks*** isn't based on natural occurrences at all—though a child presented with these books as a group might not immediately realize that. To a rhyming text ("This is the tiger who stood upside-down, / And this is the leopard who's playing the clown"), Wildsmith sets pictures of animals doing various outlandish things—few of which are even amusing, some of which are quite ridiculous (two giraffes with their long necks entwined). ***Seasons,*** to wrap up the lot, is a banal, visually unevocative reprise (flowers in the spring, bees in the summer, squirrels collecting nuts in the fall), and not a patch on dozens of other books. But this is a feeble enterprise to start with, offering nothing but the famous Wildsmith name.

Kicki Moxon Browne

SOURCE: "Looking at Animals," in *Times Literary Supplement,* No. 4069, March 27, 1981, p. 343.

When Brian Wildsmith's illustrations for children's books first appeared nearly twenty years ago, many people thought them too "difficult" for small children to appreciate. Wildsmith himself has always maintained that children are entitled to be presented with good and exciting pictures—which they do not have to "understand" if there is some emotional impact. Today no one would suggest that even for the very young there is anything difficult about Wildsmith's glowing colours and varying textures.

My test consumers (aged between three and seven) expressed no more than mild approval for a group of new picture books by Wildsmith. The books rely for their impact almost exclusively on the pictures. Visually, every page including the covers is a delight, but there is an absence of dramatic content and characterization to complement the pictures and fire the imagination.

Wildsmith has given full scope to his preoccupation with animals, which is the sole subject-matter of all five titles. ***Animal Games*** shows different animals playing children's games, but without any hint of humanized behaviour ("chimpanzees make swings", "cranes throw stones in the air and catch them", "kittens play with balls"). ***Animal Tricks*** is similar, but here the imagination runs free. We see a llama with a dozen assorted animals perched on its back, a pelican carrying a hippopotamus in its beak and a moose with birds nesting all over its horns. All the animals are at the higher end of the Wildsmith scale of realism. The effect of a group of squirrels and other furry animals looking dignified and inscrutable while doing an acrobatic balancing act is immediately funny to any child. The fact that the humour derives from purely pictorial wit may be an unappreciated bonus.

In ***Animal Shapes*** various creatures are depicted first realistically, and then, in the same position, broken down into two-dimensional blocks of colour, emphasizing the animal's colour planes. ***Animal Homes,*** aimed at slightly older picture book readers, contains fairly detailed information about not-so-common animals, such as the armadillo, kingfisher and koala and their habitat. In the illustrations Wildsmith displays his full register, the depiction of the animals ranging from the realistic yak to the fantastic snail, rainbow-coloured and beautifully decorated. The surroundings are also more elaborate—the purple, blue and green swirls of tree-bark or a great bustling beavers' lodge, almost bursting out of the double-page spread.

Seasons, also for slightly older children, has easily the most powerful impact of the group, with many exciting pictures—harvest mice, all quivering whiskers, scrambling up some wonderfully scarlet-and-fire-coloured ears of corn; the autumn wind (a comet-like manifestation with a chubby face) stirring up leaves in a forest of burning colours; hundreds and hundreds of birds of every shape and colour flocking together to fly to warmer countries; two pink-cheeked hedgehogs safe and snug in their winter sleep. The text is informative if rather dry; the pictures are quite unforgettable.

Daisy Kouzel

SOURCE: A review of *Animal Games, Animal Homes, Animal Shapes, Animal Tricks,* and *Seasons,* in *School Library Journal,* Vol. 27, No. 8, April, 1981, p. 119.

Except for the slightly steep price, these latest titles from Wildsmith have everything to recommend them: the entrancing full-page and double-spread illustrations, limned with consummate artistry and glowing with the most beautiful colors; the failsafe subject matter—animals, animals and more animals; and the simple, matter-of-fact yet not condescending text, negotiable by even the most recalcitrant learners. ***Animal Shapes*** simply presents a number of critters both in stylized and naturalistic mien. ***Animal Homes*** depicts the abodes of the eagle, wolf, wildcat and others, explaining why they live there. ***Animal Games*** shows squirrels doing somersaults, toucans fencing with their beaks, tiger cubs wrestling, etc., while ***Animal Tricks*** is a bit of whimsy (there's a penguin holding up a rhino, and a baboon with its tail in knots, for example), with the text fittingly in verse. And ***Seasons*** is a celebration of life embodied in wildflowers, birds in their nests, birds in flight, fawns in the woods, hedgehogs in their holes and a sparrow amid snowflakes. A visual feast.

Marcus Crouch

SOURCE: A review of *Animal Homes* and *Seasons,* in *The Junior Bookshelf,* Vol. 45, No. 3, June, 1981, p. 110.

Brian Wildsmith has been around now for twenty years. He first made us rub our eyes with his splendid and improbable colours in the Arabian Nights of 1961. The young genius is young no more but still one of the great masters of colour. These two little books for which the artist has provided informative but not particularly distinguished texts, demonstrate all the old virtues: the ingenious textures, the effective exaggerations of natural coloration, the bold design, the delighted exploitation of the disciplines of the page. Mr. Wildsmith is no naturalist, although he is more accurate in detail than he used to be, but he makes us look again at nature in order to match it against the grandeur of his own vision. Little books these may be—and remarkably cheap for such colour-printing—but they are the minor work of a major master of the art of book-design.

Naomi Lewis

SOURCE: "Nursery Joke," in *Times Educational Supplement,* No. 3460, October 22, 1982, p. 46.

In Oxford paperback, with stiff bright shining covers, come two inviting Brian Wildsmith picture books for the very young. The pages are in vivid self colour: orange, pink, scarlet, grey, violet, yellow, blue. ***Cat on the Mat*** shows first just what the title says. The wide mat is tomato red; the little cat is tiger-striped with green eyes. But others arrive to share the mat: dog, goat, cow, elephant, with plaintive expressive faces. Cat doesn't like them at all. Screech! she says (or something that looks like that), and off they go. You can see them, calm, on the horizon. In ***The Trunk,*** the second book, the trunk itself, a ridged brownish vertical column, almost fills each page. A squirrel arrives. Then a fox, a monkey, a tiger cub. Surprise! It isn't part of a tree at all. It's an elephant's trunk—and there at the end is the elephant himself, along a fine double spread. A proper nursery joke! Both of these wordless books are in one of Wildsmith's most likeable manners: no abstract doodlings or harlequin effects in sight.

Cliff Moon

SOURCE: A review of *All Fall Down, The Apple Bird, The Island,* and *The Nest,* in *The School Librarian,* Vol. 32, No. 1, March, 1984, pp. 41-2.

Here are four more examples of how a 'real' children's book writer/illustrator can provide far better texts for beginner readers than reading scheme designers. ***The Apple Bird*** and ***The Nest*** are wordless picture stories with amusing endings; while ***All Fall Down*** is a cumulative tale about animals piling on top of each other only to end up in a heap. ***The Island*** shows a collection of creatures climbing on to what they think is an island but turns out instead to be a hippo's back. These last two have closely matched captions accompanying the illustrations. The quality of these books in their own right and in terms of children's responses to them bears little comparison with early 'readers', yet price-wise they compare very favourably.

Margaret Carter

SOURCE: "Brian Wildsmith," in *Books for Your Children,* Vol. 14, No. 2, Summer, 1984, p. 9.

"All painting is an exploration. It's mysterious to me. The canvas takes me over. It's a religious experience—like being in a trance: a religious act where you are most at one with yourself. In the evening I'll stand back and look at the canvas I've worked on and I'm amazed at what is there!"

Brian Wildsmith is articulate, direct, cutting without preamble to the heart of a concept with formulated ordered thought. A man who knows where he's been and where he hopes to go.

For the last thirteen years he has lived in Provence, moving there with his wife and four children when the youngest, Simon, was six. *"It's the light there—somehow I can't see in England. But I'm a late developer. I've waited 25 years before I've been able to paint creatively as I'm now doing."*

In a room of his temporary English home is a vast half-finished canvas, redolent with scarlets and orange, with mingled textures of smooth and rough. *"Brian is now concentrating on real painting"* I had been told. However different the direction, one could not judge his previous work to be *"unreal"*.

It was his wife who first suggested that he should exchange teaching for book-wrapper illustration. *"Mabel George of O.U.P. took me on. She was a catalyst, an innovator—she launched us all, Ambrus, Keeping. I worked for her for three years then she asked me to illustrate an Arabian Nights. 'I've groomed you in the art of making a book' she said."*

He still remembers one review of his *Arabian Nights* illustrations and can quote it word for word:

"We have now descended to the lowest depths in Brian Wildsmith's vicious attack on the Arabian Nights. These aimless scribbles which do nothing for drawing wander aimlessly and pointlessly about the page."

His previous hurt is now tempered by a wry tolerance. *"There's no need to butcher poor devils with criticism. Best to ignore the bad—leave it alone. Although of course there's nothing worse than a bad painting."*

Perhaps it is this directness, combined with a certain stoicism, which has given him his affinity with children for they are two of the qualities most children have existing as they do in a world where imagination—the private freedom—runs like a secret stream beneath a barricade of rules dictated by dotty adults.

"I like the way children react" he says and his affection led him to recognise a need for books for the 18 month-2 years. *"The cat sat on the mat—now what could be*

drearier?" But it's a very different cat who sits on the mat in Brian Wildsmith's illustrations—a territorial possessor of a cat, proud of his mat and unwelcoming of the interlopers who, one by one, encroach on his mat. Finally there's a righteous, spitting and raising of fur and once again it's just *"the cat on the mat."*

Children accept miracles easily but with delight—*The Apple Bird* which turns into an apple. *The Trunk* which is a very strange trunk indeed. *"The explanation never matches the event"* he says, but children are used to doing without explanations—to them the event is all, and that must account for some of the popularity of his children's books, in which ***Daisy***—the story of a cow who found fame but didn't like it—is the latest. The next will be an *Oxford Book of Bedtime Stories.*

"I don't think of myself as a writer. You can dress an idea down to a few words, condense it to a sentence. ***The Hunter and His Dog*** *is a story of compassion and freedom. It's vital that children's eyes should be opened to the beauty of all that's around them. I find it sinister that 'real' education today is crippled. Our world's climate is one of polarisation and there's a need to make children aware and enlightened—knowing you can be put in cages but that freedom is in the mind and you can never be a slave if you are aware of its wonder and potential."*

For 12 months Brian Wildsmith worked in Russia on costume designs for the film of Maeterlinck's *Blue Bird* but *"eventually it became a mixture of styles with all the designs so that it never remained an entity."*

As for the future—apart from children's books—*"There are no rules in painting. One is in an unknown territory. I'd like to try to define nature in terms of modern painting—the miraculous light of Provence, the wonder of sunlight on the hills and the mystery of moonlight. I live in an ivory tower there, observing but perhaps not involved in the daily life. All painting is an invention of a theme and eventually we all end up with our own reality."*

Liz Waterland

SOURCE: A review of *Giddy Up* and *If I Were You,* in *Books for Keeps,* No. 46, September, 1987, p. 17.

The first three or four of these books broke new ground with very simple, but highly meaningful, text closely related to the equally important and artistic illustrations. The language was natural and predictable, and the whole a pleasure to read.

However, OUP seems bent on creating a 'series' and, like all series, the quality is becoming patchy. Not all writers and illustrators are able to capture the 'rightness' of ***The Trunk, Cat on the Mat*** or ***The Island*** and even Wildsmith himself seems in danger of succumbing to formula-itis.

Giddy Up is the story of a reluctant donkey being coerced to market. It required a great deal of explanation from the adult reading aloud and solo readers couldn't predict the idiosyncratic text. It was a sure sign of disappointment when no-one wanted to take this home!

If I Were You was better received. A child at the zoo wonders which animal he would like to be and what attributes he would have. The pictures are of Wildsmith's usual quality and the idea is thought-provoking . . . especially the last sentence, 'If you were me, you would be free.' There was plenty to discuss and think about here and, best of all, not just for the very young children that might at first appear to be its natural audience.

Liz Waterland

SOURCE: A review of *Animal Tricks* and *Animal Seasons,* in *Books for Keeps,* No. 72, January, 1992, p. 6.

Brian Wildsmith's picture books are always superb. His animals, in particular, manage to be both naturalistic and imaginative (often funny, too) and are therefore a welcome alternative to the cartoony or the photographic.

Here, ***Animal Seasons*** are evoked by a simple succession of creatures doing appropriate things. Few of these are original in themselves . . . squirrels gather nuts, robins hop through snow . . . but the short, clear text and Wildsmith's visual style make them interesting and fresh.

Animal Tricks is more inventive, showing a variety of creatures doing, mainly, silly things such as a penguin lifting a rhino.

It's important for very young children to talk through the difference between what animals can really do and what is just imagined. This is perhaps a weakness in presenting these two books in what appears to be a series format. Well worth exploring, however.

Margery Fisher

SOURCE: A review *Animal Tricks* and *Animal Seasons,* in *Growing Point,* Vol. 30, No. 5, January, 1992, p. 5646.

The glowing colours and vigorous shapes which spell Wildsmith whatever kind of book he is illustrating are as strong as ever in two books for small children to look at and for older reading apprentices to use, perhaps. Doggerel verse accompanies pictures of a pair of giraffes entangled by the neck, a seal balancing a toucan, a crocodile with a red panda on its nose and other weird antics performed by animals which are totally recognisable all the same. Closer to nature, the match of the seasons is explored in lavishly decorated scenes where the fancifully extended colours of a butterfly's wing, ripe corn stalks and migrating birds are balanced by accuracy in behaviour and in the matter of changeable weather patterns.

Margaret Carter

SOURCE: "Brian Wildsmith," in *Books for Your Children,* Vol. 27, No. 3, Autumn-Winter, 1992, p. 5.

Brian Wildsmith lives in the South of France—"It's the light there—somehow I can't see in England . . ."

It would be easy to imagine from that statement that it's the strong light of Provence that has inspired the brilliant colours and the stark shadows that characterise his books. Not so—2 and 2 do not always make 4—his stunning ***ABC,*** winner of the 1962 Kate Greenaway Award, was produced before his move to France, and seems not a particularly obvious result of life in Yorkshire where he grew up. Whatever his background, the colours must be inside him, although now he confesses that a few hours basking in the sun, a glass or two of wine on the terrace from which, on a clear day, he can see Corsica, does help the creative process . . . .

The 60s in England saw a quiet revolution in children's publishing, with the Oxford University Press well in the advance guard, Brian Wildsmith had already worked for some time with their children's department and was given the opportunity to join the revolution, breaking new ground with a new approach to children's books. The result was his ***ABC,*** still in print after thirty years and in its 19th American edition. It was a happy case of the right person being in the right place at the right time.

And then? "I fell in love with making children's books, finding the process exciting, ever-changing and fully enjoyable," he says. And thank goodness he did. Where would we be without some of those books—not only the illustrations to traditional texts, but the later books which he both wrote and illustrated.

"I think writing is the most difficult of the arts," he says. "I would much rather paint." Nevertheless, ***The Island*** is a small masterpiece—often quoted for its text as well as its illustrations—and it uses just fifteen words.

His excursion into children's books formulated his desire to teach through books—not to preach, but to show: to produce books which in their own right would stimulate and excite. His series of books, ***The Cat on the Mat,*** are miracles of tongue-in-cheek wit. All are not what they seem and there's usually a surprise on the last page.

"I like logic in everything I do," he says, "and I made a conscious decision to span, with the use of form, colour and words, the whole educational gamut from alphabet and numbers to human principles:—to feed the eyes and minds of children with lusciously colourful images, representative of the potential beauty of our planet and its inhabitants."

His aim could not have been more successfully achieved than in ***Over the Deep Blue Sea.*** Two children, newly arrived on an Island, make friends with a local boy. Together they explore the land and its surrounding sea. Then the island boy learns that the children are from a race that once attacked the island—and will play with them no longer. But when one child is in great danger of drowning, he is saved by the island boy, and together they learn that their ancestors, who lived thousands of years ago—were from the same lands—'we're all just sailors come ashore from the deep blue sea!' So how could they be enemies?

The lesson of humanity may be there, but it's surely also demonstrated in the depth of beauty of the paintings . . . the changing colours of the sea, its threat and its benison, the surge of waves and the splattered spume, the end of tranquillity and peace. Like all Wildsmith's books, it must be bought not borrowed. It gives a glimpse of an exotic land, at once physical and imaginary, of the underwater paradise of shape and shade, of the sea's colour and power, the dominance of the tides, and ultimately our interdependence on man and nature.

Publishers Weekly

SOURCE: A review of *Look Closer; Wake Up, Wake Up!; What Did I Find?;* and *Whose Hat Was That,* in *Publishers Weekly,* Vol. 240, No. 4, January 25, 1993, p. 85.

Rest assured—the exuberant sense of color and love of pattern that characterize Brian Wildsmith's art in such large-format books [written with daughter, Rebecca Wildsmith] as ***The Princess and the Moon*** translate superbly in these four board-book-size titles for the youngest audiences. The gorgeously dappled backgrounds and intricate designs (for example, snail shells that look like Ukrainian Easter eggs; a sun and a wrought-iron fence both rendered as rectilinear fantasies) will command attention; simple but imaginative story lines guarantee reader participation. ***Look Closer,*** for example, presents a series of pastoral scenes: "I passed wild roses and saw something move. What could it be?" reads one caption. Turn the page, and a detail from the first illustration is enlarged to show three caterpillars curled atop rose leaves. ***Wake Up*** invites readers to speculate which farmyard animal is next on the list for reveille; soberly captioned and rigidly geometrical pictures are juxtaposed with fanciful scenes in which the repeated title serves as caption in ***What Did I Find?;*** and ***Whose Hat*** conducts a geographical guessing game. A jolly introduction to the pleasures of books.

Janice Del Negro

SOURCE: A review of *Look Closer; Wake Up, Wake Up!; What Did I Find?;* and *Whose Hat Was That?,* in *Booklist,* Vol. 89, No. 14, March 15, 1993, p. 1362.

These four books [written with daughter Rebecca Wildsmith] for the very young are of varying quality both in concept and in execution. ***Look Closer*** shows a close-up view of a subject then a view from far away (for example, one page pictures a close-up of two ladybugs; the facing page shows two tiny red spots on a fence). In ***Whose Hat Was That?*** hats belonging to a group of multiethnic owners are blown off by the wind to land on some rather surprised animals—a cowboy's hat lands on a cow, an Indian's on a tiger. ***What Did I Find?*** reveals exotic animals in unlikely places at the turn of a page. The most successful of the four is ***Wake Up, Wake Up!,*** which has sequential logic as well as a coherent narrative: the sun wakes the rooster ("Cockledoodledoo!"), who wakes the goose ("Honk!"), who wakes the sheep ("Baaaa!"), etc., until the farmer is awakened to feed them all. Although the small format of the books does not always do the artwork justice, the illustrations won't fail to attract young readers and their parents with the bright colors and strong geometric designs that are a Wildsmith trademark. The absence of endpapers is problematic (the title page is on the front inside cover and its verso is on the back inside cover), but the small size works for what are essentially books meant for one-on-one sharing.

Heide Piehler

SOURCE: A review of *Look Closer; Wake Up, Wake Up!; What Did I Find?;* and *Whose Hat Was That?,* in *School Library Journal,* Vol. 39, No. 12, December, 1993, p. 97.

The strength of these board books lies in the Wildsmiths' [Brian and daughter Rebecca] bold, crisp artwork. Their small size is both a positive and a negative—they are physically accessible to little hands, but some of the picture clues are too small to identify. In ***Look Closer,*** a narrator spots tiny moving objects in various places. A turn of the page and "closer look" reveal some of the bugs and insects that inhabit our neighborhoods. This is the most visually engaging of the quartet. ***Wake Up, Wake Up*** is the most effective title. The sun wakes the rooster whose "cock-a-doodle-doo" wakes the goose whose "honk" wakes the sheep, etc. Children will enjoy the animal identification and sounds. However, this is just one of many competent farm animal books. In ***What Did I Find?*** the narrator discovers a variety of animals in unusual places—an elephant in the closet, squirrel in the lunch box, etc. At bedtime, all of the wayward creatures are tucked in the child's bed. The book seems nonsensical and pointless. ***Whose Hat Was That?*** features a playful wind blowing hats off of peoples' heads and onto animals across the globe. Eventually it blows them all to the moon. As an introduction to cultural awareness, this is a miserable failure. The ethnic images portrayed are one-dimensional and stereotypical, more insulting than enlightening. Overall, disappointing efforts that won't be missed.

Marcus Crouch

SOURCE: A review of *Look Closer; Wake Up, Wake Up!; What Did I Find?;* and *Whose Hat Was That?,* in *The Junior Bookshelf,* Vol. 58, No. 1, February, 1994, p. 21.

The pattern of these beautifully designed and printed booklets written with daughter Rebecca Wildsmith] is the same. They all depend for surprise on the turn of the page. Hence the series title 'What Next Books'. Each recto page poses a question. Turn over, and there is the answer, beautiful or funny, and often both at once. The familiar rich fabric of the Wildsmith backgrounds is mostly absent. In this context it would be distracting. Instead we have clear drawings of everyday objects, just right for identification by the youngest. The educational idea is sound; its performance carries just the right amount of detail to make the books lovely, funny and meaningful.

TITLE COMMENTARY

MAURICE MAETERLINCK'S "BLUE BIRD" (adapted by Wildsmith, 1976)

Publishers Weekly

SOURCE: A review of *Maurice Maeterlinck's "Blue Bird,"* in *Publishers Weekly,* Vol. 210, No. 7, August 16, 1976, p. 123.

Bursts of color call forth oohs and ahs on all pages; looking at the pictures is like being at Fourth of July fireworks. In a way, they distract from Wildsmith's simplified version of Maeterlinck's classic story of Mytyl and Tyltyl, the woodcutter's boy and girl who travel into fantasy country in their search for the magic blue bird. Although the book is explosive, it's far from the bomb which the movie is reported to be. Wildsmith created the graphics for the film; his illustrated retelling will probably draw a longer lasting, more satisfied audience than the star-studded flick.

Zena Sutherland

SOURCE: A review of *Maurice Maeterlinck's "Blue Bird,"* in *Bulletin of the Center for Children's Books,* Vol. 30, No. 4, December, 1976, p. 67.

First published in England, this adaptation by Wildsmith of Maeterlinck's classic is a bit heavy-handed, but his pictures, based on designs for the film, are a splendid merging of richly detailed collage and vivid painting. Two small children, Mytyl and Tyltyl, volunteer a search for the bluebird of happiness so that they may speed the recovery of the fairy Berylune's sick child. Their fantastic adventures are used as a vehicle for many concepts about truth, beauty, and happiness—not as convincingly as in the original play, but adequately. This seems too sophisticated for the K-3 audience designated by the publisher.

Joan E. Bezrudczyk

SOURCE: A review of *Maurice Maeterlinck's "Blue Bird,"* in *School Library Journal,* Vol. 23, No. 6, February, 1977, p. 59.

With artwork based upon his set designs for the movie of *The Blue Bird,* Wildsmith has created a picture-book on the classic tale of the search for happiness. Many of the subtleties of the story (e.g., the Land of Memory where Mytyl and Tytyl come upon and talk to their dead grandparents) will be lost on young independent readers for whom the book is intended. The exotic illustrations done in dazzling collage and watercolor save the generally uninspired adaptation of Maeterlinck's play to some degree. However, this will only find its way into the hands of kids who have already seen the movie.

Elaine Moss

SOURCE: "Solace for Spring," in *Times Literary Supplement,* No. 3915, March 25, 1977, p. 355.

[I]n ***Maurice Maeterlinck's "Blue Bird,"*** which Brian Wildsmith has turned into a rich and lustrous book this season, the children Mytyl and Tyltyl explore the essence of life, the soul of things, more deeply as they visit time that has gone (when their grandparents were alive) and time that is to come (where children yet unborn are preparing for life) during their quest for the blue bird which they find, bluer and more vivid because of their greater understanding of the meaning of being, in their own home when they return. The story, with its emphasis on the spirit, is not exactly a gift to the illustrator and Brian Wildsmith's picturebook jumps from naturalism, in his paintings of the woodcutter's hut, to fantasy in his representation of the spirit of, for example, milk, and geometry which he uses skillfully in colourful designs to convey his conception of the Palace of Night. In the film version of ***Blue Bird,*** on which Brian Wildsmith has been working for many years, transitional sequences will presumably help the eye to travel more easily from one kind of image to the other.

Marcus Crouch

SOURCE: A review of *Maurice Maeterlinck's "Blue Bird,"* in *The Junior Bookshelf,* Vol. 41, No. 3, June, 1977, p. 159.

Brian Wildsmith has tackled a bigger subject than usual, but he has produced something a little less than satisfactory in purely book terms. His ***Blue Bird*** designs were conceived for a film version, and, although his colour and his strong rhythmic sense are as powerful as ever, this is not enough to sustain a book which is rather longer than most picture-books and far more complex. Maeterlinck's mysticism, or whimsy—call it what you will—needs the incantation of his own words and the magic of the theatre. Mr. Wildsmith's condensed version conveys none of the poetry and little of the underlying logic of the play. It is merely a vehicle for his drawings and they, although sumptuous enough, are rather too much the rich but familiar mixture as before. Here is a great picture-book artist who desperately needs a new outlet but who has not found it here.

THE TRUE CROSS (1977)

Marcus Crouch

SOURCE: A review of *The True Cross,* in *The Junior Bookshelf,* Vol. 42, No. 3, June, 1978, p. 138.

It is giving away no secrets to say that Brian Wildsmith has been going through a bad patch. It is obviously difficult for an artist who has a runaway success to sustain the impetus. It is not so much that he has slowed down, but the others have caught up. To confuse the metaphor slightly, he needs to run rather faster to keep in the same place.

In ***The True Cross*** he has managed a short burst of speed. He has taken as his theme the Tree of Life, from which came the tree growing out of Adam which was made into the cross of Calvary. The story begins in Eden and ends in Jerusalem with the rediscovery of the true cross by St. Helena. Mr. Wildsmith's book clearly springs from a genuine religious impulse, and is informed with his love of all living things. The tree in its heyday, crammed full of birds and flowers, is in his best manner. Some of the scenes, especially those with many human figures, call for a greater technical range than he commands, and this destroys the unity which so diverse a theme badly needs. So, although this is his best book for some time, ***The True Cross*** does not allay all the fears which his greatest admirers must suffer. Here is a great maker of picture-books not quite back on the rails.

Publishers Weekly

SOURCE: A review of *The True Cross,* in *Publishers Weekly,* Vol. 214, No. 25, December 25, 1978, p. 59.

Wildsmith's unmistakable style makes his new book as personal as his signature. He illustrates this version of a medieval legend with strikingly designed paintings in shining colors and rich textures. According to the story, Jesus is crucified on a cross made from the Tree of Life which God had planted in the Garden of Eden. Lost for centuries, the holy relic is found by Helena, mother of the Roman Emperor Constantine. But with it are the two on which the robbers died at the same time as Jesus, so the Christians test each and identify the true cross by its miraculous powers.

Kirkus Reviews

SOURCE: A review of *The True Cross,* in *Kirkus Reviews,* Vol. XLVII, No. 3, February 1, 1979, pp. 122-23.

Wildsmith makes one continuous narrative out of several traditional anecdotes connected with the "the true cross," beginning in the garden of Eden where Adam's son Seth obtains a sprig from the Tree of Life to plant in his dying father's mouth. The tree that grows from it has healing power; a bridge made from its wood evokes an awed prophecy from the Queen of Sheba; her vision comes true when the wood is used for Jesus' cross; and the cross is found by Helena two centuries later when it brings a dead boy to life. It's unlikely that many children around today have grandmothers still cherishing their own tiny chips of the "true cross"; nevertheless, Wildsmith does rely on a preconditioned response to Jesus (whose story he doesn't go into) for whatever impact or resonance the chronicle might have. The illustrations also have a foregone, if not stale, quality, despite a sort of festive formality: they seem not so much responses to the story as well-made decorations.

Jane E. Gardner Connor

SOURCE: A review of *The True Cross,* in *School Library Journal,* Vol. 32, No. 2, October, 1985, p. 166.

This legend traces the True Cross back to the Garden of Eden, when Adam's son Seth placed a sprig from the Tree of Life in his father's mouth after Adam's death. The tree that grew was later worshipped by the Queen of Sheba; the wood was also used for the cross on which Jesus was crucified. Much later, a temple on Calvary was torn down to reach the cross, which was distinguished from the two others buried with it when its touch brought a dead man back to life. The text is short and crisply written, which well suits the legend. However, the story assumes that children are familiar with the Biblical figures mentioned. There are no sources cited, nor is there sufficient background information. The illustrations are rich with color and pattern that effectively sustains the mood. This expressionistic style suits the direct understated text.

WHAT THE MOON SAW (1978)

Publishers Weekly

SOURCE: A review of *What the Moon Saw,* in *Publishers Weekly,* Vol. 214, No. 21, September 20, 1978, p. 60.

Big, color-splashed and eye-filling paintings are the British author-illustrator's specialty and they excite one's imagination in this bountiful work. When Moon mentions that she has never had a good look at the world, Sun brags, "I have seen everything," and takes the night wanderer on a tour of daytime sights. With this opportunity to paint scenes familiar and exotic, the artist goes all out. Besides, he includes pictures and comments that give a child ideas of relativity—things big and small, fat and thin, etc. But at the end, Moon thanks Sun for the experience while taking a poke at the great star's claim of seeing everything. The final, sweeping panorama shows the reader what Sun has never viewed: the night sky, with millions of glittering lights adorning the velvet dark.

Janet Domowitz

SOURCE: A review of *What the Moon Saw,* in *The Christian Science Monitor,* December 4, 1978, p. B20.

The sun proves illuminating as it teaches the moon—and the reader—about some contrasts: fast and slow, outside and inside, fierce and timid, etc. Wildsmith's art is, as always, bursting with charm and bright color, but he relies on boldface type to emphasize his theme of contrasts—a stationary cheetah can't illustrate "fast" nor can a "light" bird be one-fourth the size of the facing "heavy" elephant. Let Sesame Street reinforce the teaching and be content to loll in this book's familiar beauty.

Kirkus Reviews

SOURCE: A review of *What the Moon Saw,* in *Kirkus Reviews,* Vol. XLVI, No. 24, December 15, 1978, p. 1355.

Wildsmith begins with the sun pointing out objects on earth to the moon, and his version of a city and then a village as seen from above is bright and clever. But soon he abandons the moon's perspective—a dog is seen not from the top but from both *front* and *back*—and with it any rationale for his designs. (Why, for example, is the side of the house all diamond-patterned?). Anyway, the whole demonstration soon turns into another parade of Wildsmith's animals, combined here with a study in opposites; thus, a *heavy* elephant faces a *light* bird, a *fierce* tiger a *timid* rabbit, and a giraffe with a *long* neck is next to a raccoon with a *short* one. Flashy as usual, though not uniformly so—the *weak* kitten is just that. The sun dazzles and there is a stylish lizard and a groovy acid dream of a forest—but it's all spectacle.

Eileen A. Archer

SOURCE: A review of *What the Moon Saw,* in *Book Window,* Vol. 6, No. 1, Winter, 1978, p. 17.

In this book Wildsmith has illustrated pages of "opposites". A Magnificent Sun tells the Moon about cities with "many" houses and villages with "few"; of animals that are "heavy" and those that are "light", and so on. The pictures are marvellous, full of colour, pattern and invention in true Wildsmith style. The Sun believes he has seen everything, but the Moon scores on a delightful final page when he tells the Sun about "dark".

Marcus Crouch

SOURCE: A review of *What the Moon Saw*, in *The Junior Bookshelf*, Vol. 43, No. 1, February, 1979, p. 15.

So to Wildsmith. He is not strong on story-making and draughtsmanship is not his best point. He is essentially a designer. As so often, his book would be just as good as a set of separate wall-charts or as a nursery frieze. The colour is dazzling, the patterns—although we are now just a little overfamiliar with the Wildsmith conventions—brilliant and exciting. But the thread of text which links the pictures is, to put it kindly, undistinguished.

Gemma DeVinney

SOURCE: A review of *What the Moon Saw*, in *School Library Journal*, Vol. 25, No. 6, February, 1979, p. 49.

The Moon complains to the Sun that she has never really seen the world below. The Sun is eager to show the Moon some of the things to be found in the world because after all, as the Sun boasts, "I have seen everything." Except for darkness that is, as the Moon gently reminds the Sun on the last page. Opposites such as front/back, long/short, fast/slow are revealed in the simple text. And Wildsmith's fans will be treated to an assortment of big, bright, bold illustrations that reveal the full range of the artist's drawing talent.

Zena Sutherland

SOURCE: A review of *What the Moon Saw*, in *Bulletin of the Center for Children's Books*, Vol. 32, No. 9, May, 1979, p. 166.

The brilliant hues and distinctive style of Wildsmith's paint and collage pictures are strong as ever in their appeal; here they are used to illustrate a book about contrasting terms. The Moon, complaining that she had never really seen the world below, is told all about it by the Sun: The city has *many* houses, the village has *few;* the elephant is *heavy,* a bird is *light;* the kitten is *weak,* the bear is *strong,* etc. Some of the concepts—bear and

From Goat's Trail, *written and illustrated by Brian Wildsmith.*

kitten, for example—are weakened by a lack of differentiation in the illustrations; the kitten is fully half the size of the bear and looks even more balefully from its green eyes. Some concepts are cited but not shown, as with the swift cheetah and slow tortoise. Useful as a concept book, although not always crystal-clear, and lovely to look at. Oh, yes, what the moon saw . . . something the sun never could, the dark.

HUNTER AND HIS DOG (1979)

Publishers Weekly

SOURCE: A review of *Hunter and His Dog,* in *Publishers Weekly,* Vol. 215, No. 14, April 2, 1979, p. 73.

Nimbly avoiding mawkishness, Wildsmith tells a story of improbable but perfect love. The illustrations radiate beauty and tenderness, a fairy-tale atmosphere contrasting with the realism in portrayals of animal players in the drama. A hunter trains his puppy to retrieve game by throwing sticks for him to fetch, then takes the dog on a shoot. But when the retriever finds a duck wounded by his master's gun, he hides the bird and fetches a stick to the man. In time, the dog saves an army of injured ducks which he cares for secretly. The hunter eventually discovers the truth and then what happens is unexpected as well as gently comic. In their innocence and native nobility, small children will find the deeds of a creature with their attributes quite natural.

Marcus Crouch

SOURCE: A review of *Hunter and His Dog,* in *The Junior Bookshelf,* Vol. 43, No. 4, August, 1979, p. 191.

Brian Wildsmith's new book is his best for a long time. There is not much that is new here, but he uses his old visual clichés confidently, as if they had come to him freshly this minute. The story is original and told economically and with a more successful use of words than usual. But why is his hunter dressed like Harlequin? Surely he should take some hints on protective coloration from the game he stalks. But we must forgive him much for some colourful, imaginative and humorous openings; notably an unforgettable picture of the ducks' surgery with bandages in all sorts of improbable places!

Margery Fisher

SOURCE: A review of *Hunter and His Dog,* in *Growing Point,* Vol. 18, No. 4, November, 1979, p. 3609.

Like Aesop, Wildsmith humanises the hunting dog to point the contrast between its gun-proud master and its own compassion for the wounded ducks which it hides on an island, placating the hunter with sticks till he sees the error of his ways. In spite of the moral the book is most impressive as a celebration of natural beauty—not naturalistic so much as evocative of light, colour, shape and texture in the exquisite detail of feathers, white-washed stone, a dog's fur, reeds in darkness. A brilliantly inspiriting picture-book.

Zena Sutherland

SOURCE: A review of *Hunter and His Dog,* in *Bulletin of the Center for Children's Books,* Vol. 33, No. 4, December, 1979, pp. 83-4.

Wildsmith's jewel-tone colors and the rich details of his paintings are beautiful, as always, but the text of this oversize picture book is weak, despite the positive message about kindness to animals. Trained to hunt, a dog feels compassion for the wounded ducks his master has shot; he carries a series of ducks to a small island, licks them, and brings them bread. One day his master follows the dog, sees the ducks, is ashamed, brings the ducks home (in a cart-borne cage, from an island?) and frees them when they recover after having been given tender, loving care. A nice idea, but not very convincing in execution.

Aidan Warlow

SOURCE: A review of *Hunter and His Dog,* in *The School Librarian,* Vol. 27, No. 4, December, 1979, p. 347.

Brian Wildsmith's latest picture book is one of his most enchanting. It tells a simple moral tale of a hunter who trains his dog to retrieve the ducks he shoots. The dog secretly sets up a little island hospital for the injured ducks, then converts his master to the cause of duck welfare instead of slaughter. The hunter is in fact no more than a childish *commedia dell'arte* clown figure, much better suited to his new role than his old. Wildsmith's pictures range from quite realistic line drawings to wild and almost abstract gouache colouring effects which hold the eye and give a powerful impression of the glow of ducks' feathers and the wateriness of the lakeside. The book should be made available to as many young children as possible.

PROFESSOR NOAH'S SPACESHIP (1980)

Publishers Weekly

SOURCE: A review of *Professor Noah's Spaceship,* in *Publishers Weekly,* Vol. 218, No. 26, December 26, 1980, p. 59.

Wildsmith's new book is entirely different from and, in some ways, more meaty than his popular works. While the pages are filled, as usual, with his coruscatingly colorful paintings of forest animals, he has also included views showing his expertise at draftsmanship, the plan of Professor Noah's spaceship. In the wilderness, Lion and the other creatures are suffering from bad air, bad water and spoiled food. Lion leads an expedition to find healthier surroundings and the animals meet Noah, preparing to leave Earth in search of an unpolluted planet. The animals pitch in, helping the professor's robots to finish the spacecraft and they blast off, just in time, as Earth begins to go up in flames. The surprise ending deepens the import of a timely cautionary tale.

Zena Sutherland

SOURCE: A review of *Professor Noah's Spaceship,* in *Bulletin of the Center for Children's Books,* Vol. 34, No. 6, February, 1981, pp. 123-24.

Pollution comes to the forest, fouling the air and spoiling the plants. Owl reports to the assemblage of unhappy creatures that he has seen a huge object being built, and that perhaps the clever builder can help them. He is Professor Noah, and it seems that he has been building a spaceship just so that he can rescue the animals and take them to another planet. Robots help, food for forty days and forty nights is collected, and the spaceship takes off just as the forest is consumed by flames. A dove is sent out to bring a leaf back from a tree, and it proves to be a leaf from Earth; the spaceship has travelled backward through time, and the happy animals joyfully debark on a still-verdant earth. Last comment, "There seems to have been some flooding here." A nice twist to the story of Noah and the Flood; although the writing is not distinguished, the concept of the story and the cast of animals should appeal to children. The paintings combine the beautiful and dramatic animals that Wildsmith fans will recognize and the bold use of color in geometric forms, especially triangles, that are the artist's trademark.

Celia H. Morris

SOURCE: A review of *Professor Noah's Spaceship,* in *The Horn Book Magazine,* Vol. LVII, No. 1, February, 1981, p. 46.

In a not-too-distant future time the animals of the forest begin to notice changes—air is foul, food is no longer fit to eat, and eggs are breaking before hatching. The animals consult Professor Noah, who invites them to join him in his spaceship for forty days and forty nights, traveling to a new planet where the forests "will be as beautiful as our forest once was before it was spoiled by pollution." They blast off from the now flaming Earth; Elephant, suitably garbed in a space helmet and equipped with meters and cameras strapped to his trunk, is recruited to repair the "time-zone guidance fin." When Dove is sent to retrieve a leaf, Professor Noah realizes they have gone backwards in time to their own planet Earth, "as it was in the beginning." Utilizing space, color, and geometric shapes, the author-artist carefully controls the design of the large double-page spreads. Unfortunately, the slightly choppy, heavy-handed text is not quite the equal of the artwork. Children familiar with the traditional Noah story may find it strange that the animals are not presented in pairs and may not appreciate the delightful subtlety of the last lines in which Otter comments, "Thank goodness for all the rain. There seems to have been some flooding here."

Barbara Elleman

SOURCE: A review of *Professor Noah's Spaceship,* in *Booklist,* Vol. 77, No. 12, February 15, 1981, p. 813.

In this modern Noah's tale, Wildsmith concocts a wondrous science fiction adventure against a lush, colorful backdrop. The forest animals, concerned about a world where the air is too foul to breathe, the fruit too rancid to eat, the eggshells too thin to hatch, and the forests dwindling to nothing, appeal to Professor Noah, who is building a giant spaceship to escape the earth's pollution. To hurry along construction, the animals help the busy robots, and soon they are all hurtling through space. When the time-zone guidance fin gets out of kilter, Elephant makes a space-walk adjustment; but he inadvertently twists the fin the wrong way, and they find themselves not only in reverse direction but also traveling backwards in time. It all ends happily, however, when they arrive back on earth to the clean air and bountiful land of centuries ago. Otter's final, tongue-in-cheek comment (" . . . thank goodness for all the rain. There seems to have been some flooding here") slyly ties it to the original Biblical story. The artist's splashily colored pages have an orderly flow, with well-balanced composition and arrangement. The intricacies of the space ship and the work of the animals (the monkey dangling by the tail from the robot's arm, the elephant in the huge space suit) are cleverly depicted. A good choice for teachers doing ecology units and a popular one for young science fiction fans.

Marcus Crouch

SOURCE: A review of *Professor Noah's Spaceship,* in *The Junior Bookshelf,* Vol. 45, No. 2, April, 1981, p. 60.

Brian Wildsmith has a nice story here. Noah, alarmed at the increasing pollution of the world, builds a spaceship—for which the artist provides a blueprint—and takes off with a representative collection of animals. They are looking for a planet as beautiful as earth before the polluters got to work, and have just forty days and nights to find it in. When the space-ship develops a fault, the elephant puts on his space-suit—an awesome sight!—and carries out repairs. Not surprisingly, he gets it wrong, and the ship arrives at an unscheduled destination. It could not be better. A really good idea, this, if told with less than complete felicity of words. The pictures contain no surprises. Mr. Wildsmith draws his animals as he has been doing now for eighteen years, with mannered mastery. At what stage does an individual style become a mannerism? I am not sure, but I am fairly sure that Mr. Wildsmith has within him a potential which has not yet been realised in print. Until that day let us be duly grateful for such splendid riots of colour as ***Professor Noah's Spaceship.***

Roy Foster

SOURCE: "Machine-Minded," in *Times Literary Supplement,* No. 4308, October 25, 1985, p. 1218.

Brian Wildsmith's ***Professor Noah's Spaceship,*** reissued and paperbacked, caters not only to juvenile machine-obsession but also to adult preoccupations with pollution and apocalypse. The animals who flee their defiled forest in the Professor's spaceship are told they are going to a green and habitable planet: rather a questionable proposition for the *au fait* reader. The difficulty is solved by some funny business when a time-zone guidance fin gets twisted; they return through time to a pure and unsullied Earth, just after the Flood. Some of the technical drawings are striking, but it is a little marred by a certain preciousness in text and illustration, and an air of adult knowingness which will not satisfy the demanding literal-mindedness of junior space-freaks.

BEAR'S ADVENTURE (1981)

Marcus Crouch

SOURCE: A review of *Bear's Adventure,* in *The Junior Bookshelf,* Vol. 46, No. 1, February, 1982, p. 14.

As for Brian Wildsmith, he continues on the course he started many years ago. His draughtsmanship—always the weakest point in his artistic equipment—has improved and with it his range of graphic images, but he is still essentially the master of colour. His story is longer and more complex than he has tried before, but it has no great distinction of word or idea. It provides the excuse for some splendid openings in which literally all the colours of the rainbow assault the senses. An exciting visual experience, the bear has more emotional appeal than most of Mr. Wildsmith's creation.

Margery Fisher

SOURCE: A review of *Bear's Adventure,* in *Growing Point,* Vol. 20, No. 6, March, 1982, p. 4036.

The sequence of incidents after a bear has fallen asleep in a balloon tethered in the mountains is built round certain familiar places and people—a television studio, a sports stadium, a pop group—and in each case the absurdity of a shaggy bear being mistaken for a visiting celebrity is prolonged in dazzling colour and geometrical patterns elegantly deployed; angles and perspective are manipulated to give an air of fantasy to solid objects, and the whole book has an airy quality that adds a fairy-tale touch to the comedy of incongruity.

Celia Berridge

SOURCE: A review of *Bear's Adventure,* in *The School Librarian,* Vol. 30, No. 1, March, 1982, p. 27.

Brian Wildsmith's 1981 offering is his usual combination of colourful illustrations and a pleasantly simple animal tale. The story is no great shakes. A bear climbs into the basket of a hot-air balloon and is carried away to a city where he encounters, uncomprehendingly, skyscrapers, a fancy-dress parade, a television interview, and a pop concert. This gives Mr. Wildsmith the opportunity to draw some splendid set-pieces—a luminous yellow taxicab against a mauve background, a motorbike, a helicopter, a fire engine—giving the curious impression that this is very much a picture book for boys. The pictures are psychologically interesting. Mr. Wildsmith employs the same kind of arbitrary embellishments that children use in their drawings. Parts of each picture are decorated with numerals, letters, stripes, dots, zig-zags; but, unlike a child, Mr. Wildsmith balances the busy effect thus created with large expanses of single colour, or with blocks of black. What a pity that the story is not strong enough to complement these deceptively-sophisticated, rich, lovely pictures.

Ilene Cooper

SOURCE: A review of *Bear's Adventure,* in *Booklist,* Vol. 78, No. 22, August, 1982, p. 1529.

A big brown bear crawls into a balloon basket for a nap; instead he finds himself on the airways to high adventure when he lands in the middle of a big city parade. Everyone thinks the bear is actually a man dressed in a costume, and so he gets shuffled from parade, to TV interview, to footrace, to rock concert until he miraculously winds up at home. The story has a silly infectious humor kids will adore; on another level Wildsmith is giving his audience a sly wink, commenting on people who look but don't really see. Bright vibrant circus colors highlight the amusing oversize pictures. Young gigglers will appreciate Bear looking anxiously out the window of a bright yellow taxi or being "interviewed" on TV. A rollicking journey that can be undertaken individually or with the story-hour crowd.

Nancy Palmer

SOURCE: A review of *Bear's Adventure,* in *School Library Journal,* Vol. 28, No. 10 August, 1982, p. 109.

A large, hairy brown bear crawls into the gondola of a hot-air balloon, falls asleep and floats away. A bird punctures his balloon, and he drifts down into the city to find himself leading a parade, being interviewed on TV, winning a stadium race, dancing on stage at a rock concert and, to escape his "fans," climbing a fire-truck ladder into the same hot-air balloon he started out in. When its pilots land for a mountain picnic, Bear waddles away "dazed and bewildered." Bear's retention of bear-ness through all his encounters, his essential incomprehension and our brief glimpses into his muddled ursine mind lend the ordinary text a winsome absurdity and bring Bear's circular adventure to a satisfying close. The large, vivid double spreads in watercolor, felt pen and ink are unmistakably Wildsmith: the flat forms with their bright geometric pieces, the subtle designs and various textures of backgrounds, the fine-line detailing emerging through wash or in tandem with big patches of color—the color that is everywhere, limning everything and its parts. Details that the story lacks, e.g., how Bear's balloon rises in the first place, go unnoticed in the rich mix of forms, styles and colors that fill each oversize page.

James A. Norsworthy, Jr.

SOURCE: A review of *Bear's Adventure,* in *Catholic Library World,* Vol. 54, No. 4, November, 1982, p. 183.

Sleepy bear looks for a place to take a nap and finds it in the basket of a hot air balloon. Without realizing what is happening, the balloon rises and bear has a series of adventures that are delight and surprise until he ends where he began. While this book may be effectively read on the simple story level, enough basic material is in its pages to challenge the most astute reader by asking them to go beyond the simple meaning into determining why and how things were accepted as they were. A delightful book to entertain, challenge and confront the reader in many ways. As always, Wildsmith's large, bold, graphic art presents a vivid artistic experience. Highly recommended for kindergarten through third grade.

PELICAN (1982)

Zena Sutherland

SOURCE: A review of *Pelican,* in *Bulletin of the Center for Children's Books,* Vol. 36, No. 7, March, 1983, pp. 139-40.

Wildsmith uses half-pages, in the style of John Goodall, to show changes of scene in this story of a boy who finds a large egg that proves to be a pelican and who makes a pet of the bird although it creates problems. The pelican likes fish and snatches them from fishing boats and frozen food counters—but is slow to learn how to catch fish from the river. It is useful, however, bringing groceries home in its beak and carrying lunch to the boy's father when he's working in the fields. Eventually the bird flies off to live with other pelicans, the punch line of the story being that it is disclosed that the bird, who's been referred to as "he" throughout the story, is a female. The text is adequate in structure, and the style is unexceptionable; it is, as is usually true of Wildsmith's books, the lavish and striking use of color in handsomely composed paintings that is impressive: the frozen food counter glows with magenta and royal blue, the landscape is effulgently vernal, the farmer's clothes are dazzling: yellow shirt and boots, blue pants, red and green jacket.

Publishers Weekly

SOURCE: A review of *Pelican,* in *Publishers Weekly,* Vol. 223, No. 12, March 25, 1983, p. 51.

Here's another offering from the immensely talented British artist and Kate Greenaway Medalist. Wildsmith's splashy paintings in bright and beautiful hues feature split pages that continue the action of the other side, a sure bet for enjoyment by readers of all sizes. Paul, who lives on a farm, one day finds a speckled egg inside a box and puts it beneath his hen so it will hatch. What eventually comes out is rather odd-looking, not at all like a chick, and causes immediate problems when he won't eat chicken feed. Paul's family figures out the bird's a pelican when he's caught chomping the fish they'd intended for dinner, but when Paul tries to teach him to fish for himself he can't quite get the hang of it. He wreaks all sorts of havoc, but grows to be a bit of a pet around the farm, diffusing Paul's father's threat to send him to a zoo, and he finally figures out how to catch his own dinner instead of stealing it. One day he flies off to be with other pelicans, revealing a surprise for the reader at the end: "he" is really a she and is last seen sitting happily on a newly laid egg of her own.

Kirkus Reviews

SOURCE: A review of *Pelican,* in *Kirkus Reviews,* Vol. LI, No. 8, April 15, 1983, p. 458.

A large, typically multi-colored, characteristically fanciful Wildsmith product—with split pages that supply the strung-together story with a little internal drama (and an excuse, maybe, for being as arbitrary as it is). Thus, the surprise of turning a half-page and seeing a box falling off a passing truck—with farm-boy Paul, who's watching from a tree—may keep kids from wondering how a box with a pelican egg got on that truck. And the long time it takes Paul's mother and father to recognize that this saucer-beaked, fish-loving bird is a pelican may also be overlooked, along with the incongruities that attend his learning to catch fish for himself, in the fun of turning the pages. (These people are garbed and housed like Elizabethans—but go to the supermarket and drive a tractor.) The story is negligible and old-hat any way you look at it—the pelican eventually learns to dive for fish (from watching a kingfisher), and ultimately flies away "to be with other pelicans"—but where the Wildsmith books retain their allure, the split pages will provide an extra fillip.

Ronald A. Jobe

SOURCE: A review of *Pelican,* in *Language Arts,* Vol. 60, No. 6, September, 1983, p. 775.

The end has a great beginning! A young boy's discovery of an unusually large egg, which hatched into an even more unusual looking bird, created endless problems. Raised as a chicken, he neither resembled a chicken nor shared a preference for corn; he loved fish! This love was frustrating because he just couldn't be trained to catch fish. Eventually he was recognized as a pelican and became an amusingly useful family member, until self-discovery led HER instinctively to search for the land of the pelicans!

Showing new directions in his art, Brian Wildsmith retains aspects of his earlier vibrant collages, while introducing a startling split-page concept allowing for a sense of increased action, surprise and intrigue. He is extremely successful in his use of open white space, intense black, watery blurs for an out-of-focus effect, and richly textured pages that shout to be felt. Wildsmith also accurately captures the delicate ambiance and sense of light found in a Mediterranean French village.

This is a direct well-conceived story providing insight into a boy's loving care for a pet bird. Although age-old in theme, each time a boy adopts a wild bird the feelings of love, understanding and delight are captured anew, only to be lost temporarily when the bird flies to its freedom.

Kathleen Brachmann

SOURCE: A review of *Pelican,* in *School Library Journal,* Vol. 30, No. 1, September, 1983, p. 113.

When a box falls off a passing truck, Paul opens it to find a large egg, out of which hatches a baby pelican. Because of the bird's habit of stealing fish from local fishermen, Paul teaches his pet to fish for itself, and all is well until the day the pelican, now grown, flies away to join the others of his species. The story is a simple and time-honored one: unusual pet temporarily wreaks havoc before becoming an accepted member of the family. Wildsmith's illustrations are large, bold and brightly colored, this time in a variety of styles ranging from impressionism in garish colors to detailed reality in vivid colors to muted and bold landscapes. A beguiling feature is the split-page format, where half-pages open to reveal small surprises, enabling the illustrations to tell the story even more effectively than the text. The theme and illustrations make it a natural for story-telling.

DAISY (1984)

Kirkus Reviews

SOURCE: A review of *Daisy,* in *Kirkus Reviews,* Vol. LII, Nos. 1-5, March 1, 1984, p. J-12.

Wherein Daisy the up-country cow goes to Hollywood: an overblown trifle that does, however, deliver its money's-worth of split-page visual spectacle. In a setting that might be the Tyrol (the usual quaint cottages and parti-colored costumes), Farmer Brown watches television and yearns for a tractor, while cow Daisy, watching from outside the window, yearns to see the world. When Farmer Brown forgets to close the gate, Daisy makes her way to the mountain village, walks from slope to roof, attracts a TV crew—and in short order is being cranked aboard a ship, bound for Hollywood. Naturally, she's "a big star"—amusingly, in Westerns. She's also "on the cover of all the best magazines"—and, least amusingly, she appears in a bubble-bath ad. And so it goes on, to excess—with Daisy trampling a banquet table (like some soused Roman emperor) and calling for "fresh grass and buttercups." As a vet prescribes, it's time for lonesome Daisy to go home—by open plane and parachute to a hearty welcome from Farmer Brown. When last seen, Daisy is her old self—watching her star self on TV. There's a certain match here, at least, between the contents and the form.

Zena Sutherland

SOURCE: A review of *Daisy,* in *Bulletin of the Center for Children's Books,* Vol. 37, No. 8, April, 1984, p. 158.

Brian Wildsmith uses his lush palette to full advantage in an oversize book in which half-pages are used between full pages to add a fillip to the story, in the format of so many books by John Goodall. The illustrations are perhaps the chief attraction of the book, handsome in composition and use of color, but the story should also appeal to the read-aloud audience; it describes a cow, Daisy, who succeeds not only in her desire to see the world but also becomes a famous movie star. Eventually Daisy becomes homesick and pines for her English meadow, so there's one last Hollywood film, "Daisy Come Home," that records Daisy's parachute ride to the ground and her reunion with Farmer Brown. As placid and pleasant as chewing a cud.

Ilene Cooper

SOURCE: A review of *Daisy,* in *Booklist,* Vol. 80, No. 17, May 1, 1984, p. 1255.

Wildsmith makes the most of a well-designed, oversize layout to tell the story of Daisy, a cow who becomes famous. Farmer Brown is a hard worker who enjoys spending his evenings watching TV with Daisy. His dream is to own a tractor he has seen advertised on television; Daisy's dream is to experience the exciting life she has glimpsed on the small screen. One day Daisy escapes the confines of her field and finds herself on top of the church roof. Her escapades make the news, and a famous producer gets the farmer's consent to take her to Hollywood, where she makes movies and embarks upon life in the fast lane. But as time goes on, Daisy finds she's wearying of all the excesses. Her producer parachutes her home to the farmer, who is as glad to get back his companion as Daisy is to be there. Wildsmith's message about happiness being found in your own backyard may seem didactic to adults but less obvious to little ones. Whether or not children catch the book's philosophical drift, they will enjoy the buoyant pictures that cascade with unusual shapes and carnival colors. The split pages work exceptionally well, with each cleverly revealing a new aspect of the story.

Margery Fisher

SOURCE: A review of *Daisy,* in *Growing Point,* Vol. 23, No. 2, July, 1984, p. 4295.

Using half-page flaps, Wildsmith doubles the incidents and the humour in the tale of a cow whose sense of adventure is awakened by television. Her expedition to the world beyond her mountain farm seems to be ended when the village priest sends for the farmer to bring her down from the roof which she has treated as a continuation of the hillside; fortunately for her a television crew happens to be on the spot so off she goes to Hollywood to become a star. The end is predictable: the course of the tale is irresistibly and exquisitely pursued in scenes in which tools and roofs, flowers and costume and all the impedimenta of life in city and country are blended in glowing, crowded, superbly ordered scenes.

Nancy C. Hammond

SOURCE: A review of *Daisy,* in *The Horn Book Magazine,* Vol. LX, No. 4, August, 1984, p. 463.

Daisy, a discontented cow who longs to see the world, attracts a television crew when she wanders away and walks onto the rooftops of a village nestled on a hillside. Shortly thereafter, she is starring in Hollywood Westerns, in bubble-bath ads, and on magazine covers and being feted at banquets with delicacies like caviar and smoked salmon. But the homesick cow longs for grass, buttercups, and her old field. Thus, her final movie features her homecoming as she parachutes—mooing contentedly—from the wings of a biplane into her familiar field. Now satisfied to be living "where she really belonged," she watches her adventures unfold on television. The author-artist continues to be more inspired by color than by words. Still, despite the perfunctory writing, his use of the expansive technique of half-page pictures alternately bound in with full pages creates some of his most varied and animated illustrations; dazzling colors and designs are offset by large, white spaces and by intricate, technical drawings of photographic equipment and machines.

Anne McKeithen Goodman

SOURCE: A review of *Daisy,* in *School Library Journal,* Vol. 30, No. 10 August, 1984, pp. 66-7.

After watching television through Farmer Brown's window, Daisy the cow wants to see the world. Her opportunity comes when the gate is left open and she saunters into town (which is built into a hillside) and onto a roof. While the townspeople watch the fire department rescue her, a TV cameraman captures the scene on film. Thus begins Daisy's movie career and a series of adventures—until she decides she'd rather go home and eat grass. The story is predictable but told with affection and humor. Most outstanding are the sweeping illustrations—predominately watercolors—that cover each page with vibrant color, rich texture and pattern. Each page is followed by a half page that carries the story forward and insures page-turning. The combination of visual stimuli and gentle fun equals high marks.

GIVE A DOG A BONE (1985)

Publishers Weekly

SOURCE: A review of *Give a Dog a Bone,* in *Publishers Weekly,* Vol. 228, No. 12, September 20, 1985, pp. 108-09.

Lush color and continual surprises in paintings by England's Kate Greenaway Medalist grace the story of a stray mutt, avid for a bone to crunch. Split pages invite kids to make a game of discovering how the dog snatches then loses bone after bone as he frisks through the streets of a medieval community. Wildsmith's sly inventions pile on extra giggles: the pictures include a modern street sweeper that swallows one bone, a tractor that flattens another and more jokey anachronisms in the ancient setting. Then there is the museum where a dinosaur skeleton falls on the stray when he tries to steal its leg. The curious cat who races after the homeless canine to observe the quest is another comic touch. All this japery is crowned by the finale in which the dog is a loner no longer, assured of amassing as many bones as he can gnaw.

Jane Doonan

SOURCE: "Picturing the Scene: Picture Books 1," in *Times Literary Supplement,* No. 4313, November 29, 1985, p. 1359.

In Brian Wildsmith's new split-page picture book, ***Give a Dog a Bone,*** images in uninhibited colour seem to tumble on to the page, not once but right through the

From Whose Hat Was That?, *written and illustrated by Brian Wildsmith and his daughter, Rebecca.*

entire sequence. It is carnival time in an Italianate walled city set in a necklace of hills, buzzing with quaintly costumed citizens, overrun with curious tabby cats, hit by road-works, and hosting a circus. Naturally it is a very noisy place. Enter Stray, a poor grey dog, in search of a bone. Finding one is easy; each turn of the page records her luck, but reversal swiftly follows, as mischance lies in wait to rob her, hidden behind the next half-page. On she traipses, winning and losing, hungry and resourceful. Success comes at last. The text quietens as the city is left behind, and Stray is taken by her new owners to live happily ever after in the countryside. This picture book, dedicated to all strays, is one to contemplate, explore and return to.

Martha Rosen

SOURCE: A review of *Give a Dog a Bone,* in *School Library Journal,* Vol. 32, No. 5, January, 1986, p. 62.

Wildsmith's inimitable artistic style is evident on every page of this colorful, oversized picture book. He again enlists the clever device of alternating half-page and full-page illustrations that he used in ***Pelican*** and ***Daisy.*** On each half-page are both text and picture, which elucidate and enlarge upon each incident. The story is leisurely and anecdotal, relating the adventures of an appealingly scruffy stray sort-of-terrier as she gamely pursues an elusive bone. Although Stray at times possesses an assortment of bones, she manages to lose all of them. Stray's travels from butcher shop to the dinosaur room of a museum to her "adoption" at last by a newly married couple (she goes after a bone tied to the honeymoon carriage and ends up part of the wedding entourage) offer many opportunities for lavish and lively illustrations. The time frame is a bit confusing, as Stray encounters modern machinery in the streets and at the circus, while the town scenes, people's clothing and the horse and carriage seem to belong to an earlier era. A rather tame but lovely story.

Denise M. Wilms

SOURCE: A review of *Give a Dog a Bone,* in *Booklist,* Vol. 82, No. 9, January 1, 1986, pp. 687-88.

Wildsmith's attractive illustrations elevate this simple tale of a stray dog whose lost bones finally lead to a happy home. The artist's usual intense, splashy colors are moderated here to bring forth scenes of contemporary village life in an Old World setting. Among the stucco, tile-roofed buildings, a lonely stray begs a posh poodle for a bone. The poodle obliges, but no sooner does Stray walk away with it than he barks at a cat and drops the bone only to see it crushed by a steamroller. In one contrivance after another, the poor dog gets and loses a series of bones—until Stray lands in a wedding carriage that results in a happily ever after for dogs as well as newlyweds. Half-pages are used to show the action; each turning reveals the latest disaster to befall Stray's bone. There's lots of child appeal here both in story and in bookmaking.

Ethel R. Twichell

SOURCE: A review of *Give a Dog a Bone,* in *The Horn Book Magazine,* Vol. LXII, No. 1, January-February, 1986, pp. 53-4.

Scraggly and probably flea-ridden Stray finds and loses some choice bones on a doggy romp through a town which combines the pageantry of a medieval town festival with the modern necessities of bulldozers and trucks. Between each colorful double-page spread a perfectly matched and cleverly conceived half page is inserted which can be turned to reveal a further surprise in Stray's adventures. Intent on her single-minded pursuit, Stray is all but oblivious to the panorama of activity which teems around her and of the havoc she creates from time to time. The full-color and generously scaled illustrations do full justice to the background magic of fairgrounds and the flurry of a circus parade. Even the clutter and mess of road repairs becomes merely a joyous disorder when seen through the artist's more discerning eyes. Bright and beguiling, large in conception but attentive to entertaining details and motifs, the book in every way fulfills an accomplished and painterly departure from the illustrator's earlier work with brighter, stronger colors and busily filled pages. That Stray finds her final bone attached to the horse-drawn cart of a newly married couple bodes well for her future and is a delightful conclusion for the child in all of us that longs for happy endings.

M. Hobbs

SOURCE: A review of *Give a Dog a Bone,* in *The Junior Bookshelf,* Vol. 50, No. 1, February, 1986, pp. 13-14.

Brian Wildsmith's new split-page book, ***Give a Dog a Bone,*** is quite another thing. The story-line is slight. Stray is characterised more by hairiness than sense. He is unable to keep any bone he acquires, legally or otherwise, chiefly by tangling with a series of heavy mechanical vehicles, though his choice of bone is indiscriminate: a dinosaur being taken to a museum proves little use. His last bone-mistake, however, tied to a wedding-coach on which he rides, leads him to a home. It is Wildsmith's soft colour-washes with firmer jewel colours and the gloriously detailed Italian hill-town settings which the reader will treasure and over which he will pore endlessly.

GOAT'S TRAIL (1986)

Publishers Weekly

SOURCE: A review of *Goat's Trail,* in *Publishers Weekly,* Vol. 230, No. 8, August 22, 1986, p. 96.

DING DONG, VROOM VROOM, HONK HONK, UMP-PA-PA are the sounds that lure the wild goat off his high mountain top, where he leads a dull and lonely life. Down the mountain he goes to hear the bees buzz and the wind whistle, and to seek excitement in the town below. Along the way, he is joined by some sheep, a cow, a pig and a donkey. In the end, the animals find themselves in a classroom where they create chaos and are then reunited with their owners who take them home. Satisfied with his adventure, the goat returns to his mountain top alone. Throughout the story, the sounds of the animals mingle with the sounds of the city, creating the effect of a cumulative tale. Children will enjoy the musical cadence of the text and the attractive watercolor illustrations of European country and city scapes. And they'll especially enjoy the die-cut doorways that lead the way as we follow goat and his friends on their trail.

Margery Fisher

SOURCE: A review of *Goat's Trail,* in *Growing Point,* Vol. 25, No. 5, January, 1987, p. 4747.

Wildsmith's familiar swatches, stripes and zigzags of colour support a cumulative tale about a goat who leaves his mountain fastness to take a look at the nearby town. Along the way he collects for companions sheep, cow, pig and donkey; the last member of the group obligingly pulls them all on a cart until he sits down obstinately like his kind in the middle of a crowded street. There follows a confusion of interests as one after another the owners of the animals claim them, leaving the goat to return alone to a silence that he can now appreciate. The story serves as a peg on which to hang a series of spectacular scenes, with apertures contrived on some pages (doors, windows, archways) to add drama to the sequence.

Ellen Mandel

SOURCE: A review of *Goat's Trail,* in *Booklist,* Vol. 83, No. 10, January 15, 1987, p. 789.

From a medieval-looking walled village tucked in a valley, curious sounds waft up the mountain to a lonely goat who sets off down the slopes to investigate. As he makes his way, he invites other animals to join him. The meandering goat, cow, sheep, pig, and donkey stall the city's modern-day traffic, disrupt a band's performance, and create chaos in a classroom as they discover the sources of the unfamiliar sounds. Wildsmith joyfully details the adventure in lavish, softly colored watercolors on double-page spreads. Clues identifying the noises are seen through windows or doors cut out of the illustrations; when the page is turned, the excised portion frames, for example, a perplexed shepherd or farmer left puzzling over the whereabouts of his disappeared livestock. Youngsters will enthusiastically join in the refrain of ding-dongs, ump-pa-pas, oink oinks, and whatevers as they enjoy the visual gaiety of this ludicrous escapade.

M. Hobbs

SOURCE: A review of *Goat's Trail,* in *The Junior Bookshelf,* Vol. 51, No. 1, February, 1987, p. 24.

Brian Wildsmith here uses every method available to ensure this is a book children will enjoy reading with an adult. The beauty and richness of his colours go without saying, but we have in addition a traditional-style cumulative story—the mountain goat who decides to explore the noises he can hear from the walled town below gathers as he goes sheep, a cow, a pig, a donkey and his cart—cumulative noises for the young listener to reproduce (shown in capitals), and holes in the pages which show glimpses of what lies in front and of puzzled people behind. The animals disrupt traffic, make chaos among a brass band and in a schoolroom, but then resist the goat's call to further adventures and go off home—somewhat a whimper of an ending, were it not for the final magic landscape of medieval city, wide flowery meadows with paths winding through and distant mountains.

Lee Bock

SOURCE: A review of *Goat's Trail,* in *School Library Journal,* Vol. 33, No. 7, March, 1987, p. 151.

If ever a tale was fit for reading aloud, this is it. With a delightful use of sounds, Wildsmith has created a classically styled cumulative tale. ***Goat's Trail*** opens serenely with a goat on a quiet mountain top, builds into a riotous traffic jam and schoolroom scenes, then backs down again to the quiet mountain scene. Illustrations are unmistakably Wildsmith, with large, richly detailed pages and highly stylized characters. The book offers the added bonus of cleverly placed die-cut windows on each spread. The time frame of the story is an odd mix of the medieval and modern. Much of the action, for example, occurs in a walled medieval village peopled with brightly costumed folks who may drive a donkey cart . . . or a semi-truck. There is a lot of fun waiting for the lucky folks who get their hands on ***Goat's Trail.***

Elizabeth S. Watson

SOURCE: A review of *Goat's Trail,* in *The Horn Book Magazine,* Vol. LXIII, No. 3, May-June, 1987, pp. 337-38.

A wild goat hears some new sounds from town—"DING-DONG. HONK, HONK. VROOM, VROOM. UMP-PA-PA"—and finds them far more exciting than the quiet of his mountain top. He sets out to see what life is like away from his peaceful home and soon meets some sheep. A new sound is introduced—"BAA, BAA." As the cumulative tale progresses, each new sound is added to the basic phrase as each creature joins the goat on his way to town. The sound's producer is first introduced through a cutout hole—a cow, then a pig, a donkey, an ump-pa-pa band, and, finally, a school class. Looking back through the hole, we see the people who have lost the creatures searching for them. The book is well thought out and cleverly constructed to make the most of a simple tale and minimal construction techniques. When the parade of creatures enters the schoolroom to investigate the last sound—"A . . . B . . . C"—chaos reigns. The resulting mess is shown in a delightful double-page spread. The bright colors and rhythmic text make the book a natural choice for story hours, while the multitude of details in the pictures will provide pleasure for the youngster who has more time to pore over the illustrations.

CAROUSEL (1988)

M. Hobbs

SOURCE: A review of *Carousel,* in *The Junior Bookshelf,* Vol. 53, No. 1, February, 1989, p. 11.

In Brian Wildsmith's rather sober tale, the yearly circus visits the town, and Rosie and her brother Tom ride as usual on their favourite carousel. That winter, she falls ill, and has to remain in bed a long time. On her birthday, Tom asks friends to bring her pictures of her favourite carousel rides. That night, her illness comes to a crisis, and in her delirium she imagines herself sailing out into the night to the lands they represent, from the Snowflake to the Wings of Time. Next morning her temperature has fallen, and she recovers completely in time for the fair's next visit, when she thanks the carousel as she rides on it. Most of the illustrations are a uniform two to a page, contrasting with the rich double-page spreads of Rosie's delirium and her final ride. Brian Wildsmith's colours, of course, are never uniform: from the royal blues and scarlets of the fair we pass through white and grey to the dark midnight blues of Rosie's ride, until we end with the carousel once more.

David Lewis

SOURCE: A review of *Carousel,* in *The School Librarian,* Vol. 37, No. 1, February, 1989, p. 18.

This is a handsome looking book, the first part of which tells of brother and sister, Rosie and Tom, their excitement at the arrival in town of the travelling fair and of Rosie's sickness and decline during the following winter. The tale here is illustrated with small, self-contained, pretty paintings laid out two to a page. Unfortunately these rather static tableaux fail to convey any real excitement or joy though this is clearly called for by the text. There is simply no real sense of *carnival.* During Rosie's fever-dream which occupies the second part of the book and during which Rosie is swept away and 'cured' by the carousel, Brian Wildsmith's painterly instincts take over and he swamps each double-page spread from edge to edge with his designs. The biggest disappointment here is in the snatches of verse with which the designs are annotated—they are lame to the point of banality and illustrate just how hard it is to write good text for children. Ultimately, though the colours vibrate on the page, the tale refuses to come to life.

Nancy Seiner

SOURCE: A review of *Carousel,* in *School Library Journal,* Vol. 35, No. 6, February, 1989, pp. 76-7.

A lively, colorful fantasy. The setting is a small town in which the most exciting event for children is the yearly visit of a travelling fair. When one child, Rosie, becomes ill, the doctor says that she must be given hope. Her brother plans with his friends to give Rosie something to keep her spirits up, a toy carousel and hand-drawn pictures of unusual carousel seats. The next night Rosie dreams of a magic carousel ride through the sky where she enjoys the special qualities of each seat. In the morning Rosie has made dramatic steps toward recovery. She knows that the carousel has given her hope. Wildsmith's pictures and words complement the story. In the realistic parts, the pictures are small, two to a page, and crowded with details. The town, the trucks, and the children are brightly colored, stylized, and static. The narration is simple, one or two short sentences to a picture. However, during Rosie's dream the pictures soar. Each one, spread across two pages, has motion and color. Here the story is written in rhymed couplets. This would be an excellent book to read to small groups of preschoolers, and primary grade children will enjoy reading it themselves.

Ellen Mandel

SOURCE: A review of *Carousel,* in *Booklist,* Vol. 85, No. 12, February 15, 1989, p. 1006.

Dazzling in rich, full-palette hues, Wildsmith's intricate pen-and-ink gems express the gaiety of an itinerant carnival and its carousel that particularly delights young Rosie. After taking ill in winter, Rosie remains cheerlessly confined to bed even when spring's flowering vines entwine her window. Her friends thoughtfully paint pictures of the carousel figures she adores, and her brother buys her a musical merry-go-round toy. As multicolored points of color sprinkle an air of fantasy across the pages, Rosie dreams her carousel toy transports her through the night, around the world, and into the wondrous realms represented by each of its beloved figures. In the morning Rosie awakens, her fever finally broken, her spirits lifted, her health renewed. In an explosive amalgamation of his vibrant and familiar imagery and styles, Wildsmith gives fanciful testimony to the healing power of positive suggestion.

N. Tucker

SOURCE: A review of *Carousel,* in *Books for Your Children,* Vol. 24, No. 1, Spring, 1989, p. 13.

This picture story concerns a sick child returning to health after a magical, night-time ride on the roundabout of the title. Initially a little small and cramped, Brain Wildsmith's illustrations spread out with all their usual glowing colours and swirling shapes once Rosie's marvellous journey gets under way. Prose turns to verse as fabulous beasts, exotic birds and multi-coloured courtiers crowd round her in something that resembles both a delirious dream and a book-lover's fantasy. A lovely book.

Donnarae MacCann and Olga Richard

SOURCE: A review of *Carousel,* in *Wilson Library Bulletin,* Vol. 63, No. 10, June, 1989, p. 97.

Brian Wildsmith is another legerdemainist, but he does not embrace the surrealist enigmas of Peter Sis. Instead, he incorporates in ***Carousel*** a dream state that is explainable in everyday terms, one induced by a sick child's delirium. This plot construction opens the way for imaginatively designed pages and the full expression of Wildsmith's incredible feel for color. The tale revolves around Rosie, who is laid up for the winter with an obstinate illness. Her family is advised by the doctor to strengthen the child's morale, and her brother leads the way with the purchase of a toy carousel (a replica of the one in a traveling fair that frequently visits the village). Rosie's feverish dream is populated with wondrous carousel figures who help her through her crisis.

Examples of Wildsmith's humor, tenderness, bold sense of composition, and extravagant treatment of color abound in this book. He is a daring artist because he is a tasteful one. He balances the ornate (almost baroque) sections of his paintings with great swoops of soft grays, or he stabilizes busy areas with precise, geometric drawing. We have space to mention only a few special moments: a painting that depicts a procession of bright trucks moving through the dusk; an illustration of cubist houses (each broken into light and dark geometric divisions); great, soft bed covers of blended watery colors in the scene that begins Rosie's dream; and an amazing snowflake image.

A CHRISTMAS STORY (1989)

Susan Hepler

SOURCE: A review of *A Christmas Story,* in *School Library Journal,* Vol. 35, No. 14, October, 1989, p. 45.

Spectacular illustrations show the Nativity as backdrop for a story of a small donkey whose mother carries Mary to Bethlehem. A neighbor, Rebecca, offers to care for the donkey, but he pines so for his mother that she promises to take him to her. At each stop on the road, Rebecca asks if anyone has seen a donkey and two people, and is improbably but miraculously steered in the directions of the stable. Wildsmith's illustrations are striking and vivid. His angels brightly garbed in geometric patterns alone are worth the price of the book. For children who already know the Christmas story, this is a chance to see it from another point of view, and to enjoy Wildsmith's elegant illustrations.

Margery Fisher

SOURCE: A review *A Christmas Story,* in *Growing Point,* Vol. 28, No. 4, November, 1989, p. 5258.

The deepest meaning of the Nativity story is suggested in gilding for the endpapers and in the star shining over the stable; the human aspect is seen in the attitudes of oddly toylike figures of people and animals and in a symbolically rough wooden stable. The whole book is embellished with Wildsmithian decoration—snowflake shapes, birds and animals ordinary enough (owl, cat, duck, hen) but bedecked with jewelled colours, the use of insets for the Annunciation and the conference of the three kings with Herod. The artist has used all his skill in interpreting an anecdote simple in itself (a young donkey, led by a girl, seeks the mother donkey on which Mary had ridden) but serving as an image for a universal myth.

Kirkus Reviews

SOURCE: A review of *A Christmas Story,* in *Kirkus Reviews,* Vol. LVII, No. 22, November 15, 1989, p. 1679.

From a noted British illustrator who has long been a popular favorite, one of the most beautiful books he has done in quite a while.

The unexceptional text here focuses on a little donkey—who is left behind when his mother carries the Holy Family to Bethlehem—and the neighbor girl, Rebecca, who sets out with him to find them. But the rich, dark colors, the delightful Wildsmith details (including a little tiger cat who tags along on the journey), and the unusual effects he produces with the addition of bright gold—in the stars, the angel, and even the city of Jerusalem—will appeal to a broad audience. It does seem odd, in illustrations that clearly derive inspiration from the appearance of the real Holy Land, to show both Rebecca and Mary (inconsistently) as blonde; but perhaps that license should be as forgivable as the swirling, starry snow. Regardless, this is sure to be a favorite gift book for the coming holidays.

A. R. Williams

SOURCE: A review of *A Christmas Story,* in *The Junior Bookshelf,* Vol. 54, No. 1, February, 1990, pp. 19-20.

Mary and Joseph set off for Bethlehem leaving behind the new foal of their ass. It pines for its mother. A village child takes pity on its plight and also sets out for Bethlehem with the sturdy baby, asking for directions from other travellers and country folk. Thus takes place a journey parallel to that of the Holy Family (to be). Along the way glimpses are caught of the other actors in the drama of the nativity en route or en levee. The return journey, more briefly, is similarly highlighted. The general effect is delightful. The two-page illustrations executed in Mr. Wildsmith's idiosyncratic style are not only charming but contain so much for the child of 3 or 4 to *look at* while the story is explained with or without the minimal text. It was a minor stroke of genius, one is tempted to think, to have these pictures "illuminated" in gold making them not only different but richer in colour. The passing vegetation sometimes appears odd and cats are not mentioned in the Bible but the tigerish kitten which follows the star is too witty to cavil at.

Hazel Townson

SOURCE: A review of *A Christmas Story,* in *The School Librarian,* Vol. 38, No. 2, May, 1990, p. 63.

This picture book is the perfect book to wake up to on Christmas morning. The pictures, with their special gold effects, have all the colour, mystery and splendour that children associate with Christmas, while the story, although still the original Christmas story, has its own original twist. Little Rebecca has been asked to look after a baby donkey while its mother travels with Mary and Joseph to Bethlehem. But when the baby donkey grieves, Rebecca takes it to find its mother. On their journey they pass Herod's palace, meet the shepherds, find the baby Jesus and the wise men; and the baby donkey is reunited with its mother.

THE SNOW COUNTRY PRINCE (written by Daisaku Ikeda and translated by Geraldine McCaughrean, 1990)

Publishers Weekly

SOURCE: A review of *The Snow Country Prince,* in *Publishers Weekly,* Vol. 238, No. 41, September 13, 1991, p. 79.

Winter comes early and with a bitter vengeance to the Snow Country. For young Mariko and her brother Kazuo, the harsh season signals the annual departure of their fisherman father, who must travel inland to find work until spring. But the advent of frosty weather also means that the swans come to shelter on the coastline. Mariko and Kazuo feed the helpless birds so that they won't freeze to death; in return for their kindness, the Snow Country Prince, "robed in a dazzle of frost-glory," appears to the children, offering these words of wisdom: "Whatever happens, don't give up." The universal message of this Japanese folktale is well-suited to young readers grappling with their burgeoning independence and responsibility. Wildsmith's lustrous paintings are sparked by dashes of brilliant color—in the plumage of birds, woolen hats and the Snow Prince's vestments. Despite the icy landscape, this thoughtful collaboration exudes plenty of warmth.

Donnarae MacCann and Olga Richard

SOURCE: A review of *The Snow Country Prince,* in *Wilson Library Bulletin,* Vol. 66, No. 7, March, 1992, p. 93.

In an interview with Pamela Marsh in 1969, Brian Wildsmith emphasized "soul" and "work" in his discussion of book illustration:

> You plant a way of looking—not just at books but an open way of seeing so that the child is able to look at anything and enjoy it just for itself. . . . Somehow a painting must express the soul of a thing—whatever it is that makes a thing what it is. . . .
>
> It's hard work. All the time you are watching and receiving images. Like having fleas—you just can't get away from them.

Over three decades Wildsmith has worked to share those soul qualities with children, and the images that still pursue him give ***The Snow Country Prince*** its artistic dimensions.

Daisaku Ikeda's text supplies Wildsmith with a good blend of fantasy and human drama. The author explains that the Japanese leave their fishing nets in wintertime and seek inland jobs, while migrating swans find refuge in the coastal swamplands. Some particular swans are fed and nursed to health by young Mariko and Kazuo—a care-giving endeavor that has its parallel when their mother hurries to the city to assist their injured father. Life is hard, but the Snow Country Prince, guardian of the birds, swings through the sky, sending encouragement to nature lovers: "Whatever happens," he says, "don't give up." Mariko and her brother have extraordinary reserves of tenderness as well as perseverance, and both the human and bird families are reunited.

Ikeda adds occasional poetic touches, as when he describes the winter ice sheets that "grew and ground together and growled fiercely"; but the text as a whole teeters on the brink of predictability and needs the consistent eloquence of Wildsmith's paintings.

The pages are saturated with the most exceptional fusion of light, color, pattern, and space. Everything is recognizable but imbued with the artist's own magical inventions. To carry the mood of the tale, Wildsmith paints miles and miles of sky, water, and woodland. In one episode, a sleigh is surrounded by acres of birches in different shades and sizes. The artist lets the trees recede on a snow-spattered picture plane, creating a mystical illusion of depth. In the last drawing of the injured swan, the scene implies the haunting silences of nature, yet we feel a thunderous "swoosh." At a purely emotional level, the painting's power suggests an airborne jet.

Wildsmith's concept of beauty is in the best Romantic tradition, but he is always intensely individual. His scope, skill, and awesome creativity—these are all the outcome of his coherent aesthetic. As he stated in his interview,

> You must make a book that in some strange way appeals to the child and at the same time deepens his [and her] artistic sensibility. It must have all the qualities of a work of art—the form, the color, the texture.

And he adds this advice for parents and other educators: "You must let [children] wander among good books and choose between the good . . . and the good."

THE CHERRY TREE (written by Daisaku Ikeda; translated and retold by Geraldine McCaughrean, 1991)

Publishers Weekly

SOURCE: A review of *The Cherry Tree,* in *Publishers Weekly,* Vol. 239, No. 8, February 10, 1992, p. 80.

Hope springs eternal—even in the dark aftermath of war—as seen in this picture book. After bombs have destroyed their Japanese village and killed their father, Taichi and Yumiko's broken-hearted mother must go to town and earn money shining shoes. Left to play outdoors each day, the children encounter an old man tending a brittle, dead-looking cherry tree. They help care for the tree through the harsh winter, and despite the old man's doubts, their vigilance pays off—the resulting pink blossoms rekindle the spirits of the entire village. As in ***The Snow Country Prince,*** their previous collaboration, Ikeda and Wildsmith present a tender story about the rewards of kindness. Ikeda's quiet text is infused with the innocence and curiosity embodied in his child protagonists; his message is fundamental without being didactic. Wildsmith's airy watercolors depict a Japanese countryside in the process of rebirth—indigenous animals, plants and native people in brilliant garb all come to life. A spread showing the cherry tree in its full flowering glory is breathtaking.

Hazel Rochman

SOURCE: A review of *The Cherry Tree,* in *Booklist,* Vol. 88, No. 15, April 1, 1992, pp. 1456-57.

Translated from the Japanese and illustrated by an award-winning British artist, this handsome, large-size picture book combines messages of peace and ecology. Taichi and Yumiko's world has been shattered by war. Their father is dead; their home is gone; their mother is heart-broken. But life is renewed when they help an old man save a damaged cherry tree through a harsh winter. When it blossoms again in a "froth of flowers," as it did before the war, it brings hope to all who see it. The story's predictable and a bit sentimental. Even at the start when the village lies in ruins, the pictures are of joyful natural growth, which cuts down on tension or surprise, though it does reinforce the upbeat message. Wildsmith's unframed, double-spread watercolor paintings with exquisitely detailed line drawings are awash with glowing color and light that climax in the bursting spring of the cherry blossoms.

THE PRINCESS AND THE MOON (written by Daisaku Ikeda; translated and retold by Geraldine McCaughrean, 1992)

Janice Del Negro

SOURCE: A review of *The Princess and the Moon,* in *Booklist,* Vol. 89, No. 8, December 15, 1992, pp. 745-46.

The crescent moon that watches over all children is watching Sophie, who is "always bad-tempered, never smiling, out of step at school." One night, the moon sends the Great Moon Rabbit to fetch the recalcitrant little girl and show her what people look like "through the Moon's eyes." She sees her playmates and herself in their most perfect light, with gold capes and crowns, each one a prince or princess, "Always smiling. Always cheerful. Always friendly. Always patient." She returns to earth resolved "to be like a princess all the time." The didactic nature of the text is somewhat tempered by Wildsmith's energetic, decorative illustrations. Brilliantly colored and conceptually fantastic, they depict a Great Moon Rabbit with gleaming eyes, "its long ears . . . heavy with stardust," and capture Sophie's moonbeam journey with vigorous aplomb.

Janet M. Bair

SOURCE: A review of *The Princess and the Moon,* in *School Library Journal,* Vol. 39, No. 1, January, 1993, p. 78.

A fantasy about a little girl who is taken by the Great Moon Rabbit to the moon. Sophie asks "What have I done? Is it because I'm so bad-tempered?" Her questions indirectly reveal her behavior. In the moon's country, however, Sophie is able to see herself as she can be and others as they really are. The book's rather abstract concept—that we are all princesses and princes—may well be lost on young audiences. The Moon Rabbit tells the child that we all wear crowns, but they don't show in the sunlight. After she returns to Earth, she has learned to see things with royal, bright, and caring eyes. Sophie has changed, but it is a little obscure as to how this has come about. Wildsmith's distinctive, lavishly colored pictures are the strength of this moralistic tale.

OVER THE DEEP BLUE SEA (written by Daisaku Ikeda; translated by Geraldine McCaughrean, 1992)

Hazel Rochman

SOURCE: A review of *Over the Deep Blue Sea,* in *Booklist,* Vol. 89, No. 17, May 1, 1993, p. 1604.

The people in this oversize picture book seem small against the lavish scenery in Wildsmith's double-page-spread paintings of a lush, brilliant, unpolluted island. To Akiko and Hiroshi, their new tropical home seems like paradise, especially when they make a friend in Pablo, who shows them the secrets of his island—the rich underwater world, and the wonder of sea-turtles and other creatures who've been there for millions of years. But one day they come across a wrecked ship and learn it was left over from the war. Then Pablo won't play with Akiko and Hiroshi anymore because their "kind" were the enemy that attacked Pablo's people. The resolution comes when Pablo rows out to save Hiroshi in a storm at sea and "together" they are saved by another ship. The message is spelled out ("We're all just sailors come ashore off the same deep blue sea"), but kids will be caught by the friends and enemies story. Wildsmith's sunlit paintings express the glory that could be lost.

THE EASTER STORY (1994)

Marcus Crouch

SOURCE: A review of *The Easter Story,* in *The Junior Bookshelf,* Vol. 57, No. 4, August, 1993, p. 129.

While Brian Wildsmith tells the Easter story from the point of view of the donkey, he keeps close to the Bible but in his own—not very good—words. We don't come to Wildsmith for words but for stunning colours and memorable designs. At times these powerful golds and blues throw individual characters, especially angels, into sharp relief, reminding us that, while this is the ultimate master of the picture-book in terms of colour and design, Wildsmith does not draw very well. Never mind. Here is the authentic scene of the Holy Land, its landscapes and buildings rendered with loving care. And there are many little characteristic touches, like the cat and mouse playing hide-and-seek around the steps leading to the Upper Room. Lovely stuff. And what an astonishingly low price for all that gold-leaf.

Kirkus Reviews

SOURCE: A review of *The Easter Story,* in *Kirkus Reviews,* Vol. LXII, No. 1, January 1, 1994, p. 76.

Framing his unadorned retelling of the biblical account with his own story about Jesus' donkey, ridden to Jerusalem on Palm Sunday and last seen going home with "one of Jesus' friends" after the Ascension, Wildsmith relates key events surrounding the crucifixion in some detail; but the glory of this book—even more than its companion, ***A Christmas Story***—is its illustrations. Once again, Wildsmith's full-bleed paintings burgeon with his signature motifs—the noble towers of Jerusalem tucked among hills fading from emerald to rose; dramatically arranged crowds of delicately suggested figures; blossoms, birds, and other creatures, especially appropriate to this story of rebirth. Gleaming gold is judiciously featured: behind an arch framing Jesus, filling the sky after He rises from the tomb, radiating downward from the cross and, again, from the Ascension. But it's the bright angels overseeing each scene that capture the eye; brilliantly colored, sharply defined, they are of a world more enduring than the events among the evanescent rocks below; the glorious angel poised triumphant above the dying Jesus transcends despair. A richly complex visual feast, masterfully integrated into a reverent, unusual interpretation: Wildsmith at his best.

Roger Sutton

SOURCE: A review of *The Easter Story,* in *Bulletin of the Center for Children's Books,* Vol. 47, No. 6, February, 1994, p. 182.

While the nuns never were terribly convincing in their insistence that Easter was a much more important holiday than Christmas, it remains true that the Easter story is much more complicated, narratively and theologically, than is the story of the Nativity. Wildsmith's retelling is straightforward enough, but lacks context. "Judas had betrayed his friend," says the text, but we don't know why or for what or to whom. The addition of a little donkey to the cast ("'If I only I could help him,' thought the donkey sadly") seems meant to give the story an empathetic linchpin for young listeners, but it also seems out of place against the otherwise scrupulous adaptation. Gold-accented watercolor paintings are large and theatrical and give both the human drama and the pageantry their due, with angels always watching from above.

Elizabeth Bush

SOURCE: A review of *The Easter Story,* in *Booklist,* Vol. 90, No. 11, February 1, 1994, p. 1006.

Employing a rich palette of jewel tones and metallic golds, Wildsmith offers an opulent and symbol-laden visual re-creation of Jesus' last days. The actual retelling with the superfluous and ineffective addition of a donkey who witnesses the events is simplified, yet faithful to the biblical account. But it is the artwork, not the text, that conveys the passion of the story, which Wildsmith treats "like grand opera." Gethsemane is a riotous garden of purple and gold, textured more as drapery than foliage. The great stone walls of Jerusalem loom ominously over human figures. Even the stone tomb with its altarlike slab is framed as a proscenium arch. Throughout the drama, the figure of Jesus remains relatively small, set against huge and detailed backdrops. Yet he is never overwhelmed by his setting; Jesus is carefully framed by open space, within tightly arched trees, doors, and window frames, or amid the sweeping oval of a colonnade. After death and burial, a larger, transfigured image of Jesus dominates its setting with a translucent and ethereal quality that underscores the mysteries of the Resurrection and the Ascension. A first choice for the Easter collection.

Patricia Pearl Dole

SOURCE: A review of *The Easter Story,* in *School Library Journal,* Vol. 40, No. 4, April, 1994, p. 123.

The events of Holy Week are viewed by a little donkey who carries Jesus into Jerusalem among waving palms and excited onlookers. He watches the cleansing of the Temple, peers through a window at the Last Supper, waits in the Garden of Gethsemane, and then follows the prisoner to Caiaphas's house and Pilate's court and along the Via Dolorosa to the Crucifixion. He bears Jesus' body to the garden tomb and then witnesses the Resurrection and Ascension before returning to his home. These essentials are told rather sketchily but adequately in a simple text, but the focus is on the huge panoramic double-page spreads lit by sumptuous greens, purples, blues, and reds and highlighted in gleaming gold. The city, rising starkly on its hill, is the walled, arched, and domed Jerusalem of Crusader times. The stylized figures of the angels, soldiers, followers of Jesus, and curious onlookers are splendidly and vividly costumed; and each scene is full of action and detail. The effect of regal splendor and beauty is tied to everyday life by the presence of the wistful, bewildered little donkey who gazes astounded at the events both cruel and celestial.

JACK AND THE MEANSTALK (with daughter Rebecca Wildsmith, 1994)

Roger Sutton

SOURCE: A review of *Jack and the Meanstalk,* in *Bulletin of the Center for Children's Books,* Vol. 47, No. 9, May, 1994, p. 305.

"Now we shall see how fast my vegetables grow," crows Professor Jack after subjecting his garden seeds to a collection of chemicals delivered via a mad-scientist array of tubes and vats and Bunsen burners. Whoops—up through the laboratory ceiling, up through the roof of the house, growing and growing into space climbs a wildly developing plant, no two of its many leaves the same pattern. The government tries to shoot it down, its enormous roots are toppling towns, and worse yet, a satellite sends back pictures of a big space monster making its way down the stalk to earth. While what went up does not come down (nibbling of the plant's roots by woodland creatures causes the plant to float off into space, taking the monster with it), it does go away, leaving Professor Jack a much wiser gardener. It's a slender lesson upon which to hang a tale, but the extravagant pictures of the plant growing feverishly across expansive double-spreads have their attractions—much more so, ironically, than the peaceful, pretty tomato vines Jack grows in its stead.

Rachel Fox

SOURCE: A review of *Jack and the Meanstalk,* in *School Library Journal,* Vol. 40, No. 9, September, 1994, pp. 201-02.

Professor Jack, a scientist, wants to make his garden grow faster. Things get out of hand, however, when the plant he creates in his laboratory grows so tall that it breaks through the ozone layer. At the same time, its roots are destroying everything in their path. As more and more of the area's wildlife are frightened and lose their homes, they come up with a plan—"Day after day, night after night, the burrowing animals tore at the roots with their teeth and claws," killing the monster and solving the problem for all involved. Wildsmith's vividly colored, double-page paintings embellish this simply told story that demonstrates the importance of caring about the Earth and the potential danger of trying to improve on Mother Nature.

Donnarae MacCann and Olga Richard

SOURCE: A review of *Jack and the Meanstalk,* in *Wilson Library Bulletin,* Vol. 69, No. 2, October, 1994, p. 111.

Finally we come to the Wildsmiths' "meanstalk," the plant world's fanciest, mock-scary aberration. ***Jack and the Meanstalk*** is a moral tale about the planet, quite unlike [Leo] Lionni's swipe at intellectual swaggering. But it matches the Lionni book as an artist's tour de force. Rebecca Wildsmith tells of the out-of-control vegetation, while her father, Brian, renders the havoc in brilliant, geometric patterns. He sometimes blends on

From Saint Francis, *written and illustrated by Brian Wildsmith.*

one page different art attitudes, as when hard-edged, opaque objects are juxtaposed with looser forms. For example, Professor Jack's flat-looking plants and test tubes coexist with sketchier images of the professor and his cats. There is talent to spare here. The TV crews are capriciously dressed in period costumes; massive medieval architecture is seen from hovering, toylike helicopters; and the root structure for the berserk "meanstalk" is a spectacular clash of brown, black, magenta, and raw green. Fanciful and commonplace objects are turned into comic inventions, and, as in all this month's books, the artwork is expansive and intriguingly provocative.

Alicen Geddes-Ward

SOURCE: A review of *Jack and the Meanstalk,* in *The School Librarian,* Vol. 42, No. 4, November, 1994, p. 148.

This is a humorous, contemporary version of the original fairy tale where Professor Jack grows impatient with nature, which doesn't grow fast enough for his liking. His experimental psychedelic beanstalk, designed from chemical formulas, grows so big, it smashes through his roof and goes right up to the sky and into deepest space. When a terrible monster comes to live in the meanstalk there is trouble, and finally the wild animals are the only ones with the foresight to stop the meanstalk from destroying planet earth.

This is a wacky environmental story with a difference, aimed at children aged 4 and upwards. It is relevant to today's problems and perhaps will not stand the test of time as a children's classic, but it is a valuable contribution to the heightening of environmental awareness.

NOAH'S ARK (1994)

Marcus Crouch

SOURCE: A review of *Noah's Ark,* in *The Junior Bookshelf,* Vol. 58, No. 6, December, 1994, p. 209.

When an artist of Brian Wildsmith's eminence enters the world of the pop-up something special is indicated, and so it is. While many of the effects must be credited to the paper engineer Wildsmith has plenty of his own. In particular, as ark and sea, dove and rainbow rise up from the page they can be viewed as rewardingly from the back as the front, and the utilitarian tabs which operate some of the gadgetry are in themselves small works of art. Each of the five pop-up spreads has its surprise. Pelican and elephant help to load the ark. Noah's family act as a welcoming party as the animals enter. Lightning flashes across a stormy sky. A typical Wildsmith sun breaks through the clouds as the dove returns. Sun and rainbow join in benediction over Ararat. Pop-up collectors will want this one. The price may deter the rest from a book which must necessarily have a brief life.

THE CREATION (1995)

Elaine Williams

SOURCE: "Top of the Pop-Ups," in *Times Educational Supplement,* No. 4144, December 1, 1995, p. 13.

The Creation by Brian Wildsmith matches delicious illustrations and beautifully designed, awe-inspiring pop-ups to text based on the Book of Genesis. Combining rich passages with fine, detailed drawing and bold, effective constructions, Wildsmith captures the wonder and poetry of the creation story in a book that families will treasure.

SAINT FRANCIS (1996)

Carolyn Phelan

SOURCE: A review of *Saint Francis,* in *Booklist,* Vol. 92, Nos. 9 and 10, January 1, 1996, p. 842.

This large-format picture book presents the life of St. Francis of Assisi, told from his point of view. The use of a first-person narrative is unexpectedly effective, but the storytelling never overshadows the artwork. Noted for his sensitive use of brilliant colors, Wildsmith makes good use of ink drawings here as well, creating double-page spreads that are varied in composition and effective as narrative art. A thin border of gold frames each spread, while golden highlights appear occasionally within the illustrations as a mark of spirituality. A note on the saint's life follows the story. Despite Francis' choice of poverty, Wildsmith finds visual glory in the saint's life and expresses it in a beautifully made, rather opulent-looking book.

Patricia Pearl Dole

SOURCE: A review of *Saint Francis,* in *School Library Journal,* Vol. 42, No. 2, February, 1996, p. 99.

Highlights of the gentle saint's life are told in a simple, straightforward first-person narrative, and the celestial glories of his spirituality are reflected in the lavish panoramic ink-and-watercolor double-page spreads. Framed in gold, they gleam with brilliant colors and are filled with action and detail. Francis is almost a minor figure amid the sweeping landscapes, monumental 13th-century architecture, and splendidly dressed medieval people, all depicted with precise delicacy. Clouds of birds hover, hop, and perch. A multicolored angel watches over the saint's every move, and crowds swirl about him.

Publishers Weekly

SOURCE: A review of *Saint Francis,* in *Publishers Weekly,* Vol. 243, No. 7, February 12, 1996, p. 71.

Renowned illustrator Wildsmith has turned his considerable talents to the life of the 12th-century Christian monk who renounced an affluent lifestyle and took to the streets, restoring ruined churches and preaching to animals (including human ones). Children and adults alike will delight in that story and in these colorful, detailed illustrations, each page appropriately framed in gold. The clean and intricate style of the drawings, suggestive of a gloriously enhanced Waldo book (complete with an angel to track), provides a visual feast for individual or communal meditation. The text itself requires some explanation, but in this handsome volume that will prove no chore for adults. A gorgeous book and an ideal gift, Francis teaches all of us the beauty of both the natural and the spiritual world.

Elizabeth Bush

SOURCE: A review of *Saint Francis,* in *Bulletin of the Center for Children's Books,* Vol. 49, No. 11, July-August, 1996, p. 389.

Rebellious son and gentle nature lover, suffering mystic and holy fool, the "poor man of Assisi" is arguably the most magnetic of saints, and his riches-to-rags story has appeal beyond religious circles. Tales of Francis' abandonment of class privilege, his empathy with animals, even his painful stigmata have the potential to rivet a young audience, while the medieval milieu offers Wildsmith a glorious canvas for his signature artwork. Craggy countryside, teeming harbors, and lofty church interiors are lavishly documented in finely inked line drawings washed with mottled pastels or picked out in more vibrant tones. Wildsmith's ubiquitous pied angel zealously dogs Francis' every step, sometimes boldly appearing in the forefront but sometimes camouflaged amid the densely detailed scenes. Still, the handsome illustrations never quite unify Francis' narration—snippets of legend which have been loosely stitched together. As each double-page spread focuses on a chapter in Francis' life, listeners can hardly absorb one tale before they're handed another. In Francis' laconic voice, one experience sounds much like another: "The prison was cold and damp. My fellow prisoners were sad"; "The sky was ablaze, and a vision of wonder appeared . . . I felt that the Gates of Paradise were opening for me." This visual depiction of *il poverello* and his world may delight an audience, but the fleeting narrative treatment barely illuminates so rich a legend.

AMAZING WORLD OF WORDS (also published as *Brian Wildsmith's Amazing World of Words,* 1996)

Kirkus Reviews

SOURCE: A review of *Amazing World of Words,* in *Kirkus Reviews,* Vol. LXIV, No. 24, December 15, 1996, p. 1806.

The premise is that a visiting alien, clad rather like a court jester and traveling in an extravagant Jules Verne fantasy of a spaceship, is landing on Earth and encountering for the first time its objects and creatures. Ten to twenty labeled objects and animals are illustrated around the margins of gloriously colored pen-and-ink drawings; every spread represents a different environment (space, ocean, town, market, dinosaur museum, playground, etc.), and all invite viewers to locate the border objects within the pictures. As usual with Wildsmith's work, the animals and birds are superb, but there are also some extraordinary renderings of buildings and machines, many recycled from his ***Give a Dog a Bone.*** For a younger group than the Martin Handford and Jean Marzollo/Walter Wick collaborations, this book is fully accessible to prereaders. Opportunities abound for all sorts of recognition, from colors and shapes to bird species, types of musical instruments, and forms of transport, both modern and antique. Drawbacks: There's an index for which any use is difficult to imagine, and the tab cuts on the pages will become quickly dog-eared.

Publishers Weekly

SOURCE: A review of *Amazing World of Words,* in *Publishers Weekly,* Vol. 244, No. 2, January 13, 1997, p. 75.

In this British import, each of Wildsmith's dynamic and crowded illustrations is surrounded by a swarm of small pictures that label elements in the spread. The explosively colored, kaleidoscopic "Space" scene, for example, includes an angular, abstract "sun"; a cubist, candy-colored "space capsule"; and a handful of vivid "planets." Tabs down the side of the pages enable readers to turn quickly to the spread of their choice. A brightly colored spaceship, which looks like something Willie Wonka would dream up on acid, skims through each scene to provide continuity. Wildsmith's quirky, dense style works especially well for the hectic jumble of produce and people in "Market" and for the fanciful costumes of "School Play." He is fond of housing his items in elaborately drawn architectural elements, like the vaulted arches soaring over a blue-and-purple spotted Corythosaurus and a hot pink Brachiosaurus in "Dinosaurs." Many readers may need Wildsmith's key to identify the more peculiar renderings of objects. Literal-minded children might be thrown by this unconventional take on the word book, but most are likely to enjoy poring over these odd and whimsically conceived scenes.

Prue Goodwin

SOURCE: A review of *Amazing World of Words,* in *The School Librarian,* Vol. 45, No. 1, February, 1997, p. 22.

I was delighted when I received a new book from Brian Wildsmith, having loved his work for many, many years.

Amazing World of Words has the exciting line and vibrant colours of all Wildsmith's other books, but I am not quite sure how to 'read' this one. Is it about the 'amazing world' that is being discovered by a visiting alien, or is it about the words? The character—a flamboyant space traveller—is present on each double-page spread, but there is no obvious story about him. He travels through space and time visiting places described as broadly as *Ocean* and as specifically as *School Play*. It is fun to spot the different things he finds in each place. But this book is also clearly intended to be used for reference, with a thumb index and over 300 words listed under headings such as *jungle, market* and *farm.*

Amazing World of Words is fascinating and very entertaining, but I am left wondering two things: am I missing something in the story, and why were particular words chosen? I don't usually feel a need to make such hard and fast definitions about books, so I conclude that it is principally to share and explore with a very young reader. This is a purpose it serves very well as there are plenty of things to spot and talk about on every page, and the character can be part of the fun.

Barbara Baker

SOURCE: A review of *Amazing World of Words,* in *Children's Book Review Service,* Vol. 25, No. 8, March, 1997, p. 91.

What is a reviwer to do? Like all Wildsmith books, this is a glorious splash of color and imaginative design. Unfortunately, I don't know what I would do with this book. The premise is that a space traveler visits many locations on earth. Some of the things he might see are illustrated and spelled out around the margins. The words are so varied and of such unequal reading difficulty that it would be hard to predict an audience for the words. The pictures are great. Perhaps that's a good reason to buy it.

Eunice Weech

SOURCE: A review of *Amazing World of Words,* in *School Library Journal,* Vol. 43, No. 5, May, 1997, p. 126.

A friendly traveler from outer space visits Earth and meets many children who teach him how to play. As he travels all over the planet in a spaceship, he learns many words in the process. The "I Spy" format features detailed double-page spreads devoted to such environments as a desert, jungle, market, wildlife park, playground, and farm. Small labeled drawings of objects that can be found on that page appear around each spread. An index directs readers to the locale in which each word can be traced. When the alien leaves the Earth, he trails a flag with the word "goodbye" printed in over 30 languages. The colorful, intricate drawings will keep browsers occupied for hours. An intriguing vocabulary builder.

Additional coverage of Wildsmith's life and career is contained in the following sources published by Gale Research: *Contemporary Authors New Revision Series,* Vol. 35; *Major Authors and Illustrators for Children and Young Adults; Something about the Author,* Vols. 16, 69; and *Something about the Author Autobiography Series,* Vol. 5.

CUMULATIVE INDEXES

How to Use This Index

The main reference

Baum, L(yman) Frank 1856-1919 .... **15**

list all author entries in this and previous volumes of *Children's Literature Review:*

The cross-references

See also CA 103; 108; DLB 22; JRDA MAICYA; MTCW; SATA 18; TCLC 7

list all author entries in the following Gale biographical and literary sources:

AAYA = *Authors & Artists for Young Adults*
AITN = *Authors in the News*
BLC = *Black Literature Criticism*
BW = *Black Writers*
CA = *Contemporary Authors*
CAAS = *Contemporary Authors Autobiography Series*
CABS = *Contemporary Authors Bibliographical Series*
CANR = *Contemporary Authors New Revision Series*
CAP = *Contemporary Authors Permanent Series*
CDALB = *Concise Dictionary of American Literary Biography*
CDBLB = *Concise Dictionary of British Literary Biography*
CLC = *Contemporary Literary Criticism*
CMLC = *Classical and Medieval Literature Criticism*
DAB = *DISCovering Authors: British*
DAC = *DISCovering Authors: Canadian*
DAM = *DISCovering Authors: Modules*
DRAM: *Dramatists Module;* ***MST:*** *Most-Studied Authors Module;*
MULT: *Multicultural Authors Module;* ***NOV:*** *Novelists Module;*
POET: *Poets Module;* ***POP:*** *Popular Fiction and Genre Authors Module*
DC = *Drama Criticism*
DLB = *Dictionary of Literary Biography*
DLBD = *Dictionary of Literary Biography Documentary Series*
DLBY = *Dictionary of Literary Biography Yearbook*
HLC = *Hispanic Literature Criticism*
HW = *Hispanic Writers*
JRDA = *Junior DISCovering Authors*
LC = *Literature Criticism from 1400 to 1800*
MAICYA = *Major Authors and Illustrators for Children and Young Adults*
MTCW = *Major 20th-Century Writers*
NCLC = *Nineteenth-Century Literature Criticism*
NNAL = *Native North American Literature*
PC = *Poetry Criticism*
SAAS = *Something about the Author Autobiography Series*
SATA = *Something about the Author*
SSC = *Short Story Criticism*
TCLC = *Twentieth-Century Literary Criticism*
WLC = *World Literature Criticism, 1500 to the Present*
YABC = *Yesterday's Authors of Books for Children*

CUMULATIVE INDEX TO AUTHORS

CUMULATIVE INDEX TO NATIONALITIES

Nationality Index

CUMULATIVE INDEX TO TITLES

Title Index

Title Index

Title Index

Title Index

Title Index

Title Index

Title Index

Title Index

ISBN 0-7876-2080-7
90000
9 780787 620806